T0408160

RESEARCH HANDBOOK ON PRIVACY AND DATA PROTECTION LAW

RESEARCH HANDBOOKS IN INFORMATION LAW

The volumes in the Research Handbooks in Information Law series examine the legal dimensions of issues arising out of an increasingly digitalized world. Edited by leading scholars in their respective fields, they explore such topics as data protection, advertising law, cybercrime and telecommunications, as well as many others. Taking as their common thread, the impact of information law on the world in which we live, they are unrivaled in their blend of critical, substantive analysis and synthesis of contemporary research. Each *Research Handbook* stands alone as an invaluable source of reference for all scholars interested in information law. Whether used as an information resource on key topics or as a platform for advanced study, volumes in this series will become definitive scholarly reference works in the field.

Titles in this series include:

Research Handbook on Electronic Commerce Law
Edited by John A. Rothchild

Research Handbook in Data Science and Law
Edited by Vanessa Mak, Eric Tjong Tjin Tai and Anna Berlee

Research Handbook on Big Data Law
Edited by Roland Vogl

Research Handbook on Information Law and Governance
Edited by Sharon K. Sandeen, Christoph Rademacher and Ansgar Ohly

Research Handbook on Privacy and Data Protection Law
Values, Norms and Global Politics
Edited by Gloria González Fuster, Rosamunde Van Brakel and Paul De Hert

Research Handbook on Privacy and Data Protection Law

Values, Norms and Global Politics

Edited by

Gloria González Fuster

Research Professor, Vrije Universiteit Brussel (VUB), Belgium and Co-Director of VUB's Law, Science, Technology & Society (LSTS) Research Group

Rosamunde Van Brakel

Associate Professor, Tilburg Institute for Law, Technology, and Society (TILT), Tilburg University, the Netherlands and Assistant Professor, Vrije Universiteit Brussel (VUB), Belgium

Paul De Hert

Professor, Vrije Universiteit Brussel (VUB), Belgium and Associate Professor, Tilburg Institute for Law, Technology, and Society (TILT), Tilburg University, the Netherlands

RESEARCH HANDBOOKS IN INFORMATION LAW

Cheltenham, UK • Northampton, MA, USA

Published by
Edward Elgar Publishing Limited
The Lypiatts
15 Lansdown Road
Cheltenham
Glos GL50 2JA
UK

Edward Elgar Publishing, Inc.
William Pratt House
9 Dewey Court
Northampton
Massachusetts 01060
USA

A catalogue record for this book
is available from the British Library

Library of Congress Control Number: 2022931291

This book is available electronically in the **Elgar**online
Law subject collection
http://dx.doi.org/10.4337/9781786438515

Printed on elemental chlorine free (ECF)
recycled paper containing 30% Post-Consumer Waste

ISBN 978 1 78643 850 8 (cased)
ISBN 978 1 78643 851 5 (eBook)

Printed and bound in the USA

Contents

Contributors

Mónica Arenas Ramiro is Ph.D. in Law by University of Alcalá with the Thesis "The fundamental right to personal data protection in Europe"; (National Award AEPD (2005) and Doctorate Award (2007)). Currently, Data Protection Officer (DPO) of her University. Lecturer of Constitutional Law at the University of Alcalá since 1999, and of various Masters and Courses, and external trainer of the City Council of the Community of Madrid, with a course on data protection awarded with the European Best Practices Award of European Public Administrations (2006). She has also carried out several research stays abroad (Germany, Italy and the United States), has developed numerous academic management tasks, and has participated in Congresses, Seminars, and given Conferences both nationally and internationally. Her main lines of research are fundamental and social rights, gender, immigration, political parties, media, transparency, digital society and personal data protection, on which she has published numerous works.

Tyler Blake is an associate at the law firm of Vinson & Elkins in San Francisco, where he practices in the areas of cybersecurity & data privacy and internal investigations. He received his J.D. from Washington University in St. Louis School of Law, where he graduated magna cum laude and served as Chief Commentaries Editor for the Washington University Law Review.

Maja Brkan is a Judge at the General Court of the European Union. Prior to her judicial appointment, she had been Associate Professor of European Union Law at Maastricht University (2018–2021) and Assistant Professor at the same university (2013–2018), as well as Associate Director of the Maastricht Centre for European Law (2017–2020), where she is now a Distinguished Fellow. She is also a Member of the European Centre on Privacy and Cybersecurity. Prior to her academic appointment, she served as a legal adviser (*référéndaire*) at the Court of Justice of the EU (2007–2013). She holds a Diploma of the Academy of European Law from the European University Institute in Florence and was awarded the prize 'Young Lawyer of the Year 2007' from the Union of Lawyers' Associations in Slovenia. Dr Brkan has published widely in numerous areas of European law. Her recent research focuses on EU fundamental rights, particularly on privacy and data protection, on legal questions of artificial intelligence, as well as on the impact of new technologies on society. On these topics, she lectured at various conferences and universities across Europe and beyond, including Oxford University, Yale University and University of Ljubljana. She has also been a visiting researcher at the European University Institute, at the University of California – Berkeley, at the University of Ljubljana, as well as at the Autonomous University of Barcelona. Her notable publications include a core Slovenian textbook on EU law (co-authored with Professor Dr Verica Trstenjak), a monograph on EU external relations and two edited volumes on data protection in the digital environment and procedure before the EU courts, respectively. She is also a member of the editorial board of the *European Data Protection Law Review* and of the online platform *EU Law Live*.

Damian Clifford is a senior lecturer at the Australian National University, College of Law and an associate researcher at Information Law and Policy Centre at the Institute of Advanced Legal Studies (University of London). His research focuses predominantly on data protection, privacy and the regulation of technology. Damian completed his Ph.D. at the KU Leuven Centre for IT and IP Law (CiTiP) where he was a FWO Aspirant Fellow funded by Fonds Wetenschappelijk Onderzoek – Vlaanderen (FWO) from October 2015 to October 2019.

Paul De Hert is Professor of Law at the Faculty of Law and Criminology of Vrije Universiteit Brussel. He is the Director of the research group on Fundamental Rights and Constitutionalism (FRC) and senior member of the research group on Law, Science, Technology & Society (LSTS). Paul De Hert is also associated-professor Law and Technology at the Tilburg Institute for Law and Technology (TILT).

Cécile de Terwangne is full Professor at the Faculty of Law of the University of Namur (Belgium). She is research director at the CRIDS (Research Centre for Information, Law and Society) of the University of Namur. Her courses and research focus on Human Rights and ICT, Privacy, Data Protection, Freedom of Expression and of Information, eGovernment.

Diana Dimitrova is a research assistant in the Intellectual Properties Rights Department at FIZ Karlsruhe and an affiliated researcher at LSTS/VUB. She researches and publishes on a wide variety of data protection topics. Diana defended her Ph.D. at the Vrije Universiteit Brussel on the topic of the rights of access and rectification in the Area of Freedom, Security and Justice. She is the Co-Editor of the biweekly 'Data Protection Insider' Newsletter. Diana is one of the core members of the annual CPDP (Computers, Privacy and Data Protection) Conference. Before joining FIZ Karlsruhe, Diana was a research assistant from 2012–2016 at KU Leuven, Belgium, where she researched on data protection topics in the framework of EU FP-7 research project. In 2012 she completed an internship at the EDPS in Brussels. Diana holds an LL.M. in European law at the University of Leiden, the Netherlands.

Gloria González Fuster is a research Professor at the Vrije Universiteit Brussel (VUB)'s Faculty of Law and Criminology, where holds a research position on the theme *Digitalisation and a Europe of Rights and Freedoms*, and teaches Privacy and Data Protection Law. She is the Co-Director of VUB's Law, Science, Technology and Society (LSTS) Research Group, and investigates legal issues related to privacy, personal data protection, security and fundamental rights.

Sînziana Ianc is a Managing Associate in the Linklaters antitrust and foreign investment practice. She advises international clients in all aspects of EU, German and global merger control law as well as anti-trust compliance. Her work also focuses on representing clients before both instances of the Court of Justice of the European Union.

Els J. Kindt is a lecturer, post-doc legal researcher and Associate Professor at respectively the Centre for IT and IP Law (CITIP) – iMec of KU Leuven, Belgium and eLaw of the Universiteit Leiden, the Netherlands. Her research domain comprises privacy and data protection regulation, eprivacy, health data, fundamental rights, identity management and egovernment and she has been collaborating in many European research projects. She is internationally recognized as a legal scholar on biometric technologies, is a board member at EAB and is regularly invited as expert by national and international institutions. She is heading the Biometric Law Lab (BLL) at CITIP, comprising currently six legal researchers and one post-doctoral Marie Curie legal scholar all specializing in biometric law. She is also an attorney at the Brussels Bar.

Matthias Leese is a Senior Researcher at the Center for Security Studies (CSS), ETH Zurich. His research interests are broadly located in the fields of critical security studies, surveillance studies, and science and technology studies. His works have among others been published in International Political Sociology, Security Dialogue, Critical Studies on Security, Criminology & Criminal Justice, Global Society, and Science and Engineering Ethics. With Stef Wittendorp, he is the editor of Security/Mobility: Politics of Movement (with Manchester University Press).

Milda Mačėnaitė received her Ph.D. from Tilburg Institute for Law, Technology and Society (TILT), the Netherlands. Her Ph.D. research focused on the protection of children's privacy and personal data in the digital environment. She was previously a Senior Fellow at the UNICEF Office of Research – Innocenti, Italy and a visiting researcher at the University of Ottawa, Canada.

Gianclaudio Malgieri is an Associate Professor of Law and Technology at the EDHEC Business School in Lille, France, where he conducts research at the Augmented Law Institute and teaches Data Protection Law, Intellectual Property Law, and AI Regulation. He is also the Co-Director of the Brussels Privacy Hub, a Guest Professor at Vrije Universiteit Brussel, and an Editorial Board Member of Computer Law and Security Review. He obtained a PhD in Law at the Law, Science, Technology and Society (LSTS) Research Group of the Vrije Universiteit Brussel (VUB). He obtained an LLM with honors at the University of Pisa (2016) and a JD with honors at St. Anna School of Advanced Studies of Pisa (2017). He has authored more than 55 publications, including articles in leading international academic journals. He has published editorials in top international newspapers (The New York Times, Le Monde, La Tribune, France Culture, ilSole24Ore, la Repubblica and il Corriere della Sera).

Alessandro Mantelero is Associate Professor of Private Law at the Polytechnic University of Turin. He is Council of Europe Rapporteur on Artificial Intelligence and data protection. In 2016, he was appointed expert consultant by the Council of Europe to draft the Guidelines on personal data in a world of Big Data (2017). He is member of the IPEN-Internet Privacy Engineering Network (European Data Protection Supervisor) and has served as an expert on data regulation for several institutions, including UN–ILO, EU Agency for Fundamental Rights, UN-OHCHR, American Chamber of Commerce in Italy, Italian Ministry of Justice, and Italian Communications Authority.

Ninja Marnau is a Senior Researcher at the CISPA Helmholtz-Zentrum in Saarbruecken, Germany. Together with her team she conducts interdisciplinary research on legal and computer science challenges of data protection and IT security. She works on several national and international research projects addressing basic research and real-world applications of Privacy-Enhancing Technologies and security-by-design. Before joining CISPA, she worked at the Data Protection Authority of Schleswig-Holstein (ULD), Germany, and the World Wide Web Consortium (W3C), France.

Karen McCullagh is a Lecturer in Law at the University of East Anglia where she contributes to teaching on the LLM in IT and IP Law and MSc in Cybersecurity. Her research specialism is information rights: both the commercial and fundamental rights aspects of privacy and data protection and Freedom of Information, as an aspect of public law. She is a member of the

Executive Committee of British & Irish Law, Education & Technology Association (BILETA) and the IT editor for the European Journal of Current Legal Interests (EJoCLI).

Hiroshi Miyashita is Professor of Law, Chuo University, Tokyo, Japan. Prior to this, he served for the Office of Personal Information Protection in the Cabinet Office and conducted research as a visiting scholar at Harvard Law School and at Brussels Privacy Hub, Vrije Universiteit Brussel. He published six books on privacy in Japanese.

Jonathon W. Penney is a legal scholar and social scientist based at the Faculty of Law at Osgoode Hall Law School in Toronto. He is also a Research Affiliate at Harvard's Berkman Klein Center for Internet & Society and a long-time Research Fellow at the Citizen Lab based at the University of Toronto's Munk School of Global Affairs and Public Policy. Jon's research and expertise lies at the intersection of law, technology, and human rights, with strong interdisciplinary and empirical dimensions.

Jo Pierson, Ph.D., is Professor of Digital Technologies and Public Values in the Department of Media and Communication Studies at the Vrije Universiteit Brussel (VUB) in Belgium (Faculty of Social Sciences & Solvay Business School) and Principal Investigator at the research centre SMIT (Studies on Media, Innovation and Technology). He is in charge of the research unit 'Data, Privacy and Empowerment', in close cooperation with imec (R&D and innovation hub in nanoelectronics and digital technology). He is also affiliated with Hasselt University. His main research expertise is in data privacy, digital platforms, algorithms, user innovation, and value-based design.

Priscilla M. Regan is a Professor in the Schar School of Policy and Government at George Mason University. Prior to joining that faculty in 1989, she was a Senior Analyst in the Congressional Office of Technology Assessment (1984–1989). Since the mid-1970s, Dr Regan's primary research interests have focused on the analysis of the social, policy, and legal implications of organizational use of new information and communications technologies. She is currently a co-investigator on a Social Sciences and Humanities Research Council of Canada's eQuality grant exploring big data, discrimination, and youth. Dr Regan has published over 50 articles or book chapters, as well as *Legislating Privacy: Technology, Social Values, and Public Policy* (University of North Carolina Press, 1995). She was a member of the National Academy of Sciences, Computer Science and Telecommunications Board, Committee on Authentication Technologies and their Privacy Implications. Dr Regan received her PhD in Government from Cornell University and her BA from Mount Holyoke College.

Neil Richards is the Koch Distinguished Professor in Law at Washington University in St. Louis, where he also directs the Cordell Institute for Policy in Medicine & Law. Professor Richards writes, teaches, and lectures about privacy and data protection law, free expression law, and law and technology. He is the author of two books, *Intellectual Privacy* (Oxford 2015) and *Why Privacy Matters* (Oxford 2021), and dozens of academic and popular articles. He is also a former law clerk to William H. Rehnquist, Chief Justice of the United States.

Andrew Serwin is the US Chair and Global Co-Chair of both the Data Protection, Privacy and Security Practice and the Cybersecurity Practice at the law firm of DLA Piper. He is also the author of the leading treatise on privacy and security, Information Security and Privacy: A Guide to Federal and State Law and Compliance and Information Security and Privacy: A Guide to International Law and Compliance (West 2006–2020), collectively a 6,000-page, three-volume treatise that examines all aspects of privacy and security laws, published by Thomson-West. He has published numerous other books and law review articles and routinely authors client alerts on cutting-edge privacy and cybersecurity developments.

Christoph Sorge received his Ph.D. in computer science from Karlsruhe Institute of Technology. He worked as a research scientist at NEC Laboratories Europe and as an assistant professor of network security at the University of Paderborn. Christoph Sorge joined Saarland University in 2014, where he is now a full Professor of Legal Informatics. He is an associate member of the CISPA – Helmholtz Center for Information Security, a senior fellow of the German Research Institute for Public Administration, and a board member of the German Association for Computing in the Judiciary. His research area is the intersection of computer science and law, with a focus on data protection.

Valerie Steeves, JD, PhD, is a Full Professor in the Department of Criminology at the University of Ottawa in Canada. She is the Principal Investigator of The eQuality Project, a seven-year partnership examining children's experiences of privacy and equality in networked spaces, funded by the Social Sciences and Humanities Research Council of Canada. She is also a co-investigator with the Big Data Project, also funded by the Social Sciences and Humanities Research Council of Canada.

Rosamunde Van Brakel is Associate Professor Cybercrime at Tilburg Institute for Law, Technology and Society and as Assistant Professor at the Law, Science, Technology and Society Research Group of the Vrije Universiteit Brussel. Previously, she has been managing director of the annual Computers, Privacy and Data Protection conference and co-founder and executive director of the non-profit organisation Privacy Salon between 2014 and 2021. In 2019 she was elected as co-director of the Surveillance Studies Network. She has been conducting research on the social, ethical and legal consequences of (algorithmic) surveillance technologies since 2006. Current research is focused on the governance of surveillance, cybercrime and cybersecurity. She has been co-editor of four edited volumes and has published numerous articles in national and international journals and books on surveillance and police oversight.

Karlijn van den Heuvel works as a lawyer for Stibbe in Amsterdam in the IT, IP and Data Protection department. She specializes in information law with a focus on privacy and data protection law. Before working at Stibbe, Karlijn was affiliated as a research master student with the Institute for Information Law at the University of Amsterdam and pursued her studies at the University of Utrecht, the University of Cambridge and The Benjamin N. Cardozo School of Law in New York City.

Joris van Hoboken is a Professor of Law at the Vrije Universiteit Brussels (VUB) and an Associate Professor at the Institute for Information Law (IViR), University of Amsterdam. At the VUB, he is appointed to the Chair 'Fundamental Rights and Digital Transformation', established at the Interdisciplinary Research Group on Law Science Technology & Society (LSTS), with the support of Microsoft. Previously, Van Hoboken worked at New York University and Cornell University and was a visiting researcher at Harvard University. Van Hoboken obtained his PhD from the University of Amsterdam (2012) and has graduate degrees in Law (2006) and Theoretical Mathematics (2002).

Maximilian von Grafenstein LL.M. is Full Professor of the chair Digital Self-Determination at the Einstein Center Digital Future (ECDF) affiliated to the Berlin University of the Arts (UdK). He is also co-head of the research program 'Data, Actors, Infrastructures: Governance of Data-Driven Innovation and Cybersecurity' at the Alexander von Humboldt Institute for Internet and Society (HIIG). His research focuses on the regulation of data-driven innovation and, in particular, Data Protection by Design. Max has led for four years the HIIG Startup Law Clinic, where he assisted over 100 start-up entrepreneurs in solving legal issues related to their innovations. Max is a member of the ISO/IEC JTC 1/SC 27/WG5 Identity management and privacy technologies and Vice President of the Academic Board of the European Association of Data Protection Professionals (EADPP).

Gabriela Zanfir-Fortuna is Vice President for Global Privacy for the Washington DC-based Future of Privacy Forum, where she coordinates the regional offices of FPF in Brussels, Tel Aviv and Singapore. She is also associated researcher for the LSTS Center of Vrije Universiteit Brussel. Gabriela is a member of the Reference Panel of the Global Privacy Assembly and a member of the Executive Committee of ACM's Fairness, Accountability and Transparency Conference. She has experience in working for the European Data Protection Supervisor in Brussels, dealing with enforcement, litigation and policy matters, and contributed to the work of the Article 29 Working Party. She holds a PhD in law with a thesis on the rights of the data subject from the perspective of their adjudication in civil law, and an LLM in Human Rights.

Introduction to *Research Handbook on Privacy and Data Protection Law*

Gloria González Fuster, Rosamunde Van Brakel and Paul De Hert

Research on privacy and data protection law has never been so vibrant, and so challenging. It is vibrant because its subject matter is in constant evolution. Privacy and data protection laws across the world are in a perpetually accelerating movement, and discussions about their need and their future, as well as on their gaps and limitations, appear to be forever intensifying. There is a never-ending effervescence of legislative proposals about data being put forward and debated – internationally, but also regionally; a perennial set of open questions about the ultimate effectiveness of existing and upcoming instruments; a recurrent realization of the potential need to legislate, perhaps differently, perhaps more, the processing of data and more particularly of personal data.

This continuously moving landscape makes the study of privacy and data protection law a peculiarly demanding endeavour, calling for continuous attention to a myriad of developments. Some of these events require a particularly strong commitment – if not devotion – from experts in the field. In Europe, the advent of the General Data Protection Regulation (GDPR) brought about a peculiarly hectic period for privacy and data protection law scholars and practitioners.[1] Then, just as the GDPR had become applicable in May 2018, what might be called the spring of Artificial Intelligence (AI) regulation started to firmly occupy academic and policy space, and capturing an extensive number of intellectual resources, including those of privacy and data protection law experts. Surrounding these debates, numerous other policy initiatives touching upon data, and thus, even if secondarily or accidentally, also affecting personal data, saw the light.

That, however, is not all. If research on privacy and data protection law is challenging it is, mainly, because it invites (or shall we say it obliges?) to mobilize, in addition to disparate legal perspectives, a variety of trans- and interdisciplinary insights, or modes of knowledge. Legal developments related to privacy and data protection law cannot be correctly apprehended by strictly focusing on their legal dimension. As researchers active in this area, we are firmly convinced that a multiplicity of perspectives is necessarily required to fathom the real complexity of the issues at stake. This means that in order to enter this field one must familiarize oneself with a variety of heterogenous approaches, literatures, concepts, and methodologies; one needs to learn to recognize, and when necessary, cross disciplinary borders, in addition to jurisdictional borders. Additionally, it also means that to stay up to date it is vital to keep an eye on how a whole range of thoughts, traditions and innovations are evolving. A challenging, but fascinating venture.

---

[1] See, also in this sense, Editors' Preface in Christopher Kuner, Lee A. Bygrave, and Christopher Docksey (eds), *The EU General Data Protection Regulation (GDPR): A Commentary*, Oxford University Press, 2020, p. vii.

I. GOALS OF THE BOOK

This volume aims to contribute to the study of privacy and data protection law by illustrating its many complexities, helping readers to not only obtain new knowledge on specific aspects of the current policy and legal framework, but also perceiving the variety of coexisting viewpoints on the matters at stake.

It is not a book about the GDPR, even if much of it is certainly concerned with the GDPR: it acknowledges that the coming into effect of the GDPR constituted a major step forward for the European Union (EU), with a clear potential for major international impact. At the same time, the volume builds on the many questions that still surround the GDPR, starting with the crucial one of whether the GDPR – or even more broadly, the EU data protection legal framework as such – might effectively be the answer for all the legal, ethical, and social issues arising from the widespread use of technology in an increasingly data-driven world. This question is itself deeply connected to the issue of the relation(s) between data protection and privacy, themselves looking potentially different and differently (dis)connected when approached from different geographies and/or at different moments in time.

This volume, we hope, will serve as an insightful resource for many kinds of readers with an interest in research in privacy and data protection, including most notably students wishing to obtain a general overview of a selection of important issues, caveats, and possibilities for doing research on data protection and privacy. Instead of trying to build a uniformising frame through which to apprehend privacy and data protection law, it aims at mirroring the many paths through which this field can be explored – and which sometimes cross, but sometimes lead in different directions.

II. CHAPTERS

II.1 General

This handbook brings together chapters from interdisciplinary perspectives on privacy and data protection from Europe and beyond. The volume is divided into three parts. The first section provides different jurisdictional and geographical perspectives, guided by a wish to explore how travelling across the global landscape of privacy and data protection laws impacts our perspectives on these notions. This part of the book offers different insights from Europe and outside, illustrating that there are different layers to European privacy and data protection law (Ch 1), as well as moving views on the advantages of the European framework, especially when a country transitions from being an EU Member State to being a 'third country' (Ch 2). The Europe vs. United States (US) divide is a major theme of privacy thinking and is in this part addressed from both sides of the Atlantic (Chs 3 and 4), revealing both commonalities and interesting nuances in the appraisals. There is however much more to global privacy and data protection law than Europe and the US, as the part opens up to Canadian, Japanese and Latin American viewpoints (Chs 5, 6 and 7).

The second series of chapters (Part II) discusses interdisciplinary and transdisciplinary perspectives on privacy and data protection such as from a social values privacy law and policy perspective (Ch 8), media and communication studies (Ch 9), computer science (Ch 10), and critical security studies (Ch 11), and dwells into the relations between privacy and data protection law and others fields of law, such as consumer law (Ch 12) and competition law (Ch 13).

The final part of the book discusses a number of hot topics in privacy and data protection such as the role of the courts (Ch 14), surveillance at the borders (Ch 15), big data and data protection (Ch 16), children's online privacy (Ch 17), biometric data processing (Ch 18), co-regulation and the competitive advantage in the GDPR (Ch 19) and automated decision-making specifically (Ch 20).

II.2 Geographical Perspectives on Privacy and Data Protection

Cécile de Terwange's opening chapter introduces us to European data protection by looking at it from a double prism: it is concerned with the GDPR, but also – and somehow even more strongly – with the Council of Europe's Modernised Convention 108. The chapter takes the challenge of simultaneously acknowledging both realities as important. This is as such probably an increasingly rare approach, at least in Europe, where the GDPR's attraction is peculiarly strong. De Terwange's original contribution subtly invites us to imagine a Europe in which Convention 108+ would be the main data protection reference. Interestingly, also, it discusses both major European instruments from an historical viewpoint. As such, it situates the reader in the shoes of the legislator and allows to revive some of the key dilemmas that accompanied the drafting of Convention 108 and the GDPR.

Karen McCullagh's chapter on Brexit and post-Brexit data protection takes also some distance from the GDPR, albeit for different reasons and in a different context. Her contribution offers an historically unique account of how an EU Member State started to move out of the EU data protection framework, and the connected dilemmas. Describing the transformation of the United Kindgom (UK) into a third country, it puts on the table the crucial question of what the GDPR means for third countries, and thus globally, illustrating at the same time the 'Brussels effect' and what might as well be a – very different – 'post-Brussels effect'.

'Understanding American Privacy', by Neil Richards, Andrew Serwin and Tyler Blake, hints somehow at the idea that US privacy law is often misunderstood worldwide and attempts to dispel some common misunderstandings. As such, it constitutes very much an US contribution in a way addressing the European and generally global reader, and thus offers very interesting insights of how this reader is perceived.

The chapter by Karlijn van den Heuvel and Joris Van Hoboken explores both EU and US laws, by taking as entry point into their analysis the 'justiciability' of privacy and data protection. This approach is more than a mere argumentative device to attempt to compare models but represents a real effort to question to which extent, somehow regardless of their other features, global privacy laws can make a real difference for individuals.

Penney's chapter brings in a Canadian perspective, which, in full consistence with the history of academic writing on these matters, is very much concerned with the international discussions around privacy and data protection laws. As such, this chapter tells us much about the history of convergence and divergence in the global landscape, reminding us that this history is not only necessary to understand Canadian developments, but also other regional and national situations.

Hiroshi Miyashita's chapter on data protection law in Japan zooms in more decidedly into a specific moment of a specific national legal framework. His contribution is fascinating especially insofar as it shows how seemingly minor nuances in punctual definitions can have a dramatic impact on the level of protection granted to individuals, and from there, indirectly, on the international relations and trade opportunities of a whole country. In this sense, even subtleties in translation can deeply alter the assessment of what is adequate or inadequate.

Finally, Mónica Arenas Ramiro attempts to provide a much-needed overview of the situation in Latin America. Her chapter very well illustrates the different dynamics at stake in the region, between influence of external models, international guidance, regional impetus for harmonisation and national disparities. The 'Brussels effect' is here again perceptible, together however with a variety of other forces that deserve due acknowledgment.

II.3 Interdisciplinary and Transdisciplinary Perspectives on Privacy and Data Protection

The second part of the book deals with interdisciplinary and transdisciplinary perspectives on privacy and data protection. The chapter 'Social Values and Privacy Law and Policy' by Priscilla Regan eloquently shows that privacy is not only of value to the individual as individual but also has a wider social value in a democratic society. In the legal and policy realms, privacy is still largely conceptualized as an individual interest or right. Although in Europe with the strong human rights tradition and the new data protection framework this is not as striking as in the US, which is the focus of the chapter. In the first part Regan reviews the literature on the social value of privacy to extract the central themes and their potential policy implications, in the second part policy discussions are examined to determine whether the social value of privacy has been raised in policy discussions and if so to what effect. In the final part Regan looks into the future to see how a social value of privacy can be more fully incorporated into policy debates and outcomes.

The chapter by Jo Pierson 'Media and Communication Studies, Privacy and Public Values: Future Challenges' shows how Media and Communication Studies (MCS) can enrich the research on privacy and data protection in mediated communication. As communication in society increasingly takes place via digital intermediaries in the form of digital platforms, it becomes essential to focus on how the latter take form, operate and have impact in relation to public values like privacy and data protection. The chapter takes an interdisciplinary perspective that integrates the advertising motives of these platforms, the (inter)national legal and policy environment, the affordances of the data-driven technologies and the everyday user practices of citizens. Pierson identifies and discusses how these different elements together shape the mechanisms (datafication, commodification and selection) that drive current data-driven digital platforms and argues that to safeguard fundamental public values like privacy and data protection in a future platform society, we need to address these mechanisms, integrating the levels of artefacts, practices and socio-economic arrangements. To do this Pierson suggests a number of possible pathways using notions of cooperative responsibility, empowerment by design and data literacy.

In their chapter, 'From Law to Engineering: A Computer Science Perspective on Privacy and Data Protection', Ninja Marnau and Christoph Sorge argue that the nature of computer science with regards to privacy is Janus-faced. The ever-progressing digitalization requires digital solutions for effective privacy protection. Computer science can and has to act as an enabler of privacy-friendly data processing. The role of privacy engineering and privacy-enhancing technologies by far exceeds just guaranteeing legal compliance. In fact, the crucial value of privacy engineering is to lessen the latent conflict arising from this power asymmetry by empowering the individual and building trust by giving technical privacy assurances. In this chapter the authors show that recent and ongoing research efforts in computer science have resulted in many approaches with the potential to greatly benefit individuals' privacy. Most importantly, they give individuals the power to use digital services anonymously, and they enable statistical evaluations of data without revealing too much information about individuals.

In his chapter Matthias Leese discusses how privacy and data protection are discussed in security studies. The author introduces developments in security studies as parts of the security studies community have taken a 'critical' turn, scholars have started to increasingly turn their analyses to the potential negative ramifications of security politics and practices – a scope that strongly intersects with the concepts of privacy and data protection, as they are set to protect the individual from intrusions into their private (data) sphere. The identification of new security issues, new sites of security production, and new security practices thereby lays the foundation for a review of new questions for security studies vis-à-vis privacy and data protection in the ensuing section, outlining the role of a privacy/data protection perspective for the (critical) study of security and its larger political, social, and economic ramifications. The chapter ends with a discussion of the challenges posed to privacy and data protection by securitization processes, particularly against the backdrop of a Big Data perspective on the analysis of security-relevant data.

Data Protection and consumer protection policy is a topic that has been discussed extensively in academic literature, policy making and enforcement circles. In his chapter Damian Clifford, provides a detailed descriptive and evaluative analysis of the EU data and consumer protection frameworks to provide normative insights into the potential challenges. The author illustrates that there is a complex relationship between the respective data protection and consumer protection policy agendas. By examining the protections for pre-formulated declarations of data subject consent, the analysis aims to point towards the fundamental challenges at the core of this debate. More specifically, the positioning of personal data as a counter-performance/consideration or a 'core term' and hence, the alignment of a fundamental rights orientated approach with economically focused protections are illustrative of a clear divide in thinking. Although the author sees some positive aspects about as the alignment of protections could afford citizen-consumers with more robust enforcement tools, he does question if such a development should be sought at the expense of the protections afforded in the GDPR.

The final chapter in this section is a chapter by Gabriela Zanfir- Fortuna and Sînziana Ianc on Data Protection and Competition Law. The authors give a positive message illustrating that data protection law and competition law are starting to cross paths in meaningful ways in the EU legal framework, aiming to provide a thick layer of protection to individuals as market participants whose personal data feed unexplored competition parameters as well as new, significant, and profitable markets. It provides an empirical analysis of competition adjudication cases at EU level and at national level within Member States of the EU to identify possible trends or shifts in enforcement and policymaking with regard to data protection and privacy law issues as relevant factors for the assessment of anticompetitive behaviour. Based on this analysis the authors identified three stages of the intersection between data protection law and competition law: (1) the parallel pathways for the two fields of law; (2) acknowledgment that the two fields interact and that they cannot remain in silos; and (3) the beginning of a new era, ensuring ramped up protection of the individual as data subject and participant to the digital economy, as well as of an integrated, efficient, and competitive digital market.

II.4 Hot Topics in Privacy and Data Protection

The third part of the book opens with Maja Brkan's discussion of the role of the European Courts in developing Privacy and Data Protection. The chapter starts with a disclaimer about what is not be expected: an analysis of the way the Court of Justice of the EU (CJEU) and the European Court of Human Rights (ECtHR) distinguish privacy from data protection and requires protection of both. The unique perspective that Brkan develops to make sense of the plurality of courts in Europe that guide us, is essential for our understanding of applying privacy and data protection. After a short discussion of the role of national courts of EU Member States in the fields of privacy and data protection – a role that has been strengthened by the GDPR – the author proceeds with examining the role of the CJEU and of the ECtHR in subsequent sections. The observations are subtle and fascinating. In particular, the CJEU is an actor with many particularities. In the chapter Brkan also discusses the ongoing dialogue between the national highest and the European courts as well as between the CJEU and the ECtHR. The case law on surveillance and data retention serves to prove her point; the ECtHR in *Szabó and Vissy* refers to CJEU judgements (*Digital Rights Ireland* and *Seitlinger*), but does it in general in a *non-systematic* way, whereas the CJEU refers to ECtHR case law in a *selective* way 'when it is necessary to strengthen its reasoning on issues where its own case law is lacking and thus uses the ECtHR jurisprudence to fill in the missing pieces of argumentation jigsaw'.

Diana Dimitrova's chapter 'Surveillance at the Borders' guides us in a comprehensive way through the diverse landscape of border control initiatives and laws initiated by the EU to closely monitor incoming, residing, and outgoing travellers, both EU citizens and third country nationals. Her chapter offers a rare opportunity to get acquainted with all the databases, tools and law enforcement and border guard networks set up in recent time. The section on what kind of data processing takes place before, during and after the travel is visualizing in a quite novel way and is a recommended read. The section nicely prepares the way for a more classical data protection discussion of the difficulty of combining current border control ideas and policies with the principles *and* the effective exercise of data subject rights.

Dimotrova's chapter is followed by Alessandro Mantelero on 'Big Data and Data Protection'. The author opens with a short historical timeline to remind us about when data protection rules emerged and when big data practices were first developed. Essential for understanding the tensions between the two is the following observation: 'big data analytics make it possible to infer predictive information from large amounts of data to acquire further knowledge about individuals and groups, which may not necessarily be related to the initial purposes of data collection'. This feature thwarts the basic understandings of the traditional model of personal information protection (regarding data subject remedies and the principle of purpose limitation), Mantelero writes, which explains why the author then turns to recent data protection reform at the level of the EU, the US and the Council of Europe. In the EU section, the reader will appreciate the detection of several novel elements brought to us by the GDPR that are designed to address big data challenges, and equally the critical reflections about their respective value offered by the author. One of the novelties discussed is the set of articles in the GDPR that together frame the so-called right to explanation (see also the chapter by Malgieri in this book). Mantelero underlines the importance of such a right but points equally at the weaknesses of the GDPR in creating a solid right (limitation in scope and extensive exceptions). Key is his observation that the GDPR is only a first step in the regulatory development to frame big data in a data protection respectful way.

The chapter of Valerie Steeves and Milda Macenaite on 'Data Protection and Children's Online Privacy' is the best possible illustration of the legal wisdom that perfect regulation is often impossible. Often there is a plurality of possible choices that all have pros and cons. Steeves and Macenaite offer rich comparative materials that highlight some of the regulatory options. They discuss the US Children's Online Privacy Protection Act with its child-specific sector specific approach to children's privacy and compare this approach with the more general children's privacy approach in Canada and Australia. Interesting is their finding that the US regulation is more about parents than about children: 'the focus of the legislation is on parents' rights as opposed to children's rights: in the words of the Federal Trade Commission website, the 'primary goal is to place parents in control over what information is collected from their young children online'. Troubling is their observation that the laws in Canada and Australia are partly shaped by the US approach, including the bright line rule that under 13 parental control and consent is always asked for. Still there is a distinct regulatory approach, complemented by active policymaking by both the Canadian and Australian privacy commissioners to promote children's privacy issues. That regulatory effort by data protection bodies (national data protection authorities, Article 29 Working Party, ...) is also to be found in the EU. The specific provisions of the GDPR that relate to children are concisely situated within comparative and historical context. Their contribution ends with a beautiful reflection about the lack of individual assessment of youngsters in the American and EU laws and their reliance on bright line rules.

There is no better guidance about biometrics than the one offered by Els J. Kindt in her many writings on the topic. The contribution 'Biometric Data Processing is the legislator keeping up or just keeping up appearances?' contains an excellent overview of the many regulatory issues with this new technology, which is receiving more and more specific attention in recent law making. Kindt identifies many tensions with fundamental rights caused by the use of biometrics. This is followed by a technical discussion of the main biometrical relevant novelties in the GDPR. A simple question such as whether pictures taken by an amateur fall under these provisions seemingly gets no easy answer. Thorny questions about the collection of data, the (non-)use of templates and the central storage of biometrical data are avoided, squashing all hopes of fundamental rights lawyers to address the main threatening aspects of this technology. Kindt ends her contribution with a discussion of three outstanding issues (in the section 'legal politics') and a useful reminder of some of the legal obligations on the authorities and private parties to respect fundamental rights.

Max von Grafenstein in his contribution on 'Co-Regulation and the Competitive Advantage in the GDPR' discusses a topic closely related to a general discussion in law about self-regulation as an alternative of or complement to top-down control-based regulation, for instance, through laws. Companies increasingly make use of certification to demonstrate their good faith in the application of laws and regulations. The GDPR testified the importance of certification (and the linked activity of accreditation) in its Articles 42 and 43. Closer analysis reveals a complex system with roles for private certification bodies, national data protection authorities, the European Data Protection Board (EDPB) and the European Commission. The system is designed in such a way that by adding enforceable elements of control by data protection authorities, it waters down self-regulatory elements. In his detailed contribution, Von Grafenstein goes in depth into this regulatory tool (identified as a co-regulatory instrument rather than a self-regulatory instrument) that he situates in a regulatory dilemma about uncertainty and the need to leave openness to safeguard innovation. His conclusion is positive about the potential to 'solve' the dilemma between certainty in law and innovation. Under certain conditions co-regulatory instruments like certification can overcome the divide.

In the chapter on 'Automated Decision-making and Data Protection in Europe', Gianclaudio Malgieri examines the regulation of profiling algorithms and automated decision-making as omnipresent features of our data-driven society. Both the GDPR and Convention 108+ are now recognizing rights to receive/access meaningful information about logics and effects of automated decision-making processes and shield the individual against automated decision-making with additional safeguards. Perhaps the GDPR was too early for mature regulation and its innovations have been the object of many academic debates. Malgieri discusses these debates and the relevant guidance by the Article 29 Working Party. Clearly, not all outstanding issues are solved, but it is manifest that the risks of algorithms and automated decision-making are not ignored in the regulatory capitals of Europe.

A *Research Handbook on Privacy and Data Protection Law: Values, Norms and Global Politics* can mean several things, and would probably have another outlook in the hands of others. In the view of the editors of this Handbook, the current collection of contributions will be a good reference point for starters and experts in data protection and privacy law, policy, and related developments throughout the world.

PART I

GEOGRAPHICAL PERSPECTIVES

1. Privacy and data protection in Europe: Council of Europe's Convention 108+ and the European Union's GDPR

Cécile de Terwangne

I. INTRODUCTION

Two main texts deserve particular attention in Europe: Council of Europe's Convention 108, and the European Union (EU) General Data Protection Regulation (GDPR). The presentation and analysis of these texts is of great interest since EU Member States are bound by both. Furthermore, Convention 108, ratified by States both within and outside the Council of Europe, is in the process of becoming the main international legally binding instrument in the field of data protection. Its influence reaches far beyond European boundaries, making it worth discovering its provisions. A modernized version of Convention 108, known as Convention 108+, is currently available for signature and ratification. The EU GDPR also has a far-reaching geographical scope, and many actors will have to comply with it in different parts of the world. Both texts present in consequence a great interest for lawyers in Europe and abroad.

The following pages discuss them jointly. A joint presentation of Convention 108+ and GDPR has been considered preferable in order to avoid excessive repetitions, since their content is similar on many points. Divergences or specificities are of course clearly indicated. This chapter will first present a general overview of the European legal landscape (section II) before highlighting the fundamental rights dimension attributed in Europe to the issue of the protection of personal data (section III). Section III is dedicated to clarifying the main notions and the material and geographical scope of the European texts. Section IV presents the basic general principles of the data protection, whereas section V is devoted to the specific regime offering a higher protection to sensitive data. The remarkable list of data subjects' rights is presented in section VI, and the duties and obligations imposed to data controllers and processors are detailed in section VII. The rules to respect in case of transborder data flows outside European borders are examined in section VIII. A last section presents the specialized supervisory authorities put in place to monitor the respect of the whole protection regime, and to provide advice on these matters.

II. GENERAL SETTING

In Europe, two regional organizations have taken action in the field of data protection: the Council of Europe and the EU.

The **Council of Europe** adopted one of the first international texts on the subject on 28 January 1981: Convention 108 for the Protection of Individuals as Regards the Automatic

Processing of Personal Data. This Convention is the only legally binding text in the field with an international scope. All 47 member States of the Council of Europe have ratified it. This text has moreover the particularity of being open to signature for non-European States. At this stage,[1] it has been ratified by Argentina, Cabo Verde, Uruguay, Mauritius, Mexico, Morocco, Senegal and Tunisia, and Burkina Faso has also been invited to accede, which is the first stage before becoming party to the Convention.

As any international convention, the text contains high-level principles. It was further supplemented in 2001 by an Additional Protocol Regarding Supervisory Authorities and Transborder Data Flows (ETS No. 181).

A Convention committee (named T-PD) gives orientations to face the challenge of applying Convention 108 in an ever-moving reality. This committee has published recommendations about the application of the Convention in particular contexts such as the police sector,[2] insurance,[3] social security,[4] but also about the processing of medical data,[5] or statistics.[6]

In 2016, a modernizing process launched six years earlier to take account of the new technological and societal landscape lead to a substantive rewriting of the text.[7] The modernization notably melted the content of the original Convention and that of its mentioned Additional Protocol. Overall, it has brought the changes needed in our connected world to better balance the data subjects' rights and interests and those of the person or entity processing personal data about them. The Modernised Convention[8] was finally adopted by the Committee of Ministers of the Council of Europe on 18 May 2018, and opened for signature on 10 October 2018.[9] It has already been ratified by fifteen States Parties to Convention 108, including two non-European States (Mauritius and Uruguay) and signed by twenty-eight others.

The EU had found it necessary to adopt a set of more precise rules as regards data protection than those included in Convention 108. The latter left a margin of manoeuvre to the Parties that had brought divergences between national legislations, and such divergences inhibited the free flow of personal data through the EU.

A first attempt to harmonize European national legislations took place in 1995 with Directive 95/46/EC of 24 October 1995.[10] The adaptation of this text, 15 years later, to the

---

[1] November 2020.

[2] Recommendation No. R(87) 15, regulating the use of personal data in the police sector, 17 September 1987.

[3] Recommendation No. CM/Rec(2016)8 on the processing of personal health-related data for insurance purposes, including data resulting from genetic tests, 26 October 2016.

[4] Recommendation No. R(86) 1, on the protection of personal data for social security purposes, 23 January 1986.

[5] Recommendation CM/Rec(2019)2 on the protection of health-related data, 27 March 2019.

[6] Recommendation No. R(97) 18, on the protection of personal data collected and processed for statistical purposes, 30 September 1997.

[7] See the consolidated text of the modernisation proposals of Convention 108 for the Protection of Individuals with Regard to the Processing of Personal Data finalised by the CAHDATA, meeting of 15–16 June 2016.

[8] Modernised Convention for the Protection of Individuals with Regard to the Processing of Personal Data (Convention 108+).

[9] Protocol amending the Convention for the Protection of Individuals with regard to Automatic Processing of Personal Data, Council of Europe Treaty Series (CETS) No. 223, 10 October 2018.

[10] Directive 95/46/EC of the European Parliament and of the Council of 24 October 1995 on the protection of individuals with regard to the processing of personal data and on the free movement of such data [1995] OJ L281/31.

new connected reality that has brought 'a profound change of scale in terms of the role of personal data in our economies, societies and daily lives'[11] proved to be necessary and led to the adoption on 27 April 2016 of the GDPR.[12] The change from a directive to a regulation aimed at achieving a greater uniformization of the European legal landscape in the field of data protection. However, certain possibilities of disparities remained: for example, for data processing in the public sector[13] or to reconcile the right to the protection of personal data with the right to freedom of expression and information, including processing for journalistic purposes and the purposes of academic, artistic or literary expression.[14] [15] Besides this specific instrument, Article 8(1) of the Charter of Fundamental Rights of the EU provides that everyone has the right to the protection of personal data concerning him or her.[16] This Charter, legally binding since 2009, was the first regional catalogue of human rights that proclaimed the right to data protection. The two European data protection regimes are convergent. The Council of Europe's Convention contains high-level principles, while the EU GDPR is a set of detailed rules, but both texts have been elaborated having in mind a total compatibility to avoid that Parties having to comply with both texts would be submitted to conflicting requirements. Before presenting the main elements of this double European data protection regime, it is necessary to highlight what characterizes the European approach of this topic: its fundamental rights dimension.

III. THE PROTECTION OF PERSONAL DATA IN EUROPE: A FUNDAMENTAL RIGHTS APPROACH

In Europe, the right to data protection has been considered a fundamental right, primarily derived from the right to privacy and later recognized as an autonomous right in the EU Charter of Fundamental Rights. This approach differs from the one that considers data protec-

---

[11] The OECD Privacy Framework, 2013, Foreword.

[12] Regulation (EU) 2016/679 of the European Parliament and of the Council of 27 April 2016 on the protection of natural persons with regard to the processing of personal data and on the free movement of such data, and repealing Directive 95/46/EC (General Data Protection Regulation) [2016] OJ L119/1. Another text was adopted simultaneously, regarding data processing in the field of police and justice: Directive (EU) 2016/680 of the European Parliament and of the Council of 27 April 2016 on the protection of natural persons with regard to the processing of personal data by competent authorities for the purposes of the prevention, investigation, detection or prosecution of criminal offences or the execution of criminal penalties, and on the free movement of such data, and repealing Council Framework Decision 2008/977/JHA [2016] OJ L119/89. This text is not analysed in the present contribution.

[13] Art. 6(2) GDPR.

[14] Art. 85 GDPR.

[15] Cécile de Terwangne, Karen Rosier and Bénédicte Losdyck, 'Le règlement européen relatif à la protection des données à caractère personnel: quelles nouveautés ?', *Journal de droit européen*, 2017/8, 302.

[16] Art. 8 of EU Charter of Fundamental Rights states:
Protection of personal data: Art. 8(1) Everyone has the right to the protection of personal data concerning him or her. Art. 8(2) Such data must be processed fairly for specified purposes and on the basis of the consent of the person concerned or some other legitimate basis laid down by law. Everyone has the right of access to data which has been collected concerning him or her, and the right to have it rectified. Art. 8(3) Compliance with these rules shall be subject to control by an independent authority.

tion concerns a matter of consumer protection. Autonomy, in the sense here of informational self-determination, and dignity are the main values underlying the legal protection of individuals as regards the processing of their personal data. They should help to re-balance the relationship between humans, on the one hand, and machines or algorithms, on the other. The intention is obviously not to stop progress, but to accompany it and surround it.

III.1 Data Protection as a Right to Informational Self-determination

At the level of the Council of Europe, it has been stated that a major objective of Convention 108 is 'to put individuals in a position to know about, to understand and to control the processing of their personal data by others. Accordingly, the Preamble expressly refers to the right to personal autonomy and the right to control one's personal data, which stems in particular from the right to privacy'.[17] The revised version of the Preamble of Convention 108 affirms that:

> it is necessary to secure the human dignity and protection of the human rights and fundamental freedoms of every individual and, given the diversification, intensification and globalization of data processing and personal data flows, personal autonomy based on a person's right to control of his or her personal data and the processing of such data.[18]

Convention 108 is about data protection notably as a right of control guaranteed to the individuals based on his or her personal autonomy or personal self-determination.[19] Data protection is indeed here an offshoot of the right to privacy taken in this dimension of personal autonomy rather than in the sense of a confidentiality requirement traditionally attached to the notion of privacy. The right to data protection is linked to a right to 'informational self-determination' that has been recognized as part of the right to privacy.[20]

At EU level, while Directive 95/46/EC stated that '[i]n accordance with this Directive, Member States shall protect the fundamental rights and freedoms of natural persons, and in

---

[17] Explanatory Report to the Protocol amending the Convention for the Protection of Individuals with regard to Automatic Processing of Personal Data, para. 10 (hereafter Explanatory Report).

[18] Modernised Convention 108, Preamble.

[19] For the explicit recognition of a *right* to self-determination or to personal autonomy contained in the right to respect for private life under Art. 8, see: *Evans v. UK* App no 6339/05 (ECHR, 10 April 2007); *Tysiac v. Poland* App no 5410/03 (ECHR, 20 March 2007); *Daroczy v. Hungary* App no 44378/05 (ECHR, 1 July 2008); *Satakunnan Markkinapörssi oy and Satamedia oy v. Finland* App no 931/13 (ECHR, 27 June 2017).

[20] *Satakunnan Markkinapörssi oy and Satamedia oy*, para. 137:

> [...] Article 8 of the Convention thus provides for the right to a form of informational self-determination, allowing individuals to rely on their right to privacy as regards data which, albeit neutral, are collected, processed and disseminated collectively and in such a form or manner that their Article 8 rights may be engaged.

It is worth highlighting here that lessons deriving from the European Court of Human Rights case-law present a great interest also to enlighten the understanding of Arts 7 and 8 of the European Union Charter of Fundamental rights (providing the right to privacy and the right to data protection). Art 52.3 of this Charter states:

> In so far as this Charter contains rights which correspond to rights guaranteed by the Convention for the Protection of Human Rights and Fundamental Freedoms, the meaning and scope of those rights shall be the same as those laid down by the said Convention.

particular their right to privacy with respect to the processing of personal data',[21] the GDPR no longer mentions the right to privacy, but refers to the right to data protection.[22] Following its first recital: 'The protection of natural persons in relation to the processing of personal data is a fundamental right'.

III.2 Data Protection and Human Dignity

Convention 108 – in its original version of 1981 – does not mention the protection of human dignity. The evocation of human dignity in the new Preamble has been introduced as a reminder of the fact that human beings are subjects, and should not be reduced to mere objects of surveillance and control.[23] It follows from the idea that human beings should not be subjected to a machine, but that, instead, machines should be at their service and shall not undermine individuals' core values. This proclamation of the fundamental value of dignity as underlying data protection is without doubt necessary in view of certain uses of technology. Information systems are increasingly carrying out comprehensive monitoring of individuals and whole populations, creating systems based on people's transparent behaviour, which may be contrary to human dignity. Similarly, when profiling leads to deriving information without the knowledge of data subjects in order to take all sorts of decisions concerning them, it can seriously impair the dignity of the profiled persons. The GDPR does not expressly mention human dignity, but in the very first recitals of the text the EU legislator included a statement indirectly evocating this value and the idea that data processing should be at the service of human beings: 'The processing of personal data should be designed to serve mankind'.[24]

IV. DEFINITIONS AND SCOPE OF EUROPEAN DATA PROTECTION LEGISLATIONS: KEY ELEMENTS

IV.1 Definition of Personal Data

'Personal data' means 'any information relating to an identified or identifiable individual ("data subject")'.[25] Article 4(1) of the GDPR specifies that:

> an identifiable natural person is one who can be identified, directly or indirectly, in particular by reference to an identifier such as a name, an identification number, location data, an online identifier or to one or more factors specific to the physical, physiological, genetic, mental, economic, cultural or social identity of that natural person.[26]

---

[21] Art. 1(1) of Directive 95/46/EC.

[22] Art. 1(2) GDPR: 'This Regulation protects fundamental rights and freedoms of natural persons and in particular their right to the protection of personal data'.

[23] Explanatory Report, para. 10.

[24] Recital 4 GDPR.

[25] Art. 2(a) Convention 108; Art. 4(1) GDPR (which mentions 'natural person' instead of 'individual').

[26] On the notion of personal data within the EU, see also: Article 29 Working Party, *Opinion 4/2007 on the concept of personal data*, WP 136, 20 June 2007; Case C-434/16 *Peter Nowak v. Data protection Commissioner* [2017]; Case C-582/14 *Breyer v. Germany* [2016].

The Explanatory Report of Convention 108+ provides that an individual shall not be regarded as 'identifiable' if his or her identification requires unreasonable time, effort or means.[27] Recital 26 of GDPR goes in the same direction. Both texts specify that to determine whether somebody is identifiable account should be taken of the available technology at the time of the processing and technological developments,[28] since technological and other developments may change what qualifies as 'unreasonable' time, effort or means.[29] In addition – and this new element is particularly important in the current context – 'identifiable' does not only refer to the individual's civil identity, but also to whatever may allow singling out somebody,[30] or distinguish one person amongst others, such as an identification number, geolocation data, an IP address,[31] etc. This singling out may occur by referring to a person, but also to an access point (computer, mobile phone, connected objects, etc): individualization is possible both in relation to a person and to equipment.[32]

IV.2 Definition of Data Processing

Convention 108 originally relied on the concept of 'automated data file', which had a dated technological connotation. The term was eventually abandoned and replaced in the modernised Convention by terminology used by Directive 95/46/EC. The concept of 'data processing' appears thus in Convention 108+. Under its Article 2(c), data processing means:

> any operation or set of operations which is performed upon personal data, such as the collection, storage, preservation, alteration, retrieval, disclosure, making available, erasure, or destruction of, or the carrying out of logical and/or arithmetical operations on such data; where automated processing is not used, data processing means an operation or set of operations performed upon personal data within a structured set of such data which are accessible or retrievable according to specific criteria.

This definition presents a noticeable difference with the prior text: it includes data processing not involving any automated means, the so-called 'manual processing'. Indeed, it seems appropriate to include such processing under the scope of protection, especially if the Convention is to be adopted by countries where manual processing operations are still numerous.

The revised Convention is in line with the definition of the GDPR, which states that processing means:

> any operation or set of operations which is performed on personal data or on sets of personal data, whether or not by automated means, such as collection, recording, organisation, structuring, storage, adaptation or alteration, retrieval, consultation, use, disclosure by transmission, dissemination or otherwise making available, alignment or combination, restriction, erasure or destruction.[33]

---

27 Explanatory Report, para. 17.

28 Recital 26 GDPR.

29 Explanatory Report of Convention 108, para. 17. See also: Article 29 Working Party, *Opinion 05/2014 on anonymisation techniques*, WP 216, 10 April 2014.

30 Recital 26 GDPR; Explanatory Report of Convention 108, para 18: 'The notion of 'identifiable' does not only refer to the individual's civil or legal identity as such, but also to what may allow to "individualise" or single out (and thus allow to treat differently) one person from others'.

31 Frederik J Zuiderveen Borgesius, 'The Breyer Case of the Court of Justice of the European Union: IP Addresses and the Personal Data Definition', *EDPL*, 2017/1.

32 Explanatory Report of Convention 108, para. 18; Recital 26 GDPR.

33 Art. 4(2) GDPR.

As mentioned earlier, it was considered highly desirable that both texts be coherent, not to have EU Member States subject to contradictory rules or heterogenous notions.

IV.3 Definition of the Main Actors: Controller and Processor

The main actors are named controller and processor in Convention 108+ and the GDPR. The definitions of these actors are quite similar in both texts.

Regarding the controller, Convention 108+ refers to the person or body having decision-making power over the processing of personal data,[34] whether this power derives from a legal designation or from factual circumstances.[35] According to Article 4(7) of the GDPR, the:

> 'controller' is the natural or legal person, public authority, agency or other body which, alone or jointly with others, determines the purposes and means of the processing of personal data; where the purposes and means of such processing are determined by EU or Member State law, the controller or the specific criteria for its nomination may be provided for by Union or Member State law.

As to the notion of 'processor', it receives a quasi-identical definition in both texts and means a natural or legal person, public authority, agency or other body which processes personal data on behalf of the controller.[36]

IV.4 Scope of the Instruments

The two analysed texts apply to the processing of personal data wholly or partly by automated means. If no automated means are used, they still apply where the data are part of a structured set or are to become part of such a structured set.[37]

In its 1981 version, Convention 108 states that its purpose is to offer protection to personal data 'in the territory of each Party for every individual, whatever his nationality or residence' (Art. 1). The 2018 version opted for a criterion different than territory. The protection will apply on the basis of the 'jurisdiction' of the Parties. The revised Article 3 provides that 'Each Party undertakes to apply this Convention to data processing subject to its jurisdiction in the public and private sectors, thereby securing every individual's' right to protection of his or her personal data'. Convention 108+ applies thus when data processing is carried out within the jurisdiction of a Party, be it in the public or private sector. All data processing in the public sector falls directly within the jurisdiction of the Party, including data processing carried out for national security purposes. This all-encompassing scope of Convention 108+ is wider than that of GDPR.[38] Data processing carried out in the private sector falls within the jurisdiction

---

[34] Art. 2(d) of the revised Convention: '"Controller" means the natural or legal person, public authority, service, agency or any other body which, alone or jointly with others, has the decision-making power with respect to data processing'.

[35] Explanatory Report, para. 22.

[36] Art. 2(f) of the revised Convention 108; Art. 4(8) GDPR.

[37] Article 2(1) GDPR; Art. 3(1) of the revised Convention 108.

[38] See the restriction of GDPR scope in its Art. 2(2)(a), (b) and (d): the GDPR applies neither to the processing of personal data in the course of activities which fall outside the scope of Union law, nor to processing linked to the EU common foreign and security policy, nor to processing by competent authorities for the purposes of the prevention, investigation, detection or prosecution of criminal offences or the

of a Party when there is a sufficient connection with the territory of that Party. It is left to the Party to determine the criteria of this connection. For instance, there could be a sufficient link if the controller is established within the territory of that Party.

The GDPR kept, for the determination of its territorial scope, a criterion from Directive 95/46/EC that referred to processing in the context of the activities of the establishment of the controller, but extending this criterion to cover also the establishment of the processor. The GDPR thus applies to the processing of personal data in the context of the activities of an establishment in the EU of a controller or a processor, regardless of whether the processing itself takes place in the EU or not.[39] What is important to trigger the GDPR applicability is that data are processed in the framework of the activities of an establishment which is in the territory of the EU. The location of processing activities or the place of storage of the data do not matter.

The GDPR also applies in certain cases where personal data are processed by a controller or a processor not established in the EU, thus extending the territorial scope of the GDPR potentially far beyond European borders.

First,[40] the EU instrument applies when the processing activities relate to the offering of goods or services – for free or against payment – to data subjects in the EU. To determine whether a controller or processor is offering goods or services to data subjects who are in the EU, the mere accessibility of their website in the Union is not sufficient; however, 'factors such as the use of a language or a currency generally used in one or more Member States with the possibility of ordering goods and services in that other language, [...] may make it apparent that the controller envisages offering goods or services to data subjects in the Union'.[41]

Secondly, the GDPR also applies when the processing of data relates to the monitoring of the data subjects' behaviour (e.g., the tracking of their activities on the Internet) in so far as their behaviour takes place within the EU.[42]

IV.4.1 Limitation of the scope: Activities exclusively for personal purposes

In its 1981 version, Convention 108 had left it open to States Parties to exclude certain data processing operations from its scope. This was changed in the modernized version of the Convention, which excludes from its scope of application any 'data processing carried out by an individual in the course of purely personal or household activities'.[43] The GDPR provides a scope limitation in almost the same terms.[44] The justification of this exclusion lies in that it aims 'at avoiding the imposition of unreasonable obligations on data processing carried out by individuals in their private sphere for activities relating to the exercise of their private life',[45] as well as on the supposed low level of risk that such processing activities represent.

---

execution of criminal penalties, including the safeguarding against and the prevention of threats to public security. In this latter case, Directive (EU) 2016/680 (cited in note 12 *supra*) applies instead of GDPR.

[39] Art. 3(1) GDPR.

[40] Art. 3(2)(a) GDPR. See also Recital 23.

[41] Recital 23 GDPR.

[42] Art. 3(2)(b) GDPR. See also Recital 24.

[43] Art. 3(2) of the revised Convention.

[44] Art. 2(2)(c) GDPR: 'This Regulation does not apply to the processing of personal data by a natural person in the course of a purely personal or household activity.'

[45] Explanatory Report, para. 27.

The scope of this limitation, however, must take into account the major changes in the delimitation of public and private spheres on the Internet. As pointed out by Douwe Korff, reflecting on whether a middle way should be found:

> [t]he overall problem is that the granting of a full exemption from data protection requirements to anyone who uploads materials to the Internet as a private individual would lead to easy circumvention of the rules and, in an age of user-generated content, would fundamentally undermine data protection (and privacy) itself; yet the full imposition of the law to all such individuals would seem excessive and, because of the sheer numbers, would be largely unenforceable.[46]

The personal sphere can be defined according to various criteria. It is the nature of the circle of recipients of the data that matters: '[T]he private sphere encompasses notably the family, a restricted circle of friends or a circle which is limited in its size and based on a personal relationship or a particular relation of trust.'[47]

Recital 18 of the GDPR notes that a purely personal activity has no connection with a professional or commercial activity.[48] As examples of personal activities, it mentions correspondence and the holding of addresses, or social networking and other online activities undertaken within that context.

The Court of Justice of the EU (CJEU) has stated that the personal or household limitation should not apply when data are made available to an undetermined number of people, as it is the case for publication on the Internet.[49] It has interpreted strictly this limitation of the scope of application: if the personal or household activity extends – even only partially – to the public space (like a private camera in a house filming part of the street), the limitation will not apply.[50]

IV.4.2 Other limitations of the scope

The GDPR foresees certain additional limitations of its scope.[51] It does not apply to the processing of personal data related to activities falling outside the scope of EU law, such as activities concerning national security. Nor does it apply to the processing of personal data by the Member States when carrying out activities in relation to the EU's Common Foreign and Security Policy (CFSP). It does not apply either to processing activities for the purposes of the prevention, investigation, detection or prosecution of criminal offences or the execution of criminal penalties by 'competent authorities'.[52]

---

[46] Douwe Korff, *New challenges to data protection study - Working Paper No. 2: Data protection laws in the EU: The difficulties in meeting the challenges posed by global social and technical developments*, European Commission Directorate-General Justice, Freedom and Security Report (2010).

[47] Explanatory Report, para. 27 *in fine*.

[48] Recital 18 GDPR.

[49] Case C-101-01 *Lindqvist* [2003], paras 46–47; Case C-73/07 *Satamedia* [2008].

[50] Case C-212/13 *František Ryneš* [2014].

[51] Art 2(2)(a), b) and d) GDPR; Recital 16 GDPR.

[52] The latter processing activities fall under the scope of directive (UE) 2016/680 of the European Parliament and of the Council of 27 April 2016 on the protection of natural persons with regard to the processing of personal data by competent authorities for the purposes of the prevention, investigation, detection or prosecution of criminal offences or the execution of criminal penalties, and on the free movement of such data, and repealing Council Framework Decision 2008/977/JHA.

V. BASIC PRINCIPLES

The fundamental principles of data protection have not changed for several decades. The principles laid down in the 1981 version of Convention 108 and in Directive 95/46/EC have demonstrated their capacity to stand the test of time. They have proved to be generally appropriate and efficient also in evolving technological and societal contexts. Thus, they were maintained both in Convention 108+ and in the GDPR, which only brought adjustments and complements where necessary.

V.1 Principle of Proportionality

One noticeable 'new principle' was added in Convention 108+: the principle of proportionality. According to this principle, data processing should not constitute a disproportionate interference with the data subject's or society's interests in light of the controller's interest in processing the data.

The case-law of the European Court of Human Rights (ECtHR) requires that a fair balance between public and private interests at stake be taken into account in the implementation of data processing. In the case *S. and Marper*,[53] for instance, the Court emphasized that data processing must be proportionate, that is to say, appropriate in relation to the legitimate aims pursued and necessary in the sense that there are no other appropriate and less intrusive measures with regard to the interests, rights and freedoms of data subjects or society. Moreover, it should not lead to a disproportionate interference with these individual or collective interests in relation to the benefits expected from the controller.

The EU Court of Justice has also ruled[54] that to be admissible a legal obligation to process personal data (*in casu*, to publish personal data on the beneficiaries of EU agricultural funds) must respect the principle of proportionality (which lies in the requirement for a legitimate purpose, see hereunder). The Court has checked the respect of this principle of proportionality in several cases,[55] one of the most famous being the *Digital Rights Ireland* case,[56] where the Court also found that the principle had not been respected.

In the original version of Convention 108, only the proportionality of the data collected and processed was evoked, but not that of the processing itself. It thus appeared imperative to the modernisers of the Convention to incorporate an explicit requirement of proportionality of data processing at all stages. This can serve as a bulwark against risks associated to technical developments (including unexpected processing abounding on the Internet) and to the generalized reliance on data subjects' consent to process their data. The balancing of interests and verification of the achieved balance provides a welcome backup when one considers the defects often attached to inappropriate reliance on consent (insufficient information given to the data subject, consent inferred from the non-change of the default settings, etc.).

As a result, Article 5(1) of Convention 108+ states: 'Data processing shall be proportionate in relation to the legitimate purpose pursued and reflect at all stages of the processing a fair

[53] *S and Marper v. UK*, App no 30562/04, 30566/04 (ECHR, 4 December 2008).

[54] Joined cases C-92/09 and 93/09 *Volker and Markus Schecke GbR and Hartmut Eifert v. Land Hessen* [2010], paras 86 and 89.

[55] All those cases were based on Directive 95/46/EC mentioned *supra*.

[56] Joined cases C-293/12 and C-594/12 *Digital Rights Ireland* [2014].

balance between all interests concerned, whether public or private, and the rights and freedoms at stake.'

V.2 Lawfulness, Fairness and Transparency Principle

Personal data is to be processed lawfully, fairly and in a transparent manner.[57]

Data processing must be lawful to the effect that it respects all applicable legal requirements (even outside the scope of data protection regulation, such as, e.g., the obligation of professional secrecy, if applicable).

The principle of lawful processing is however also understood as requiring the consent of the data subject or another legitimate ground provided in the data protection legislation. Article 6 of the GDPR, dealing with such legitimate grounds for processing, is entitled 'Lawfulness of processing', instead of 'Criteria for making data processing legitimate' as in Directive 95/46/EC. It lists all the grounds which can render processing personal data admissible as lawful. This, however, does not free processing from needing to be compliant also with the other aspects of the lawfulness requirement.[58]

The principle of fair processing[59] implies that personal data shall not be obtained nor otherwise processed through unfair means, by deception or without the data subject knowing.[60] Nor should personal data be processed in ways which would be completely unexpected or unforeseeable to the data subject.

The GDPR explicitly includes the transparency principle together with the requirement that data be processed lawfully and fairly, even though some commentators had attached till now such a transparency requirement to the notion of fairness.[61] This transparency principle is explained in a long Recital 39 which starts by clarifying that it 'should be transparent to natural persons that personal data concerning them are collected, used, consulted or otherwise processed'. The recital specifies that natural persons should be made aware of risks and safeguards in relation to the processing of their personal data. The transparency principle is further developed in Article 8 of Convention 108+ and in Articles 12–14 of the GDPR.

V.3 Purpose Limitation Principle

Presented for 35 years as the true cornerstone of data protection and as a prerequisite for almost all other fundamental requirements, the purpose limitation principle[62] requires data to be collected for specified, explicit and legitimate purposes (the 'purpose specification' dimension),[63] and not further processed in a manner that is incompatible with those purposes

---

[57] Art. 5(3) and 5(4)(a) revised Convention 108; Art. 5(1)(a) GDPR.

[58] *Contra*, Jef Ausloos, 'Giving meaning to Lawfulness under the GDPR', Centre for IT and IP (CITIP) Blog, 2 May 2017.

[59] Art 5(4)(a) of the revised Convention 108; Art. 5(1)(a) GDPR.

[60] See for a case of unfair processing: *KH and others v. Slovakia,* App no 32881/04 (ECHR, 28 April 2009).

[61] 'Fair processing means transparency of processing, especially vis-à-vis data subjects.' (European Union Agency for Fundamental Right (FRA), European Court of human rights, Council of Europe, *Handbook on European data protection law,* 2014, https://rm.coe.int/16806b294a, p. 76).

[62] Art. 5(4)(b) of the revised Convention 108; Art. 5(1)(b) GDPR.

[63] Article 29 Working Party, *Opinion 03/2013 on purpose limitation*, WP 203, 2 April 2013, 11–12.

(the 'compatible use' dimension).[64] The purposes for which the processing of personal data is to occur should be determined from the very beginning, when personal data are collected. The processing of personal data for undefined or unlimited purposes is unlawful, since it does not enable delimiting precisely the scope of the processing. The purposes of data processing must also be unambiguous, clearly expressed, and never kept hidden.[65]

Finally, the purposes must be legitimate and proportionate, which means that they shall not entail a disproportionate interference with the rights, freedoms and interests at stake in the name of the interests of the data controller.[66] The Explanatory Report of Convention 108+ notes:

> What is considered a legitimate purpose depends on the circumstances as the objective is to ensure that a balancing of all rights, freedoms and interests at stake is made in each instance; the right to the protection of personal data on the one hand, and the protection of other rights on the other hand, as, for example, between the interests of the data subject and the interests of the controller or of society.[67]

In all cases, data processing serving an unlawful purpose (that is contrary to the law) cannot be considered to be based on a legitimate purpose.[68]

The second dimension of the purpose limitation principle implies that one may perform on these data all the operations that can be considered to be compatible with the initial purposes. This notion of 'compatible' processing of data has raised numerous questions in practice. The EU legislator and the modernizers of Convention 108 considered it necessary to clarify the requirement. They thus offered a series of criteria allowing to determine whether the processing for a purpose other than that for which the personal data have been collected is to be considered as compatible with this initial purpose.[69] Account should be taken of the possible link between both purposes, of the context in which the personal data have been collected, in particular regarding the relationship between data subjects and the controller, of the nature of the personal data, ordinary or sensitive, of the possible consequences of the intended further processing for data subjects, and of the existence of appropriate safeguards.[70]

'Further processing for archiving purposes in the public interest, scientific or historical research purposes or statistical purposes'[71] is considered as compatible – and thus admissible – if subject to appropriate safeguards. A clarification of what is meant by scientific and historical research purposes and by statistical purposes can be found in Recitals 159, 160 and 162 of the GDPR, on the one hand, and in a Recommendation of the Council of Europe, on the other hand.[72]

---

[64] *Ibid.*, 12–13.

[65] *Ibid.*, 39.

[66] Marie-Hélène Boulanger et al., 'La protection des données à caractère personnel en droit communautaire', *Journal des Tribunaux droit européen* [1997] 41.

[67] Explanatory Report of Convention 108+, para. 48.

[68] Article 29 Working Party, WP 203 (n 63).

[69] Art. 6(4) GDPR; Explanatory Report of Convention 108+, para. 49. This list is based on the one elaborated by the Article 29 Working Party (see Opinion 3/2013 WP 203, 40).

[70] See also Recital 50 GDPR.

[71] Art. 5(4)(b) Convention 108; Art. 5(1)(b) GDPR.

[72] Explanatory Memorandum to Recommendation No. R (97) 18 of the Committee of Ministers to Member States, 30 September 1997, concerning the protection of personal data collected and processed for statistical purposes, §§ 11 and 14 and Appendix, para. 1.

Finally, the processing of personal data for a purpose other than that for which it had been collected is allowed in certain circumstances even if the new purpose is not compatible with the first one. The GDPR allows it in two cases: if the data subject consents to the new incompatible purpose, or if the processing is based on a Union or Member State law.[73]

V.4 Minimization and Quality of Data

According to the data minimization principle, personal data undergoing processing must be adequate, relevant and not excessive (or limited to what is necessary[74]) in relation to the purposes for which they are processed.[75] The data minimization principle requires in particular that personal data should only be processed if the purposes cannot reasonably be fulfilled by other means.[76] Furthermore, the 'not excessive' or 'limited to what is necessary' criterion not only refers to the quantity, but also to the quality of personal data. It is thus clear that one may not process an excessively large number of data (e.g., asking an employee his complete medical file to assess their capacity to work). But one may not process a single data either if this would entail a disproportionate interference in the data subject's rights and interests (e.g., collecting information about private drugs consumption from a job applicant).[77]

The accuracy principle requires that data be accurate and, where necessary, kept up to date.[78] All inaccurate data should be rectified or erased. The controller must take every reasonable step to ensure respect of the accuracy principle. The GDPR clarifies that any requested rectification must be done without delay.

The storage limitation principle prohibits storing personal data in a form that permits identification of data subjects beyond the time necessary to achieve the purposes of processing.[79] Controllers are invited to establish time limits for erasure or for a periodic review.[80] This would ensure that the personal data are not kept longer than necessary. Article 25 GDPR is to be taken into account here since it mandates that controllers implement appropriate technical and organizational measures for ensuring notably that, by default, the legitimate period of storage of personal data be respected. Such measures could be expiry dates determined for each category of personal data.

Besides, the storage limitation principle admits storage of personal data for longer periods if for archiving purposes in the public interest, scientific or historical research purposes or statistical purposes and subject to implementation of appropriate technical and organizational measures in order to safeguard the rights and freedoms of the data subject.

---

[73] Art. 6(4) GDPR.
[74] Terms of Art. 5(1)(c) GDPR.
[75] Art. 5(4)(c) Convention 108+.
[76] Explanatory report, para. 52; Recital 39 GDPR.
[77] In this way, see the explanation given for the notion of 'excessive' data in the Explanatory Report, para. 52.
[78] Art. 5(4)(d) revised Convention 108; Art. 5(1)(d) GDPR.
[79] Art. 5(4)(e) revised Convention 108; Art. 5(1)(e) GDPR.
[80] Recital 39 GDPR.

V.5 Security – Data Breaches

In the GDPR the security requirement appears in the list of the basic data protection principles under the title of 'integrity and confidentiality' principle.[81] Besides, in both the GDPR and Convention 108+, the security requirement is developed in specific provisions.[82] While the security requirement has been provided since the emergence of data protection legislation, it is especially crucial today. Cybercrime (including hacking, identity theft, computer fraud, extortion, phishing, virus, malwares, and so on) has increased to staggering levels.[83] In response to these security concerns, both European legal texts require that personal data be processed in a manner that ensures their appropriate security, 'including protection against unauthorised or unlawful processing and against accidental loss, destruction or damage, using appropriate technical or organisational measures'.[84]

This security duty includes, and this is new compared to previous texts (Directive 95/46/EC and the initial version of Convention 108), the requirement to notify personal data breaches to the supervisory authority and in certain cases to the data subjects too. An additional paragraph has been added to Article 7 of Convention 108+ on the security of data. It concerns those security problems known as 'data breaches'. It provides that the controller must notify, without undue delay, at least the supervisory authorities of those data breaches which may seriously interfere with the rights and fundamental freedoms of data subjects. Article 33.1 of the GDPR is slightly more precise, as it states that:

> In the case of a personal data breach, the controller shall without undue delay and, where feasible, not later than 72 hours after having become aware of it, notify the personal data breach to the supervisory authority competent [...], unless the personal data breach is unlikely to result in a risk to the rights and freedoms of natural persons.[85]

Illegal access to personal data falls within the scope of this obligation, as well as situations in which personal data has been lost (e.g., on CD-ROMs, USB sticks or other portable devices), or communicated to third parties in breach of the purpose principle. A threshold is set to trigger the notification obligation, corresponding in Convention 108+ to a serious interference with the rights and freedoms of the data subject, and in the GDPR to a potential risk to the rights and freedoms of natural persons. The aim is not to overburden data controllers, nor to drown supervisory authorities with trivial messages that would blunt the alert function. If the personal data breach is likely to result in a high risk to the rights and freedoms of natural persons, the controller must communicate it to the data subject in addition to the notification to the supervisory authority.[86]

---

81 Art. 5(1)(f) GDPR.

82 Art. 7 revised Convention 108; A whole section (Section 2. Security of personal data) of Chapter IV dedicated to controllers and processors develops this security duty: Arts 32–34 GDPR.

83 European Commission, *Joint Communication to the European Parliament and the Council: Resilience, Deterrence and Defence: Building strong cybersecurity for the EU*, JOIN(2017) 450 final, 13 September 2017; McAfee & Centre for Strategic and International Studies, *Net losses: Estimating the global cost of cybercrime*, 2014; Europol, *Serious and organised crime threat assessment*, 2017.

84 Art. 5(1)(f) GDPR.

85 See also: Céline van Waesberge, and Stéphanie De Smedt, 'Cybersecurity and Data Breach Notification Obligations Under the Current and Future Legislative Framework', *EDPL*, 2016/3.

86 Art. 34 GDPR. See also Explanatory report, para. 66.

V.6 Accountability Principle

The last principle of the European data protection regime is the accountability principle according to which controllers are not only responsible for ensuring compliance with all the legal requirements, but they must also be in a position to demonstrate that they have taken all appropriate measures and that the processing is compliant with the applicable legal rules.[87] Accountability has been strengthened in the GDPR and in the new version of Convention 108. Both texts, in compensation, have reduced the existing notification and approval procedures in order to remove needlessly burdensome bureaucracy on data controllers.

The obligations linked to the accountability principle are further developed below, in the section about the duties of the actors.

VI. SENSITIVE DATA

Certain categories of data are recognized as deserving greater protection since the processing of this data is linked to an increased risk of harm for individuals. It is mainly the risk of illegal or arbitrary discrimination that is at stake, or of injury to an individual's dignity or physical integrity, as well as the risk of affecting the most intimate sphere of individuals or where processing of data could affect the presumption of innocence.

The new Article 6(1) of Convention 108+ provides the following:

> The processing of:
> - genetic data;
> - personal data concerning offences, criminal convictions and related security measures;
> - biometric data uniquely identifying a person;
> - personal data for the information they reveal relating to racial origin, political opinions, trade-union membership, religious or other beliefs, health or sexual life shall only be allowed where the applicable law provides appropriate safeguards, complementing those of the present Convention.

The major difference compared to the text of 1981 lies in the fact that without sacrificing the drawing of a predetermined list, it is proposed to take into account the context of use of data. Some data follow the pattern of 1981: they are considered sensitive in all circumstances and simply because they are subject to processing, regardless of its purpose, the more protective regime will be applicable (i.e., genetic data[88] and personal data concerning offences, criminal convictions and related security measures). However, for other categories of data the new text presents a list of data identified as sensitive but triggering the protection regime only if it is the

---

[87] Art. 10, § 1 revised Convention 108; Art. 5(2) and 24 GDPR. The accountability principle had already been mentioned in the very first international text on data protection: the OECD Guidelines of 22 September 1980, article 14. See also Article 29 Working Party, *Opinion 3/2010 on the principle of accountability*, WP 173, 13 July 2010.

[88] In the *S and Marper* case, para. 75, the ECtHR states that genetic data raise particular concern with regard to the protection of privacy. DNA profiles contain a significant amount of unique and irrefutable personal data that allow authorities to go beyond a neutral identification (to search the genetic relationships between individuals, for instance). Moreover, genetic data can reveal things the individual wishes not to know.

sensitive element of the data that is specifically sought and processed. Biometric data appears now in the list but is to be considered as sensitive only when it is processed for identifying an individual.[89]

It should be noted that the new text of Convention 108+ brings some specification about the 'appropriate safeguards' that States must take to allow sensitive data to be processed. These safeguards are already mentioned in the current Article 6 of the Convention, but nothing was added to clarify them. This time, two clarifications are made:[90] The appropriate safeguards must come in addition to the safeguards put in place by the Convention; and the appropriate safeguards are those likely to prevent the serious risk that the processing of sensitive data presents as regards the interests and rights of the data subject, notably the risk of discrimination. The Explanatory Report adds that appropriate safeguards must be adapted to the risks at stake and to the interests, rights and freedoms needing protection. Examples of appropriate safeguards are:

> alone or cumulatively, the data subject's explicit consent, a law covering the intended purpose and means of the processing or indicating the exceptional cases where processing such data would be permitted, a professional secrecy obligation, measures following a risk analysis, a particular and qualified organisational or technical security measure (data encryption for example).[91]

The GDPR also presents a list of categories of data to be considered as sensitive and deserving higher protection. This list is nearly identical to the one of Convention 108: sensitive data are 'personal data revealing racial or ethnic origin, political opinions, religious or philosophical beliefs, or trade union membership, and the processing of genetic data, biometric data for the purpose of uniquely identifying a natural person, data concerning health or data concerning a natural person's sex life or sexual orientation'.[92] The GDPR addresses separately 'personal data relating to criminal convictions and offences or related security measures'. Their higher protection is provided, in a separate provision but also linked to the higher risk such data present, notably a risk of discrimination.[93] The processing of all these categories of data is prohibited except in the circumstances listed in GDPR provisions.[94]

VII. RIGHTS OF THE DATA SUBJECT

Rights have been recognized by the Council of Europe to data subjects since 1981, such as the right of access to data, the right to rectify or erase them and the right to remedy (Art. 8, b, c, and d of the Convention 108). These rights are strengthened in the modernized text of the Convention while new ones complete the list of safeguards offered to data subjects. As for GDPR, it offers the most elaborate catalogue of rights among data protection legal instru-

---

[89] Catherine Jasserand, 'Legal nature of biometric data: From 'generic' personal data to sensitive data', *EDPL*, 2016/3; Els Kindt, *Privacy and Data Protection Issues of Biometric Applications* (Springer 2013).

[90] Art. 6(2) revised Convention 108.

[91] Explanatory Report, para. 56.

[92] Art. 9 GDPR.

[93] Art. 10 GDPR.

[94] Arts 9(2) and 10 GDPR.

ments, in line with the rights listed in the new Article 8 of the Convention, but deeply further developed.

These rights are presented in the paragraphs below, following the order of Article 8 of Convention 108+. This order aims at highlighting the values linked to these rights: at first human dignity (machines cannot dominate human beings) and then autonomy, that implies individuals must know and understand what is being done with the data about them, by whom and for which purpose, and that implies the right to object, to rectify and to erase. In case of difficulties in exercising these rights, a right to remedy is granted to data subjects. The GDPR adds a new right to this list: the right to data portability.[95]

The right to receive information from the controller about the processing of personal data will be evoked *infra* under the section devoted to the controllers' duties. These rights are not absolute. Exceptions are admitted for each of them. In both texts, a provision is specially dedicated to the exemptions that Parties have the possibility to adopt as regards the main provisions on data subject rights of the Convention[96] and of the GDPR.[97] To be admissible these exemptions must be provided for by law and must constitute a necessary measure in a democratic society for the protection of certain public or private interests.

VII.1 Right not to be Subject to an Automated Decision

It appeared imperative to the reviewers of Convention 108 to guarantee to any person the right 'not to be subject to a decision significantly affecting him or her, based solely on an automated processing of data without having his or her views taken into consideration'[98]. Presented now as the first right of the data subject, this right ensues from the will that a human being be not entirely subject to a machine. It is not desirable that a decision imposed on a person depends on the sole findings of a machine. This right is the expression of the pre-eminence to be given to human dignity.

The right was already present in Directive 95/56/EC[99] and it appears also in Article 22 of the GDPR, which states in similar terms: 'The data subject shall have the right not to be subject to a decision based solely on automated processing, including profiling, which produces legal effects concerning him or her or similarly significantly affects him or her.' Automated decisions are admitted however in a contractual process or with the data subject's consent, but in both cases the data subject must have the right to obtain human intervention on the part of the controller, to express his or her point of view, and to contest the decision.[100] Individuals are not explicitly granted these rights if the automated decision is authorized by a law. However, that law must lay down suitable measures to safeguard the data subject's rights and freedoms and legitimate interests.[101]

---

[95] Art. 20 GDPR; See Article 29 Working Party, *Guidelines on the right to data portability*, WP 242, 13 December 2016.

[96] Art. 11 of the revised Convention 108.

[97] Art. 23 GDPR.

[98] Art. 9(a) of the revised Convention 108.

[99] Art. 12(a) of Directive 95/46/EC.

[100] Art. 22(2)(a) and (c) and Art. 22(3) GDPR.

[101] Art. 22(2)(b) GDPR; Explanatory Report, para 73 *in fine*.

VII.2 Enriched Right of Access

Authors of the modernization of Convention 108 as well as of GDPR have expanded the right of access so as to broaden the information that should be communicated to the data subject exercising their right. Beside the communication 'in an intelligible form of the data processed'[102] or of 'a copy of the personal data undergoing processing',[103] the right of access implies also access to the purposes of the processing, to the preservation period and to the origin of data.[104] This latter information is indeed crucial because one often questions the source of the data (how did they get this information, who did provide it?). In addition, information on the origin of the data allows to verify the legality of the communication or collection of it and to possibly 'stop the bleeding' if the first holder of the data unlawfully transmits it. In case of problems with data quality and a need of correction, it becomes possible as soon as information is obtained as to the source of the data to make these corrections at the source, preventing the further spread of errors.

VII.3 Right to Know the Reasoning Underlying the Data Processing

In today's technological context, there is a right of great interest, particularly with regard to the exponential phenomenon of profiling where one relies on 'profiles' to make decisions about a person or predict their preferences, behaviour and personal attitudes. This is the right to know the reasoning underlying a data processing the results of which are applied to someone.

Faced with a refusal of credit, a failure at a multiple-choice question examination, the targeting as suspected fraudster, etc., it is clear that one may wish to understand the assessment or the decision by accessing to the reasoning underlying the data processing. We can legitimately want to know the criteria used and the weight given to each of these criteria.[105] This right is a key right largely contributing to transparency and therefore to individuals' informational self-determination, because it allows them not only to know what is happening with their data, but also to understand it.

This right, first guaranteed in Directive 95/46/EC,[106] was logically taken over in GDPR.[107] As exposed in this text, the right to receive information as well as the right of access include the right to know the existence of automated decision-making, including profiling, and, at least in those cases, meaningful information about the logic involved, as well as the significance and the envisaged consequences of such processing for the data subject.

As for the Council of Europe, the reviewers of Convention 108 have it considered mostly appropriate to enshrine this right within the Convention. They have consequently added to the list of guarantees offered to data subjects the right of every individual to 'obtain, on request, knowledge of the reasoning underlying data processing where the results of such processing are applied to him or her' (new Art. 8, d).

---

[102] Art. 8(b) of the revised Convention 108.

[103] Art. 15(3) GDPR.

[104] Art. 8(b) of the revised Convention 108; Art. 15(1)(a, c, d, g) GDPR.

[105] See Joshua A. Kroll et al., 'Accountable algorithms', *University of Pennsylvania Law Review* [2017] 165.

[106] Art. 12(a) of Directive 95/46/EC.

[107] Arts 13(2)(f), 14(2)(g) and 15(1)(h) GDPR.

Like with other data subject rights, this right is not absolute and may be limited by national laws in accordance with the conditions laid down in Article 9 of the Convention 108+ and in Article 23 of the GDPR.

VII.4 Right to Object

Both European texts[108] include the right to object to processing of data in order to enable individuals to exercise control over what happens to the data about them. Individuals are entitled to object at any time, on grounds relating to their situation, to the processing of personal data concerning them unless the controller demonstrates legitimate grounds for the processing which override the data subject's interests or rights and fundamental freedoms.

This right is particularly relevant where data processing is not based on the data subject's consent. It may be used in cases where the controller has weighed up the interests at stake beforehand and has concluded that the result is balanced, and that they could legitimately process the data.[109] Thanks to the right to object, the data subject has an opportunity to challenge the outcome of that weighing up, at least in their personal case. The burden of proof rests on the controller who has to demonstrate that their legitimate interests in processing the data prevail over the rights and interests of the data subject.

VII.5 Right to Correct and Erase – Right to be Forgotten

The right to obtain rectification of inaccurate data and erasure of data which have been processed contrary to data protection rules has been granted to data subjects since the adoption of the very first European text.[110] This right has not changed and is protected under the modernized Convention 108,[111] as well as in the GDPR.[112]

In the GDPR, the right to erasure is presented associated with the 'right to be forgotten'. In the Internet environment, this right has appeared as an appropriate answer to the problems raised by the eternal electronic memory (creating an 'eternity effect') combined with the retrieving and gathering power of search engines (and the de-contextualization of the data that ensues).[113] Like the other data subject rights, this right to erasure/to be forgotten is not absolute and limitations are admitted. Contrary to the other rights, some of these limitations are embedded in Article 17 GDPR itself.

Convention 108 does not provide for an explicit inclusion of a 'right to be forgotten'. It was felt by the group of modernizers of the Convention that the existing safeguards (the limited length of time of data storage, and the right of rectification or erasure of data) combined with an effective right of opposition would offer adequate protection. T-PD members intend to

---

[108] Art. 9(1)(d) of the revised Convention 108; Art. 21 GDPR.

[109] Art. 6(1)(f) GDPR.

[110] Art. 8(c) of Convention 108.

[111] Art. 9(1)(e) of the revised Convention 108.

[112] Arts 16 and 17 GDPR.

[113] See Cécile de Terwangne, 'The right to be forgotten and informational autonomy in the digital environment', in Alessia Ghezzi, Ângela Guimarães Pereira and Lucia Vesnić-Alujević (eds) *The Ethics of Memory in a Digital Age: Interrogating the Right to be Forgotten* (Palgrave 2014); EUCJ (G.C.), 13 May 2014, *Google Spain SL, Google Inc. v. Agencia Española de Protección de Datos (AEPD), Mario Costeja González,* C-131/12.

specifically address this issue through a future recommendation on social networks because it is mainly – although not exclusively – in this context that the question of the right to be forgotten is arising today.

VII.6 Right to Data Portability

Article 20 of the GDPR creates a new right to data portability that allows for data subjects to receive the personal data that they have provided to a controller, in a structured, commonly used and machine-readable format, and to transmit those data to another data controller, or to have it directly transferred.[114] The purpose of this new right is to empower the data subject and give them more control over the personal data concerning them.[115] By facilitating data subjects' ability to transfer personal data easily from one IT environment to another, without hindrance, data portability provides consumer empowerment and prevents 'lock-in'.[116]

VIII. DUTIES OF THE ACTORS

Besides the security obligation mentioned above (see section V.5), a range of other duties and obligations are incumbent on data controllers and processors. Some new obligations implement the 'accountability principle' in concrete measures, such as the obligation to establish internal mechanisms to demonstrate the compliance of the processing with the national law or with the GDPR,[117] to carry out a risk analysis,[118] and to design processing in such a way as to minimize risks for data subjects.[119]

As regards the obligation to conduct data protection impact assessments, this is a new tool in order to assess the risk before one starts with data processing.[120] Such assessment is required whenever data processing is likely to result in a high risk to the rights and freedoms of individuals. The GDPR mentions three specific situations where this is the case: when a company evaluates systematically and extensively personal aspects of an individual (including profiling); when it processes sensitive data on a large scale; and where it systematically monitors public areas on a large scale. National data protection authorities have to draw a list of additional cases requiring a data protection impact assessment.

The duty of 'privacy by design' has long existed as a concept before becoming part of a legal requirement with the GDPR. The GDPR states that the controller shall implement appropriate technical and organisational measures in order to meet its requirements and to protect the rights of data subjects.[121]

---

[114] Art. 20 GDPR; see also Article 29 Working Party, WP 242rev.01.

[115] *Ibid.*, 3–4.

[116] *Ibid.*

[117] Art. 10(1) of the revised Convention 108; Art. 24 GDPR.

[118] Art. 10(2) of the revised Convention 108; Art. 35 GDPR.

[119] Art. 10(3) of the revised Convention 108; Art. 25 GDPR. See: Lee A. Bygrave, 'Hardwiring privacy', in Roger Brownsword, Eloise Scotford and Karen Yeung (eds), *The Oxford Handbook of the Law and Regulation of Technology* (Oxford University Press 2017).

[120] Atanas Yordanov, 'Nature and ideal steps of the Data Protection Impact Assessment under the General Data Protection Regulation', *EDPL*, 2017/4.

[121] Art. 23 GDPR.

A transparency duty has been imposed on controllers by EU law since Directive 95/46/EC. It was taken over in GDPR (where it is connected to data subject rights)[122] and in the revised version of Convention 108.[123] It is indeed imperative, given the particularly opaque current information systems, to provide for active transparency requirements. Data subjects may not be willing to exert their rights as regards a data processing if they do not even suspect their data to be processed. It is therefore of utmost importance to require controllers to spontaneously inform data subjects about what they are doing with their data:

> Each Party shall provide that the controller informs the data subjects of: a) his or her identity and habitual residence or establishment, b) the legal basis and the purposes of the intended processing, c) the categories of personal data processed, d) the recipients or categories of recipients of the personal data, if any, and e) the means of exercising the rights set out in Article 8, as well as any necessary additional information in order to ensure fair and transparent processing of the personal data (Art. 8 of the revised Convention).

Given that the Convention, as an international treaty, should not enter into too much detail, there is no indication as to when and how information must be provided by the controller.

The GDPR, on the contrary, foresees a detailed transparency obligation. Controllers are required to communicate a series of information pieces to the data subject, and to do it in a clear manner. In addition to the information listed in the new version of the Convention 108, they must also indicate 'the contact details of the data protection officer', 'the legitimate interests, if any, pursued by the controller or by a third party', 'where applicable, the fact that the controller intends to transfer personal data to a third country or international organisation and the existence or absence of adequate protection for the data in that case, the period of storage of the data, the existence of automated decision-making, including profiling, and meaningful information about the logic involved, as well as the significance and the envisaged consequences of such processing for the data subject.[124] The controller must provide all this information to the data subject in a concise, transparent, intelligible and easily accessible form, using clear and plain language.[125] The GDPR specifies that the information must be provided in writing, and, where appropriate, by electronic means.

When personal data are not collected from the data subjects, the controller is not required to provide the information where it is impossible or would involve disproportionate effort. The impossibility may be of a practical or legal nature (e.g., professional secrecy). The second exception is granted where the processing is expressly prescribed by law. But this is valid only if the law is sufficiently precise and provides the necessary information to ensure fair information of data subjects.[126]

Finally, a last duty consists in appointing a Data Protection Officer (DPO). While this is just a suggestion linked to the accountability requirement in the Explanatory Memorandum of the Convention 108 in order to help to reach compliance,[127] it is mandatory in the GDPR in cases

[122] Arts 13–14 GDPR. See: Merle Temme, 'Algorithms and transparency in view of the new General Data Protection Regulation', *EDPL*, 2017/4.

[123] Art. 8 of the revised Convention 108.

[124] Arts 13 and 14 GDPR.

[125] Art. 12(1) GDPR.

[126] Arts 14(5)(b) and (c) GDPR; Art. 8(3) of the revised Convention 108.

[127] Explanatory Report, para. 87.

where the processing is carried out by a public authority or body, and for those controllers and processors whose core activities consist of processing on a large scale sensitive data or data relating to criminal convictions and offences or consist of processing operations which require regular and systematic monitoring of data subjects on a large scale.[128] [129] The DPOs must be independent[130] and appointed on the basis of professional qualities and, in particular, expert knowledge on data protection law and practices.[131]

IX. TRANSBORDER DATA FLOWS

Although there is no definition of a transborder data flow or transborder transfer of personal data in the GDPR,[132] one can find one in the Explanatory Memorandum of Convention 108+. The latter states: 'A transborder data transfer occurs when personal data is disclosed or made available to a recipient subject to the jurisdiction of another State or international organisation'.[133]

The issue of transborder data transfers was key in the modernization process of Convention 108+. The new provisions revise the existing provisions on flows of personal data to other Parties (Art. 12 of the current Convention) and to non-Parties (Art. 2 of the 2001 additional Protocol[134]). Between Parties, the rule is still that of free flows unless the sending Party is 'bound by harmonised rules of protection shared by States belonging to a regional international organisation'.[135] In this case, a transfer of data may nevertheless take place if it is governed by ad hoc or standardized measures. Freedom of flows is thus not systematic among Parties to Convention 108+. This is due to the necessity to coordinate the two European legal spheres and to take into account the constraints from the European Union legal regime.

Transfers to recipients not subject to the jurisdiction of a Party to the Convention can only occur where an appropriate level of data protection based on the principles of the Convention is guaranteed.[136] This appropriate level of protection can be ensured by the law of that State or international organization, including the applicable international treaties or agreements. If no such law offers appropriate protection, protection can be guaranteed by several mechanisms: it can be ensured by 'ad hoc or approved standardised safeguards provided by legally binding and enforceable instruments adopted and implemented by the persons involved in the transfer

---

[128] Art. 37(1) GDPR.

[129] Fanny Coton and Jean-François Henrotte, 'Everything you always wanted to know about DPO (but were afraid to ask)', *Cahier du juriste*, 2017/2.

[130] Art. 38(3) GDPR.

[131] Art. 37(5) GDPR.

[132] Gloria González Fuster, 'Un-mapping personal data transfers', *EDPL*, 2016/2.

[133] Explanatory Report, para. 102. See also the definition given by the European Data Protection Supervisor (EDPS) in its position paper *The transfer of personal data to third countries and international organisations by EU institutions and bodies*, 14 July 2014, 7. See also: González Fuster (n 132).

[134] Additional Protocol to the Convention for the Protection of Individuals with regard to Automatic Processing of Personal Data, regarding supervisory authorities and transborder data flows, 8 November 2001 (ETS no. 181).

[135] Art. 14(1) revised Convention 108.

[136] Art. 14(2) revised Convention 108.

and further processing'.[137] Contractual clauses or binding corporate rules are examples of such mechanisms.

As for the GDPR, it does not change the existing regime much, but it brings interesting light and precision, and it enlarges the list of legal instruments that can be used to provide for appropriate safeguards and thus to allow transborder data transfers. Chapter V takes over the rules regulating the question. It integrates the legal tools that have appeared since 1995 to protect personal data once they cross EU borders. Transfers of data outside the EU are forbidden unless the third country or the international organization has been recognized by the European Commission as ensuring an adequate level of protection to the data, or unless the sending party offers itself an adequate protection through appropriate safeguards.

These safeguards can be provided for by binding corporate rules in accordance with the GDPR provision[138] dedicated to this instrument, or by standard contractual clauses adopted by the European Commission, or by ad hoc clauses authorized by a national supervisory authority.[139] New legal tools can be used such as administrative arrangements between public authorities or bodies, and codes of conduct or standardization mechanisms approved by a supervisory authority. In the absence of an adequacy decision or of appropriate safeguards, derogations to the forbidding of transborder transfers of personal data are foreseen, allowing them in specific situations: with the data subject's explicit consent, if necessary for a contract or for important reasons of public interest, if necessary for the defence of legal claims or to protect a vital interest, and if the transfer is made from a public register, under certain conditions.[140]

X. SUPERVISORY AUTHORITIES

Specialized supervisory authorities are an integral part of the European system of protection of personal data. All over the European territory, national supervisory authorities are responsible for monitoring compliance with all the data protection rules outlined in the previous paragraphs. Both Convention 108+ and the GDPR set up data protection authorities (DPAs)[141], see to the independence of these authorities[142] and to their dialogue, cooperation and mutual assistance[143].[144]

National DPAs are established to enforce data protection rules, and to offer guidance. They supervise, through investigative and corrective powers,[145] the application of data protection rules. They handle complaints lodged against violations of these rules.[146] Moreover, they provide expert advice on data protection issues.[147] DPAs have now significant enforcement

---

137 Art. 14(3) revised Convention 108.
138 Art. 47 GDPR.
139 Art. 46(2)(c) and (d) and Art. 46(3)(a) GDPR.
140 Art. 49(1) GDPR.
141 Art. 15 revised Convention 108; Art. 51(1) GDPR.
142 Art. 15(5) revised Convention 108; Art. 52 GDPR.
143 Art. 17 revised Convention 108; Arts 60–61 GDPR.
144 Andra Giurgiu and Tine A Larsen, 'Roles and powers of national data protection authorities', *EDPL*, 2016/2.
145 Art. 57(1)(h) GDPR.
146 Art. 57(1)(f) GDPR.
147 Art. 57(1)(c) GDPR.

powers, including the ability to impose substantial fines on controllers and processors in view of a better implementation of the rules. Those fines can go up to EUR 20 million or, in the case of a company, 4 per cent of the worldwide annual turnover.[148]

Each DPA can only exercise its powers on the territory of its own State, but this may affect processing that occurs in other States. In the EU, a 'one-stop-shop' mechanism has been put in place to prevent organizations with several establishments in the EU that might be confronted with inconsistent decisions by various local supervisory authorities. The one-stop-shop mechanism means that, as a main rule, organizations carrying out cross-border processing activities[149] will only have to deal with one supervisory authority, acting as the 'lead supervisory authority'.[150] This 'lead supervisory authority' has the primary responsibility for dealing with cross-border data processing activities and for coordinating any investigation for which it might have to involve other 'supervisory authorities concerned'.[151]

The GDPR establishes the European Data Protection Board (EDPB),[152] that comprises representatives of each of the national data protection authorities in the EU,[153] and whose functions include to advise EU institutions and to issue guidelines, recommendations and best practices – including binding decisions – in order to ensure consistent application of the GDPR.[154] The EDPB will replace the Working Party on the Protection of Individuals with regard to the Processing of Personal Data (referred as 'Article 29 Working Party') that was established under the Data Protection Directive.

XI. CONCLUSION

Europe's advanced data protection architecture may serve as a model and have an outreach beyond European boundaries. Convention 108 is the only legally binding instrument presenting a unique potential of becoming a universal standard as concerns the protection of personal data. The revision of this text occurred at a time where sharing common core principles around the world to protect individuals as regards the processing of their personal data had become an absolute necessity. The process of revision of the Convention introduced key elements reinforcing the protection of individuals. The first of such key elements is the explicit formulation of the principle of proportionality to be respected at any stage of data processing and for all the operations done with the data.

Other major improvements correspond to elements of the protection that are also present in the GDPR. They concern the rights granted to data subjects, notably the right not to be submitted to an exclusively automated decision (human beings should never be submitted to a machine), the right to object to the processing and the right to know the reasoning underlying

---

148 Art. 83 GDPR.

149 See the explanations on 'cross-border processing of personal data' in Article 29 Working Party, *Guidelines for identifying a controller or processor's lead supervisory authority*, WP 244rev01, 5 April 2017, 3–4.

150 Art. 56 GDPR; see: Article 29 Working Party, *Guidelines for identifying a controller or processor's lead supervisory authority*, WP 244rev01, 5 April 2017, 4–10.

151 Art. 60 GDPR. For a definition of 'supervisory authorities concerned' see Art. 4(22) GDPR.

152 Art. 68(1) GDPR.

153 Art. 68(3) GDPR.

154 Art. 70(1) GDPR.

a processing. Informational self-determination means not only the right to know but also the right to understand what is done with one's data. Already existing rights have been enriched such as the right to access and, especially in the GDPR, the right to erasure linked to the right to be forgotten. GDPR has also introduced the new right to data portability. New duties have appeared in both European texts, such as the important duty of active transparency (presented as a right to receive information in the GDPR), that of implementing privacy by design and taking measures linked to the accountability principle, and that of notifying data breaches. Certain of these new obligations are incumbent upon controllers as well as processors.

The picture resulting from the revision work in Strasbourg and from the adoption of the GDPR by the EU legislator is certainly an enhanced one as regards the protection of individuals in Europe. The general nature of the text of the Convention does not allow to offer a view as precise as that resulting from the EU texts. But contrary to the EU GDPR, Convention 108+ covers all the activities of the private as well as of the public sector. This is an essential asset of this legal instrument.

REFERENCES

Article 29 Working Party *Opinion 4/2007 on the concept of personal data*, WP 136, 20 June 2007

Article 29 Working Party *Opinion 3/2010 on the principle of accountability*, WP 173, 13 July 2010

Article 29 Working Party *Opinion 03/2013 on purpose limitation*, WP 203, 2 April 2013

Article 29 Working Party *Opinion 05/2014 on anonymisation techniques*, WP 216, 10 April 2014

Article 29 Working Party *Guidelines on the right to data portability under Regulation 2016/679*, WP 242rev.01, 27 October 2017

Article 29 Working Party *Guidelines for identifying a controller or processor's lead supervisory authority*, WP 244rev.01, 5 April 2017

Ausloos J, 'Giving meaning to Lawfulness under the GDPR', Centre for IT and IP (CITIP) Blog, 2 May 2017

Boulanger M H et al., 'La protection des données à caractère personnel en droit communautaire', *Journal des Tribunaux droit européen* (1997) 41

Bygrave L A, 'Hardwiring Privacy', in R Brownsword, E Scotford and K Yeung (eds), *The Oxford Handbook of the Law and Regulation of Technology* (Oxford University Press 2017)

Coton F and J F Henrotte, 'Everything you always wanted to know about DPO (but were afraid to ask)' (2017) 2 *Cahier du juriste*

De Terwangne C, 'The right to be forgotten and informational autonomy in the digital environment', in A Ghezzi, Â Guimarães Pereira and L Vesnić-Alujević (eds) *The Ethics of Memory in a Digital Age: Interrogating the Right to be Forgotten* (Palgrave 2014)

De Terwangne C, K Rosier and B Losdyck, 'Le règlement européen relatif à la protection des données à caractère personnel : quelles nouveautés ?' (2017) 8 *Journal de droit européen*

European Commission, *Joint Communication to the European Parliament and the Council: Resilience, Deterrence and Defence: Building strong cybersecurity for the EU*, JOIN(2017) 450 final, 13 September 2017

European Data Protection Supervisor (EDPS), *Position paper: The transfer of personal data to third countries and international organisations by EU institutions and bodies*, 14 July 2014

Giurgiu A and TA Larsen, 'Roles and powers of national data protection authorities', *EDPL*, 2016/2

González Fuster G, 'Un-mapping personal data transfers' (2016) 2 *EDPL*

Jasserand C, 'Legal nature of biometric data: From 'generic' personal data to sensitive data' (2016) 3 *EDPL*

Kindt E, *Privacy and Data Protection Issues of Biometric Applications* (Springer 2013)

Korff D, *New challenges to data protection study - Working Paper No. 2: Data protection laws in the EU: The difficulties in meeting the challenges posed by global social and technical developments*, European Commission Directorate-General Justice, Freedom and Security Report (2010)

Kroll J A et al., 'Accountable algorithms' (2017) *University of Pennsylvania Law Review* 165
Kuner Ch., Bygrave L. ,Docksey Ch. (ed.), and Drechsier L. (ass. ed.), *The EU General Data Protection Regulation (GDPR) – A Commentary* (Oxford University Press, Oxford, 2020).
McAfee & Centre for Strategic and International Studies, *Net losses: Estimating the global cost of cybercrime*, 2014
Temme M, 'Algorithms and transparency in view of the new General Data Protection Regulation' (2017) 4 *EDPL*
Van Waesberge C and S De Smedt, 'Cybersecurity and data breach notification obligations under the current and future legislative framework' (2016) 3 *EDPL*
Yordanov A, 'Nature and ideal steps of the Data Protection Impact Assessment under the General Data Protection Regulation' (2017) 4 *EDPL*
Zuiderveen Borgesius FJ, 'The Breyer Case of the Court of Justice of the European Union: IP addresses and the personal data definition' (2017) 1 *EDPL*

2. Post-Brexit data protection in the UK – leaving the EU but not EU data protection law behind[1]

Karen McCullagh

1. INTRODUCTION

On 31 January 2020 the United Kingdom (UK) formally left the European Union (EU) after 47 years of membership, following the outcome of the historic 'Brexit' referendum on 23 June 2016 in which a majority of eligible voters in the UK voted to 'Leave' the EU.[2] As the decision to leave the EU (the world's largest trading bloc[3] and the UK's largest trading partner)[4] – was momentous one might have expected the UK government to have engaged in contingency planning and to have decided on the nature and degree of future trading relationship it would seek with the EU and other countries prior to the referendum but the UK government did not take these actions because it did not expect the 'leave' vote to win the referendum.

Consequently, it was unprepared for the outcome and a great deal of political turmoil ensued – including the resignation of two prime ministers, and the UK requesting postponement of its departure from the EU on three occasions in the next three years because of disagreements amongst UK government ministers over the scope and terms of the withdrawal agreement, before the EU and UK eventually agreed the terms of a Trade and Cooperation Agreement on 24 December 2020, a mere seven days before the UK would have 'crashed out' of the EU on a 'no deal' basis.

The government's failure to plan for Brexit included a failure to give any thought to data protection arrangements, that is, whether it would continue to comply with EU data protection law as it had since Directive 95/46/EC came into force, or whether it would seek to diverge

[1] The author thanks Mr Jon Baines, Mr Neil Brown, Prof Morten Hviid, Prof David Mead, Mr Daragh O'Brien, Dr Katherine O'Keefe, Prof Claudina Richards, and the anonymous reviewer for their comments on earlier drafts.

[2] Brexit is a neologism of British and Exit coined in 2012 by Peter Wilding which expresses the UK's withdrawal from the EU; http://www.bbc.com/culture/story/20190314-how-brexit-changed-the-english-language accessed 19 April 2021; Brexit is the outcome of a referendum held on 23 June 2016 across the UK and Gibraltar about whether or not the UK should remain a member of the EU. A majority of eligible voters (17.41 million people; 51.9 per cent of all voters) voted to leave the EU; Electoral Commission, 2016, EU referendum results, https://www.electoralcommission.org.uk/find-information-by-subject/elections-and-referendums/past-elections-and-referendums/eu-referendum/electorate-and-count-information accessed 19 April 2021; Prime Minister's Office, Prime Minister's letter to Donald Tusk triggering Art 50, 29 March 2017, https://www.gov.uk/government/uploads/system/uploads/attachment_data/file/604079/Prime_Ministers_letter_to_European_Council_President_Donald_Tusk.pdf accessed 19 April 2021.

[3] European Commission, 'EU position in world trade,' 9 February 2019, https://ec.europa.eu/trade/policy/eu-position-in-world-trade/index_en.htm accessed 19 April 2021.

[4] House of Commons Library,' Research Briefing: Statistics on UK-EU trade,' 10 November 2020 https://commonslibrary.parliament.uk/research-briefings/cbp-7851/ accessed 19 April 2021.

either in the immediate or longer term. Accordingly, the objective of this chapter is to trace how the UK data protection framework evolved from the time of the Brexit referendum to the adoption by the Commission of an EU-UK adequacy decision, and to explain why the UK has, for the time being, decided not to diverge from EU data protection law.

The chapter begins by explaining why the UK decided to comply with the GDPR before becoming a third country for EU data protection purposes and then illustrates that the Brussels effect, that is, 'multinational companies voluntarily extend[ing] the EU rule to govern their global operations',[5] influenced the UK's decision to continue to comply with EU data protection standards after it became a third country. It also discusses why the UK initially sought to pursue an exceptionalism strategy – seeking a bespoke data agreement outside the scope of the GDPR adequacy framework before eventually conceding that it would need to seek an adequacy decision from the European Commission (the Commission) to facilitate EEA-UK personal data transfers. Thereafter, it demonstrates that although the UK has secured an adequacy decision it may prove unstable. Finally, it considers whether longer-term divergence is likely or not and concludes that whilst a degree of friction and divergence is likely, multi-national data controllers are unlikely to call for the UK government to completely diverge from the GDPR if it continues to meet their needs because divergence would result in further compliance burdens which would be an unwelcome business cost. Therefore, EU data protection advocates have rightly framed the UK's continued compliance with the GDPR as early evidence of the EU's ability, through its trade and regulatory power, to 'export' its laws and standards to third countries by offering unrestricted access to its large and valuable marketplace of personal data in return for confirmation of legal compliance, via an adequacy assessment.[6] However, for the EU to be assured that the GDPR standards become and remain the global norm, it must ensure that it remains fit for purpose, which is why it is trite to say that the UK has left the EU but not EU data protection law behind, for now, at least.

2. DATA PROTECTION DURING THE NEGOTIATION PERIOD (2016–2020)

The UK government knew that the GDPR would supersede Directive 95/46/EC and be directly applicable in all EU member states and EEA countries, including the UK, from 25 May 2018 until the end of the transition period on 31 December 2020.[7] Failure to give effect to and to fully comply with the GDPR would have left the UK in breach of its member state obligations during that period (31 January 2020 – 31 December 2020) and could have led to disruption

---

[5] Anu Bradford, *The Brussels Effect: How the European Union Rules the World*, (OUP, 2012), XIV.

[6] A. Bendiek and M. Römer, M. (2019) 21(1) 'Externalizing Europe: the global effects of European data protection' (2019) *Digital Policy, Regulation and Governance* 32-43, 33 and 35; Patrick Müller and Gerda Falkner 'The EU as a policy exporter? The conceptual framework', in Gerda Falk ner and Patrick Müller (eds), *EU Policies in a Global Perspective: Shaping or Taking International Regimes?* (London: Routledge, 2014), 11–12.

[7] The period was referred to as the transition period in the Withdrawal Agreement and called the implementation period by the UK government. Art 288(2) TFEU; An EEA Joint Committee Decision of 6 July 2018 incorporated the GDPR, a text with EEA relevance, into the EEA Agreement, and it entered into force in all three EFTA-EEA States on 20 July 2018; Decision of the EEA Joint Committee, No 154/2018, OJ No L 183/23, 19.7.2018.

in personal data flows if the Commission prohibited transfers from EU member states to the UK.[8] It therefore enacted the Data Protection Act 2018 (hereafter DPA 2018) to repeal and replace the Data Protection Act 1998 and give effect to national derogations permitted by the GDPR before exit from the EU on 31 January 2020, and during the transition period for two interrelated reasons,[9] the first of which was legal and economic necessity.

A second reason for maintaining compliance with the GDPR during the transition period was that the UK government had not planned for a 'leave' vote and attendant consequences before the referendum, so it did not have an alternative ready to 'roll out'. The easiest option, therefore, was to maintain the status quo until it had evaluated the merits of diverging from the GDPR which was hailed as a clarion call for a new global digital gold standard of data protection,[10] particularly as the GDPR would continue to have extra-territorial application to UK data controllers offering goods or services to individuals or monitoring the behaviour of individuals in EEA countries, thereby necessitating ongoing compliance with the GDPR.[11] Divergence before then would merely have increased the compliance burden of data controllers and been an unwelcome business cost.

The Withdrawal Agreement therefore specified that the GDPR would continue to apply (with the exception of Chapter VII – co-operation & consistency) in the UK during the transition period (31 January 2020 – 31 December 2020) in relation to personal data transferred between the EEA and the UK[12] and that data received from the UK would not be treated differently to data received from EU member states even though the UK had left the EU.[13] In essence, it created a 'GDPR-envelope' that applied to personal data processed in the UK during the transition period, and would continue to be processed in the UK in reliance of these arrangements after the transition period ended thereby ensuring that personal data of individuals residing in EEA countries would not lose GDPR protection once the transition period ends if an adequacy decision was not in place by then.[14]

Confirmation that UK-based data controllers and processors could continue to receive personal data from EEA countries during the transition period without needing to put in place Chapter V transfer mechanisms (e.g., model clauses or binding corporate rules, or rely on one of the derogations) was welcomed by many data protection experts because 'it could only

---

[8] Art 45, Recital 107 GDPR It could, subject to an infringement action by the Commission, eventually result in pecuniary sanctions (Arts 258 and 260 TFEU) but the Commission might decide not to pursue this course of action in respect of the UK because it is a lengthy and time-consuming process – one that might prove futile in respect of a member state in the process of exiting the EU.

[9] For a detailed analysis of the national derogations to the GDPR in the Data Protection Act 2018 see: Karen McCullagh, 'The UK Data Protection Act 2018,' E-Conference on National Adaptations to the GDPR (*Blogdroiteuropéen*, 4–6 June 2018), https://blogdroiteuropeen.files.workdpress.com/2018/06/karen.pdf accessed 19 April 2021.

[10] EDPS, The EU GDPR as a clarion call for a new global digital gold standard, 1 April 2016, https://edps.europa.eu/press-publications/press-news/blog/eu-gdpr-clarion-call-new-global-digital-gold-standard_en accessed 19 April 2021; The DPA 2018 provides for two separate regimes for general processing: one for processing that falls within the scope of the GDPR and a separate, broadly equivalent regime for processing that falls outside the scope of the GDPR (the 'applied GDPR').

[11] Art 3 GDPR 2016/679.

[12] Arts 71 and Art 127.

[13] Art 73.

[14] Art 71 (a) and (b).

have the effect of making transfers easier'.[15] However, a few data protection experts reacted with concern to the 'GDPR-envelope' because it would allow the UK to temporarily avoid compliance with the *Schrems* criteria i.e., fundamental rights limitations on surveillance.[16] In my view, drafting and implementation of Chapter V compliance measures e.g., contractual arrangements would have been a costly, time-consuming, and onerous exercise that would have unfairly penalised small- and medium-sized enterprises, causing harm to both the EU and UK economies, which both parties were keen to avoid, particularly as an adequacy decision could well be in place before the other mechanisms were finalised. The pragmatic 'fudge' minimised economic harm by ensuring that EEA/EU-UK personal data transfers continued unimpeded during the transition period.

In the interests of seamless continuity, the Withdrawal Agreement stipulated that the CJEU would have jurisdiction to settle questions of interpretation raised by the UK courts regarding data protection law and the UK would abide by CJEU decisions during the transition period. Likewise, UK-based data controllers and processors, including those from non-EEA countries e.g., the US that had established a base in the UK for the purpose of trading in the EU single market continued to benefit from the One-Stop-Shop (OSS) principle. As such, they were able to continue to designate the UK national supervisory authority, the Information Commissioner's Office (ICO), as their lead supervisory authority to coordinate actions and complaints regarding cross-border processing (e.g., a complaint originating in France or Germany), with the help of other 'concerned DPAs' (i.e., other data protection authorities in member states affected by the processing), thereby minimising the administrative burden of compliance.

However, as Chapter VII of the GDPR did not apply under the terms of the Withdrawal Agreement the ICO ceased to be a full member with voting rights of the European Data Protection Board (EDPB), as of 31 January 2020. Instead, the ICO had 'observer' status, that is, it was permitted to attend (by invitation) but could vote in meetings of the EDPB during this period.[17]

3. DIVERGENCE V CONTINUED ALIGNMENT: THE BRUSSELS EFFECT?

As alluded to above, the UK government did not have an agreed vision about the nature or extent of the trade deal it wished to secure with the EU or other countries when it triggered Article 50, to commence the process of leaving the EU.[18] Nor did it have an agreed vision regarding data protection.

---

[15] Jon Baines, Mischon de Reya, quoted in Sam Clark, 'No SCCs needed for data controllers governed by GDPR, ICO lawyer suggests' (*Global Data Review Blog* 12 October 2018), https://globaldatareview.com/data-privacy/no-sccs-needed-data-controllers-governed-gdpr-ico-lawyer-suggests accessed 19 April 2021.

[16] Cybermatron, Data protection in the EU-UK Withdrawal Agreement - Are we being framed?, (*Cybermatron Blog*, 15 November 2018) http://cybermatron.blogspot.com/2018/11/data-protection-in-eu-uk-withdrawal.html accessed 19 April 2021.

[17] Arts 70 and 128(5).

[18] The UK Prime Minister invoked Art 50 of the Treaty on European Union (TEU) which commenced the UK's withdrawal, commonly known as Brexit, from the EU; Prime Minister's Office, Prime

One might have expected the UK government to immediately declare an intention to maintain compliance with EU data protection laws given that this would ensure that the UK provides an essentially equivalent level of protection and increase the likelihood of securing and thereafter retaining an adequacy decision to facilitate personal data-enabled services exports from the EU to the UK – they were worth approximately £42bn (€47bn) whilst exports from the UK to the EU were worth £85bn (€96bn) in 2018.[19] However, there were calls for Brexit to be used as an opportunity to diverge from the EU standard by those who viewed the GDPR standards as being too high[20] and contended that lower, less onerous standards would give the UK leverage when engaging in trade deals with other countries.[21]

The House of Lords EU Home Affairs Sub-Committee considered how the UK government might meet its objective of ensuring 'unhindered and uninterrupted data flows with the EU' and facilitating transfers to non-EEA countries e.g., the US. It heard evidence that the UK and EU economies are currently very heavily integrated – three-quarters of the UK's cross-border data flows are with EU countries – and forecast to remain so for decades to come. Business representatives were particularly cognisant of the trade power of the EU. For example, Antony Walker of TechUK emphasised that 'we have to remember the size of the UK market versus the size of the European market',[22] which means that 'we will have to do that very much in partnership with the European Union, rather than simply boldly striking out by ourselves and hoping others will follow'.[23] Business representatives also made implicit mention of the Brussels effect, that is, the regulatory 'race to the top' whereby the most stringent standard has an appeal to companies operating across multiple regulatory environments as it makes global production and exports easier.[24]

> If you are running [a] global operation, you will want to have consistent processes across your businesses. What we are seeing is that global firms based outside of the EU are taking the GDPR as the norm for their business and are building their processes around it, so, for very large companies, there is no desire to diverge from the GDPR—the opposite, because they worry about falling between the gaps.[25]

In short, the Sub-Committee was advised that there was little appetite in the business sector for wholescale divergence from the EU data protection standard.

Minister's letter to Donald Tusk triggering Art 50, 29 March 2017, https://www.gov.uk/government/uploads/system/uploads/attachment_data/file/604079/Prime_Ministers_letter_to_European_Council_President_Donald_Tusk.pdf accessed 19 April 2021.

[19] Estimated by the UK government's Department for Digital, Culture, Media and Sport by applying the UN definition of digitally deliverable services (DDS) to UK Office for National Statistics data; cited in DCMS, Explanatory Framework for Adequacy Discussions, Section A: Cover Note, 13 March 2020, 1.

[20] Federation of Small Businesses, 'Manifesto European Elections 2014' (February 2014).

[21] Daniel Castro, 'Brexit Allows UK to Unshackle Itself from EU's Cumbersome Data Protection Rules' (Centre for Data Innovation, 20 July 2016) https://www.datainnovation.org/2016/07/brexit-allows-uk-to-unshackle-itself-from-eus-cumbersome-data-protection-rules/ accessed 19 April 2021.

[22] Ibid., para 129.

[23] Ibid.

[24] Anu Bradford, 'The Brussels effect,' (2012) *NW U Law Rev*, 107(1), 1–68, 9.

[25] House of Lords, European Union Committee, 'Brexit: the EU data protection package,' 3rd Report of Session 2017–19 – published 18 July 2017 – HL Paper 7, para 128.

Evidently the EU is able, through its '*trade power*,' to 'export' its laws and standards to other countries by offering improved access to its large and valuable market in return for legal compliance.[26] And, the UK's application for an adequacy decision exemplifies that an adequacy decision is often made in the context of an asymmetrical power relationship, with the EU wielding significantly more economic power than the third country, and this dynamic allows the EU to *de facto* impose its legislative framework onto a third country which is seeking to strengthen or, in the case of the UK, dependent upon and seeking to maintain strong economic ties with the EU. The 'behaviour of market actors' also drives this externalisation of EU regulatory policy, an impact Bradford labelled the 'Brussels effect' when describing the EU's 'unilateral regulatory globalisation', that is, the extension of EU regulatory norms and practices beyond the EU territory but outside the structures and institutions of hierarchical public rule-making.[27] As Bradford and Walker have highlighted, multinational corporations are obliged to comply with the GDPR to gain access to the EU market, and as these multinational companies prefer to deal with as few legislative frameworks as possible, they promote through compliance with it, the GDPR as the global regulatory standard, not least to avoid the additional costs of compliance with multiple rules and to gain the economies of scale achieved by promoting compliance with the GDPR. Consequently, trade and market forces were drivers of the UK's continued compliance with EU data protection law, post Brexit.

3.1 Bespoke Data Agreement v Mutual Adequacy Decisions

The Sub-Committee was further advised that the UK, as a third country, would not benefit from *de jure* recognition of its data protection laws as providing an adequate standard of protection to facilitate EEA-UK personal data transfers, and it therefore considered alternative mechanisms for effectuating such transfers.[28] Specifically, it considered whether post-transition EEA-UK data flows would be best facilitated by either seeking either a partial adequacy decision or a whole country adequacy decision from the European Commission.[29] The Committee also considered, in the alternative, the merits of requiring individual data controllers and processors to adopt their own compliance measures such as model clauses or binding corporate rules.

Expert witnesses confirmed that the UK-established data controllers favoured a whole country (as opposed to sectoral) adequacy decision and continued harmonisation with the EU data protection framework because it would be the 'least burdensome' option and offer 'stability and certainty for businesses', particularly small- and medium-sized UK-based data controllers and processors that could not easily absorb the legal costs associated with drafting

---

[26] Bendiek and Röme (n 6); Müller and Gerda (n 6), 11–12.

[27] Bradford (n 24), 3.

[28] Art 45, GDPR.

[29] An (whole country) adequacy decision confirm with binding effects on EEA countries that the level of data protection in the UK is 'essentially equivalent' to that in EU member states such that additional safeguards would not be required nor would UK-based data controllers in be required to individually show compliance with the GDPR to facilitate transfers of personal data from EEA countries to the UK, whereas a partial or sectoral adequacy decision applies only to a particular sector e.g., the commercial sector. See Arts 45(3) and 93(2) of the GDPR for further information on implementing acts.

and obtaining approval for model clauses or other legal mechanisms to effectuate transfers.[30] It also reported that if the UK were to obtain an adequacy decision from the Commission to facilitate EEA-UK personal data transfers it would have regulatory implications for data transfer agreements between the UK and other third countries because compliance with the onward transfer principle in the GDPR would necessitate restrictions on transfers of personal data of individuals in EEA countries from the UK to countries that do not meet EU data protection standards.

Whilst the Sub-Committee rightly focused on economic considerations, the government also had to give due weight to political considerations to build and maintain government support for the trade negotiations so that Parliament would ratify any deal reached. Some Brexiteers had, in the run up to the Brexit referendum, claimed Brexit would offer a unique opportunity to restore sovereignty by 'freeing' the UK from EU laws and institutions and data protection framework, and that this would be beneficial because 'the EU had imposed data protection requirements' which are 'against British interests',[31] and 'ECJ [European Court of Justice] judgments on data protection issues hobble the growth of internet companies',[32] and were therefore loath to accept EU institutions having any continuing jurisdiction.

In this regard, an adequacy decision would be an anathema as it would necessitate the UK accepting oversight by various EU institutions, for instance, the Commission having the ability to withdraw an adequacy decision, and member states' national data protection authorities having the power to order the suspension of data flows to the UK. The UK would also have to accept the jurisdiction of the European Data Protection Board as a 'rule-taker', that is, the UK would have to accept decisions of the EDPB without representation on the Board, a position likely to be quite unpalatable to those who view Brexit as a complete divorce from EU institutions.[33] And should the UK fail to accept any decision of the EDPB, it may lose its adequacy status.

Relatedly, the UK would also have to accept indirect oversight roles by the Council and Parliament because these bodies may at any time request that the Commission amend or withdraw an adequacy decision on the grounds that its enactment exceeds the implementing powers provided for in the GDPR.[34] Moreover, as the EU is an autonomous legal order, any EU-UK adequacy decision made by the Commission could be subject to challenge before the

---

[30] House of Lords, European Union Committee, 'Brexit: the EU data protection package (n 25), Paper 7, Chapter 3, paras 112–115.

[31] Michael White, 'Why John Whittingdale is politically tone deaf and 30 years out of date,' (*The Guardian Blog*, 9 March 2016), https://www.theguardian.com/politics/blog/2016/mar/09/why-john-whittingdale-is-politically-tone-deaf-and-30-years-out-of-date accessed 19 April 2021.

[32] Michael Gove, 'Why I'm backing Brexit' (*The Spectator,* 20 February 2016), <https://www.spectator.co.uk/article/michael-gove-why-i-m-backing-brexit accessed 19 April 2021.

[33] Andrew Murray, 'Data transfers between the EU and UK post Brexit?,' (2017) *International Data Privacy Law*, 7 (3), 149–164, 151.

[34] European Commission, 'How the EU determines if a non-EU country has an adequate level of data protection,' https://ec.europa.eu/info/law/law-topic/data-protection/international-dimension-data-protection/adequacy-decisions_en accessed 19 April 2021; For example, a non-binding resolution by the Committee on Civil Liberties, Justice and Home Affairs (LIBE Committee) of the European Parliament that the Commission suspend the EU-US. Privacy Shield unless and until corrective actions were taken by the US Department of Commerce prompted amendments to the operation of the Privacy shield before a second annual review of the scheme by the Commission.

CJEU which holds itself out as the guardian of fundamental rights.[35] Acceptance of this oversight role would represent a major concession by the UK government as it had made ending the jurisdiction of the CJEU a 'red line' issue in early statements on the UK's withdrawal from the EU.[36]

Efforts to reconcile conflict between the UK's economic and political objectives led the UK government to initially pursue a strategy of exceptionalism. It proposed that the UK should receive preferential treatment in the form of a free trade deal with the EU and close cooperation on inter alia law enforcement and criminal justice matters and on security and defence matters, with mutual recognition of each other's data protection laws in the absence of an adequacy assessment.[37] The UK further proposed to deal with data protection disputes through provisions in the trade and cooperation agreement, should one be agreed, instead of the GDPR oversight and enforcement mechanisms; the underlying motivations were to prevent the EU from having the power to unilaterally rescind an adequacy decision thereby immediately halting EU-UK data transfers should the UK be found to be substantially in breach of the GDPR. Various factors were cited in support of these bespoke proposals including compliance with EU data protection laws during the transition period and retention of the GDPR in UK law thereafter.[38]

The exceptionalism approach was roundly and repeatedly rejected by the EU for several reasons, not least because construction of the single market has been accomplished not only through the elimination of barriers to the flow of capital, goods, services and labour, but also by the development of a legal order and corresponding range of measures to regulate economic activity within and across borders, including the GDPR, which regulates data protection in all member states.[39] If the Commission unilaterally agreed to a bespoke data agreement with weaker obligations it could give a third country a competitive trade advantage, and ultimately undermine the single market itself. Accordingly, although the Commission has drafted 'non-negotiable horizontal provisions for cross-border data flows and for personal data protection' for inclusion in trade agreements with the aim of reducing barriers to trade, such as forced

---

[35] *Schrems* and *Opinion 1/15* confirm that if the Commission were to enter into an EU-UK adequacy agreement on terms contrary to primary law, including the Charter, then it could be struck down by the ECJ. For a discussion of the crucial role of the CJEU both in negotiating international agreements and in developing the European model of personal data protection and respect for private life. See, Christopher Kuner, A. Court of Justice International agreements, data protection, and EU fundamental rights on the international stage: Opinion 1/15, EU-Canada PNR, (2018) *CML Rev,* 55(3) 857–882; Olivia Tambou, Opinion 1/15 on the EU-Canada Passenger Name Record (PNR) Agreement: PNR Agreements Need to Be Compatible with EU Fundamental Rights, (2018) *European Foreign Affairs Review,* 23 (2), 187–202; Vagelis Papakonstantinou and Paul De Hert, 'The PNR Agreement And Transatlantic Anti-Terrorism Co-Operation: No Firm Human Rights Framework On Either Side Of The Atlantic' (2009) *CML Rev*, 46(3) 885–919.

[36] European Parliament, LIBE Committee, Briefing: Personal data protection achievements during the legislative term 2014–2019: the role of the European Parliament, April 2019, https://www.europarl.europa.eu/RegData/etudes/BRIE/2019/608870/IPOL_BRI(2019)608870_EN.pdf accessed 19 April 2021, 4.

[37] DexEU, The exchange and protection of personal data - a future partnership paper, 24 August 2017, https://assets.publishing.service.gov.uk/government/uploads/system/uploads/attachment_data/file/639853/The_exchange_and_protection_of_personal_data.pdf accessed 19 April 2021.

[38] Ibid., 8.

[39] Mitchell P. Smith, 'Single market, global competition: regulating the European market in a global economy,' (2010) *Journal of European Public Policy*, 17(7), 936–953.

data localisation in a state's territory, it envisages only using them in situations where under the data protection track an adequacy decision cannot be realistically adopted,[40] and instead advocates that trade negotiations and applications for an adequacy assessment follow separate but parallel tracks.[41] This approach allows the EU to achieve its goal of promoting the GDPR as the global standard, whilst simultaneously ensuring that its integrity and competitiveness is not undermined.

Unsurprisingly, Michel Barnier, the then chief negotiator for the EU, dismissed the UK's proposal for bespoke data protection arrangement, saying:

> The transfer of personal data to the UK will only be possible if the UK provides adequate safeguards. One example to ensure that adequate safeguards are in place is an 'EU adequacy decision'. This is an autonomous EU decision. There can be no system of "mutual recognition" of standards when it comes to the exchange and protection of such data.[42]

Mr Barnier's comments about no system of mutual recognition pre-date a landmark agreement between the EU and Japan to pursue mutual adequacy recognition and must be understood in the context of the UK's proposal for a bespoke adequacy agreement outside the scope of the GDPR adequacy criteria and procedure. His point about an adequacy decision being an autonomous decision remains valid.

The UK government subsequently proposed a new agreement between the EU and UK, that would 'build on a standard adequacy arrangement' and conceded that the Commission would 'conduct an assessment to assure itself that we meet the essential equivalence test provided for in the GDPR'[43] but the UK did not specify how any disputes would be resolved. Unsurprisingly, a few days later, Mr Barnier once again rejected the UK's proposals. He said that the UK's plans posed 'real problems' and raised a number of legal questions, specifically:

> Who would launch an infringement against the United Kingdom in the case of misapplication of GDPR? Who would ensure that the United Kingdom would update its data legislation every time the EU updates GDPR? How can we ensure the uniform interpretation of the rules on data protection on

---

[40] European Commission, Letter on cross-border data flows and EU trade agreements, 1 Mar. 2018, http://data.consilium.europa.eu/doc/document/ST-6687-2018-INIT/en/pdf; Art 216 (1) TFEU allows authority for the conclusion of an international agreement to be 'provided for in a legally binding Union act', which would allow EU legislation to set out criteria for data protection agreements with third countries; For more information on the inclusion of horizontal clauses in EU trade agreements see: Svetlana Yakovleva and Kristina Irion, 'Pitching trade against privacy: reconciling EU governance of personal data flows with external trade' *International Data Privacy Law*, (2020).

[41] In 2018 the European Commission endorsed horizontal provisions for inclusion in trade agreements that allow the EU to tackle protectionist practices in third countries in relation to digital trade while ensuring that trade agreements cannot be used to challenge the high level of protection guaranteed by the EU Charter of Fundamental Rights and the EU legislation on the protection of personal data; European Commission, EU horizontal provisions on *Cross-border data flows and protection of personal data and privacy* in the Digital Trade Title of EU trade agreements, http://trade.ec.europa.eu/doclib/docs/2018/july/tradoc_157130.pdf.

[42] European Commission, Speech by Michel Barnier at Business Europe Day 2018, Brussels, 1 March 2018, http://europa.eu/rapid/press-release_SPEECH-18-1462_en.htm accessed 19 April 2021, 8.

[43] HMG, Framework for the UK-EU partnership Data protection, 25 May 2018, 16–17.

> both sides of the Channel? ... [He concluded] the UK must understand that the only possibility for the EU to protect personal data is through an adequacy decision.[44]

He insisted that a post-Brexit data protection agreement could not be divorced from the EU's GDPR rules and procedure on adequacy assessment; the UK would have to agree to submit to an adequacy assessment, and by implication, the UK would have to agree to periodic review of an adequacy decision and oversight by the CJEU.

Thereafter, the UK government published a Technical Note on the benefits of a new data protection agreement in which repeated the case for a bespoke legally binding agreement on the basis that:

> a key benefit of such an agreement, over a standard Adequacy Decision, is that we can negotiate the right governance mechanisms for our future data relationship. This could include an agreed approach to the standards applied and their interpretation, and to enforcement and dispute resolution.[45]

It proposed to resolve disputes using the terms of a bespoke agreement with the explicit aim of avoiding a *Schrems*-like scenario, that is, the Commission would not be able to unilaterally suspend or repeal an adequacy decision thereby halting EU-UK data transfers. Subsequently, the UK government published a further paper in which it repeated its proposals but added that, 'The UK is ready to begin preliminary discussions on an adequacy assessment so that a data protection agreement is in place by the end of the implementation period at the latest.'[46]

Given the Commission's consistent refusal to offer the UK a bespoke data protection agreement outside the scope of the GDPR adequacy criteria and procedure, the UK's Exiting the EU Committee proposed a pragmatic solution. It recommended that the UK begin the process of applying for an adequacy decision without delay while continuing to explore the possibility of a bespoke agreement that could ultimately replace an adequacy decision.[47]

The UK pursued this course of action – the political declaration outlined an intention by the UK to seek an adequacy assessment during the transition period with the EU confirming an intention to adopt an adequacy decision by the end of the transition period 'if the applicable conditions are met',[48] that is, should the UK satisfy the 'essentially equivalent' level of protection test. In effect, the trade negotiations and adequacy assessment were conducted on separate, parallel tracks, something the EU could insist upon as the stronger economic party in the negotiations. The EU insisted on this course of action to ensure that the UK could not seek to lower EU data protection standards during any trade negotiations. The Commission takes the

---

[44] European Commission, Speech by Michel Barnier at the 28th Congress of the International Federation for European Law (FIDE), Lisbon, 26 May 2018, SPEECH/18/3962, http://europa.eu/rapid/press-release_SPEECH-18-3962_en.htm accessed 19 April 2021.

[45] HM Government, Technical Note: Benefits Of A New Data Protection Agreement, 7 June 2018, https://assets.publishing.service.gov.uk/government/uploads/system/uploads/attachment_data/file/714677/Data_Protection_Technical_Note.pdf accessed 19 April 2021, para 6.

[46] HMG response to the Committee on Exiting the European Union Seventh Report of Session 2017–18, The progress of the UK's negotiations on EU withdrawal: Data (HC 1317, 6 Sept. 2018) https://publications.parliament.uk/pa/cm201719/cmselect/cmexeu/1564/156402.htm accessed 19 April 2021, para 3.

[47] Ibid., para 9.

[48] Political declaration setting out the framework for the future relationship between the European Union and the United Kingdom, OJ 2019 C 384 I/02.

view that they should be kept separate 'to keep trade deals uncontroversial',[49] particularly as 'For the EU, privacy is not a commodity to be traded. Data protection is a fundamental right in the EU'[50] and protection of fundamental rights is non-negotiable.[51] By divorcing the adequacy assessment from trade talks, the EU maintained a strategic competitive advantage while simultaneously defending its own regulatory principles. And it did so, because as Lynskey observes:

> in data protection law, although there is no reference to mutual trust in the GDPR or the 1995 Directive, it is the assumed mutual respect for fundamental rights standards (provided for in EU secondary legislation) that facilitates the 'free movement' of personal data within EU Member States, without need for formal adequacy findings.[52]

Such trust does not automatically exist in relation to third countries, rather it must be built through formal legal relationships; and as Lynskey notes, it is this change in status i.e., from trusted member state to third country that explains why 'on the eve of the end of the transition period the UK is de facto "adequate" as an EU Member State while the following day it is not'.[53] The UK applying for and obtaining an adequacy decision would restore that trust.

The need to build trust through a legal mechanism also explains why the Political Declaration further stated that the UK 'will take steps to ensure comparable facilitation of personal data flows to the [European] Union' signalling an intention on the part of the UK to pursue mutual adequacy recognition arrangements.[54] The UK, as sovereign state, is equally entitled to assess the adequacy of protection provided by EU member states and any other country seeking to engage in data transfers with it.

4. THE TRADE AND COOPERATION AGREEMENT

On 24 December 2020, after ten rounds of negotiations during an eight-month period, and a mere seven days before the Transition Period was due to end, after which the UK would have commenced trading with the EU on a 'no-deal' basis, that is on World Trade Organisation terms that would have been very economically damaging for both parties, the UK and EU agreed upon the terms of a Trade and Cooperation Agreement (TCA). The TCA was signed

---

[49] Jakob Hanke Vela, Joanna Plucinska and Hans von der Burchard, 'EU trade, the Martin Selmayr way' (*Politico*, 21 Feb. 2018).

[50] Ibid.

[51] The EU similarly excluded data protection from the remit of the Transatlantic Trade and Investment Partnership (TTIP) negotiations (on a proposed trade agreement between the EU and the US), at least in part because of concerns that the talks would put downward pressure on European standards, something the Commission was been unwilling to countenance; James Fontanella-Khan, 'Data protection ruled out of EU-US trade talks', (*Financial Times*, 4 November 2013); Jakob Hanke Vela, Joanna Plucinska and Hans von der Burchard, 'EU trade, the Martin Selmayr way,' (*Politico*, 21 Feb. 2018).

[52] Orla Lynskey, Extraterritorial Impact in Data Protection Law through an EU Law Lens, *DCU Brexit Institute Working Paper* Series – No 8/2020, 12.

[53] Ibid., 6.

[54] HMG, Political Declaration Setting Out The Framework For The Future Relationship Between The European Union And The United Kingdom, (19th October 2019) https://assets.publishing.service.gov.uk/government/uploads/system/uploads/attachment_data/file/840656/Political_Declaration_setting_out_the_framework_for_the_future_relationship_between_the_European_Union_and_the_United_Kingdom.pdf accessed 19 April 2021.

by both parties on 30 December 2020. On that date the UK Parliament approved it and it was implemented into UK law by the enactment of the European Union (Future Relationship) Act 2020. It was applied on a provisional basis within the EU from 1 January 2021 until it entered into force on 1 May 2021 after ratification, by the Council of the EU and the EU Parliament.[55]

While it is less wide-ranging than many had hoped for, it does at least provide a measure of certainty in some respects – not least in relation to the avoidance of tariffs or quotas on goods passing between the UK and the EU. It also provides for limited mutual market access in services (subject to further negotiations on certain aspects e.g., equivalence for financial services), as well as for cooperation mechanisms in a range of policy areas, including data protection and transitional provisions about EU access to UK fisheries, and UK participation in some EU programmes.

More specifically, Title III sets out the basis for the EU and the UK to cooperate on digital trade, i.e., trade carried out by 'electronic means'.[56] It is based on a reaffirmation by each party of their respect for the Universal Declaration of Human Rights and other international human rights treaties to which they are parties.[57] And there is an express affirmation of the commitment of each party to high levels of personal data protection, alongside a commitment to work together to promote high international standards and to engage in dialogue, the exchange of expertise, and cooperation on enforcement.[58] The TCA also states that both the UK and the EU agree not to restrict cross border data flows. There is a list of the types of provisions that would count as a restriction – ranging from data localisation provisions, through to requirements to use locally certified or approved computing facilities.[59]

One element of the TCA that drew criticism was the failure by the Commission to faithfully reproduce in the text of TCA horizontal EU provisions on cross-border data flows and protection of personal data and privacy in the Digital Trade Title of EU trade agreements endorsed by the European Commission in 2018.[60] The relevant clauses in the TCA do not state that data protection is a fundamental right which could lead to arguments that it does not warrant the same level of protection as other fundamental rights, not least because a second clause contains wording that could give rise to conflict if EU laws protecting privacy and related to data protection were challenged in a trade dispute as the EU would need to justify its data protection and privacy laws under strict tests based on Article XIV of the General Agreement on Trade in Services.[61]

Whilst the Commission's actions, in 'watering down' the horizontal clauses were expedient in bringing UK-EU trade negotiations to a conclusion, and are moot now that the UK has

---

[55] Art 217 TFEU; The European Parliament voted by a majority of 655 in favour of the TCA on 27 April 2021. On 29 April 2021, the Council adopted a decision on the conclusion of the agreement, the final step in the EU's ratification process.

[56] Art DIGIT.2, TCA.

[57] Art COMPROV.4, TCA.

[58] COMPROV.19, TCA

[59] The provision is to be reviewed three years; Art 6, TCA.

[60] European Commission, 'Horizontal Provisions on Cross-border Data Flows and Personal Data Protection' (news release of 18 May 2018) http://ec.europa.eu/newsroom/just/item-detail.cfm?item_id=627665 accessed 31 May 2021; See also: European Commission, EU proposal for provisions on Cross-border data flows and protection of personal data and privacy, http://trade.ec.europa.eu/doclib/docs/2018/july/tradoc_157130.pdf accessed 31 May 2021.

[61] Title X.

secured an adequacy decision and data transfers have been brought under the GDPR framework, the Commission's approach could prove short-sighted should other third countries such as Australia who are engaging in trade negotiations with the EU seek to negotiate the inclusion of similarly broad horizontal provisions in any trade agreement it secures with the EU. Repeated inclusions of such clauses in trade negotiations could have the effect of 'watering down' the EU's high standards of data protection over time, if the third country did not also proceed to seek an EU adequacy assessment. Unsurprisingly, the European Data Protection Supervisor expressed regret and concern that 'In amending the legal wording of the horizontal provisions, the TCA unnecessarily creates legal uncertainty as to the Union's position on the protection of personal data in connection with EU trade agreements and risks creating friction with the EU data protection legal framework.'[62] In an effort to calm the waters and reassert the EU's commitment to high standards of data protection the EDPS has invited the Commission to 'clearly reiterate its commitment to the horizontal provisions as the only basis for future trade agreements by the EU with other third countries, and [to confirm] that personal data protection and privacy rights will not be up for negotiation'.[63]

4.1 TCA Transitional Data Protection Arrangements

The Trade and Cooperation Agreement does not, however, include an adequacy decision to facilitate EEU-UK personal data transfers. A Declaration attached to the TCA recorded the European Commission's intention to 'promptly launch the procedure for the adoption of adequacy decisions with respect to the UK under the General Data Protection Regulation', once the adequacy assessment process was complete.[64] The TCA is silent on adequacy because as explained above, an adequacy assessment is a separate process. And although the Commission had agreed to commence its assessment of UK adequacy, using the powers conferred to it by Article 45(3) of the GDPR, in parallel with the trade negotiations, the assessment was not complete by the time the negotiations ended.

To avoid a data protection 'cliff-edge' the TCA contained further transitional arrangements to facilitate EEA-UK transfers pending the outcome of the adequacy assessment. It provided that the UK would not be treated as a third country for GDPR purposes for a 'specified period' that began on 1 January 2021 and would end either on the date on which an adequacy decision in relation to the UK was adopted by the European Commission under Article 45(3) of the GDPR, or after four months (i.e., until 1 May 2021), a period which could be extended by

---

62 EDPS, EDPS Opinion on the conclusion of the EU and UK trade agreement and the EU and UK exchange of classified information agreement, Opinion 3/2021, (22 February 2021), https://edps.europa.eu/system/files/2021-02/2021_02_22_opinion_eu_uk_tca_en.pdf, 8.

63 Ibid., 10–11; See also: Svetlana Yakovleva, Kristina Irion, 'Pitching trade against privacy: reconciling EU governance of personal data flows with external trade' (2020) International Data Privacy Law, 10(3), 201–221.

64 Declarations referred to in the Council Decision on the signing on behalf of the Union, and on a provisional application of the Trade and Cooperation Agreement and of the Agreement concerning security procedures for exchanging and protecting classified information, Declaration on The Adoption of Adequacy Decisions with Respect to The United Kingdom, Official Journal of the European Union L 444/1475, 31.12.2020.

two months by agreement, i.e., until 1 July 2021, if extra time were needed to complete the assessment.[65]

However, the transition period was conditional on the UK not amending its data protection legislation or exercising 'designated powers' such as recognising other third countries as adequate for data transfer purposes, or approving new codes of conduct, certification mechanisms, binding corporate rules, standard contractual clauses or administrative arrangements during the 'specified period,' since changes could jeopardise a finding of adequacy.[66] The only permitted changes were those made to ensure alignment with rules applicable in the EU, for example recognising the new Standard Contractual Clauses (SCC), when adopted by the EU.[67] If the UK otherwise changed its data protection laws or exercised any of the designated powers without consent, the bridging mechanism and specified period would automatically end.

5. POST-TRANSITION DATA PROTECTION IN THE UK AND ADEQUACY REGULATIONS

Given the need for close alignment with the GDPR to initially secure an adequacy decision, and to maximise the likelihood of renewal of an adequacy decision in due course, it should come as no surprise that the UK data protection law is in essence a facsimile of the GDPR. When the transition period ended the GDPR was incorporated into UK law by virtue of regulations made pursuant to the European Union (Withdrawal) Act 2018. The Data Protection, Privacy and Electronic Communications (Amendments etc) (EU Exit) Regulations 2019 (hereafter DPPEC Regulations) renamed the GDPR as the 'EU GDPR' and generated a 'UK GDPR' by making numerous changes to the GDPR text to allow it to be retained as UK domestic law.[68] For instance, references to EU institutions and procedures were removed and replaced with appropriate post-transition terms e.g., references to 'Union or Member State law' were replaced with references to 'domestic law', and references to decisions made by the EU Commission were replaced with references to decisions made by the UK government. The DPA 2018 was similarly revised.[69] The fundamental principles, obligations on data controllers and processors, and rights for individuals remain the same.

As for transfers of personal data outside the UK they are only permissible if an adequacy decision or appropriate safeguard is in place, or, where a derogation applies. To this end, the DPPEC Regulations provide that derogations continue to be available, and all Binding Corporate Rules (BCRs) authorised, and EU Standard Contractual Clauses issued by the EU before the end of the transition period continue to be recognised as valid by the UK, but any new SCCs must be submitted to the ICO or respective EU supervisory authorities. Likewise, a BCR-holder is required to transfer to the appropriate lead authority and appoint a representative, in the relevant jurisdictions.

---

[65] Art FINPROV.10A (1) and (2), TCA.

[66] Art FINPROV.10A (3), TCA.

[67] EU Commission, 'Data Protection -Standard Contractual Clauses for Transferring Personal Data to Non-EU Countries (Implementing Act)' (*Have your say*) https://ec.europa.eu/info/law/better-regulation/have-your-say/initiatives/12741-Commission-Implementing-Decision-on-standard-contractual-clauses-for-the-transfer-of-personal-data-to-third-countries accessed 19 April 2021.

[68] SI 419/2019, Schedule 1.

[69] Ibid., Schedule 2.; Withdrawal Agreement, Art 128(5).

The UK also ensured that data flows could continue by preserving all EU adequacy decisions adopted by the EU prior to the end of the transition period (e.g., in respect of Andorra, Japan and New Zealand), and by specifying that all EEA countries, EU institutions and bodies are considered to provide an adequate level of protection on a transitional basis. Gibraltar has also been recognised as offering an adequate level of protection, no doubt because Gibraltar is a British overseas territory.

These steps offer certainty and continuity of data flows in the short term, but in recognition of the UK's 'reclaimed' regulatory autonomy, power is conferred on the UK Secretary of State for Digital, Culture, Media and Sport (DCMS) to conduct its own adequacy assessments in respect of transfers outside the UK.[70] Little information is available on the criteria the UK intends to use to assess adequacy apart from public statements that it intends to adopt an outcomes-based risk assessment approach in the hope that they will be concluded more speedily than adequacy assessments by the EU.[71] What is known is that an adequacy assessment will involve four phases, the first of which is 'gatekeeping', that is, the process by which a specific team within DCMS will consider whether to commence an assessment of a third country (territory or sector therein) or international organisation for adequacy purposes. This phase will be followed by an 'assessment',[72] that is, the programme of work associated with collecting and analysing information relating to the level of data protection in another country, which will be followed by the third phase, namely a recommendation to the secretary of state, and finally a 'procedural phase', during which an *adequacy regulation* (the UK equivalent of an adequacy decision) will be drafted and laid before the Westminster parliament. The ICO and DCMS are expected to meet for discussions at various intervals during the assessment process, and the secretary shall consult the ICO (and other persons they consider to be appropriate) but the secretary of state has ultimate responsible for issuing adequacy regulations and is not bound by the views of the ICO. [73]

The secretary of state will maintain a list of countries, territories, sectors and organisations deemed adequate. If the secretary of state determines that a country does not provide an adequate level of protection, then data flows could be restricted – through a refusal to make an adequacy regulation or the revocation of an existing *adequacy regulation* if one exists.[74]

---

[70] Section 17A, DPA 2018; See also the Memorandum of Understanding between the Secretary of State for Digital, Culture, Media & Sport and the UK Information Commissioner's Office with respect to new UK adequacy assessments following the UK's departure from the European Union, signed on 19 March 19, 2021, https://www.gov.uk/government/publications/memorandum-of-understanding-mou-on-the-role-of-the-ico-in-relation-to-new-uk-adequacy-assessments/memorandum-of-understanding-mou-on-the-role-of-the-ico-in-relation-to-new-uk-adequacy-assessments accessed 19 April 2021.

[71] Statement made by Oliver Patel, Head of Inbound Data Flows, Department for Digital, Culture, Media and Sport (DCMS) at Commercial data transfers between UK and EU and the adequacy decision, Cross DPN Online Workshop, 22 April 2021.

[72] Art 45 UK GDPR.

[73] Section 182(2) of the DPA 2018; Art 36(4) of the UK GDPR.

[74] DCMS, Memorandum of Understanding on the role of The ICO in relation to New UK Adequacy Assessments, 19 March 2021, https://ico.org.uk/media/about-the-ico/mou/2619468/uk-adequacy-assessments-ico-dcms-memorandum-of-understanding.pdf.

6. AN 'UNSTABLE' ADEQUACY DECISION

As outlined above, the UK's application for an adequacy assessment was not finalised by the time the TCA was concluded. It was continuing as a separate, parallel process. The UK government had to demonstrate to the Commission that the UK provides an adequate i.e., essentially equivalent level of protection to that in the EU by meeting the criteria in Article 45 of the GDPR and elaborated on in the EDPB's 'adequacy referential,'[75] and corresponding CJEU case law. When assessing adequacy, the Commission was not merely concerned with assessing whether the UK had an appropriate legislative framework regarding data protection, it also had to make a normative judgment about the UK's political structures and values, including respect for the rule of law and respect for human rights and fundamental freedoms. This necessitated an assessment inter alia of UK data protection law and derogations therein, an assessment of data protection procedures and practices and oversight and enforcement measures, a review of surveillance powers in the Investigatory Powers Act 2016, and of provisions to facilitate onward transfers of EEA data from the UK to third countries. To this end, the UK government submitted to the Commission a series of policy documents entitled the 'Explanatory Framework for Adequacy Discussions',[76] covering a wide range of topics, including the legislative framework, restrictions and processing conditions, and the role and effectiveness of the ICO, in which it set out its case for a finding of adequacy.

Many deficiencies in UK laws and practices that could prove a bar to a finding of adequacy were identified, including an overly broad immigration exemption in the UK's Data Protection Act 2018, the UK government's decision not to retain the EU Charter in UK law and declarations of an intention to 'opt out' of parts of the European Convention on Human Rights, or at least from interpretations of the Convention by the European Court of Human Rights,[77] and concerns that the Investigatory Powers Act 2016 does not contain substantive limits and safeguards powers regarding retention of and access to bulk data for national security purposes to be compatible with EU fundamental rights law,[78] and relatedly that UK membership of the Five Eyes Intelligence Sharing Alliance posed problems in relation to onward transfers of data from EEA countries to the US especially, but also to other third countries without an adequacy decision in place.[79]

---

[75] Article 29 Working Party, 'Adequacy Referential' (2018), wp254rev.01.

[76] HMG, Explanatory framework for adequacy discussions, (13 March 2020) https://www.gov.uk/government/publications/explanatory-framework-for-adequacy-discussions accessed 31 May 2021.

[77] Owen Bowcott, *UK government plans to remove key human rights protections*, *The Guardian*, (13 September 2020), https://www.theguardian.com/law/2020/sep/13/uk-government-plans-to-remove-key-human-rights-protections accessed 31 May 2021.

[78] Ian Brown and Douwe Korff, The inadequacy of UK data protection law Part One: General inadequacy, https://www.ianbrown.tech/wp-content/uploads/2020/10/Korff-and-Brown-UK-adequacy.pdf accessed 19 April 2021, and The inadequacy of UK data protection law in general and in view of UK surveillance laws, Part Two: UK Surveillance, https://www.ianbrown.tech/wp-content/uploads/2020/11/Korff-Brown-Submission-to-EU-re-UK-adequacy-Part-Two-DK-IB201130.pdf, accessed 19 April 2021 and Case C-623/17, Privacy International v Secretary of State for Foreign and Commonwealth Affairs and Others, ECLI:EU:C:2020:790.

[79] Ibid.; See also: Oliver Patel and Dr Nathan Lea, 'EU-UK Data Flows, Brexit and No-Deal: Adequacy or Disarray? UCL European Institute, August 2019, https://www.ucl.ac.uk/european-institute/sites/european-institute/files/eu-uk_data_flows_brexit_and_no_deal_updated.pdf, accessed 31 May 2021.

Given these deficiencies, the EU Commission's announcement on 19 February 2021 that it had completed its assessment and publication of a draft adequacy decision in which it found that the UK provides an adequate level of protection[80] was met with consternation in some circles, particularly amongst those who had called for the Commission to adopt a pure or strict approach to interpretation of the legal provisions and standards.[81] Those of us who have followed the Commission's work in the field, in particular its track record of adopting of two deficient adequacy decisions in respect of the US, were less surprised that once again the Commission took account not only of data protection considerations but also political and economic considerations when conducting its assessment.[82]

Thereafter the European Data Protection Board (EDPB) was asked to provide its opinion on UK adequacy. It noted 'strong alignment' on key areas between the EU and UK data protection frameworks on core provisions such as lawful and fair processing for legitimate purposes, purpose limitation, special categories of data, and on automated decision-making and profiling. It also noted the UK's stated intention to diverge from the GDPR and, on that basis, welcomed the Commission's proposal to limit an adequacy decision to four years and to closely monitor developments in the UK in the interim. As regards surveillance powers and concomitant oversight powers and safeguards, the EDPB opinion welcomed the creation of the UK's Investigatory Powers Tribunal and its ability to review access to data by UK national security agencies, and the establishment of the Judicial Commissioners in the Investigatory Powers Act 2016 to ensure better oversight, and to provide individuals with opportunities to seek redress. Nevertheless, the EDPB opinion raised concerns related to national security monitoring, bulk interceptions, independent oversight related to the use of automated processing tools, and the lack of safeguards under UK law related to overseas disclosure of data, especially for national security exemptions, and recommended that the Commission further assess and/or closely monitor these deficiencies.[83]

A few weeks later, MEPs passed a resolution in the European Parliament on the draft adequacy decision in which they asked the Commission to modify its draft decision that the UK data protection provides an adequate level of protection and concomitantly that data can safely be transferred there pending rectification of several deficiencies.[84] Several MEPs made

---

[80] European Commission, Draft Commission Implementing Decision pursuant to Regulation (EU) 2016/679 of the European Parliament and of the Council on the adequate protection of personal data by the United Kingdom, https://ec.europa.eu/info/sites/info/files/draft_decision_on_the_adequate_protection_of_personal_data_by_the_united_kingdom_-_general_data_protection_regulation_19_feb_2020.pdf accessed 19 April 2021.

[81] Douwe Korff, The inadequacy of the EU Commission's Draft GDPR Adequacy Decision on the UK, (03.03.2021) https://www.ianbrown.tech/2021/03/03/the-inadequacy-of-the-eu-commissions-draft-gdpr-adequacy-decision-on-the-uk/ accessed 31 May 2021.

[82] Karen Mc Cullagh, 'EU-UK Trade Deal: Implications for Personal Data Transfers' Blogdroiteuropeen, (06.01.21) https://blogdroiteuropeen.com/2021/01/06/eu-uk-trade-deal-implications-for-personal-data-transfers-by-karen-mc-cullagh/ accessed 31 May 2021.

[83] EDPB, Opinion 14/2021 regarding the European Commission Draft Implementing Decision pursuant to Regulation (EU) 2016/679 on the adequate protection of personal data in the United Kingdom, Adopted on 13 April 2021, https://edpb.europa.eu/sites/edpb/files/files/file1/edpb_opinion142021_ukadequacy_gdpr.pdf_en.pdf accessed 19 April 2021.

[84] European Parliament, Press Release: Data protection: MEPs urge the Commission to amend UK adequacy decisions (21.05.21) https://www.europarl.europa.eu/news/en/press-room/20210517IPR04124/data-protection-meps-urge-the-commission-to-amend-uk-adequacy-decisions accessed 31 May 2021.

reference to a research paper that identified deficiencies including shortcomings in the implementation of EU data protection standards linked to the immigration exemption, the overly broad definition of personal data in the Digital Economy Act 2017, weak enforcement of data protection rules by the UK Information Commissioner's Office, potential liberal onward transfer of data to the US, the UK's wavering commitment to EU data protection and human rights standards i.e., stated intention to diverge, and UK surveillance laws and practices pertaining to bulk surveillance and data retention practices that do not comply with CJEU and ECtHR law.[85]

Shortly thereafter the Court of Appeal in England and Wales ruled in *R (Open Rights Group and the 3million) v Secretary of State for the Home Department and Others*, that an exemption in the UK Data Protection Act 2018 which disapplied many data subject rights such as the right of subject access or erasure when personal data was processed for 'the maintenance of effective immigration control' or the 'investigation or detection of activities that would undermine the maintenance of effective immigration control' – at least to those matters which would be prejudiced by complying with the data subject rights, was unlawful because it was overly broad and therefore incompatible with Article 23 of the GDPR and, by extension, the UK GDPR.[86]

These criticisms prompted the Commission to make some changes to its draft adequacy decision prior to adoption on 28 June 2021, a mere two days before the expiration of the TCA bridging mechanism facilitating EEA-UK personal data transfers. Significantly, the adequacy decision does not, at present, cover transfers of personal data to the UK for immigration control purposes, in response to the Court of Appeal judgment which ruled that the immigration exemption in the DPA 2018 is unlawful. The Commission has, however, indicated a willingness to reassess this exclusion once it has been remedied under UK law.[87]

As regards surveillance measures, the Commission stated in a press release accompanying the adequacy decision that it was satisfied the UK system provides an adequate level of protection because the collection of data by UK intelligence authorities is limited to what is strictly necessary to achieve the legitimate objective in question, subject to prior authorisation by an independent judicial body, and individuals have the ability to seek redress via the UK Investigatory Powers Tribunal.[88] Nevertheless, criticism has been expressed that the Commission did not properly scrutinise UK law to ensure compliance with EU law, such that it could be the subject of a legal challenge and suffer a similar fate to the Safe Harbor and its successor Privacy Shield, adequacy decisions, that is, revoked.[89]

---

[85] European Parliamentary Research Service, EU-UK private-sector data flows after Brexit: Settling Adequacy, PE 690.536 – April 2021, https://www.europarl.europa.eu/RegData/etudes/IDAN/2021/690536/EPRS_IDA(2021)690536_EN.pdf accessed 19 April 2021.

[86] *The Open Rights Group & Anor, R (on the Application of) v The Secretary of State for the Home Department & Anor* [2021] EWCA Civ 800. The Court deferred a decision as to appropriate relief, pending further submissions from the parties. It may well be that the DPA 2018 will now need to be amended.

[87] European commission, Press Statement: Data protection: Commission adopts adequacy decisions for the UK, 28 June 2021.

[88] European Commission, Commission Implementing Decision of 28.6.2021 pursuant to Regulation (EU) 2016/679 of the European Parliament and of the Council on the adequate protection of personal data by the United Kingdom, C(2021) 4800 final, https://ec.europa.eu/info/files/decision-adequate-protection-personal-data-united-kingdom-general-data-protection-regulation_en, para 275.

[89] Korff contends inter alia that the decision completely fails to assess (or even note) the UK's intelligence agencies' actual surveillance practices; Douwe Korff, The inadequacy of the

The adequacy decision may prove unstable for another reason, namely that adequacy decisions are 'living' documents that need to be 'closely monitored and adapted when developments affect the level of protection ensured by the third country'.[90] To this end, the adequacy decision provides an automatic review of the UK legal regime within four years, and it will automatically expire on 27 June 2025 if the Commission has not made a renewed finding of adequacy by then.[91] This reflects the Commission's awareness that as a third country the UK could seek to diverge from the GDPR, and its other international obligations. As Věra Jourová, Vice-President of the Commission for Values and Transparency, explained, 'we have listened very carefully to the concerns expressed by the Parliament, the Member States and the European Data Protection Board, in particular on the possibility of future divergence from our standards in the UK's privacy framework'.[92] The Commission is undoubtedly aware of the UK's vacillating and contradictory statements on the European Convention on Human Rights,[93] as in the statement accompanying the draft decision the Commission stated: 'the UK is – and has committed to remain – party to the European Convention on Human Rights and to Convention 108 of the Council of Europe…Continued adherence to such international conventions is of particular importance for the stability and durability of the proposed adequacy findings'.[94] Clearly, withdrawal from the European Convention on Human Rights and/or the ambit of the associated court, or other changes to the UK's legal framework e.g., regarding surveillance laws, or onward transfers to third countries, or drifting judicial interpretation by UK courts of core concepts such as the definition of personal data, or failure to revise the DPA 2018 in light of ECtHR and CJEU judgments such that the UK no longer provides an adequate level of protection, could prompt early review of the adequacy decision and its revocation or non-renewal.

EU Commission Draft GDPR Adequacy Decision on the UK, Executive Summary, (3 March 2021) KORFF-The-Inadequacy-of-the-EU-Commn-Draft-GDPR-Adequacy-Decision-on-the-UK-Executive-Summary-210303final accessed 19 April 2021 and Douwe Korff, The inadequacy of the EU Commission Draft GDPR Adequacy Decision on the UK, (3 March 2021) KORFF-The-Inadequacy-of-the-EU-Commn-Draft-GDPR-Adequacy-Decision-on-the-UK-210303final accessed 19 April 2021; Vincent Manancourt, 'UK data flows get Brussels' blessing, with caveats,' (*Politico*, 17 April 2021), Two campaigners, speaking on the condition of anonymity, told *Politico* that they were looking to raise funds for a potential legal challenge.

[90] European Commission, 'Communication from the Commission to the European Parliament and the Council, Exchanging and Protecting Personal Data in a Globalised World' (Communication No COM (2017) 7 Final, European Commission, 10 January 2017, 8–9.

[91] European Commission, Commission Implementing Decision of 28.6.2021 pursuant to Regulation (EU) 2016/679 of the European Parliament and of the Council on the adequate protection of personal data by the United Kingdom, C(2021) 4800 final, https://ec.europa.eu/info/files/decision-adequate-protection-personal-data-united-kingdom-general-data-protection-regulation_en, accessed 31 May 2021, para 289.

[92] European Commission, Press Release: Data protection: Commission adopts adequacy decisions for the UK, 28 June 2021, https://ec.europa.eu/commission/presscorner/detail/en/ip_21_3183 accessed 31 May 2021.

[93] Owen Bowcott, *UK government plans to remove key human rights protections*, *The Guardian*, (13 September 2020), https://www.theguardian.com/law/2020/sep/13/uk-government-plans-to-remove-key-human-rights-protections accessed 31 May 2021.

[94] European Commission, Press Release: Data protection: European Commission launches process on personal data flows to UK, 19 February 2021, https://ec.europa.eu/commission/presscorner/detail/en/ip_21_66>1 accessed 31 May 2021.

7. LONGER-TERM: CONTINUED ALIGNMENT V DIVERGENCE

Evidently, Brexit has added to the complexity of the UK, and indeed, global data protection landscape. And, as Celeste astutely observed,

> Brexit does not achieve its long-awaited objective of freeing UK data protection law from the bridles of EU law. In the TCA, the parties reiterate multiple times their independence, especially from a regulatory point of view, but the data protection reality tells us a different story. The UK legal framework is inexorably put in a position of dependence.[95]

Indeed, whilst the UK government's announcement that it 'intends to expand the list of adequate destinations in line with our global ambitions and commitment to high standards of data protection',[96] will be welcomed by those seeking evidence of the UK reclaiming its sovereignty and boldly seeking to forge new or stronger trade links with countries beyond the EU, it is important to note that the UK's own adequacy status (i.e., adequacy decision facilitating EEA-UK personal data transfers), could be imperilled if the UK were to make a finding of adequacy in respect of countries that the EU has not found adequate and allow such adequacy regulations to be used as a 'back door' for onward transfers of data from EEA countries that would breach GDPR requirements.

Likewise, although the UK can, as a sovereign third country, revise the UK GDPR and DPA 2018, significant divergence could jeopardise the EU-UK adequacy decision and/or impede its renewal. The power to diverge is therefore best described as illusory. And, as the ICO can only participate as an 'observer' in EDPB meetings, Brexit has in fact reduced the UK to a 'rule taker' instead of a rule-maker in respect of EU data protection law. Not only that, but Brexit has made the data protection landscape more onerous for multinationals operating in both jurisdictions because both the UK GDPR and the GDPR have extra-territorial effect. Consequently, the compliance burden for data controllers and processors that process data in both jurisdictions has increased because of the need to appoint a representative in each jurisdiction. Relatedly, a data breach that has a multi-country dimension may require notification of both the ICO and at least one EU supervisory authority of the breach, and a supervisory authority in both jurisdictions could investigate and impose sanctions e.g., fines. This change has already prompted some US-owned companies such as Facebook and Google to transfer all their UK users into user agreements with the corporate headquarters in California, to avoid potential legal action in both the EU and UK.[97] These restrictions and dependencies have

---

[95] Edoardo Celeste, 'Cross-border data protection after Brexit', *DCU Brexit Institute Working Paper Series*, No 4/2021, 12.

[96] ICO and DCMS, Joint Statement: Secretary of State for the Department for Digital, Culture Media and Sport and the Information Commissioner sign Memorandum of Understanding on data adequacy, 19 March 2021 https://ico.org.uk/about-the-ico/news-and-events/news-and-blogs/2021/03/secretary-of-state-for-the-department-for-dcms-and-the-information-commissioner-sign-memorandum-of-understanding/ accessed 19 April 2021.

[97] Joseph Menn, 'Exclusive: Facebook to move UK users to California terms, avoiding EU privacy rule, (*Reuters*, US Legal News, 15 December 2020), https://www.theguardian.com/technology/2020/dec/15/facebook-move-uk-users-california-eu-privacy-laws accessed 19 April 2021; Joseph Menn, 'Exclusive: Google users in UK to lose EU data protection – sources, (*Reuters, Technology News*, 19

prompted some to question whether the UK should, in the longer term, strive for regulatory divergence.

The PM has indicated such an intention in a written statement: 'The UK will in future develop separate and independent policies in areas such as [...] data protection.'[98] Likewise, the UK's Secretary of State for Digital, Culture, Media and Sport Oliver Dowden MP observed that:

> The EU doesn't hold the monopoly on data protection. So, having come a long way in learning how to manage data risks, the UK is going to start making more of the opportunities. Right now, too many businesses and organisations are reluctant to use data – either because they don't understand the rules or are afraid of inadvertently breaking them. That has hampered innovation and the improvement of public services and prevented scientists from making new discoveries. Clearly, not using data has real-life costs.[99]

Comments of this nature have fuelled speculation that the UK will seek to forge its own data protection path. One proposal suggests replacing the UK GDPR with a new 'framework for data protection' that would inter alia reduce reliance on consent by placing greater emphasis 'on the legitimacy of data processing', and removing Article 22, focusing instead on 'whether automated profiling meets a legitimate or public interest test', on the basis that it would reduce onerous compliance burdens and improve the UK's ability to innovate using personal data.[100]

The UK is not alone in expressing frustration with the GDPR. A review conducted two years after its implementation found that 'some stakeholders report that the application of the GDPR is challenging especially for small- and medium-sized enterprises (SMEs)',[101] a concern that was also identified in the UK National Data Strategy.[102] And, Axel Voss, MEP, one of the strongest proponents of the GDPR has asserted that 'the GDPR is not made for blockchain, facial or voice recognition, text and data mining [...] artificial intelligence'.[103] He claims that the GDPR:

> makes it impossible to properly use or even develop these technologies – AI needs access to data for training purposes, yet the vast majority of data is being stored outside the EU, which risks making

---

February 2020), https://www.reuters.com/article/us-google-privacy-eu-exclusive-idUSKBN20D2M3 accessed 19 April 2021.

[98] PM Statement, UK / EU relations: Written statement – HCWS86, 3 February 2020.

[99] Oliver Dowden, 'New approach to data is a great opportunity for the UK post-Brexit' (*Financial Times* 27 February 2021), https://www.ft.com/content/ac1cbaef-d8bf-49b4-b11d-1fcc96dde0e1 accessed 19 April 2021.

[100] The Taskforce on Innovation, Growth and Regulatory Reform (TIGRR), Independent Report, (16 June 2021), https://assets.publishing.service.gov.uk/government/uploads/system/uploads/attachment_data/file/994125/FINAL_TIGRR_REPORT__1_.pdf accessed 19 April 2021, 49–53.

[101] European Commission, Communication from The Commission To The European Parliament And The Council, Data protection as a pillar of citizens' empowerment and the EU's approach to the digital transition – two years of application of the General Data Protection Regulation, COM (2020) 264 final, Brussels, 24.6.2020 https://eur-lex.europa.eu/legal-content/EN/TXT/HTML/?uri=CELEX:DC0264&from=EN accessed 19 April 2021.

[102] DCMS, Policy Paper, National Data Strategy, 9 December 2020, https://www.gov.uk/government/publications/uk-national-data-strategy/national-data-strategy accessed 19 April 2021.

[103] Javier Espinoza, "EU must overhaul flagship data protection laws, says a 'father' of policy," (*Financial Times*, 3 March 2021).

it impossible for us to be competitive in any form of digital innovation, undermining our future economic prosperity.[104]

He has also asserted that 'the coronavirus pandemic also highlighted how the GDPR has prevented better health management, as its provisions hampered the use of tracing apps or even the exchange of data between local authorities for contacting potential vaccine recipients'.[105]

In my view, some of these criticisms are unfounded, or at least a indicate misunderstanding of how data can be processed in compliance with the GDPR.[106] As acknowledged by the Commission, SMEs should be offered additional support e.g., templates, hotlines, and appropriate training to help them understand and meet their GDPR obligations.[107] As for the GDPR impeding innovation, it must be noted that the GDPR does contain lots of 'white spaces' including wide exemptions for research which, if properly developed, will support the UK's world-leading research.[108] If the initial 'teething problems' regarding support for SMEs can be overcome, and the ICO develops guidance explaining how UK-based data controllers and processors can and should interpret the derogations and 'white spaces' in the GDPR, then multi-national data controllers are unlikely to call for the UK government to significantly diverge from the GDPR if it continues, on the whole, to meet their needs because significant divergence could lead to revocation or failure to renew the EU-UK adequacy decision resulting in additional compliance burdens which would be an unwelcome business cost. Accordingly, significant UK divergence from the GDPR would not necessarily be an appropriate response given that customers increasingly value high levels of data protection,[109] and multi-national companies operating in both the EU and UK are likely to promote continued compliance with the GDPR than a multiplicity of different standards.

If the UK were to diverge from the GDPR in the future, such divergence could take several forms. For instance, the UK could follow the US approach in seeking a partial adequacy decision) akin to the US-EU Privacy Shield (e.g., in respect of only the digital and financial sectors of the UK economy), and a different lower standard e.g., Convention 108+ for other personal

[104] Axel Voss, 'How to bring GDPR into the digital age,' (*Politico*, 25 March 2021) https://www.politico.eu/article/gdpr-reform-digital-innovation/ accessed 19 April 2021.

[105] Ibid.

[106] For instance, the ICO has produced guidance for health and social care organisations explaining how personal data may be processed during the coronavirus pandemic, along with guidance for employers conducting workplace testing and for businesses collecting personal data for contact tracing <https://ico.org.uk/global/data-protection-and-coronavirus-information-hub/data-protection-and-coronavirus/> accessed 19 April 2021.

[107] European Commission, Communication from the Commission to the European Parliament and the Council: Data protection as a pillar of citizens' empowerment and the EU's approach to the digital transition - two years of application of the General Data Protection Regulation, COM (2020) 264 final, Brussels, 24.6.2020, 9.

[108] For example, scholars have already developed a concept of functional anonymisation in order to allow greater use to be made of personal data for research purposes. Elliot, M, O'Hara, K, Raab, C, O'Keefe, C.M., Mackey, E, Dibben, C, Gowans, H, Purdam, K and McCullagh, K., 'Functional anonymisation: Personal data and the data environment,' (2018) *Computer Law & Security Review*, 34 (2) 204-221.

[109] Information Commissioner's Office Information Rights Strategic Plan: Trust and Confidence, July 2020.

data processing, given that the UK has ratified this convention already.[110] However, doing so would require at least two parallel standards of privacy and data protection in the UK e.g., a high level, the GDPR-compliant protection for data that is the subject of EU-UK adequacy decision transfers and a separate, lower (e.g., modernised-Council of Europe Convention 108) level of protection for other data. The UK could alternatively seek to diverge wholly from the GDPR and focus on complying with Convention 108+. If the UK (and other countries were to pursue this course of action the GDPR could lose influence over time.[111] But, in my view calls for divergence from the EU standard are not likely to be loud or pressing for as long as the EU remains an important trading partner of the UK, and multi-nationals operating on a global basis support compliance with the EU standard.

8. CONCLUSIONS

This chapter opened by arguing that UK's departure from the EU would serve as an acid test not only of the EU's influence as a trade power and global regulator in general, but more specifically, whether the GDPR has any realistic prospect of becoming the 'global digital gold, standard of data protection'.

Despite protracted and at times rancorous negotiations the parties did eventually agree the terms of a trade and cooperation agreement and the UK retained the GDPR in domestic law and applied for an EU adequacy decision under the GDPR framework having conceded that its request for bespoke arrangements would not be entertained, so in that respect the GDPR adequacy framework can be considered a success. Not only that, but the extra-territorial provisions and mutual adequacy obligations in both the UK GDPR and GDPR have created the conditions for synergy and continued alignment between the two data protection frameworks, with the benchmark of protection being the high standard set in the GDPR, at least for so long as each want to facilitate 'free flows' of data to the other.

Whilst Brexiteers are likely to be disappointed at this outcome given their vociferous calls to restore complete sovereignty, data protection advocates will extol the UK's continued com-

[110] Technically, Convention 108+ is formed of the original Convention 108 (Convention for the Protection of Individuals with regard to Automatic Processing of Personal Data (ETS 108). The Convention is complemented by a supplementary protocol setting out further requirements as regards data protection regulation and transborder personal data flows. See Additional Protocol to the Convention for the Protection of Individuals with regard to Automatic Processing of Personal Data, regarding supervisory authorities and transborder data flows (ETS 108)) and an amending instrument, namely, Protocol amending the Convention for the Protection of Individuals with regard to Automatic Processing of Personal Data (CETS 223). As per Article 37 of that Protocol it will only generally apply once all Parties to Convention 108 have ratified it or on or after 11 October 2023 so long as there are at least 38 Parties to this amending protocol: Council of Europe, *Convention 108+: Convention for the Protection of Individuals with Regard to the Processing of Personal Data* (2018), <https://rm.coe.int/convention- 108-convention-for-the-protection-of-individuals-with-regar/16808b36f1> accessed 19 April 2021.

[111] Greenleaf has observed that CoE Convention 108 is of increasing importance in a world in which the majority of data privacy laws already come from countries outside Europe; Graham Greenleaf, 'Renewing Convention 108: The CoE's 'GDPR Lite' Initiatives,' (2017) UNSW Law Research Paper No. 17-3, 2.

pliance with the GDPR as early evidence of the influence of the GDPR and its effectiveness in in ensuring high standards of data protection in third countries around the world.

Having said that, continued compliance by the UK with the GDPR should not be taken for granted. Rather, it must remain fit for purpose. Accordingly, the EU should not ignore the concerns raised that it hampers innovation and competitiveness. If such concerns are not addressed trade and market forces could act as drivers for divergence from EU data protection law in the longer term. If that were to occur then the EU may not realise its goal of the GDPR becoming the 'global digital gold, standard of data protection'.

In sum, EU data protection advocates have rightly framed the UK's continued compliance with the GDPR as early evidence of the potential for the EU to set the standard of data protection laws and encouraging harmonisation on a global basis, but its longer-term future is not so certain as the GDPR could lose influence over time if it is not fit for purpose. Hence, the UK has left the EU but not EU data protection law behind, for now, at least.

3. Understanding American privacy

Neil Richards, Andrew Serwin and Tyler Blake

I. INTRODUCTION

It is frequently suggested, particularly by European observers, that the United States (US) lacks much in the way of privacy law. Some American consumers, lawyers, and academics also lament that their personal information receives little protection in the law once it is collected and placed 'out there'. Foreign regulators and lawyers trained in European notions of data protection may also look at the American system and see an absence of an overarching generally applicable data protection statute and conclude that American privacy law is either nonexistent or woefully inadequate.

The lack of a European-style data protection law in the US should not be the end of the analysis. American privacy law is not perfect, but US privacy law exists, it provides substantial regulatory effect, and it is surprisingly complex, particularly once the full ramifications of state-level laws are considered. American privacy law is not as easy to appreciate as other bodies of law that have, for example, a general statute that is interpreted by a thick body of cases, and understanding American privacy law therefore must require a wider lens. That does not mean that American privacy law is not real, or that it is insignificant. In fact, in some areas, American law is both denser and more regulatory than its European counterpart, and in some ways state law has driven global privacy laws, such as in the area of data breach laws. The US also has an active and aggressive plaintiffs' bar, and a number of state and federal privacy regulators who are also quite willing to bring enforcement actions. In many ways, companies in the US face more regulatory oversight because of the multiple layers of laws and the numerous regulators they must be concerned with.

This chapter offers a basic roadmap to American privacy law for the uninitiated. Because of the nuances of American privacy law, including the substantial state privacy and security laws, our roadmap is not top-down, but thematic. In order to understand American privacy, we believe that it is important to understand five of its guiding principles. First, American privacy law is *bifurcated* into two discrete regulatory regimes – one covering the government and the other covering the private sector of individuals, corporations, and other institutions. Second, American privacy law takes a *sectoral* or *sectorized* approach, meaning that rather than having a federal omnibus privacy or data protection law, US law regulates particular sectors of human activity in a way that is both piecemeal and more specific where it applies. Third, it is impossible to understand American privacy without taking account of the role of the Federal Trade Commission (FTC), a consumer protection regulator that is more than a century old, and which functions something like a data protection authority with a limited but general authority over trade practices that are unfair or deceptive. Fourth, American privacy law is *federalized*: both the national government and the 50 state governments have passed privacy laws. In this regime, national ('federal') law is supreme where it applies, but the state privacy laws remain very important, particularly those of California which has been an aggressive privacy regulator. Fifth, and finally, questions of *privacy harm* run throughout American privacy law, both as a threshold question required for private litigants to sue, again at the level of damages, as well as in the class certification process for private enforcement in the US.

Once these five principles are appreciated, the body of American privacy law – its system of protections for personal information, as well as the numerous enforcement avenues that exist – become much easier to appreciate, and American privacy law becomes much more comprehensible.

II. BIFURCATION

Privacy law in the US is schematically very different from privacy law in Europe. American privacy and security law is bifurcated into two separate, distinct regulatory schemes; one covering the government and the other covering the private sector. While some laws cross over, affecting both the government and the private sector,[1] most laws address one or the other. While this chapter will focus primarily on regulation in the commercial sphere, it is important to understand that American privacy laws constrain the government as well.

Before one can understand what American privacy law is, one must first understand what privacy is, particularly in the legal or regulatory context. Privacy is a societal norm, often expressed in law,[2] that reflects a society's concern over the collection, protection, processing, and deletion of data regarding an individual. It is not concerned with other forms of data, such as that about an entity, and it does not focus on the activities of third parties who should not have the data, such as identity thieves, but rather on what a person or entity that is authorized to have an individual's data does with it.

Modern American privacy law has often reflected the influence of three different sources of law: the Fair Information Practices, the US Constitution, and federal statutory law. In 1973, the Department of Health, Education, and Welfare (the precursor agency to the modern Department of Health and Human Services) released a report, titled *Records Computers and the Rights of Citizens*, looking at electronic recordkeeping and data storage practices in the United States.[3] The HEW Report proposed that the federal government enact a 'Code of Fair Information Practice', centred on five basic principles:

1. There must be no personal data record-keeping systems whose very existence is secret.
2. There must be a way for an individual to find out what information about him is in a record and how it is used.
3. There must be a way for an individual to prevent information about him that was obtained for one purpose to be used or made available for other purposes without his consent.

---

[1] E.g., the Electronic Communications Privacy Act of 1986, 18 U.S.C. § 2501 et seq., which regulates wiretapping and access to electronic communications by both government and private actors.

[2] The most famous early expression of this concept is, of course, the famous Warren and Brandeis Article, Samuel D Warren and Louis D Brandeis, 'The Right to Privacy', 4 *Harv. L. Rev.* 193 (1890). It was not the first discussion of privacy rights in American law, which has protected privacy rights (though often in other names and guises) for much longer. See: Neil M Richards and Daniel J Solove, 'Privacy's Other Path: Recovering the Law of Confidentiality', 96 *Geo. L. J.* 123 (2007).

[3] Department of Health, Education and Welfare, *Records Computers and the Rights of Citizens* (July 1973).

4. There must be a way for an individual to correct or amend a record of identifiable information about him.
5. Any organization creating, maintaining, using, or disseminating records of identifiable personal data must ensure the reliability of the data for their intended use and must take reasonable precautions to prevent misuse of the data.[4]

These principles, collectively referred to as the Fair Information Practices (or FIPs), are reflected in many of the sectoral laws that govern American privacy and security law.[5] The FIPs are fundamentally based on the concept of 'notice and choice', or the idea that fair information collection and use should provide the consumer with notice about what information is being collected and a choice about whether to agree to the collection or not. However, this principle has been subject to wide-ranging criticism by scholars writing in American privacy law.[6]

The FIPs form the basis of the Privacy Act of 1974, which regulates the collection, use, dissemination, and destruction of personal information held by federal government agencies.[7] The Act was passed in response to rising concerns about the federal government's surveillance and collection of personal data on private citizens, and it was broadly aimed to give citizens the right to access and correct personal information held about them and to restrict the ability of the federal agencies holding these records to disseminate that information.[8]

Other statutes that constrain the US government include the Freedom of Information Act (FOIA)[9] and the Foreign Intelligence Surveillance Act (FISA).[10] FOIA permitted individual citizens to request information from various government agencies, and required agencies to post certain frequently-requested information publicly.[11] FISA is most notable for creating the Foreign Intelligence Surveillance Court (FISC), a secret court which is empowered to authorize surveillance on US persons who are deemed to be operating as 'agents of a foreign power' as long as foreign intelligence gathering is a 'significant purpose' of the investigation.[12]

The US Constitution also plays a significant role in shaping how the government can act with respect to privacy issues for US citizens and 'persons', primarily based on the First and Fourth Amendments. The Fourth Amendment, which protects citizens against unreasonable searches and seizures by law enforcement, has been the primary driver of privacy rights in the

---

4 Ibid.

5 Daniel J Solove and Paul M Schwartz, *Consumer Privacy and Data Protection* (Aspen Publishers 2015), 19–20.

6 E.g., Neil Richards and Woodrow Hartzog, 'Taking Trust Seriously in Privacy Law', 19 *Stanford Technology Law Review* 431 (2016); Aleecia M. McDonald and Lorrie Faith Cranor, 'The Cost of Reading Privacy Policies', 4 I/S*: J. L. Pol'y Info. Soc'y* 543 (2009); Daniel J Solove, 'Introduction: Privacy Self-Management and the Consent Dilemma', 126 *Harv. L Rev.* 1879 (2013); Daniel J Solove and Woodrow Hartzog, 'The FTC and the New Common Law of Privacy', 114 *Colum. L. Rev.* 583 (2014); Julia Angwin, 'Dragnet Nation: A Quest for Privacy, Security, and Freedom in a World of Relentless Surveillance: Chapter 1: Hacked.' *Colo. Tech. LJ* 12 (2014).

7 *Overview of the Privacy Act of 1974: Introduction*, United States Department of Justice, https://www.justice.gov/opcl/introduction.

8 *Overview of the Privacy Act of 1974: Policy Objectives*, United States Department of Justice, https://www.justice.gov/opcl/policy-objectives.

9 5 U.S.C. § 552.

10 50 U.S.C. § 1801 *et seq.*

11 *What is FOIA?*, United States Department of Justice, https://www.foia.gov/about.html.

12 50 U.S.C. § 1804.

criminal law sphere. The landmark Supreme Court case *Katz v. United States* established the modern touchstone for Fourth Amendment application in criminal law – the defendant's 'reasonable expectation of privacy'.[13] In the modern context, the Court has interpreted the Fourth Amendment to prohibit the warrantless use of GPS tracking devices on automobiles[14] and the search of data on a cell phone incident to a lawful arrest.[15] The First Amendment, in particular the freedom of association clause, has also seen use as a source by the Supreme Court for enforcing the privacy rights of citizens against the government.[16]

Two important statutes that apply to both the government and the private sector are the Electronic Communications Privacy Act (ECPA) and the Computer Fraud and Abuse Act (CFAA). ECPA itself is divided into three substantive parts – the Wiretap Act,[17] the Stored Communications Act (SCA),[18] and the Pen Register Act.[19] The Wiretap Act prohibits the interception of any 'wire, oral, or electronic communication' by any person, including US government agents and employees.[20] It contains both civil and criminal penalties for violations, including jail time. The Stored Communications Act prohibits accessing stored electronic communications of all forms, including emails stored on a serves, internet service provider (ISP) records, subscriber records, and metadata.[21] Like the Wiretap Act, the SCA provides both civil and criminal penalties for violation, and protects against intrusion by both governmental and private actors.[22] To access emails and other stored communications less than 180 days old, the government must acquire a warrant.[23] Under the statute, communications older than 180 days required only a subpoena or court order to obtain. However, some courts have held that this lower standard is unconstitutionally permissive and that a warrant is required to access these communications as well.[24] Finally, the Pen Register Act permits law enforcement officials to attach a device (called a 'pen register' or a 'trap and trace device') to a telephone line that logs outgoing calls made by a particular telephone. This provision of ECPA applies only to law enforcement and telephone company personnel.

---

[13] 389 U.S. 347 (1967).

[14] *Jones v. United States*, 565 U.S. 400 (2012).

[15] *Riley v. California*, 134 S. Ct. 2473 (2014).

[16] *See National Association for the Advancement of Colored People v. State of Alabama*, 357 U.S. 449 (1958) (*NAACP*). In *NAACP*, the Court held that a state cannot compel an association to disclose its membership list to the state absent a substantial showing of need by the state. For an explanation of the relationship between the First Amendment and privacy, see generally Neil Richards, *Intellectual Privacy: Rethinking Civil Liberties in the Digital Age* (Oxford University Press 2015).

[17] 18 U.S.C. § 2510 *et seq.*

[18] 18 U.S.C. § 2701 *et seq.*

[19] 18 U.S.C. § 3121 *et seq.*

[20] 18 U.S.C. § 2511. Government employees, such as law enforcement officers, can intercept communications covered by the Wiretap Act after going through an extensive warrant process. *See* 18 U.S.C. §§ 2516, 2518.

[21] 18 U.S.C. §§ 2510, 2701.

[22] 18 U.S.C. §§ 2510, 2701, 2707.

[23] 18 U.S.C. § 2703.

[24] *See Warshak v. United States*, 631 F.3d 266 (6th Cir. 2010). In *Warshak*, the US Court of Appeals for the Sixth Circuit held that individuals have a reasonable expectation of privacy in the contents of emails that are stored with or sent through a commercial ISP. Ibid., at 288. In the October 2017 term, the Supreme Court will address whether a warrant is required to access historical cell phone location data under the SCA in *Carpenter v. United States*. *See* Amy Howe, *Justices to tackle cellphone data case next term*, SCOTUSBLOG (June 5, 2017).

The other major statute that covers acts both by the government and the private sector is the Computer Fraud and Abuse Act. The CFAA was passed in 1984, inspired in part by then-President Ronald Reagan's reaction to the 1983 film *WarGames*, starring Matthew Broderick.[25] Reagan is believed to have said to his advisers, 'I don't understand these computers very well, but this young man obviously did. He had tied into NORAD!'[26] The CFAA, originally enacted to protect critical government and military infrastructure (like NORAD), expanded through a series of amendments to include expanded criminal jurisdiction, increased penalties for criminal offenders, a civil cause of action, and an expansive definition of computer than now covers almost every computer in the US.[27] The CFAA, at its core, makes it illegal to access a computer (1) without authorization or (2) beyond the scope of prior granted authorization for a variety of illicit purposes.[28] The CFAA has been used extensively by both federal prosecutors seeking to prosecute a wide variety of computer-related crimes and by private litigants, particularly employers seeking damages for employee theft of sensitive or confidential business information.[29]

III. SECTORIZATION

Unlike its European counterparts, as noted above, the US does not have a federal omnibus privacy or data protection law. Instead, the federal government has taken a sectoral approach by enacting laws that regulate privacy and data security by focusing on a particular sector of the economy, or particular groups of people, such as children 12 and under who use the internet. Many of the most important federal privacy laws are sector-specific: the Fair Credit Reporting Act (FCRA), for example, focuses on companies that compile individual credit scores, the Health Insurance Portability and Accountability Act (HIPAA) focuses on health care data, the Gramm-Leach-Bliley Act focuses on financial information, and so on.

There are advantages and drawbacks to this approach. Sector-specific regulation allows for greater context specificity and a more detailed approach to the privacy and data security issues that are problematic in a particular industry. However, on the whole, the sectoral approach can leave major gaps in the overall privacy scheme. For example, HIPAA is aimed at regulating the use of health information created by a health care provider (or their business associate) that relates to the condition, provision of care, or payment for care.[30] The particular focus

---

[25] Declan McCullagh, *From 'WarGames' to Aaron Swartz: How U.S. anti-hacking law went astray*, CNET (Mar. 13, 2013). In *WarGames*, a teenage hacker played by Matthew Broderick hacks into the US strategic aerospace defense command using a personal computer and almost inadvertently starts a thermonuclear war. A House Committee Report on the CFAA explicitly references the film as a realistic representation of a personal computer's capacity. *See* 1984 U.S.C.C.A.N. 3689, 3696.

[26] Lou Cannon, The Reagan Presidency: Every night at the movies: White House: A creature of Hollywood, Ronald Reagan drew his reality from the films he watched, not from his aides or his briefing books, *L.A. Times*, April 28, 1991.

[27] McCullagh, *supra* note 25. For a more comprehensive look at the amendments to the CFAA and their effects on the law, see Office of Legal Education, *Prosecuting Computer Crimes*, Executive Office for United States Attorneys 2–3 (2010).

[28] 18 U.S.C. § 1030 *et seq.*

[29] Andrew B Serwin, *Information Security and Privacy: A Guide to Federal and State Law and Compliance* Vol. 1 173–74 (2016).

[30] Ibid.

of HIPAA has permitted regulators to address issues particular (such as those dealing with clinical laboratories and student vaccination records) to the health care field with specificity.[31] However, the law is not a comprehensive medical privacy law because it does not cover data when it is not generated by the specific types of entities that are covered by HIPAA. As new technologies create and share health data outside HIPAA, it is likely that this phenomenon will increase.

Another sectoral federal privacy law, the Video Privacy Protection Act (VPPA), offers a good example of a law that is effective at regulating the conduct described, but it is narrowly tailored. The VPPA makes it a federal crime for a video tape service provider to knowingly disclose any personally identifiable information concerning a customer, and also offers civil remedies for people whose statutory rights have been violated.[32] This law was quickly enacted after a Washington, DC-area newspaper obtained and published Supreme Court nominee Robert Bork's family's video rental records in the 1980s.[33] The VPPA requires law enforcement to obtain a warrant before obtaining protected records, and provides a civil cause of action for any person aggrieved by the knowing disclosure of protected records.[34] While the VPPA has proven effective in protecting access to customers' video rental records, it does not protect other datasets that are related, including some of those that might be described as implicating 'intellectual privacy'.[35] Many states protect reader privacy, however, often in the context of library records.[36]

IV. THE FEDERAL TRADE COMMISSION

The US government agency that has been most involved in privacy regulation across sectors at the national level has been the FTC. The FTC sets the agenda for consumer protection in the US, and privacy is a prominent part of this agenda. Despite its now central role in consumer protection, the FTC was established in the early 20th century and focused on unfair competition by businesses. These origins of the FTC, including its original jurisdictional scope, required Congress to significantly amend the Federal Trade Commission Act (FTCA) to provide the FTC with authority to address harms to consumers. This was achieved by giving the FTC expanded ability to act to stop 'deceptive' and 'unfair' acts or practices. Over time, both the courts and the FTC have clarified the FTC's jurisdiction to protect consumers, and the FTC has taken an increased role in privacy enforcement, first through cases alleging deception, and then through cases relying upon the FTC's unfairness authority.[37]

The FTC has become the lead privacy enforcer in the US, and has expanded its portfolio in recent years to focus on international cooperation in privacy and consumer protection.

---

[31] Ibid., 962.

[32] Ibid.

[33] Neil M Richards, 'The Perils of Social Reading', 101 *Geo. L.J.* 689, 694–96 (2013).

[34] Ibid.

[35] Ibid., 691. Included in the broader concept of intellectual privacy is that the media materials an individual consumes, whether it be in video, print, or audio form, should be protected from disclosure. See generally, Richards (2015) (n 16).

[36] Richards (2013) (n 33) 693.

[37] Andrew B Serwin, 'The Federal Trade Commission and Privacy: Defining Enforcement and Encouraging the adoption of best practices', 48 *San Diego L. Rev.* 809 (2011).

International enforcement and policy cooperation also has become more important with the proliferation of complex cross-border data flows and cloud computing. To protect consumers in this rapidly changing environment, the FTC participates in various international policy initiatives, including those in multilateral organizations such as the OECD and the Asia-Pacific Economic Cooperation forum (APEC), as well as international cooperation between consumer protection regulators.

Within the OECD, the FTC has participated in the Working Party on Information Security and Privacy, which led the development of the 2007 OECD Council's Recommendation on Cross-border Co-operation in the Enforcement of Laws Protecting Privacy. In APEC, the FTC has been actively involved in an initiative to establish a self-regulatory framework governing the privacy of data transfers throughout the APEC region.

While Section 5, discussed below, is the main focus of the FTC's enforcement power, this was not its first foray into consumer privacy – in the 1970s the FTC was given authority to enforce under the FCRA. Now, while the FTC still enforces under the FCRA, Section 5 is the most common basis of enforcement.

The FTC's deception power was articulated in its 1983 'Policy Statement on Deception', and later discussed in the case of *In re Cliffdale Associates*. The FTC will find an act or practice deceptive if (1) 'there is a representation, omission, or practice' that is (2) 'likely to mislead the consumer acting reasonably in the circumstances' and (3) the representation, omission, or practice is material. In determining whether a practice is deceptive, the FTC will consider the statements from the perspective of a reasonable consumer. Moreover, in the FTC's view, it does not need to prove that the statement need not actually mislead consumers, but rather that it is likely to mislead consumers.

The FTC's unfairness authority was first addressed in *FTC v. Sperry & Hutchinson Co.*, and those principles have been refined over time. In response to a Congressional inquiry, the FTC issued a policy statement that is now known as its 'Unfairness Statement'. Congress also amended the FTC Act to address some of these issues, and ultimately the FTC's view of its unfairness authority can be boiled down to the following: an act or practice is unfair if the injury it causes, or is likely to cause, is (1) substantial, (2) not outweighed by other benefits, and (3) not reasonably avoidable.

The most prominent case addressing the scope of the FTC's unfairness and deception powers in the context of privacy and data security is the Third Circuit's decision in *Federal Trade Commission v. Wyndham Worldwide Corporation*.[38] In *Wyndham*, the FTC brought unfairness and deception charges against the Wyndham hotel chain based upon allegations related to alleged failures of data security. The Third Circuit held that the FTC's unfairness power did extend to cover data security issues, rejecting a challenge brought by the hotel chain which had suffered a series of data breaches.[39]

The FTC has traditionally relied more heavily on its deception power to regulate privacy and information security cases, although it has increasingly offered unfairness as an independent theory for regulation, particularly in data security cases.[40] Deception can be an easier route for the FTC because it avoids the harm analysis that is imbedded in the unfairness analysis;

---

[38] 799 F.3d 236 (2015).

[39] Ibid., 246.

[40] Daniel J Solove and Woodrow Hartzog, 'The FTC and the New Common Law of Privacy', 114 *Colum. L. Rev.* 583, 599 (2014).

in a deception case, by contrast, a material false statement is sufficient to violate the FTC Act. The FTC has averaged about ten such complaints per year for the last couple of decades, although that number seems to be increasing to some extent.[41]

The FTC cases are not published decisions from courts, but a few scholars view FTC consent decrees as the 'new common law of privacy'.[42] While this may overstate the effect that FTC orders and consent decrees play in regulating privacy, primarily because they are only binding on the parties named in the order, and frequently contain provisions expressly stating that the company does not admit any of the conduct or alleged violations, privacy lawyers advising companies in the US certainly consider consent decrees at some level when advising clients. It should be noted that some have criticized the FTC's use of consent decrees to 'fence in' companies that deal with consumer data as arbitrary and unpredictable.[43]

V. PRIVACY FEDERALISM

In the US, state law and state attorneys general play a major role in the development of privacy and data security law. While federal law has taken the lead in sector-specific laws relating to various segments of the economy (such as the Gramm-Leach Bliley law's focus on financial services and HIPAA's focus on healthcare), state legislatures and attorneys general have led the way in other areas, particularly in the area of data breach notification. Data breach notification laws in various states make up a large component of the privacy regulatory burden that companies operating in the US must face and California started this trend by enacting the first data breach law in the world. We now see this trend picked up in many countries, including in Europe. In order to give an overview of some of the elements of state data breach notification laws, it is helpful to look at three examples: California, Massachusetts, and Nevada.

In 2003, California became the first state to enact a data breach notification statute.[44] Today, 48 US states and the District of Columbia have enacted some form of data breach notification law.[45] These state laws, not federal law, drive many of the obligations that companies operating in the US must meet in the event of an inadvertent disclosure of personal data. Under California law, any person or entity who owns or licenses computer data must disclose the breach of their data systems to any consumer whose data the entity knows or reasonably believes has been compromised by the breach.[46] The disclosure must be made as soon as reasonably possible and must include the type(s) of information believed to be disclosed by the breach, the approximate date of the breach (if known), a general description of the incident that resulted in the breach, and the contact information of the person or entity that lost the data in question.[47] California's notification statute also includes a wide definition of personal

---

41 Ibid., 599.

42 See generally ibid.

43 Ibid., 608.

44 Serwin (2016) (n 29) 432–33.

45 National Conference of State Legislatures, *Security Breach Notification Laws*, http://www.ncsl.org/research/telecommunications-and-information-technology/security-breach-notification-laws.aspx accessed 19 November 2021.

46 Serwin (2016) (n 29), 432–33.

47 Ibid., 435. Other types of disclosures may be required by statute depending on which types of information were exposed by the breach. For example, the entity issuing the notification is required to

information, including medical information and health insurance information, as well as user-name and password for certain accounts.[48] In addition, the California Department of Consumer Affairs' Office of Privacy Protection has distributed a list of best practices for companies to follow in the event that their databases have been breached and notification is required, including adopting written procedures for documenting data security incidents, designating specific individuals to coordinate specific elements of a data breach response, and ensuring third parties that can access data adopt similar practices.[49] Any consumer who is harmed by a violation of the California breach notification statute is authorized to bring suit against the breaching entity for damages.[50]

Massachusetts is another example of a robust state data breach notification law. However, the requirements under the Massachusetts breach notification statute are different from California's. Under Massachusetts law, in the event of a qualifying breach, the entity that was breached must contact not only the affected consumers, but also the state Attorney General's office and the Office of Consumer Affairs and Business Regulation.[51] The timing requirements are similar to the California data breach notification laws. Unlike California, which requires a general description of the incident that led to the data breach, Massachusetts prohibits companies from including this information in their notification.[52] The Massachusetts law also requires that the state Attorney General, not a private citizen, bring any suit authorized by the notification statute.[53]

The Nevada data breach notification statute is similar in scope to the California and Massachusetts laws with respect to the definitions of personal information and the timing requirements for notifying Nevada residents affected by the breach.[54] The Nevada data breach notification law also requires that the entity holding the data provide notices to national consumer reporting agencies if at least 1,000 Nevada residents are affected by the breach.[55] Nevada also permits companies to maintain their own notification procedures as part of a comprehensive information security policy and holds that companies will be in compliance with the law as long as they follow their own notification procedures (and are otherwise in compliance with the statute's timing requirements).[56] Nevada permits both private citizens and the state Attorney General to bring suits in response to a violation of the data breach notification statute.[57]

California has led the way in other areas of privacy law as well. In 2003, California passed the Online Privacy Protection Act (Cal OPPA).[58] Cal OPPA, among other important provisions,

provide the phone numbers for the major credit reporting agencies if the breach involved the loss of Social Security, driver's license, or California identification numbers.

48 Ibid., 434.
49 Ibid., 439.
50 Ibid., 437–38.
51 Ibid., 506.
52 Ibid., 508.
53 Ibid., 511.
54 Ibid., 538–40.
55 Ibid., 538.
56 Ibid., 540.
57 Ibid., 541.
58 Ibid., 62.

required websites that collect personal information on its users to display a privacy policy.[59] The privacy policy that Cal OPPA requires must include, at a minimum, the categories of information the site collects, the categories of third parties with whom the information will be shared, the process by which the operator allows consumers to review and request changes to the information held by the operator, the process by which consumers will be notified to any changes in the privacy policy, and the policy's effective date.[60] Another California-specific data security law, known as the Shine the Light Law, requires companies that collect personal information provide an 'opt-out' clause that allows consumers to prevent companies from sharing their data with third parties for the purposes of direct marketing.[61]

In addition to state statutes, state attorneys general play an important role both as independent policy makers and enforcement agencies and through the reinforcement of federal privacy standards. State attorneys general can use their 'soft' powers to encourage companies to comply with privacy regulations and adopt sound privacy and data security practices, such as engaging business and community leaders on privacy issues, offering to review companies' privacy policies, and offering 'best practices' documents, which provide companies with a list of procedures to follow while also keying them into the views and interpretations that the attorney general's office may take with respect to various provisions in their states' privacy laws.[62] Of course, the power of state attorneys general to bring enforcement actions against violators when gentler measures fail to provide adequate security or privacy is ever-present. In many cases, state attorneys general coordinate efforts by bringing multiple suits against a single target, then sharing information and engaging in joint negotiations.[63] The actions of various state attorneys general have been critical in setting norms in a wide variety of privacy and data security areas, including transparency of data use, data breach notification, use restrictions, and others.[64] In addition to creating policy and norms through state statutes, policies, and enforcement actions, state attorneys general can use their positions to help reinforce federal privacy and data security norms. State attorneys general have brought actions against private entities for failing to comply with HIPAA, FCRA, COPPA, and other federal privacy statutes.[65] State attorneys general have also emulated the FTC's enforcement approach in their use of an enforcement tool known as an 'assurance of voluntary compliance', similar to the FTC's use of settlements and consent decrees to address unfair and deceptive trade practices.[66]

Rather than engage in costly and time-consuming state-by-state analysis and compliance efforts, companies may simply choose to comply with the rules set by the most restrictive state (or states) and thereby ensure compliance with the rest. This gives large states immense power in setting privacy and data security regulations. Sometimes known as the 'California effect',

---

59 Ibid., 63. This is an important contribution to privacy and data security regulation for a number of reasons, not the least of which being that the FTC has based much of its privacy-based deceptive trade practice litigation on failing to live up to standards a company has announced in its privacy policies (see generally Section III *supra*).

60 Serwin (2016) (n 29), 63.

61 Ibid., 77–80.

62 Danielle Keats Citron, 'The Private Policymaking of State Attorneys General', 92 *Notre Dame L. Rev*. 747, 758–60 (2016).

63 Ibid., 761–62.

64 Ibid., 763–78.

65 Ibid., 778–80.

66 Ibid., 761–62, 781.

the power of these large marketplaces to set regulations and policies that companies then follow across the board can exert tremendous influence on privacy and data security behaviours both nationally and internationally.[67] All of these state-imposed obligations show that companies operating in the US cannot afford to ignore the states' roles in creating and shaping American privacy and data security law. Entities who ignore the role of state legislatures and attorneys general do so at their own peril.

VI. THE HARM PROBLEM

One final problem that data privacy advocates have encountered when attempting to enforce privacy standards in US courts has been the problem of proving a legally recognizable harm. This is a significant problem for claimants that has both conceptual and practical dimensions. Conceptually, under Article III of the US Constitution, the federal courts are limited to hearing matters that involve 'cases or controversies'. Over time, this has given rise to the concept of 'standing', or the idea that the plaintiff in a case must be the right person or entity to bring the case before the court – they must have legal 'standing' to bring the claim against the defendant. At the most fundamental level, a plaintiff must prove three elements to show they have standing: (1) they must show an injury-in-fact that is either actual or imminent (in other words they must show 'harm'), (2) they must show that injury is fairly traceable to the defendant's conduct, and (3) they must show that it is likely that their injury will be reduced or eliminated by a favourable court decision.[68] An injury-in-fact must be both 'concrete' and 'particularized'.[69] For an injury to be concrete, it must be real, i.e., not an abstract injury.[70] To be particularized, it must impact the plaintiff in a 'personal and individual way'.[71] While Congress has the power to create legally protected interests by statute that did not exist at common law, this does not mean that they can authorize a plaintiff to bring suit in federal court if they do not meet the minimum constitutional requirements for standing.[72] A 'bare procedural violation', or the mere violation of a statute without proof of actual harm, is not enough.[73]

In practice, in the privacy and data security context, plaintiffs have struggled to meet the 'injury in fact' requirement, the first element of this fundamental test. Traditionally, harm has been characterized as either economic harm or deprivation of fundamental rights, and absent a showing of economic harm courts have been reluctant to confer standing upon privacy plaintiffs. In *Clapper v. Amnesty International*,[74] for example, the Supreme Court held that the likelihood that the federal government would intercept the plaintiffs' communications, and the cost of implementing protective measures to defend against such interception, were insufficient to confer standing.[75] Another case that exemplifies the difficulties of showing

[67] Ibid., 762.
[68] *Lujan v. Defenders of Wildlife*, 504 U.S. 555, 560-61 (1993).
[69] *Spokeo, Inc. v. Robins*, 136 S.Ct. 1540, 1548 (2015).
[70] Ibid.
[71] Ibid.
[72] Ibid., at 1549
[73] Ibid.
[74] 133 S.Ct. 1138 (2013).
[75] In *Clapper*, the plaintiffs were a group of lawyers, human rights advocates, and other non-profit organizations that, in the course of their work, had contact with individuals overseas who they believed were targets of the National Security Agency's electronic surveillance programs. Ibid., at 1145–°46.

privacy harm in the context of a data breach is *Bell v. Acxiom Corporation.*[76] In *Bell*, April Bell filed suit against Acxiom, a databank that stores personal information for corporate clients, after a gap in Acxiom's database security allowed a third party to access, download, and sell information located on multiple Acxiom-managed databases to a marketing company that used the illegally-downloaded information to advertise via direct mailings.[77] The plaintiff alleged as her harm that the theft of data from Acxiom (which held her personal information) created an increased risk of receiving unwanted direct mailings and an increased risk of identity theft.[78] In dismissing Ms. Bell's claim, the court stated that the mere risk of identity theft was 'too speculative' to sustain standing.[79]

Even if plaintiffs can get past the harm requirement for standing in US courts, the inability to prove the costs of inadequate data security may prevent plaintiffs from recovering. Plaintiffs will need to be able to prove damages in order to 'win' privacy cases in any meaningful sense, and as long as courts remain hostile to recognizing noneconomic harm in privacy and data security cases. While Article III standing is not a privacy-specific issue, it is one that is frequently litigated in privacy cases given the abstract and sometimes ephemeral harms that are alleged in most privacy cases. Ultimately, this issue is one that is embedded in the United States Constitution, and thus the burdens plaintiffs must meet are unlikely to change in the near term because changes to the United States Constitution are uncommon, whether by amendment or by changes in the interpretation given to the Constitution by the federal Courts.

VII. CONCLUSION

The American law of privacy is not without its complexities or ambiguities, and it can at times be confusing or even bewildering to the uninitiated. Nevertheless, the idea that American law does not protect privacy is a fallacy. Much of the failure to appreciate American privacy can come from a failure to appreciate its key features – Bifurcation, Sectorization, the FTC, Privacy Federalism, and the importance of Privacy Harm. Some of these features are unique to American law, and others are unique (or have special resonance) in US privacy law. Nevertheless, when these features are considered, we believe that the existence and nature of American privacy law can be better appreciated. This is not to say that American privacy law is perfect, or that it has no complexity, ambiguity, and even gaps. However, it would be false to maintain that American privacy law is nonexistent, or that, properly understood, it does not regulate the processing of personal data to a meaningful degree.

---

[76] 2006 WL 2850042 (E.D. Ark. Oct. 3, 2006).

[77] Ibid., at *1.

[78] Ibid., at *2.

[79] Ibid, in a case cited in the footnotes, the US District Court for the District of Arizona stated that in order to obtain standing, a plaintiff must show '1) significant exposure of sensitive personal information, 2) a significantly increased risk of identity theft as a result of that exposure and 3) the necessity and effectiveness of credit monitoring in detecting, treating, and/or preventing identity fraud.' *Stollenwerk v. Tri-West Healthcare Alliance, Inc.*, 2005 WL 2465906 at *4 (D. Ariz. Sept. 6, 2005).

REFERENCES

Angwin J, 'Dragnet Nation: A Quest for Privacy, Security, and Freedom in a World of Relentless Surveillance: Chapter 1: Hacked.' *Colo. Tech. LJ* 12 (2014).
Department of Health, Education and Welfare, Records Computers and the Rights of Citizens (July 1973).
Keats Citron D, 'The Private Policymaking of State Attorneys General', 92 *Notre Dame L. Rev.* 747, 758–60 (2016).
McCullagh D, *From 'WarGames' to Aaron Swartz: How U.S. anti-hacking law went astray*, CNET (Mar. 13, 2013).
McDonald A M and L F Cranor, 'The Cost of Reading Privacy Policies', 4 I/S*: J. L. Pol'y Info. Soc'y* 543 (2009).
Office of Legal Education, *Prosecuting Computer Crimes*, Executive Office for United States Attorneys 2–3 (2010).
Richards N, 'The Perils of Social Reading', 101 *Geo. L.J.* 689, 694–96 (2013).
Richards N, *Intellectual Privacy: Rethinking Civil Liberties in the Digital Age* (Oxford University Press 2015).
Richards N M and D J Solove, 'Privacy's Other Path: Recovering the Law of Confidentiality', 96 *Geo. L. J.* 123 (2007).
Richards N and W Hartzog, 'The FTC and the New Common Law of Privacy', *114 Colum. L. Rev*. 583, 599 (2014).
Richards N and W Hartzog, 'Taking Trust Seriously in Privacy Law', 19 *Stanford Technology Law Review* 431 (2016).
Serwin A B, 'The Federal Trade Commission and Privacy: Defining Enforcement and Encouraging the adoption of best practices', 48 *San Diego L. Rev*. 809 (2011).
Serwin A B, *Information Security and Privacy: A guide to Federal and State Law and Compliance* Vol. 1 173-74 (2016).
Solove D J, 'Introduction: Privacy Self-Management and the Consent Dilemma', 126 *Harv. L Rev*. 1879 (2013).
Solove D J and P M Schwartz, *Consumer Privacy and Data Protection* (Aspen Publishers 2015).
Daniel J Solove and Woodrow Hartzog, 'The FTC and the New Common Law of Privacy', 114 *Colum. L. Rev.* 583 (2014).
Warren S D and L D Brandeis, 'The Right To Privacy', 4 *Harv. L. Rev*. 193 (1890).

4. The justiciability of data privacy issues in Europe and the US

Karlijn van den Heuvel and Joris van Hoboken

I. INTRODUCTION

The differences between European Union (EU) and United States (US) data privacy law are a complex issue to navigate for privacy scholars and practitioners, and continue to cause tension, litigation and high-level political discussion. Because of the dependency on transatlantic data transfers in the economic and security realm, there is a clear political interest in interoperability, in convergence when possible, and in pragmatic approaches to deal constructively with the more fundamental differences.

In this chapter, the differences and tensions between US and EU approaches to data privacy are discussed through the lens of the justiciability of privacy issues.[1] Over the years, the differences in approaches and the possibility of bridging these differences have been discussed from a variety of perspectives. Whitman, for example, analysed the cultures of privacy on both sides of the Atlantic, offering an historical account of the European emphasis on human dignity, and on the US approach to liberty.[2] Bignami offered a comparative account of the legal treatment of counterterrorism data mining, concluding that the European system may place greater restrictions on such data processing by the government, and providing thus nuance to the popular claim that the US privacy culture reflects more distrust in government than the European.[3] Bamberger and Mulligan analysed the regulation of data privacy through an analysis of privacy governance in corporate practice, concluding that some convergence between Europe and the US can be found at this level, especially between Germany and the US.[4] Bennett and Raab offered a discussion of the emergence of data privacy as a policy issue and the different approaches that have emerged in the US, Europe and elsewhere, from a global perspective.[5] Bygrave discussed the US sectoral approach to privacy, in contrast to the comprehensive approach followed in Europe's and most other countries in the world, as well as the US' emphasis on self-regulation.[6] Schwartz has provided an in-depth analysis of the

---

1 The research for this chapter was finalized in Fall 2017.

2 James Q Whitman, 'The Two Western Cultures of Privacy: Dignity versus Liberty' (2004) 113(6) *Yale Law Journal* 1151.

3 Francesca Bignami, 'European Versus American Liberty: A Comparative Privacy Analysis of Antiterrorism Data Mining', (2007) 48 *Boston Comparative Law Review* 609, accessed electronically at http://lawdigitalcommons.bc.edu/bclr/vol48/iss3/3 accessed 15 October 2021.

4 Kenneth A Bamberger and Deirdre K Mulligan, *Privacy on the Ground: Driving Corporate Behavior in the United States and Europe* (MIT Press 2015).

5 Colin J Bennett and Charles D Raab, *The Governance of Privacy: Policy Instruments in Global Perspective* (2nd edn, MIT Press 2006).

6 Lee A Bygrave, *Data Privacy Law: An International Perspective* (Oxford University Press 2014).

institutional mechanisms that have emerged to address the tension between the two regulatory systems,[7] more recently diving deeper into the differences in regulatory cultures.

This chapter aims to add to the literature on the EU-US privacy divide by taking a look through the lens of a fundamental question from a legal perspective. To what extent do individuals have the right to sue for privacy wrongs in the EU and the US respectively? That the two legal systems differ in this regard is well known,[8] but a more systematic analysis of their differences is missing. We have chosen to focus in particular on enforcement of data privacy law in civil courts. This means that administrative routes of enforcement, including judicial review of decisions of regulators such as the US Federal Trade Commission and European Data Protection Authorities, are only mentioned in passing.

We approach the question about the ability to sue for privacy wrongs in two steps. First, we focus on the disparity between the material scope of privacy law in the EU versus the US. We analyse differences in opportunities for finding a cause of action for privacy issues. Second, the conditions under which private individuals have standing to sue will be analysed. This part involves a discussion of standing and procedural aspects of European data protection law on the one hand, and the question of Article III standing in the US, on the other hand. In the US, a number of Supreme Court judgments, including *Spokeo* and *Clapper*, have brought the question of Article III standing to the fore.[9] Through the discussion of a selection of examples of data privacy issues in the private and public sector, we provide an overview of key differences in this regard.

The research is comparative in the sense that we aim to explore the differences between the possibilities of enforcing a data privacy law in civil court in the US and the EU respectively. We also take note of the increasing attention in the field of data privacy law for convergence, which adds to the purpose of finding more common legal ground between the US and EU systems of data privacy law.[10] The importance of this flows from the increased economic and technological reliance on transatlantic data transfers. The decision by the Court of Justice of the European Union (CJEU) in the *Schrems* case is a poignant example of the discrepancy between the legal and actual reality.[11]

The comparison we make is mostly horizontal as we look at legal systems at the national level, but it is far from a perfect comparison, due to the differences in the legal systems involved. They are notably different in the degree of federalism. The US has a federal government that serves as the national government, whilst the different States also have legislative power. The different European countries are independent, but have concluded several

---

[7] Paul M Schwartz, 'The EU-U.S. Privacy Collision: A Turn to Institutions and Procedures' (2013) 126(1) *Harvard Law Review* 1966. Paul M Schwartz 'The Value of Privacy Federalism' in Beate Roessler and Dorota Mokrosinska (eds), *Social Dimensions of Privacy: Interdisciplinary Perspectives* (Cambridge University Press 2015).

[8] Paul M Schwartz and Karl-Nikolaus Pfeifer, 'Structuring Transatlantic Data Privacy Law' (2017) *Georgetown Law Journal* (forthcoming).

[9] Daniel J Solove and Danielle Keats Citron, 'Risk and Anxiety: A Theory of Data Breach Harms' (2017) 96 *Texas Law Review* 737; GWU Law School Public Law Research Paper No. 2017-2; GWU Legal Studies Research Paper No. 2017-2; U of Maryland Legal Studies Research Paper No. 2017-3 https://ssrn.com/abstract=2885638 accessed 16 January 2017.

[10] Ibid.; Schwartz, 'The EU-U.S. Privacy Collision: A Turn to Institutions and Procedures' (n 7); Schwartz 'The Value of Privacy Federalism' (n 7).

[11] Case C-362/14 *Maximillian Schrems v Data Protection Commissioner* EU:C:2015:650.

transnational agreements that shape and restrict their sovereignty. A discussion of EU data privacy law therefore necessarily includes supranational law like EU law and the European Convention on Human Rights (ECHR or 'Convention').

We show that in the US, compared to the EU, a private litigant often needs to overcome extra hurdles in order to sue for privacy wrongs. Due to the patchwork-like structure of US privacy laws, finding a cause of action that can remedy a privacy wrong can be difficult. In the EU, finding a cause of action is generally easy due to the fundamental right status of privacy and personal data protection coupled with laws that protect personal data across the board. However, we suggest that the relatively open norms of data protection law can be a challenge for the justiciability of privacy wrongs in the EU, too. We point out that relevant standing requirements do exist at the boundary of EU data privacy law and procedural law at national level. This has placed them on the margins of the discussion on data privacy in the EU, even though they raise unanswered legal questions that warrant further analysis and research.

In the US, the doctrine of Article III standing filters out cases at a preliminary level. In particular, the requirement that the plaintiff needs to have suffered an injury-in-fact proves difficult to satisfy. There is no equivalent doctrine in the EU that requires a showing of injury at a preliminary stage in order to obtain access to the judiciary or to a Data Protection Authority (DPA). In the EU, the hurdles that need to be overcome to obtain access to the judiciary are therefore lower. Increasingly, however, a complex administrative and self-regulatory privacy governance framework (responsibility, data protection by design, the risk-based approach and the data protection impact assessment) is shaping the justiciability of privacy wrongs. Despite easy access to the courts, little judicial action is taken, especially compared to the increasing amount of privacy litigants in the US. We conclude that the wide applicability of EU data protection and the increase in litigation over data privacy in Europe, which may see a sharp increase after the coming into force of the GDPR, may also more sharply raise the question of which elements of this privacy governance framework a privacy litigant should be able to invoke in court.

II. FINDING A RIGHT

Here, we focus on the disparity between the material scope of privacy law in the EU versus the US. More specifically, we will provide an overview of the system of privacy law in the EU and the US respectively from the perspective of finding a right to address a privacy wrong, i.e., a cause of action. By analysing the different opportunities for finding a cause of action for privacy issues, we will see that the EU system provides more extensive protection compared to the US. Hereafter we will first discuss the European system of privacy law, focusing on fundamental rights protection and secondary EU law. This is followed by a discussion of data privacy law in the US, discussing constitutional, common law and statutory sources of data privacy law. At the end we will give some concluding remarks before we continue to the next part of our research concerning the question of standing.

II.1 The European System of Data Privacy Law

In Europe, the system of data privacy law is characterized by fundamental rights protection and broad data protection laws. Essential roles are reserved for the ECHR and the Charter of Fundamental Rights of the European Union (CFREU or 'Charter'). The Data Protection Directive (DPD or 'Directive'),[12] replaced by the General Data Protection Regulation (GDPR or 'Regulation')[13] on 25 May 2018, is at the core of EU data privacy law and policy. Other legal instruments that shape the field of data privacy law in the EU include CoE Convention 108,[14] the e-Privacy Directive,[15] and the Directive on data processing by police and justice for criminal matters.[16] Taken together, these legal instruments create a comprehensive protection of privacy interests in Europe as they arise from the collection and use of personal data.

II.1.1 Fundamental rights to privacy and protection of personal data

Both the ECHR and the CFREU protect the fundamental right to privacy in Article 8 ECHR and Article 7 of the Charter respectively. Stated in full, this concerns the right to respect for private and family life, home and correspondence. In addition to this, the Charter also explicitly recognises the right to protection of personal data as a distinct and separate fundamental right in Article 8 of the Charter, whereas such protection exists under the ECHR only implicitly and in limited circumstances. The protection of privacy and personal data at the level of fundamental rights is of great significance, because the entire system of European privacy law is framed by these rights; it is rights-based.

The right to privacy covers issues concerning the collection, storage and disclosure of personal data, access to personal data, secret surveillance and search and seizure powers of the government. The scope and meaning however goes beyond data privacy law. It for example also includes issues concerning the physical and moral integrity of the person, gender identification, procreation, euthanasia and the environment.[17] The Convention's right to privacy has been substantiated by case law from the European Court of Human Rights (ECtHR) over the years since its establishment in 1959. This case law is important for the Charter rights also, as Article 52(3) of the Charter states that where Charter rights 'correspond to rights guaranteed by the [ECHR], the meaning and scope of those rights shall be the same as those laid down by the said Convention'. However, this is but a minimum standard for the Charter rights, as more extensive protection (compared to the ECHR) is explicitly reserved in the last sentence of Article 52(3) of the Charter. Through this mechanism, the relatively young Charter rights

---

[12] Directive 95/46/EC of the European Parliament and of the Council of 24 October 1995 on the protection of individuals with regard to the processing of personal data and on the free movement of such data [1995] OJ L281/0031.

[13] Regulation (EU) 2016/679 of the European Parliament and of the Council of 27 April 2016 on the protection of natural persons with regard to the processing of personal data and on the free movement of such data, and repealing Directive 95/46/EC (General Data Protection Regulation) [2016] OJ L119/1.

[14] Convention for the Protection of Individuals with regard to Automatic Processing of Personal Data, Council of Europe, CETS No 108, 1981.

[15] Directive 2002/58/EC of the European Parliament and of the Council of 12 July 2002 concerning the processing of personal data and the protection of privacy in the electronic communications sector (Directive on privacy and electronic communications) [2002] OJ 2 201/0037.

[16] Directive (EU) 2016/680 of the European Parliament and of the Council of 27 April 2016 on the protection of natural persons with regard to the processing of personal data by competent authorities for the purposes of the prevention, investigation, detection or prosecution of criminal offences or the execution of criminal penalties, and on the free movement of such data, and repealing Council Framework Decision 2008/977/JHA [2016] OJ 2 119/89.

[17] David J Harris et al., *Law of the European Convention on Human Rights* (3rd edn, Oxford University Press 2014), 536–589.

already have a clear substance. We say relatively young because the Charter was proclaimed in 2000, 50 years after the ECHR and became legally binding with the entering into force of the Lisbon Treaty in 2009.[18] The scope of application of the Charter is limited to 'institutions and bodies of the Union' and 'Member States only when they are implementing Union law'.[19]

Article 8 of the EU Charter provides the newly codified fundamental right to protection of personal data.[20] There is no explicit counterpart of this right in the ECHR. The ECtHR has recognized protection of personal data as being a part of the right to private life in certain instances, but this implicit right to protection of personal data is narrower than the explicit right in the Charter. As Gellert and Gutwirth explain, the right to protection of personal data is a distinct right that is both narrower and broader than the right to private life.[21] It is narrower because it only deals with the protection of personal data, whilst the right to private life covers other subject matter including for example, bodily integrity and gender.[22] At the same time it is broader, because the right to protection of personal data is broader also covers processing of personal data that does not infringe upon privacy in the strict sense.[23] It for instance also applies to personal data that has been lawfully made public and personal data that has no private nature.[24]

The recognition of the protection of personal data as a fundamental right in the Charter was an innovative move, as at the time only a few countries recognized it as such in their national constitution.[25] The Charter, proclaimed in 2000, became binding with the entering into force of the Lisbon Treaty in 2009. The latter treaty has been influential for data protection law in Europe also because it codified the right to data protection in Article 16(1) TFEU. Article 16(2) TFEU provides a specific legal basis for rules relating to the protection of individuals' personal data and recognizes the need for independent supervisory authorities in line with Article 8(3) ECHR. The specified legal basis, which was used for the recent reform of EU data protection law, can be contrasted with the general internal market legal basis on which the DPD was formed,[26] although fundamental rights perspective has been present in EU data protection from the very beginning.[27]

---

[18] Art 6(1) Treaty on European Union (The Lisbon Treaty).

[19] Art 51 Charter.

[20] See on this topic: Gloria González Fuster, *The Emergence of Personal Data Protection as a Fundamental Right of the EU* (Springer International Publishing 2014); Orla Lynskey, *The Foundations of EU Data Protection law* (Oxford University Press 2015).

[21] Raphaël Gellert and Serge Gutwirth, 'The Legal Construction of Privacy and Data Protection', (2013) 59(5) *Computer Law & Security Review* 522.

[22] Ibid., 526.

[23] Ibid.

[24] Gellert has argued that the notion of data protection law should be fully disentangled from privacy, because the former is concerned with managing risks stemming from the use of personal data rather than being a part of notions of privacy and self-determination. See Raphaël Gellert, 'Data Protection: A Risk Regulation? Between the Risk Management of Everything and the Precautionary Alternative' (2015) 5(1) *International Data Privacy Law*, 3.

[25] Paul De Hert and Serge Gutwirth, 'Data Protection in the Case Law of Strasbourg and Luxemburg: Constitutionalisation in Action' in Serge Gutwirth et al. (eds), *Reinventing Data Protection?* (Springer Science Dordrecht 2009) 11–12.

[26] Art 95 EC (at the time of adoption Art 100a EC).

[27] Peter Hustinx, 'EU Data Protection Law: the Review of Directive 95/46/EC and the Proposed General Data Protection Regulation' https://www.law.ox.ac.uk/sites/files/oxlaw/oscola_4th_edn_hart_2012.pdf accessed 17 May 2017, 44.

Despite being a relatively young right, the fundamental right to protection of personal data has gained increasing prominence in the European legal landscape. It gives legitimacy to the European data protection framework.[28] As such, Article 8 of the Charter and Article 16(1) TFEU are mentioned in Recital 1 of both the GDPR and the new Directive on processing of personal data in the context of criminal matters. Moreover, Article 8 of the Charter is now frequently appearing the CJEU's most significant rulings. Examples of this include the *Digital Rights Ireland* case[29] in which the Data Retention Directive was invalidated, the *Google Spain* case on the right to request delisting of personal data in search engine results, and the *Schrems* case,[30] invalidating the safe harbour decision for transfers of personal data to the US.

II.1.2 Secondary EU legislation: the DPD and GDPR

The DPD was adopted in 1995. It has been an increasingly influential piece of legislation, inspiring lawmakers both within and outside the EU.[31] The Directive combined elements from the different national traditions that existed at the time, resulting in a 'patchwork' of data protection rules.[32] Article 1 of the Directive states its two-fold objective: protecting fundamental rights, in particular the right to privacy, and ensuring the free flow of data between the Member States. On the one hand the DPD creates obligations and conditions for those that process personal data, and on the other it creates rights for those whose data is being processed. It also creates a system of independent oversight by Data Protection Authorities (DPAs) as codified in Article 8(3) of the Charter.[33]

In 2016 the GDPR was adopted, and it entered into force, replacing the DPD, on 25 May 2018. The GDPR continues the two-fold aim of the DPD and maintains its core definitions and principles. Substantively, main changes include the introduction of the principle of accountability[34] and new subjective rights for individuals.[35] The GDPR also incorporates the risk-based approach into data protection law for example, by introducing a mandatory data protection impact assessment for data processing that creates a high risk for individuals.[36] Furthermore noteworthy is that the GDPR includes more extensive administrative enforcement mechanisms compared to the DPD, including fines.[37]

The adoption of a Regulation rather than a Directive for the protection of personal data has significant consequences for interpretation and enforcement of the rules. The GDPR is directly applicable in all Member States and need not be implemented in national law first. This leaves less room for variation between the Member States and ideally leads to a higher degree of har-

---

28 De Hert and Gutwirth (n 25), 8.

29 Joined Cases C-293/12 and C-594/12 *Digital Rights Ireland* EU:C:2014:238.

30 Case C-362/14 *Maximillian Schrems v Data Protection Commissioner* EU:C:2015:650.

31 Schwartz, 'The EU-U.S. Privacy Collision: A Turn to Institutions and Procedures' (n 7), 2–3.

32 Ibid., 6.

33 On this topic, the CJEU has held various times that the requirement of Art 28(1) DPD that a DPA 'shall act with complete independence' means that a DPA should be free from any external influence in exercising its function. Case C-518/07 *Commission v Germany* [2010] ECR I-01885, paras 25, 30; Case C-614/10 *Commission v Austria* EU:C:2012:631, para 41; Case C-288/12 *Commission v Hungary* EU:C:2014:237, para 51; Case C-362/14 *Maximillian Schrems v Data Protection Commissioner* EU:C:2015:650, paras 40–41.

34 Art 5(2) GDPR.

35 Arts 12–23 GDPR. Cf. Arts 10–12 DPD.

36 Arts 35–36 GDPR.

37 Arts 51–78 GDPR. Cf. Arts 28–30 DPD.

monisation. As De Hert and Papakonstantinou point out, the choice of legal instrument signals an important qualitative change:

> [D]ata protection is no longer perceived as a local phenomenon, to be regulated according to local legislation with an EU Directive only issuing high-level instructions and guidelines (…) [rather] data protection is considered from now on an EU concern, to be regulated directly at EU level in a common manner for all Member States through a Regulation.[38]

As a consequence of regulating data protection by means of a Regulation, the entire field of law is forced from the legislative hands of Member States to the EU.[39] During the drafting of the GDPR, Paul Schwartz warned that this institutional change of power may be detrimental to the further development of EU data protection law and may upset the current legal status quo between the US and EU, leaving little to no room for experiments and developments at the national level, similar to the US interplay between Congress and State legislators.[40]

Like the DPD, the GDPR is a so-called omnibus law or data protection law, to be contrasted with the sectoral privacy laws and consumer protection laws that characterize the US system of privacy law.[41] This means that the DPD and GDPR protect data privacy by regulating the processing of personal data *across the board*, regardless of the exact circumstances or parties involved. The material and territorial scope of the GDPR is thus broad. In essence, it applies to 'the processing of personal data wholly or partly by automated means' that is done 'in the context of an establishment of a controller or processor in the Union, regardless whether the processing takes place in the Union or not' or 'by a controller or processor not established in the Union' provided certain additional circumstances are present.[42] As all the key concepts are defined very broadly, the application of the GDPR is very easily triggered.

To start, 'personal data' means 'any information relating to an identified or identifiable natural person ("data subject")'.[43] According to the Article 29 WP, this includes so-called singling out, whereby one person can distinguished from a group.[44] It is important to realize that the European concept of personal data is objective rather than subjective, meaning that it includes any information regarding an individual regardless of the source of the information.[45] According to the Article 29 WP, in order to consider that the data 'relate' to an individual, the information needs not be strictly *about* a person. It can also be sufficient if a purpose element (i.e., the information will or can be used in relation to the person) or a result element (i.e., the information is likely to have an impact on the rights and freedoms of the person) is present.[46]

---

[38] Paul De Hert and Vagelis Papakonstantinou, 'The New General Data Protection Regulation: Still a Sound System for the Protection of Individuals?' (2016) *Computer Law Security Review* 32(2) 179, 182.

[39] Ibid.

[40] Schwartz, 'The EU-U.S. Privacy Collision: A Turn to Institutions and Procedures' (n 7). Schwartz 'The Value of Privacy Federalism' (n 7).

[41] William McGeveran, *Privacy and Data Protection Law* (Foundation Press 2016), 257.

[42] Art 2(1) GDPR, Art 3(1) and 3(2) GDPR.

[43] Art 4(1) GDPR.

[44] Article 29 Data Protection Working Party, 'Opinion 4/2007 on the concept of personal data' (20 June 2007), 14.

[45] Case C-582/14 *Patrick Breyer v Bundesrepublik Deutschland* EU:C:2016:779, paras 25, 31–49.

[46] Article 29 Data Protection Working Party, 'Opinion 4/2007 on the concept of personal data' (20 June 2007), 13.

'Processing' covers practically anything that is done with personal data, whether or not by automated means, including storage, collection (from public sources), deletion, alteration and alignment or combination.[47] The 'controller' is the person who is mainly responsible for the processing of personal data; a natural or legal person that determines the purposes and means of the processing of personal data, alone or jointly with others.[48] Also bearing some responsibilities for the (secure and lawful) processing is the 'processor': a natural or legal person that processes personal data on behalf of the controller.[49]

As mentioned already, the GDPR imposes an interrelated set of obligations on the side of the controller and/or processor, and a set of rights on the side of the individuals whose data are being processed ('data subjects'). The intention of this design is not to prevent or limit the processing of personal data per se, but to give adequate safeguards whenever personal data are processed in the form of protection against improper and/or disproportionate processing and by giving control to individuals over information concerning them.[50] Because of the wide application of the GDPR – due to the broad material and territorial scope in combination with broad definitions of key concepts – many organizations will qualify as controller or processor. As such, they need to comply with the obligations set out in the GDPR. The DPAs are entrusted with the task of monitoring and enforcing these obligations.[51]

The core obligation for controllers is to process data in a fair, transparent and lawful manner. The GDPR sets out a myriad of requirements on how to achieve this. The key principles can be found in Article 5 GDPR. Firstly, processing of personal data is only lawful if it is based on a legal basis, with six possibilities exhaustively listed in Article 6 GDPR. Secondly and thirdly, collection of personal data is only allowed for (predetermined) specified, explicit and legitimate purposes, and the amount of personal data processed must be adequate, relevant and limited to what is necessary for those purposes. Fourthly and fifthly, the personal data must be accurate and kept up to date, and kept in a form that allows identification of the individuals no longer than is necessary for the purposes for which the personal data is processed. Sixthly, processing must be done in a manner that ensures appropriate security of personal data. Lastly, the controller must be able to demonstrate compliance with all these principles. The principles enumerated in Article 5 GDPR are elaborated in other GDPR provisions. For example, the principle of transparency is further clarified in provisions on information obligations in Articles 12–14 GDPR.

The GDPR broadens rights that already existed, and new rights are added or stipulated in more detail and more explicitly. Chapter III of the GDPR provides various data subject rights, namely: a right to information about the processing of his or her personal data, a right of access, a right of rectification or erasure, a right to restriction of processing, a right to data portability, a right to object to processing and a right not to be subject to a decision based solely on automated decision making. It is the controller that is responsible for the handling of requests on the basis of these rights, and for facilitating the exercise of data subject rights.[52]

---

[47] Art 4(2) GDPR.

[48] Art 4(7) GDPR.

[49] Art 4(8) GDPR.

[50] Peter Hustinx, 'EU Data Protection Law: the Review of Directive 95/46/EC and the Proposed General Data Protection Regulation' https://www.law.ox.ac.uk/sites/files/oxlaw/oscola_4th_edn_hart_2012.pdf accessed 17 May 2017, 44, 1–2.

[51] Art 57 GDPR.

[52] Art 12(1), (2) and (5) GDPR.

Requests should be responded to free of charge, without undue delay and in principle at the latest within one month, and a refusal to comply with a request must be accompanied with reasons explaining the refusal.[53] In case a processor is involved, it should assist the controller in its compliance with this obligation where possible.[54]

Besides these rights, other data subject rights can be found elsewhere in the GDPR. For instance, the data subject has the right to withdraw consent where the processing of his or her personal data is based on consent.[55] Another example is the right to lodge a complaint with the DPA, and, in case the complaint is dismissed, the right to an effective judicial remedy against the DPA.[56] Regardless of whether requests are filed with the controller and/or a complaint lodged with the DPA, any data subject also has the right to start civil proceedings against a controller or processor where he or she considers his or her rights infringed as a result of unlawful processing.[57] This private right of action will be further discussed below.

II.2 US Data Privacy Law

The US system of data privacy law consists of an array of laws that regulate a particular element of privacy or protection of personal data. The US system is harm-based rather than rights-based, meaning that there is no all-encompassing fundamental right or law that protects privacy and personal data, but rather a system of diverse legal and regulatory acts that cover specific privacy interests and situations that cause cognizable harm. The US system is also more oriented towards market-based approaches to ensuring data privacy interests than the rights-based approach of the EU. At first glance the US system of privacy law may seem obscure and much less straightforward than the European system. Once one finds a way through the diverse range of legal possibilities however, the US system may turn out to provide more precise and clear-cut legal guidance than European privacy and data protection law which contains numerous open norms and broad concepts. Nevertheless, it is abundantly clear that US privacy law, by lack of a general data privacy right and/or law, leaves many gaps compared to EU privacy law. It has been argued by American scholars that US law should recognize more privacy harms and wrongs in law.[58]

Sources of US data privacy law include the US Constitution – although there is no constitutionally protected right to privacy or protection of personal data as such – common law (privacy torts) and federal and State statutory law. Consumer protection law plays a significant role in protecting privacy interests in the context of commercial transactions, with oversight and enforcement at the national level by the Federal Trade Commission (FTC). Whereas constitutional law and common law privacy torts used to provide the most significant protection for privacy interests, the focus has since shifted to statutory and regulatory sources.[59] Also

---

53 Art 12(3) and (4) GDPR
54 Art 28(3)(e) GDPR.
55 Art 7(3) GDPR.
56 Arts 77–78 GDPR.
57 Art 79 GDPR.
58 Joel R Reidenberg, 'Privacy Wrongs in Search of Remedies' (2002) 54(4) *Hastings Law Journal* 877; Solove and Keats Citron (n 9).
59 William McGeveran, *Privacy and Data Protection Law* (Foundation Press 2016), 165.

discernible is the growth of privacy statutes at the State level whilst consolidation at the federal level still remains mostly absent, leading to statutory variations across the country.[60]

In the following paragraphs we will provide an overview of the various sources of US data privacy law mentioned. This discussion is not meant to be an exhaustive review, as this clearly goes above and beyond the scope of our undertaking in this chapter. In line with our research focus, we will pay particular attention to the rights of individuals within the system of US data privacy law.

II.2.1 Constitutional protection

Although in the US there is no constitutionally protected right to privacy or to the protection of personal data, the US Constitution does play a significant role in US privacy law. In particular the Fourth Amendment, which protects individuals from unwarranted intrusion in private affairs by the government, functions as an important privacy safeguard. The First Amendment, which protects free speech, may both limit and enhance the protection of data privacy. Another constitutional doctrine of privacy follows from the substantive due process clause of the Fourteenth Amendment, though protections derived from this clause are narrow and pertain to specific topics such as family, marriage and procreation.

An important restriction on the scope of constitutional (privacy) law is the state action doctrine. Under this doctrine, restrictions that flow from the US Constitution apply to government action only.[61] Therefore, there cannot be a violation of a constitutionally protected right without some type of action from a state actor.[62] Exceptions to this rule do exist, but its general effect is that private entities are not affected by constitutional restrictions. In the US, the Constitution is seen as regulating 'public' power and therefore does not regulate other, 'private' sources of power.[63] This can be contrasted with the approach in Europe, where fundamental rights create both negative and positive obligations for States, and where private parties may invoke constitutional rights against each other in a horizontal fashion.

II.2.1.1 Fourth Amendment

The Fourth Amendment protects individuals from unwarranted intrusion in private affairs by the government. More specifically, it provides a right against unreasonable searches and seizures by government officials. Save for certain exceptions, 'unreasonable' generally means without a warrant. Hence, where a search or seizure by a government official is held to be in violation with the Fourth Amendment, most of the time the decision will not constrain what law enforcement may do, but rather which actions require a warrant beforehand.[64] A court will provide such a warrant where authorities have sufficiently described the scope of the intended search and demonstrated 'probable cause'.[65]

The constitutional inquiry under the Fourth Amendment consists of two questions: (1) was there a search or seizure; and (2) was this search or seizure unreasonable? Especially the first

---

[60] Schwartz 'The Value of Privacy Federalism' (n 7), 333–334.

[61] McGeveran (n 59), 18.

[62] Harvard Law Review, 'Developments in the Law: State Action and the Public/Private Distinction' (2010) 123(5) *Harvard Law Review* 1248, 1255.

[63] Richard S Kay, 'The State Action Doctrine, the Public-Private Distinction, and the Independence of Constitutional Law' (1993) 10(2) *Constitutional Commentary* 329, 330.

[64] McGeveran (n 59), 42.

[65] Ibid., 17.

question has created considerable case law before the US Supreme Court. What qualifies as a search is more complicated than one might expect. Advancements in technology provide more and better possibilities for the government to conduct searches and seizures in the lives of individuals, and this requires a constant re-evaluation of what counts as one. For example, if the government places a GPS tracking device on a car and tracks the car movements 24/7 for a month, is the government conducting a search?[66] This type of government intrusion into (relatively) private affairs has only recently become available, so that it is not immediately clear how it should be qualified and whether Fourth Amendment protection is available.

The question of what qualifies as a search is, as many questions, a lot easier when considered in hindsight, when the (then new) technology has been around for a while and is firmly established in society. In 1928, the majority of the Supreme Court held in *Olmstead v United States* that a phone wiretap was *not* a search or seizure within the meaning of the Fourth Amendment, because there was no physical trespass in the private property of the complainant. In the words of Chief Justice Taft: 'The reasonable view is that (...) the [telephone] wires beyond [someone's] house, and messages while passing over them, are not within the protection of the Fourth Amendment'. What was required was a search of material and private things, like a house or a sealed letter in the mail. A phone wiretap does not amount to such a thing, because authorities merely listened in by placing a device on a public part of the telephone wires. Nothing was physically searched or seized. Nowadays the outcome of this case seems strange.[67]

It was not until 1967, in *Katz v United States*, that a phone wiretap was held to be a 'search' within the meaning of the Fourth Amendment. The case is well-known for Justice Harlan's concurrence, in which he formulated the 'reasonable expectation of privacy'-test. This test has two prongs: (1) a person has exhibited an actual (i.e., subjective) expectation of privacy; (2) the expectation is one that is reasonable in the eyes of society. The idea of a reasonable expectation of privacy has been influential ever since, also in Europe.

As mentioned above, a search or seizure is 'reasonable' when a warrant based on probable cause and subject to judicial review has been obtained beforehand. There are exceptions to this rule. For example, when there are so-called 'exigent circumstances' like search upon lawful arrest.[68] Another important exception is the third-party doctrine. Under this doctrine, an individual no longer has a reasonable expectation of privacy when information is shared with a third party that might further disclose this information. This includes disclosures to institutional third parties like a bank (financial information) or telecommunications company (telephone records), so that authorities can search and seize this information without obtaining a warrant first.[69] Other exceptions include the 'plain view' and 'open fields' doctrine, both dealing with the boundaries of perception from and onto a lawful (public) place, and the special needs doctrine for searched conducted for specific government needs.

---

[66] *Jones v United States,* 565 U.S. 400 (2012).

[67] At the time, Justice Brandeis gave a prescient dissent in which he argued that every unjustifiable intrusion by the government upon the privacy of the individual, whatever the means employed, must be deemed a violation of the Fourth Amendment.

[68] Cases dealing with this exclusionary rule include: *Weeks v United States*, 232 U.S. 383 (1914); *Chimel v California*, 395 U.S. 752 (1969); *United States v Robinson*, 414 U.S. 218 (1973); *United States v Chadwick*, 433 U.S. 1 (1977); *Arizona v Gant*, 556 U.S. 332 (2009); *Riley v California*, 573 U.S. __ (2014).

[69] See e.g., *California v Greenwood*, 486 U.S. 35 (1988).

II.2.1.2 First Amendment

The First Amendment protects, amongst other things, freedom of speech. This affects the protection of privacy both negatively and positively. In the US, free speech is protected strongly under the First Amendment.[70] Therefore, when privacy interests clash with free speech interests, the latter tend to prevail. This can be contrasted with Europe, where both free speech and privacy are fundamental rights, so that when a conflict occurs, the involved interests need to be balanced against each other. Insightful case law by the ECtHR on this topic include the *Von Hannover* cases involving Princess Caroline of Monaco.[71] An example of the effect of the First Amendment on legislative attempts to protect privacy is *Sorell v IMS Health Inc.* In that case, the Supreme Court found a Vermont law that limited the disclosure of physician-prescriber data to pharmaceutical companies by pharmacies for marketing purposes to be unconstitutional. The marketing by the pharmaceutical companies to the doctors constituted protected speech that the Vermont law unconstitutionally limited.

Besides limiting privacy protection, the First Amendment can also enhance it. *Stanley v Georgia* involved a criminal prosecution for possession of obscene material (films) that police found in the defendant's house when searching for evidence of bookmaking. The court held that the right to receive information and ideas is protected by the First Amendment, and that 'a State has no business telling a man, sitting alone in his own house, what books he may read of what films he may watch'. Therefore, the mere possession of obscene material by an individual in the privacy of their own home could not be made a crime; the State's power to regulate obscenity does not extend that far. Another example is *McIntyre v Ohio Elections Commission*, in which an Ohio statute prohibiting the distribution of anonymous campaign literature was held to be in violation with the First Amendment. The court recognized a right to remain anonymous, as 'anonymous pamphleteering is not a pernicious, fraudulent practice, but an honourable tradition of advocacy and of dissent'.

II.2.1.3 Fourteenth Amendment

The last source of US constitutional privacy law is the substantive due process clause of the Fourteenth Amendment, which reads that 'no state shall [...] deprive any person of life, liberty, or property, without due process of law'. The question under this constitutional clause is whether the deprivation of an individual's life, liberty or property is justified by a sufficient purpose.[72] The privacy protection derived from this is however narrow and mostly pertains to topics such as family, marriage, procreation, motherhood and child rearing. Famous examples include the Supreme Court decisions *Griswold v Connecticut*; *Roe v Wade*; and *Obergefell v Hodges*, dealing with marital privacy and contraception, abortion and same-sex marriage respectively.

II.2.2 Common law: privacy torts, other torts and contract

Samuel D Warren's and Louis Brandeis' 'The Right to Privacy', published in the *Harvard Law Review* in 1890, is a seminal article that is often cited as the beginning of privacy law in

---

[70] See e.g., *New York Times Co v US*, 403 U.S. 713 (1971).

[71] *Von Hannover v Germany (No 1)* App No 59320/00 (ECHR, 24 June 2004); *Von Hannover v Germany (No II)* App No 40660/08 and 60641/08 (ECHR, 7 February 2012); *Von Hannover v Germany (No 3)* App No 8772/10 (ECHR 19 September 2013) (only published in French).

[72] Erwin Chemerinsky, 'Substantive Due Process' (1999) 15(4) *Touro Law Review* 1501, 1501.

the US. In this article, they called for protection of privacy as the right 'to be *let* alone'.[73] It is important to realize that Warren and Brandeis did not call for an overall right to privacy as one might nowadays expect from a right called 'the right to privacy'. Rather, the tort they envisaged was aimed at maintaining certain social norms and values in a changing society where the press, aided by inventions like the portable photo camera, was 'overstepping in every direction the obvious bounds of propriety and of decency'.[74] [75]

Ten years later, Georgia was the first State to recognize the right to privacy in *Pavesich v New England Life Insurance Co.*, a case involving a complaint by Pavesich whose picture was used without his knowledge or consent for a life insurance advertisement.[76] This case set a precedent for courts of other States to follow, which most (eventually) did.[77] Soon other types of privacy torts developed under a variety of other theories, resulting in other types of privacy torts including those that were later coined intrusion upon seclusion and misappropriation.[78]

The next major development for privacy torts was the categorization of case law into four distinct privacy torts by William Prosser in 1960. As Neil Richards writes: 'If Warren and Brandeis gave tort privacy its name and guiding principles, Prosser gave it form and credibility'.[79] Prosser's privacy torts are the following:[80]

1. Intrusion upon the plaintiff's seclusion or solitude, or into his private affairs;
2. Public disclosure of embarrassing private facts about the plaintiff;
3. Publicity which places the plaintiff in a false light in the public eye;
4. Appropriation, for the defendant's advantage, of the plaintiff's name or likeness.

Each of the four torts has its own elements and corresponding case law developing these further.[81] It is important to realize, first, that, though Prosser's torts remain a leading model of privacy tort law, not every tort is available to every privacy litigant, and that sources of privacy tort liability vary across States. For example, the State of New York only recognizes the misappropriation tort. California, on the other hand, a State known for its extensive protection of privacy, accepts all four. Second, the torts are limited in scope and therefore available only in very specific instances, so that a successful claim is relatively rare. Third, although Prosser's privacy torts have been very influential in developing protection of privacy in the US, their importance has decreased with the rise of statutory privacy law (especially at State level) and consumer protection law coupled with enforcement by the FTC.[82]

---

[73] Samuel D Warren and Louis D Brandeis, 'The Right to Privacy' (1890) 4(5) *Harvard Law Review* 193, 195.

[74] Ibid., 196.

[75] See for interesting discussions on the historical placement of the article: Randall P Bezanson, 'The Right to Privacy Revisited: Privacy, News and Social Change, 1890-1990' (1992) 80(5) *California Law Review* 1133; Neil Richards, *Intellectual Privacy: Rethinking Civil Liberties in the Digital Age* (Oxford University Press 2015), 15–26.

[76] *Pavesich v New England Life Insurance Co.*, 50 S.E. 68 (Ga 1905).

[77] William L Prosser 'Privacy' (1960) 48(3) *California Law Review* 383, 386–387.

[78] Neil Richards, *Intellectual Privacy: Rethinking Civil Liberties in the Digital Age* (Oxford University Press 2015), 23.

[79] Richards (n 75), 24; Neil Richards and Daniel Solove 'Prosser's Privacy Law: A Mixed Legacy' (2010) 98 *California Law Review* 1887, 1888.

[80] Prosser (n 77), 383; Restatement (Second) of Torts (1977) §652B–E.

[81] And it has been done by others, see e.g., McGeveran (n 41), Chapter 2.

[82] Ibid., 87, 165.

Besides the specific privacy torts, other parts of the common law may be relevant for privacy litigants also. Depending on the circumstances of the case, one or more of these torts may be relevant: negligence, breach of confidentiality, defamation, intentional or negligent infliction of emotional distress and possibly even trespass. Again, depending on the circumstances, breach of contract may be a claim worth pursuing also.

II.2.3 Statutory privacy law, including consumer (data privacy) law

Statutory sources of US privacy law have been developed more recently compared to constitutional and common law sources. We can make a rough divide between consumer law protection measures and sectoral privacy laws. The former is distinctive because of its breadth and mainly administrative enforcement structure through the FTC, whereas the latter is characterized by a sector-specific and hence more narrow scope coupled with both administrative and civil enforcement.

The US deals with many privacy issues via consumer protection law. The field of consumer protection law is obviously much broader and protects consumers in commercial transactions against a wide variety of harms. Enforcement of these laws is done mainly by various public regulators, and the FTC is the principal regulator in the field of privacy and security. The FTC's authority to supervise commercial entities in these areas derives from Section 5 of the Federal Trade Commission Act, which gives them competence to act against unfair and deceptive business practices. The FTC also derives powers from several sector specific privacy laws, including the Children's Online Privacy Protection Act, the Fair Credit Reporting Act and the Gramm-Leach-Bliley Act. The role of the consumer in this administrative structure is limited to filing a complaint with the FTC. This corresponds to some degree with the power of data subjects in the EU to file a complaint with a Data Protection Authority.

There exist in the US a myriad of different rules for particular entities and particular types of information and activities, and only specific instances of privacy wrongs are recognized. Below, we will only include federal statutes, but bear in mind that other laws may exist at the State level.[83]

The advantages of sector specific statutes, as McGeveran explains, are that the rules are tailored to specific instances and specialized regulators can oversee compliance.[84] Because of the wide scope of privacy and data protection law in Europe, the rules are necessarily more generic and contain open norms, which may lead to diverging interpretations resulting in confusion on what compliance actually requires. In terms of oversight, something can be said for having one specialized regulator dealing with all issues relating to personal data processing also: it provides clarity to all actors involved and signifies the importance of privacy and data protection whilst also leaving room for further guidance and advice to specific industries.

The drawbacks of the US system of sectoral privacy laws are that, as mentioned, they give rise to a fragmented and complex area of law. Each statute has its own scope of application and delineate their own definitions. Adding to the complexity is that some statutes are complemented by further regulations. For example, the HIPAA (Health Insurance Portability and Accountability Act) is complemented by additional regulations from the Department of Health and Human Services (HIPAA Privacy Rule and HIPAA Security Rule) and supplemented by the HITECH Act (Health Information Technology for Economic and Clinical Health

---

[83] For a more comprehensive overview, see ibid., Part 3.

[84] Ibid., 549.

Act). Also, it is possible that for certain entities the statutory obligations overlap, resulting in potential for confusion, duplication and overregulation, whilst certain troubling activities may fall through the cracks.[85] While the more focused approach of US data privacy law has the advantage of directing regulation towards the most important issues, another drawback is that, with its precise definitions and scope of application, US statutory privacy law is not very flexible in light of changing practices and technologies.

As regards the statutory definitions and scope of application, each statute has its own (material) scope. This pertains to the *entities* that are regulated, the *personal information* and the *processing activities* that are covered. This approach is very much unlike in the EU, where a few key definitions function as a catch-all, rendering it unlikely that a particular type of processing remains untouched by the law. In the US the default is the opposite, i.e., anything goes save for the specific instances that are regulated.

HIPAA is an example of how only particular entities are regulated. It regulates the use and disclosure of 'protected health information' – a definition we will ignore here – by 'covered entities', but only a limited group of entities is regulated under HIPAA, namely 'health plans' (e.g., health insurers), 'health care providers' (e.g., doctors and hospitals) and 'health care clearinghouses' (e.g., billing services). HIPAA does not aim to regulate the use and disclosure of medical data in general, but specifically regulates the healthcare industry. New players in this industry like mobile applications or other devices that handle data pertaining to individuals' health are out of scope. Other examples of regulated entities under different US statutory privacy laws include 'consumer reporting agencies' (Federal Credit Reporting Act, FCRA), 'business associates' (HITECH Act) and 'video tape service provider' (Video Privacy Protection Act, VPPA).

As for the different types of information that are regulated, several statutes include terms like 'personal information' or 'personally identifiable information' but attribute different meanings to it. For example, the Children Online Privacy Protection Act (COPPA) defines 'personal information' as 'individually identifiable information about an individual collected online', and includes a list of identifiers such as name, address, username, telephone number and more. By contrast, the VPPA defines 'personally identifiable information' as including 'information which identifies a person as having requested or obtained specific video materials or services from a video tape service provider'. Another possibility is that the rules only apply to particular records that contain specific information, like 'consumer report' in the FCRA, 'education record' in Family Educational Rights and Privacy Act (FERPA) or a 'record' contained in a 'system of records' with information about an individual maintained by a federal agency in the Privacy Act. A miscellaneous category remains, for example, statutes regulating 'genetic information' (GINA) or 'nonpublic personal information' (Gramm-Leach-Bliley Act).

Lastly, the processing activities that are covered by the federal privacy statutes vary also. To take HIPAA as an example again, the only processing activities regulated are use and disclosure of 'protected health information' by 'covered entities'.[86] HIPAA does not concern itself with the collection of this data. COPPA on the other hand focuses on the collection stage especially. The Privacy Act is an example of a law offering more comprehensive coverage, regulating the collection, maintenance, use and dissemination.

---

[85] Ibid.

[86] Office of Civil Rights, U.S. Dept. of Health and Human Services, 'Summary of the HIPAA Privacy Rule' (May 2003).

This brings us to the question whether a federal privacy statute contains a private right of action or not. Some, but not all of the privacy statutes rely on private rights of action for enforcement. Often this is in combination with a public regulator that also has competences for enforcing against companies or other actors that are regulated, for example the FTC or FCC. Examples of statutes that do not contain private rights of action include the COPPA, the FERPA, the C-SPAM Act, the HIPAA and the GLB-Act. Enforcement of those acts is exclusively reserved for public regulators like the FTC or a US government department. Other acts, including the FCRA, VVPA, TCPA, CCPA and Privacy Act, do contain a private right of action. It is however not the case that a violation of one of those acts automatically means that an individual can enforce related private rights. Other requirements must be satisfied in the US system of privacy law, namely standing requirements.

III. FINDING STANDING TO SUE

How do the different standing requirements in the US and Europe impact privacy litigants seeking to enforce obligations imposed on entities collecting and using personal data and/or related privacy rights of individuals? Let us imagine a company that neglects to take adequate security measures, as a result of which a hacker is able to extract customer data. Names, addresses and payment information of thousands of customers are ‘stolen’. Could customers of this company sue for negligence? The answer to this question very much depends on standing requirements. Another example: a company collects and sells personal information to third parties. When someone finds out that their personal details are wrong or inaccurate, this may result in harm. Can this person sue the company? Again, this depends on the particulars of standing in the legal system.

We will first discuss the concept of standing in general, and thereafter focus on the question of whether standing is an issue for privacy litigants in the US and the EU. For the US we will focus on so-called ‘Article III standing’. This is a constitutional doctrine developed by the courts that poses requirements for plaintiffs seeking access to federal courts. The requirements for Article III standing are difficult to satisfy for litigants in different areas of privacy law, affecting constitutional, common law and statutory claims. In the EU, by contrast, standing does not seem to be such an issue for privacy litigants; discussing the standing required for the civil routes of enforcement in EU data privacy law, we will explain why, in the EU, privacy litigants practically always have an enforceable privacy right of action.

III.1 On the Concept of Standing

Standing to sue means that a person has a right to bring a case before a court. In Latin, *locus standi* literally means ‘place to stand’. In law, the doctrine of standing functions as a so-called ‘rationing device’: it seeks to ensure that only those who are sufficiently connected to the dispute are entitled to have their case adjudicated.[87] It also functions to avoid abuses, reduce the

[87] Carol Harlow and Richard Rawlings, *Law and Administration* (3rd edn, Cambridge University Press 2009), 694; Xavier Groussot, ‘The EC System of Legal Remedies and Effective Judicial Protection: Does the System Really Need Reform?’ (2003) 30(3) *Legal Issues of Economic Integration* 221, 223.

number of cases and ensure efficiency.[88] In other words, standing is concerned with whether a particular person is entitled to have a dispute or issue decided and (possibly) remedied by the court. It is a matter of deciding which parties are allowed entry.[89] Different legal systems have formulated distinct standing requirements that are generally part of procedural law. It usually comes down to showing a particular connection between the party responsible for an event or action that causes some type of harm and the party seeking to challenge this action.

Another way of looking at the role of standing in a legal system is from the perspective of the powers of the judiciary. Standing requirements are a means of deciding which parties are allowed entry to court. The underlying rationale for any particular set of standing requirements can be traced to the competence of the judiciary in a particular legal system. Rather than framing standing as a matter of which parties are allowed entry to court, we can also consider it as a matter of which issues the courts may decide, or how far do the court's powers reach. Therefore, standing requirements are closely linked to constitutional law. Their function is to focus and shape the power of the judiciary in relation to other branches of government.

It is helpful to consider here the difference between private and public rights. The law creates rights and duties that are allocated to particular (groups of) people. Not everyone can sue for any wrong, it needs to be *your* wrong in one way or another. Only those who are entitled to enforce a particular right can access legal remedies or, in short, 'remedies are correlative with rights'.[90] The question of who has standing to sue is therefore concerned with to whom legal duties are owed or, conversely, who can enforce a particular right. This is often clear for private rights, held by a particular individual, but less so for public rights, which are owed to the public collectively.[91]

Let us consider an example of a private right: if A is hurt by B in a car accident, it is A who can sue B for this injury to *her* property and body, and not anyone else. Enforcement of public rights is more complex: imagine a company is under a statutory obligation to follow a certain procedure with regard to the processing of personal data. Who may sue this company when it fails to meet this obligation? Is enforcement solely a matter for a public regulator and/or can affected and concerned individuals also enforce this obligation through private litigation? These are the questions on which standing debates have traditionally focused, in the context of environmental protection, the levying of taxes, or the performance of agreements on nuclear weapons.[92]

A last feature of standing to highlight is that it functions as a preliminary inquiry. It either opens or shuts the door to court. A case dismissed for standing will not legally require a discussion on the merits of the case. The specific requirements for standing are thus essential for the question of whether a wrong can be remedied in court.

---

[88] Idem.

[89] Ann Woolhandler and Caleb Nelson, 'Does History Defeat Standing Doctrine' (2004) 102(4) *Michigan Law Review* 689, 689.

[90] Christopher F Forsyth and William Wade, *Administrative Law*, (11th edn, Oxford University Press 2014), 584.

[91] Andrew Hessick, 'Standing, Injury in Fact and Private Rights' (2008) 93(2) *Cornell Law Review* 275, 279–280; Woolhandler and Nelson (n 89), 693 (referring to William Blackstone).

[92] *Lujan v Defenders of Wildlife,* 504 U.S. 555 (1992); *Regina v Commissioners of Inland Revenue* [1996] STC 681; HR (Dutch Supreme Court) 21 December 2012, NJ 2002, 217 (*Kernwapens*).

III.2 Standing Doctrine in the US

In the US, federal courts derive their competence to decide cases from Article III of the US Constitution, and this part of the Constitution is proving to be an issue for privacy litigants. We will first start with a short discussion of Article III of the US Constitution and how standing has emerged alongside other justiciability doctrines, looking at various standing requirements and scholarly critiques. Thereafter we look at one standing requirement – the injury-in-fact requirement – in more detail and in relation to privacy cases specifically. We will see how this particular Article III standing requirement is proving to be a difficult hurdle to overcome in different areas of privacy law. Even when a litigant can find a cause of action to remedy a privacy wrong, it is not automatically guaranteed that this right is enforceable in court.

Article III of the US Constitution deals with the judicial branch of the federal government; the federal courts. Section 1 states that there will be a Supreme Court and that Congress can create inferior courts. Our interest here goes to Section 2, which is where Article III standing originates. It states, in part: '[t]he judicial power shall extend to all cases (…) [and] controversies'. This clause thus delineates the powers of the federal judiciary, or, put differently, it deals with the justiciability of cases. Justiciability refers to which matters are suitable for federal courts to hear and decide on the merits.[93] The Supreme Court itself has admitted that the term 'justiciability' is uncertain in meaning and scope, and that therefore it is mostly characterized by what it is not.[94] Accordingly, the Supreme Court has developed various legal doctrines that limit the competence of the federal courts to deciding 'cases' and 'controversies'. By the words of Justice Warren in *Flast v Cohen*:

> [N]o justiciable controversy is presented when the parties seek adjudication of only a political question, when the parties are asking for an advisory opinion, when the question sought to be adjudicated has been mooted by subsequent developments, and when there *is no standing to maintain the action* (emphasis added).[95] [96]

The doctrine of Article III standing thus belongs to a set of justiciability doctrines that also encompasses other doctrines such as ripeness and mootness.[97] Altogether these doctrines aim to achieve that federal power only extends to deciding 'cases' and 'controversies'.

Article III standing requires that a plaintiff seeking access to a federal court has: (1) suffered an injury in fact; that is (2) fairly traceable to the challenged action; and (3) likely to be redressed by a favourable outcome.[98] Without a showing of all three elements, a case will

---

[93] *Wex Legal Dictionary*, https://www.law.cornell.edu/wex/justiciable accessed 16 October 2021.

[94] *Flast v Cohen*, 392 U.S. 83, 95 (1968).

[95] Ibid.

[96] Some authors have a more extensive list of justiciability doctrines, e.g., Jonathan R Siegel, 'A Theory of Justiciability' (2007) 86(1) *Texas Law Review* 73, 76–77.

[97] These doctrines both deal with *when* a case is ready for adjudication. The doctrine of ripeness excludes cases that rest upon 'contingent future events that may not occur as anticipated, or indeed may not occur at all', *Texas v United States,* 523 U.S. 296, 300 (1998) (internal quotation marks omitted). The doctrine of mootness excludes cases that legal proceedings cannot affect, because there is no actual controversy anymore. See e.g., *North Caroline v Rice,* 404 U.S. 244 (1968); *DeFunis et al. v Odegaard et al.,* 416 U.S. 312 (1974).

[98] *Lujan v Defenders of Wildlife,* 504 U.S. 555, 560–61 (1992); *Spokeo v Robins*, 578 U.S. ___, 136 S. Ct. 1540, 1547 (2016).

be dismissed for lack of standing. Even when these constitutional requirements are satisfied, a case can be refused on the basis of so-called prudential limits.[99] The Supreme Court considers the constitutional standing requirements to be a minimum threshold that needs to be satisfied in every case, whereas the prudential limitations can be overcome by statute or disregarded by the court in exceptional circumstances.[100] The classification as 'prudential limit' is not set in stone, as they can be 'relabelled' as being part of the constitutional inquiry.[101]

The US doctrine of standing has been (and still is) subject to much criticism and debate.[102] It is considered to be the most controversial justiciability doctrine[103] and has been described by judges and scholars as 'a word game played by secret rules',[104] and 'ill-matched to the task that it is asked to perform'.[105] The standing doctrine has also generated a string of (confusing) case law at the Supreme Court level and continues to confound lower courts.[106] Critique is expressed towards all justiciability doctrines. Professor Siegel calls them 'fundamentally misconceived'[107] and argues that courts have wrongly interpreted the text of Article III as imposing purposeless constraints on judicial power.[108] In essence, these critiques discuss questions of judicial policy: what is the appropriate role of the judiciary in a (democratic) society?

Narrowing the discussion to privacy law cases, we discuss the first Article III standing requirement, i.e., injury-in-fact. This requirement of Article III standing, in simplified terms, requires that the plaintiff demonstrates that they were harmed because of the challenged action. Without harm or injury, the plaintiff has no standing to sue in federal court. In exact terms, to satisfy the injury-in-fact requirement, the plaintiff needs to demonstrate that there has been an invasion of a legally protected interest or injury that is 'concrete and particularized' and 'actual or imminent, not conjectural or hypothetical'.[109] The injury-in-fact requirement

---

[99] *Gladstone, Realtors v Village of Bellwood*, 441 U.S. 91, 99–100 (1979) (naming the prudential limits: zone of interest, generalized grievances and third-party rights).

[100] *Warth v Seldin*, 422 U.S. 490, 500-501 (1975); *Craig v Boren*, 429 U.S. 190, 193-194 (1976).

[101] *Lexmark International, Inc. v Static Control Components Inc.*, 572 U. S. ____ (2014) (Fn 3 on p 8: The zone-of-interests test is not the only concept that we have previously classified as an aspect of 'prudential standing' but for which, upon closer inspection, we have found that label inapt. Take, for example, our reluctance to entertain generalized grievances (...). While we have at times grounded our reluctance to entertain such suits in the 'counsels of prudence', we have since held that such suits do not present constitutional 'cases' or 'controversies.') (internal quotations omitted).

[102] E.g., William A Fletcher 'The Structure of Standing' (1988) 98(2) *The Yale Law Review* 221; Cass R Sunstein 'What's Standing After Lujan? Of Citizen Suits, "Injuries" and Article III' (1992) 91(2) *Michigan Law Review* 163; Siegel (n 96); William A Fletcher 'Standing: Who Can Sue to Enforce a Legal Duty' (2013) 65(2) *Alabama Law Review* 277. Cf. Woolhandler and Nelson (n 89), 689.

[103] Siegel, ibid., 86–87.

[104] *Flast v Cohen*, 392 U.S. 83, 129 (1968) (Harlan J., dissenting).

[105] Fletcher 'The Structure of Standing' (n 102), 221.

[106] E.g., *Lujan v Defenders of Wildlife,* 504 U.S. 555, 560-61 (1992); *Clapper v Amnesty International USA et al.*, 568 U. S. ____ (2013); *Spokeo v Robins*, 578 U.S. ___ (2016).

[107] Siegel (n 96), 75 (his remark was about all the justiciability doctrines).

[108] Ibid.

[109] *Spokeo v Robins*, 578 U.S. ___, 136 S. Ct. 1540, 1548 (2016); *Clapper v Amnesty International USA et al.*, 568 U. S. ____, 10 (2013).

is regarded as the most important of the three constitutional standing requirements.[110] It is the focus point of several cases before the Supreme Court, including some regarding privacy issues.[111] One can easily see why privacy litigants struggle to demonstrate injury as required, as privacy harms are often intangible, hard to measure and subjective.[112] As such, they are not easily recognized by courts as sufficient for the purpose of showing Article III standing. In the following paragraphs we will discuss the elements of injury-in-fact, including relevant privacy cases and scholarly critiques.

III.2.1 Concrete and particularized

The injury-in-fact needs to be both 'concrete and particularized'. The Supreme Court emphasized in *Spokeo, Inc v Robins* that these requirements are distinct and cumulative.[113] First, particularization requires that the plaintiff is injured in a personal and individual way. This also means that it is not possible to sue over a 'general grievance', i.e., lawsuits that involve harm to the public at large.[114] For example, a concerned citizen claims she is harmed because a particular law is not properly applied. This is a generalized grievance, as proper application of laws is every citizen's interest. Second, a concrete injury is one that is *de facto*, i.e., that is real; exists. This does not however mean that the injury needs to be tangible per se; an intangible injury may also satisfy the concreteness requirement. This can occur where the injury has a close relationship to a type of injury traditionally recognized by the courts or when Congress has (within constitutional limits) identified it as a cognizable injury.[115] Risk of injury may also satisfy the concreteness requirement under certain circumstances.

---

[110] *Steel Co. v Citizens for Better Environment*, 523 U.S. 83, 103 (1998):

> The 'irreducible constitutional minimum of standing' contains three requirements. First and foremost, there must be alleged (and ultimately proved) an 'injury in fact'—a harm suffered by the plaintiff that is 'concrete' and 'actual or imminent, not "conjectural" or "hypothetical"'.

Spokeo v Robins, 578 U.S. ___, 136 S. Ct. 1540, 1547 (2016).

[111] *Flast v Cohen*, 392 U.S. 83 (1968); *Sierra Club v Morton*, 405 U.S. 727 (1972); *United States v Scrap*, 412 U.S. 669 (1973); *Valley Forge College v Americans United*, 454 U.S. 464 (1982); *Los Angeles v Lyons*, 461 U.S. 95 (1983); *Allen v Wright* 468 U.S. 737 (1984); *Lujan v Defenders of Wildlife*, 504 U.S. 555 (1992); *Hollingsworth v Perry*, 570 U.S. ___ (2013), 133 S.Ct. 2652; *Clapper v Amnesty International USA et al.*, 568 U. S. ____ (2013) (constitutional challenge against government surveillance powers under Section 702 FISA); *Spokeo v Robins*, 578 U.S. ___, 136 S. Ct. 1540 (2016) (concerning a claim under a federal privacy statute, the FCRA).

[112] Ryan Calo 'The Boundaries of Privacy Harm' (2010) 86(3) *Indiana Law Journal* 1131, 1133 (breaking down privacy harms in 'objective' and 'subjective' harm, the latter category described as 'unwelcome mental states—anxiety, for instance, or embarrassment accompany the belief that one is or will be watched or monitored.') Ryan Calo, 'Privacy Harm Exceptionalism' (2014) 12(2) *Colorado Technology Law Journal* 361, 363 (calling privacy harms 'ethereal'); Solove and Keats Citron (n 9) (their remarks about the 'intangible, risk-oriented and diffuse' nature of privacy harms relate to data breach harms).

[113] *Spokeo v Robins*, 578 U.S. ___, 136 S. Ct. 1540, 1548 (2016) ('We have made it clear time and time again that an injury must be both concrete *and* particularized').

[114] *Lujan v Defenders of Wildlife*, 504 U.S. 555, 573–574 (1992):

> We have consistently held that a plaintiff raising only a generally available grievance about government—claiming only harm to his and every citizen's interest in proper application of the Constitution and laws, and seeking relief that no more directly and tangibly benefits him than it does the public at large—does not state an Article III case or controversy.

Lexmark International, Inc. v Static Control Components Inc., 572 U. S. ____ (2014) (see fn 3 on p 8).

[115] *Spokeo v Robins*, 578 U.S. ___, 136 S. Ct. 1540, 1549 (2016).

A Supreme Court case dealing with the 'concrete and particularized' is section of the injury-in-fact requirement is *Spokeo, Inc v Robins*. The facts of the case are as follows. Robins complained that Spokeo, a 'people search engine', acted in violation of the Fair Credit and Reporting Act (FCRA) by generating and disseminating a profile about him that contained several inaccuracies. In particular, his profile falsely stated that 'he is married, has children, is in his 50's, has a job, is relatively affluent and holds a graduate degree'.[116] The injury alleged by Robins was that the inaccurate information in his profile had a detrimental effect on his job prospects during the time he was unemployed, as it made him look too good. Based on the profile, potential future employers would find him to be overqualified, expecting a higher salary, and less mobile because of family responsibilities. A central issue in this case was whether these allegations of injury were sufficient for the purpose of Article III standing.

The Supreme Court discussed the standing doctrine and the requirements of particularization and concreteness specifically. It vacated and remanded the Ninth Circuit's judgment, because their standing analysis was incomplete. The Ninth Circuit had only considered whether the injury alleged by Robins was *particularized*, without discussing whether the injury was also *concrete*. In the words of Justice Alito, the Ninth Circuit 'did not address the question framed by our discussion, namely, whether the particular procedural violations alleged in this case *entail a degree of risk sufficient to meet the concreteness requirement*' (emphasis added).[117] The majority did however not take a position on whether the injury alleged by Robins was concrete enough. Justice Ginsburg, joined by Justice Sotomayor, dissented. According to her, Robins' allegations of harm were concrete enough.[118] She did not see utility in remanding the case to the Ninth Circuit to show what was already clear, namely that Spokeo's misinformation caused actual harm to Robins' employment prospects.[119]

An aspect of this case that is important to the potential future of US privacy law is how the constitutional doctrine of standing relates to the power of Congress to create legally enforceable rights by statute. *Spokeo, Inc. v Robins* concerned an action under a federal statute, the FCRA, that contains a private right of action for individuals in case its provisions are violated.[120] In this case, the Supreme Court held that, although Congress' judgment is instructive when determining which intangible harms are sufficiently concrete to establish Article III standing, Congress cannot create a private right of action that automatically grants standing whenever statutory provisions are violated.[121] Therefore, also a party that invokes a statutory private right of action will need to demonstrate all standing requirements, including a con-

---

116 Ibid., at 1546.

117 Ibid., at 1550.

118 Ibid., at 1555 (Ginsburg J., dissenting) ('Judged by what we have said about "concreteness," Robins' allegations carry him across the threshold').

119 Ibid., at 1556 (Ginsburg J., dissenting).

120 §1681n(a) FCRA:

> '[a]ny person who willfully fails to comply with any requirement [of the Act] with respect to any [individual3] is liable to that [individual]' for, among other things, either 'actual damages' or statutory damages of $100 to $1,000 per violation, costs of the action and attorney's fees, and possibly punitive damages.

121 *Spokeo v Robins*, 578 U.S. ___, 136 S. Ct. 1540, 1549 (2016):

> Congress' role in identifying and elevating intangible harms does not mean that a plaintiff automatically satisfies the injury-in-fact requirement whenever a statute grants a person a statutory right and purports to authorize that person to sue to vindicate that right. Article III standing requires a concrete injury even in the context of a statutory violation.

crete injury.[122] In sum, Congress cannot override the constitutional standing requirements by statute. Because the Constitution limits the judicial power of the federal courts, the Supreme Court reasons, courts are not capable of enforcing rights that do not adhere to justiciability requirements. Interesting in this regard is Justice Thomas' concurrence, who indicates that, if the Ninth Circuit identifies the FCRA right as a private right, a bare procedural violation would be sufficient for standing purposes.[123]

The inflexible attitude of the Supreme Court's majority towards the constitutional doctrine of standing has serious ramifications in general, but also for privacy law in particular. As seen in section II, US privacy law has increasingly become a matter of statutory law. The relevance of constitutional law and common law privacy torts has decreased. As a result, individuals rely on statutory sources of privacy law. Some of these laws, though not all, purport to grant individuals a private right of action. The *Spokeo* ruling concerned the FCRA, but as scholars have pointed out, many other privacy statutes rely on private rights of action as the only or an important enforcement mechanism.[124] Examples include the Video Privacy Protection Act, the Wiretap Act and the Telephone Consumer Protection Act.[125] Privacy harms are however often intangible and hard to demonstrate. Privacy wrongs often cause emotional harm, for example anxiety and distress over a loss of control over one's personal data. It is especially difficult therefore for privacy litigants to satisfy the demands of Article III standing. The fact that Congress cannot elevate this burden is unfortunate for the protection of individuals' privacy in the US. It means that even where an individual has a right under a statute, it may not be able to enforce this right in court due to a lack of standing.

There are elaborate critiques on this particular feature of the Article III standing doctrine. Professor Siegel argues that courts should always permit actions if Congress authorizes them, regardless of whether the constitutional requirements of Article III are satisfied in a particular case.[126] Fletcher argues that the abstract procedural structure of standing should be abandoned in favour of a substantive approach. According to him: 'Standing (...) [should be] a question of substantive law, and the answers to standing questions will vary as the substantive law

---

Solove explains it nicely in his blog on TechPrivacy. For an explanation of this part of the court's judgment: Daniel Solove, 'When is a Person Harmed by a Privacy Violation: Thoughts on Spokeo v. Robins' (*TechPrivacy*, 17 May 2016) https://www.teachprivacy.com/thoughts-on-spokeo-v-robins/ accessed 29 March 2017 'This opinion is like an M C Escher painting. It keeps on begging questions and sending the reader around and around in impossible loops.'

[122] *Spokeo v Robins*, 578 U.S. ___, 136 S. Ct. 1540, 1549 (2016) ('Article III standing requires a concrete injury even in the context of a statutory violation.').

[123] Ibid., at, 1553 (Thomas J., concurring) ('If Congress has created a privacy duty owed personally to Robins to protect *his* information, then the violation of the legal duty suffices for Article III injury in fact').

[124] Brief of Information Privacy Law Scholars in *Spokeo*, *Spokeo v Robins*, 578 U.S. ___, 136 S. Ct. 1540 (2016). Accessed electronically 29 March 2017, <http://ssrn.com/abstract=2656482> 27–29.

[125] Ibid., at 29.

[126] Siegel (n 96), 77 and 127 (In particular, Siegel argues that US federal courts should embrace the 'public rights model' instead of the 'private rights model'. Under the former, it is one of the court's primary tasks to articulate norms and policing other branches of government. Under the latter the court's task is restricted to resolving disputes. According to Siegel, by embracing a public rights model courts would serve 'the purpose of promoting the rule of law and fulfilling the Constitution's vision of establishing justice by requiring government to behave lawfully'. The public rights model is basically the current approach under UK law, where any 'concerned citizen' can challenge public wrongs).

varies'.[127] Professor Hessick also criticizes the one-size-fits-all nature of Article III standing doctrine, noting it has the effect that plaintiffs have to demonstrate factual harm regardless of the underlying cause of action, even if their private rights are violated.[128] In those cases, Hessick argues, the plaintiff should be required only to establish a violation of the right, and nothing more.[129] Other authors support these or similar views.[130]

If the Supreme Court at some point leaves its rigid interpretation of Article III standing, allowing Congress to confer standing on plaintiffs by statute, this will have beneficial effects for privacy litigants seeking access to federal court. For the time being, we can however conclude that each privacy litigant seeking access to federal court needs to show that he has suffered an injury that is particularized, i.e., directly connected to him in particular, and concrete, i.e., an actually existing, legally cognizable injury.

III.2.2 Actual or imminent

We now move to the second criterion, the 'actual or imminent' criterion. This can be seen as a temporal requirement for the concrete and particularized injury as it relates to whether the injury is presently occurring or about to happen. If the injury is not *actual*, i.e., existing in the present, it needs to be *imminent*. The Supreme Court has clarified that, '[a]lthough imminence is concededly a somewhat elastic concept, it cannot be stretched beyond its purpose, which is to ensure that the alleged injury is not too speculative for Article III purposes – that the injury is certainly impending'.[131] Therefore, allegations of possible future injury are insufficient for Article III purposes.[132] Further guidance from the *Lujan* court teaches that:

> [the concept of imminence] has been stretched beyond the breaking point when, as here, the plaintiff alleges only an injury at some indefinite future time, and the acts necessary to make the injury happen are at least partly within the plaintiff's own control. In such circumstances we have insisted that the

---

[127] Fletcher 'The Structure of Standing' (n 102), 290–291.

[128] Andrew Hessick, 'Standing, Injury in Fact and Private Rights' (2008) 93(2) *Cornell Law Review* 275, 277.

[129] Ibid., 325.

[130] See e.g., Harvard Law Review, 'Class Action Standing: Spokeo, Inc. v. Robins' (2016) 130(1) *Harvard Law Review* 437, 446:

> Because the Court has no particular basis for displacing Congress's judgment that the publication of misinformation inflicted and injury worthy of a federal case, the court would have been better served to avoid such consequences by deferring to the will of Congress and the protection of individual rights.

Lexi Rubow, 'Standing in the Way of Privacy Protections: The Argument for a Relaxed Article III Standing Requirement for Constitutional and Statutory Causes of Action' (2014) 29(4) *Berkeley Law Technology Journal* 1007, 1009 (arguing the same as Hessick, i.e., that a violation of the underlying cause of action should be sufficient for standing purposes ('merging standing with substance' 1041) in the particular context of privacy law, because 'the abstract and context-specific nature of privacy harm does not fit well with current, rigid judicial conceptualizations of injury-in-fact').

[131] *Lujan v Defenders of Wildlife*, 504 U.S. 555, 565–564, footnote no 2 (1992). Cited with approval in *Clapper v Amnesty International USA et al.*, 568 U. S. ____ (2013).

[132] *Whitmore v Arkansas,* 495 U.S. 149, 158 (1990). Cited with approval in *Clapper v Amnesty International USA et al.*, 568 U. S. ____ (2013). See also: See also *Lujan v Defenders of Wildlife,* 504 U.S. 555, 567 footnote 3 (1992); *DaimlerChrysler Corp. v Cuno*, 547 U.S. 332, 345 (2006); *Friends of the Earth, Inc. v Laidlaw Environmental Services (TOC) Inc.*, 528 U.S. 167, 190 (2000); *Babbitt v Farm Workers*, 442 U.S. 289, 298 (1979).

> injury proceed with a high degree of immediacy, so as to reduce the possibility of deciding a case in which no injury would have occurred at all.[133]

The 'actual or imminent' section of the injury-in-fact requirement may also affect the second constitutional requirement for standing, namely that the injury is fairly traceable to the challenged action. If the alleged injury has not yet occurred, it may also be less clear that the challenged action will turn out to be the source of the injury.[134]

In privacy law, two types of cases have shown to struggle with the actual or imminent criterion, namely government surveillance cases and data breach cases. For the first category, the Supreme Court decision in *Clapper v Amnesty International* provided valuable insights. Respondents in this case, a group of attorneys and human rights, labour, legal and media organizations, complained that Section 702 of the Foreign Intelligence Surveillance Act (FISA) was unconstitutional.[135] In short and simplified, Section 702 authorizes secret surveillance of foreigners located outside the US. Respondents argued that their work caused them to engage in sensitive and sometimes privileged communications with individuals that are likely targets of surveillance under Section 702.[136] They alleged to have suffered harm because of this (threat of) surveillance, because their ability 'to locate witnesses, cultivate sources, obtain information, and communicate confidential information to their clients' was compromised.[137] Second, respondents also ceased engaging in certain telephone and email communications, instead incurring costs to travel abroad for in-person conversations.[138] Third, they also declared to have undertaken costly and burdensome measures to protect the confidentiality of their sensitive communications.[139]

According to the majority of the Supreme Court, in an opinion written by Justice Alito, respondents' theory of standing was based on a '*highly speculative fear*' that their communications would in fact be targeted by the government. They relied on a '*highly attenuated chain of possibilities*', and therefore failed to show that their alleged injury was *actual* or *certainly impending*. Furthermore, even if they would be targeted by government surveillance and therefore suffered actual injury, it was unclear whether the government would base their surveillance on Section 702, so that the injury was not fairly traceable to the challenged action. Because the harm against which they sought to protect themselves was not certainly impending, the costly and burdensome measures that they undertook in order to protect the confidentiality of their communications did not qualify as actual injury. In the words of Justice Alito: 'the cost that [respondents] have incurred to avoid surveillance are simply the product of their fear of surveillance'. Respondents' argument that they should be held to have standing because

---

133 *Lujan v Defenders of Wildlife*, 504 U.S. 555, 565-564, footnote no 2 (1992).

134 *Clapper v Amnesty International USA et al.*, 568 U. S. ____ (2013) (clear example of this relation).

135 The group sought a declaration that section 702 violates the Fourth Amendment (protection against unlawful searches and seizures by the government), the First Amendment (protection of free speech), Article III and separation-of-powers principles. They also sought a permanent injunction against the use of section 702. Their case was dismissed for lack of standing because they did not demonstrate an injury that is certainly impending or fairly traceable to section 702 FISA.

136 *Clapper v Amnesty International USA et al.*, 568 U. S. ____, 7 (2013).

137 Ibid.

138 Ibid.

139 Ibid.

otherwise nobody could challenge the constitutionality of Section 702 did not convince the majority either.

The outcome of this case, decided by a five-to-four vote, was controversial. Justice Breyer, leading the dissent, found that it was likely that respondents would be harmed under section 702 FISA. The dissenters were convinced that there was a very highly likelihood that at least some of the respondents' communications would be intercepted by the government.[140] The threatened harm alleged by respondents therefore was not too speculative. This is not equal to saying that the threatened harm was certainly impending either, but according to the dissenting opinion, there is a sufficient or reasonable degree of certainty for at least some of the plaintiffs to have standing.[141]

Data breach cases present a second category of cases for which the 'actual or imminent' section of injury-in-fact has shown to be difficult to surmount.[142] The typical fact pattern of these cases is that, due to inadequate security, personal data are stolen and possibly misused. In cases of actual identity theft resulting from a data breach and causing, for example, monetary harm, it will not be difficult to show a concrete and actual injury-in-fact.[143] This is less clear however when there is no proof that the stolen personal data is actually used in a harmful way. The harm generally alleged in such cases is an increased risk of identity theft, emotional harm in the form of anxiety and distress and incurred costs for monitoring services to protect against possible identity theft. Whether such injuries are sufficient for Article III divides the courts. The Sixth, Seventh and Ninth Circuit have recognized injury-in-fact based on increased risk of identity theft,[144] whilst the First, Third and Fourth Circuit refused to recognize such injury as sufficient for standing purposes.[145] The Supreme Court has not (yet) decided the issue.

A good example of the stricter approach to injury-in-fact in a data breach case is *Reilly v Ceridian Corp.*, a case decided by the Third Circuit in 2011. The facts of the case are as follows. Ceridian, a payroll processing company, suffered a security breach of its IT systems. An unknown hacker potentially gained access to personal and financial information of almost 30,000 people. It was unknown whether the hacker had read, copied or understood the data. Appellants sued for negligence and breach of contract. As harm they alleged increased risk of

---

[140] Ibid. (Breyer J., dissenting) ('several considerations, based upon the record along with common-sense inferences, convince me that there is a very high likelihood that Government, acting under the authority of §1881a, will intercept at least some of the communications just described. First ...').

[141] Ibid. (Breyer J., dissenting):

> In sum, as the Court concedes (...) the word 'certainly' in the phrase 'certainly impending' does not refer to absolute certainty. As our case law demonstrates, what the Constitution requires is something more akin to 'reasonable probability' or 'high probability.' The use of some such standard is all that is necessary here to ensure the actual concrete injury that the Constitution demands. The considerations (...) make clear that the standard is readily met in this case.) (internal quotations omitted).

[142] See for a discussion hereof: John L Jacobus and Benjamin B Watson, 'Clapper v. Amnesty International and Data Privacy Litigation: Is a Change to the Law "Certainly Impending"?' (2014) 21(1) *Richmond Journal of Law and Technology*.

[143] To prevent this, companies often undertake to reimburse monetary harm caused by identity theft.

[144] *Galaria v Nationwide Mut. Ins. Co.*, No. 15-3386, 2016 WL 4728027, at footnote 3 (6th Cir. Sept. 12, 2016); *Remijas v Neiman Marcus Group LLC*, 794 F.3d 688, 692, 694–95 (7th Cir. 2015); *Krottner v Starbucks Corp.*, 628 F.3d 1139, 1142–43 (9th Cir. 2010), *Pisciotta v Old Nat'l Bancorp*, 499 F.3d 629, 632–34 (7th Cir. 2007).

[145] *Katz v Pershing LLC*, 672 F.3d 64, 80 (1st Cir. 2012); *Reilly v Ceridian Corp.*, 664 F.3d 38, 40, 44 (3d Cir. 2011) *Beck v McDonald* (4th Cir. 2017).

identity theft, incurred costs to monitor their credit activity, and emotional distress. The Third Circuit dismissed the complaint for lack of standing, because it found the allegations of harm to be merely hypothetical and future-based; there was no actual harm nor imminent threat of harm. Because of this, the costs incurred to prevent harm in the future were not the result of any injury either. Rather, '[appellants] prophylactically spent money to ease fears of future third-party criminality. Such misuse is only speculative – not imminent'. This rationale is the same as used by the Supreme Court in *Clapper* to dismiss incurred costs to protect against surveillance.

In early 2017, the Fourth Circuit dismissed a data breach case for lack of standing for similar reasons. *Beck v McDonald* involved claims against the government for violations of the Privacy Act and the Administrative Procedure Act.[146] Two data breaches had occurred at a medical facility. First, a laptop with unencrypted data containing personal data of approximately 7,400 patients was stolen. Second, four boxes of medical reports were misplaced or stolen. The plaintiffs, veterans, alleged harm in the form of increased risk of identity theft and incurred costs for protecting against this risk. According to the Fourth Circuit, these allegations were insufficient to establish a substantial risk of harm.

American privacy scholars are critical of the functioning of Article III standing in data breach cases. Solove and Keats Citron have argued that courts are too dismissive of data breach harm.[147] They admit that data breach harms are difficult, because they are intangible, risk-oriented and diffuse, but argue that this should not confound courts, because similarly difficult types of harms have already been recognized in other areas of law. They therefore urge courts to recognize data breach harm and show how the existing legal state of affairs supports this. In a broader attack on Article III standing, professor Hessick has argued that federal courts should recognize all probabilistic or threatened injuries. According to him, the 'minimum-risk requirement', i.e., that *a risk* of harm must be real and imminent, is unwarranted, because any risk or threat of injury establishes a personal interest that is justiciable.[148] The recent ruling of the Fourth Circuit in *Beck* however shows that courts remain reluctant to find sufficient injury-in-fact in data breach cases.[149]

The requirements of Article III standing can thus be a difficult hurdle to overcome in different areas of privacy law. Even when a privacy litigant can find a cause of action to remedy a privacy wrong (as discussed in Section II), it is only possible to gain access to the court when he or she can also demonstrate that the requirements for standing are satisfied. Because of the Supreme Court's rigid interpretation of Article III of the US Constitution, it also creates a significant hurdle for Congress to create privacy statutes that include an actually enforceable private right to action.

III.3 Standing Doctrines in Europe

In contrast to the US, standing requirements generally do not seem to pose a problem for privacy litigants in Europe. Access to the court for privacy wrongs is relatively easy to achieve

---

146 *Beck v McDonald*, No. 15-1395 (4th Cir. 2017).

147 Solove and Keats Citron (n 9).

148 Andrew Hessick, 'Probabilistic Standing' (2012) *Northwestern University Law Review* 106(1) 55, 65.

149 *Beck v McDonald*, No. 15-1395 (4th Cir. 2017).

for individuals whose personal data is being processed ('data subjects'). The question central to this final part of this chapter is why standing is *not* an issue for privacy litigants in Europe. We will consider what is required from individuals to obtain standing for civil enforcement of data privacy law in Europe. First, we discuss the role of the two supranational courts, the Court of Justice of the EU and European Court of Human Rights, for data privacy litigation. Second, we discuss standing at the national level of EU Member States, in particular in the Netherlands, and how this relates to the substantive data privacy law framework.

III.3.1 Standing before the CJEU and ECtHR

Both the CJEU and the ECtHR are supranational courts that serve a secondary role in enforcing the obligations in EU law and the ECHR respectively, with national courts fulfilling the primary role.

As explained in Section II, the ECHR creates obligations for States. This means that a data privacy litigant is only able to sue a contracting State before the ECtHR, in cases where they have failed to fulfil their obligations with regard to Article 8 ECHR. It is not possible for two private parties to have a case between them adjudicated by the ECtHR. It must be a question of whether a State has infringed a Convention right without proper justification. This can involve a violation of a negative obligation, meaning the obligation of States not to interfere with the Convention rights.[150] For example, a case concerning a complaint by an individual about government surveillance. Also possible are violations of positive obligations, meaning that the government failed to take measures to guarantee Convention rights in horizontal relations between private parties also.[151] An example hereof is the *Von Hannover* case law involving the princess of Monaco suing the German government because the German courts rejected her privacy claims against a tabloid.[152]

Articles 34 and 35 ECHR provide the admissibility criteria for applications by individuals to the ECtHR.[153] Besides individual complaints, inter-State proceedings are also allowed before the ECtHR. The admissibility requirements can be seen as the standing requirements for the ECtHR. In short: the ECtHR is competent to decide applications made by any person that claims to be a victim of a violation of a Convention right by a contracting State. There are some procedural demands such as the requirement that all domestic remedies must have been exhausted and that the application must be made within six months of the final decision.[154] More substantive grounds of refusal can be found in Article 35(2) and (3) of the Convention.

Relevant to our research is that an application will be declared inadmissible in a case where there is no significant disadvantage to the applicant.[155] At first glance, this demand seems to resemble the injury-in-fact requirement in the US. Looking more closely, however, the resemblance fades. The background to introducing this admissibility requirement is to permit the court to work more effectively by only focusing on cases that raise important human rights

---

150 Harris et al. (n 15), 504.

151 Ibid.

152 *Von Hannover v Germany (No. 1)* App No 59320/00 (ECHR, 24 June 2004); *Von Hannover v Germany (No. II)* App No 40660/08 and 60641/08 (ECHR, 7 February 2012); *Von Hannover v Germany (No. 3)* App No 8772/10 (ECHR 19 September 2013) (only published in French).

153 Harris et al. (n 15), Chapter 2: Admissibility of Applications.

154 Art 35(1) ECHR.

155 Art 35(3)(b) ECHR.

issues.[156] The idea of this admissibility requirement, which has only existed since 2010,[157] is that a violation of a Convention right, however real from a legal point of view, must attain a level of severity in order to warrant consideration by the ECtHR.[158] It is a means to achieve judicial efficiency. Compared to the injury-in-fact requirement, it is a much less rigid rule. Even where there is no significant disadvantage to the individual, the court may still consider the case if respect for the Convention rights requires an examination of the merits of the application. Furthermore, a case may not be rejected for a lack of significant disadvantage in the event that it has not been duly considered by a domestic tribunal.

Another relevant requirement is that a violation of a Convention right must have occurred, which the applicant must prove. The applicant must demonstrate facts proving the interference with the Convention right beyond a reasonable doubt,[159] which is a high burden of proof.[160] For data privacy law, an issue that comes to mind is secret surveillance by the government; how can anyone prove such an interference when it is cloaked in secrecy? We have already seen the problems this can cause for litigants in the US when discussing the *Clapper* case involving a challenge to Section 702 of FISA. By contrast, the approach of the ECtHR is to award standing more easily. With regard to laws and practices permitting secret surveillance, the court has repeatedly held that *the mere existence* of such laws and practices is enough to give rise to an interference with Article 8 ECHR. The applicants need therefore only show that the legislation *could* apply to them.[161]

With regard to standing before the CJEU, it is important to understand that the EU is characterized by a system of indirect administration under which the proper administration and implementation of EU law is a responsibility of the Member States (Art 4(3) TEU).[162] National courts play a vital role in fulfilling this obligation.[163] Therefore, even though the CJEU is the highest court in matters concerning EU law, in practice it has a secondary role in the administration of EU law. The primary route via which the CJEU becomes involved in data privacy cases is when a national court asks preliminary questions regarding the interpretation or validity of EU law.[164] This is a referral from one court to another, and the decision to do so lies with the referring court.[165] The parties to the case have no decisive power in this regard, though they

---

[156] Antoine Buyse, 'Protocol 14 Enters into Force', (*ECHR Blog*, 1 June 2010) http://echrblog.blogspot.nl/2010/06/protocol-14-enters-into-force.html accessed 24 June 2017.

[157] Harris et al. (n 15), 67.

[158] Ibid., 68.

[159] Ibid., 531.

[160] Ibid.

[161] *Klass and Others v Germany* App No 5029/71 (ECHR 6 September 1978), par. 41 ('In the mere existence of the legislation itself there is involved, for all those to whom the legislation could be applied, a menace of surveillance (...)').

[162] Olivier Dubos, 'The Origins of the Proceduralisation of EU Law: A Grey Area of European Federalism' (2015) 8(1) *Review of European Administrative Law* 7, 17–18; Schwartz 'The Value of Privacy Federalism' (n 7), 334–335.

[163] Case C-567-13 *Nóra Baczóet al. v Raiffeisen Bank Zrt* EU:C:2015:88, para 41:

> it is for the domestic legal system of each Member State, in accordance with the principle of the procedural autonomy of the Member States, to designate the courts and tribunals having jurisdiction and to lay down the detailed procedural rules governing actions for safeguarding rights which individuals derive from EU law.

[164] Art 267 Treaty on the Functioning of the European Union (TFEU).

[165] See EU summary of legislation for an explanation of the procedure for preliminary rulings of the CJEU: http://eur-lex.europa.eu/legal-content/EN/TXT/?uri=URISERV%3Al14552.

may make a request for a referral.[166] The rules about which cases can or must be referred to the CJEU focus on whether the question relates to the interpretation of EU law; these are not standing requirements.[167] Important data privacy cases like *Lindqvist*; *Digital Rights Ireland*; and *Schrems* have found their way to the CJEU via this route.[168]

Another way in which the CJEU can become involved with disputes is when an individual starts proceedings directly before the CJEU. This is however only possible in limited circumstances. Article 263 paragraph 4 TFEU is concerned with individual standing. Put shortly and simplified, a measure of general application, like a Regulation or Directive, can be challenged if the plaintiff can show *direct and individual concern*. The criterion of direct concern requires that the measure affects the applicant's legal situation.[169] 'Individual concern' is more complicated. According to the Plaumann formula, the measure must affect the individual's position 'by reason of certain attributes peculiar to them, or by reason of a factual situation which differentiates them from all other persons and distinguishes them individually in the same way as the addressee'.[170] This criterion has generated a string of case law.[171]

So far, we have discussed issues of standing at the level of the CJEU and ECtHR. We have seen that these courts play a secondary (but important) role in the enforcement of the rights contained in EU legal instruments and the Convention. Data privacy litigants will virtually always turn to the national courts first (and independent regulatory authorities) for enforcement of their rights under EU data privacy law.

III.3.2 Standing before national courts

Standing requirements are usually part of the laws of procedure in a national legal system. Adding to the fragmentation of this field of law, procedural law varies strongly between different countries. It has been called to be the most 'ethnocentric' branch of law, meaning that it is strongly marked by national traditions.[172] Moreover, not only do rules of procedure differ, also whether rules are deemed as part of procedural or substantive law varies.[173] All Member States must respect the fundamental right to an effective remedy for violations of EU law and violations of fundamental rights (Art 47 EU Charter and Art 13 ECHR). This fundamental right seeks to guarantee that substantive rights are coupled with an effective administrative or judicial remedy.[174] Amongst other things, the effectiveness of a remedy depends on the range of powers attributed to the judicial or administrative body that has been given the task

---

166 See, ibid.

167 Parties have already established standing before a national court.

168 Case C-101/01 *Bodil Lindqvist* [2003] ECR I-12971; Joined Cases C-293/12 and C-594/12 *Digital Rights Ireland* EU:C:2014:238; Case C-362/14 *Maximillian Schrems v Data Protection Commissioner* EU:C:2015:650 Case C101/01.

169 Groussot (n 87), 223–224.

170 Case 25/62 *Plaumann v Commission* [1963] ECR 95, para 107.

171 See for a discussion: Groussot (n 87), 221, 225 and onwards.

172 Dubos (n 162), 8.

173 Ibid.

174 European Union Agency for Fundamental Rights and Council of Europe, *Handbook on European Law Relating to Access to Justice* (Publications Office of the European Union 2016) 99–100. See also Gerards, Janneke H., and Lize R. Glas. 'Access to justice in the European Convention on Human Rights system' (2017) 35(1) *Netherlands Quarterly of Human Rights* 11–30.

to provide a remedy for a right.[175] In this sense, strict standing requirements may contravene the right to an effective remedy for violations of rights granted to individuals in the GDPR or violations of the fundamental right to privacy and/or protection of personal data. Thus, the fundamental rights nature of data privacy laws at the EU level limits the possibility for national level standing requirements.

To take the Netherlands as a case study for standing requirements at the national level, we see that standing requirements find their origin in the Dutch Constitution (*Grondwet*). Article 112 of the Constitution decides the competence of the judiciary.[176] The allocation of judicial competence is two-fold. First, disputes involving private rights and debt claims are entrusted to the judiciary exclusively.[177] Second, the legislature is competent to decide who is entrusted with other types of disputes.[178] The decisive factor to decide whether a civil court is competent is *which law* the plaintiff invokes for protection (the so-called '*objectum-litis* doctrine'). Irrelevant is the underlying legal relationship of the parties and the nature of the law that the defendant invokes. In practice, this translates into the requirement of showing 'sufficient interest' (Art 3:303 of the Dutch Civil Code, *Burgerlijk Wetboek*).

According to case law on the topic of sufficient interest, it is not a high threshold. The existence of sufficient interest is rarely explicitly discussed and generally presumed to exist.[179] This means that a private litigant obtains access to court relatively easily. Depending what remedies are claimed, it may be required to demonstrate injury or harm at a later stage in the proceedings during a discussion of the merits, for example when damages are claimed. This is different for a declaration of law, which you can obtain without a showing of injury or harm. According to Professor Vranken, the quick and generally implicit assumption of sufficient interest is consistent with the general assumption in (Dutch) case law and literature that a declaration of law is a means to achieve greater judicial efficiency.[180] In this fashion, questions of liability can be answered first, before moving onto questions of injury and related inquiries.[181] The same can be said for injunctions. Case law in the field of data privacy law shows that an injunction to remove personal data from a website because its processing is unlawful does not require a discussion (at least not an explicit one) of injury or harm.[182]

---

[175] EU Agency for Fundamental Rights and Council of Europe, *Handbook on European Law Relating to Access to Justice*, ibid.

[176] See for an English translation of Art 112 *Grondwet*: http://www.denederlandsegrondwet.nl/9353000/1/j9vvihlf299q0sr/vgrnf8w664zn.

[177] The constitution itself does not define which courts belong to the judiciary. This task is left to the legislature (Art 116 of the *Grondwet*). Accordingly, Art 2 of the Judiciary Organisation Act (*Wet RO*) provides that the district courts, courts of appeal and the Supreme Court belong to this category.

[178] The legislature may entrust these matters to the judiciary also, or to other (special) courts. There are currently three administrative courts that do not belong to the judiciary that deal with disputes (mostly appeals), but otherwise administrative cases are adjudicated by a branch of the judiciary. These courts are: *Centrale Raad van Beroep, het College van Beroep voor het bedrijfsleven en de Afdeling bestuursrechtspraak van de Raad van State.*

[179] Dutch Supreme Court (*Hoge Raad*) 27 March 2015, ECLI:NL:HR:2015:760 (*AIG/X*), para 4.1.2. Note also the commentary by Prof. Vranken para 5 (own translation):

> [Empirical research] shows that a request for a declaratory decision, mostly in combination with other claims, is completely integrated and that in case law it is apparently quickly, often implicitly, assumed that the plaintiff has sufficient interest with the claimed declaration of law.

[180] Jan B M Vranken, case note HR 27 March 2015, NJ 2016/77, para 6.

[181] Ibid.

[182] See District Court of Rotterdam, 24 March 2009, ECLI:NL:RBROT:2009:BH7631.

III.3.3 Standing for civil enforcement of privacy laws

With regard to civil enforcement of data privacy law, an individual can invoke their fundamental right to privacy or data protection and/or rely on secondary EU data privacy law. Individuals in Europe can indeed also sue for privacy wrongs directly on the basis of their fundamental right to privacy and/or protection of their personal data. Unlike the US, where the State action doctrine limits constitutional protection to violations by the government, fundamental rights in Europe can be applied 'horizontally'. This means that, although originally construed as protection against government action, fundamental rights also apply, or perhaps better, shape the rights and obligations between private parties. In the case of data protection, a detailed legislative framework has been set up to give meaning and effect to the right to data privacy in horizontal relations, giving the right a regulatory character.[183]

Also possible are claims based on secondary EU data privacy law like the GDPR. As discussed above, procedural law is a field of law that typically belongs to the legislative competence of Member-States and which is therefore not harmonized. This is because the EU has no express competence to harmonize procedural law. In the system of indirect administration, Member States may choose themselves *how* to administer EU law. Amongst other things, this means that procedures to be followed before the national courts remain a matter of national law, including standing requirements.[184] Despite all this, so-called 'proceduralisation' of EU law is actually ongoing.[185] This means that some procedural requirements can be found in EU secondary law. As Dubos writes, '[f]rom the mid-1980s onwards, proceduralisation spread in order to bolster the effectiveness of subjective rights conferred by Community law and, thereby, legal actions brought on that basis'.[186] Member-State procedural law is therefore supplemented by some European procedural rules.

The GDPR is no exception to this trend. Chapter VIII contains a variety of procedural provisions on remedies, liabilities and penalties. In our interest in particular is Article 79 GDPR, which provides the data subject with a private right of action against a controller or processor.[187] The GDPR also allows a data subject to mandate a representative body to exercise this right and to receive compensation where this is allowed under national laws, i.e., collective actions.[188] Besides this civil route of enforcement, the data subject can also pursue an administrative route, which consists of lodging a complaint with a DPA coupled with a right to judicial review when the DPA makes a legally binding decision that concerns the data subject and with which he or she does not agree.[189] Although not specified as such in the GDPR, the latter will usually consist of proceedings before an administrative court of a Member State. The GDPR furthermore provides that the data subject has a right to compensation of material and non-material damage that has been suffered as a result of the infringement of the GDPR.[190] Compared to the DPD, the GDPR expanded rules on procedural aspects, though some authors

---

183 Raphael Gellert et al., 'A Comparative Analysis of Anti-Discrimination and Data Protection Legislation' in Custers et al. (eds) *Discrimination and Privacy in the Information Society: Data Mining and Profiling in Large Databases* (Springer 2013).

184 Dubos (n 162), 18.

185 Ibid., 7.

186 Ibid., 13.

187 Art 79 GDPR.

188 Art 80 GDPR.

189 Arts 77 and 78 GDPR.

190 Art 82 GDPR.

have argued that the GDPR could and should have gone further, for example by harmonising the possibility of summary proceedings.[191]

The broad substantive scope of the GDPR is thus coupled with broad procedural rights of action. The private right of action exists for any data subject that 'considers that *his or her rights* under this Regulation have been infringed as a result of the processing of his or her personal data in non-compliance with this Regulation' (emphasis added). The DPD used similar wording in Article 22. This is different from the criterion of Article 77 GDPR on the right to lodge a complaint with a DPA, which is that the data subject 'considers that the processing of personal data relating to him or her infringes this Regulation'. By not requiring that the data subject's rights are infringed, the right to lodge a complaint seems to be broader than the private right of action, meaning that the scope of the administrative route of enforcement is broader than the civil route of enforcement. In other words, data subjects may have more room to complain with a DPA than to start proceedings directly against the controller and/or processor or personal data.

It is however not exactly clear what is meant with the words 'his or her rights' in Article 79 GDPR. One may question whether this is limited to the Chapter III data subject rights, or whether it extends to other provisions also. The GDPR establishes a complex co-regulatory privacy governance framework, but it is not clear whether all of its requirements can be directly invoked by data subjects. The interpretation of this private right of action will therefore greatly affect enforcement opportunities for data subjects. Nevertheless, the fact that the GDPR contains a private right of action does indicate that, once the criterion is satisfied, data subjects should have access to the court to have the merits of their case considered. National standing requirements that make the GDPR rights illusory are most likely not allowed.

Illustrations of the fact that standing rights are broad in EU data privacy law can be found in the CJEU's case law. For example, in the *Schrems* case, Mr. Schrems requested the Irish Data Protection Commissioner to prohibit Facebook Ireland from transferring his personal data to the US, because he found US law not to adequately protect his personal data against surveillance activities by the US government. This case ended up before the CJEU via a referral by the High Court and resulted in the invalidity of the Safe Harbor agreement. In the US, this case would probably have failed for reasons of standing as was the case in *Clapper*. The same can be said about the *Digital Rights Ireland* case involving a challenge to the (now invalid) Data Retention Directive and its implementations in UK and German law. Another example is the *Google Spain* case, in which Mr. Costeja González complained that Google refused to remove a search result that linked to an old newspaper article reporting on his financial troubles. Notably, the CJEU clarified that the question of actual harm is irrelevant for the exercise of the right to request delisting of results. In the words of the CJEU: 'it must be pointed out that it is not necessary in order to find such a right that the inclusion of the information in question in the list of results causes prejudice to the data subject'.[192] This can be contrasted to the *Spokeo* case. There, it was not enough that Spokeo made and sold an inaccurate report about Mr. Robins, in violation of their obligations under the FCRA to do adequate reporting; Mr. Robins also needed to show an injury-in-fact.

---

[191] Antonella Galetta and Paul De Hert, 'The Proceduralisation of Data Protection Remedies under EU Data Protection Law: Towards a More Effective and Data Subject-oriented Remedial System?' (2015) 8(1) *Review of European Administrative Law* 125, 148.

[192] See consideration 96 of the Court in *Google Spain*.

IV. CONCLUSION

We set out to find out to what extent individuals have the right to sue for privacy wrongs in the EU and the US respectively, with a focus on enforcement before civil courts. First, we focused on the material scope of data privacy law in both legal systems, seeking to find out which situations involving (perceived) privacy wrongs are actually regulated and thereby giving individuals rights. Second, we focused on the opportunities for individuals to enforce the rights found in substantive law in court. This involved a discussion of Article III standing doctrine for the US, and an exploratory inquiry into (the lack of) standing issues in the EU.

With regard to the first part, we found that it is generally harder for a private litigant to find a cause of action to remedy a (perceived) privacy wrong in the US than in the EU. The EU data privacy framework is based in fundamental rights to privacy and personal data protection, coupled with strong secondary legislation from the European Union harmonizing European data privacy law. This results in an all-encompassing field of law that applies to all types of entities (both natural and legal) processing personal data. Because of the broad material and territorial scope, it is difficult to think of a situation involving processing of personal data sufficiently related to the EU that is left unregulated. The GDPR creates a multitude of obligations for those processing personal data on the one hand and rights for those whose data is being processed on the other. By contrast, the US system is harm-based and inherently fragmented. US data privacy law consists of an assemblage of laws including constitutional law, common law torts and statutory law. When comparing what the two systems substantively cover, it is clear that the US leaves many gaps. In the US, fewer privacy wrongs are actually recognised in law as such compared to the EU. It is therefore harder for an individual to find a legal right that can be invoked in order to remedy a (perceived) privacy wrong. An individual seeking privacy protection therefore has more opportunity to do so in the EU than in the US.

In the second part we examined the US Article III standing doctrine first, because this has shown to cause issues for privacy litigants. This constitutional doctrine originates from the US Constitution and filters out cases at a preliminary level. The injury-in-fact requirement of the Article III standing doctrine is in particular proving to be difficult to satisfy for privacy litigants for different reasons. The injury may not be 'concrete and particularized' and/or 'actual or imminent'. The *Spokeo* case shows the difficulty of demonstrating facts that a privacy wrong has produced a concrete injury. Privacy harms are often intangible, hard to measure and subjective and therefore difficult to prove. Furthermore, this case shows the difficult relationship between Article III standing and Congress' attempt to create legally enforceable private rights by statute. The *Clapper* and *Reilly* cases furthermore show how it may be hard to demonstrate facts that an injury, though if proven concrete and particularized, is actual or imminent. With regard to the surveillance in *Clapper* the problem lie with the secrecy cloaking FISA. With regard to Reilly the difficulty lies with US courts not recognizing a risk of harm and damage flowing from there as an injury sufficient for the purpose of Article III standing, forcing privacy plaintiffs to wait for damage to be done or very certain to occur.

There is no equivalent doctrine in the European legal system that requires a demonstration of injury at a preliminary stage in order to obtain access to the judiciary or a Data Protection Authority. The roles of the supranational courts, i.e., the ECtHR and CJEU, are of a secondary nature because they function as the highest appellate court in their legal fields and provide a safety net for privacy violations not properly adjudicated at the national level. Relevant standing requirements are a matter of national law. In the case study of the Netherlands we showed that standing requirements for civil litigants are much lower compared to the US, with only the requirement of showing a sufficient interest to the case. This requirement is generally not even explicitly discussed but assumed to exist. Furthermore, in the Netherlands it is possible to obtain remedies such as a declaration of law or even an injunction without a discussion of injury or harm (or at least not an explicit one). In data privacy law plaintiffs can invoke fundamental rights and/or secondary EU law in private lawsuits. The former is possible because of the doctrine of horizontal application of fundamental rights, which makes direct application more or less possible. The latter, in the case of the future GDPR, is possible due to a harmonized private right of action contained in Article 79 GDPR. The exact scope of this right of action is however not clear; it remains to be seen whether this will be constructed narrowly or broadly by courts, and this will have serious ramifications for individuals seeking to enforce EU data privacy law.

Overall, we can conclude that in the US, compared to the EU, a privacy litigant needs to overcome extra hurdles in order to sue for privacy wrongs both with regard to material and procedural aspects of data privacy law. In the EU there are more opportunities for individuals to seek a remedy before a court. We would like to end with the observation that, despite this easy access to the courts, in fact little judicial action is taken in the EU, especially compared to the amount of privacy litigants in the US. This is remarkable given the outcome of our research. Nevertheless, the interest in civil enforcement seems to be increasing in the EU also. Privacy litigation may furthermore see a sharp increase now that the GDPR has entered into force. We know that the GDPR, in comparison with the DPD, places a bigger focus on co- and self-regulatory obligations of the controller (e.g., the principle of accountability and responsibility, data protection by design, the risk-based approach and the data protection impact assessment). An increase in privacy litigation will therefore also raise the question of which elements of this privacy governance framework a privacy litigant should be able to invoke in court. The scope of the private right of action contained in the GDPR should then become clearer, which also provides clarity about the litigation opportunities for individuals in the EU.

REFERENCES

Article 29 Data Protection Working Party, 'Opinion 4/2007 on the concept of personal data' (20 June 2007)

Bamberger K A and Mulligan D K, *Privacy on the Ground: Driving Corporate Behavior in the United States and Europe* (MIT Press 2015).

Bennett C J and Raab C D, *The Governance of Privacy: Policy Instruments in Global Perspective* (2nd edn, MIT Press 2006).

Bezanson R P, 'The Right to Privacy Revisited: Privacy, News and Social Change, 1890–1990' (1992) 80(5) *California Law Review* 1133.

Bignami F, 'European Versus American Liberty: A Comparative Privacy Analysis of Antiterrorism Data Mining', (2007) 48 *Boston Comparative Law Review* 609, accessed electronically at http://lawdigitalcommons.bc.edu/bclr/vol48/iss3/3.

Brief of Information Privacy Law Scholars in *Spokeo*, *Spokeo v Robins*, 578 U.S. ___, 136 S. Ct. 1540 (2016) http://ssrn.com/abstract=2656482 accessed 29 March 2017.

Buyse A, 'Protocol 14 Enters into Force' (*ECHR Blog*, 1 june 2010) http://echrblog.blogspot.nl/2010/06/protocol-14-enters-into-force.html accessed 24 June 2017.

Bygrave L A, *Data Privacy Law: An International Perspective* (Oxford University Press 2014).

Calo R, 'Privacy Harm Exceptionalism' (2014) 12(2) *Colorado Technology Law Journal* 361.

Calo R, 'The Boundaries of Privacy Harm' (2010) 86(3) *Indiana Law Journal* 1131.

Carol Harlow and Richard Rawlings, *Law and Administration* (3rd edn, Cambridge University Press 2009).
Chemerinsky E, 'Substantive Due Process' (1999) 15(4) *Touro Law Review* 1501.
De Hert P and Gutwirth S, 'Data Protection in the Case Law of Strasbourg and Luxemburg: Constitutionalisation in Action' in Serge Gutwirth et al. (eds), *Reinventing Data Protection?* (Springer Science Dordrecht 2009).
De Hert P and Papakonstantinou V, 'The new General Data Protection Regulation: Still a Sound System for the Protection of Individuals?' (2016) 32(2) *Computer Law Security Review* 179.
Dubos O, 'The Origins of the Proceduralisation of EU Law: A Grey Area of European Federalism' (2015) 8(1) *Review of European Administrative Law* 7.
European Union Agency for Fundamental Rights and Council of Europe, *Handbook on European Law Relating to Access to Justice* (Publications Office of the European Union 2016).
Fletcher W A, 'Standing: Who Can Sue to Enforce a Legal Duty' (2013) 65(2) *Alabama Law Review* 277.
Fletcher W A, 'The Structure of Standing' (1988) 98(2) *The Yale Law Review* 221.
Forsyth C F and Wade W, *Administrative Law*, (11th edn, Oxford University Press 2014).
Galetta A and De Hert P, 'The Proceduralisation of Data Protection Remedies under EU Data Protection Law: Towards a More Effective and Data Subject-oriented Remedial System?' (2015) 8(1) *Review of European Administrative Law* 125.
Gellert R and Gutwirth S, 'The Legal Construction of Privacy and Data Protection' (2013) 59(5) *Computer Law & Security Review* 522.
Gellert R et al., 'A Comparative Analysis of Anti-Discrimination and Data Protection Legislation' in Custers et al. (eds) *Discrimination and Privacy in the Information Society: Data Mining and Profiling in Large Databases* (Springer 2013).
Gellert R, 'Data Protection: A Risk Regulation? Between the Risk Management of Everything and the Precautionary Alternative' (2015) 5(1) *International Data Privacy Law* 3.
Gellert R, 'We Have Always Managed Risks in Data Protection Law: Understanding the Similarities and Differences Between the Rights-Based and Risk-Based Approaches to Data Protection' (2016) 4(2) *European Data Protection Law Review* 481.
Gellert R, 'Why the GDPR Risk-based Approach is About Compliance Risk, and why it's not a Bad Thing', in E Schweighofer et al. (eds), *Trends and Communities of Legal Informatics: IRIS – 2017 – Proceeding of the 20th International Leg Informatics Symposium* (Austrian Computer Science).
Gerards, Janneke H, and Lize R Glas, 'Access to justice in the European Convention on Human Rights System' (2017) 35(1) *Netherlands Quarterly of Human Rights* 11–30.
González Fuster G, *The Emergence of Personal Data Protection as a Fundamental Right of the EU* (Springer International Publishing 2014).
Groussot X, 'The EC System of Legal Remedies and Effective Judicial Protection: Does the System Really Need Reform?' (2003) 30(3) *Legal Issues of Economic Integration* 221.
Harris DJ et al., *Law of the European Convention on Human Rights* (3rd edn, Oxford University Press 2014).
Harvard Law Review, 'Class Action Standing: Spokeo, Inc. v. Robins' (2016) 130(1) *Harvard Law Review* 437.
Harvard Law Review, 'Developments in the Law: State Action and the Public/Private Distinction' (2010) 123(5) *Harvard Law Review* 1248.
Hessick A, 'Probabilistic Standing' (2012) 106(1) *Northwestern University Law Review* 55.
Hassick A, 'Standing, Injury in Fact and Private Rights' (2008) 93(2) *Cornell Law Review* 275.
Hustinx P, 'EU Data Protection Law: the Review of Directive 95/46/EC and the Proposed General Data Protection Regulation' https://www.law.ox.ac.uk/sites/files/oxlaw/oscola_4th_edn_hart_2012.pdf accessed 17 May 2017.
Jacobus J L and Watson B B, 'Clapper v. Amnesty International and Data Privacy Litigation: Is a Change to the Law "Certainly Impending"?' (2014) 21(1) *Richmond Journal of Law and Technology*.
Kay R S, 'The State Action Doctrine, the Public-Private Distinction, and the Independence of Constitutional Law' (1993) 10(2) *Constitutional Commentary* 329.
Lynskey O, *The Foundations of EU Data Protection Law* (Oxford University Press 2015).
McGeveran W, *Privacy and Data Protection Law* (Foundation Press 2016).

Prosser W L, 'Privacy' (1960) 48(3) *California Law Review* 383.
Reidenberg J R, 'Privacy Wrongs in Search of Remedies' (2002) 54(4) *Hastings Law Journal* 877.
Richards N and Solove D 'Prosser's Privacy Law: A Mixed Legacy' (2010) 98 *California Law Review* 1887.
Richards N, *Intellectual Privacy: Rethinking Civil Liberties in the Digital Age* (Oxford University Press 2015).
Rubow L, 'Standing in the Way of Privacy Protections: The Argument for a Relaxed Article III Standing Requirement for Constitutional and Statutory Causes of Action' (2014) 29(4) *Berkeley Law Technology Journal* 100.
Schwartz P M and Pfeifer K, 'Transatlantic Data Privacy Law' (2017) 106(1) *Georgetown Law Journal* 115.
Schwartz P M, 'The EU-U.S. Privacy Collision: A Turn to Institutions and Procedures' (2013) 126(1) *Harvard Law Review* 1966.
Schwartz P M, 'The Value of Privacy Federalism' in Beate Roessler and Dorota Mokrosinska (eds), *Social Dimensions of Privacy: Interdisciplinary Perspectives* (Cambridge University Press 2015).
Siegel J R, 'A Theory of Justiciability' (2007) 86(1) *Texas Law Review* 73.
Solove D, 'When is a Person Harmed by a Privacy Violation: Thoughts on Spokeo v. Robins' (*TechPrivacy*, 17 May 2016) https://www.teachprivacy.com/thoughts-on-spokeo-v-robins/ accessed 29 March 2020.
Solove D J and Keats Citron D, 'Risk and Anxiety: A Theory of Data Breach Harms' (2017) 96 *Texas Law Review* 737; GWU Law School Public Law Research Paper No. 2017-2; GWU Legal Studies Research Paper No. 2017-2; U of Maryland Legal Studies Research Paper No. 2017-3. https://ssrn.com/abstract=2885638 accessed 16 January 2020
Sunstein C R, 'What's Standing After Lujan? Of Citizen Suits, "Injuries" and Article III' (1992) 91(2) *Michigan Law Review* 163.
Vranken J B M, case note HR 27 March 2015, NJ 2016/77.
Warren S D and Brandeis L D, 'The Right to Privacy' (1890) 4(5) *Harvard Law Review* 193.
Whitman JQ, 'The Two Western Cultures of Privacy: Dignity versus Liberty' (2004) 113(6) *Yale Law Journal* 1151.
Woolhandler A and Nelson C, 'Does History Defeat Standing Doctrine' (2004) 102(4) *Michigan Law Review* 689.

5. Canadian privacy law and the post-war freedom of information paradigm

Jonathon W. Penney

I. INTRODUCTION

A widely held assumption among lawyers and scholars is that technology drive changes in privacy and data protection laws. This is not surprising. As Colin Bennett and Charles Raab note, the 'task' of the 'privacy policy community' has always involved addressing new technologies:

> It has become trite to observe that information and communication technologies are being innovated and applied with astonishing speed and creativity. The task of the privacy policy community has always been to comprehend these emerging technologies, to study their impact on privacy and to formulate appropriate responses whether regulatory, political, or technological.[1]

Similarly, Canadian lawyer R.L. David Hughes writes:

> Perhaps more than any other single issue, the way in which judges and lawmakers respond to the privacy challenges brought about by the evolution of technology will determine the values and the type of society in which our children will grow up. Thus, as Justice Moldaver has recognized, the task of updating our privacy laws is truly a profoundly important one.[2]

---

1 Colin Bennett and Charles Raab, *Governance of Privacy: Policy Instruments in Global Perspective* (Ashgate 2003) 4.
2 R.L. David Hughes, 'Two Concepts of Privacy' (2015) 31 *Computer L Security Rev* 527, 528.

This common assumption is actually quite pervasive,[3] and not just limited to privacy lawyers and experts in Canada.[4] And, as Lisa Austin has noted, this assumption is neither new nor novel.[5] This overemphasis on technology and its impact on privacy and data protection law has neglected other important factors, ideas, and norms. Moreover, as Bennett and Raab note, privacy scholarship remains largely 'ahistorical' and the field would be 'enriched' by new historical treatments relevant to privacy issues and risks today and tomorrow.[6] On this count, despite the fact that privacy and access to information are often seen as inextricably linked legislatively,[7] no work has specifically examined the impact that ideas and norms associated information access—that is, freedom of information and the free flow of data so common in the decades after the Second World War—have had on Canada's privacy laws historically.[8]

---

[3] For just a few examples among Canadian legal scholars, see: Ronald J. Krotoszynski, *Privacy Revisited: A Global Perspective on the Right to Be Left Alone* (OUP 2016) 64; Paul D.M. Holden, 'Flying Robots and Privacy in Canada' (2016) 14 *CJLT* 65, 66; Graham Mayeda, 'My Neighbour's Kid Just Bought a Drone . . . New Paradigms for Privacy Law in Canada' (2015) 35 *NJCL* 59, 65–68; Tamir Israel, 'Foreign Intelligence in an Inter-Networked World' in Michael Geist (ed) *Law, Privacy and Surveillance in Canada in the Post-Snowden Era* (University of Ottawa Press 2015) 73; Craig Forcese, 'Law, Logarithms, and Liberties: Legal Issues Arising From CSE's Metadata Activities' in Michael Geist (ed) *Law, Privacy and Surveillance in Canada in the Post-Snowden Era* (University of Ottawa Press 2015) 137; Arthur J. Cockfield, 'Protecting the Social Value of Privacy in the Context of State Investigations Using New Technologies' (2007) 40 *UBCLR* 41; Avner Levin and Mary Jo Nicholson, 'Privacy Law in the United States, the EU and Canada: The Allure of the Middle Ground' (2005) 2:2 *UOLTJ* 357, 361; Lisa Austin, 'Privacy and the Question of Technology' (2003) 22:2 *Law & Philosophy* 119. Also, compare these two statements from the Canadian Privacy Commissioner almost 25 years apart: Privacy Commissioner of Canada, 'Time to Break Out of Technological Trance, says Commissioner' (Remarks by Privacy Commissioner of Canada regarding 10th Annual Report to Parliament, Ottawa, 13 July 1993) https://www.priv.gc.ca/en/opc-news/news-and-announcements/archive/02_05_b_930713/ accessed 18 October 2021; Privacy Commissioner of Canada, 'Statement' (Remarks by Privacy Commissioner of Canada regarding 2015–2016 Annual Report to Parliament, Ottawa, 27 September 2016) https://www.priv.gc.ca/en/opc-news/speeches/2016/s_d_20160927/ accessed 18 October 2021.

[4] See, e.g.: Rolf H Weber, 'The Digital Future – A Challenge for Privacy?' (2015) 31 *Computer L Security Rev* 234; Gehan Gunasekara, 'Paddling in Unison or Just Paddling? International Trends in Reforming Information Privacy Law' (2014) 22:2 *IJLIT* 141; Theresa Payton and Ted Claypoole, *Privacy in the Age of Big Data: Recognizing Threats, Defending Your Rights, And Protecting Your Family* (Rowman & Littlefield 2014).

[5] Austin (n 3), 121–122.

[6] Bennett and Raab (n 1), 5; Lawrence Cappello, 'Big Iron and the Small Government: On the History of Data Collection and Privacy in the United States' (2017) 29:1 *Journal of Policy History* 177, 178–179. There are exceptions: See, e.g.: Colin J Bennett, 'The Formation of a Canadian Privacy Policy: The Art and Craft of Lesson-drawing' (1990) 33:4 *Canadian Public Administration* 551; Colin J. Bennett and David Lyon, *Playing the Identity Card: Surveillance, Security, and Identification in Global Perspective* (London 2008); David H. Flaherty, *Protecting Privacy in Surveillance Societies: The Federal Republic of Germany, Sweden, France, Canada, and the United States* (Chapel Hill 1989); David H Flaherty, 'Reflections on Reform of the Federal Privacy Act' (Publication of the Office of the Privacy Commissioner of Canada 2008) https://www.priv.gc.ca/media/2044/pa_ref_df_e.pdf accessed 18 October 2021. Other treatments offering historical perspective: Bennett and Raab, (n 1); David H. Flaherty, *Privacy and Government Data Banks* (Mansell 1979).

[7] Flaherty (2008) (n 6), 10–11.

[8] See Jonathon W. Penney, 'Internet Access Rights: A Brief History and Intellectual Origins' (2011) 28 *William Mitchell L Rev* 10, 21–24. See generally also: Jonathon W Penney, 'The Cycles of Global Telecommunications Censorship and Surveillance' (2015) 36:3 *U Pa J Int'l L* 693.

The chapter aims to fill that void through a case study examining how ideas and norms tied to a broader Post War paradigm impacted on Canada's most important early privacy laws. Beyond some privacy protections in the Canadian Charter of Right and Freedoms, the primary privacy and data protection laws in Canada are statutory.[9] This case study will examine three foundational such enactments: (1) the 1977 enactment of Part VI of the Canadian Human Rights Act, which was the first statutory provisions on privacy enacted in Canada; (2) the 1983 enactment of the federal Privacy Act, which regulates how the federal government can use personal information gathered about citizens; and (3) the 2000 enactment of the Personal Information Protection and Electronic Documents Act (PIPEDA), which regulates how private sector companies can collect and use personal information.[10] Overall, the case study suggests that despite concerns being raised about privacy threats posed by technology at the time of each of the enactments, those concerns were often overshadowed by predominant concerns with freedom of information and related ideas and norms consistent with a broader international trend in those same years.[11] Through this case study, this chapter also offers insights as to Canada's overall privacy and data protection regulatory scheme and its development over time.

II. THE POST-WAR FREEDOM OF INFORMATION PARADIGM

Understanding early Canadian privacy laws requires understanding a broader historical context—involving a global shift toward freedom of information—in which they were enacted. In the decades since the Second World War there has been a 'global wave' of countries' freedom of information (FOI) laws.[12] As of 2006, there were over 66 such states with laws granting citizens greater access to government information.[13] There are a myriad of reasons for this 'explosion' in innovative transparency laws, but two central ones include international pressure to keep up with this emerging global paradigm, as well as domestic political pressure due to public concerns about the need for greater government accountability.[14]

In terms of the emerging global paradigm, freedom of information and radio jamming were major international issues after World War II. This salience was not only due to US

---

[9] Hughes (n 2), 528; Levin and Nicholson (n 3), 378–380; Miguel Bernal-Castillero, 'Canada's Federal Privacy Laws' (Library of Parliament Research Publication 2013) https://lop.parl.ca/Content/LOP/ResearchPublications/2007-44-e.htm accessed 18 October 2021; Tariq Ahmad, 'Online Privacy Law: Canada' (U.S. Library of Congress 2012) https://www.loc.gov/law/help/online-privacy-law/canada.php accessed 18 October 2021.

[10] Hughes, ibid., 528–529; Levin and Nicholson, ibid., 378–380; Bernal-Castillero, ibid.; Ahmad, ibid.

[11] John M. Ackerman and Irma E. Sandoval-Ballesteros, 'The Global Explosion of Freedom of Information Laws' (2006) 58 *Admin L Rev* 85, 85; Donald C. Rowat, 'The Right to Governmental Information in Democracies' (1981) 2 *J Media L & Prac* 314, 314. See also: Lotte E. Feinberg, 'Managing the Freedom of Information Act and Federal Information Policy' (1986) 46:6 *Public Administration Review* 615; Harold C. Relyea, 'Freedom of Information, Privacy, and Official Secrecy: The Evolution of Federal Government Information Policy Concepts' (1980) 7:1 *Social Indicators Research* 137.

[12] Ackerman and Sandoval-Ballesteros, ibid., 85.

[13] Ibid.

[14] Ibid., 115–119, 121–123. See Penney (2011) (n 8); Penney (2015) (n 8).

influence, but also developments during the war itself.[15] Both war propaganda and state censorship—enabled through extensive radio jamming—were pervasive during the war and posed significant threat to guaranteeing enduring peace and stability.[16] For example, newly developed shortwave radio technology, which made transnational propagation of radio broadcasts possible, led countries like Germany to use information warfare strategies like 'broadcast defense'—widespread and systematic jamming of foreign and transnational radio broadcasting.[17]

All this led to a strong Post War Period consensus on an international policy framework centred on the 'free flow of information' doctrine, promoted largely by the US and its allies in the West.[18] The doctrine involved the promotion of unrestricted flow of information and ideas across country borders internationally. The free flow doctrine, at least in theory, offered a single solution to pressing 'dual' problem of state propaganda and radio jamming experienced during the war; with information flowing freely across borders, both propaganda and jamming would be undercut by ensuring citizens would have a diversity of information sources from which draw information.[19] The consensus on the free flow doctrine was reflected in the substantial reduction of radio jamming after the war, as well as a wide range of international conventions, declarations, and treaties that would codify the doctrine's principles, like the right to 'seek, receive, and impart information' enshrined in Article 19 of the United Nations' 1948 Universal Declaration of Human Rights and its 1946 Declaration on Freedom of Information—which declared freedom of information a 'fundamental human right'—adopted unanimously in the very first session of the UN General Assembly.[20] This international consensus and the emerging 'freedom of information' paradigm, and the governments (namely the Americans), civil society groups, and international organizations that helped promote it, would exact substantial pressures on countries to similarly codify its principles with domestic legislation in the years following.[21]

This emerging international paradigm was strengthened by related domestic concerns in the West, about the growing secrecy of government bureaucracies in the Post-War period. Again, the US played a key role here. As the US promoted the free flow doctrine abroad, it wrestled with issues of bureaucratic growth and secrecy at home.[22] Both early 20th Century 'New Deal' policies and the War itself led to a significant expansion of the US federal bureaucracy.[23] Concerned about executive branch secrecy and encroachment on its legislative and constitutional authority, Congress began to push back starting only years after the war, with passage of the Administrative Procedure Act (APA) in 1946.[24] The aim of the APA was to force federal

[15] Penney (2011), ibid., 21–23.

[16] Ibid.

[17] James G Savage and Mark W Zacher, 'Free Flow versus Prior Consent: The Jurisdictional Battle Over International Communications' (1987) 42 *International Journal* 342, 344–347.

[18] Penney (2011) (n 8), 23; see generally Savage and Zacher, ibid., 348.

[19] Penney (2011), ibid., 22–23.

[20] Ibid., 23–30; Cees J Hamerlink, *The Politics of World Communication: A Human Rights Perspective* (Sage 1994) 60; Savage and Zacher (n 17), 348 ('Immediately after the end of the war jamming was virtually absent from the air waves...').

[21] Ackerman and Sandoval-Ballesteros (n 11), 115–119, 121–123. Penney (2011), (n 8), 21–23.

[22] Ackerman and Sandoval-Ballesteros, ibid., 116.

[23] Ibid., 117; Feinberg (n 11), 615.

[24] Ibid.; Feinberg, ibid., 615.

agencies to be more transparent about its processes, particularly decisions and rule-making.[25] The American Freedom of Information Act, passed in 1966, grew out of that same 'distrust' for government administrative agencies and likewise aimed to reduce their secrecy through greater freedom of, and access to, information in government.[26] These acts, particularly the Freedom of Information Act, would serve as models for similar legislation elsewhere, contributing to this global freedom of information movement.[27]

Yet, this freedom of information paradigm would also influence privacy and data protection laws internationally.[28] In Canada, the influence would prove even more significant—arguably commencing, enabling, and shaping the country's most significant early legislative efforts to protect privacy far more than any technological change or technology-related threat to privacy.

III. SHAPING CANADA'S FIRST MAJOR PRIVACY SCHEME: THE CANADIAN HUMAN RIGHTS ACT, PART IV

It is often said that Canada's privacy and data protection laws have historically been 'undeveloped', due to the fact there was little public concern and no 'dramatic event' similar to US Congressional hearings on national databanks, to 'focus' public attention on the threats to privacy posed by technology.[29] Yet, that is not quite true, at least with respect to the years leading to the enactment of Part IV of the Canadian Human Rights Act in 1977 and the 1983 Privacy Act, the first major privacy laws of general application in Canadian history. In fact, there were several high profile and widely covered events, scandals, and stories, involving technological threats to privacy—electronic surveillance— beginning in the late 1960s, and continuing through the 1970s.

During this period, the use of electronic surveillance technology, especially by police, was a 'major source of controversy'.[30] In 1965, the *Toronto Daily Star* reported it had become 'common practice' for car dealers to 'bug' their salesrooms and in 1965 that 'four and one-half million dollars' worth of listening device technology had been sold in Canada.[31] *The Star Weekly* also reported in 1965 that a Hamilton detective was fined for 'tapping' the telephone of a client's estranged wife.[32] In November 1966, an officer with the Pulp and Paper Workers union went public with allegations that union meetings at a Vancouver meeting had been 'bugged' with electronic surveillance devices.[33] Both a former Royal Canadian Mounted Police (RCMP) detective, working for a rival union, was involved in 'planting' the listening

---

[25] Ibid., 117–118.

[26] Ibid., 118; Feinberg (n 11), 616.

[27] Ibid., 85; Relyea (n 11), 137.

[28] See the discussion: Rowat (n 11), 326–331.

[29] Flaherty (1979) (n 6), 231; Bennett (1990) (n 6), 551 (noting '…low salience in public opinion'); Canadian Department of Communications/Department of Justice, *Privacy and Computers: A Report of the 1972 Task Force* (Ottawa 1972) 10; Flaherty (1979) (n 6), 231; Flaherty (1989) (n 6), 246.

[30] Robert W. Cosman, 'A Man's House Is His Castle-Beep: A Civil Law Remedy for the Invasion of Privacy' (1971) 29 *Fac L Rev* 3, 19.

[31] David A. Cornfield, 'The Right to Privacy in Canada' (1967) 25 *Fac L Rev* 103, 104–105.

[32] Ibid., 105.

[33] Peter Burns, 'The Law and Privacy: The Canadian Experience' (1976) 54 *Can B Rev* 1, 29; Stanley M Beck, 'Electronic Surveillance and the Administration of Criminal Justice' (1968) 46 *Can B Rev* 643.

devices, as were two officers employed in the RCMP's Security and Intelligence Branch.[34] There were also multiple stories in 1966 and 1967, uncovering police plans, from Victoria, to Saskatoon, to Oakville, of police using electronic surveillance devices to listen in on prison inmate conversations, including confidential discussions with their lawyers.[35] In fact, as of 1967, the RCMP and 'every major police force' in Canada admitted to using electronic surveillance, including press coverage of stories with police maintaining permanent wiretapping and electronic surveillance installations in major hotels.[36]

These incidents and national press coverage led to multiple public inquiries and national committees including the Sargent Royal Commission in BC in 1966, the Ouimet Committee on Criminal Justice and Corrections in 1969, and a House of Commons Standing Committee on Justice and Legal Affairs inquiry in 1970.[37] The issue would also provoke a 'wealth' of legal and academic commentary on point, including work examining the challenges electronic surveillance technology posed to privacy and the law.[38]

Eventually, Parliament would respond with the enactment of the Protection of Privacy Act (PPA) in 1974.[39] The Act would prohibit private use of electronic surveillance technology and devices to intercept or listen in on private communications, while at the same time both authorizing and regulating police use. Given there was absolutely no law or regulations impeding electronic surveillance before the PPA, the Act *did* provide a measure of privacy protection. But it would also be strongly criticized for doing far too little, particularly in terms of constraining law enforcement. Two prominent legal experts argued the PPA was 'official sanctioning of the immoral act of eavesdropping' and constituted an 'erosion of freedom as we know it'.[40] Others, citing judge-shopping and rubber stamping by magistrates, argued its

---

[34] Burns, ibid., 29; Beck, ibid.

[35] Cornfield (n 31), 106.

[36] Ibid.

[37] Norman MacDonald, 'Electronic Surveillance in Crime Detection: An Analysis of Canadian Wiretapping Law' (1987) 10 *Dalhousie LJ* 141, 144–145; Yoni Rahamim, 'Wiretapping and Electronic Surveillance in Canada: The Present State of the Law and Challenges to the Employment of Sophisticated and Intrusive Technology in Law Enforcement' (2004) 18 *Windsor Rev Legal & Soc Issues* 87, 90. For reports, see: Government of British Columbia, *Report of the Commission of Inquiry Into Invasion of Privacy* (Victoria 1967) ('Sargent Report'); Solicitor General of Canada, *Report of the Canadian Committee on Corrections—Toward Unity: Criminal Justice and Corrections* (Ottawa 1969) ('Ouimet Report').

[38] Rosemary Cairns Way, 'The Law of Police Authority: The McDonald Commission and the McLeod Report' (1985) 9 *Dalhousie L.J.* 683, 701n64. See e.g.: Cornfield (n 31); Beck (n 33); Tom MacKinnon, 'The Right to Privacy in British Columbia Before and After the Privacy Act' (1970) 5 *UBCLR* 228; Cosman (n 30); Morris Manning, *The Protection Against Privacy Act* (Butterworths 1974); Peter Burns, 'Electronic Eavesdropping and the Federal Response: Cloning a Hybrid', 10 *U. Brit. Colum. L. Rev.* 36 (1975); E. P. Craig, 'Electronic Surveillance: Setting the Limits', 24 *UNBLJ* 29 (1975); Burns (1976) (n 33) 29; M. Manning and C. Branson, 'Wiretapping: the Morality of Snooping' (1977) 1:5 *Can Lawyer* 24; Morris M. Title, 'Canadian Wiretap Legislation: Protection or Erosion of Privacy' (1978) 26 *Chitty's LJ* 47; Peter Burns, 'A Retrospective View of the Protection of Privacy Act: A Fragile Rede is Recked' (1979) 13 *U Brit Colum L Rev* 123; Francis M. Valeriote, 'Judicial Authorization for Wiretap: An Illusory Protection' (1980) 12 *Ottawa L Rev* 215; Stanley A. Cohen, 'Invasion of Privacy: Police and Electronic Surveillance in Canada' 1982 27:4 *McGill L J* 619.

[39] MacDonald (n 37), 145; Nathan Forester, 'Electronic Surveillance, Criminal Investigations, and the Erosion of Constitutional Rights in Canada: Regressive U-Turn or a Mere Bump in the Road towards Charter Justice' (2010) 73 *Sask L Rev* 23, 36.

[40] Manning and Branson (n 38).

provisions, including judicial pre-authorization, offered privacy only 'illusory protections'[41] and its capacity to deter police abuse 'seriously questioned'.[42] The Canadian Civil Liberties Association strongly opposed the legislation, particularly provisions allowing illegally obtained evidence to be admitted to court.[43]

One of the stronger criticisms was that the PPA provided a legal basis for, and legitimated, wider police use of electronic surveillance.[44] This criticism would ring true, with *The Globe and Mail* reporting in 1978 that not only did PPA amendments not deter police, but emboldened as Canadian law enforcement were 'seven times more likely' to engage in electronic surveillance when doing criminal investigations than their American counterparts.[45] Moreover, the PPA also opened the door to expansive electronic surveillance for the purposes of crime detection and intelligence gathering. In addition to amending the Criminal Code, the PPA also amended the Official Secrets Act, not in order to provide greater privacy protections, but to authorize electronic eavesdropping and surveillance for these purposes offered 'virtually no safeguards at all'.[46] All that the PPA required was that the Solicitor General be satisfied that an 'interception is necessary for the security of Canada'.[47] Noted privacy scholar Peter Burns, after an extensive analysis in 1979, would conclude that the PPA's name was a 'complete misnomer' given its privacy protections were 'small indeed'.[48] Even the Supreme Court of Canada would ruefully remark in 1980 that the PPA's effect was mainly to 'regulate the method of breach' of privacy, rather than deter or prevent it.[49] In short, the PPA failed to address privacy concerns raised by electronic surveillance technologies. More needed to be done.

In light of all this, it might have been expected these issues would be addressed in the first major federal legislation on privacy enacted only years later in 1977, being Part IV to the Canadian Human Rights Act. Not so. Though Section 2 described the Act's purpose as both prohibiting discrimination as well as protecting the 'privacy of individuals', nothing in the Act would address privacy concerns raised by electronic surveillance.[50] Nor did it address any concerns about electronic eavesdropping and intelligence gathering, nor any of the other concerns raised during wide-ranging debates concerning electronic surveillance technologies in the years leading up to enactment.

Now, it might be suggested that Part IV and the Act aimed to tackle privacy concerns raised by a different technology—emerging federal information systems, databases, and computerization of government records.[51] But this point also rings hollow, as commentators and academics had long made important links between government electronic surveillance practices ill-addressed by the PPA and these newly emerging computerized databases—combined, these

---

[41] Valeriote (n 38), 216.
[42] Title (n 38), 48.
[43] Dominique Clément, 'Privacy' (*Canada's Human Rights History*, 2018) https://historyofrights.ca/encyclopaedia/main-events/privacy/ accessed 18 October 2021.
[44] Douglas Camp Chaffey, 'The Right to Privacy' (1993) 108:1 *Political Science Quarterly* 117, 128.
[45] Forester (n 39), 37.
[46] MacDonald (n 37), 159; Cohen (n 38), 667.
[47] MacDonald, ibid., 159.
[48] Burns (1979) (n 38), 156.
[49] *R v Goldman* [1980] 1 SCR 976, 994.
[50] Inger Hansen, 'The Canadian Human Rights Act, Part IV' in John D McCamus (ed), *Freedom of Information: Canadian Perspectives* (Butterworths 1985) 249.
[51] Bennett (n 6), 556, 558 (noting that the Act was 'partly' a response to the 1972 Task Force on Computers and Privacy that focused on the 'computerization' of personal information systems).

technologies posed even greater threats to privacy, allowing for Orwellian surveillance and, through databases, storage and linkage to individuals over time. Alan Westin's influential work Privacy and Freedom published in 1967, would discuss these issues at length, capturing this important point in his concept of 'data surveillance'.[52] Prominent Canadian experts like Stanley Beck, David Cornfield, Peter Burns, and E.P. Craig would cite Westin's work, along with Orwell's warnings from his classic novel 1984, on privacy concerns raised by new surveillance and data storage technologies in commentaries before 1977.[53] And the 1972 federal Task Force on Computers and Privacy linked, in its discussion of new privacy concerns, data gathering technology like electronic surveillance with powerful new data storage and dissemination capacities.[54]

The more likely reason these issues were ignored, consistent with the broader Post-War paradigm, was that the drafters of the legislation were far more preoccupied freedom of information concerns. In fact, Section 2 defined 'privacy' in relation to a 'right of access to records containing personal information' as well as rights to 'ensure accuracy and completeness' in those records[55] and ideas of freedom of information and provisions implementing it are evident throughout Part IV. Section 52 set out basic rights of access and record correction, including rights to inquire as to records about a person are used by the government for 'administrative purposes', as well as rights to examine and correct records.[56] Section 52(2) placed limits on use of personal information provided to the government inconsistent with the original purpose the information was tendered.[57] Sections 53 and 54 set out exemptions, such as for certain federal databanks from, access rights.[58] Although Part IV did include important privacy measures like the establishment of a privacy commissioner's office (though with important limits as critics like David Flaherty pointed out) overall the scheme emphasized 'publicity and access'.[59] In the words of the first Privacy Commissioner Inger Hansen, the law 'embraced' the 'freedom of information concept'.[60]

In retrospect, this development was not surprising. Indeed, parallel to the public debates and press coverage surrounding privacy threats posed by electronic surveillance and related technology was another contentious debate over access to government information.[61] The debate began with academic writings in the 1960s and 1970s and was sustained through an 'influential' Task Force Report released in 1969, entitled 'Known and Be Known', as well as ongoing pressure from Conservative politicians tendering private members bills in Parliament.[62]

Adding greatly to this momentum was international pressure tied to the aforementioned global trends towards freedom of information, particularly the US, which had been moving to

---

[52] Alan F. Westin, *Privacy and Computers* (Atheneum 1967) 6.

[53] Beck (n 33), 650–651; Burns (1976) (n 33), 10–11, 31; Cornfield (n 31), 104; Craig (n 38), 29–30, 32.

[54] Report of the 1972 Task Force (n 29), Ch 10–11.

[55] Hansen (n 50), 249.

[56] Ibid., 251.

[57] Ibid.

[58] Ibid., 251–252.

[59] Bennett (1990) (n 6), 558; David Flaherty, 'Commentary' in John D McCamus (ed), *Freedom of Information: Canadian Perspectives* (Butterworths 1985) 262.

[60] Hansen (n 50), 251–252.

[61] Bennett (1990) (n 6), 558.

[62] Ibid., 559; Colin J Bennett, 'How States Utilize Foreign Evidence' (1991) 11:1 *Journal of Public Policy* 31, 43–52.

address government secrecy through freedom of information reforms in the Post War Period, accentuated by Watergate and Pentagon Paper scandals in the 1970s.[63] In fact, concerns about government secrecy raised by Americans had also been raised in Canada.[64] Colin Bennett has extensively documented the influence that the US Freedom of Information Act of 1966 had on Canada, including encouraging law-makers to kick start reforms, creating pressure to legislate, and serving as a model for Canada's own law.[65] Even the 1972 Task Force Report on Computers and Privacy, ostensibly aimed at addressing privacy risks, emphasized that any new privacy laws must not 'interfere with the free flow of information', otherwise they would 'constitute a cure worse than the original ill'.[66]

In short, a preoccupation with freedom of information, consistent with (and spurned on by) a broader international free flow of information paradigm, led to a first major federal privacy enactment that emphasized freedom of information over privacy concerns for surveillance and technology.[67] But Part IV would not last long—its provisions did not fit well in the context of the Canadian Human Rights Act—and compared to legislative efforts elsewhere, it was modest and only experimental legislation.[68] Reform was coming, but freedom of information would remain a central focus.

IV. IMPACT ON REFORMS: THE FEDERAL PRIVACY ACT, 1983

The first major reforms to Canadian federal privacy legislation would not be driven by privacy, but predominant federal efforts to enact more comprehensive freedom of information legislation. These efforts would intensify in 1979 with the election of the Progressive Conservatives led by Joe Clarke.[69] The new Prime Minister made access to information a top priority, putting 'considerable pressure' on federal public servants to produce a draft bill.[70] Although the Conservative Government would fall by December with the Trudeau Liberals returned to power in 1980, key parts of Conservative proposals for government information access would find expression in a Cabinet Discussion Paper published by the Justice Department in 1980.[71] That Paper's proposals would form the basis for new comprehensive freedom of information legislation.[72]

Privacy law was literally an afterthought to freedom of information priorities. Changes to Part IV were only included in the draft legislation 'at the behest' of public servants.[73] This

---

63 Bennett (1990) (n 6), 559.

64 See e.g.: James Eayrs, *Diplomacy and its Discontents* (Toronto 1971) 33; E.Z. Friedenberg, *Deference to Authority: The Case of Canada* (ME Sharpe 1980); Robert J Hayward, 'Federal Access and Privacy Legislation and the Public Archives of Canada' (1984) 18 *Archivaria* 47, 47.

65 Bennett, (1991) (n 61), 43–52.

66 Report of the 1972 Task Force (n 29), 178.

67 Flaherty (1989) (n 6), 243; Bennett (1990) (n 6), 558.

68 Flaherty (1989), ibid., 245; Bennett, ibid., 559.

69 Flaherty (1989), ibid.; Flaherty (2008) (n 6), 6–7; Bennett, ibid.

70 Flaherty (1989), ibid.; Flaherty (2008) ibid.7; Bennett ibid., 560.

71 Ibid.

72 Ibid.

73 Flaherty (1989), ibid.

was likely to avoid problems the US experienced implementing its 1966 FOI Act.[74] That law's information access rights led to conflicts with federal legislation enacted in 1974 regulating disclosure of personal information.[75] The new Liberal Government's draft Bill C-43 would repeal Part IV and enact two new statutes—the Access to Information Act and a Privacy Act.[76] However, the House of Commons Standing Committee on Justice and Legal Affairs, tasked with a 'clause-by-clause' review of the draft legislation spent nearly all of its time reviewing the access to information proposals.[77] The review of the Privacy Act came in a 'last minute, marathon session' in June 1982.[78] Bill C-43 would eventually come into force in July 1983.[79]

Although the new Privacy Act was marginal in this reform process, and inextricably tied to broader freedom of information trends, it *did* offer important improvements to the Part IV scheme. At its core, the new Act regulated how the federal government could use and disclose personal information gathered about citizens.[80] Overall, the Privacy Act codified the same 'fair information practices' formulated in the US and Europe, and employed in similar data protection regulations internationally.[81] Those fair information practices concerned rules and regulations on the collection, retention, disposal, and protection of government held personal information.[82] The Act also had important innovations, most notably provisions giving the Office of the Privacy Commissioner a more active and independent role in investigating and enforcing the Act while also allowing for recourse to courts, something specifically precluded in the Americans' own Privacy Act of an earlier decade.[83]

But there would be important consequences to the Privacy Act being only an afterthought to freedom of information reforms—it failed to address important privacy concerns raised by new electronic surveillance technologies, and related data tracking, collection, and storage capacities. These concerns, as we have seen, were not new. The aforementioned public commentary and academic discussion on point that began in the 1960s and 1970s would continue well into the 1980s as new technologies continued to emerge.[84] This oversight was compounded by the fact that extensive press coverage of RCMP misconduct through 1977 would lead the Liberal Government to establish a Royal Commission, known as the McDonald Commission, to investigate illegal activities by officers in the RCMP's 'Security Services' Branch.[85] The Commission would issues several reports, the final one issued in 1981.[86] Among the RCMP's Security Services' illegal activities it documented was illegal, abusive, and over-reaching

---

[74] Hansen (n 50), 251; Bennett (1990) (n 6), 42.

[75] Hansen, ibid.; Bennett ibid. For an analysis of these conflicts, see: Thomas M Susman, 'The Privacy Act and the Freedom of Information Act: Conflict and Resolution' (1988) 21 *J Marshall L Rev* 703.

[76] Flaherty (1989) (n 6), 245.

[77] Ibid; Flaherty (2008) (n 6),. 7; Bennett (1990) (n 6), 560.

[78] Flaherty (1989), ibid., 5; Flaherty (2008), ibid.; Bennett, ibid.

[79] Ibid.

[80] Ibid., 560–561; Flaherty (1989) (n 6), 253.

[81] Bennett (1990) (n 6), 561–562; Flaherty, ibid.

[82] Ibid.

[83] Flaherty (1989) (n 6), 246–247.

[84] See works cited footnote 38.

[85] Cairns (n 38), 683; Iain Cameron, 'Commission of Inquiry concerning Certain Activities of the Royal Canadian Mounted Police. Second Report: Freedom and Security under the Law' (1985) 48:2 *Modern Law Review* 201.

[86] Cairns, ibid., 684.

electronic surveillance, bugging, and wiretapping, with targets ranging from political parties, activists, trade unions, minority groups, academics, and even Members of Parliament.[87] While the Liberal Government would respond to the McDonald Commission Report in 1983 with legislation to abolish the RCMP's Security Services and establish a new national security agency—the Canadian Security Intelligence Services—which would have new surveillance and intelligence gathering powers, creating new privacy concerns.[88]

The Privacy Act reforms constituted an opportunity for a comprehensive federal scheme addressing not only fair information practices, but also new privacy concerns raised by these developments as well as a range of then emerging technological threats including new forms of electronic surveillance, computer matching, micro-computing technology, and trans-border data flows.[89] In fact, a comprehensive report issued in 1987 by the House of Commons Standing Committee on Justice and Solicitor General would make extensive recommendations for Privacy Act revisions to deal with these and other issues.[90] None were acted on by the then Conservative Government.[91]

Once again, privacy concerns about surveillance and technology were 'subordinated' to freedom of information.[92] And less than five years after its enactment, commentators were calling for the Privacy Act's 'modernization' particularly due to its failure to address 'new surveillance challenges'.[93] Yet, changes would not come soon.

V. ENDURING LEGACY: PRIVACY REFORMS, FIPS, AND BEYOND

Beyond these noteworthy historical case studies, the enduring impact freedom of information norms have had on Canadian privacy and data protection laws is apparent in two additional ways today. First, the Privacy Act, in being closely linked to the Access to Information Act when passed, has likely deterred meaningful reforms to the legislation over the years.[94] David Flaherty makes this point, noting that subsequent governments 'hostility' to the Access to Information Act likely also discouraged Privacy Act reform, seeing the two laws as compan-

---

[87] Cameron (n 85), 202–203.

[88] As Stuart Farson would observe in 1985, while the legislation may add some checks on CSIS, the 'system as a whole is enabling' quoted in Geoffrey R. Weller, 'The Canadian Security Intelligence Service Under Stress' (1988) 31:2 *Canadian Public Administration* 279, 293–294. See also Peter H. Russell, 'The Proposed Charter for a Civilian Intelligence Agency: An Appraisal' (1983) 9:3 *Canadian Public Policy* 326, 326, 328, 330.

[89] These issues would all be covered only a few years later in a comprehensive report issued by the House of Commons Standing Committee on Justice and Solicitor General in 1987: Privacy: Flaherty (2008) (n 6), 9–10.

[90] See House of Commons, Standing Committee on Justice and Solicitor General, *Open and Shut: Enhancing the Right to Know and the Right to Privacy: Report of the Standing Committee on Justice and Solicitor General on the Review of the Access to Information Act and the Privacy Act* (Ottawa 1987); Flaherty (2008), ibid.

[91] Ibid., 10.

[92] Flaherty (1989) (n 6), 243; Bennett (1990) (n 6), 558.

[93] Flaherty, ibid., 297.

[94] Flaherty (2008) (n 6), 10.

ion legislation.[95] Canada's Privacy Commissioner from 1991–2000 Bruce Phillips similarly argues that federal public servants tend to treat the laws as one and the same notwithstanding the fact the two laws concern largely separate spheres of government activity.[96] This may be one reason why, as Canada's present Privacy Commissioner Daniel Therrien has recently noted, the federal Privacy Act has largely sat 'dormant' while 'second and third generation' privacy laws have been enacted provincially and internationally since 1983.[97]

A second way freedom of information norms continue to impact Canadian privacy law is through the fair information practices finding expression in the federal Privacy Act of 1983 and then later, more comprehensively, in the Protection of Personal Information and Electronic Document Act (PIPEDA).[98] Canada's last major data protection law, PIPEDA, was enacted in 2000 and regulates the collection, use, and disclosure of personal information in the Canadian private sector.[99] PIPEDA largely codifies the same fair information practices formulated and widely used internationally.[100]

Although seen as central to an internationalization of data protection norms, those fair information practices (FIPs) were also shaped by freedom of information norms. The FIPs are generally understood to have originated in a well-known Report on Records, Computers, and the Rights of Citizens issued in 1973 by the Advisory Committee to the US Secretary for Health, Education, and Welfare.[101] But in the 1970s, America was far more concerned with promoting freedom of information than privacy.[102] Internationally, it was promoting the flow of information doctrine as foreign policy,[103] and legislating freedom of information at home, including its landmark FOI Act in 1966.[104] In fact, many Americans at this time regarded 'data protection' sceptically, as a Trojan horse for barriers to trade and the free flow of information across borders.[105] Meeting transcripts for the HEW Advisory Committee, which led to the Report, reflect this broader context, including tensions between privacy protections and

---

[95] Ibid.

[96] Ibid.

[97] Office of the Privacy Commissioner, 'Privacy Act Reform in an Era of Change and Transparency: Summary of Recommendations' (Letter to the Standing Committee on Access to Information, Privacy and Ethics, 22 March 2016).

[98] Lisa Austin, 'Is Consent the Foundation of Fair Information Practices? Canada's Experience under PIPEDA' (2006) 56:2 *UTLJ* 181, 181; Christopher Berzins, 'Protecting Personal Information in Canada's Private Sector: The Price of Consensus Building' (2002) 27 *Queen's LJ* 609, 620–621; Colin J Bennett, 'Adequate Data Protection by the Year 2000: The Prospects for Privacy in Canada' (2000) 11:1 *International Review of Law, Computers & Technology* 79, 80 (speaking to how the OECD Guidelines were the 'starting point' for the CSA Code).

[99] Austin, ibid., 181.

[100] Ibid., 198–200; Berzins (n 98), 620–621; Bennett (2000) (n 98).

[101] Robert Gellman, 'Willis Ware's Lasting Contribution to Privacy: Fair Information Practices' 12 IEEE Security and Privacy 51; Robert Gellman, 'Fair Information Practices: A Basic History' SSRN Working Paper (10 April 2017) https://papers.ssrn.com/sol3/papers.cfm?abstract_id=2415020 accessed 19 October 2021; Colin J Bennett, *Regulating Privacy: Data Protection and Public Policy in Europe and the United States* (Cornell 1992) 96–97.

[102] Bennett, ibid., 137; Ackerman and Sandova-Ballesteros (n 11), 116.

[103] Penney (2011) (n 8) 23; see generally Savage (n 17), 348.

[104] Ackerman and Sandova-Ballesteros (n 11), 116; Bennett (1992) (n 101), 137.

[105] See, e.g.: John M Eger, 'Emerging Restrictions on Transnational Data Flow: Privacy Protection or Non-Tariff Trade Barriers?' (1978) 10 *Law and Policy in International Business* 1055; Robert Bigelow, 'Transborder Data Flow Barriers' (1979–1980) *Jurimetrics* 20. See also Bennett (n 101) 137.

freedom of information.[106] In fact, 1973 HEW Report itself reflects those tensions too—the forward, written by then HEW Secretary Caspar Weinberger, heralds not privacy or data protection, but the 'innovations' destined to come in government and private industry thanks to newly emerging 'high-speed telecommunications networks'.[107]

However, the influence of freedom of information norms on FIPs is even clearer with their most important and well-known expression in the OECD's Guidelines on the Protection of Privacy and Transborder Flows of Personal Data.[108] The OECD Guidelines, in the words of Colin Bennett, represent a 'fundamental statement' of 'international consensus' on communications policy and FIPs, a product of a 'fascinating' process of international policy convergence in 1970s.[109] The OECD Guidelines have been 'tremendously influential', with 'direct impact' on legislative harmonization on FIPs globally,[110] while also serving as the 'foundation' for privacy laws in Canada, particularly PIPEDA.[111]

Although today the OECD Guidelines are most often associated with data protection, they were drafted by an OECD expert group originally formed to address not privacy but *barriers* to the free flow of information internationally.[112] As Michael Kirby, the chair of that expert group, would later point out, the OECD was always an organization primarily concerned with 'economic efficiency' and free movement and sharing of information necessary for free markets and democracy to prosper.[113] And it viewed differences and inconsistencies in new laws being enacted internationally on data protection and new computing technologies as threats to the free flow of information and data across borders.[114] These concerns prompted the OECD to form the expert group— to 'contribute to' and 'defend' trans-border data flows.[115]

Freedom of information norms are clearly seen in the Guidelines themselves. The preface warns about the 'danger' that "disparities national legislations" might 'hamper the free flow of

---

[106] See Chris Hoofnagle, who first released the transcripts, notes the '…[t]ensions among interests in efficiency, law enforcement, cost, access to knowledge and freedom of information…' in the committee meetings: Chris Hoofnagle 'The Origin of Fair Information Practices: Archive of the Meetings of the Secretary's Advisory Committee on Automated Personal Data Systems (SACAPDS)' SSRN Working Paper (16 July 2014) https://papers.ssrn.com/sol3/papers.cfm?abstract_id=2466418 accessed 19 October 2021.

[107] Advisory Committee to the United States Secretary of Health, Education, and Welfare, *Records, Computers, and the Rights of Citizens: Report of the Secretary's Advisory Committee on Automated Personal Data Systems* (Washington 1973) v.

[108] OECD, *Guidelines on the Protection of Privacy and Transborder Flows of Personal Data*, Annex to Recommendation of the Council (23 September 1980) http://www.oecd.org/sti/ieconomy/oecdguidelinesontheprotectionofprivacyandtransborderflowsofpersonaldata.htm accessed 19 October 2021; Bennett (n 101), 138–139.

[109] Bennett (n 101), 138.

[110] Berzins (n 98), 616; Bennett (n 101), 138–139; Austin (n 98), 194.

[111] Nancy Holmes, 'Canada's Federal Privacy Laws' (Library of Parliament Research Publication 2008) 2 http://epe.lac-bac.gc.ca/100/200/301/library_parliament/backgrounder/2008/can_federal_privacy-e/prb0744-e.pdf accessed 19 October 2021.

[112] Michael Kirby, 'The History, Achievement and Future of the 1980 OECD Guidelines on Privacy' (2011) 1:1 *International Data Privacy Law* 6. See also David Wright, Paul de Hert, and Serge Gutwith, 'Are the OECD guidelines at 30 showing their age?' (2011) 54:2 *Communications of the ACM* 119.

[113] Kirby, ibid., 8; Wright, De Hert and Gutwirth, ibid., 120; Andrew Clearwater and Trevor J Hughes, 'In the Beginning... An Early History of the Privacy Profession' (2013) 74:6 *Ohio State Law Journal* 897, 902–903.

[114] Kirby, ibid.; Clearwater and Hughes, ibid.

[115] Kirby, ibid; Bennett (1992) (n 101), 137.

personal data across frontier'.[116] It also indicates the Guidelines were developed to 'harmonise' privacy legislation in a way that would not needlessly cause 'interruptions' in international flows of data.[117] The OECD Council recommendations include a commitment to 'advance the free flow of information between Member countries'. All of Part Three of the Guidelines is dedicated to these free flow aims.[118]

These elements of FIPs have surely led to fewer restrictions on global data flows over the years, but that reality—and new forms of surveillance—have also created significant privacy challenges.[119] Indeed, some of the earliest and most enduring criticisms for FIPs are tied to these free flow norm influences. Critics like James Rule called the FIPs principles 'efficiency' principles more concerned with the smooth and efficient operation of data processing and information flows than curtailing surveillance and other threats to privacy.[120] In providing largely only procedural rights, FIPs do nothing *substantively* to limit the growth or development if new forms of data collection and surveillance.[121] Graham Greenleaf argues these challenges still remain at the heart of FIPs today, asking to what extent do data protection laws based on FIPs actually 'limit and control the expansion of surveillance systems' beyond rendering 'personal information systems' more 'efficient'?[122] And Fred Cate, in a work entitled *The Failure of Fair Information Practices Principles*, takes aim at the narrow definitions of protected information and consent at the heart of FIPs, arguing these provisions offer only the 'illusion' of privacy protection in practice, as consumer 'choice' or citizen 'consent' is rarely that.[123]

Not surprisingly, these same sorts of critiques have been levied at Canada's PIPEDA, which essentially codified FIPs as defined by the OECD Guidelines. Echoing Graham Greenleaf and James Rule criticisms of FIPs more generally, Lisa Austin has argued that the 'consent-based privacy model' at the heart of PIPEDA is 'inadequate in addressing contemporary information practices' particularly the growing 'corporate–state nexus that has created such a striking surveillance infrastructure on the internet'.[124] And Samantha Bradshaw (et al) likewise argues that PIPEDA fails to properly address a range of new privacy threats and challenges posed by 'big data', that will have 'far-reaching consequences if not properly addressed' with reforms.[125]

---

[116] OECD Guidelines.

[117] Ibid.

[118] Ibid.

[119] Wright et al (n 112), 119 (noting 'Global data flows have elevated the risks to privacy'). See also Jonathon Penney, 'Internet Surveillance, Regulation, and Chilling Effects Online: A Comparative Case Study' (2017) 6:2 *Internet Policy Review* https://policyreview.info/articles/analysis/internet-surveillance-regulation-and-chilling-effects-online-comparative-case accessed 19 October 2021.

[120] James Rule, et al., *The Politics of Privacy: Planning for Personal Data Systems as Powerful Technologies* (Elsevier 1980) 93; Woodrow Harzog, 'The Inadequate, Invaluable Fair Information Practices' (2017) 76 *Md L Rev* 952, 964.

[121] Harzog, ibid., 964.

[122] Graham Greenleaf, *Asian Data Privacy Laws: Trade & Human Rights Perspectives* (Oxford 2014) 61; Hartzog, ibid., 964–965.

[123] Fred Cate, 'The Failure of Fair Information Practices Principles' in Jane K Winn (ed) (Ashgate 2006) 344.

[124] Lisa Austin 'Enough About Me: Why Privacy is About Power, Not Consent (or Harm)' in Austin Sarat (ed.) *A World Without Privacy* (Cambridge 2014) 41.

[125] Samantha Bradshaw, Kyle Harris, and Hyla Zeifman, 'Big Data, Big Responsibilities: Recommendations to the Office of the Privacy Commissioner on Canadian Privacy Rights in a Digital Age' CIGI Policy Brief 6/2013 (Balsillie School 2013) 7.

Indeed, as the Colin Bennett (et al) has shown in *Transparent Lives: Surveillance in Canada*, private sector surveillance has grown considerably since PIPEDA was enacted.[126]

And as with FIPs more generally, PIPEDA has also been criticized for overemphasizing process rights. Consumer groups have criticized PIPEDA as not being 'kind to consumers', and calling for 'major reforms' promoting norms favourable to consumer privacy, rather than PIPEDA's procedural standards.[127] Similar to Cate's concerns, Austin argues PIPEDA's 'all-or-nothing' regulatory approach fails to account for definitional difficulties with new forms of data, collection, and 'identifiable' information,[128] while also not necessarily providing people with meaningful choice or consent when it comes to their privacy and personal information.[129] All of these criticisms and the challenges and shortcomings they have identified have led to numerous calls for major reforms of PIPEDA, though none yet have come.[130] The legacy of Post War freedom of information ideas and norms remain with Canada's privacy and data protection scheme through FIPs and PIPEDA—and with that legacy, persistent difficulties remain.

VI. MOVING FORWARD

This historical case study has examined Canada's earliest and most important privacy and data protection laws, including Part VI of the Canadian Human Rights Act of 1977, the Privacy Act of 1983, and PIPEDA of 2000, with the latter two still in force today. This analysis has suggested that while technological changes certain did play a factor in privacy enactments and reforms, a pre-occupation with freedom of information and the trans-border free flow of data was an important driver of legislative agendas and change.

Analysing whether the influence of freedom of information on Canadian privacy is definitively positive or negative would take us far beyond the scope of this chapter, including into more empirically oriented work testing privacy outcomes. Nevertheless, there would appear to be both positive and negative aspects to the influence of freedom of information in Canada's privacy law story. On the one hand, without interest and pre-occupation with freedom of

---

[126] Colin J Bennett, Kevin D Haggerty, David Lyon, and Valerie Steeves (eds) *Transparent Lives: Surveillance in Canada* (Athabasca 2014) 8–9, 19–39.

[127] Public Internet Advocacy Centre, *Report: Consumer Privacy Under PIPEDA: How Are We Doing?* (PIAC, Ottawa 2004) 3.

[128] Lisa M Austin, 'Reviewing PIPEDA: Control, Privacy and the Limits of Fair Information Practices' (2006) 44 *Can Bus LJ* 21, 28.

[129] See, generally: Austin, ibid.

[130] See, e.g.: Teresa Scassa, 'It is time to overhaul Canada's data protection —your rights are at stake' *MacLean's Magazine* (Ottawa, 2 February 2018) http://www.macleans.ca/opinion/it-is-time-to-overhaul-canadas-data-protection-your-rights-are-at-stake/ accessed 19 October 2021; Susan Krashinsky Robertson, 'Calls grow for Canada to Modernize Privacy Laws Amid EU Changes' *The Globe and Mail* (Ottawa, 24 July 2017) https://www.theglobeandmail.com/report-on-business/industry-news/marketing/calls-grow-for-canada-to-modernize-privacy-laws-amid-eu-changes/article35778176/ accessed 19 October 2021; Office of the Privacy Commissioner, 'The Case for Reforming the Personal Information Protection and Electronic Documents Act' (Report of Office of the Privacy Commissioner of Canada, May 2013) https://www.priv.gc.ca/en/privacy-topics/privacy-laws-in-canada/the-personal-information-protection-and-electronic-documents-act-pipeda/r_o_p/pipeda_r/pipeda_r_201305/ accessed 19 October 2021; Flaherty (2008) (n 6), 33.

information ideals among Canada policy-makers and broader international trends towards the same, it is unlikely Canada would have acted as early as it did to enact privacy legislation or possibly fallen further behind in subsequent years. The history surrounding the passage of the federal Privacy Act in 1983, in particular, suggests had it not been enacted as a companion statute to the new Access to Information Act, it may have been years before a comparable statute was passed.

Fair information practices remain foundational to Canada's privacy laws today, for good or ill, in still finding clear expression in both the Privacy Act and PIPEDA, and thus the legacy of freedom of information will remain with us for some time, though the privacy law landscape continues to evolve slowly by surely. Of course, federal and provincial legislatures are now not alone in shaping core Canadian privacy and data protection rights and norms. Although the Canadian Charter of Rights and Freedoms does not include an express constitutional right to privacy, the Supreme Court of Canada has held that certain privacy interests are protected by its provisions, including the 'right to life, liberty, and security of the person' as well as right against 'unreasonable search and seizure'.[131] In *R v Dyment*, Justice LaForest set out a 'seminal' statement on the importance of privacy under the Charter, including finding that privacy had bodily, territorial, and informational dimensions.[132] In doing so, he would cite neither fair information practices, nor OECD guidelines, nor the 'free flow' of information. Rather, he would cite Alan Westin's landmark privacy text and then tie privacy to people's 'physical and moral autonomy' and 'well being'.[133]

REFERENCES

Ackerman J.M. and I.E. Sandoval-Ballesteros, 'The Global Explosion of Freedom of Information Laws' (2006) 58 *Admin L Rev* 85.

Advisory Committee to the United States Secretary of Health, Education, and Welfare, *Records, Computers, and the Rights of Citizens: Report of the Secretary's Advisory Committee on Automated Personal Data Systems* (Washington 1973).

Ahmad T., 'Online Privacy Law: Canada' (U.S. Library of Congress 2012).

Austin L., 'Privacy and the Question of Technology' (2003) 22:2 *Law & Philosophy* 119.

Austin L., 'Reviewing PIPEDA: Control, Privacy and the Limits of Fair Information Practices' (2006) 44 *Can Bus LJ* 21.

Austin L., 'Is Consent the Foundation of Fair Information Practices? Canada's Experience Under PIPEDA Information Practices' (2006) 56:2 *UTLJ*.

Austin L.,'Enough About Me: Why Privacy is About Power, Not Consent (or Harm)' in Austin Sarat (ed.) *A World Without Privacy* (Cambridge 2014).

Beck S.M., 'Electronic Surveillance and the Administration of Criminal Justice' (1968) 46 *Can B Rev* 643.

Bennett C.J., 'The Formation of a Canadian Privacy Policy: The Art and Craft of Lesson-drawing' (1990) 33:4 *Canadian Public Administration* 551.

Bennett C.J., 'How States Utilize Foreign Evidence' (1991) 11:1 *Journal of Public Policy* 31, 43–52.

Bennett C.J., *Regulating Privacy: Data Protection and Public Policy in Europe and the United States* (Cornell 1992) 96.

131 Hughes (n 2), 528–529; Levin and Nicholson (n 3), 378–380; Bernal-Castillero (n 9); Ahmad (n 9).

132 [1988] 2 SCR 417, 427.

133 Ibid., 427.

Bennett C.J., 'Adequate Data Protection by the Year 2000: The Prospects for Privacy in Canada' (2000) 11:1 *International Review of Law, Computers & Technology* 79.
Bennett C.J. and C. Raab, *Governance of Privacy: Policy Instruments in Global Perspective* (Ashgate 2003).
Bennett C.J. and D. Lyon, *Playing the Identity Card: Surveillance, Security, and Identification in Global Perspective* (London 2008).
Bennett C.J., K.D. Haggerty, D. Lyon, V. Steeves (eds) *Transparent Lives: Surveillance in Canada* (Athabasca 2014).
Bernal-Castillero M., 'Canada's Federal Privacy Laws' (Library of Parliament Research Publication 2013).
Berzins C., 'Protecting Personal Information in Canada's Private Sector: The Price of Consensus Building' (2002) 27 *Queen's LJ* 609.
Bigelow R., 'Transborder Data Flow Barriers' (1979–1980) *Jurimetrics* 20.
Bradshaw S., K. Harris, and H. Zeifman, 'Big Data, Big Responsibilities: Recommendations to the Office of the Privacy Commissioner on Canadian Privacy Rights in a Digital Age' CIGI Policy Brief 6/2013 (Balsillie School 2013).
Burns P., 'Electronic Eavesdropping and the Federal Response: Cloning a Hybrid' (1975) 10 *U. Brit. Colum. L. Rev.* 36.
Burns P., 'The Law and Privacy: The Canadian Experience' (1976) 54 *Can B Rev* 1, 29.
Burns P., 'A Retrospective View of the Protection of Privacy Act: A Fragile Rede is Recked' (1979) 13 *U Brit Colum L Rev*.
Cairns Way R., 'The Law of Police Authority: The McDonald Commission and the McLeod Report' (1985) 9 *Dalhousie L J* 683.
Cameron I., 'Commission of Inquiry concerning Certain Activities of the Royal Canadian Mounted Police. Second Report: Freedom and Security under the Law' (1985) 48:2 *Modern Law Review* 201.
Canadian Department of Communications/Department of Justice, *Privacy and Computers: A Report of the 1972 Task Force* (Ottawa 1972).
Cappello L., 'Big Iron and the Small Government: On the History of Data Collection and Privacy in the United States' (2017) 29:1 *Journal of Policy History* 177.
Cate F., 'The Failure of Fair Information Practices Principles' in Jane K Winn (ed) (Ashgate 2006).
Chaffey D.C., The Right to Privacy' (1993) 108:1 *Political Science Quarterly* 117.
Clearwater A. and T.J. Hughes, 'In the Beginning... An Early History of the Privacy Profession' (2013) 74:6 *Ohio State Law Journal* 897.
Clément D., 'Privacy' (*Canada's Human Rights History*, 2018).
Cockfield A.J., 'Protecting the Social Value of Privacy in the Context of State Investigations Using New Technologies' (2007) 40 *UBCLR* 41.
Cohen S.A., 'Invasion of Privacy: Police and Electronic Surveillance in Canada' (1982) 27:4 *McGill L J* 619.
Cosman R.W., 'A Man's House Is His Castle-Beep: A Civil Law Remedy for the Invasion of Privacy (1971) 29 *Fac L Rev* 3, 19.
Cornfield D.A., 'The Right to Privacy in Canada' (1967) 25 *Fac L Rev* 103.
Craig E.P., 'Electronic Surveillance: Setting the Limits' (1975) 24 *UNBLJ* 29.
Eayrs J., *Diplomacy and its Discontents* (Toronto 1971).
Eger J.M., 'Emerging Restrictions on Transnational Data Flow: Privacy Protection or Non-Tariff Trade Barriers?' (1978) 10 *Law and Policy in International Business* 1055.
Feinberg L.E., 'Managing the Freedom of Information Act and Federal Information Policy' (1986) 46:6 *Public Administration Review* 615.
Flaherty D.H., *Privacy and Government Data Banks* (Mansell 1979).
Flaherty D.H., 'Commentary' in John D McCamus (ed), *Freedom of Information: Canadian Perspectives* (Butterworths 1985).
Flaherty D.H., *Protecting Privacy in Surveillance Societies: The Federal Republic of Germany, Sweden, France, Canada, and the United States* (Chapel Hill 1989).
Flaherty D.H., 'Reflections on Reform of the Federal Privacy Act' (Publication of the Office of the Privacy Commissioner of Canada 2008).

Forester N., 'Electronic Surveillance, Criminal Investigations, and the Erosion of Constitutional Rights in Canada: Regressive U-Turn or a Mere Bump in the Road towards Charter Justice' (2010) 73 *Sask L Rev* 23.
Friedenberg E.Z., *Deference to Authority: The Case of Canada* (ME Sharpe 1980).
Geist M., (ed) *Law, Privacy and Surveillance in Canada in the Post-Snowden Era* (University of Ottawa Press 2015).
Government of British Columbia, *Report of the Commission of Inquiry Into Invasion of Privacy* (Victoria 1967) ('Sargent Report').
Greenleaf G., *Asian Data Privacy Laws: Trade & Human Rights Perspectives* (Oxford 2014).
Gunasekara G., 'Paddling in Unison or Just Paddling? International Trends in Reforming Information Privacy Law' (2014) 22:2 *IJLIT* 141.
Hamerlink C.J., *The Politics of World Communication: A Human Rights Perspective* (Sage 1994).
Hansen I., 'The Canadian Human Rights Act, Part IV' in John D McCamus (ed), *Freedom of Information: Canadian Perspectives* (Butterworths 1985).
Harzog W, 'The Inadequate, Invaluable Fair Information Practices' (2017) 76 *Md L Rev* 952.
Hayward R.J., 'Federal Access and Privacy Legislation and the Public Archives of Canada' (1984) 18 *Archivaria* 47.
Holden P.D.M., 'Flying Robots and Privacy in Canada' [2016] 14 *CJLT* 65.
Holmes N., 'Canada's Federal Privacy Laws' (Library of Parliament Research Publication 2008).
Hoofnagle C., 'The Origin of Fair Information Practices: Archive of the Meetings of the Secretary's Advisory Committee on Automated Personal Data Systems (SACAPDS)' SSRN Working Paper (16 July 2014).
House of Commons, Standing Committee on Justice and Solicitor General, *Open and Shut: Enhancing the Right to Know and the Right to Privacy: Report of the Standing Committee on Justice and Solicitor General on the Review of the Access to Information Act and the Privacy Act* (Ottawa 1987).
Hughes R.L.D., 'Two Concepts of Privacy' (2015) 31 *Computer L Security Rev* 527.
Tamir Israel, 'Foreign Intelligence in an Inter-Networked World' in Michael Geist (ed) *Law, Privacy and Surveillance in Canada in the Post-Snowden Era* (University of Ottawa Press 2015).
Kirby M., 'The History, Achievement and Future of the 1980 OECD Guidelines on Privacy' (2011) 1:1 *International Data Privacy Law*.
Krashinsky Robertson S., 'Calls Grow for Canada to Modernize Privacy Laws Amid EU Changes' *The Globe and Mail* (Ottawa, 24 July 2017).
Krotoszynski R.J., *Privacy Revisited: A Global Perspective on the Right to Be Left Alone* (OUP 2016).
Levin A. and M.J. Nicholson, 'Privacy Law in the United States, the EU and Canada: The Allure of the Middle Ground' (2005) 2:2 *UOLTJ* 357.
MacDonald N., 'Electronic Surveillance in Crime Detection: An Analysis of Canadian Wiretapping Law' (1987) 10 *Dalhousie LJ* 141.
MacKinnon T., 'The Right to Privacy in British Columbia before and after the Privacy Act' (1970) 5 *UBCLR* 228.
Manning M., *The Protection Against Privacy Act* (Butterworths 1974).
Manning M. and C. Branson, 'Wiretapping: the Morality of Snooping' (1977) 1:5 *Can Lawyer* 24.
Mayeda G., 'My Neighbour's Kid Just Bought a Drone . . . New Paradigms for Privacy Law in Canada' (2015) 35 *NJCL* 59.
Office of the Privacy Commissioner, 'The Case for Reforming the Personal Information Protection and Electronic Documents Act' (Report of Office of the Privacy Commissioner of Canada, May 2013).
Office of the Privacy Commissioner, 'Privacy Act Reform in an Era of Change and Transparency: Summary of Recommendations' (Letter to the Standing Committee on Access to Information, Privacy and Ethics, 22 March 2016).
Payton T. and T. Claypoole, *Privacy in the Age of Big Data: Recognizing Threats, Defending Your Rights, And Protecting Your Family* (Rowman & Littlefield 2014).
Penney J.W., 'Internet Access Rights: A Brief History and Intellectual Origins' (2011) 28 *William Mitchell L Rev* 10.
Penney J.W., 'The Cycles of Global Telecommunications Censorship and Surveillance' (2015) 36:3 *U Pa J Int'l L* 693.

Penney J.W., 'Internet Surveillance, Regulation, and Chilling Effects Online: A Comparative Case Study' (2017) 6:2 *Internet Policy Review*.
Privacy Commissioner of Canada, 'Time to Break Out of Technological Trance, says Commissioner' (Remarks by Privacy Commissioner of Canada regarding 10th Annual Report to Parliament, Ottawa, 13 July 1993).
Privacy Commissioner of Canada, 'Statement' (Remarks by Privacy Commissioner of Canada regarding 2015–2016 Annual Report to Parliament, Ottawa, 27 September 2016).
Public Internet Advocacy Centre, *Report: Consumer Privacy Under PIPEDA: How Are We Doing?* (PIAC, Ottawa 2004).
Rahamim Y., 'Wiretapping and Electronic Surveillance in Canada: The Present State of the Law and Challenges to the Employment of Sophisticated and Intrusive Technology in Law Enforcement' (2004) 18 Winds*or Rev Legal & Soc Issues* 87.
Relyea H.C., 'Freedom of Information, Privacy, and Official Secrecy: The Evolution of Federal Government Information Policy Concepts' (1980) 7:1 Social Indicators Research 137.
Rowat D.C., 'The Right to Governmental Information in Democracies' (1981) 2 *J Media L & Prac* 314.
Rule J., et al., *The Politics of Privacy: Planning for Personal Data Systems as Powerful Technologies* (Elsevier 1980).
Russell P.H., 'The Proposed Charter for a Civilian Intelligence Agency: An Appraisal' (1983) 9:3 *Canadian Public Policy* 326.
Savage J.G. and M.W. Zacher, 'Free Flow versus Prior Consent: The Jurisdictional Battle Over International Communications' (1987) 42 *International Journal* 342.
Scassa T., 'It is Time to Overhaul Canada's Data Protection —your rights are at stake' *MacLean's Magazine* (Ottawa, 2 February 2018).
Solicitor General of Canada, *Report of the Canadian Committee on Corrections—Toward Unity: Criminal Justice and Corrections* (Ottawa 1969) ('Ouimet Report').
Susman T.M., 'The Privacy Act and the Freedom of Information Act: Conflict and Resolution' (1988) 21 *J Marshall L Rev* 703.
Title M.M., 'Canadian Wiretap Legislation: Protection or Erosion of Privacy' (1978) 26 *Chitty's LJ* 47.
Valeriote F.M., 'Judicial Authorization for Wiretap: An Illusory Protection' (1980) 12 *Ottawa L Rev* 215.
Weber R.H., 'The Digital Future – A Challenge for Privacy?' (2015) 31 *Computer L Security Rev* 234.
Weller G.R., 'The Canadian Security Intelligence Service Under Stress' (1988) 31:2 *Canadian Public Administration* 279.
Westin AF, *Privacy and Computers* (Atheneum 1967).
Wright D., P. de Hert and S. Gutwith, 'Are the OECD Guidelines at 30 showing their age?' (2011) 54:2 *Communications of the ACM* 119.

6. Data protection laws in Japan

Hiroshi Miyashita

I. GLOBAL WAVE OF DATA PROTECTION LAW REFORM

We live in a global wave of data protection law reforms from Europe and North America to the Asia-Pacific, Latin America and Africa. According to some estimates, 145 jurisdictions had enacted their own data privacy legislations as of 2020.[1] In Japan, the Act on the Protection of Personal Information, originally enacted in 2003, was amended in 2015 and subsequently amended in 2020 and 2021. One of the purposes of the amending Act is, among other things, to confirm the international consistency of Japan's data protection laws. In particular, the amendment process consciously aimed for an adequate level of protection based on the EU standard in light of Article 45 of the General Data Protection Regulation (GDPR). As a result, Japan successfully obtained EU adequacy decision in the private sector on 23 January 2019.[2] This chapter first provides an overview of the amendments to the Act and compares it with the EU data protection framework. Then the chapter suggests several future tasks for the Japanese law to enhance its international consistency, particularly in light of the EU GDPR.

II. LAW REFORMS FOR BIG DATA AND DIGITAL SOCIETY

II.1 Basic Framework of Data Protection

Data protection is not explicitly provided by the Constitution of Japan. However, Japanese academic literature has introduced the right to privacy and data protection legislation since 1960s. For instance, Masami Ito, who later became a Supreme Court Justice, advocated the right to privacy, stating that it is the social and cultural conditions, not just the legal text, that protect the right to privacy in Japan.[3] Under the Japanese 'shame cultures',[4] privacy violation is not just about the legal issues, but also a matter of trust and reputation.

In practice, the Supreme Court has also acknowledged and interpreted the right to privacy. In this sense, the Court has stated 'Article 13 of the Constitution protects … that every individual has the freedom not to make personal information disclosed nor publicized to the third party without good reason'.[5] The Court has also found privacy interests in the context of

---

[1] Graham Greenleaf, 'Global data privacy laws 2021: Despite Covid delays, 145 laws show GDPR dominance' (2021) 169 *Privacy Laws & Business International Report* 3.

[2] Commission, 'Commission Implementing Decision (EU) 2019/419 of 23 January 2019 pursuant to Regulation (EU) 2016/679 of the European Parliament and of the Council on the adequate protection of personal data by Japan under the Act on the Protection of Personal Information' C [2019] 304.

[3] Masami Ito, *The Right to Privacy [Puraibashii no Kenri]*, Iwanamishoten (1963) 7.

[4] Ruth Benedict, *The Chrysanthemum and the Sword* (Houghton Mifflin 1946) 223.

[5] Judgement of the Supreme Court on 6 March 2008, Minshu vol.62 no. 3 p.665 (Juki-net (residential network system) case).

criminal procedures against unreasonable 'entries, searches and seizures' in the case of GPS tracking without a warrant under Article 35 of the Constitution.[6] Thus, protection of personal data in Japan is guaranteed by the Constitution as well as data protection laws.

The Civil Code also protects the so-called 'right to personality' including the right to privacy in case law. For instance, the Tokyo District Court first recognized in 1964 privacy right as 'the legal protection or the right so as not to be disclosed of private life'.[7] The Court has also protected the right to personality against the publication of a private person's criminal history in a novel after a passage of time,[8] and has supported the legal protection of private information which must not be disclosed to a third party without consent.[9] On the other hand, the Court did not recognize the 'right to be forgotten' in a claim of delisting in a search engine by using the existing framework of balancing between free speech and privacy.[10]

The protection of personal data has been the subject of special legislation, namely the Act on the Protection of Personal Information (APPI) in 2003. The basic principles enumerated in the APPI dependably reflect the OECD Privacy Guidelines of 1980. The Act covers the basic principles and lists the obligations of business entities in the private sector. At the time the Act was drafted in the early 2000s when small government was a political trend, an independent supervisory authority had not been established; instead, each Ministry had its own power to enforce the Act, with some Ministries having issued guidelines.

In the public sector, repealing the 1988 Act on the Protection of Personal Information Pertaining to Electronic Data Processing Held by Administrative Organs, the two different Acts were introduced in 2003; namely, the Act on the Protection of Personal Information Held by the Administrative Organs (such as Ministries) and the Act on the Protection of Personal Information Held by the Incorporated Administrative Organs (such as national universities and national hospitals). Since the 1970s, for instance, with Kunitachi city's ordinance on the operation of electronic calculation processing in 1975, local governments have their own ordinances on the protection of personal information held by the local governments.

In addition, the Act on the use of numbers to identify the specific individuals in the administrative procedures, also known as the ID Number Act or My Number Act (hereafter 'ID Number Act'), was passed in the Diet (the Japanese Parliament) in May 2013 in order to realize a fair society, to promote administrative efficiency in the use of identification numbers on social security and taxation and to enhance convenience for the citizens. The Next Generation Medical Infrastructure Act was also enacted in 2017 to promote big data analytics for medical and drug research by using anonymous processing of medical information. It should be noted

---

[6] Judgement of the Supreme Court on 15 March 2017 (GPS tracking case). Art. 35 of the Constitution provides: 'The right of all persons to be secure in their homes, papers and effects against entries, searches and seizures shall not be impaired except upon warrant.'

[7] Tokyo District Court, Judgment on 28 September 1964, Hanreijiho vol. 385 p. 12 ('Utage-no-Ato' (After the Banque) case).

[8] Judgement of the Supreme Court on 8 February 1994, Minshu vol.48 no.2 p.149 ('Gyakuten' ('Reverse') case).

[9] Judgement of the Supreme Court on 12 September 2003, Minshu vol.57 no.8 p.973 (Kotakumin lecture case).

[10] Decision of the Supreme Court on 31 January 2017, Minshu. vol.71 no.1 p.63 (Google search result case).

here that the government has also promoted Artificial Intelligence and the internet of things in the Basic Act on the Advancement of Public and Private Sector Data Utilization.[11]

This public-private distinction was the Japanese feature of approaching to protection of personal information. Traditionally, constitutional rights are to protect individuals from arbitrary power of the public institutions, while private disputes cannot be directly settled by constitutional law. However, as discussed later, the 2021 amendments to the Act dramatically changed the public-private distinction in order to integrate one comprehensive personal information protection Act.

II.2 Main Issues in the Reforms

Debate on law reform began in June 2013 when the government of Japan publicized the 'Declaration to be the World's Most Advanced IT Nation', which recognized that the guidelines for personal information protection should be reviewed. There was a strong demand from the business side to utilize personal data for data analytics, in particular because of perceived 'overreaction' (namely excessive protection of personal data) after the APPI entered into effect in 2005; for instance, in some cases the personal information was not shared even in cases of natural disasters and earthquakes. Such debates surrounding personal information protection in Japan always entail the need to protection and the demand of utilization.

The contents of a series of law reforms in 2015, 2020 and 2021 can be summarized in the following five points.[12]

II.3 Scope of Personal Information

First, the scope of personal information was clarified. Personal information thus means 'information that is identifiable of the individuals by names, birthdate and the other descriptions including the documents, drawings, electromagnetic records or voices, motions and the other means' (Art.2 (1)). In addition, the reform mentioned a personal identification code, including letters, numbers, marks and the other codes to identify a specific individual from a bodily feature and from the service codes (Art. 2 (2)). It is however still contestable, as it was discussed during the Parliament debate, if a customer's IDs which are assigned by a company can be categorically regarded as 'personal identifiers' under the law because of the diverse and different types of services. Sensitive data, known as 'special care required personal information', which was not listed before the amendments, is explicitly defined as 'race, creed, social status, medical history, criminal record, fact of having suffered damage by a crime, or other descriptions etc.' (Art. 2 (3)).

II.4 Anonymous/Pseudonymous Data

Second, for the purpose of enhancing Big Data analytics, the Act provided a definition of 'anonymous processing information' in the 2015 amendments and 'pseudonymous processing

---

[11] Act No. 103 of December 14, 2016. English translation is available at http://www.japaneselawtranslation.go.jp/law/detail_main?re=02&vm=04&id=2975 accessed 20 October 2021.

[12] The Amended Act, Cabinet Order and PPC rule in English translation can be available at: https://www.ppc.go.jp/en/legal/ accessed 19 October 2021.

information' in the 2020 amendments. Anonymous information is information that is not able to identify the individual and is not able to restore such identification by (1) deleting the descriptions containing the personal information or (2) deleting all the personal identifiers containing the personal information (Art.2 (6)). On the other hand, pseudonymous information can be reidentified by matching with the original information. Those who use anonymous processing information must apply the security measures even if they use anonymous information (Art. 43 (2)). The Personal Information Protection Commission (PPC) also published guidelines on anonymous processing information to clarify that anonymous processing means that the standard of not being able to restore the personal information is judged by the ability and means of ordinary people and ordinary business.

In July 2013 data from 43 million IC cards of JR East (a railway company), used on public railroads and buses, but which can also be used in convenience stores and vending machines, were sold to a data analytics company in July 2013. This was done for marketing purposes to promote the commercial facilities around stations. In the process of selling the information, the railroad company deleted the names and the dates of birthdates of the users by assigning them ID numbers. However, immediately after this press release, users expressed fierce criticism. In the end, the railway company, JR East, apologized for its project and accepted that the users should be able to opt-out from the scheme.

From a legal point of view, processing ID numbers and deleting only a part of personal data can be understood as the use of 'pseudonymous data' rather than of 'anonymous data'. A lesson that can be drawn from this incident is that it is necessary to properly understand the scope of 'identification or identifiability', particularly of what it means to be 'readily collated with other information and thereby identify a specific individual' (APPI Art. 2 (1) (i)).

II.5 Transparency and Accountability

Third, in terms of transparency and accountability, some new provisions were added to the amendments. For instance, prohibition of inappropriate utilization was incorporated in the 2020 amendments. In 2020, the PPC first issued an order against the two unknown companies in the case of bankrupt mapping where the PPC ordered the deletion of the locations of bankrupt persons in the Google map whose information was originally available at the Official Gazette.[13] Such an improper utilization of personal data infringes the personality and hinders rehabilitation of bankrupt persons. Thus, a substantive regulation of personal information utilization by 'a method that has the possibility of fomenting or prompting unlawful or unfair act' (Art. 19).

A major data scandal is a data breach incident that occurred in 2014. The former contractor of the education company, Benesse's former contractor, sold a total of 48.58 million sets of customer personal data, including the personal data of many children, to at least three data brokers.[14] There were no direct criminal sanctions for stealing the data under the APPI, so the

---

[13] PPC, 'Regarding the administrative response under the Act on the Protection of Personal Information', 29 July 2020 https://www.ppc.go.jp/files/pdf/200729_meirei.pdf accessed 19 October 2021.

[14] Benesse Holdings, Inc., 'Investigation report by the data breach incident investigation committee', 25 September 2014 p.5 (in Japanese). A total of 35.04 million items (some cases of a single item including several personal data) were leaked.

former contractor was prosecuted for unlawfully acquiring a trade secret of the Act on Unfair Competition Prevention and was sentenced to an imprisonment of two and a half years and a fine of 3 million yen.[15]

From the point of data protection, the supervision over trustee and sanction were not enough as a lesson of this case. The use of smart phones in the system room was not prohibited, and the alert system for transferring massive amounts of data from the system did not work in this case, which shows that the legal standard for security measures, particularly with regard to data processors or contractors, should be reviewed. In the end, it demonstrated that penalties or sanctions for data stealing should be included, which were realised in the 2015 amendments.

Furthermore, data controllers must keep records of sending and receiving personal data in order to enhance transparency, and to address the improper data sharing with data brokers (Arts 29 and 30). Under these requirements, business operators must keep the records for three years except for a retention period of one year in specified situations (PPC rules Art. 14). In addition, personal information handling entities can use an opt-out for marketing or purposes only when they notify or publicize this to data subjects and notify it to the PPC (Art. 27 (2)). As previously mentioned in the Benesse case, the activities of data brokers for the purpose of acquiring an illegal profit by providing or stealing a database of the personal information shall be punished by imprisonment of up to one year or a fine of up to 100 million yen (Arts 179 and 184).

Along with these developments, there have been intensive discussions in the Japanese government to regulate artificial intelligence in the wake of an incident regarding recruiting services in 2019. Rikunabi, an online platform operator, sold the scores of job-hunting applicants without consent to the companies. The scores are marked on the possibility of declining job offers based on the AI analytics of web behaviours in the Rikunabi platform.

The PPC issued recommendations and instructions, stating that the Rikunabi service was extremely inappropriate as it circumvented the law. Emerging technologies such as facial recognition and emotional AI which are used in Japan make the policymakers reconsider the existing framework of protecting personal data, which led to the 2020 amendments. The Rikunabi case justified a necessity of regulation toward human-centric data protection approach toward the artificial intelligence in Japan.[16]

II.6 International Data Transfer

Fourth, international cooperation and cross-border data transfer were clearly incorporated in the amended Act. For instance, the Act introduced a similar provision regarding data transfers to the third countries as in the EU GDPR and Data Protection Directive. This means that business operators cannot transfer personal data to a third country unless its country ensures 'the equivalent level of protection' as Japan (Art. 28). The PPC can list those equivalent countries (Commission rules Art.11), and it already mentioned, in the PPC's guidelines that the international frameworks as ensuring an equivalent level of protection with proper and reasonable

---

[15] Tokyo High Court, Judgement on 21 March 2017, Hanrei Times vol. 1443 p.80.

[16] The Cabinet Office of Japan publicized 'Report on Artificial Intelligence and Human Society', 24 March 2017 http://www8.cao.go.jp/cstp/tyousakai/ai/summary/aisociety_en.pdf accessed 19 October 2021. See Hiroshi Miyashita, 'Human-centric Data Protection Laws and Policies: A Lesson from Japan', (2021) 40 *Computer Law & Security Review* 105487.

measures include the OECD Privacy Guidelines and the APEC Cross-Border Privacy Rules (CBPR).[17] Japan is a member of the APEC CBPR and JIPDEC (Japan Information Processing and Development Center) as a certification organization, was accredited as Accountability Agent under the APEC CBPR system. This means that Japan may possibly use a certification scheme to data transfers to the APEC economies. However, the EU adequacy decision explicitly excluded using APEC CBPR as a tool for onward transfer,[18] which may vex the data flow of Japanese companies in the Asia-Pacific area.

In the context of global business, the issue of foreign government access to private data was raised in the LINE case in 2021. LINE is a leading social media in Japan with its approximately 86 million users and is widely used by both the national and local governments. Some of the contents of LINE were accessed by a Chinese software company and stored in South Korea. A serious concern was raised for possible access to the contents by foreign governments. The PPC issued an instruction against LINE, requiring LINE to supervise the trustee. However, before the 2020 amendments which enters into force in 2022, there was no requirement for the business operators to list the third country's name for exporting personal data. Thus, the LINE case was not just a single company's problem, rather it is a critical issue concerning the Japanese data strategy of 'Data Free Flow with Trust'.[19]

II.7 Power of PPC

Last, but most importantly, the PPC which was restructured from the Commission supervising only the national ID number (My number) system is now the key player for enforcing the data protection Act in Japan. The PPC, consisting of a chairperson and eight Commissioners each with a five-year term, started its operation in January 2016 in the private sector and the part of public sector for the use of de-identification data. The PPC has the power to provide guidance and advice (Art. 147) and issue orders and recommendations (Art. 148) including onsite inspection (Art. 146). A lack of an independent supervisory authority may have resulted in weak enforcement in the past, so this was a major improvement.

In the 2021 amendments, the scope of the PPC's power was expanded to the entire public sector including the government access to private data. In the adequacy decision, the European Data Protection Board expressed a concern regarding the voluntary access to private data by law enforcement agencies. For instance, the several newspaper articles published the facts that the Prosecutor's Office was in possession of a list containing approximately 290 companies that give customers' data to the Office on a voluntary basis.[20] Access right is exempted for the purpose of law enforcement activities, and transparency report by corporations is not common in Japan. Thus, it is important for the PPC to supervise the government access to private data under the amended Act.

---

[17] PPC, 'Guidelines on the Protection of Personal Information (Transfer to the third party in the foreign country)' November 2016 (last amended January 2021) 8–9. https://www.ppc.go.jp/files/pdf/210101_guidlines02.pdf accessed 29 October 2021.

[18] Commission, (n.2) para 79.

[19] G20 Osaka Leaders' Declaration, 28–29 June 2019 https://www.mofa.go.jp/policy/economy/g20_summit/osaka19/en/documents/final_g20_osaka_leaders_declaration.html accessed 19 October 2021.

[20] 'Acquisition of customers' information without warrant' *Tokyo Newspaper*, 3 January 2019 p.1.

III. JAPANESE LAW AND GDPR IN COMPARISON

During the legislative process of amending the Act in Japan, it was clearly recognized that an adequacy decision by European Commission would be desirable for the global Japanese businesses. Then-Minister Shunichi Yamaguchi expressed in the House of Representatives that 'the government will proceed to obtain the adequacy finding from EU in order to improve the Japanese business environment in EU after the bill passes through'.[21] The Minister explained in the Diet that the amendment bill contained some improvements for obtaining an adequacy finding such as (1) establishment of the independent authority, (2) inclusion of sensitive data, (3) abolition of the exemptions for SMEs, (4) data transfer restrictions, and (5) the right to disclosure. While these five elements may have been updated, there seems to be, as a matter of degree, some differences between the Japanese and EU systems. This section focuses on the following three issues by comparing the new Japanese Act with EU General Data Protection Regulation.

III.1 Scope of Personal Data and Sensitive Data

It was repeatedly discussed during the legislative process that the Japanese Act limited the scope of personal data by comparing the Japanese approach with the EU definition of personal data. In the EU, personal data is broad enough to include dynamic IP addresses,[22] handwritten examination scripts[23] and other directly or indirectly personally identifiable information.[24] The Japanese Act includes information that allows a specific individual to be identified. Here it is important to understand that personal information includes those 'which can be easily collated with other information and thereby identify a specific individual' (Art. 2(1)). While the meaning of 'easily' collated with other information is frequently questioned, the Act intends to exclude the information which requires excessive effort to identify the individual with other information. During the legislative process, some grey zones were discussed, such as customer IDs, IP addresses and unique ID identifier, which are not considered personal information.

In addition to the general definition of personal data, one can also find the differences between the scope of sensitive data. In the GDPR, data revealing racial or ethnic origin, political opinions, religious or philosophical beliefs, or trade union membership, genetic data, biometric data, health data and sex life or sexual orientation are explicitly provided as special categories of personal data (Art. 9). On the other hand, the Japanese Act limits the special care required personal information to cover information concerning 'race, creed, social status, medical history, criminal record, fact of having suffered damage by a crime, or other descriptions etc.' (Art. 2(3) and Cabinet Order Art. 2). Trade union membership, genetic data and sex life or sexual orientation are not listed under the Japanese Act.[25] It should be well recognized

---

[21] Plenary Session, House of Representatives, Diet 189, 23 April 2015, Minister Shunichi Yamaguchi.

[22] Case 582/14 *Patrick Breyer v Germany*, [2016] OJ C 2016/779.

[23] Case 434/16 *Peter Nowak v Data Protection Commissioner*, [2017] OJ C 2017/582.

[24] Article 29 Data Protection Working Party, 'Opinion 4/2007 on the concept of personal data' 12.

[25] Some guidelines define broader scope of sensitive data to include member of labour union, family origin, permanent domicile, medial treatment of health and sexual life. See: PPC & Financial Services Agency, 'Guidelines on the Protection of Personal Information in the Credit Sectors' (2017) https://www.fsa.go.jp/common/law/kj-hogo-2/01.pdf accessed 19 October 2021 and PPC & Ministry of Justice,

that sensitivity in personal data is different from one culture to another; for example, the criminal records which directly relate to honour are protected in Japan, whereas publication of the criminal record of the accused is a matter of free speech in the United States.[26]

Furthermore, under Japanese law there is no distinction between 'controller' and 'processor'. The Act generally provides for a series of obligations for business entities 'handling' personal information. Here 'handling' includes both controlling and processing, however it does not clarify the contents of these concepts, in particular in the context of platform business. The differences in the scope of personal data and sensitive data and the definition of 'processing' may lead to conflict, just as it was the case in the EU-US dialogue on the processing of personal data by the security agencies.[27]

III.2 Rights-oriented Approach Versus Duties-oriented Approach

The Charter of Fundamental Rights in the EU explicitly protects the fundamental right to personal data. As to secondary law, the GDPR contains a series of innovative rights for the data subjects, such as the right to information, the right to be forgotten, the right to data portability right, and the right to object to profiling. There is no doubt that the Court of Justice of the EU also protects the right to personal data a part of fundamental right, as can be seen in the *Google Spain* case[28]or the *Digital Rights Ireland* case.[29]

The amended Japanese Act includes rules on the possibility to 'request' to disclose, rectify and suspend to use personal data (Arts 33–35). Here it is important to understand that the word 'demand' (seikyu) was changed from 'ask for' (motome), but there is still no mention of a 'right' for disclosure, rectification and suspension of use. In addition, these articles are located in the chapter of 'obligations of business operators handling personal information'. The Japanese Act provides for 'fundamental duties' for controllers and processors rather than 'fundamental rights' for data subjects. To prove this, the fee is admissible as complying with the duties when the business operators respond to data subjects' access to retained personal data. Furthermore, there is an exemption clause under the Cabinet Order regarding access to personal data in the context of law enforcement activities. As the European Data Protection Board observed, APPI has a restrictive provision regarding data subjects' access rights without balancing under necessity and proportionality test.[30] In this sense, for instance, the Tokyo District Court judgement denied the 'demand' of disclosure of personal data under the

---

'Guidelines on the Protection of Personal Information in the Debt Collection Sectors' (2017) https://www.ppc.go.jp/files/pdf/saikenkaisyu_GL.pdf accessed 19 October 2021.

[26] Dan Rosen, 'Private Lives and Public Eyes: Privacy in the United States and Japan' (1990) 6(1) *Florida Journal of International Law* 141.

[27] 'For the EU, data acquisition is synonymous with data collection and is a form of processing of personal data ... under US law, the initial acquisition of personal data does not always constitute processing of personal data; data is "processed" only when it is analysed by means of human intervention'. See: Report on the Finding by the EU Co-chairs of the ad hoc EU-US Working Group on Data Protection, 27 November 2013.

[28] Case 131/12, *Google Spain v Agencia Española de Protección de Datos (AEPD)* [2014] OJ C 2014/317.

[29] Case 293/12 & Case 594/12, *Digital Rights Ireland* [2014] OJ C 2014/238.

[30] European Data Protection Board, 'Opinion 28/2018 regarding the EU Commission Draft Implementing Decision on the adequate protection of personal data in Japan' 7.

APPI owing to the structure of the law.[31] The key case concerns the right to be forgotten in Japan; such a right cannot be derived from erasure 'demand' under the APPI, rather it is an interpretative matter of the right to personality in civil law though, as previously mentioned, the Supreme Court is in favour of free speech over privacy in the Google search case.[32] The amended Act clarified, according to the explanation by the government, the nature of right of data subjects, which remain to be an open question for the court to decide.

The same is true of the short-term personal information. Under the APPI before the 2020 amendments, personal information which retains shorter than six months was excluded, due to low risk of harm, from retained personal data for data subject to access. In the process of adequacy decision, the European Parliament accurately pointed out this harm-based approach under the APPI may not be compatible with the EU's rights-based approach.[33] The notion of this short-term personal information, however, was abolished, quite possibly as a result of the European Parliament's resolution, in the process of 2020 amendments.

One may be able to categorize the EU regime as a rights-oriented approach, whereas the Japanese system is rather a duties-oriented approach. This is just a relative comparison, as possibly a matter of degree, because the EU regime surely provides a series of duties for data controllers and processors and the Japanese system no doubt protects right to personality based on the civil law jurisprudence. This comparison may illuminate the philosophical differences between the EU and Japan in the context of protecting personal data. 'Human dignity', embedded in the Charter of Fundamental Rights, can be described as the cornerstone of the EU data protection regime, whereas the Japanese philosophy of privacy comes from the etiquette of not interfering with the private life of others, which is now expressed as 'respect' under the Constitution (Art. 13) and the basic philosophy of the APPI (Art. 3).

III.3 Enforcement Mechanism

The so-called competent Minister system, which means the competent Minister which issues orders and recommendations in each business field, was the former enforcement mechanism in Japan. However, it was not efficient for the business to identify which Ministry was their supervisor, or to overlap different business sectors so that they had to obey the multiple guidelines issued by different Ministries. In addition, the lack of an independent supervisory authority resulted in the weak enforcement without independent and technical supervision for protecting personal data.[34] A series of amendments overcame the lack of an efficient enforcement mechanism.

Yet, several issues remain for the future. First, the 2021 amendments expand the power of the PPC to the public sector. Before these amendments, the Ministry of Internal Affairs and Communications had the power to implement public sector legislation. However, as

---

31 Tokyo District Court, Judgement on 27 June 2007, Hanrei Times vol.1275 p.323.

32 An article that business entities must 'delete the personal data without delay when such use has become unnecessary' (Art. 22) is also a part of 'obligations of a personal information handling business operator'.

33 European Parliament, 'Resolution of 13 December 2018 on the adequacy of the protection of personal data afforded by Japan' (2018/2979(RSP)) para 13.

34 Graham Greenleaf, 'Independence of Data Privacy Authorities (Part II): Asia-Pacific Experience' (2011) 28 *Computer Law & Security Review* 126. See also Graham Greenleaf, *Asian Data Privacy Laws* (Oxford University Press 2014) 263.

Japan failed to obtain an adequacy decision with regard to the public sector, the government introduced the necessity of independent supervisory authority in the public sector in the 2021 amendments. It is an open question, due to a lack of resources, whether the PPC will effectively monitor the public institutions including the government access by law enforcement agencies. Second, as to the stringency of enforcement, the PPC has not yet given a bark with a fine. There have been only recommendations, instructions or an order over data breach cases. Third, the 2015 amendments allow for the supervision of the law to be transferred from the PPC back to the Ministries (Art. 150, Cabinet Order Art. 12). This delegated power from the PPC to the Ministries is allowed only in the case of 'emergency and predominant issues for the proper protection of personal information'. It is confirmed, according to the explanations by the Minister during the parliamentary debate, that the PPC has the authority to interpret the law in order to avoid the multiple reports by multiple Ministries.[35] However it is not yet clear how the enforcement mechanism in Japan will function in practice.

Furthermore, in terms of independence, most of the staff of the PPC are temporarily posted from different Ministries. Complete independence under the EU standard requires that their staff and resources as well as their power which should be free from any direct and indirect external influence that could affect the performance of their duties or decision-making processes.[36] The new PPC in Japan has been modelled on the EU independent supervisory authorities, which surely results in learning from the EU experiences.

As for an effective remedy for data breaches, as the Benesse case illustrates the use of unfair competition prevention law instead of data protection law in light of the fact that the APPI failed to give consumers a direct and effective remedy. The Supreme Court of Japan held in 2017 that the lower courts should take into account the mental distress and its degree for the individuals affected.[37] Previous lower court judgments generally agree with the compensation of mental distress in the cases of data breach.[38] It should also be noted here that the data breach of over one million pension records which occurred during the legislative process in 2015 proved that there is a lack of effective remedy with no compensation concerning breaches in the public sector. The 2021 amendments drastically abandoned the traditional public-private divide in order to concentrate the powers of the PPC to include public sector supervision. It is essential for the PPC to gain its trust from the citizens to investigate and enforce the law in the public sector including the government access to private data. Providing an effective remedy in the case of data breaches and enforcement action in the public sector are the next step for bridging Japanese law closer to the GDPR and the judgements of the CJEU.[39]

---

35 Plenary Session, House of Representatives, Diet 189, 23 April 2015, Minister Shunichi Yamaguchi.

36 C-518/07 *Commission v. Germany*, [2010] OJ C 2010/125; C-614/10, *Commission v. Austria*, [2012] OJ C 2012/631.

37 Judgement of the Supreme Court on 23 October 2017, Hanreijiho vol.1442 p.46.

38 For instance, Osaka High Court, Judgement on 25 December 2001, 2001WLJPCA12259004 (holding 10,000 yen for data breach case in Uji city); Tokyo High Court, Judgement on 28 August 2007, Hanrei Times, vol.1264 p.299 (holding 30,000 yen for data breach case in TBC Aesthetic salon).

39 C-498/16, *Maximilian Schrems v Facebook Ireland Ltd* [2018] OJ C2018/37.

IV. THE MUTUAL ADEQUACY WITH 'MINDING THE GAP'

It is commonly understood that data protection cannot be negotiable as a matter of trade or commerce because the protection of personal data is different from the protection of a commodity. Yet, the motivation of enhancing the level of protection of personal data sometimes originates in trade negotiation with an economic incentive, as we have seen between EU and Japan in the Economic Partnership Agreement (EPA) to remove barriers and to shape the global trade rules without protectionism.[40]

On 10 January 2017, the European Commission publicized the Communication on *Exchanging and Protecting Personal Data in a Globalised World.* In this Communication, the Commission expressed its interest in potentially issuing further adequacy findings, 'starting from Japan and Korea in 2017'.[41] In addition, the Joint Declaration by the Japanese Prime Minister and the President of the European Commission on 6 July 2017 mentioned that 'the EU and Japan have further increased the convergence between their two systems' with 'a simultaneous finding of an adequate level of protection by both sides'. Finally, on 23 January 2019, the European Commission, as a symbol of 'the world's largest area of safe data flows',[42] issued an adequacy decision to the Japanese APPI together with Supplementary Rules and assurance by the Japanese government officials. On the same day, the PPC listed 31 EEA countries as ensuring an equivalent level of protection as the APPI.[43] Thus, both the EU and Japan agreed to ensure free flow of data in the private commercial sectors nearly one week before the EU-Japan EPA's entry into force.

In the context of these dialogues, the Japanese PPC made an effort to publicize its Supplementary Rules on handling personal data transferred from the EU under an adequacy finding.[44] They contain the five elements, in an effort to 'mind the gap' between the EU law and the Japanese law. These elements include the categories of sensitive data or personal information requiring special care; the fact that a retention period does not influence the definition of retained personal data in spite of the law; specification of the purpose of use and its limitation; restrictions on onward transfers, and the definition of the anonymous processing of personal information.

Taking an optimistic view, it is a good sign that both the EU and Japan value data protection, and that the Japanese amended Act is becoming closer to the EU regime. From a pessimistic view, the two systems between the EU and Japanese systems may still have some differences which may require further 'gaiatsu' (external impetus) to change the Japanese data protection

---

[40] Marija Bartl and Kristina Irion, 'The Japan EU Economic Partnership Agreement: flows of personal data to the land of the rising sun', 25 October 2017 https://ssrn.com/abstract=3099390 accessed 19 October 2021.

[41] Commission, 'Communication: Exchanging and Protecting Personal Data in a Globalised World', COM/2017/07 final, 10.

[42] Commission, 'European Commission adopts adequacy decision on Japan, creating the world's largest area of safe data flows' (press release), 23 January 2019.

[43] PPC, 'The framework for mutual and smooth transfer of personal data between Japan and the European Union has come into force', 23 January 2019 https://www.ppc.go.jp/en/aboutus/roles/international/cooperation/20190123/ accessed 19 October 2021.

[44] PPC, 'Supplementary Rules under the Act on the Protection of Personal Information for the Handling of Personal Data Transferred from the EU based on an Adequacy Decision' January 2019.

system.[45] It is true that an adequacy finding does not require an 'identical' law, but the Japanese law should be 'essentially equivalent' to the EU legal order.[46] It is beyond the scope of this contribution to assess both systems in a comprehensive manner.[47] However, one thing is clear: the EU has successfully exported its data protection philosophy, in the name of the 'Brussels effect',[48] also to Japan in the process of the amendments of its the data protection law.

REFERENCES

Article 29 Data Protection Working Party, 'Opinion on the concept of personal data' 20 June 2007.
Bartl M and K Irion, *The Japan EU Economic Partnership Agreement: flows of personal data to the land of the rising sun*, 25 October 2017, https://papers.ssrn.com/sol3/papers.cfm?abstract_id=3099390.
Benedict R, *The Chrysanthemum and the Sword* (Houghton Mifflin 1946).
Bradford A, 'The Brussels Effect' (2012) 107 *Northwestern University Law Review* 1.
European Commission, 'Communication: Exchanging and Protecting Personal Data in a Globalised World', 10 January 2017.
EU Co-chairs of the ad hoc EU-US Working Group on Data Protection, 'Report on the Finding by the EU Co-chairs of the ad hoc EU-US Working Group on Data Protection' 27 November 2013.
European Data Protection Board, 'Opinion 28/2018 regarding the EU Commission Draft Implementing Decision on the adequate protection of personal data in Japan' 5 December 2018.
European Parliament, 'Resolution of 13 December 2018 on the adequacy of the protection of personal data afforded by Japan' (2018/2979(RSP)).
Greenleaf G, 'Independence of Data Privacy Authorities (Part II): Asia-Pacific Experience' (2011) 28 *Computer Law & Security Review* 121.
Greenleaf G, *Asian Data Privacy Laws* (Oxford University Press 2014).
Greenleaf G, 'Global data privacy laws 2021: Despite Covid delays, 145 laws show GDPR dominance', (2021) 169 *Privacy Laws & Business International Report* 1.
Ito M, *The Right to Privacy [Puraibashii no Kenri]*, Iwanamishoten (1963) 7.
Miyashita H, 'EU-Japan Mutual Adequacy Decision' in Nakanishi Y and Tambou O (eds), *EU-Japan Relations* (Collection Open Access Book 2020).
Miyashita H, 'Human-centric Data Protection Laws and Policies: A Lesson from Japan', (2021) 40 *Computer Law & Security Review* 105487.
Personal Information Protection Commission, *Guidelines on the Protection of Personal Information (Transfer to the third party in the foreign country)*, November 2016 (last amended January 2021).
Personal Information Protection Commission, *Supplementary Rules under the Act on the Protection of Personal Information for the Handling of Personal Data Transferred from the EU based on an Adequacy Decision* January 2019.
Rosen D, 'Private lives and public eyes: Privacy in the United States and Japan' (1990) 6(1) *Florida Journal of International Law*.
Suda Y, 'Japan's Personal Information Protection Policy under Pressure' (2020) 60 *Asian Survey* 510.

---

[45] Yuko Suda, 'Japan's Personal Information Protection Policy under Pressure' (2020) 60 *Asian Survey* 510, 524.
[46] C-362/14 *Maximilian Schrems v Data Protection Commissioner* [2015] OJ C:2015:650; C-311/18 *Data Protection Commissioner v Facebook Ireland Limited and Maximillian Schrems* [2020] ECLI:EU: C:2020:559.
[47] See Hiroshi Miyashita, 'EU-Japan Mutual Adequacy Decision' in Yumiko Nakanishi and Olivia Tambou (eds), *EU-Japan Relations* (Collection Open Access Book 2020) 72.
[48] Anu Bradford, 'The Brussels Effect' (2012) 107 *Northwestern University Law Review* 1.

7. Data protection in Latin America

Mónica Arenas Ramiro

I. INTRODUCTION

This chapter discusses the regulation of the processing of personal data in Latin America. First, we analyse the recognition of the right to data protection in the region, referring to its guarantee mechanisms, especially to supervisory authorities. Afterwards, we examine the principles that govern the legal regulation of personal data processing, from the different standards approved in each of the Latin American countries to the criteria included in the Standards that aim at creating a unified data processing regime in Ibero-America.

Technological advances facilitate the transfer and exchange of personal information, but they also generate new and potential threats for people's privacy. This reality has triggered among States a preoccupation to achieve the right balance between the protection of the rights of their citizens, on the one hand, and, at the same time, guaranteeing the transfer of personal information and supporting the digital economy. For these reasons, many States have made important efforts to raise awareness about the importance of protecting personal information, as well as the need to guarantee the international transfer of personal data in order to favour – in the context of the digital and globalized market in which we are – the digital economy. Each State, however, has elaborated its own legal framework according to the notion of privacy and private life that it has. And since there is no unambiguous concept of privacy, the mechanisms to regulate and protect the right vary from one region to another, and from one country to another.

We could differentiate two large models to protect the privacy of individuals and, therefore, their personal information. On the one hand, we have the American model, followed in the United States (US), characterized by betting on self-regulatory mechanisms. In the US, privacy is not expressly recognized in its constitutional text, but derives from the Fourth Amendment, considering it a fundamental right that must be protected against threats from public authorities and on the other hand is considered that this right must be regulated by the private sector with the norms approved sectorally for regulating data processing. On the other side, we have the European model, which guarantees privacy based on the protection of the right and on the regulation of the treatment of data as foreseen, on the one hand, in international treaties such as the European Convention on Human Rights of 1950 (ECHR), or in Convention 108, of the Council of Europe of 1981, on the protection of individuals with respect to the automated processing of their personal data; and, on the other hand, in EU instruments such as the Charter of Fundamental Rights of the European Union (CDFUE) – which guarantees the right to privacy and data protection in Articles 7 and 8, respectively – and the current Regulation (EU) 2016/679 General Data Protection Regulation (GDPR), which replaced Directive 95/46/

EC on the protection of personal data and came into force in May 2018.[1] The European model is characterized by establishing a standard and uniform model for the processing of personal data in order to guarantee the personal data flow, recognizing the right to the processing of personal data as a fundamental right. With the approval of the GDPR, of direct application in EU Member States, without the need for transposition and leaving little margin for States to react, the uniform application of data protection regulations in Europe was reinforced and the rights of the data subjects were strengthened. The data protection was made to revolve around a proactive model, favouring the European digital single market.

Between these two models we find the model followed in Latin America, based essentially on the constitutional recognition of the fundamental right to *habeas data* and influenced, especially, by the European model, without ignoring American influences when betting on models of self-regulation. Latin America, unlike Europe, does not have a horizontal regional law on the protection of personal data; and, unlike the US model, many Latin American States recognize the right to privacy in their Constitutions. However, the standards approved by the different Latin American States have tended to follow the European model (especially since the adoption of the GDPR and its application in 2018) in order to comply with an adequate level of data protection in order to guarantee an exchange of data between Europe and Latin America. But the fact of being a region composed of a great plurality of languages and cultures causes the appearance of different privacy laws, which, inevitably, has its consequences in the commercial and business field, which is forced to adapt its strategies to the peculiarities of each country, with the difficulties that this implies.

In general terms, the Latin American States have been regulating the processing of personal data in such a way that we can group them into three large groups, bearing in mind that at the present all States have either a rule governing the processing of personal data or a draft thereof, with a few exceptions:

(a) States that protect expressly the right to protection of personal data as a constitutional right, as a right to *habeas data*, and have rules about data protection (or drafts). Among these states are: Colombia, Mexico and Dominican Republic, and Chile and Ecuador with drafts.
(b) States that do not have approved data protection laws, but recognize a *habeas data* action, as is the case in Honduras, Paraguay and Venezuela.
(c) Other States that, through other constitutionally recognized rights such as privacy, access to information, secrecy of communications, or even the action of *habeas data*, guarantee the privacy of citizens and have, in addition, data protection laws or drafts thereof. This is the case, for example, if Costa Rica and Uruguay; and with draft data protection laws, El Salvador and Guatemala, or Bolivia (which also has an action of *habeas data*).

---

[1] Together with the GDPR, Directive (EU) 2016/680 of the European Parliament and of the Council of 27 April 2016 on the protection of individuals with regard to the processing of personal data by the competent authorities for the purpose of the prevention, investigation, detection or prosecution of criminal offences or the execution of criminal penalties and on the free movement of such data and repealing Council Framework Decision 2008/977/JAI was adopted as part of the EU data protection legislative package.

Despite the tendency of the Latin American States to follow the European model, it is evident, as we have said, that at the present moment there is a lack of harmonization between the different States that make up the region, not only in the way of recognizing the right, but also in the way of regulating the processing of personal data. This makes it difficult to face the new challenges presented by the technological revolution and globalization in which we find ourselves immersed. For this reason, in the Latin American region, in recent years, significant efforts have been made to approve criteria or standards that will help unify the matter in the region and raise the level of protection of personal information of its citizens in order to not establish barriers to the free flow of personal data and thus favour the commercial activities not only between the States of the region, but with other States.

In this regard, at the end of June 2017, the so-called Standards for Personal Data Protection for the Ibero-American States, or 'Ibero-American Standards', were approved, so that in Ibero-America the laws currently in force, as well as future ones, follow homogeneous rules and principles that guarantee uniform protection for citizens and their personal information. These Ibero-American Standards are the result of the work that the Ibero-American Data Protection Network (RIPD, after its acronym in Spanish) has been developing in this field.[2]

The RIPD emerged as a result of the agreement reached by 14 Ibero-American countries at the Ibero-American Meeting on Data Protection held in La Antigua, Guatemala in June 2003. This agreement had its political support at the XIII Summit of Heads of State and Government of Latin American countries held in Santa Cruz de la Sierra, Bolivia, on November 14 and 15, 2003, when States were aware of the importance of recognizing and guaranteeing the right to protection of personal data as a fundamental right, as well as establishing legal regulations for the processing of personal data in accordance with uniform and agreed criteria.

II. THE RECOGNITION OF THE RIGHT TO DATA PROTECTION IN LATIN AMERICA

II.1 The Recognition Process in the Latin American Region

The protection of personal data is a universal and fundamental human right recognized globally in international and European texts, expressly or in connection with the protection of

---

[2] About the RIPD, vid. http://www.redipd.es/index-ides-idphp.php. At present, the Latin American States that compose the RIPD, as members, are: Argentina, Chile, Colombia, Costa Rica, Mexico, and Uruguay. And as observers: the Ombudsman's Office of the City of Buenos Aires (Argentina), the General Ombudsman of the Union of the Ministry of Transparency, the Oversight and General Control of the Union (Brazil), the Transparency and Social Control Function (FTCS) (Ecuador), the Institute for Access to Public Information (IAIP) (El Salvador), the Office of the Ombudsman Procurator (Guatemala), the Institute of Transparency, Public Information and Personal Data Protection of the State of Jalisco (ITEI), the Institute of Access to Public Information of the State of Chiapas (IAIPCHIAPAS), the Veracruz Institute for Access to Information and Personal Data Protection (IVAI), the Commission of Transparency and Access to Information of the State of Nuevo Leon (CTAINL) and the Coahuilense Institute of Access to Public Information (ICAI) (México), the Institute for Access to Public Information (IAIP) (Honduras), the Ministry of Public Administration (Paraguay), the General Directorate of Ethics and Government Integrity (DIGEIG) (Dominican Republic). For the European Union, the European Data Protection Supervisor (EDPS), and for the Council of Europe, the Advisory Committee on Convention 108.

privacy. As already said, at international level, the Universal Declaration of Human Rights of 1948 (UDHR) specifically protects private life against any type of arbitrary interference (Art 12). And in the same way, also at the international level, the International Covenant on Civil and Political Rights (ICCPR) does (Art 17). With binding force, we find the European Convention on Human Rights of 1950 (The Convention) (Art 8), an international treaty although of regional scope. However, any country that wants to join the Council of Europe will have to ratify the said Convention and respect the rights recognized in it.

Taking these international texts as models, in Latin America the right to data protection is regulated, in general terms, as a constitutional guarantee; in most Ibero-American legal systems, within the framework of the aforementioned '*habeas data*'.

The *habeas data* action was born linked to the privacy or intimacy of the subjects. It was born as a constitutional guarantee or an action against all actions that produce a use of abusive, inaccurate or harmful personal information for people. With the action of habeas data, access to public and private data registers and files is allowed, with the purpose of adapting, updating, rectifying, cancelling or preserving the information of the citizen to whom is related said information.

The right to a private life free from interference is also recognized by the American Declaration of the Rights and Duties of Man,[3] as well as in the American Convention on Human Rights or 'Pact of San José'.[4] Likewise, in general, the possibility of accessing personal information, as well as updating or rectifying it, was recognized by the Inter-American Commission on Human Rights in 2000 in its Declaration of Principles on Freedom of Expression.[5]

In addition, the Member States of the RIPD have affirmed that the essence of their respective regulatory systems is the recognition of the right to personal data protection as a fundamental right.[6] In this sense, the aforementioned Ibero-American Standards also start from the consideration of the right to data protection as a fundamental right, 'that is recognized with maximum rank in the majority of the Political Constitutions of the Ibero-American States, in the form of the right to the protection of personal data or habeas data, and that in some cases has been defined jurisprudentially by its Courts or Constitutional Courts.'[7]

In this context, the *habeas data* action was recognized in the different Latin American States and it was recognized as a right of access and control over personal data. The *habeas*

---

[3] The American Declaration of the Rights and Duties of Man was adopted at the Ninth International American Conference, held in Bogotá, Colombia, 1948. Art V, under the rubric 'Right to protection of honour, personal reputation and private and family life', guarantees that 'Everyone has the right to the protection of the Law against abusive attacks on his honour, reputation and private and family life.'

[4] American Convention on Human Rights, signed at the Inter-American Specialized Conference on Human Rights (B-32) of the Organization of American States, held in San José, Costa Rica, from November 7–22, 1969, in which Art 11.2 on the Protection of Honour and Dignity states that: 'No one may be subjected to arbitrary or abusive interference with his privacy, that of his family, his home or his correspondence, nor to unlawful attacks on his honour or reputation.'

[5] Declaration of Principles on Freedom of Expression of the Inter-American Commission on Human Rights of the Organization of American States (OAS), adopted by the Inter-American Commission on Human Rights at its 108th regular session, held from 2–20 October 2000, Principle nº 3.

[6] Declaration of the XV Meeting of the Ibero-American Data Protection Network, in Santiago de Chile on 22 June 2017: 'The application of international standards and the harmonization of national legislation in the framework of the defence of fundamental rights.'

[7] Ibero-American Standards, p. 7.

data action is included in most of the Constitutions of the Ibero-American States. When the *habeas data* action is not recognized in the constitutional text, there are provisions that guarantee the privacy of citizens. Thus, we can cite as examples the Brazilian Federal Constitution of 1988 (Art 5), the Political Constitution of Colombia (Art 15), the Political Constitution of the Republic of Ecuador of 2008 (Art 92), the Constitution of Honduras of 1982 (Art 182), that of Peru (Art 200), or that of Paraguay of 1992 that incorporated the *habeas data* in the constitutional text.

In conclusion, we may say that the inclusion of personal data protection in the Constitutions of the countries of Latin America appeared with particular intensity in the 1980s and was consolidated in the 1990s and during the first decade of the 21st century. Along with this constitutional recognition, more and more Latin American countries started, at the same time, passing laws and specific rules to guarantee this right, or protect the private life or the honour of citizens. In this sense, in the Final Declaration of the XVIII RIPD Meeting of December 4, 2020, it was stated to recognize 'the need to promote regulatory convergence' through common principles included in the Ibero-American standards or in the OAS Principles (pto. 6).

However, we must also say that of all the provisions, only in the Chilean, Mexican, and in the Ecuadorian Constitution, is explicitly included the recognition of a right to the protection of personal data (Art 19.4º, Section 6, and Art 66.19, respectively), and in the Colombian and Dominican Constitution the right to data protection is recognized indirectly (Art 15 and Art 44.2, respectively).

II.2 The Grounds of the Right

The right to the personal data protection, as we have seen, is closely linked to the protection of privacy of individuals, including the protection of their honour or their self-image. In Latin America, as in most democratic States, while these rights are considered personal rights, and are related to the essence of personal development, they are also linked to human dignity.

Thus, the right to data protection or *habeas data* action is ultimately based on guaranteeing the free development of the personality and the personal dignity of citizens.

II.3 Holders and Obligated Persons

The holders of the right to the personal data protection or of the action of *habeas data* are, as a general rule, everybody, or 'every person'. Being a constitutionally recognized right, the right will enjoy the same ownership rules as the other rights, as recognized in the respective national Constitutions, especially with regard to legal persons.

Furthermore, this right obliges, according to constitutional texts natural or legal persons, most of the time, only public persons. However, the legal developments of the different Ibero-American States can stipulate that are they obliged to respect and guarantee the right to the protection of personal data, private legal persons. Also, subjects must respect the rights of the others.

If different Ibero-American Constitutions recognize this fundamental right, in the majority of the occasions they recognize that all people have the right to their personal and family privacy and to their good name, and that the State must respect these rights and enforce them. Therefore, the State is also bound.

II.4 Content and Limits

In the Latin American constitutional texts, in order to protect privacy, honour and self-image or, more expressly, the right to data protection, is defined the content and the limits of control of personal information. In this way the faculties that make up the right are recognized.

Thus, for example, is recognized the right of access to data stored in public and private databases (Argentina, Colombia, or Mexico), or data stored only in public databases (Argentina or Dominican Republic).

In addition, the right to inform the holder of the right to personal data protection is also recognized and also recognized is the right to know the use of the data (cf. Argentina; about the period of validity of the file or database, see Ecuador).

Other constitutional texts also expressly guarantee what is known as the right of rectification, that is, the right to demand the updating of data (Argentina, Colombia) or its correction (Colombia, Ecuador).

Finally, among the faculties of the holders of the right to personal data protection, the so-called right of cancellation is also recognized, that is, the right to request the elimination or destruction of data (Bolivia, Paraguay); or the so-called right of opposition to the processing of personal data (Mexico). And in relation to these cases, in some States reference is made to a blocking obligation for the sole purpose of determining possible responsibilities in relation to their treatment (Nicaragua).

As to obligations, some of constitutional texts recognize, within the security measures applicable to personal data, the obligation of confidentiality of personal information (Argentina).

II.5 Guarantees

Currently, at international and European level, and also at Latin American level, there are mechanisms to protect the rights derived from privacy, such as the right to personal data protection.

The right to personal data protection is guaranteed in Latin America through the *habeas data* action, which gives the holders of the right the possibility to file an action with the relevant legal mechanisms at the national level to know the data referred to them, as well as the purpose of the processing, at the same time that it allows to demand the data's rectification, suppression or cancellation. This specific right is *inter alia* recognized in the Argentine Constitution (Art 43) or in the Constitution of Peru (Art 200) or in that of the Dominican Republic (Art 70). Or in the Bolivian Constitution that recognizes the 'action of protection of privacy' (Art 130).

In many Latin American States, such as the case of Argentina, together with the protection granted by *habeas data*, there is the amparo and the habeas corpus. Interesting is also the case of Brazil (cf. Art 5.LXXII and LXXVII, which recognize the gratuity of said actions).

In addition, together with the guarantees inherent in any constitutionally guaranteed right, this right enjoys its own institutional guarantees, such as those called in this area, the 'Control Authorities' or data protection authorities. However, we must point out that, despite the region's regulatory advances in this area, not all Latin American States have a control authority, and this is one of the most controversial issues that can even paralyse the drafting of data protection laws (cf. the case of Chile). And many other States do not have authorities that deal expressly with the subject, but rather with related matters such as Bolivia's AGETIC (Agency of the Electronic Government and Information Technologies), which is more focused on the development and implementation of e-government and information and communication technologies; the Council of Citizen Participation and Social Control (CPCCS) with the Secretariat of Transparency and Fight against Corruption in Ecuador; or the Panama´s National Authority of Transparency and Access to Information (ANTAI). Likewise, we cannot forget the role that in Latin America the Ombudsmen play in the defense of this right, such as the Human Rights Ombudsman's Office of Guatemala, and more specifically within the Ombudsman's Office, the Secretariat for Access to Public Information (SECAI).

Among the States that have bodies to control the processing of personal data, can be mentioned:

- In Argentina, the Agency of Access to the Public Information (AAIP), which oversees the application of both the Argentine Data Protection Act as well as the Argentina Freedom of Information Act and the National 'Don't Call' Registry. The AAPI is a decentralized entity spinning off the Chief of Staff. In this country, is also relevant the fact that in the city of Buenos Aires there is as control body the Ombudsman of the City of Buenos Aires, although only competent for the data processing activities done by the Government of that city.[8]
- In Brazil, the National Data Protection Authority (ANPD), which is part of the Presidency of the Republic.[9] This Authority is to exclusively interpret the Brazilian Data Protection Law (Law 13.709/2018) and will only impose sanctions arising from the violation of said law. Its structure was approved and developed by Decree No. 10.474/220, which came into force on November 6, 2020.
- In Chile, there is no supervisory authority specifically charged with protecting the right; for the time being, the Transparency Council is the body with competence in this area. In 2017 a draft Law on data protection was presented and provides for a Data Protection Agency, which will see the light of day when the text is approved. Meanwhile, the Council for Transparency of Chile deals with the protection of privacy and its conflicts with transparency.[10]
- In Colombia, is competent the Superintendence of Industry and Commerce (SIC), through the Delegation for the Protection of Personal Data.[11] Although according to Statutory Law No. 1.266 the general control Authority is the aforementioned SIC, the Superintendence of Finance (SOF) is also mentioned, although it supervises only the financial authorities.
- In Costa Rica, the Agency for the Protection of Data of Inhabitants (Prodhab), attached to the Ministry of Justice and Peace, is considered as the Control Authority.[12]

---

8 Cf. https://www.argentina.gob.ar/aaip accessed 20 October 2021. This Agency was created by Law no 27.275, with functions in data protection by Decree no 746, of 25 September 2017.

9 The Authority was created by Law 13,709 of 14 August 2019, the General Law on Data Protection, but its implementation was vetoed. Its creation and implementation was again provided for by Executive Order 869/18 of 28 December, which became Law 13,853 of 8 July 2019.

10 Cf. https://www.consejotransparencia.cl/ accessed 20 October 2021.

11 Cf. http://www.sic.gov.co/delegatura-para-la-proteccion-de-datos-personales accessed 20 October 2021.

12 Cf. http://prodhab.go.cr/ accessed 20 October 2021.

- In El Salvador, the Institute for Access to Public Information (IAIP) has competence over the processing of personal data as provided for in the Law on Access to Public Information (Decree no 534/2013).[13]
- In Honduras, although there is no right to data protection or a law that regulates it, the Law of Transparency and Access to Public Information (Legislative Decree no 170-2006), regulates the guarantee of *habeas data* and entrusts its protection to the Institute of Access to Public Information (IAIP).[14]
- In Mexico, the Control Authority is the National Institute of Transparency, Access to Public Information and Protection of Personal Data (INAI), which was granted constitutional autonomy in 2004.[15]
- In Nicaragua, the Control Authority is the Directorate of Personal Data Protection attached to the Ministry of Finance and Public Credit Law No. 787 of 29 March 2012 provides for its creation (Art 28).
- In Paraguay, the control authorities are the Central Bank of Paraguay and the Secretariat for Consumer and User Defense (established by art. 20 Law No. 6.534/2020 on the Protection of Personal Credit Data), although it only deals with controlling credit and consumer reports.
- In Peru, the body in charge of controlling the right to data protection is the National Authority for the Protection of Personal Data is the Ministry of Justice, through the National Directorate of Justice[16] or the National Directorate for the Protection of Personal Data within the General Directorate of Transparency, Access to Public Information and Protection of Personal Data (APDP).
- In the Dominican Republic, the control body is the Superintendency of Banks, although it only deals with controlling credit reports,[17] as established by Law No 172-13 on Data Protection (Art 29).
- In Uruguay, we find the Agency for the Development of the Government of Electronic Management and the Society of Information and Knowledge (AGESIC)[18] and the Regulatory and Personal data control unit (URCDP).

Regarding data protection authorities, we must point out that, to date, the Authorities that exist at the Latin American level and are part of the aforementioned RIPD as members are those of Argentina (AAIP), Chile (CT), Colombia (SIC-DPD), Costa Rica (PRODHAB), Mexico (INAI, InfoDF, INFOEM), and Uruguay (URCDP), to which are joined those of Spain (AEPD, and the regional APDCAT and AVPD) and also Andorra (APDA), which is not part of Latin America.

---

13 Cf. https://www.iaip.gob.sv/ accessed 20 October 2021.
14 Cf. https://web.iaip.gob.hn/ accessed 20 October 2021.
15 Cf. http://inicio.inai.org.mx/SitePages/ifai.aspx accessed 20 October 2021.
16 Cf. https://www.minjus.gob.pe/dgtaipd/ accessed 20 October 2021.
17 Cf. http://www.sb.gob.do/ accessed 20 October 2021.
18 Vid. https://www.gub.uy/unidad-reguladora-control-datos-personales/ accessed 20 October 2021.

III. THE LEGAL REGULATION OF THE RIGHT TO PERSONAL DATA PROTECTION IN LATIN AMERICA

We have already seen how the Latin American region has been strongly influenced when it comes to recognizing the right to personal data protection by international treaties and European norms that guarantee and protect human rights. This same influence is manifest regarding the model for regulating the processing of personal data in the region.

The norms approved by the different Latin American States have been influenced by both the North American and the European systems, although different States of the region followed this last model in order to be able to establish commercial relations with Europe, requiring a level of 'adequate protection'. This European model will be governed both by the current European Data Protection Regulation (the GDPR), as well as by the Convention No. 108 of 1981, of the Council of Europe, modernized today through an Additional Protocol, known as Convention 108+, opened for signature in October 2018.[19] If we bear in mind that Convention 108+ is overall governed by the same principles as those of the GDPR, its entry into force will result in the existence of data protection principles on a global scale, which will allow a better flow of personal data from all the States that have ratified it.[20]

Although the European model is a benchmark for Latin America, we cannot forget the membership of some Latin States to the Forum of Asia-Pacific Economic Cooperation (APEC), which forces them to assume their Framework of Privacy and compliance with the privacy system of the APEC, based on a certification model, if they want to negotiate with the countries within the Asia-Pacific region.

With this same commercial purpose, more than as a guarantee of the right to personal data protection, the Guidelines on the subject of the Organization for Economic Cooperation and Development (OECD) approved in 1980, have also been a reference in the region.[21] In this sense, the OECD currently brings together almost 40 countries, among which, from Latin America are Chile or Mexico, so these Guidelines are a benchmark beyond the EU and the US.

Taking into account these references, the RIPD has been emphasizing the need for the Latin American region to comply with a common denominator, taking into account, especially, that data processing is not an issue that can be limited by the traditional limits of space and time, especially due to the advancement of the Internet and new technologies.

For these reasons, and with the aim of establishing international standards applicable to the protection of personal data, the RIPD approved in 2007, at the V Ibero-American Meeting on Data Protection, the so-called Guidelines for the Harmonization of Data Protection in the Ibero-American Community,[22] also known as the Lisbon Guidelines, recommending, in the Declaration of Lisbon resulting from this meeting, the adhesion by the members of the Network to the Convention no 108 of the Council of Europe, in its quality of international

[19] The Protocol or Convention 108+ was adopted by the Committee of Ministers of the Council of Europe on 18 May 2018, and opened for signature on 10 October 2018.

[20] Of all the Latin American States, the first to sign it on 10 October 2018 was Uruguay, followed by Argentina on 19 September 2019. Council of Europe sources reported that Chile, Costa Rica and Brazil could be next.

[21] OECD Guidelines on privacy protection and cross-border flows of personal data. They are set out in the Recommendation adopted by the OECD Council on 23 September 1980.

[22] Held in Lisbon, Portugal, on 8 and 9 November 2007.

regulatory instrument in the matter. This recommendation was reiterated a year later in the Declaration of Cartagena de Indias of 2008.

The universal standards approved at the XXXI International Conference of Data Protection and Privacy Authorities in 2009, known as the 'Madrid Resolution', seeking universal international criteria that would serve as a reference for all States that would like to approve their rules for processing personal data or modernize existing ones, must also be mentioned. The Madrid Resolution is a benchmark in that the standards it contains can be applied to any State, regardless of their conception of privacy or protection of personal data and regulatory models followed.

This was further agreed in June 2016, at the XIV Meeting of the RIPD that took place in Colombia. It was the Authority of Control of Mexico, the INAI who was responsible for drafting the aforementioned Standards, which led to the aforementioned 'Ibero-American Standards' in June 2017. It is the opinion of the members of the RIPD that, 'the homogenization of rules, principles, rights and duties, derived from the application of the criteria included in the approved Standards, in the respective national legislations, will allow reaching new levels of international cooperation, will facilitate the cross-border flows of data and, ultimately, will ensure effective protection of the right to protection of personal data.'[23]

In the same way, in the Strategic Guidelines of the RIPD for 2020[24] the RIPD considered it necessary to provide itself with guidelines or standards that would serve as a parameter for future regulations or for the revision of existing ones in the Latin American region.

Thus emerged the Ibero-American Standards.[25] These Standards were approved in accordance with the manifestation held at the XXV Ibero-American Summit of Heads of State and Government, with the aim of adopting not only 'guarantees that generate confidence in current technological developments ... not only harmonized criteria ... but also an intense and reinforced cooperation action to promote the development of good practices at the international level'.[26]

Among the objectives of the Ibero-American Standards are: to establish a set of common principles and rights for the protection of personal data; guarantee the effective exercise and guarantee the right to personal data protection; facilitate the flow of personal data between Ibero-American States and beyond their borders; and favouring international cooperation among the control authorities the following.[27]

In this regard, we cannot forget the work carried out not only by the RIPD, but also by the Ibero-American Observatory of Data Protection, especially through different 'declarations' or documents that have been approved as a result of their meetings. The Observatory, which was born in 2013, is the result of a meeting forum whose main purpose was to extend the culture of privacy and data protection in Latin America. The exchange of experiences and opinions are

---

[23] Declaration of the XV Meeting of the Ibero-American Data Protection Network, in Santiago de Chile on 22 June 2017: 'The application of international standards and the harmonization of national legislation in the framework of the defence of fundamental rights'.

[24] Cf. at: https://www.redipd.org/sites/default/files/inline-files/DOCUMENTO_RIPD_2020.pdf accessed 20 October 2021.

[25] The version resulting from the work carried out during the close session on the Cartagena de Indias workshop was unanimously approved and it was formally proclaimed in the Open Session held at the XV Ibero-American Data Protection Meeting, held from 20–22 June 2017 in Santiago de Chile.

[26] RIPD 2020.

[27] Ibero-American Standards.

thus reflected in the different declarations that are published after the corresponding meetings. There are notably the Declarations of Lima,[28] Barranquilla,[29] Buenos Aires,[30] Santiago de Chile,[31] La Plata,[32] Riobamba (Ecuador),[33] Panamá,[34] México,[35] and San José (Costa Rica).[36] Throughout all the Declarations, and because there is a component of internationality and universality in the Network, what is emphasized is that the different national legislations alone cannot give an adequate response to the data protection problems. For instance, there must be coordinated action to prevent companies moving to 'data paradises', that is, countries that do not offer adequate levels of privacy protection.

Finally, and in this line of seeking a unique and universal model for the Latin American region, we must highlight the draft Inter-American Model Law on Personal Data Protection prepared within the Organisation of American States (OAS).[37] The proposal, as a Model Law, is aimed at establishing general parameters, guidelines, so that the States can then incorporate them into their internal legislation.[38] The Project, the roots of which date back to June

---

[28] The Declaration of Lima, towards the unification of normative criteria on data protection and privacy in Ibero-America, elaborated from the initiative of the Ibero-American Data Protection Observatory, presented in the city of Lima (Peru) on 12 April 2013.

[29] The Barranquilla Declaration, towards the unification of instruments for the protection of privacy in Ibero-America, drafted on the initiative of the Ibero-American Data Protection Observatory, was presented in the city of Barranquilla (Colombia) on 1 June 2013.

[30] The Declaration of Buenos Aires, towards the unification of educational criteria for the protection of privacy in Ibero-America, drawn up by the initiative of the Ibero-American Data Protection Observatory, was presented in the Autonomous City of Buenos Aires (Argentina) on 11 July 2013.

[31] The Santiago Declaration, towards a unification of criteria on security and data protection on the Internet, drawn up from the initiative of the Ibero-American Data Protection Observatory, presented in the city of Santiago (Chile) on 12 September 2013.

[32] The Declaration of La Plata, towards the unification of criteria in the protection of personal data of children and adolescents, drafted on the initiative of the Ibero-American Data Protection Observatory, was presented in the City of La Plata, on Wednesday 20 November 2013.

[33] The Declaration of Riobamba, towards the unification of criteria and security measures in data protection, elaborated from the initiative of the Ibero-American Data Protection Observatory, was presented at the University of Chimborazo (city of Riobamba of the Republic of Ecuador), on 29 March 2014.

[34] The Declaration of Panama City, towards the unification of criteria and guarantees for the protection of digital identity and the right to forget, prepared by the initiative of the Ibero-American Data Protection Observatory, was presented at Harmodio Arias Auditorium of the National Bar Association of Panama, on 23 July 2014.

[35] The Declaration of Mexico City, towards the implementation of guarantees for privacy in Big Data treatments, drawn up on the initiative of the Ibero-American Data Protection Observatory, was presented on Saturday 23 August 2014.

[36] The Declaration of San José, towards the implementation of a Seal on the processing of personal data in Ibero-America, prepared on the initiative of the Ibero-American Data Protection Observatory, presented in the city of San José (Costa Rica) on 15 March 2016.

[37] The aforementioned OAS was created in 1948, following the signing of the OAS Charter in Bogota, Colombia, which entered into force in 1951, becoming the first governmental, political, legal and social forum in Latin America, composed of 35 independent States in the region. To see the States that make up the OAS, see http://www.oas.org/es/estados_miembros/default.asp accessed 20 October 2021.

[38] We highlight here, e.g., the Model Inter-American Law on Access to Public Information, approved on 8 June 2010 by the OAS General Assembly which was expanded and updated, being approved on October 21, 2020 as the Inter-American Model Law 2.0 on Access to Public Information. See http://www.oas.org/es/sla/ddi/docs/AG-RES_2607_XL-O-10_esp.pdf accessed 20 October 2021.

1996,[39] is essentially based on the study prepared by the Department of International Law of the OAS, presented in October 2011,[40] and on the Document prepared by the Inter-American Juridical Committee of the OAS (CJI) on the Proposed Declaration of Principles on Privacy and Personal Data Protection in the Americas, presented in March 2012.[41] and the Legislative Guide on Privacy and Data Protection in the Americas, approved in 2015.[42] Thus, on the basis of these documents, especially on the 12 principles presented in the 2012 Declaration,[43] work was carried out on a Draft Model Law.[44] However, on April 9, 2021, the update of the aforementioned Privacy and Data Protection Principles with annotations was approved by the OAS. These Updated Principles recognize the importance of promoting legal development and harmonization, as well as transparency in data processing, accountability, security of sensitive data, streamlining domestic and international trade, and empowering citizens.[45]

IV. CURRENT NATIONAL REGULATORY FRAMEWORKS

In Latin America, in addition to the recognition of the right to data protection, we can find States that have their data protection Act, to which can be added in some cases specific or sectorial regulatory developments on the subject (Argentina, Brazil, Colombia, Costa Rica,

---

[39] On 7 June 1996, the OAS General Assembly issued a resolution requesting the Inter-American Juridical Committee (CJI) to attach importance in its studies and projects to the protection of personal data and its situation in the OAS Member States.

[40] Cf. *Preliminary Principles and Recommendations on Data Protection (The Protection of Personal Data)*, presented by the Department of International Law of the OAS Secretariat for Legal Affairs (CP/CAJP-2921/10 rev.1 corr.1), on 17 October 2011 (http://www.oas.org/es/sla/ddi/docs/CP-CAJP-2921-10_rev1_corr1_esp.pdf accessed 20 October 2021).

[41] See *Proposed Declaration of Principles on Privacy and Personal Data Protection in the Americas*, presented by the CJI (CJI/RES. 186 (LXXX-O/12), 9 March 2012 (http://www.oas.org/es/sla/cji/docs/CJI-RES_186_LXXX-O-12.pdf accessed 20 October 2021).

[42] Vid. Legislative Guide on Privacy and Data Protection Personal in the Americas (http://www.oas.org/en/sla/iajc/docs/personal_data_protection_CJI_Legislative_Guide_2015.pdf accessed 12 December 2021).

[43] These principles are intended to prevent illegal use of personal data and are as follows: 1. Legitimate and Fair Purposes; 2. Clarity and Consent; 3. Relevance and Need; 4. Limited Use and Retention; 5. Duty of Confidentiality; 6. Protection and Security; 7. Fidelity of Information; 8. Access and Correction; 9. Sensitive Information; 10. Responsibility; 11. Cross-Border Flow of Information and Responsibility; and 12. Publicity of Exceptions.

[44] We highlight here, in the process of elaboration of the Model Law, the reports presented by David P. Stewart as rapporteur of the topic, on 25th February 2014 (*Privacidad y protección de datos,* CJI/doc.450/14), and on 26 March 2015 (CJI/doc.474/15 rev 2), version adopted by the CJI on 27 March 2015. See, respectively: http://www.oas.org/es/sla/ddi/docs/proteccion_datos_personales_documentos_referencia_CJI_doc_450-14.pdf; and https://www.redipd.org/sites/default/files/inline-files/Informe_CJI-doc_474-15_rev2_26_03_15.pdf both accessed 20 October 2021. Stewart found it more convenient and practical to develop a Legislative Guide based on the 12 principles of the 2012 Declaration, rather than a Model Law.

[45] See http://www.oas.org/es/sla/cji/docs/CJI-doc_638-21.pdf accessed 12 December 2021. These updated principles are now thirteen: 1. Legitimate and fair Purposes; 2. Transparency and Consent; 3. Relevance and Necessity; 4. Limited Processing and Retention; 5. Confidentiality; 6. Data Security; 7. Data Accuracy; 8. Access, Rectification, Cancellation, Opposition and Portability; 9. Sensitive personal data; 10. Accountability; 11. Transborder Data Flow and Liability; 12. Exceptions; and 13. Data Protection Authorities.

México, Nicaragua, Panamá, Perú, Dominican Republic or Uruguay). However, we also find States that are preparing it (Bolivia, Chile, Ecuador, El Salvador or Guatemala), as well as States that do not have any reference norm (Honduras, Paraguay or Venezuela).

In any case, national legislations tend to move towards the criteria established in the Ibero-American Standards, on the understanding that only with the adoption of common criteria by all States can a correct treatment of personal data be guaranteed. In addition, the fact that most Latin American countries, with the exception of Argentina and Uruguay,[46] do not offer an 'adequate level of protection' as recognized by Europe means that Latin American States seek to comply with common criteria that facilitate exchange and transfers of information with Europe.

- Argentina. This State, in addition to having the constitutional recognition of the *habeas data* action (s 43), has the Law no 25.326, of November 2, 2000, on Data Protection, as well as a Decree on the development thereof, the Decree no 1558/2001, or the creation of the National Registry 'Don't call', created by Law No. 26,951 of 2 July 2014. The Argentinian legislation stands out for having a comprehensive and specific regulation of the matter and for being one of the Ibero-American States that have the recognition of having an adequate level of protection to carry out international transfers with Europe.[47] It was also one of the first Latin American States to sign the aforementioned Convention 108+ in September 2019. In this sense, Argentina has become the main recipient of personal data transferred from Spain to Latin American countries. Together with these norms, we must highlight the provisions issued by its Control Authority, the Agency of Access to the Public Information (AAIP).
- Bolivia. In addition to constitutionally recognizing the guarantee of privacy (Article 21) and the *habeas data* action called 'action of protection of privacy' (Art 130), it guarantees the processing of personal data not through a specific rule, but of sectoral laws such as, for example, the Law no 28.168 of 18 May 2005, on Access to Information of the Executive Power (which recognizes in its Art 19 the request for habeas data), or the Law no 164, of 8 August 2011, on General Telecommunications, Information and Communication Technologies, whose Development Decree (Supreme Decree no 1793, of 13 November 2013) recognizes, for example, the right to the protection of personal data (Art 56). We also highlight the Digital Citizenship Law (Law no 1080 of 11th July 2018) which provides for the processing of personal data limited to the legally established purpose (Art 12) and which opened up the need for a new data protection law in Bolivia at the II Internet Governance Forum, held in Bolivia in December 2018. Since that same year, in 2018, a first proposal for a Personal Data Protection Law was presented, and in May 2019 the proposal for a Citizens' Law on Privacy and Data Protection in Bolivia. They are still pending approval.
- Brazil. Along with constitutional recognition of the *habeas data* action (Art 5 LXXII and LXXVII), Brazil was the first State to have a specific regulation on the matter or a control authority based on the GDPR, and that also has sectoral regulations such as, for example,

[46] Adequate level of protection granted to Argentina by Commission Decision 2003/490/EC of 30 June 2003 and to Uruguay by Commission Decision 2012/484/EU of 21 August 2012.

[47] Adequate level of protection granted to Argentina by Commission Decision 2003/490/EC of 30 June 2003.

the Law no 9.507, of 12 November 1997, which recognizes and regulates the action of habeas data (Article 1), or the Law no 12.527, of 8 November 2011, about Access to the Information, that limits the right of access to personal information to transparent and privacy-aware access (Art 31). Also, in Brazil the Internet Civil Framework was approved (Law no 12.965, of 23 April 2014), known as the 'Internet Constitution' in order to guarantee freedom and privacy in the Internet, establishing, among other things, the general prohibition of exchanging personal data with third parties without their express consent. This legislation, together with the reference of the European GDPR, served as a reference for a new personal data Law: The General Data Protection Law (Law no 13.709 of 14 August 2018, LGPD) which provides for a Supervisory Authority, the Brazilian National Data Protection Authority (ANPD), created by Executive Order No. 869/2018, of 27th December, converted into Law no 13.853 of 8 July 2019, which provides for the entry into force of data protection regulations by August 2020. In this way, Brazil becomes the first country in Latin America to have a rule that follows the model of the GDPR as can be seen, for example, in the extraterritorial effectiveness of the law or in the requirement of an adequate level of protection for data transfers outside the country, although it contains aspects that differ from this rule such as the fact of notifications in the event of security breaches, where the Brazilian law does not establish any time limit to inform.

- Chile. Although Chile is a benchmark in the treatment of personal information to comply with the obligation of transparency, Chile does not have a general rule on Personal Data Protection or a Control Authority, although in the absence thereof, the Council for Transparency is competent to ensure respect for privacy on the part ('only') of the State Administration. Chile constitutionally recognizes the right to privacy (Art 19) and expressly the right to data protection (Art 19.4, since Law 21.096, of 5 June 2018), which is also guaranteed by the Law 19.628, of 28 August 1999, on the Protection of Private Life; and, in addition, it has an important list of sectoral rules on the matter, such as the Law 19.223, of 7 June 1993 on Computer Crimes, or the Law. However, at present, since mid-2016, work is being done on a standard that corrects the deficiencies in data protection in this country, as well as the recognition and creation of a National Directorate for Data Protection. In September 2019 a project was presented, which is in the final phase in the Senate's Constitution Commission, but which is paralyzed, specifically, by the discussion on the creation of a new control authority or the splitting into two Chambers of the Council for Transparency with functions of transparency and personal data protection, respectively. The project proposes to adapt Law 19.628 to international and European standards and to perfect the bases of legitimacy of the processing of personal data, and to reinforce the principle of security by linking it to the duty of diligence.
- Colombia. In addition to the constitutional recognition of the right to privacy and proper use of personal data (Art 15), Colombia has a specific regulation on the processing of personal data, such as the Statutory Law no 1.581 of 17 October 2012, by which General Provisions for the Protection of General Data are enacted, or the Statutory Law no 1.266, of 31 December 2008, by which General Provisions on Habeas Data are issued and the handling of information contained in databases personal information; and, in addition, a sectoral legislation supplemented to the general one already mentioned, such as, for example, the Decree no 886 of 13 May 2014, about the National Register of Databases, or the Law no 1.712 of 6 March 2014, on Transparency and Right of Access to National Public Information. We must point out here that the Colombian Constitutional Court has

played a very important role in the work of both the recognition of the right to data protection and in the regulation of the treatment of personal data, establishing the rules for the processing of personal data, especially those that refer to financial or credit information. This has resulted in draft laws on financial habeas data of July 2019, which will amend Law no 1.266 on Habeas data.

- Costa Rica. In addition to guaranteeing the right to privacy constitutionally (Article 24), there is a general Law on data protection, the Law no 8.968, of 7 July 2011, on Protection of the Person against the processing of their personal data, and its Development Regulation (Executive Decree no 37.554-JP, of 30 October 2012). This Decree was amended in 2019 by Executive Decree no 41.582 of 21 February 2019, in order to guarantee the right to informational self-determination and the role of its Supervisory Authority (Prodhab).
- Ecuador. It is one of the few Ibero-American States that expressly recognizes in its constitutional text the right to data protection (Art 66.19) and differentiated from the right to privacy (Art 66.20) or the action of habeas data (Art 94), but does not have a General Law of personal data protection. Ecuador regulates the processing of personal data with sectoral regulations, such as the Law no 162 of 31 March 2010 on the National Public Data Registration System, or the Organic Law no 24 of 18 May 2004 of Transparency and Access to Public Information. In October 2016 a bill was presented to protect the right to privacy and the personal data, which proposes the creation of a 'National Directorate for the Registration of Public Data', which is still under study. Once again, in September 2019 the aforementioned project was promoted before the National Assembly within the proposal of the Ministry of Telecommunications presented in May 2019 called 'Digital Ecuador' aimed at digitalizing public administration, and which provides for the existence of a National Personal Data Protection Register and a Data Protection Authority attached to the Presidency.
- El Salvador. It contains nothing more than a constitutional guarantee of privacy (Art 2) and sectoral laws on the matter, focusing more specifically on transparency and access to public information, such as the Law on Access to Public Information (approved by Decree no 534, of 30 March 2011), in which the Title III regulates the protection of personal data; the Law regulating the Information Services on the Credit History of Persons (approved by Legislative Decree no 695, of 27 July 2011); or Decree no 133 of 1 October 2015, which, in a new way in Latin America, approved the Electronic Signature Law, offering definitions such as personal data and sensitive personal data, including among such data those relating to the marital status of the person (Art 3) or collecting the rights of rectification and cancellation of personal data (Art 5). In November 2019, the Legislative Assembly's Economy Committee began to study different proposals aimed at approving a new data protection Law that is expected to come into force before the end of 2020, but which raises doubts as to whether the Control Authority should be the aforementioned IAIP or the Consumer Ombudsman's Office.
- Guatemala. This country constitutionally recognizes access to public records and archives (Art 31) and the right to privacy (Art 26), and sectoral regulates the processing of personal data, such as, for example, with the Law on Access to Public Information (approved by Decree no 57-2008, of 22 October 2008), or with the Criminal Code (approved by Decree no 17-1973, of 27 July), whose Art 274.D) establishes as a cybercrime the creation of databases that may affect the privacy of individuals. Since 2009, a draft law on personal data protection (Initiative 4090/2009) has been under study, in which the conflicting issue

is the creation of a decentralized Directorate for Personal Data Protection within the Office of the Human Rights Ombudsman.

- Honduras. The constitutional text of Honduras guarantees both the right to privacy (Art 76) and the habeas data action (Art 182, after constitutional amendment carried out by Legislative Decree no 381-2005, of 20 January 2006). But Honduras does not have a general rule on data protection, but regulates the matter in a sectoral manner, such as, for example, through the Law on Transparency and Access to Public Information (approved by the Decree no 170-2006, of November), which regulates the action of *habeas data* in its Chapter III.
- México. Of all the Ibero-American countries, together with Argentina, Brazil or Chile, México is one of the States in the region that has evolved the most when it comes to regulating the processing of personal data. Thus, together with Ecuador and Chile, it is the only other country that expressly recognizes in its constitutional text a right to the protection of personal data (Arts 6 and 16 since constitutional reform by Decree of 1 June 2009), not forgetting Colombia and the Dominican Republic, which recognize it indirectly. And it also has a new specific rule to regulate the processing of personal data such as the Federal Law on Protection of Personal Data Held by Private Parties (of 13 December 2016, published in the Official Gazette of the Federation, on 26 January 2017), and with the provision of its supervisory Authority already mentioned, the National Institute of Transparency, Access to Information and Protection of Personal Data (INAI). These specific rules are completed, for example, with the regulations on transparency in the country, guaranteed by the Federal Law on Transparency and Access to Government Public Information (published in the Official Gazette of the Federation, June 11, 2002). In addition to this federal regulation, the Mexican States also have their rules on the subject, although we have to say that most of them focus on regulating transparency and access to information rather than the processing of personal data. As an exception we find the data protection Laws of the States of Campeche, Colima, the Federal District, Guanajuato, Mexico, Oaxaca and Tlaxcala. Mexican regulations have become one of the most solid in the region, highlighting, in addition, being a flexible regulation that is easily adaptable to the online environment due to the way in which it regulates the consent requirement.
- Nicaragua. It also expressly recognizes in its constitutional text the right to privacy and the habeas data action (Art 26). Although it does not expressly recognize the right to data protection, it does expressly regulate the processing of personal data through the Law no 787, of 21 March 2012, of Protection of Personal Data, as well as its implementing regulations, approved by Decree no 36-2012 of 17 October 2012.
- Panama. In addition to the recognition of the habeas data action (Arts 42–44), Panama has had a data protection Act since 2019: the Law no 81, of 26 March 2019, on Personal Data Protection. This norm lives with sectoral regulations, such as for example, the Law no 6, of 22 January 2002, on Transparency and Access to Public Information that develops the aforementioned *habeas data* action (Arts 3, 13 and 17), or through the Law no 24, of 22 May 2002, on the Credit history Arts 23 and 30.
- Paraguay. In Paraguay there is no general law on the subject, although the *habeas data* action is expressly guaranteed in its Constitution (Art 135), as well as the right to privacy (Art 33). The processing of personal data is regulated through sectoral laws such as, for example, the Law no 1.682 of 16 January 2001, on Private Information, which regulates the right of every person 'to collect, store and process personal data for strictly private

use'; or, through the Law no 4.989, of 9 August 2013, by which the National Secretariat of Information and Communication Technologies (SENATIC) is created, responsible for formulating all ICT development policies. On October 27, 2020, was passed the Law No. 6.534/2020 on the Protection of Personal Credit Data, and the aforementioned Law 1.682/2001 was repealed (art. 30). The new Law is limited to credit data, leaving all other personal data unprotected. Therefore, on April 30, 2021, the draft D-2162170 on Data Protection Law was presented during an event organized by the Science and Technology Committee of the Parliament in order to promote a comprehensive protection of personal data.

- Peru. In addition to constitutionally guaranteeing access to personal information and the *habeas data* action (Arts 2 and 200, respectively), it has a Law on data protection, the Law no 29.733 of 3 July 2011, on the Protection of Personal Data, and a Regulation of its development (approved by Supreme Decree no 003-2013-JUS, published on 22 March 2013). The case of Peru stands out because in addition to paying special attention to the treatment of the minors' personal data and the information published in the media, it is part of the APEC Forum, thus accepting the measures for guaranteeing privacy provided by it. Peru also has a large number of sectoral regulations in banking and insurance, health, public safety, telecommunications and transport, such as Law no 30.024 creating the National Registry of Electronic Medical Records (of 22 May 2013).
- Dominican Republic. It is one of the few States in the region that, in addition to constitutionally recognizing the right to data protection (Art 44) and the *habeas data* action (Art 70), contains a specific rule for the processing of personal data, the Organic Law 172-13, (of 'Protection of Personal Data'), which aims at the comprehensive protection of personal data held in archives, public registers, data banks or other technical means of data processing intended for reporting purposes, whether public or private. This norm is completed with other sectoral regulations such as the provisions of the General Law 200-04, of 28 July 2004, on Free Access to Public Information or the General Law 310-14, which regulates the sending of unsolicited commercial e-mails (*spam*).
- Uruguay. Although the Uruguayan Constitution does not contain an express mention of the processing of personal data, but only protection of honour, address and correspondence (Arts 7, 11 and 13), Uruguay expressly regulates the treatment of personal data through the Law no 18.331, of 11 November 2008, on Protection of Personal Data and Habeas Data Action, which is completed by the Law no 18.381, of 7 November 2008, which regulates Access to Information public, in addition to other sectoral regulations, such as, for example, the Law no 19.030, of 7 January 2013, which approves the aforementioned Convention no 108 of the Council of Europe; the Decree no 664/008 of 22 December 2008, created by the Register of Personal Data Bases; or the Decree no 396/003, of 20 September 2003, on Personal data relating to health. The data protection regulation of Uruguay stands out, because as happened with the case of Argentina, from the EU it recognized that said legislation guaranteed a level of data protection equivalent to the European,[48] and because it was the first State in the region to sign Convention 108+, as soon as it was opened for signature on 10 October 2018.

[48] Adequate level of protection granted to Uruguay by Commission Decision 2012/484/EU of 21 August 2012.

- Venezuela. The Venezuelan constitutional text protects private life (Art 60) and includes the *habeas data* action (Arts 28 and 281), but there is no specific rule that develops the processing of personal data, although it is currently in draft. What we can find in this State are sectoral regulations such as, for example, the Law on Access to and Electronic Exchange of Data, Information and Documents between State Bodies and Entities (approved by Decree No. 9.051 of June 15, 2012).

As we can see from the norms approved in the different Ibero-American States, while some States have developed their own laws for the protection of privacy or protection of personal data (like Chile with its Law no 19.628 of 1999), others have focused on a sectoral regulation of the matter, like Guatemala or Paraguay. However, all follow a pattern of more or less common characteristics.

V. GENERAL CHARACTERISTICS

While it is true that there are differences between Latin American states because not everyone recognizes the right to data protection or *habeas data* and not all have a regulation of the matter, States that have rules on the matter confirm some general criteria.

It can be said that the differences between existing norms are subtle. Thus, for example, in some States legal persons are protected, as in Argentina, while in the majority of States they are excluded from the concept of personal data protection. But the greatest differences are found, for example, in the recognition of the principle of consent and in the requirement of its express or implicit nature, as well as in relation to the principle of purpose limitation, which is not recognized by all States; in the criteria for an international transfer of personal data, not recognized by all States, as is the case of Chile; in the regulation of data processing and the rights of individuals when processing occurs on the Internet, to which very few States pay attention; in relation to security measures, where security is usually left to the free disposal of the controller as Costa Rica, or is followed by a system of levels, as in Peru, or is not established any measure as in Nicaragua; or in relation to the sanctioning regime, where the sanctions range from the possible warning to the penalties of deprivation of liberty as in Mexico.

However, the criteria that follow the existing standards have been captured and included in the aforementioned Ibero-American Standards, in order to harmonize the regulation for the protection of personal data in the sector, so that they can serve as an example to the States that do not count with rules on the processing of personal data or for the States that have them, adapt them to achieve greater homogeneity.

In relation to the principles that should govern all processing of personal data, the Ibero-American Standards recognize the principles of legitimacy, legality, loyalty, transparency, purpose limitation, proportionality, quality, responsibility, security and confidentiality. At this point, the legality or lawfulness of the treatment, based mainly on consent, requires the person responsible to demonstrate 'in an indubitable way that holder granted its [sic] consent, whether through a clear representation or affirmation', which will be reflected by a clear affirmative action or declaration, omitting any reference to an implicit consent. On the other hand, special emphasis is placed on the principle of transparency in the processing of data, requiring those responsible to inform the owner of the treatment carried out so that he can make informed decisions in this regard, as in the principle of responsibility or accountability, requiring that the mechanisms established to comply with this principle of responsibility be permanently reviewed and evaluated.[49]

In relation to the rights of the holders of personal data protection, the Ibero-American Standards, in addition to recognizing the traditional rights of access, rectification, cancellation and opposition, recognizes the right to portability of the data, although curiously, the right to be forgotten is not mentioned, although it is recognized in some Latin American States such as Costa Rica, Nicaragua or Uruguay. There is also no reference to the processing of data over the Internet (except in a timely manner in its *Consideranda*), which is causing considerable controversy in the region and which would have been convenient to harmonize.[50]

In relation to the security measures to be implemented to protect any data processing that occurs, they must be homogeneous enough to allow the interoperability of security protocols, networks and systems in a globalized world. The Ibero-American Standards establish a series of factors to determine the administrative, physical and technical measures necessary to guarantee the confidentiality, integrity and availability of the data. These factors include both the state of the art and the purposes of the treatment or previous violations occurred, in addition to establishing that the measures implemented should be monitored and reviewed continuously. In connection with security measures, the obligation to report security incidents or breaches is highlighted. Given that in Colombia, companies must inform their Control Authority, but in Mexico or Uruguay only the data owner must be informed and there is no uniformity in the matter, the Ibero-American Standards require notification both to the Control Authority and to the headlines without any delay.[51] We highlight here the Brazilian standard that will come into force in 2020 and that indicates, as a measure to ensure the integrity and preservation of personal data, that companies should evaluate the adoption of more robust security management through ISO standards, such as the ISO 27.001, which provides for the creation of specific security policies.

In relation to international transfers of personal data, while in some States such as Argentina they sometimes require anonymization of confidential data to be transferred and in others they prohibit transfers to those States that do not comply with an adequate level of protection, the Ibero-American Standards include certain rules general that may be limited for reasons of 'national security, public safety, protection of public health, protection of the rights and freedoms of third parties, as well as issues of public interest'.[52] In this area, cooperation with APEC is particularly important in order to promote economic growth and harmonize interoperability between the different legal systems, adapting to the Transboundary Protection Rules approved by APEC in 2011. From the Standards of Privacy of APEC is promoted not only the fulfilment of its principles but the collaboration between the Control Authorities of the States parties of the APEC and the Ibero-American States.

In relation to the sanctions system, the Ibero-American Standards recognize the right of the holder of data protection rights to claim before the National Control Authority, being the Ibero-American States the ones that must establish the corresponding regime for this to be possible. Likewise, a harmonizing criterion is needed for sanctions to set the maximum limit

---

[49] About the Principles, cf. Cap. II Ibero-American Standards.

[50] About the Rights, cf. Cap. III Ibero-American Standards.

[51] About Security Measures, cf. Standards 21–23 Ibero-American Standards.

[52] About International transfers, cf. Cap. V Ibero-American Standards.

and the objective criteria by which they are set, being able to take into account the nature of the infraction, the seriousness, the duration and its consequences.[53]

In relation to Control Authorities, since not all States have this protection mechanism, the Ibero-American Standards require their recognition, as well as a homogenization of their functions.[54] Some States, such as México, do not require the registration of those responsible for the data processing in their Control Authorities and other States strengthen their sanctions system as the Peruvian Authority, and therefore is set general criteria. The Ibero-American Standards in addition to demanding the existence of these Authorities, demand the independence in their powers, as well as their appointment by a transparent system and the powers of investigation, supervision, resolution, promotion, sanction and others that are necessary to guarantee the effective fulfilment and protection of the right to data protection.[55] In many cases, these Authorities have been responsible for the defence of both the right of access to public information and the right to data protection, with some States even modifying their regulations to this end (as in the case of Argentina, through Decree no 746, of 25 September 2017). However, it is a complex issue that has come to paralyze many of the existing legislative projects, as in the case of Chile.

Finally, we must point out that in addition to these general criteria, the Ibero-American Standards set specific criteria in relation to the treatment of personal data of children and adolescents, privileging the best interests of the minor, as well as promoting their education with respect to the use of their personal information, as can be seen in the Recommendations on Personal Data and Childhood approved by the Argentine Supervisory Authority on May 21, 2021. The Standards also highlight the need to apply proactive measures in the processing of personal data such as privacy by design and by default, self-regulation mechanisms, impact assessments, and the appointment of a Personal Data Protection Officer (DPO).[56]

REFERENCES

Stewart, D.P., *Privacidad y protección de datos*, 25th February 2014, CJI/doc.450/14.
Stewart, D.P., *Privacidad y protección de datos personales*, 27 March 2015, CJI/doc.474/15 rev 2.

---

[53] About Complaints and Penalties, cf. Cap. VIII Ibero-American Standards.

[54] This subject was concluded with special attention at the XVII Ibero-American Data Protection Meeting, held in Naucalpan de Juárez (México), on 21st June 2019. Vid. https://www.redipd.org/sites/default/files/2020-01/declaracion-final-xvii-encuentro.pdf accessed 20 October 2021. To analyze the regulatory framework of the Control Authorities and their degree of compliance with the provisions of Standard 42 of the Ibero-American Standards, regarding their autonomy and impartiality; their profile, appointment procedure and causes for dismissal; their powers; their jurisdictional control; and their human and material resources, cf. AECID (2021) "Marco regulatorio de autoridades de protección de datos personales en Iberoamérica, un estudio comparado 2020" (https://www.redipd.org/sites/default/files/inline-files/marco-regulatorio-autoridades-protecci%C3%B3n-datos-personales-iberoamerica-un-estudio-comparado-2020%20_0.pdf accessed 12 December 2021), and its Annex (https://www.redipd.org/sites/default/files/inline-files/anexo-unico.pdf accessed 12 December 2021).

[55] About Control Authorities, cf. Cap. VII Ibero-American Standards.

[56] About these proactive measures, cf. Cap. VI Ibero-American Standards.

PART II

INTER- AND TRANS-DISCIPLINARY PERSPECTIVES ON PRIVACY AND DATA PROTECTION

8. Social values and privacy law and policy

Priscilla M. Regan

I. INTRODUCTION

Since the 1990s privacy scholars have recognized the social value of privacy – that privacy is not only of value to the individual as individual but also has wider social value in a democratic society. Although this recognition is widespread in academic and legal communities, it has not yet been well incorporated into privacy law and policy. In the legal and policy realms, privacy is still largely conceptualized as an individual interest or right. This is truer in the common law countries (US, Canada and England) than it is in the European civil law countries with their stronger human rights traditions undergirded now by the shared legal framework of the European Community. Across these countries it has been difficult to shift policy and legal attention from the individual rights perspective to a social value perspective.

This chapter will explore these issues in three parts, with particular focus on policy thinking and action in the US; other chapters in this volume explore European developments in more detail. First, the literature on the social value of privacy will be reviewed to extract the central themes and their potential policy implications. In order to organize relevant scholarship, this review will use the framework of privacy's common value, public value, and collective value.[1] Second, policy discussions primarily in the US will be examined to determine whether the social value of privacy has been raised in policy discussions and if so to what effect. Finally, the conclusion will evaluate what the near future might bring to incorporating a social value of privacy more fully into policy debates and outcomes.

II. SOCIAL VALUE OF PRIVACY – THEORETICAL PERSPECTIVES[2]

Modern thinking about the importance of privacy was shaped by Warren and Brandeis' 1890 *Harvard Law Review* article defining privacy as the 'right to be let alone'. Alan Westin in his seminal book *Privacy and Freedom* adopted this individual rights view of privacy, defining it as the right 'of the individual to decide for himself, with only extraordinary exceptions in the interests of society, when and on what terms his acts should be revealed to the general public'.[3] This focus on the individual right and the emphasis on individual control dominated much of liberal legal and philosophical thinking about privacy during the late 1960s and through the 1980s – a time when information and communication technologies transformed the ways that

---

1 Priscilla M. Regan *Legislating Privacy: Technology, Social Values, and Public Policy* (University of North Carolina Press 1995).

2 A more complete development of the following discussion on theoretical perspectives can be found in Regan (2015) from which parts of the following discussion are derived.

3 Alan Westin *Privacy and Freedom* (Atheneum 1967) 42.

businesses, governments and individuals collected, retained, analysed and transferred information about individuals.

A different discourse about privacy as a component of a well-functioning society was developing at the same time by sociologists but received less attention among most philosophers and legal scholars, particularly those writing for both academic and policy audiences. Robert Merton in *Social Theory and Social Structure* stated that '"Privacy" is not merely a personal predilection; it is an important functional requirement for the effective operation of social structure'.[4] Although this passage was quoted by Westin in *Privacy and Freedom*[5], Merton's thinking was not incorporated by legal scholars or by philosophers writing at that time. Other social scientists, however, adopted Merton's thinking about privacy with Erving Goffman, a sociologist, in *The Presentation of Self in Everyday Life*[6] and Irwin Altman, a social psychologist, viewing privacy as a social phenomenon.[7] Goffman and Altman distinguished privacy as important not just for individual self-development and freedom but also as important to the society more generally.

Starting in the 1970s, a group of philosophers began to consider a broader social value of privacy. In a compendium of essays,[8] Carl Friedrich and Arnold Simmel both acknowledged that privacy has some broader social importance. Friedrich wrote that he was 'not concerned... with the private aspect of this privacy, individualistic and libertarian, but with the political interest that may be involved'.[9] Simmel argued that privacy is 'part and parcel of the system of values that regulates action in society' but then ultimately defined the drawing of boundaries of self, family and social organization as involving 'conflicts over the rights of individuals'.[10] A series of articles in *Philosophy and Public Affairs* in 1975 also raised the possibilities of the social importance of privacy. Judith Jarvis Thomson, Thomas Scanlon and James Rachels each considered how to broaden the interest in privacy beyond traditional liberal thinking in order to expand and revitalize its importance.[11]

Ferdinand Schoeman, in an anthology on privacy[12] and a later book,[13] began a more serious scholarly discussion about the social importance of privacy. Drawing upon Goffman's thinking, Schoeman argued 'that respect for privacy enriches social and personal interaction by providing contexts for the development of varied kinds of relationships and multiple dimensions of personality'.[14] He concluded 'it is important in a society for there to be institutions in which people can experience some of what they are without excessive scrutiny. Privacy is such an

---

[4] Robert K. Merton *Social Theory and Social Structure* (The Free Press 1957) 375.

[5] Alan Westin (1967) 32

[6] Erving Goffman *The Presentation of Self in Everyday Life* (Doubleday 1959).

[7] Irwin Altman *The Environment and Social Behavior* (Brooks/Cole, 1975).

[8] Roland J. Pennock and John W. Chapman, eds *Privacy,* Nomos Series 13, *Yearbook of the American Society for Political and Legal Philosophy* (Atherton Press, 1971).

[9] Carl J. Friedrich 'Secrecy versus Privacy,' in Pennock and Chapman, ibid., 115.

[10] Arnold Simmel 'Privacy is not an Isolated Freedom,' in Pennock and Chapman, ibid., 71, 87.

[11] *See* Judith Jarvis Thomson 'The Right to Privacy,' *Philosophy and Public Affairs* 4 (1975) 295–314; Thomas Scanlon 'Thomson on Privacy,' *Philosophy and Public Affairs* 4 (1975) 315–22; James Rachels 'Why Privacy is Important,' *Philosophy and Public Affairs* 4 (1975) 323–33.

[12] Ferdinand Schoeman 'Privacy and Intimate Information,' in Schoeman (ed.), *Philosophical Dimensions of Privacy* (Cambridge University Press 1984).

[13] Ferdinand Schoeman. *Privacy and Social Freedom* (Cambridge University Press 1992).

[14] Schoeman (1984), 413.

institution'.[15] In his 1992 book, Schoeman 'situates privacy in a social process' (2) and argues for 'the form and function of privacy in promoting *social* thinking' [emphasis in original] (2). He viewed 'the practice of privacy, not as a right but as a system of nuanced social norms, modulates the effectiveness of social control over an individual'.[16]

Increasingly, privacy scholars at that time recognized that a narrow individual rights justification for and basis of privacy was inadequate to the actual importance of privacy in modern life. Spiros Simitis argued that privacy should not be regarded as a 'tolerant contradiction' but a 'constitutive element of a democratic society'.[17] Richard Hixson suggested that personal privacy thrives in community where there is mutual self-regard, not in isolation.[18] Legal scholars, such as Robert Post, began to shape arguments that privacy's value to society could be found in tort law's recognition of the importance of both the community and the individual.[19] In 1995, I argued that privacy is not only of value to the individual but also to society in general and suggested three bases for the social importance of privacy: privacy as a common, a public and a collective value.[20]

The early-2000s witnessed growing interest in the social value, role and importance of privacy. Daniel Solove emphasized a pragmatic value of privacy based on the common good and on the value of privacy in specific situations.[21] Valerie Steeves drew upon the earlier writings of Westin, Altman and George Herbert Mead to recapture the social aspects of privacy; she argued that privacy is 'a social construction that we create as we negotiate our relationships with others on a daily basis'.[22] Interested in exploring the concept of 'privacy in public'[23] and drawing upon the earlier philosophical thinking of Schoeman and the sociological thinking of Goffman, Helen Nissenbaum argued that different social contexts are governed by different social norms that govern the flow of information within and out of that context.[24] Protecting privacy entails ensuring appropriate flows of information between and among contexts. Key to Nissenbaum's framework is the construct of 'context-relative informational norms' which express 'entrenched expectations' regarding flows of information.[25]

Interest in articulating the social importance of privacy continues. Below the literature developing the social importance of value will be reviewed more fully using the framework

---

[15] Ibid., 415–6.

[16] Schoeman (1992), 6.

[17] Simitis Spiros 'Reviewing Privacy in an Information Society,' *University of Pennsylvania Law Review* 135 (March 1987): 707–746, 732.

[18] Richard F. Hixson *Privacy in a Public Society: Human Rights in Conflict* (Oxford University Press 1987) 130.

[19] Robert Post 'The Social Foundations of Privacy: Community and Self in the Common Law Tort,' *California Law Review* 77(5) 1989 957–1010.

[20] Priscilla M. Regan *Legislating Privacy: Technology, Social Values, and Public Policy* (University of North Carolina Press 1995).

[21] Daniel Solove *Understanding Privacy* (Harvard University Press 2008).

[22] Valerie Steeves 'Reclaiming the Social Value of Privacy,' pp. 191–208, in Ian Kerr, Valerie Steeves and Carole Lucock (eds), *Lessons from the Identity Trail: Anonymity, Privacy, and Identity in a Networked Society* (Oxford University Press 2009) 193.

[23] Helen Nissenbaum 'Toward an Approach to Privacy in Public: The Challenges of Information Technology,' *Ethics and Behavior* 7(3) (1997) 207–219.

[24] Helen Nissenbaum *Privacy In Context: Technology, Policy and the Integrity of Social Life* (Stanford University Press 2010).

[25] Ibid., 129.

of privacy's common, public, and collective value. At the outset, it is important to note that this literature is highly interdisciplinary with scholars from philosophy, history, sociology, psychology, political science, economics, computer science, and law all finding interest in this topic and contributing valuable insights to our understanding of the social importance of privacy.

II.1 Common Value

The common value of privacy is based on the notion that all individuals value some degree of privacy and have some common perceptions about privacy.[26] As John Stuart Mill pointed out, privacy is important for the development of a type of individual that forms the basis for the contours of society that we share in common. Mill's concern was echoed by John Dewey in his claim that the perception of the 'public' arises from the perception of broader consequences – 'concern on the part of each in the joint action and in the contribution of each of its members to it'.[27] Although individuals may have different definitions of privacy and may draw dissimilar boundaries about what they regard as private and public, they all recognize privacy as important. There is an analogy here to freedom of conscience – individuals may believe in different religions or no religion, but they similarly acknowledge the importance of freedom of conscience.[28] In the same way that one need not agree on the particulars of religious beliefs, one need not agree on the particulars of privacy beliefs to accept that privacy is essential to one's individual and social existence.

This traditional liberal view of privacy as important for self-development and for the particular kind of society liberal theory values is strengthened when joined by the sociological arguments of Goffman and Altman. Valerie Steeves reclaims the social value of privacy by focusing on the social interactions individuals undertake to negotiate the personal boundaries in their relationships.[29] Social psychologists[30] and communication scholars[31] have provided valuable analyses for understanding individual behaviour in groups. For example, Petronio in her Communication Privacy Management typology proposed five criteria that individuals use in developing privacy rules – cultural, gendered, motivational, contextual and risk-benefit – and suggests that individuals set such boundaries differently depending on the stage of their lives (child, adolescent, adult, elderly).[32]

The concept of the self as 'socially constructed' provides substantial support for the social importance of privacy. Julie Cohen identifies a 'dynamic theory of individual autonomy' where the individual is valued 'as an agent of self-determination and community-building' and

---

26 Regan (1995).

27 John Dewey *The Public and its Problems* (Swallow Press 1927) 181.

28 Regan (1995).

29 Steeves (2009), 191–208.

30 Jacquelyn Burkell and Alexandre Fortier 'Privacy Policy Disclosures of Behavioural Tracking on Consumer Health Websites' *Proceedings of the Association for Information Science and Technology* 50(1) (2013) 1–9.

31 Sandra Petronio *Boundaries of Privacy: Dialectics of Disclosure. SUNY series in communication studies* (State University of New York Press 2002).

32 Ibid., 24–27.

where 'productive expression and development … have room to flourish'.[33] Without the space privacy protects to engage in the 'conscious construction of the self',[34] individuals' beliefs and desires are more likely to track with the mainstream and expected. As Cohen elaborates in her 2012 book, the modern individual is widely recognized as a socially constructed, 'situated, embodied being',[35] and privacy plays an important role in protecting against the tyranny of the majority and allowing individuality and creativity to flourish.[36] Similarly, Beate Rossler argues that 'the true realization of freedom, that is a life led autonomously, is only possible in conditions where privacy is protected'.[37]

Helen Nissenbaum's emphasis on 'social context' provides support for a commonly held value of privacy at a more practical level. Nissenbaum views privacy as a social norm that specifies what information is appropriate to reveal and how that information should move in different social contexts with the understanding that as members of society we share certain understandings of the normative values that govern different social contexts. Privacy has a social value because it serves to maintain different social contexts and the values of these different contexts. For Nissenbaum, privacy is a 'shared collective value of a community' and a 'legitimate reason for accepting or rejecting a given socio-technical system'.[38] This is quite similar to Daniel Solove's view that privacy 'is itself a form of social control that emerges from the norms and values of society' and that privacy is protected 'because we recognize that a good society protects against excessive intrusion and nosiness into people's lives'.[39]

II.2 Public Value

Many scholars recognized that privacy is important to the democratic political system. In most of the legal and constitutional writing about privacy and democracy in the US literature, privacy is seen as an instrumental right particularly important in two respects – furthering the exercise of First Amendment rights and providing constraints on the use of government power, especially in Fourth Amendment terms. But privacy is also independently important to the democratic process as the development of commonality, essential to the construction of a 'public' or Arendt's 'community of one's peers,' required privacy so that people were not over-differentiated.[40] The use of personal information for targeting political messages, for example, can be viewed as violating the integrity of the electoral process because such messages not only fragment the body politic but also, as a result of this panoptic sorting,[41] discriminates among voters allocating options and messages on the basis of selected characteristics.

---

33 Julie Cohen 'Examined Lives: Informational Privacy and the Subject as Object,' *Stanford Law Review* 52(5) (2000) 1377.

34 Ibid., 1424.

35 Julie E. Cohen *Configuring the Networked Self: Law, Code, and the Play of Everyday Practice* (Yale University Press 2012) 6.

36 Ibid., 110–111.

37 Beate Roessler *The Value of Privacy* (Polity Press 2005) 72.

38 Nissenbaum (2010), 66.

39 Daniel Solove 'The Meaning and Value of Privacy,' in Beate Roessler and Dorota Mokrosinska, *Social Dimensions of Privacy: Interdisciplinary Perspectives* (Cambridge University Press 2015) 80.

40 Regan (1995), 226–7.

41 Oscar Gandy *The Panoptic Sort: A Political Economy of Personal Information* (Westview Press 1993).

The writings of Paul Ohm, Paul Schwartz and Daniel Solove on the legal side and Beate Rossler and Kirsty Hughes on the philosophical side also develop the public value of privacy. Roessler notes how the 'public realm is turned into an "Arendtian nightmare" that no longer has anything to do with civic commitment to public welfare, or indeed with any notion of "public".'[42] Paul Schwartz anchors a public value of privacy in civic republicanism and the importance of democratic deliberation and of individual self-determination:

> The need is to insulate an individual's reflective facilities from certain forms of manipulation and coercion. Privacy rules for cyberspace must set aside areas of limited access to personal data in order to allow individuals, alone and in association with others, to deliberate about how to live their lives.[43]

Schwartz is critical of viewing an individual right to privacy as a right of control over data use because 'it has not proved capable of generating the kind of public, quasi-public, and private spaces necessary to promote democratic self-rule'.[44]

As governments began to extend the use of more generalized surveillance of the public, for example using video or CCTV technologies,[45] the theoretical interests of surveillance studies scholars, adopting Michel Foucault's concern with anonymous surveillance as a technique of discipline and control,[46] joined the interests of legal scholars in limitations on the reasonableness of government searches and seizures. Paul Ohm, among other Fourth Amendment scholars, reminds readers that:

> the Fourth Amendment was originally intended and is better interpreted to ensure not privacy but liberty from undue government power. For more than two hundred years, privacy has served as a pretty good proxy for this value, but the rise of the surveillance society will break the connection between privacy and liberty from power and will force us to protect the core value of the Fourth Amendment through other means.[47]

Kirsty Hughes similarly notes that society benefits because 'privacy precludes the dissent into a totalitarian regime' and that 'one of the core values of privacy is that it allows individuals to have distance from the state: no democracy can flourish where individuals have no privacy from the state. It is a prerequisite to a non-totalitarian state'.[48]

---

[42] Roessler (2005), 170.

[43] Paul M. Schwartz 'Privacy and Democracy in Cyberspace,' *Vanderbilt Law Review* 52(6) (1999) 1653.

[44] Schwartz (1999) 1660.

[45] Clive Norris 'From Personal to Digital: CCTV, the Panopticon, and the Technological Mediation of Suspicion and Control,' in *Surveillance as Social Sorting: Privacy, Risk and Digital Discrimination*, David Lyon ed. (Routledge 2003).

[46] Michel Foucault *Discipline and Punish: The Birth of the Prison,* translated by Alan Sheridan (Pantheon 1977).

[47] Paul Ohm 'World Without Privacy,' *Mississippi Law Journal* 81(5) (2012) 1312.

[48] Kirsty Hughes 'The Social Value of Privacy,' in *Social Dimensions of Privacy: Interdisciplinary Perspectives* Beate Roessler and Dorota Mokrosinska (eds) (Cambridge: Cambridge University Press 2015) 226–229.

II.3 Collective Value

The collective value of privacy is based on the argument that technology and market forces are making it harder for any one person to have privacy without all persons having a similar minimum level of privacy. Privacy was in effect a 'collective or public good', as used in economics,[49] for three reasons. First, privacy is not a 'private good' in that one cannot effectively buy back or establish a desired level of privacy because of the non-voluntary nature of many record-keeping relationships. If individuals exited these relationships in order to protect their privacy not only would they make their own lives more complicated to live, they would also make the functioning of a modern economy and society more complicated and less efficient. These developments arguably make privacy less of a 'private good', where one could buy back or establish a desired level of privacy, and more of a 'collective good', where one's level of privacy affects not only others' level of privacy but also the functioning of the institutions whose activities might implicate privacy.

Second, the market will not produce an optimal supply of privacy and is an inefficient mechanism for supplying privacy. It is widely recognized, and borne out by experience, that the calculus of any organization – private, public or non-profit – will be to collect as much information as possible about individuals to reduce any risk of decision-making about that individual. An organization will rationally be privacy invasive in its information gathering and use. But for individuals, the rational calculus is often to not see the privacy implications of their decisions to release information. Privacy choices are often hidden transaction costs; the individual is focused on the purchase or service being negotiated – not focused on the opportunity or need to make a decision about privacy. Both the organizational calculus and the individual calculus thus result in less privacy – a suboptimal supply both because the quality of the information flowing within the system may be degraded and because trust in the system may be compromised. Left to its own devices, privacy invasions are the result of market failures.

And third, the complexity and interrelatedness of the computer and communication infrastructure make it more difficult to divide privacy. The idea that the complexity and interrelatedness of the communication infrastructure made it more difficult to divide privacy was supported by the agreement that the design of the overall system determines what is possible. As Lawrence Lessig noted in 1999, 'code is law' and defaults built into the system architecture establish the floor for what is possible on the system.[50] A focus on the technological infrastructure has also aligned the concerns of privacy scholars with those of surveillance studies scholars, many of who are trained in interdisciplinary fields such as science, technology and society (STS) and media studies.

The collective value of privacy has become more profoundly evident as a result both of the ubiquity and complexity of the communications systems on which much of modern life occurs and of the 'big data' that results from and fuels those systems. The idea that one can individually set one's own privacy level unaffected by others is undermined by social networking sites (SNS) in which others may, knowingly or unknowingly, reveal information that implicates the privacy of others. Barocas and Nissenbaum refer to this as the 'tyranny of the minority' whereby 'the volunteered information of the few can unlock the same information about the

---

[49] Ronald Coase 'The Lighthouse in Economics,' *Journal of Law and Economics* 17(2) (1974) 357–376.

[50] Lawrence Lessig *Code and Other Laws of Cyberspace* (Basic Books 1999).

many'.[51] Moreover, the methods of collecting, analysing and using 'big data' have become far removed from the point at which an individual consciously provides information about herself and similarly obviate the possibility of setting one's privacy level. Paul Ohm points out that the correlations that result from big data techniques make it 'difficult to know that we are in the presence of risky data, the kind of data that will likely lead to privacy harm'.[52]

III. LAW AND POLICY

As seen from the above, the philosophical and legal writing about privacy provides a rich basis for thinking about the social values of privacy – and provides thoughtful rationales for why policy should protect these social values of privacy. The following sections analyse whether policy discussions have incorporated these scholarly insights.

III.1 Common Value

Public opinion surveys and the actions people take provide continued support for privacy as a common value. People take numerous public and private actions to carve out and protect privacy in ways that demonstrate common views about privacy's meaning and importance. Evidence for this is illustrated by continued recognition of the sensitivity of medical information as we move health files into electronic systems and of the need to protect financial records as security breach notification laws, as well as growing concern with tracking online transactions and GPS monitored physical space. Debates over privacy on social networking sites, especially Facebook, present concrete empirical evidence that privacy is viewed as similarly important among users.

To some extent sectoral privacy legislation, as is common in the US, is evidence that people have common views about privacy's meaning and value with respect to certain kinds of information, e.g., education, financial, tax, cable, etc. But it is not accurate or appropriate to view these laws as representing an actual social value of privacy as they rely not on a truly common understanding of privacy or on social institutions or mechanisms for enforcement but instead on a particular interpretation of aggrieved individuals who have the means and knowledge to bring cases to court. The 'data protection' approach, as found in most European statutes and the EU directives, reflects a common value of privacy that is more appropriately categorized as a social value as the onus is on the institutions handling the information to comply with legal requirements.

Difficulties in moving beyond this more individual rights view of the value of privacy is illustrated in the 2012 policy discussions following the Obama administration's Consumer Privacy Bill of Rights which incorporated a new principle of 'respect for context' that appeared to reflect Nissenbaum's emphasis on the importance of context and contextual

---

[51] Solon Barocas and Helen Nissenbaum 'Big Data's End Run Around Anonymity and Consent,' 44–75 in Julia Lane, Victoria Stodden, Stefan Bender and Helen Nissenbaum (eds), *Privacy, Big Data, and the Public Good* (Cambridge University Press 2014) 61.

[52] Paul Ohm 'Changing the Rules: General Principles for Data Use and Analysis,' 96–111 in Julia Lane, Victoria Stodden, Stefan Bender and Helen Nissenbaum (eds), *Privacy, Big Data, and the Public Good* (Cambridge University Press 2014) 101.

integrity. As Nissenbaum points out context can be interpreted in at least four different ways – as technology platform or system, as sector or industry, as business model or practice, or as social domain – and the 'only interpretation of context that marks a meaningful departure for business as usual'[53] is context as social domain, which was not the interpretation stakeholders or policymakers brought to policy discussions. She goes on to say that 'Contextual integrity reveals the systematic dependencies of social values on appropriate information flows, once-and-for-all challenging the fallacy of privacy as valuable for individuals alone.'[54]

III.2 Public Value

Policy support for the public value of privacy is hinted at in recent Supreme Court decisions regarding the Fourth Amendment as a means of restricting the use of government power. In *United States v Jones* the Court ruled that a GPS device placed by law enforcement on a car requires a warrant. Justice Sotomayor, in a concurring opinion, argued that:

> The net result is that GPS monitoring – by making available at a relatively low cost such a substantial quantum of intimate information about any person whom the Government, it its unfettered discretion chooses to track – may alter the relationship between the citizen and government in a way that is *inimical to democratic society*.[55]

The European Court of Human Rights appears to be following a path similar to that of the US Supreme Court in that it also, as Kirsty Hughes carefully analyses, has primarily emphasized the individualistic basis of privacy's importance in cases involving privacy's importance to democracy.[56] This is true in state surveillance cases where the Court has found that surveillance activities might violate the privacy rights in Article 8 of the European Convention on Human Rights but 'has not developed a strong notion of the role of privacy as a bulwark against totalitarianism comparable to that which has appeared in the academic scholarship'.[57] Although the Court has protected privacy, 'it never directly addresses the role of privacy in preserving democracy and preventing the demise into a surveillance state'.[58]

In neither the US nor Europe have courts recognized privacy's role in democracy in the way they have for the right to freedom of expression. In the US, the Supreme Court's seminal ruling in *Buckley v Valeo* enshrined that 'free speech' should not be compromised and that disclosure of donor information serves public purposes in deterring corruption and aiding in enforcement of anti-corruption laws, as well as providing useful information to voters.[59] With the widespread availability of this information on the Internet, as well as the ability to data mine public records and other information, scholars are beginning to question whether the original goals of 'public records' and 'public disclosure' are being served.[60] The Court's more recent decisions

[53] Helen Nissenbaum 'Respecting Context to Protect Privacy: Why Meaning Matters,' *Science and Engineering Ethics* (2015) 5.

[54] Ibid., 19.

[55] Emphasis added, *United States v Jones* (132 S. Ct. 945, 2012) 956.

[56] Hughes (2015).

[57] Ibid., 234.

[58] Ibid., 235.

[59] *Buckley v Valeo* (1976).

[60] Deborah G. Johnson, Priscilla M. Regan and Kent Wayland 'Campaign Disclosure, Privacy and Transparency,' *William and Mary Bill of Rights Journal* 19 4 (2011) 959–982; Daniel Solove, 'Access and Aggregation: Public Records, Privacy and the Constitution,' *Minnesota Law Review* 86 (2002) 1137.

in *Citizens United v FEC* and *McCutcheon v FEC* have further exacerbated debates about the public value of information about campaign contributions by permitting rather unfettered corporate and non-profit campaign spending without public disclosure.[61]

Perhaps the most telling evidence for the public value of privacy can be found in how candidates, political parties, and interest groups are collecting, analysing, and using personal information to foster the polarization and partisanship in today's electorate.[62] The empirical effects are obvious in the US with the reapportionment of congressional seats into safe districts where votes are pre-determined by the demographics and likely voting patterns. It is similarly illustrated in political races where candidates carefully couch their messages and positions to particular segments of the electorate rather than to the electorate as a whole. Recognition of a public value of privacy as justification for restricting collection and disclosure of voters' specific views on an issue would inhibit the reach and specificity of targeted political messages, enable the development of a more unified sense of the public, and quite possibly reduce political polarization. Questions about Russian meddling in the 2016 American presidential election, as well as meddling in European elections, and the revelations about activities of Facebook and Cambridge Analytica, provide further evidence of the importance of a public value of privacy.

III.3 Collective Value[63]

Given modern networks of computerized databases, sophisticated algorithms, and high-speed global communications systems, the concepts of 'record' and individual privacy harms are somewhat anachronistic. As an illustration, the data breach that a US chain store experienced during November and December 2013 involved the personal data of about 110 million customers – a number more characteristic of a collective harm than discrete individual harms. Dennis Hirsch likens the effects of such data breaches to oil spills, causing broad wide-spread harm to the social environment.[64] Greenwood et al point out that when data are accessible over networks 'the traditional container of an institution makes less and less sense' and the complex ways in which data travel between services has 'become too complex for the user to handle and manage'.[65]

There is also growing recognition that our complex organizational systems are more fundamentally socio-technical systems and that in some cases, such as Google and Facebook, these systems are exhibiting attributes of public infrastructures.[66] Marwick and Boyd view these

---

[61] *Citizens United v FEC* (2010); *McCutcheon v FEC* (2013).

[62] Ibid.

[63] A more complete development of the ideas in this section and in the section below on the collective value in law and policy can be found in Priscilla M. Regan, 'Reviving the Public Trustee Concept and Applying to Information Privacy Policy,' in the *University of Maryland Law Review* (2017) from which parts of these discussions are derived.

[64] Dennis D. Hirsch 'The Glass House Effect: Big Data, the New Oil, and the Power of Analogy,' *Miami Law Review* (2014).

[65] Daniel Greenwood, Arkadiusz Stopczynski, Brian Sweatt, Thomas Hardjono and Alex Pentland 'The New Deal on Data: A Framework for Institutional Controls' in Julia Lane, Victoria Stodden, Stefan Bender and Helen Nissenbaum (eds) *Privacy, Big Data and the Public Good* (Cambridge University Press 2014) 192–210 200.

[66] Deborah G. Johnson and Priscilla M. Regan (eds) *Transparency and Surveillance as Sociotechnical Accountability: A House of Mirrors* (Routledge 2014) 162–184.

technological shifts in the information and cultural landscape as creating 'networked publics' and necessitating a conceptualization of privacy 'from an individualistic frame to one that is networked'.[67] In a networked public, it is hard for any one person to have a level of privacy without all other persons in that network having a similar level of privacy. Instead privacy is established as part of the network and the various databases and interconnections that compose the network, and is shared collectively by those in the network.

Recently a number of scholars have begun rethinking how the current status of personal privacy might best be conceptualized in a way that moves policy beyond the individual rights and FIPs approach. At least four lines of analysis are being pursued. The first is to stress the negative externalities that result from the way that personal information currently is collected, used, and exchanged and thus to explore how the tools and practices of environmental protection might be incorporated into personal information protection.[68] A second is to view the personal information landscape as experiencing a 'tragedy of the commons'. I have argued elsewhere that personal information can be viewed as a 'common pool resource',[69] whose value to any one user is curtailed by other users because the common pool resource system is *overloaded* in that the collection of more personal information drives up the costs to both data subjects and users, is *polluted* in that inaccurate, irrelevant and out-of-date information contaminates the resource pools, and is *over-harvested* in that more users take similar pieces of information from the pool, reducing the unique value of that information for any one user.[70] Somewhat similarly, a third way of conceptualizing a public good value of privacy is to draw attention to how the personal information landscape has resulted in the 'tragedy of the trust commons'.[71] Finally a fourth is to use tools and analysis from behavioural and experimental economics to identify the negative externalities or spillovers that individuals create in their own actions and to empower groups to protect privacy.[72]

The prevailing policy approach in the US has been one of limited government regulation over both classic market conditions (entry, exit, price) and over privacy protections. But there is increasingly recognition that competition on the Internet has actually concentrated power in the hands of a few key actors – particularly ISPs and what are referred to as edge intermediaries, such as Facebook and Google. Likewise, there is increasingly recognition that self-regulation has not worked effectively to protect online privacy – and that a privacy market has not evolved, instead individuals' private information has been commodified and, through online advertising, provides the foundation for 'free' websites. As Frank Pasquale similarly points out:

---

[67] Alice E. Marwick and Danah Boyd 'Networked Privacy: How Teenagers Negotiate Context in Social Media' *New Media & Society* 16(7) (2014) 1052.

[68] A. Michael Froomkin 'Regulating Mass Surveillance as Privacy Pollution: Learning from Environmental Impact Statements,' *University of Illinois Law Review* (2015) 1713–1790; Dennis Hirsch 'Protecting the Inner Environment: What Privacy Regulation Can Learn from Environmental Law,' *Georgia Law Review* 41(1) (2006) 1–63.

[69] Elinor Ostrom *Governing the Commons: The Evolution of Institutions for Collective Action.* (Cambridge University Press 1990).

[70] Priscilla M. Regan 'Privacy as a Common Good,' *Information, Communication and Society*, 5(3) (2002) 382–405.

[71] Dennis D. Hirsch 'Protecting the Inner Environment: What Privacy Regulation Can Learn from Environmental Law,' *Georgia Law Review* 41(1) (2006) 1–63.

[72] Joshua A.T. Fairfield and Christoph Engel 'Privacy as a Public Good' *Duke Law Journal* 65 (2015) 385.

> It would be nice to believe that market forces are in fact promoting optimal levels of privacy. It would also be comforting if antitrust law indirectly promoted optimal privacy options by assuring a diverse range of firms that can compete to supply privacy at various levels (and in various forms). But this position is not remotely plausible.[73]

With respect to large Internet actors, particularly the ISPs as well as Apple, Google and Facebook, the key policy question is how best to characterize the roles they currently play.

Pasquale argues that these firms are:

> less services than they are *platforms* for finding services (and occasionally, goods). Facebook, Google, and even Internet service providers ('ISPs') might be thought of less as sellers of particular end services than as advisors or gatekeepers, or connectors between users and what they want. In this intermediary role, Internet companies are far closer to health insurers or mortgage brokers than they are to sellers of products or services.[74]

Deborah Johnson and I similarly raised questions about the status of both Google and Facebook.[75] We noted that if Google is a search engine with a mission of delivering knowledge, then we might consider Google as something like a public utility or quasi-public trust. However, it is important to acknowledge that, at the same time as delivering 'free' knowledge to the users, Google is also delivering users as products to its paying customers, i.e., advertisers.[76] With respect to Facebook, we asked whether it is 'the Ma Bell of the twenty-first century – and should it be regulated as such?...has Facebook become public space, and should it be regulated in accordance with public trustee principles?'.[77]

In 2016 testimony before the Senate Committee on Commerce, Science, and Transportation, Paul Ohm provided four justifications for requiring ISPs to provide a higher standard of protection for information privacy: the history of common carriers' responsibility to respect the privacy of the information they carried; the relative lack of choice consumers have; the privileged place ISPs have in the network (gatekeeper, bottleneck); and the sensitivity traditionally accorded information such as communications, reading habits, and location.[78] Ohm pointed out that other online entities demonstrate some of the same characteristics such as social networking sites that 'carry exceptionally sensitive information and exhibit network effects and insufficient data portability that limit customer choice and exit'.[79]

Between 2012 and 2016, there was some interest on Capitol Hill, in the regulatory agencies and in the states in revisiting how to classify these firms and what policy approach is warranted given their size and scale. Congressional committees held a number of hearings on a possible antitrust approach to Google in September 2012. In February 2012, 36 state attorneys general addressed the dominant position that Google has in both the search engine and email environments and the difficulties consumers have as follows: 'It rings hollow to call their ability

---

73 Frank Pasquale 'Privacy, Antitrust, and Power,' *George Mason Law Review* 20(4) (2013) 1010.

74 Ibid., [72] 1015.

75 Johnson and Regan (2014).

76 Ibid., 167.

77 Ibid., 168–9.

78 Paul Ohm 'How Will the FCC's Proposed Privacy Regulations Affect Consumers and Competition?', *Statement Before the US Senate Committee on Commerce, Science and Transportation* (July 12 2016) 2–5.

79 Ibid., 9.

to exit the Google products ecosystem a "choice" in an Internet economy where the clear majority of all Internet users use – and frequently rely on – at least one Google product on a regular basis.'[80] Both the FTC and FCC considered imposing more regulations on these large actors as illustrated by the FTC's antitrust investigations of Google and the FCC consideration of whether its net neutrality rules empowered it to impose requirements on Google, Facebook and other Internet companies, as well as ISPs.[81] Neither the FTC nor the FCC took any action.

The Europeans are having very similar policy discussions about Google and Facebook's role but are more willing to take regulatory action. As Jonathan Taplan points out:

> The Europeans seem to be more resistant to Google's lobbying power, perhaps because they have far more restrictive campaign finance laws. In addition, Europeans have been far more skeptical about the surveillance capitalism that Google and Facebook practice, in which your every move is part of their data record of your life. (Witness the 'right to be forgotten,' a European legal innovation)[82]

IV. CONCLUSION

Although legal and philosophical writing has provided and continues to provide rich analyses of the social values of privacy, law and policy has not embraced such analyses instead largely justifying privacy protections based on privacy's value to the individual. This is truer in the US than in Europe or Canada. There are some factors that signal more widespread recognition of the social value of privacy and provide support for policy changes reflecting that value. The most prominent are those associated with a broader understanding of a collective interest in technological systems and platforms that protect or enable, not threaten, privacy. Revelations that the Facebook data of up to 87 million users may have been improperly shared during the 2016 election with a political consulting firm connected to the Trump campaign, Cambridge Analytica, provoked public outcry and congressional hearings. These revelations also illustrate the common value of privacy in that public opinion was united in viewing this as inappropriate,[83] the public value of privacy in that the incident may have affected the outcome of the election, and the collective value of privacy in that Facebook as a major social platform was a key player. Although many members of Congress have either introduced bills requiring more regulation of Facebook or promised to investigate what legislation may be necessary, it is also possible that if Facebook takes proactive steps to protect privacy through self-regulation that may stave off further legislative action until public and congressional interest wanes.

Given the scale and reach of technological changes generated by big data and the Internet of Things, it is certainly possible, if not highly likely, that there will be similar incidents involving misuses of data leading to questionable or discriminatory decisions, more data breaches involving millions of people, or misbehaving devices. Such occurrences, combined with more privacy protective policies in Europe and Canada, will continue to keep privacy on the policy

---

[80] Rebecca DiLeonardo 'State Attorneys General Concerned about Google Privacy Policy,' *JURIST: Paper Chase* (February 23 2012).

[81] Edward Wyatt 'FCC, in a Shift, Backs Fast lanes for Web Traffic,' *New York Times* (April 2014).

[82] Jonathan Taplan 'Why Europe Got Tough on Google But the U.S. Couldn't' *Washington Post* (June 28 2017).

[83] Natasha Singer 'Creepy or Not Your Privacy Concerns Probably Reflect Your Politics' *New York Times* (April 30 2018).

agenda in the US and continue to foster appreciation of privacy as a social, and not only individual, value in need of policy protection.

REFERENCES

Altman I., *The Environment and Social Behavior* (Brooks/Cole, 1975).

Barocas S. and H. Nissenbaum, 'Big Data's End Run Around Anonymity and Consent,' pp. 44–75 in J. Lane, V. Stodden, S. Bender and H. Nissenbaum (eds), *Privacy, Big Data, and the Public Good.* (Cambridge University Press 2014).

Coase R., 'The Lighthouse in Economics,' *Journal of Law and Economics* 17(2) (1974) 357.

Cohen J., 'Examined Lives: Informational Privacy and the Subject as Object,' *Stanford Law Review* 52(5) (2000) 1377.

Cohen J., *Configuring the Networked Self: Law, Code, and the Play of Everyday Practice* (Yale University Press 2012

Dewey J., *The Public and its Problems* (Swallow Press 1927).

DiLeonardo R., 'State Attorneys General Concerned about Google Privacy Policy,' *JURIST: Paper Chase* (February 23 2012).

Fairfield J.A.T. and C. Engel, 'Privacy as a Public Good,' *Duke Law Journal* 65 (2015) 385.

Foucault M., *Discipline and Punish: The Birth of the Prison,* translated by Alan Sheridan (Pantheon 1977).

Friedrich C.J., 'Secrecy versus Privacy,' in R.J. Pennock and J.W. Chapman (eds), *Privacy*, Nomos Series 13, Yearbook of the American Society for Political and Legal Philosophy (Atherton Press 1971).

Froomkin A.M., 'Regulating Mass Surveillance as Privacy Pollution: Learning from Environmental Impact Statements,' *University of Illinois Law Review* (2015) 1713.

Gandy Jr O., *The Panoptic Sort: A Political Economy of Personal Information* (Westview Press 1993).

Goffman E., *The Presentation of Self in Everyday Life* (Doubleday 1959).

Greenwood D., A. Stopczynski, B. Sweatt, T. Hardjono and A. Pentland, 'The New Deal on Data: A Framework for Institutional Controls' pp. 192–210 in J. Lane, V. Stodden, S. Bender and H. Nissenbaum (eds) *Privacy, Big Data and the Public Good* (Cambridge University Press 2014).

Hirsch, D.D., 'Protecting the Inner Environment: What Privacy Regulation Can Learn from Environmental Law,' *Georgia Law Review* 41(1) (2006) 1–63.

Hirsch, D.D., 'The Glass House Effect: Big Data, the New Oil, and the Power of Analogy,' *Miami Law Review* (2014).

Hixson R.F., *Privacy in a Public Society: Human Rights in Conflict* (Oxford University Press 1987).

Hughes K., 'The Social Value of Privacy,' pp 225–243 in B. Roessler and D Mokrosinska (eds) *Social Dimensions of Privacy: Interdisciplinary Perspectives* (Cambridge: Cambridge University Press 2015).

Jarvis Thomson, J., 'The Right to Privacy,' *Philosophy and Public Affairs* 4 (1975) 295–314.

Johnson D.G. and P.M. Regan (eds), *Transparency and Surveillance as Sociotechnical Accountability: A House of Mirrors* (Routledge 2014).

Johnson D.G., P.M. Regan and K. Wayland 'Campaign Disclosure, Privacy and Transparency,' *William and Mary Bill of Rights Journal* 19(4) (2011) 959–982.

Lessig L., *Code and Other Laws of Cyberspace* (Basic Books 1999).

Marwick A.E. and D. Boyd, 'Networked Privacy: How Teenagers Negotiate Context in Social Media' *New Media & Society* 16(7) (2014) 1051.

Merton R.K., *Social Theory and Social Structure* (The Free Press 1957).

Nissenbaum H., 'Respecting Context to Protect Privacy: Why Meaning Matters,' *Science and Engineering Ethics* (2015) 5.

Nissenbaum H., 'Toward an Approach to Privacy in Public: The Challenges of Information Technology,' *Ethics and Behavior* 7(3) (1997) 207.

Nissenbaum H., *Privacy In Context: Technology, Policy and the Integrity of Social Life* (Stanford University Press 2010).

Norris C., 'From Personal to Digital: CCTV, the Panopticon, and the Technological Mediation of Suspicion and Control,' in David Lyon (ed) *Surveillance as Social Sorting: Privacy, Risk and Digital Discrimination* (Routledge 2003).
Ohm P., 'Changing the Rules: General Principles for Data Use and Analysis,' pp. 96–111 in J. Lane, V. Stodden, S. Bender and H. Nissenbaum (eds), *Privacy, Big Data, and the Public Good* (Cambridge University Press 2014).
Ohm P., 'How Will the FCC's Proposed Privacy Regulations Affect Consumers and Competition?', *Statement Before the US Senate Committee on Commerce, Science and Transportation* (July 12 2016) 2.
Ohm P., 'The Fourth Amendment in a World Without Privacy,' *Mississippi Law Journal* 81(5) (2012) 1309.
Ohm P., 'World Without Privacy,' *Mississippi Law Journal* 81(5) (2012) 1312.
Ostrom E., *Governing the Commons: The Evolution of Institutions for Collective Action.* (Cambridge University Press 1990).
Pasquale F., 'Privacy, Antitrust, and Power,' *George Mason Law Review* 20(4) (2013) 1009.
Pennock R.J. and J.W. Chapman (eds) *Privacy,* Nomos Series 13, Yearbook of the American Society for Political and Legal Philosophy (Atherton Press, 1971).
Petronio S., *Boundaries of Privacy: Dialectics of Disclosure. SUNY series in communication studies* (State University of New York Press 2002).
Post R., 'The Social Foundations of Privacy: Community and Self in the Common Law Tort,' *California Law Review* 77(5) (1989) 957.
Rachels J. 'Why Privacy is Important,' *Philosophy and Public Affairs* 4 (1975) 323.
Regan P.M., 'Privacy as a Common Good,' *Information, Communication and Society*, 5, 3 (2002) 382–405.
Regan P.M., 'Reviving the Public Trustee Concept and Applying to Information Privacy Policy,' *University of Maryland Law Review* (2017) 1025–1043.
Regan P.M., *Legislating Privacy: Technology, Social Values, and Public Policy* (University of North Carolina Press 1995).
Roessler B., *The Value of Privacy* (Polity Press 2005).
Scanlon T., 'Thomson on Privacy,' *Philosophy and Public Affairs* 4 (1975) 315.
Schoeman F., 'Privacy and Intimate Information,' in F. Schoeman (ed.), *Philosophical Dimensions of Privacy* (Cambridge University Press 1984).
Schoeman F., *Privacy and Social Freedom* (Cambridge University Press 1992).
Schwartz P.M., 'Privacy and Democracy in Cyberspace,' *Vanderbilt Law Review* 52(6) (1999) 1609–1702.
Simmel A., 'Privacy is not an Isolated Freedom,' in J.R. Pennock and J.W. Chapman (eds), *Privacy*, Nomos Series 13, Yearbook of the American Society for Politica and Legal Philosophy (Atherton Press 1971) 71–87.
Singer N., 'Creepy or Not Your Privacy Concerns Probably Reflect Your Politics' *New York Times* (April 30 2018).
Solove D., 'Access and Aggregation: Public Records, Privacy and the Constitution,' *Minnesota Law Review* 86 (2002) 1137–1218.
Solove D., 'The Meaning and Value of Privacy,' pp. 71–82 in B. Roessler and D. Mokrosinska (eds) *Social Dimensions of Privacy: Interdisciplinary Perspectives* (Cambridge University Press 2015) 80.
Solove D., *Understanding Privacy* (Harvard University Press 2008).
Spiros S., 'Reviewing Privacy in an Information Society,' *University of Pennsylvania Law Review* 135 (March 1987): 707–746.
Steeves V. 'Reclaiming the Social Value of Privacy,' pp. 191–208, in I. Kerr, V. Steeves and C. Lucock (eds), *Lessons from the Identity Trail: Anonymity, Privacy, and Identity in a Networked Society* (Oxford University Press 2009).
Taplan J. 'Why Europe Got Tough on Google But the U.S. Couldn't' *Washington Post* (June 28 2017).
Warren S. and L. Brandeis, 'The Right to Privacy' (1890) *Harvard Law Review* **IV**(5) 1093–220.
Westin A., *Privacy and Freedom* (Atheneum 1967).
Wyatt E. 'FCC, in a Shift, Backs Fast lanes for Web Traffic,' *New York Times* (April 2014).

9. Media and communication studies, privacy and public values: Future challenges

Jo Pierson

I. KEY DEBATES IN MEDIA AND COMMUNICATION STUDIES

To thoroughly understand developments in privacy and data protection we need to involve the study of technologies and systems that mediate interaction and communication between people in society. This type of 'mediated communication' or 'mediation' is at the core of the field of Media and Communication Studies (MCS).

MCS became a separate area of research from the 1930s onwards, starting in the US and then taken up in the UK and in the rest of the world. The domain investigates human and social communication through media as well as from person to person. Generally, two main streams of research are identified: 'communication studies' and 'media studies'. The foundations can be found in social sciences (for communication studies, with an origin in the US in the 1930s) and in humanities (for media studies with an origin in the UK in the 1970s). Another influential input for MCS came from information science as developed by Shannon and Weaver, dealing with the technological efficiency of communication channels for carrying information. The authors started from a simple transmission model, which defines communication as the intentional transfer of information from sender to receiver by way of physical channels which are influenced by noise and interference.

In the beginning MCS were foremost concerned with the sociology of mass communication in the US, pioneered by Paul Lazersfeld. The term 'mass' in 'mass communication' is essential, starting from the (monocausal) belief that masses could be easy manipulated via broadcasting media like radio and later television, based on the experiences of the World War and the propaganda of the Third Reich in Germany. Therefore, one of the first aims was to investigate the linear effects that media messages had on a mass population. This perspective was later re-adjusted by the reception approach by taking more into account the people themselves and the way they receive, process and interpret the broadcasted messages. A next phase was to also take the socio-cultural context more seriously, by exploring the production and reinforcement of culture through communication and interpreting media by people in the everyday life. This was the start of the media studies stream in the UK, which was closely related with the so-called cultural studies tradition and with Stuart Hall and Raymond Williams as key scholars. From the 1960s onwards also critical theories (based on Marxism) of the production side in the media industry and communication infrastructures became very influential. A perspective pioneered by Max Horkheimer and Theodor Adorno of the Frankfurt School in the 1930s and later followed up by scholars like Jürgen Habermas with his work on the public sphere and Dallas Smythe on the political economy of communication.

A key notion in MCS is 'mediation', which refers to the mediated interconnection that is part of the infrastructure of most people's lives in the internet age.[1] In studying the problems associated with the nature and effects of mediation, Garnham differentiates between three types: human agents, systems of symbolic representation and technological tools.[2] Mediation by other human agents on people themselves as mediators. This refers, for example, to the concept of 'gate keepers' in journalism and news production. In order to understand the role of these human mediators and their role in the communication process, we need to look at issues like the journalism training, deontology, newsroom routines or how media industry shareholder structures and business models have an influence. The second way of mediation goes through systems of symbolic representation. This refers to the use of language and symbols as also being studied in linguistics and semiotics: how humans produce ('encode') and consume ('decode') text and what happens with meaning when it is transported through language and culture. The third way is mediation by means of (technological) tools. Here we investigate the role and meaning of media systems and related technologies, which fits best with the research on privacy and data protection. For the purpose of this chapter we focus on the study of communication mediated between people via so-called new media and computers, also indicated as 'computer-mediated communication' (CMC).[3]

'New media' or 'digital media' as technological tools are currently a focal point in MCS. Lievrouw and Livingstone define new media as information and communication technologies and their associated social contexts, incorporating three inextricable and mutually determining components:

1. The artefacts or devices that enable and extend our abilities to communicate or convey information;
2. The communication practices or activities we engage in to design and use these devices;
3. The socio-economic arrangements or organizational forms that form around the artefacts and practices.[4]

This means MCS explores the ways in which digital media configure communication and, at the same time, how they are being shaped by society through artefacts, practices, and socio-economic arrangements. Each of the three perspectives offers a particular value for better understanding and investigating privacy in technologically mediated communications. The mutual articulation between these components also helps in broadening the scope and better grasping the context of privacy and data protection law in society.

As these digital media are technological tools, the MCS discipline has also increasingly integrated insights from the related discipline of Science and Technology Studies (STS).[5] The central idea of STS – as opposed to technological determinism – is that technologies are

---

1 Roger Silverstone, *Why study the media?* (SAGE 1999).

2 Nicholas Garnham, *Emancipation, the media, and modernity: arguments about the media and social theory* (Oxford University Press 2000) 64.

3 Caroline A. Haythornthwaite and Barry Wellman, 'The Internet in everyday life' in Barry Wellman and Catherine A. Haythornthwaite (eds), *The Internet in everyday life* (Blackwell 2002).

4 Leah A. Lievrouw and Sonia Livingstone, 'Introduction: the social shaping and consequences of ICTs' in Leah A. Lievrouw and Sonia Livingstone (eds), *The handbook of new media* (SAGE 2002).

5 Tarleton Gillespie, Pablo J. Boczkowski and Kirsten A. Foot (eds), *Media technologies: essays on communication, materiality, and society* (Inside technology, MIT Press 2014); Pablo J. Boczkowski and Leah A. Lievrouw, 'Bridging STS and communication studies: scholarship on media and information

not neutral, but represent the outcome of social, cultural, economic, and political processes. This interdisciplinary school of thought typically investigates how the technological objects are being constructed and take shape in society. However, STS has increased its scope of investigation over the years, starting with scientific knowledge and expanding to artefacts, methods, materials, observations, phenomena, classifications, institutions, interests, histories, and cultures.[6]

Given the integrated perspective of MCS and STS, this chapter fundamentally takes a socio-technological perspective based on a critical stance with regard the co-construction of digital media and technological systems.[7] The chapter touches upon the urgency of safeguarding public values like privacy and data protection in data-driven societies. This will help us to set out the state-of-the art research agenda on privacy and data protection from the perspective of a quickly evolving media technology landscape. For this we will first sketch recent developments in (digital) media, more in particular their transformation into digital technology platforms.

II. TRANSITION FROM DIGITAL MEDIA TO DIGITAL PLATFORMS

The original introduction of the 'privacy' concept in law was prompted by the emergence of a – at that time – 'new' technology in media: the portable camera. The seminal essay 'The Right to Privacy' by Warren and Brandeis was aimed at invasive photography used by journalists.[8] The relationship between media technologies and privacy has since then been germane.[9] Especially with the proliferation of 'next internet' primary technological systems (that is convergence of cloud computing, big data analytics and the Internet of Things), the significance of addressing issues of privacy and data protection from an MCS perspective has only augmented.[10]

The latter is also supported by the observation that technological intermediaries in the form of digital platforms are becoming deeply embedded in a broad range of social and public activities. In that way they have started to play a vital role in the fulfilment of fundamental public values associated with these activities. These values do refer to privacy and data protection, but also relate to concerns of diversity, freedom of expression and information, public safety, transparency, non-discrimination and socio-economic equality. We define digital platforms as *socio-technical architectures that enable and steer interaction and communication between*

technologies' in Edward J. Hackett and others (eds), *The handbook of science and technology studies* (3rd edn, MIT 2008).

[6] Edward J. Hackett and others, 'Introduction' in Edward J. Hackett and others (eds), *The handbook of science and technology studies* (3rd ed., MIT Press).

[7] Andrew Feenberg, *Questioning technology* (Routledge 1999); Robin Mansell, *Imagining the Internet: communication, innovation, and governance* (Oxford University Press 2012); José van Dijck, *The culture of connectivity: a critical history of social media* (Oxford University Press 2013).

[8] Samuel Warren and Louis D. Brandeis, 'The right to privacy' (1890) *4 Harvard Law Review* 69.

[9] Jo Pierson and Ine Van Zeeland, 'Privacy from a media studies perspective' in Bart van der Sloot and Aviva de Groot (eds), *Handbook privacy studies: an interdisciplinary introduction* (Amsterdam University Press 2018).

[10] Vincent Mosco, *Becoming digital* (1st edn, Emerald Publishing 2017) 4.

users through the collection, processing and circulation of user data.[11] These intermediaries can be general-purpose platforms for social (media) communication and information sharing (e.g., Facebook, Snapchat ...) or specific platforms in various sectors like health, transportation, education and hospitality (e.g., PatientsLikeMe, Lyft, Coursera, Airbnb ...).

The particular role digital platforms play in society is closely related to long-term changes in mediated communication as investigated in MCS. Traditionally, *mass media*, like newspapers and television, control communication over their channels according to certain motives and values, related to pluralism, neutrality, objectivity, commercial appeal and so on. This form of 'curating' (or editing) is reflected in the selection of news, programme scheduling, right of reply, must-carry obligations, advertising placement and other activities. Both public broadcasting media and private media can be held responsible through media laws and government supervision for how they exercise these functions. In addition, the traditional media landscape is characterized by *interpersonal media*, such as telecommunication and postal mail, which typically only 'facilitate' (or 'host') communication between two parties. Typically, interpersonal media have no right to interfere with communication, except on certain legal grounds (e.g., criminal investigation). Given the digitization and convergence of media in past decades we have now entered the age of what Castells calls 'mass self-communication'. On the one hand 'mass communication' because user can potentially reach a worldwide internet audience through digital platforms. On the other hand, it is a form of 'self-communication' because content production is typically self-generated, the potential receiver(s) definition is self-directed and the message or content retrieval is self-selected. This means that the boundaries between mass and interpersonal communication have fundamentally blurred, which has led to the folding of the roles of 'curator' and 'facilitator'.[12]

With this transition in mediated communication, digital platforms tend to explain their role in the organization of economic activity and public communication differently depending on the actors involved. They are, as Gillespie points out, '(...) carefully positioning themselves to users, clients, advertisers and policymakers, making strategic claims for what they do and do not do, and how their place in the information landscape should be understood'.[13] Towards advertisers they stress their powerful curating abilities as editors, steering, selecting and targeting their users in a fine-grained manner. Yet, towards policy makers and the general public they claim to be mere facilitators or hosts of user activity, thereby empowering users and enabling social and public benefits. Critically reflecting on these explanations, it is above all important to note that most platforms are owned and technologically developed by large corporations, which have strong commercial interests in how public activities take shape on their platforms. As such, platform corporations fundamentally shape how users express themselves, connect with each other, and exchange goods. And in this sense, it becomes increasingly clear that platforms have an important responsibility for the content, the user activity and social dynamics in relation to the surrounding policy and regulation.

[11] Natali Helberger, Jo Pierson and Thomas Poell, 'Governing online platforms: from contested to cooperative responsibility' (2018) 34 *The Information Society* 1, 1.

[12] Manuel Castells, *Communication power* (Oxford University Press 2009).

[13] Tarleton Gillespie, 'The politics of 'platforms' (2010) 12 *New Media & Society* 347: 347.

Given events like algorithmic discrimination via software,[14] fake news on Facebook during US elections,[15] inappropriate placement of ads on Youtube[16] and privacy infringements by Uber[17] it has become clear how mediated communication via digital platforms can have a negative impact on society. This is especially true when they become embedded in key domains of that society. It is for that reason that digital platforms face more vocal calls to address the issues mentioned, from policy makers, civil society, users, and the press. In this sense, Gillespie speaks about regulation *of* and *by* platforms.[18] The regulation *of* platforms refers to the policies in liberal democracies that have emerged specifying platforms' liabilities (or lack thereof) for the user content and activity they host. The flipside is then regulation *by* platforms, with digital platforms taking the responsibility of curating the content and policing the activity of their users. As stated by Gillespie: 'The regulatory framework we impose on platforms, and the ways in which the major platforms enact those obligations and impose their own on their users, are settling in as the parameters for the how public speech online is and will be privately governed.'[19]

Addressing the regulation *of* platforms starts from the premise that digital platforms are certainly not neutral, but that they are designed to invite and shape interaction and participation toward particular ends.[20] This fits with the much broader notion that 'artifacts do have politics', as established by Langdon Winner and in the related scholarly field of STS.[21] Given their increasingly steering capacity in many fields of society, public authorities have started to demand that accountability from these platforms. However as they are seen as so-called 'online intermediaries' (at least in US information policy) they are to some extent also exempted from being responsible for what happens on their platform.[22] In Europe there is the (in this

---

[14] *See* e.g., Julia Angwin, Jeff Larson, Surya Mattu and Lauren Kirchner, 'Machine bias: There's software used across the country to predict future criminals – And it's biased against blacks' (*ProRepublica*, 23 May 2016) https://www.propublica.org/article/machine-bias-risk-assessments-in-criminal-sentencing accessed 15 December 2019.

[15] *See* e.g., Craig Timberg, Elizabeth Dwosking, Adam Entous and Karoun Demirjian , 'Russian ads, now publicly released, show sophistication of influence campaign' *The Washington Post* (1 November 2017) https://www.washingtonpost.com/business/technology/russian-ads-now-publicly-released-show-sophistication-of-influence-campaign/2017/11/01/d26aead2-bf1b-11e7-8444-a0d4f04b89eb_story.html?utm_term=.97988fac4fdf accessed 15 December 2019.

[16] *See* e.g., Olivia Solon, 'Google's bad week: YouTube loses millions as advertising row reaches US' *The Guardian* (25 March 2017) https://www.theguardian.com/technology/2017/mar/25/google-youtube-advertising-extremist-content-att-verizon accessed 15 December 2019.

[17] *See* e.g., Tim Bradshaw, 'Uber settles FTC suit over privacy violations: Ride-hailing group will submit to 20 years of audits after claims it misled customers' *Financial Times* (15 August 2017) https://www.ft.com/content/4d94f714-81d4-11e7-a4ce-15b2513cb3ff accessed 15 December 2019.

[18] Tarleton Gillespie, 'Regulation of and by platforms' in Jean Burgess, Alice Marwick and Thomas Poell (eds), *The SAGE handbook of social media* (SAGE 2017).

[19] Ibid., 255.

[20] Ibid.

[21] Langdon Winner, 'Do artifacts have politics?' (1980) 109 *Daedalus* 121; in Edward J. Hackett and others (eds), *The handbook of science and technology studies* (3rd ed., MIT Press).

[22] NN, 'Eroding exceptionalism: Internet firms' legal immunity is under threat - Platforms have benefited greatly from special legal and regulatory treatmen' *The Economist* https://www.google.com/url?client=internal-element-cse&cx=013751040265774567329:ylv-hrexwbc&q=https://www.economist.com/business/2017/02/11/internet-firms-legal-immunity-is-under-threat&sa=U&ved=2ahUKEwjR0Z-x57nmAhUa7KYKHcHGCcwQFjAAegQICRAC&usg=AOvVaw25OAQdyMk4H-yw7u0xwfSe (11 February 2017) accessed 16 December 2019.

case unhelpful) black and white differentiation between 'host' (with little responsibility) and 'editor' (with full responsibility). The new reality where these platforms do have agency to steer but are not fully in control (e.g., like mass media) demand a new conceptual framework for the governance of the public role of platforms. For this we can build on the concept of *cooperative responsibility* for the realization of critical public policy objectives (see below).[23]

The perspective of regulation *by* platforms acknowledges how platforms steer user interaction via algorithms. As communication becomes increasingly mediated, the in-between medium in a digitized world most often takes the form of an 'interface'. This can be a machine-to-person interface in the form of a Graphical User Interface (GUI), or this can be a machine-to-machine interface in the form of an Application Programming Interface (API).[24] In any case these types of programmable interface give leverage and power to the programmers to steer the actions of both the producers and users by (not) building certain affordances in a particular way. The programmability also enables the inclusion of an algorithm that will run the communication and interaction in less or more predictable way. In that way, mediated communication through digital platforms curate social interaction in addition to facilitating it. However, many users do not really know how platforms intervene in their social communication. At the same time platforms often downplay these interventions, except when it is beneficial for them to stress them.[25] Nevertheless, these interventions are an essential and underexamined part of what platforms do. We need to understand that platforms matter, with their algorithms, business models and community guidelines carefully curating the content of users. As stated by Gillespie: '(...) social media platforms pick and choose, based on explicit and implicit norms, cultural presumptions about taste and etiquette, at the behest of offended users or concerned lawmakers, and in ways that best suit their economic aims'.[26] It is for that reason that fundamental values like privacy and data protection are often made subordinate to economic reasoning.[27] We therefore need to understand how platforms govern and operate communication.

III. DIGITAL PLATFORMS OPERATING COMMUNICATION

In order to understand how digital platforms and human communication are interrelated, some scholars have referred to a number of key mechanisms. The latter define the deep entanglement of platform technologies, economic models, and user practices with the activities of different social and political actors.[28] van Dijck, Poell and de Waal identify three essential

---

[23] Natali Helberger, Jo Pierson and Thomas Poell, 'Governing online platforms: from contested to cooperative responsibility' (2018) 34 *The Information Society* 1, 1.

[24] Shreeharsh Kelkar, 'Engineering a platform: The construction of interfaces, users, organizational roles, and the division of labor' (2017) 20 *New Media & Society* 2629: 2630.

[25] Tarleton Gillespie, 'Platforms Intervene' (2015) 1 *Social Media + Society* 1.

[26] Ibid., 2.

[27] See for more extensive analysis: Shoshana Zuboff, *The age of surveillance capitalism: The fight for a human future at the new frontier of power* (PublicAffairs - Hachette Book Group 2019); Nick Couldry and Ulises A. Mejias, *The costs of connection: How data is colonizing human life and appropriating it for capitalism* (Stanford University Press 2019).

[28] Tarleton Gillespie, 'The relevance of algorithms' in Tarleton Gillespie, Pablo J. Boczkowski and Kirsten A. Foot (eds), *Media technologies: essays on communication, materiality, and society*

mechanisms to gain insight in the complex way these platforms and the underlying algorithms are operating: datafication, commodification and selection.[29]

III.1 Datafication

Datafication refers to the ability of digital platforms to convert online and offline interactions and activities into data.[30] Besides the ubiquitous capturing it is also about circulating these data via GUI and API, which includes the daily use of platform data by users and the way their actions are influenced by the data circulation. In that way platforms not only measure what users do, think and feel, but also simultaneously configure their behavior.

The datafication process happens on two levels: people and environment. Datafication of social activities of *people* relates for example to social media usage, location of people, picture sharing, amounts of steps made during a day (gathered via a wearable device), and so on. The personal data of people are typically divided in volunteered data (status updates, declared interests, …), observed data (browser history, location data, …) and inferred data (future consumption patterns, health data, …).[31] From a MCS perspective it is crucial to re-contextualize these data and give them meaning, in order to avoid analysis and prediction only based on proxies and correlation. Datafication related to the *environment* of people corresponds for example with real-time data streams as meteos, open street maps, air pollution data and data gathered via citizen sciences initiatives. The proliferation of the Internet of Things and sensors is especially seen as a key technological development for increased datafication, for example in the context of Smart Cities.[32] The everyday life of users consists more and more of densely available (often mobile) computational and communication resources that are assembled in heterogeneous ways.[33] 'Ubiquitous computing' (ubicomp) or the disappearance of the infrastructure in the background, as predicted by Mark Weiser,[34] is not fulfilled, though the ubiquitous presence of sensing devices in the form of Internet of Things is getting realistic.[35]

Datafication also builds on the notion of the 'capturing' of human activities, as put forward by Philip Agre.[36] He contrasts two cultural models of privacy issues: the surveillance model

(MIT Press 2014); José van Dijck, Thomas Poell and Martijn de Waal, *The platform society: Public values in a connective world* (Oxford University Press 2018). Pierson, Jo (2021) Digital platforms as entangled infrastructures: addressing public values and trust in messaging apps. In: European Journal of Communication (Special Issue on "Governing Institutions in European Platform Societies") 36(4), 349–361 (https://doi.org/10.1177/02673231211028374).

[29] José van Dijck, Thomas Poell, Martijn de Waal, *De platformsamenleving: strijd om publieke waarden in een online wereld* (Amsterdam University Press 2016).

[30] Viktor Mayer-Schonberger and Kenneth Cukier, *Big data: a revolution that will transform how we live, work and think* (John Murray 2013).

[31] Mireille Hildebrandt, *Smart technologies and the end(s) of law: novel entanglements of law and technology* (Edward Elgar 2015): 52; WEF, *Personal data: the emergence of a new asset class* (World Economic Forum 2011).

[32] Rob Kitchin and Sung-Yueh Perng, *Code and the city* (Routledge 2016).

[33] Paul Dourish and Genevieve Bell, *Divining a digital future: mess and mythology in ubiquitous computing* (MIT Press 2011).

[34] Mark Weiser, 'The computer for the 21st century' (1991) September *Scientific American* 94.

[35] Dourish and Bell, *Divining a digital future: mess and mythology in ubiquitous computing.*

[36] Philip Agre, 'Surveillance and capture: two models of privacy' (1994) 10 *The Information Society* 101.

and the capture model. The former derives from historical experiences (of secret policy) and employs visual metaphors (like 'Big Brother'), while the latter stems from information technologists and hinges upon linguistic metaphors (like 'grammar'). The prototype situation, presented for capturing, is the deliberate reorganization of industrial work activities to allow computers to track them in real time. Agre's capture model describes '(...) the situation that results when grammars of action are imposed upon human activities, and when the newly organized activities are represented by computers in real time'.[37] 'Grammars of action' are the way that the computer aims to model human behavior, which means maintaining a set of data structures that aims to 'mirror' the day-to-day activities of people.

III.2 Commodification

Commodification entails the conversion of objects, actions and ideas into tradable goods or commodities. On the one hand this means the selling and buying of physical goods via digital platforms. However these platforms also have the capacity of marketing informal space, goods and interactions by transforming them into data.[38] All kinds of social behavior, emotions and activities become increasingly measurable and tradable, like linking, friending, preferences, talking about health, places to stay, moving around, exchanging opinions and so forth. From a political economy of media perspective[39] it is about how digital platforms enable the increase in conversion of use value into exchange value of goods, services and human activities in a way that was not possible before.

Commodification also refers to the users who promote and market themselves and their activities via all kind of platforms. This fits in with a shift from mass media and interpersonal communication to 'mass self-communication'[40] as described above. The latter is happening by various private and professional users, like journalists via Twitter, influencers via Youtube, academics via ResearchGate or jobseekers via Linked-In.

Finally, commodification by digital platforms is also upending the traditional economic model in the media world. While in the past (mass) media outlets were essential gateways to consumer attention in two-sided markets[41] this has changed due to datafication. Instead of commodifying media products and media audiences, digital media platforms of all kinds are now able to give access to consumers by commodifying user data via (most often) 'free' services. We observe a trend where a few dominant platforms are becoming the central hub on which other organizations (e.g., in mobility, news, entertainment, government) and users become dependent for their everyday professional and private activities. This leads to an unbalanced situation where the platform owners control the interfaces and algorithms that

---

[37] Ibid., 109.

[38] José van Dijck, Thomas Poell and Martijn de Waal, *De platformsamenleving: strijd om publieke waarden in een online wereld.*

[39] Vincent Mosco, *The political economy of communication* (2nd ed. edn, SAGE 2009); Dwayne Roy Winseck, 'Introductory essay: The political economies of media and the transformation of the global media industrie" in Dwayne Roy Winseck and Dal Yong Jin (eds), *The political economies of media: the transformation of the global media industries* (Bloomsbury Academic 2011).

[40] Castells, *Communication power.*

[41] Jean-Charles Rochet and Jean Tirole, 'Platform competition in two-sided markets' (2003) 1 *Journal of the European Economic Association* 990.

steer the data flows and commodification, and hence get a preponderance that is highly difficult to counterbalance by public values.

III.3 Selection

The two former mechanisms of datafication and commodification then heavily influence selection. Platforms are able to content-wise steer communication by selecting relevant topics and actors. While in the past it was foremost experts (journalists, scientists, art critics and so on) that determined the selection, we see how in digital media and platforms users take a more prominent role. The shift toward mass self-communication also entails more user control. However – as with the other mechanisms – the final selection is an outcome of the interplay between user practices, socio-economic context and technological set-up. The enhancement of user preferences by way of algorithms also leads to more personalized information flows, with the related risk of the so-called filter bubble or echo chamber effect.[42] Besides increased personalization, also virality is a key characteristic of the interplay, as being important for the business model of most social media platforms. In that sense facts and truths are in principle of no importance for the business model of commercial digital platforms. This is one of the reasons why for example fake news can circulate so easily, as viral content interactions generate a win-win for the content creators and the digital platforms.

Despite the crucial role of algorithms, their impact on selection is however most often very opaque as (commercial) platform tend to treat them as trade secrets, which are not open for inspection or discussion. In that sense a big part of the reasoning and decisions behind selection is black-boxed.[43] Given the proliferation of these type of algorithms in many spheres of life (communication, mobility, employment, finance, and so on) scholars, policy makers and society at large are demanding more transparency, fairness and accountability regarding these selection mechanisms.[44] More broadly the question is then how society and citizens can take back control of digital platforms.

IV. SOCIETY TAKING CONTROL OF DIGITAL PLATFORMS

The outcome of these three mechanisms has major implications for how public values and fundamental issues like privacy and data protection take form. In order to mitigate possible

---

[42] Eli Pariser, *The filter bubble: what the Internet is hiding from you* (Penguin Press 2011); Cass R. Sunstein, *Republic.com 2.0* (Princeton University Press 2007).

[43] Frank Pasquale, *The black box society: the secret algorithms that control money and information* (Harvard University Press 2015).

[44] Solon Barocas and Andrew D. Selbst, 'Big Data's disparate impact' (2016) 104 *California Law Review* 671; Tal Zarsky, The trouble with algorithmic decisions: An analytic roadmap to examine efficiency and fairness in automated and opaque decision making' (2016) 41 *Science, Technology, & Human Values* 118; Christian Sandvig and others, 'Auditing algorithms: Research methods for detecting discrimination on Internet platforms' ("Data and Discrimination: Converting Critical Concerns into Productive Inquiry," a preconference at 64th Annual Meeting of the International Communication Association (ICA)). See also initiatives like FAccT ACM Conference on Fairness, Accountability, and Transparency (https://facctconference.org), FAT/ML (https://www.fatml.org) and Partnership on AI (https://www.partnershiponai.org/#s-partners both accessed 19 October 2021).

negative outcomes and to support positive impact, we propose interdisciplinary MCS research on three main strategies, linked with the set-up of media and communication in society. They would focus on socio-economic arrangement, technology and user practices, referring respectively to cooperative responsibility, empowerment by design and data literacy. These strategies are aimed at taking more control of digital platforms in data-driven societies.

IV.1 Cooperative Responsibility

Given their increasing embeddedness in public activities, digital platforms are also deeply linked with public values and policy objectives associated with these activities. Situated on the level of socio-economic arrangements, Helberger, Pierson and Poell have developed a conceptual framework for the governance of the public role of platforms.[45] For this they introduce the notion of *cooperative responsibility*. It argues that the realization of public values in platform-based public activities cannot be adequately achieved by allocating responsibility to one central actor (as is currently often the case) but should be the outcome of dynamic interaction of different stakeholders, foremost digital platforms, users and public authorities. This builds on the observation that digital communication and content is increasingly the result of the interplay between these stakeholders. The challenge is then to find an agreement on the appropriate division of labour with regard to managing responsibility for their role in public space.

The current debate on the responsibility of platforms is often framed black or white, whether or not platforms can be held accountable, legally or morally, for what is 'shared' through them. However, this does not reflect the reality because:

> multiple actors are effectively responsible, including: the platform owners that develop the technological infrastructures through which users interact with each other; the users who choose to share particular content; and, as we will argue, state institutions that must create the legal and policy framework in which these parties operate.[46]

For this we build on the notion of the *problem of many hands*, as developed in political science by Thompson.[47] This refers to a situation in which different actors contribute in diverse ways to (the solution to) a problem, where it is difficult to recognize who is responsible for which actions and what consequences. Therefore, we cannot easily allocate responsibility accordingly.[48] Typical examples are climate change, cybercrime and financial crises. The problem of many hands can also be understood as a 'wicked problem', as defined by Rittel and Webber.[49] They start from the observation that societal problems cannot be addressed on the basis of the classic (rational) paradigm of science and engineering because they are inherently 'wicked'.

---

[45] Helberger, Pierson and Poell, 'Governing online platforms: from contested to cooperative responsibility'.

[46] Ibid., 2–3.

[47] Dennis F. Thompson, 'Moral responsibility of public officials: The problem of many hands' (1980) 74 *The American Political Science Review* 905.

[48] Neelke Doorn, 'Responsibility ascriptions in technology development and engineering: Three perspectives' (2012) 18 *Science and Engineering Ethics* 69.

[49] Horst W.J. Rittel and Melvin M. Webber, 'Dilemmas in a general theory of planning' (1973) 4 *Policy sciences* 155.

The latter term refers to a class of social system problems which are ill-formulated, where the information is confusing, where there are many stakeholders with conflicting values, and where the consequences for the whole system are thoroughly confusing.[50] The issues under discussion will be framed according to the preferences, ideas, interests and values of the various actors involved, which leads to a multitude of stakeholder-specific definitions of and solutions to the problem at hand.[51] In that way problems of many hands and wicked problems clearly also apply to digital platforms, when dealing with issues like hate speech, fake news and media diversity. The possible solution to this type of situation lies in finding an adequate and fair balance of distributing responsibility among the stakeholders involved, heavily depending on the available capabilities and the specific (sector) context.

Individual users have a responsibility to behave in a decent way according to prevailing values and norms, taking into account social, cultural and institutional differences. Institutions and companies of course need to comply with the legal requirements, while they should also create the conditions that allow individual users to comply with their responsibilities. The latter can be done by awareness creation and educational initiatives (e.g., via community guidelines), but also by designing their systems and infrastructures in such a way, that they uphold the expected values and legal obligations. This is in line with the suggestion by Thompson that we need to shift our perspective from the responsibility for outcomes to the responsibility for the design of institutions and systems, which he coined as 'prospective design responsibility'.[52] In that way users and other stakeholders are (more) likely to take up their responsibilities. For digital platforms this means that architectural design choices take over some role in identifying and allocating responsibility. Privacy by design and by default is a clear example of that approach. Other examples are review and flagging mechanisms, the configuration of recommendation algorithms, constraining algorithmic amplication, the availability of, and incentives for users to engage with content, and so on. Finally, also governments have a role to play by implementing sensible legal regulations, by providing guidance and benchmarks, as well as by creating effective oversight and enforcement mechanisms and other mechanisms for monitoring the fair allocation of responsibilities.[53]

IV.2 Empowerment by Design

When we take it to the level of artefacts and building further on the notion of 'prospective design responsibility', we need to investigate in what way we can have an impact on how technological media artefacts are constructed. It has been established since long, in particular in the STS field, that artefacts and technological infrastructures do have steering capacity.[54]

---

[50] C. West Churchman, 'Guest editorial: wicked problems' (1967) 14 *Management Science* 141.

[51] Jan H. Kwakkel, Warren E. Walker and Marjolijn Haasnoot, 'Coping with the wickedness of public policy problems: approaches for decision making under deep uncertainty' (2016) 142 *Journal of Water Resource Planning and Management*.

[52] Dennis F. Thompson, 'Responsibility for failures of government: The problem of many hands' (2014) 44 *The American Review of Public Administration* 259.

[53] Ibid.; David A. Moss, 'A brief history of risk management policy' in Jacob S. Hacker and Ann O'Leary (eds), *Shared responsibility, shared risk: government, markets and social policy in the twenty-first century* (Oxford University Press 2012).

[54] Lawrence Lessig, *Code: version 2.0* (2nd edn, Basic Books 2006); Langdon Winner, 'Do artifacts have politics?' (1980) 109 *Daedalus* 121.

Within MCS there has been a shift from investigating separate media conduits to a more overall approach of infrastructures. Originally for scholars of media interested in conduit and not content, each medium was a technology and also a surrounding 'environment'.[55] This has led to separate traditions of inquiry: television studies, radio studies, film studies, telecommunication studies, and internet studies. Due to convergence and digitization, in combination with the proliferation of internet, researchers in MCS turned to new concepts to acknowledge the heterogeneity of media. This has spurred the domain of infrastructure studies containing and characterizing the new digital objects of study in the media landscape.[56] As this domain emerged from STS and information science, it also stresses the socio-technical nature of (media) technologies. As expressed by Star and Bowker:

> (...) the most important thing is for the user of the infrastructure to first become aware of the social and political work that the infrastructure is doing and then seek ways to modify it (locally or globally) as need be. Infrastructures subtend complex ecologies: their design process should always be tentative, flexible and open.[57]

This call for modifying infrastructures and the plea for their design process to be tentative, flexible and open, also fits in with the notions of data protection by design and data protection by default in the European General Data Protection Regulation (GDPR).[58] However if we aim to safeguard public values and norms in digital platforms that go beyond privacy and data protection, we should extend this notion to 'empowerment by design'. The latter is defined as the exercise of building infrastructures and systems in such a way that citizens and organized civil society have agency to safeguard and strengthen public values and norms in society.[59] Agency is seen from the perspective of having an influence on the infrastructure design as well as the enactment of citizenship. A basic question in this regard is to first identify whose values and interests we aim to safeguard. Once that question is answered, the main challenge is then 'how to infrastructure' in order to give agency to citizens and civil society organizations and thereby strengthening public values.[60] Based on insights from STS this preferably happens in the early phase of technology design and development. As indicated by Winner:

> By far the greatest latitude of choice exists the very first time a particular instrument, system, or technique is introduced. Because choices tend to become strongly fixed in material equipment, economic

---

[55] Joshua Meyrowitz, 'Shifting worlds of strangers: medium theory and changes in "them" versus "us"' (1997) 67 *Sociological Inquiry* 59: 60.

[56] Jean-Christophe Plantin and others, 'Infrastructure studies meet platform studies in the age of Google and Facebook' (2016) *New Media & Society* 1.

[57] Susan L. Star and Geoffrey C. Bowker, 'How to infrastructure' in Leah A. Lievrouw and Sonia Livingstone (eds), *The handbook of new media: Social shaping and social consequences of ICTs (Updated Student Edition)* (SAGE 2006): 242.

[58] Regulation (EU) 2016/679 of the European Parliament and of the Council of 27 April 2016 on the protection of natural persons with regard to the processing of personal data and on the free movement of such data, and repealing Directive 95/46/EC (General Data Protection Regulation), OJ 2016 L 119/1: 48

[59] Jo Pierson and Stefania Milan, 'Empowerment by design: Configuring the agency of citizens and activists in digital infrastructure' (IAMCR Conference 'Transforming Culture, Politics & Communication: New media, new territories, new discourses', 17 July 2017).

[60] Star and Bowker, 'How to infrastructure'.

> investment, and social habit, the original flexibility vanishes for all practical purposes once the initial commitments are made.[61]

This means that we need to intervene *before* the black box closes, instead of having to fight the black box *after* it has been closed.

IV.3 Data Literacy

On the level of user practices a major challenge is the need to develop and further a particular form of media literacy among citizens, that includes a data analytics perspective.[62] Media literacy is typically defined as '(…) the ability to access, analyze, evaluate and create messages in a variety of forms'[63] and is central to empowerment of users in our complex mediated and data-driven societies. Due to the proliferation of digital platforms with their specific mechanisms, we need to upgrade media literacy to also include data literacy. The latter involves increasing awareness, building attitudes, enhancing capabilities and adjusting behavior among users regarding (personal) data collection, processing and (re)use in the area of social media technologies and digital platforms. It extends media literacy by incorporating understandings of the material conditions and technological affordances of the proprietary control of personal data.[64] The growing imbalance between those who generate data and those who convert these data into value, creates a need to open up new forms of digital literacies, such as privacy literacies, code literacies and algorithmic literacies. This fits in with the broader perspective of 'data infrastructure literacy', referring to the: '(…) ability to account for, intervene around and participate in the wider socio-technical infrastructures through which data is created, stored and analysed'.[65] It is through these types of literacy that citizens can act with agency in the face of data power.[66]

However, in order for data literacy to have a real impact, we are faced with major challenges. The latter refers to the role that platforms are playing in public and private life of people. These media platforms have been able to make themselves indispensable for many kinds of information sharing and interpersonal communication, especially for younger people. Figures in Flanders (northern part of Belgium) indicate that 61 per cent of the population indicate feeling dependent on social media, spending too much time. The social media dependency is much more prevalent among Flemings younger than 44 years old. The latter group also experiences the most conflicts in time spent on social media and time spent on their careers, their families,

---

[61] Winner, 'Do artifacts have politics?', 127.

[62] Nick Couldry, 'Inaugural: A necessary disenchantment: myth, agency and injustice in a digital world' (2014) 62 *The Sociological Review* 880.

[63] Sonia Livingstone, 'Media literacy and the challenge of new information and communication technologies' (2004) 7 *The Communication Review* 3: 5.

[64] John Naughton, 'Why we need a 21st-century Martin Luther to challenge the church of tech' *The Guardian* https://www.theguardian.com/technology/2017/oct/29/why-we-need-a-21st-century-martin-luther-to-challenge-church-of-technology-95-theses (29 October 2017) accessed 15 December 2019; Evgeny Morozov, *To save everything, click here: the folly of technological solutionism* (1st edn. PublicAffairs 2013).

[65] Jonathan Gray, Carolin Gerlitz and Liliana Bounegru, 'Data infrastructure literacy' (2018) 5 *Big Data & Society* 1, 1.

[66] Helen Kennedy, Thomas Poell and José van Dijck, 'Data and agency' (2015) July–December *Big Data & Society* 1, 5.

hobbies, and so on.[67] In MCS this process of dependency and fully absorbing media technologies into the everyday life of people has been defined as 'domestication'.[68] This refers to the gradual process by which media are consumed and 'tamed' within the socio-cultural context of the home environment and beyond. People adapt their media consumption behavior according to the requirements of the (new) technology, while they simultaneously also aim to adapt the technology to their user wishes. The end result is that domesticated ICT disappear and dissolve into the everyday of people, as they are not perceived as technologies anymore but as a natural extension of face-to-face interactions and communication. This gives these platforms a self-evident character, which makes it difficult to reflect on them and hence to critique them on how they operate and the role they have.

The process of domestication is reinforced by the change in mediated communication and the related politics of platforms, as explained above.[69] Human 'connectedness' via social media is increasingly translated into automated 'connectivity' for commercial purposes.[70] 'Connectivity' is defined as the automated process behind real-life connections via social media platforms, generating a profitable form of 'connectedness'.[71] Therefore, it would be better to use the term 'connective media' instead of 'social media'. As stated by van Dijck:

> What is claimed to be 'social' is in fact the result of human input shaped by computed output and vice versa – a sociotechnical ensemble whose components can hardly be told apart. The norms and values supporting the 'social' image of these media remain hidden in platforms' technological textures.[72]

As these platforms tend to emphasize their social role, while playing down their monetization of data, they appear to be media that just facilitate social interactions and are henceforth easily domesticated, just like other media in the past. However given the obfuscated character of data monetization, it is not obvious for everyday users to become aware and understand how these platforms really operate.[73] The latter requires an enhanced effort to extend media literacy with data (infrastructure) literacy, in order to be able to act upon the increased risk of (unwanted) disclosure of private information to third parties.

The combined effect of platform domestication and the intensified conversion of human 'connectedness' into monetized 'connectivity' leads to user disempowerment.[74] Empowerment refers to the process of strengthening individuals, by which they get a grip on their situation

---

[67] Karel Vandendriessche, Eva Steenberghs, Ann Matheve, Annabel Georges and Lieven De Marez, imec.digimeter 2020: Digitale trends in Vlaanderen (imec, 2020): 47.

[68] Roger Silverstone and Leslie Haddon, 'Design and domestication of information and communication technologies: technical change and everyday life' in Robin Mansell and Roger Silverstone (eds), *Communication by design: the politics of information and communication technologies* (Oxford University Press 1996); Merete Lie and Knut H. Sorensen (eds), *Making technology our own? Domesticating technology into everyday life* (Scandinavian University Press 1996).

[69] Gillespie, 'The politics of 'platforms'.

[70] van Dijck, *The culture of connectivity: a critical history of social media.*

[71] Jo Pierson, 'Privacy and empowerment in connective media' in Thanassis Tiropanis and others (eds), *INSCI 2015 - Lecture Notes in Computer Sciences (LNCS)*, vol 9089 (Springer International Publishing 2015).

[72] van Dijck, *The culture of connectivity: a critical history of social media*: 13–14.

[73] Rob Heyman and Jo Pierson, 'Social media, delinguistification and colonization of lifeworld: Changing faces of Facebook' (2015) 1 Social Media + Society 1.

[74] Jo Pierson, 'Online privacy in social media: a conceptual exploration of empowerment and vulnerability' (2012) *4thQ Communications & Strategies (Digiworld Economic Journal)* 99.

and environment, through the acquisition of more control, sharpening their critical awareness and the stimulation of participation.[75] Empowerment in relation to digital media: '(...) is dependent on knowledge of *how mechanisms operate [artefacts]* and *from what premise [socio-economic arrangements]*, as well as on the *skills to change them [practices]*' [own emphasis and addition].[76] The user becomes disempowered from the moment that the platform is sufficiently domesticated to leverage the user acceptance of extensive collecting, processing and (re)use of (personal) data. We call this occurrence 'digital seepage' or 'data seepage',[77] which signifies that the platform has become an 'obligatory passage point'[78] for private interactions and where users have no real possibility – from a social perspective – to oppose their data from being processed in an opaque and uncontrollable way.

This is what for example is happening with messaging apps.[79] People were accustomed to use texting via SMS as a convenient way of communicating via telecommunication networks. The platforms have introduced ways to replace this type of telecom connection by a datafied internet connection.[80] This happened gradually through the rising popularity of messaging apps that send messages via the internet protocol instead of the wireless telecom protocol (e.g., Messages on Apple iOS operating system). Several messaging apps have been spun existing digital platforms and then decoupled from them, like Facebook Messenger, which has become separated from the Facebook platform. There are also applications that were established as separate messaging services (such as WhatsApp and Telegram) and have built up their own customer base. Some of these apps are acquired by larger players, like WhatsApp and Instagram being bought by Facebook. Other apps aim to survive as independent companies offering particular features, as contenders of the bigger digital platforms, like Snapchat offering disappearing pictures and augmented reality filters. The latter are then copied by their (bigger) competitors. Figures show how youth has started to use messaging much more for private communication, while the social network platforms (like Facebook) are increasingly perceived as public communication channels less fit for so-called 'original sharing'.[81] The latter refers to posts by people about themselves and their personal lives, as opposed to articles they are liking and sharing from elsewhere on the web. This has led to data seepage as it helps to leverage the intense everyday use of these messaging apps for data harvesting and

[75] Marc Zimmerman and Julian Rappaport, 'Citizen participation, perceived control and psychological empowerment' (1988) 16 *American Journal of Community Psychology* 725.

[76] van Dijck, *The culture of connectivity: a critical history of social media* 171.

[77] Jo Pierson, 'Conclusie: sociale media en empowerment' in Rob Heyman and others (eds), *Hier vloekt men niet, Facebook ziet alles - Sociale netwerken ontrafeld* (Davidsfonds Uitgeverij 2013).

[78] Bruno Latour, 'Where are the missing masses? The sociology of a few mundane artefacts' in Wiebe Bijker and John Law (eds), *Shaping technology - Building society: Studies in sociotechnical change* (MIT Press 1992): 158.

[79] Pierson, Jo (2021) Digital platforms as entangled infrastructures: addressing public values and trust in messaging apps. In: European Journal of Communication (Special Issue on "Governing Institutions in European Platform Societies"). 36(4), 349–361 (https://doi.org/10.1177/02673231222028374).

[80] Cara McGoogan, 'End of SMS? WhatsApp and Facebook messages outstrip texts by three times' *The Telegraph* (22 April 2016) http://www.telegraph.co.uk/technology/2016/04/22/end-of-sms-whatsapp-and-facebook-messages-outstrip-texts-by-thre/ accessed 15 December 2019.

[81] Will Oremus, 'Facebook isn't the social network anymore: It's losing the intimacy that once addicted us. So it's becoming something different—and much bigger' (Slate, 24 April 2016) https://slate.com/technology/2016/04/facebook-isnt-the-social-network-anymore-so-what-is-it.html accessed 15 December 2019.

processing with commercial aims. The latter however is most often invisible and too complex to understand for lay people. And even if people are aware of this, they mostly have no choice of to accept this otherwise they cannot use the (free) service.

Given the data seepage, it is no surprise that a large number of people are resigned to giving up their data, indicated as 'digital resignation'.[82] Turow, Hennessy and Draper state that:

> Resignation occurs when a person believes an undesirable outcome is inevitable and feels powerless to stop it. Rather than feeling able to make choices, Americans believe it is futile to manage what companies can learn about them. Our study reveals that more than half do not want to lose control over their information but also believe this loss of control has already happened.[83]

This type of resignation occurs even more among respondents that know more about ways marketers can use their personal data, as they observe and know how difficult it is to live your social life in a seamless way without giving up a lot of personal data. We observe a similar pattern in Flanders (Belgium) where 68 per cent of the people are defeatist, saying they do not have control any more over which personal data about them is being collected and used.[84]

This means that extending media literacy with data literacy is necessary but not sufficient for solving issues of user disempowerment. Literacy initiatives and related policies often over-estimate the role of the individual citizens in their knowledge and capabilities to uncover and understand the working of online data exchanges, and their choices to act on this.[85] Therefore we also need interventions on the levels of technology and policy, which among others means changes in the infrastructures as enforced by internet governance measures and data protection regulation. In addition, strengthening civil society organizations on digital rights and privacy also plays a major role in addressing these challenges and hence empowering citizens. Only in that way are we able to safeguard the balance between strengthening the empowerment – or mitigating disempowerment – of users while at the same time unburdening the users with respect to their responsibility.

V. CONCLUSION

The transition in mediated communication towards digital platforms generates profound inter-disciplinary research challenges for privacy and data protection. Research in MCS has shown how (mostly commercial) digital intermediaries in the form of general purpose and sector

---

[82] Nora A. Draper and Joseph Turow, 'The corporate cultivation of digital resignation' (2019) 21 *New Media & Society* 1824.

[83] Joseph Turow, Michael Hennessy and Nora Draper, *The tradeoff fallacy: how marketeers are misreprenting American consumers and opening them up to exploitation* (University of Pennsylvania 2015) 3.

[84] Karel Vandendriessche, Eva Steenberghs, Ann Matheve, Annabel Georges and Lieven De Marez, imec.digimeter 2020: Digitale trends in Vlaanderen (imec, 2020): 114.

[85] Leo Van Audenhove and others, 'Media Literacy and Internet Governance: A necessary marriage, exemplified by the case of the Belgian State versus Facebook' (Pre-conference 'Power, communication, and technology in Internet governance' for the International Communication Association (ICA) 2016, organized by GigaNet (Global Internet Governance Academic Network), hosted by Kanazawa Institute of Technology (Tokyo campus), supported by Internet Corporation for Assigned Names and Numbers (ICANN), and Department of Communication, University of Illinois at Chicago).

specific digital platforms are becoming deeply involved in a wide range of public activities. In that sense they become indispensable for all types of societal and economic activities, with sometimes no genuine alternatives. For example (young) people in the West very much complicate their social life if they abstain from using any kind of Meta/Facebook platform (like Facebook, WhatsApp or Instagram) for social interaction and communication. The same accounts for organizations. For example, in times of budgetary hardship for education, universities have a difficult time resisting commercial offerings by platform giants (like Alphabet/Google or Microsoft) for taking over their mail systems or learning management systems. These Software-as-a-Service (SaaS) offerings are often more user friendly and cheaper (if not gratis) in comparison to the expensive maintenance and upgrading of an own (legacy) system. All this of course in return for access to data and a lucrative market of potential customers. In that way the platform proliferation has a significant role in how the landscape of privacy and data protection takes form.

However, in order to genuinely understand the impact of these developments, we first need to get a grasp of the underlying forces in these platforms. For this we have explained three main mechanisms by which digital platforms operate (datafication, commodification and selection). In order to safeguard fundamental public values like privacy and data protection in a future platform society, we need to address each of these mechanisms in a threefold way, integrating the levels of artefacts, practices and socio-economic arrangements.

First, in order to avoid undesirable datafication and capturing of (personal) data we need artefacts and systems that are designed to minimize the exposure to infringement of privacy and data protection, while also ideally empowering citizens as data subjects. This would mean that we extend the notion of data protection by design to empowerment by design. Intensified initiatives on data literacy should help people to be better comprehend how current systems work and what they do. In that sense they need to be made aware of how they are datafied online (e.g., via tracking and profiling) as well as offline (e.g., via sensors and CCTV). Governments have the role via the data protection authorities (DPA) to keep an eye and enforce data minimization and purpose limitation, based on the European GDPR regulation.[86]

Secondly, excessive commodification also undermines privacy, data protection and other public values. Therefore, a public debate is needed on how to reach a fair distribution and (re) organization of responsibilities among the main stakeholders, in the first place platform corporations, public authorities and citizens. This approach of cooperative responsibility should lead to a more sustainable governance of the public role of platforms, regarding the realization of critical public policy objectives. This also requires systems to be built in a transparent and accountable way, so that the public and public authorities can better assess potential economic and financial interests or bias in the design and operations of the system. By setting up a dialogue with the stakeholders involved and building systems that explain their decision, also the citizens should have a better understanding of why platforms operate as they do.

Thirdly, selection in and via platforms is the outcome of an interplay between technology, people and regulation. This is not only essential for privacy and data protection, but also in other issues like surveillance practices and non-discrimination. The selection algorithms need to be transparent and accountable for the way they operate. Therefore, these systems need to

---

[86] Regulation (EU) 2016/679 of the European Parliament and of the Council of 27 April 2016 on the protection of natural persons with regard to the processing of personal data and on the free movement of such data, and repealing Directive 95/46/EC (General Data Protection Regulation), OJ 2016 L 119/1.

make clear why particular content and advertising is shown, based on what type of (personal) data and what kind of profiling. In that way people are more aware of the reasoning of selection behind the information they see. Besides privacy preservations, public authorities could for example also demand that systems strengthen authenticity and diversity in online news distribution.

Combining all these different perspectives will help to monitor, analyse and possibly correct undesirable or even unlawful future developments regarding privacy and data protection.

REFERENCES

Agre P., 'Surveillance and capture: two models of privacy' (1994) 10 *The Information Society* 101.

Angwin J., J. Larson, S. Mattu and L Kirchner, 'Machine bias: There's software used across the country to predict future criminals - And it's biased against blacks' (*ProRepublica*, 23 May 2016) https://www.propublica.org/article/machine-bias-risk-assessments-in-criminal-sentencing accessed 15 December 2019.

Barocas S. and A.D. Selbst, 'Big Data's disparate impact' (2016) 104 *California Law Review* 671.

Boczkowski P.J. and L.A. Lievrouw, 'Bridging STS and communication studies: scholarship on media and information technologies' in Edward J. Hackett and others (eds), *The handbook of science and technology studies* (3rd edn, MIT 2008).

Bradshaw T., 'Uber settles FTC suit over privacy violations: Ride-hailing group will submit to 20 years of audits after claims it misled customers' *Financial Times* (15 August 2017) https://www.ft.com/content/4d94f714-81d4-11e7-a4ce-15b2513cb3ff accessed 15 December 2019.

Castells M., *Communication power* (Oxford University Press 2009).

Couldry N., 'Inaugural: A necessary disenchantment: myth, agency and injustice in a digital world. (2014) 62 *The Sociological Review* 880.

Couldry N. and U.A. Mejias, *The costs of connection: How data is colonizing human life and appropriating it for capitalism* (Stanford University Press 2019).

Doorn N., 'Responsibility ascriptions in technology development and engineering: Three perspectives' (2012) 18 *Science and Engineering Ethics* 69.

Dourish P. and G. Bell, *Divining a digital future: mess and mythology in ubiquitous computing* (MIT Press 2011).

Draper N.A. and J. Turow, 'The corporate cultivation of digital resignation' (2019) 21 *New Media & Society* 1824.

Feenberg A., *Questioning technology* (Routledge 1999).

Garnham N., *Emancipation, the media, and modernity: arguments about the media and social theory* (Oxford University Press 2000) 64.

Gillespie T., 'Platforms intervene' (2015) 1 *Social Media + Society* 1.

Gillespie T., 'The politics of 'platforms' (2010) 12 *New Media & Society* 347: 347.

Gillespie T., 'The relevance of algorithms' in T. Gillespie, P.J. Boczkowski and K.A. Foot (eds), *Media technologies: essays on communication, materiality, and society* (MIT Press 2014).

Gillespie T., 'Regulation of and by platforms' in Jean Burgess, Alice Marwick and Thomas Poell (eds), *The SAGE handbook of social media* (SAGE 2017).

Gillespie T., P.J. Boczkowski and K.A. Foot (eds), *Media technologies: essays on communication, materiality, and society* (Inside technology, MIT Press 2014).

Gray J., C. Gerlitz and L Bounegru, 'Data infrastructure literacy' (2018) 5 *Big Data & Society* 1, 1.

Hackett E.J. and others, 'Introduction' in Edward J. Hackett and others (eds), *The handbook of science and technology studies* (3rd ed., MIT Press).

Haythornthwaite C.A. and B. Wellman, 'The Internet in everyday life' in B. Wellman and C.A. Haythornthwaite (eds), *The Internet in everyday life* (Blackwell 2002).

Helberger N., J. Pierson and T. Poell, 'Governing online platforms: from contested to cooperative responsibility' (2018) 34 *The Information Society* 1, 1.

Heyman R. and J. Pierson, 'Social media, delinguistification and colonization of lifeworld: Changing faces of Facebook' (2015) 1 *Social Media + Society* 1.
Hildebrandt M., *Smart technologies and the end(s) of law: novel entanglements of law and technology* (Edward Elgar 2015): 52.
Kelkar S., 'Engineering a platform: The construction of interfaces, users, organizational roles, and the division of labor' (2017) 20 *New Media & Society* 2629: 2630.
Kennedy H., T. Poell and J. van Dijck, 'Data and agency' (2015) July–December *Big Data & Society* 1, 5.
Kitchin R. and S-Y. Perng, *Code and the city* (Routledge 2016).
Kwakkel J.H., W.E. Walker and M. Haasnoot, 'Coping with the wickedness of public policy problems: Approaches for decision making under deep uncertainty' (2016) 142 *Journal of Water Resource Planning and Management*.
Latour B., 'Where are the missing masses? The sociology of a few mundane artefacts' in W. Bijker and J. Law (eds), *Shaping technology – Building society: Studies in sociotechnical change* (MIT Press 1992): 158.
Lessig L., *Code: version 2.0* (2nd edn, Basic Books 2006).
Lie M. and K.H. Sorensen (eds), *Making technology our own? Domesticating technology into everyday life* (Scandinavian University Press 1996).
Lievrouw L.A. and S. Livingstone, 'Introduction: the social shaping and consequences of ICTs' in L.A. Lievrouw and S. Livingstone (eds), *The handbook of new media* (SAGE 2002).
Livingstone S., 'Media literacy and the challenge of new information and communication technologies' (2004) 7 *The Communication Review* 3: 5.
Mansell R., *Imagining the Internet: communication, innovation, and governance* (Oxford University Press 2012).
Mayer-Schonberger V. and K. Cukier, *Big data: a revolution that will transform how we live, work and think* (John Murray 2013).
McGoogan C., 'End of SMS? WhatsApp and Facebook messages outstrip texts by three times' *The Telegraph* (22 April 2016) http://www.telegraph.co.uk/technology/2016/04/22/end-of-sms-whatsapp-and-facebook-messages-outstrip-texts-by-thre/ accessed 15 December 2019.
Meyrowitz J., 'Shifting worlds of strangers: medium theory and changes in "them" versus "us"' (1997) 67 *Sociological Inquiry* 59: 60.
Morozov E., *To save everything, click here: the folly of technological solutionism* (1st edn. edn, PublicAffairs 2013).
Mosco V., *Becoming digital* (1st edn, Emerald Publishing 2017) 4.
Mosco V., *The political economy of communication* (2nd ed. edn, SAGE 2009).
Moss D.A., 'A brief history of risk management policy' in J.S. Hacker and A. O'Leary (eds), *Shared responsibility, shared risk : government, markets and social policy in the twenty-first century* (Oxford University Press 2012).
Naughton J., 'Why we need a 21st-century Martin Luther to challenge the church of tech' *The Guardian* (https://www.theguardian.com/technology/2017/oct/29/why-we-need-a-21st-century-martin-luther-to-challenge-church-of-technology-95-theses (29 October 2017) accessed 15 December 2019'.
NN, 'Eroding exceptionalism: Internet firms' legal immunity is under threat – Platforms have benefited greatly from special legal and regulatory treatment' *The Economist* https://www.google.com/url?client=internal-element-cse&cx=013751040265774567329:ylv-hrexwbc&q=https://www.economist.com/business/2017/02/11/internet-firms-legal-immunity-is-under-threat&sa=U&ved=2ahUKEwjR0Z-x57nmAhUa7KYKHcHGCcwQFjAAegQICRAC&usg=AOvVaw25OAQdyMk4H-yw7u0xwfSe (11 February 2017) accessed 16 December 2019.
Oremus C., 'Facebook isn't the social network anymore: It's losing the intimacy that once addicted us. So it's becoming something different—and much bigger' (Slate, 24 April 2016) https://slate.com/technology/2016/04/facebook-isnt-the-social-network-anymore-so-what-is-it.html accessed 15 December 2019.
Pariser E., *The filter bubble: what the Internet is hiding from you* (Penguin Press 2011).
Pasquale F., *The black box society: the secret algorithms that control money and information* (Harvard University Press 2015).

Pierson J., 'Online privacy in social media: a conceptual exploration of empowerment and vulnerability' (2012) *4thQ Communications & Strategies (Digiworld Economic Journal)* 99.

Pierson J. and I. Van Zeeland, 'Privacy from a media studies perspective' in B. van der Sloot and A. de Groot (eds), *Handbook privacy studies: an interdisciplinary introduction* (Amsterdam University Press 2018).

Pierson J. and S. Milan, 'Empowerment by design: Configuring the agency of citizens and activists in digital infrastructure' (IAMCR Conference 'Transforming Culture, Politics & Communication: New media, new territories, new discourses', 17 July 2017).

Pierson J., 'Conclusie: sociale media en empowerment' in Rob Heyman and others (eds), *Hier vloekt men niet, Facebook ziet alles - Sociale netwerken ontrafeld* (Davidsfonds Uitgeverij 2013).

Pierson J., 'Privacy and empowerment in connective media' in T. Tiropanis and others (eds), *INSCI 2015 - Lecture Notes in Computer Sciences (LNCS)*, vol 9089 (Springer International Publishing 2015).

Pierson, J. (2021) Digital platforms as entangled infrastructures: addressing public values and trust in messaging apps. In: *European Journal of Communication (Special Issue on "Governing Institutions in European Platform Societies")* 36(4), 349–361 (https://doi.org/10.1177/02673231211028374).

Plantin J-C. and others, 'Infrastructure studies meet platform studies in the age of Google and Facebook' (2016) *New Media & Society* 1.

Rittel H.W.J. and M.M. Webber, 'Dilemmas in a general theory of planning' (1973) 4 *Policy sciences* 155.

Rochet J-C. and J. Tirole, 'Platform competition in two-sided markets' (2003) 1 *Journal of the European Economic Association* 990.

Sandvig C. and others, 'Auditing Algorithms: Research Methods for Detecting Discrimination on Internet Platforms' ("Data and Discrimination: Converting Critical Concerns into Productive Inquiry," a preconference at 64th Annual Meeting of the International Communication Association (ICA)).

Silverstone R. and L. Haddon, 'Design and domestication of information and communication technologies: technical change and everyday life' in R. Mansell and R. Silverstone (eds), *Communication by design: the politics of information and communication technologies* (Oxford University Press 1996).

Silverstone R., *Why study the media?* (SAGE 1999).

Solon O., 'Google's bad week: YouTube loses millions as advertising row reaches US' *The Guardian* (25 March 2017) https://www.theguardian.com/technology/2017/mar/25/google-youtube-advertising-extremist-content-att-verizon accessed 15 December 2019.

Star S.L. and G.C. Bowker, 'How to infrastructure' in L A Lievrouw and S Livingstone (eds), *The handbook of new media: Social shaping and social consequences of ICTs (Updated Student Edition)* (SAGE 2006): 242.

Sunstein C.R., *Republic.com 2.0* (Princeton University Press 2007).

Thompson D.F., 'Moral responsibility of public officials: The problem of many hands' (1980) 74 *The American Political Science Review* 905.

Thompson D.F., 'Responsibility for failures of government: The problem of many hands' (2014) 44 *The American Review of Public Administration* 259.

Timberg C., E. Dwosking, A. Entous and K. Demirjian, 'Russian ads, now publicly released, show sophistication of influence campaign' *The Washington Post* (1 November 2017) https://www.washingtonpost.com/business/technology/russian-ads-now-publicly-released-show-sophistication-of-influence-campaign/2017/11/01/d26aead2-bf1b-11e7-8444-a0d4f04b89eb_story.html?utm_term=.97988fac4fdf accessed 15 December 2019.

Turow J., M. Hennessy and N. Draper, *The tradeoff fallacy: how marketeers are misreprenting American consumers and opening them up to exploitation* (University of Pennsylvania 2015): 3.

Van Audenhove L. and others, 'Media literacy and internet governance: A necessary marriage, exemplified by the case of the Belgian State versus Facebook' (Pre-conference 'Power, communication, and technology in Internet governance' for the International Communication Association (ICA) 2016, organized by GigaNet (Global Internet Governance Academic Network), hosted by Kanazawa Institute of Technology (Tokyo campus), supported by Internet Corporation for Assigned Names and Numbers (ICANN), and Department of Communication, University of Illinois at Chicago).

van Dijck J., *The culture of connectivity: a critical history of social media* (Oxford University Press 2013).

van Dijck J., T. Poell and M. de Waal, *De platformsamenleving: strijd om publieke arden in een online wereld* (Amsterdam University Press 2016).
van Dijck J., T. Poel and M. de Waal, *The platform society: Public values in a connective world* (Oxford University Press 2018).
Vandendriessche, K., Steenberghs, E., Matheve, A., Georges, A. and De Marez, L., imec.digimeter 2020: Digitale trends in Vlaanderen (imec, 2020): 63.
Warren S. and L.D. Brandeis, 'The right to privacy' (1890) 4 *Harvard Law Review* 69.
WEF, *Personal data: the emergence of a new asset class* (World Economic Forum 2011).
Weiser M., 'The computer for the 21st century' (1991) September *Scientific American* 94.
West Churchman C., 'Guest editorial: wicked problems' (1967) 14 *Management Science* 141.
Winner L., 'Do artifacts have politics?' (1980) 109 *Daedalus* 121.
Winseck D.R., 'Introductory essay: The political economies of media and the transformation of the global media industries' in D.R. Winseck and D. Yong Jin (eds), *The political economies of media: the transformation of the global media industries* (Bloomsbury Academic 2011).
Zarsky T., 'The trouble with algorithmic decisions: An analytic roadmap to examine efficiency and fairness in automated and opaque decision making' (2016) 41 *Science, Technology, & Human Values* 118.
Zimmerman M. and J. Rappaport, 'Citizen participation, perceived control and psychological empowerment' (1988) 16 *American Journal of Community Psychology* 725.
Zuboff S., *The age of surveillance capitalism: The fight for a human future at the new frontier of power* (PublicAffairs – Hachette Book Group 2019).

10. From law to engineering: A computer science perspective on privacy and data protection

Ninja Marnau and Christoph Sorge

I. INTRODUCTION: COMPUTER SCIENCE AS A RISK AND ENABLER FOR PRIVACY

Privacy and data protection regulation try to strike a balance between legitimate data use and the right to personal privacy. Nevertheless, the advances in computer science pose new challenges to this careful balance. Data-driven analytics as well as resulting data use and business models e.g., for machine learning, big data and automated decision-making threaten to make individuals, their behaviour and their decision-making completely transparent and predictable, deepening the power asymmetry between individuals and data controllers.

The nature of computer science with regards to privacy is, however, Janus-faced. The ever-progressing digitalisation also requires digital solutions for effective privacy protection. Computer science can and has to act as an enabler of privacy-friendly data processing. The role of privacy engineering and privacy-enhancing technologies far exceeds just guaranteeing legal compliance. In fact, the crucial value of privacy engineering is to lessen the latent conflict arising from this power asymmetry, by empowering the individual and building trust by giving technical privacy assurances. In this chapter, we discuss the core concepts of privacy engineering, provide some examples of the state of the art, and discuss the relation between privacy principles and technical measures.

II. INTERPLAY OF SECURITY AND PRIVACY GOALS – POTENTIAL SYNERGIES AND CONFLICTS

In order for privacy engineering to act as the envisioned enabler for privacy-friendly digitalisation, those complex social, legal and ethical paradigms have to be translated into system requirements. To this end, computer scientists, lawyers and social scientists have to establish a common understanding and language to communicate risks of data use and goals for privacy engineering as well as computer science research. The various global privacy and data protection legislations are not designed to be readily operationalised for engineering objectives. For computer scientists and engineers to technically implement privacy features within their system design, the societal agreement that are privacy rights have to be translated into a workable framework of reachable objectives.

Computer scientists have for a long time agreed upon the main principles guiding system design choices for IT security. The CIA Triad of the principles Confidentiality, Integrity, and

Availability (CIA) is the core concept of IT security.[1] These three principles may be referred to as protection goals, security properties or security criteria, but there is a common understanding in computer science and industry as to what they each require regarding IT security and secure system design. The goals are defined as follows:

- Confidentiality is the property that information is not made available or disclosed to unauthorised individuals, entities, or processes (ISO 27000).
- Integrity is the property that accuracy and completeness of information is protected (ISO 27000).
- Availability is the property that information or systems are accessible and usable when an authorised entity demands access (ISO 27000).

The international privacy community, scientists, authorities and standardisation bodies, have tried to come up with a comparable framework of privacy or data protection goals to guide privacy-friendly or even privacy-enhancing system design in a similar way as the triad does for IT security. An agreed upon framework of those goals would not only allow an easier evaluation and comparison of products and services. Such a framework could be integrated into the curriculum for future computer scientists and engineers to raise awareness for privacy engineering and enhance the overall quality of IT systems with regards to individual rights.

In the following sections, we will detail the most influential of these efforts and analyse their impact on computer science and on its established protection goals.

II.1 Privacy by Design (PbD)

Probably the most well-known of these frameworks is the concept of Privacy by Design (PbD). The concept originates from a 1995 paper of a team operating around Ann Cavoukian, former Information and Privacy Commissioner of the Canadian province of Ontario.[2] She has ever since been the most enthusiastic and passionate supporter of PbD, and gained global renown for the concept. PbD aggregates design principles from global and – until then – fragmented privacy engineering initiatives and experiences. The concept aims at embedding privacy measures and privacy enhancing technologies (PETs) in the design process for IT systems and services.

Based on seven foundational principles,[3] PbD attempts to extend the more technology- and engineering-focused ideas of PETs with a concept also including organisational and business practices. PbD could thus 'be understood as PETs plus privacy enhancing processes'.[4]

---

[1] There have been several proposals to extend the classic triad with additional protection goals such as accountability, non-repudiation, authenticity or freshness. While most computer scientists do not doubt the value of these additional goals, these do not fit well within the triad of the three core protection goals.

[2] Henk van Rossum, Huib Gardeniers, John J Borking, Ann Cavoukian, John Brans, Noel Muttupulle and Nick Magistrale *Privacy-enhancing Technologies: The Path To Anonymity* (Den Haag 1995).

[3] Ann Cavoukian *Privacy by Design – The 7 Foundational Principles*, https://www.ipc.on.ca/wp-content/uploads/Resources/7foundationalprinciples.pdf, accessed 25 October 2021.

[4] Martin Rost and Kirsten Bock, *Privacy by Design and the New Data Protection Goals*, http://www.datenschutzgeschichte.de/pub/privacy/BockRost_PbD_DPG_en_v1f.pdf, accessed 25 October 2021.

The first principle *Proactive not Reactive; Preventive not Remedial* highlights that privacy risks have to be identified and prevented before they materialise. This principle could be addressed by consulting privacy experts or even a data protection officer from the start of a project, jointly identifying potential risks and deciding on effective countermeasures within the design.

The second principle, *Privacy as the Default Setting*, ensures that even when the individual does not make any choices, the maximum degree of privacy is guaranteed by the default settings of the system. The individual does not have to take action; the system is designed to protect her privacy. In contrast, deviations from this default maximum privacy setting require an action of the individual, e.g., in the form of consent by voluntarily choosing different settings.

The third principle, *Privacy Embedded into Design,* emphasises that privacy protection must not be an add-on to the system but should rather be regarded as an 'essential component of the core functionality'. Privacy does not diminish functionality, it is an integral part of the functionality.

The fourth principle, *Full Functionality – Positive-Sum, not Zero-Sum,* aims to reconcile 'false dichotomies, such as privacy vs. security'. PbD encourages designers to aim at accommodating all legitimate interests of the involved parties and scrutinise conventional trade-offs.

The fifth principle, *End-to-End Security – Full Lifecycle Protection,* emphasises that system security is the basis for the effective protection of privacy. This security has to extend throughout the whole lifecycle of the collection, processing and deletion of private data. End-to-End security in this context must not be confused with the concept of end-to-end encryption but comprises all IT security measures.

The sixth principle, *Visibility and Transparency – Keep it Open,* asks for a system design that allows independent verification, certification or audit of the adherence to these principles. This can be achieved via transparency towards the users or documentation and auditing by a trusted third party.

The seventh principle, *Respect for User Privacy – Keep it User-Centric,* emphasises that users' interests and choices should be at the centre of all design decisions. The users should be informed and empowered whenever possible.

The concept of PbD has often been criticised as being too vague to be appropriable by computer scientists and engineers.[5] PbD appears to be more of mind-set than a set of actually measurable and enforceable principles. These high-level principles need the further joint interpretation and application by experts in privacy and engineering in addition to 'contextual analysis, and a balancing of multilateral security and privacy interests'.[6]

In spite of this criticism, PbD had and still has a great impact on the international discussions on privacy legislation and privacy engineering. Its influence even reached the European

---

[5] Jeroen van Rest, Daniel Boonstra Maarten Everts Martin van Rijn and Ron van Paassen *Designing Privacy-by-Design*, in: Bart Preneel and Demosthenes Ikonomou (eds) Privacy Technologies and Policy. APF 2012. Lecture Notes in Computer Science, vol 8319. Springer, Berlin, Heidelberg; Seda Gürses, Carmela Troncoso and Claudia Diaz *Engineering Privacy by Design Reloaded*, Amsterdam Privacy Conference, Amsterdam 2015, https://software.imdea.org/~carmela.troncoso/papers/Gurses-APC15.pdf, accessed 25 October 2021.

[6] Gürses, Troncoso and Diaz, ibid.

General Data Protection Regulation (GDPR), which includes the similar concept of Data Protection by Design in its Article 25(1) GDPR.

II.2 OECD Privacy Principles

Another international, highly influential privacy framework is delineated by the OECD Privacy Principles. The Organisation for Economic Co-operation and Development's (OECD) Privacy Principles are part of the OECD Guidelines on the Protection of Privacy and Transborder Flows of Personal Data, which were developed in the late 1970s and first adopted in 1980. In 2013 the OECD then published a revision of those guidelines,[7] due to the call of the 2008 Seoul Declaration for the Future of the Internet Economy to assess the OECD Guidelines in light of 'changing technologies, markets and user behaviour, and the growing importance of digital identities'.[8]

The OECD Privacy Principles closely mirror the European Union's (EU) cultural expectations on privacy as a fundamental right, and in part reference its legislation and legal terms. They consist of eight principles. These principles outline the rights and obligations of individuals in the context of processing of personal data, and the rights and obligations of those who engage in such processing. They are meant to set a minimum standard for the protection of personal data in system design and provide guidance for national legislation. With regard to computer science, the OECD Privacy Principles are more of a rudimentary policy framework than an actual design and engineering framework. Nevertheless, they can be translated into system design requirements. Many of these system design requirements closely mirror requirements that are also incorporated within the GDPR.

The *Collection Limitation Principle* requires the data controller to obtain personal data in a limited, lawful and fair manner, relying on notice and consent of the individual wherever appropriate. The *Data Quality Principle* emphasises that all personal data should be accurate, complete, up-to-date and relevant for the purpose. In addition to those two, the *Purpose Specification Principle* and *Use Limitation Principle* require the purpose for the data collection and use to be specified, and any later change of processing purpose or disclosure being either compatible with the original purpose or legitimised by consent or national laws.

Compared to the OECD Principles, the GDPR implements these four principles in the 'Principles relating to processing of personal data' in Article 5(1) GDPR, namely (a) lawfulness and fairness, (b) purpose limitation, (c) data minimisation, and (d) accuracy. The GDPR, nevertheless, is stricter than the OECD Guidelines, in the sense e.g., that it specifies in which way the collection should be limited ('limited to what is necessary in relation to the purposes').

The *Security Safeguards Principle* emphasises the requirement to implement reasonable security safeguards against risks for the triad goals of confidentiality, integrity and availability. This OECD Principle is mirrored by Article 5(1)(f) GDPR.

The *Openness Principle* introduces the concept of a 'general policy of openness about developments, practices and policies with respect to personal data'.[9] This openness is a pre-

[7] OECD *The OECD Privacy Framework* (2013), http://www.oecd.org/sti/ieconomy/oecd_privacy_framework.pdf, accessed 25 October 2021.

[8] OECD 2008 Seoul Declaration for the Future of the Internet Economy, https://www.oecd.org/sti/40839436.pdf, accessed 25 October 2021.

[9] Ibid., [7].

requisite for the Individual Participation Principle as it provides the individual e.g., with readily available information on the identity of the processor and the processing activities. The *Individual Participation Principle* then establishes the individual's rights to information about her data and to challenge the data. These two principles are at the core of the GDPR and, therefore, are reflected in Articles 12–23, which detail data subject's rights. These rights under the GDPR are more extensive the OECD Principles and include additional rights such as 'data portability' (Art 20).

Finally, the *Accountability Principle* requires the data controller to be accountable for giving effect to all Principles. This again is mirrored in Article 5(2) GDPR, that requires the controller to be able to demonstrate to the competent authority compliance with all principles of Article 5(1) GDPR.

All of these principles could be implemented via technical measures. As with privacy by design, however, the interpretation and application for specific processing activities would benefit from the early involvement of a privacy or data protection expert in the planning.

Other international frameworks such as the Asia-Pacific Economic Cooperation (APEC) Privacy Framework[10] are similarly far from appropriable goals for computer science and engineering. Due to the different cultural background, the framework concentrates on actual or potential harm as a result of misuse or disclosing of information instead of individuals' rights to privacy.

II.3 ISO/IEC Privacy Framework

The International Organisation for Standardisation (ISO) and the International Electrotechnical Commission (IEC) published an international standard on a 'Privacy Framework' in 2011.[11] While there are several ISO standards on IT security (ISO/IEC 27000 and consecutive standards) ISO 27018, ISO/IEC 29100 focuses on the processing of personal identifiable information (PII), which is slightly narrower than the EU concept of personal data. Where privacy and data protection legislation exist, the standard is meant to be complementary.

The standard is aimed at organisations, assisting and supporting them in identifying their privacy safeguarding requirements. It aims at enhancing today's security standards by the privacy perspective whenever personally identifiable information is processed. The content of the standard specifies a common privacy terminology, defines actors and their roles in PII processing, identifies considerations for privacy safeguarding, and provides references to corresponding IT security principles.

ISO/IEC can serve as a globally applicable baseline for privacy-sensitive system design and engineering. As other ISO standards it focuses on processes, governance and management rather than engineering. Nevertheless, the standard is especially useful for the set-up of a company internal PII management and governance system, or the globally relevant certification of PII processing system.

---

[10] APEC Privacy Framework, https://www.apec.org/Publications/2005/12/APEC-Privacy-Framework, accessed 25 October 2021.

[11] ISO/IEC 29100:2011 Information technology – Security techniques – Privacy framework, https://www.iso.org/standard/45123.html, accessed 25 October 2021.

II.4 The German 'Standard-Datenschutzmodell'

The most recent framework, already taking into account the requirements of the EU GDPR, is the German Standard-Datenschutzmodell (Standard Data Protection Model – SDM),[12] which was developed by the German Data Protection Authorities (DPAs) as a methodology and catalogue of measures for unified data protection goals. The SDM was published in November 2016, and has since been updated several times.

At the heart of the SDM is a methodology for assessing privacy risks of processing activities, and choosing and evaluating appropriate technical data protection and security measures. To this end, the SDM aims to assist companies in planning, implementing and reviewing their data protection and security measures and additionally harmonise how German DPAs assess these measures.

The SDM translates the GDPR's legal requirements into 'data protection goals'. These goals extend the classic security triad of *confidentiality, integrity* and *availability* with complementary and more data protection-oriented goals, *data minimisation, transparency, unlinkability* and *intervenability*,[13] which are aimed at the protection of the data subject's fundamental rights to privacy and reflect the legal GDPR requirements on system design in a more operationalised form. Similar to PbD the SDM protection goals have to be taken into account proactively, as principles of data protection-friendly design.

By establishing technical goals very similar to the security triad, the SDM could enable a more flawless integration with the well-established engineering practices, information security standards and risk assessments. From these data protection goals the DPAs have derived a catalogue of technical and organisational measures (including PETs) that cater to each of the seven data protection goals. They expect that this standardised catalogue could also provide a basis for the data protection certifications the GDPR stipulates (Art 42(2)).

The SDM uses these data protection goals to transfer the legal requirements of the GDPR into a catalogue of technical and organisational measures, which the regulation itself requires. With this reference catalogue of data protection measures it is possible to review the effectiveness of the measures. Such standardised catalogues of measures further provide a well-suited basis for the specific data protection certifications promoted by the GDPR.

The principle of *data minimisation* may be a uniquely European requirement of data protection legislation and is therefore harshly criticised by some researchers.[14] It serves as the overarching fundamental protection goal for the SDM. The GDPR requires personal data to be 'adequate, relevant and limited to what is necessary in relation to the purposes for which they are processed' (Art 5(1)(c)). The German DPAs agree that the data minimisation principle has utmost importance in the age of explorative processing of large data sets. Data minimisation

[12] The Standard Data Protection Model—A method for Data Protection advising and controlling on the basis of uniform protection goals, Version 2.0b (English version), 2021, https://www.datenschutz-mv.de/static/DS/Dateien/Datenschutzmodell/SDM-Methode_V20b_EN.pdf, accessed 25 October 2021.

[13] Some data protection laws of the German federal states had established further protection goals prior to the GDPR that are not listed among the protection goals of the SDM such as *authenticity* and *revisability*. However, the DPAs have decided that these can be derived from the seven fundamental protection goals.

[14] Tal Zarsky, 'Incompatible: The GDPR in the Age of Big Data', *Seton Hall Law Review* (2017) 47 42.

operationalises the legal principle of necessity, which requires to not collect, process, use, transfer, disclose or store more personal data than necessary for the purpose of the processing.

The protection goal of *unlinkability* describes the requirement that data should be only processed for a purpose, and not combined or linked with other data collected and processed for different purposes or with publicly available data sets. While the GDPR enables processing for further purposes if these are not incompatible with the original purpose, those larger data sets increase the potential for abuse and accidental misuse. Therefore, the GDPR requires safeguards for the rights and freedoms of the data subjects in the case of further processing via technical and organisational measures, namely PETs such as anonymisation and pseudonymisation.

The term *unlinkability* is also used by computer scientists with a slightly different meaning: Unlinkability in this other sense is achieved if a link (or, in other words, a relation) between subjects and/or objects cannot be detected. For example, in a communication network, unlinkability might mean that an attacker cannot detect who communicates with whom. Such different uses of the same word are not uncommon, and probably unavoidable in interdisciplinary research. They are not an issue *per se*, as long as those using the term (both actively and passively) are aware of the interpretation in the respective context.

The protection goal of *transparency* refers to the requirement for processing activities (including the categories of data, the purposes, the data use, potential transfers and systems utilised) to be understandable for data subjects, controllers, processors and the competent supervisory authorities to varying degrees. Transparency enables the informed choice of the user, the controller's accountability and option to intervene, as well as the oversight of the competent authority. The term is another example of a word used with a different meaning in computer science (referring to systems that are not noticed, as one can 'see through' them).

The protection goal of *intervenability* requires appropriate system safeguards for the data subject's rights to notification, information, correction and erasure. The controller has to be able to intervene in the processing and grant those rights throughout the processing lifecycle.

These protection goals have to be implemented in the system design via a risk assessment process to choose appropriate safeguards from the catalogue of technical and organisational measures. While the aim is to fulfil each of the goals at minimum to the appropriate degree, the goals may to some extent contradict each other in edge cases, as detailed in the following section. Nevertheless, of all proposed frameworks the SDM currently seems to be the most manageable and appropriate concept to bridge the gap between legislation and engineering.

II.5 Potential Conflicts

In general, IT security can be seen as a prerequisite for compliant processing of personal data and, furthermore, for privacy-friendly system design. But although data protection and security goals for engineering mostly complement each other and can be mutually beneficial, there are some cases of conflict. Oftentimes, these conflicts arise when personal data is used for purposes of IT security. One could, for example, think of network monitoring within a company for the purpose of intrusion detection (processing personal data of the employees), a website monitoring user behaviour to detect fraud (processing personal data of users) or a public body logging each database event their administrators trigger (also processing personal data of the employees). In these cases, the classic triad of IT security goals – confidentiality, integrity and availability – is in conflict with the data protection goals of data minimisation and unlinkability. Likewise, in the case of blockchain and distributed ledger technology the exceptional integrity and guarantees that result from the underlying cryptographic protocols may render the data subject's right to be forgotten or to correct her data ineffective. While potential remedies to 'redact' the blockchain in order to meet those data protection rights have already been proposed,[15] these consequently reduce the integrity guarantees of the distributed ledger.

To solve these conflicts, engineers and system designers still have to find an appropriate balance between their legitimate interest with regard to the security of their systems and networks and the data subject's rights. The principle of necessity and thus data minimisation has to act as guidance. Often the aim of the intended security measure can also be achieved with anonymous data (e.g., anonymised IP addresses or cookies), or the necessary personal data could be reduced step by step in a tiered process and pseudonymised and aggregated as soon as possible.

II.6 Relation to PETs

The relation between these proposed frameworks and PETs is that of goals and a toolbox to achieve these goals. The frameworks provide an overall strategy and goals for system design and PETs are part of the specific set of measures to choose from to achieve these goals.[16] For each framework of privacy or data protection goals the corresponding privacy design patterns and appropriate PETs should be leveraged to design and build an overall privacy preserving system. In the next section, we will look into principles of PETs and concrete instantiations.

III. PRIVACY-ENHANCING TECHNOLOGIES (PETS)

To understand the principles of computer science research in PETs, one can start with the basic principles of data protection.

Firstly, data protection law only applies to personal data, i.e., data about an identified or identifiable natural person. As a consequence, PETs often encompass data minimisation techniques such as data anonymisation or pseudonymisation. While the goal of anonymisation is to eliminate the risk of identifiability completely, pseudonymisation is considered as a less effective protection of privacy, potentially leaving individuals still identifiable. Consequently, pseudonymous data is still regulated by the GDPR, while anonymous data is not.

Secondly, data protection law is based on the concept of informational self-determination. Therefore, any tools supporting the decisions of individuals with regards to their personal data, and any tools supporting the implementation of these decisions, can be considered as PETs. This includes the specification of policies, the description of allowed information flows

---

[15] Giuseppe Ateniese, Bernardo Magri, Daniele Venturi and Ewerton Andrade, 'Redactable Blockchain – or – Rewriting History in Bitcoin and Friends', *Proceedings of the 2nd IEEE European Symposium on Security and Privacy* (EuroS&P 2017).

[16] Jaap-Henk Hoepman, 'Privacy Design Strategies' in: Nora Cuppens-Boulahia, Fréderik Cuppens, Sushil Jajodia, Anas Abou El Kalam and Thierry Sans (eds), *ICT Systems Security and Privacy Protection*, volume 428 of IFIP Advances in Information and Communication Technology, (Springer 2014) 446–459.

in IT systems, and the establishment of transparency about the use of personal data (e.g., by designing user interfaces).

Thirdly, data protection laws – in particular, the GDPR – contain a number of additional principles and rights of individuals with respect to their personal data, and there is a wide range of PETs supporting these principles and rights.

Privacy can also be protected by more general IT security measures. For example, institutions dealing with personal data are expected to encrypt the data when transmitting them, and to use firewalls to protect against attacks on their computer networks. As these measures are not specific to personal data, we do not consider them as PETs.

PETs can also be classified in a different manner; for example, Heurix et al.[17] distinguish between the aspects (general targets) of identity, content and behaviour. While the authors refer to identity as 'the primary aspect of privacy', one should note that protection of identities is not always feasible. However, the concepts of identity protection can be generalised to many applications; we therefore focus on these in the following three subsections. Afterwards, we discuss smart metering as an application example.

III.1 Anonymisation and Identity Management

Anonymisation techniques exist in a large number of application domains. Sometimes, the challenge just lies in anonymisation itself. For example, to generate statistics about a population, one only has to make sure that no information about an individual is contained. Other applications require partial identities – some of the information about an individual (a subset of attributes) is needed in a specific situation. The precise information needed may vary. For example, when it comes to the use of online services, some services may require only the user's approximate age, while others provide a service based on location. A privacy-aware (user-centric) identity management solution will make exactly the required attributes available to each service and prevent the creation of user profiles across different services (and, sometimes, even within one service). In other words, it manages a user's partial identities.

Ideally, an identity management solution should achieve at least three goals:

- Security, i.e., any claims made about a user's identity should be true; in particular, this includes secure authentication of the user.
- Privacy, i.e., only the attributes required by a service are revealed to that service, and the creation of user profiles is prevented.
- Comfort, i.e., a user does not have to handle multiple user accounts, passwords, or hardware tokens. One way to achieve comfort are 'single-sign-on' solutions, in which a user authenticates to a so-called 'identity provider'. Service providers then receive all required attributes of a user from that identity provider, and there are mechanisms in place which ensure authenticity of the user (i.e., the service provider is dealing with the same user who has previously been authenticated by the identity provider).

Achieving all goals at the same time is a challenging task. Cryptography can play an important role in identity management solutions. Some cryptographic schemes achieve surprising results

---

[17] Johannes Heurix, Peter Zimmermann, Thomas Neubauer and Stefan Fenz, 'A Taxonomy for Privacy Enhancing Technologies', *Computers & Security*, (2015) 53, 1–17.

and are not well-known outside the cryptographic research community. We describe some examples below.

III.2 Special Cryptographic Building Blocks

Authentication is one of the most essential issues in identity management, and even in IT security in general. There is a large number of authentication protocols available. Many are based on shared secrets; others use public-key cryptographic schemes (in which the user proves possession of a private cryptographic key, which can be verified using the corresponding public key). Most authentication protocols require a permanent identifier, such as a user name with the corresponding password, or a public key. As a consequence, the creation of user profiles (albeit under a pseudonym) cannot be prevented.

Anonymous credential schemes[18] are an alternative to these traditional authentication methods. Using such a scheme, a user can prove that she belongs to a specific group (e.g., group of users who have paid for a certain service), but without revealing her full identity. The detailed properties of anonymous credential schemes vary. For example, a specific scheme may or may not allow a service to recognise returning users (while this is never allowed across services).

Group signature schemes[19] are related to anonymous credential schemes. They allow a user to sign documents on behalf of a group. The group is managed by a group manager, who decides whether or not to allow users into the group. Each user has her own private key to generate signatures. A signature can be verified using a group public key, but does not reveal which of the private keys was used for signing. As for anonymous credentials, there are numerous schemes available whose properties differ in important details. Most importantly, some allow the group manager to revoke participants' anonymity, i.e., to identify which private key was used for generating a signature.

Ring signatures[20] allow similar applications. The main difference is that ring signatures do not use group managers. Instead, to generate a signature, a group member uses her own private key and all of the group members' public keys. The signature can be verified using all these public keys – but, as with group signatures, the individual signatory cannot be identified. Since there is no group manager, anonymity cannot be revoked.

Modern cryptography also offers a large variety of potential building blocks for PETs that are not related to authentication. One example are homomorphic encryption schemes, which allow computations on encrypted data – making it possible to outsource certain computations without revealing personal data to the entity processing them. While fully homomorphic encryption (which allows arbitrary computations) is still too inefficient for most practical applications, simplified versions (e.g., limited to aggregation of individual values) are already

---

[18] As an example, see Jan Camenisch and Anna Lysyanskaya, 'An Efficient System for Non-transferable Anonymous Credentials with Optional Anonymity Revocation' in *Advances in Cryptology — EUROCRYPT* (Springer 2001) 93–117.

[19] An example is presented by Dan Boneh, Xavier Boyen and Hovav Shacham, 'Short Group Signatures', in: *Advances in Cryptology - CRYPTO 2004, 24th Annual International Cryptology Conference, Proceedings*, (Springer 2004) 41–55.

[20] Ronald Rivest, Adi Shamir and Yael Tauman, 'How to Leak a Secret', in: Proceedings of the 7th International Conference on the Theory and Application of Cryptology and Information Security: Advances in Cryptology (ASIACRYPT '01) Colin Boyd (ed) (Springer 2001) 552–565.

practical. Secure multiparty computation[21] is another example, making it possible for several parties to compute the result of a function (e.g., computing the average of the participants' inputs) without revealing the individual inputs to those functions.

Availability of such building blocks, however, is only the first step towards improving the privacy of individuals. Enabling actual privacy-preserving applications and infrastructure components requires an additional engineering effort and may sometimes contradict the assumptions underlying currently available services. For example, there is no general awareness (even among computer scientists) that checking an authorisation to use a service does not require knowledge about the users' identity. Consequently, authentication is often assumed to be a necessary first step that precedes authorisation.

III.3 Anonymous Communication

Anonymous communication networks can be considered as an important foundation for privacy on the Internet. Even if an identity management solution is in place, any provider of web-based services (among others) communicates with its customers using the Internet Protocol (IP). The customers' IP addresses are required for this communication to work, but in many cases, such addresses have to be considered as unique identifiers.

An anonymous communication network allows the use of online services, such as websites, without revealing one's IP address (or any other unique identifier). The most prominent example is the Tor[22] network, whose basic principle is quite simple. Instead of sending data directly to the respective service, the data packets are routed through a number of intermediate nodes, the so-called onion routers. The appropriate use of encryption ensures that each of these onion routers knows only its direct predecessor and its direct successor in the communication path, and none of them is aware of the link between the communication partners (the service and its user). The service learns only the IP address of the last onion router in the path, so the user stays anonymous towards the service.

III.4 Anonymous Payment

Another important basic service is anonymous payment. A proposal for an anonymous payment system had already been made in the 1980s.[23] In essence, the approach uses random numbers as 'coins'. These numbers are generated by the user who intends to make anonymous payments. A special cryptographic scheme (a so-called 'blind signature') is used to enable a bank to sign these coins without knowing what it signs (i.e., the random numbers). When sending the signed coins back to the user, the corresponding amount is deducted from the user's normal bank account. In essence, this first step is equivalent to buying physical coins from a traditional bank, but without the bank being able to see any information about the coin except its value.

---

[21] Ronald Cramer, Ivan Bjerre Damgård and Jesper Buus Nielsen, *Secure Multiparty Computation and Secret Sharing* (Cambridge University Press 2015).

[22] Roger Dingledine, Nick Mathewson and Paul F. Syverson, 'Tor: The Second-Generation Onion Router' in *Proceedings of the 13th USENIX Security Symposium*, 2004.

[23] David Chaum 'Security Without Identification: Transaction Systems to Make Big Brother Obsolete' *Communications of the ACM* (1985) 28(10) 1030–1044.

In the next step, the user pays a merchant by sending him the signed coins, corresponding to a specific value. The merchant then forwards the coins to the bank, which enters them into a database of spent coins. If the coins have not been spent before, the merchant receives the corresponding amount in his bank account. A more advanced version of the protocol does not require the merchant to communicate at the time of the transaction but allows this clearing to take place at a later time.

III.5 Anonymity in Databases

So far, we have focused on PETs in the context of communication and online service provision. Especially when considering the current trend towards 'big data', information stored in databases has to be considered by PETs as well. In many cases, a database contains information about identified individuals, but the data are used for statistical and research purposes that do not depend on identities. The challenge is thus to remove all potentially identifying information, while trying to interfere with the purpose of the database usage as little as possible. Simply removing obvious identifiers (such as name and address) is usually insufficient. As an example, consider a database that contains income data about the population of a small town, and lists just the profession and income of each person – all other attributes have been removed. For most persons, this anonymisation will be sufficient, but if the profession is something more unique such as 'mayor', that person may be easily identified.

A well-known concept for anonymisation in databases is k-anonymity.[24] To decide whether a database is k-anonymous, the first step is to identify attributes which can be used to identify an individual in conjunction with background information. These attributes are called a 'quasi-identifier'. In our example, the profession is a quasi-identifier, as the profession of a person is usually public knowledge. In the next step, one has to make sure that at least k rows ('tuples') in the database are identical in the quasi-identifier attributes. For example, if k=3, then each profession must appear at least three times in the database. This way, no person can be uniquely identified. There is more than one way to achieve k-anonymity; for example, attributes can be generalised (age 33 becomes '30 to 39', 'mayor' becomes 'public service').

The concept of k-anonymity has its drawbacks. In our example, assume there are three general practitioners in the town who, by coincidence, all have the same approximate income. Even though k-anonymity ensures that no individual general practitioner can be identified (i.e., nobody knows which row in the database corresponds to which person), the sensitive attribute is still revealed.

In real-world databases, which contain a lot more attributes, another problem becomes apparent: It is often impossible to determine in advance which of the attributes can be used to identify someone in conjunction with background knowledge. It is already difficult for an individual to find out which personal data about him is stored in various databases; anticipating the stored information about all persons represented in the database – and which may be used as background knowledge for de-anonymisation – can be considered as nearly impossible for non-trivial examples.

---

[24] Latanya Sweeney, 'K-anonymity: A Model for Protecting Privacy', *International Journal of Uncertainty, Fuzziness and Knowledge-Based Systems* (2002) 10(5) 557–570.

Therefore, a number of more advanced concepts for privacy-friendly use of databases have been proposed. The most prominent one is Differential Privacy.[25] Its focus is on statistical queries (e.g., for the number of women contained in the database with an income over 100,000 Euro). The Differential Privacy model compares two situations. In the first, the queries use the whole database as an input; in the second, the data of one person are removed. Differential privacy means that each possible output occurs with approximately the same probability in both situations. This must hold for any user, not just a particular one. In other words, the influence of a single person on the query results should be very small.

Obviously, this means that the queries cannot always give precise results. Instead, randomised algorithms are used – in other words, noise is added to the results. The concept has been adapted to cover different scenarios. The choice of parameters, however, remains a challenge; in particular, one has to define by how much the results are allowed to differ between both situations.

III.6 Application Example: Smart Electricity Meters

With a continuously increasing amount of applications that process personal data, more and more application-specific PETs are also being developed. Electricity metering has become such an application in recent years. Traditional electricity meters are manually read about once a year, but current 'smart' electricity meters transmit their readings about every 15 minutes. This represents an opportunity for attackers to create detailed profiles about the presence/absence of persons in a household, and even to identify some electrical appliances. For example, the consumption patterns of washing machines or dryers are easily identified in a household's overall electricity consumption.

In addition to security measures such as encryption, a number of PETs have been suggested which allow electricity suppliers to analyse the overall consumption of their customers or specific customer groups, but which hide individual household's consumption patterns. Some core concepts in the field include:

- Using a battery to 'even out' the electricity consumption of a household.[26]
- Anonymising the individual readings and using anonymous credentials to ensure authorisation of each smart meter to send a reading.
- Adding random noise to the data, which 'averages out' when aggregating over large groups of customers.[27]
- Using homomorphic encryption to aggregate encrypted smart meter readings before they can be decrypted by the electricity supplier.[28]

---

[25] Cynthia Dwork, 'Differential Privacy', *Proceedings of the 33rd International Conference on Automata, Languages and Programming Part II* (Springer 2006).

[26] Michael Backes and Sebastian Meiser, 'Differentially Private Smart Metering with battery recharging', *Data Privacy Management and Autonomous Spontaneous Security* (Springer 2014).

[27] Jens-Mathias Bohli, Christoph Sorge, Osman Ugus, 'A privacy model for Smart Metering', in: *Proceedings of the First IEEE International Workshop on Smart Grid Communications* (2010).

[28] Félix Gomez Marmol, Christoph Sorge; Ronald Petrlic Osman Ugus, Dirk Westhoff, Gregorio Martinez Perez 'Privacy Enhanced Architecture for Smart Metering', *International Journal of Information Security*, (2013) 12(2) 67–82.

These are only a few examples,[29] which nevertheless show the large bandwidth of PETs in just one application domain. PETs as building blocks for Data Protection by Design can help to bring the above-mentioned frameworks to life, and resolve potential conflicts between security and data protection goals. However, even with cryptographic building blocks and privacy models available, the development of PETs for a new application still requires a significant effort. Adoption is still not guaranteed; for example, despite hundreds of research papers in the field of smart meter privacy, only very basic mechanisms are currently in use.

IV. GDPR COMPLIANCE AND THE ROLE OF COMPUTER SCIENCE

The EU General Data Protection Regulation (GDPR), or Regulation (EU) 2016/679, came into force on 25 May 2016 and has been applicable in all EU Member States since 25 May 2018.

Privacy engineering and its further evolution plays a key role for GDPR compliance as Article 25 establishes the paradigms of Data Protection by Design (Art 25(1)) and Data Protection by Default (Art 25(2)) as legal requirements for system design with regard to processing of personal data. This article could potentially foster tremendous innovation efforts by companies and government, which are now legally required to consider the above-mentioned frameworks and PETs. Whether we will see such an innovation boost and growth in privacy-friendly system design will to a large extent depend on the DPAs. They have to offer guidance on how to operationalise Data Protection by Design and by Default on national and European level. As of today, the most promising approach for such a framework bridging the gap between legislation, research and engineering are the protection goals of the new German Standard-Datenschutzmodell. But whether these will be widely accepted within the EU or even internationally has yet to be seen. Additionally, the DPAs will have to give guidance to companies who want to set best practice examples, harmonise certifications, and enforce Article 25 GDPR effectively. The next years will show whether the DPAs are sufficiently staffed and have the necessary expertise to allow Article 25 GDPR to take full effect. In addition, computer science research has to strengthen the focus on privacy engineering to develop more practical solutions for privacy-friendly system design and improve PETs.

Apart from privacy engineering, IT security plays a key role in the GDPR with regard to compliance. Articles 5 and 32 GDPR provide essential requirements on the security of the processing of personal data. While Article 5 GDPR lists the principles for data processing (lawfulness, fairness and transparency; purpose limitation; data minimisation; accuracy; storage limitation; integrity and confidentiality), Article 32 GDPR calls specifically for the implementation of technical and organisational security measures to ensure a level of security appropriate to the risk of varying likelihood and severity for the rights and freedoms of natural persons.

Article 32 GDPR explicitly names the IT security triad goals of confidentiality, integrity and availability, and extends these goals with requirements for resilience, business continuity and regular review, assessment and evaluation of the effectiveness of those implemented technical and organisational measures. The only two specific technical measures to achieve these goals

---

[29] For a survey of many more approaches, see Soren Finster and Ingmar Baumgart, 'Privacy-Aware Smart Metering: A Survey', IEEE Communications Surveys & Tutorials, (2014) 16(3) 1732–1745.

mentioned by the GDPR are pseudonymisation and encryption, which both have a prominent role throughout the Regulation. Due to the Regulation being mostly technology-neutral, companies can achieve compliance by assessing the risks that come with their legitimate processing activity and choose from the various standards and guidelines of state-of-the-art security measures (e.g., the ISO/IEC 27000 ff. standards).

V. CONCLUSION

Digitalisation is often – and with good reason – considered as a major threat to the privacy of individuals. Personal data about nearly everyone is stored in hundreds of databases; communication habits of the 21st century enable surveillance and profiling on a scale that was previously unthinkable. Computer science has created these threats; is there a chance that computer science will provide the solutions?

In this chapter, we have shown that recent and ongoing research efforts have in fact resulted in many approaches with the potential to greatly benefit individuals' privacy. Most importantly, these approaches give individuals the power to use digital services anonymously, and they enable statistical evaluations of data without revealing too much information about individuals. Additional efforts are required to make these privacy-enhancing technologies available in more application domains. Even foundational research is still required; for example, current approaches do not yet allow to fulfil all the promises of the big data paradigm while ensuring individuals' privacy as rigorous anonymisation techniques for large and dynamic data sets are still insufficient.[30]

However, computer science research will not solve all privacy challenges on its own. Even where this research is very mature, actual implementations of privacy enhancing technologies are rare. How to overcome the gap between research and practice?

Several attempts have been made to establish frameworks and measurable goals for privacy engineering, meeting legislative requirements while incorporating privacy-enhancing solutions in practice. Most of these frameworks have failed to bridge the gap between legal concepts and computer science, being either too much of a policy framework, or too much of a technical standard. An internationally agreed upon framework for privacy engineering could allow for more comparability and measurement of quality in personal data processing systems and services. It could foster technical engineering standards and advance computer science education in a similar way as IT security does.

However, the international privacy research community is very aware of the need for privacy engineering guidelines and further research on PETs and fosters the interdisciplinary and international dialogue.[31] These are exciting times for computer scientists working in the fields of security and privacy.

---

[30] The Madrid Privacy Declaration of the 31st annual meeting of the International Conference of Privacy and Data Protection Commissioners from 3rd November 2009 recommended "comprehensive research into the adequacy of techniques that deidentify data to determine whether in practice such methods safeguard privacy and anonymity". http://thepublicvoice.org/TheMadridPrivacyDeclaration.pdf, accessed 25 October 2021.

[31] Future Privacy Forum: Workshop on Privacy Engineering Research, https://fpf.org/2017/08/30/privacy-engineering-research-gdpr-trans-atlantic-initiative/, accessed 25 October 2021.

REFERENCES

APEC Privacy Framework, https://www.apec.org/Publications/2005/12/APEC-Privacy-Framework.

Ateniese G, B Magri, D Venturi and E Andrade, Redactable 'Blockchain – or – Rewriting History in Bitcoin and Friends, *Proceedings of the 2nd IEEE European Symposium on Security and Privacy* (EuroS&P 2017).

Backes M and S Meiser, *Differentially Private Smart Metering with Battery Recharging, Data Privacy Management and Autonomous Spontaneous Security* (Springer 2014).

Bohli J-M, Sorge C and O Ugus, 'A Privacy Model for Smart Metering', in: *Proceedings of the First IEEE International Workshop on Smart Grid Communications* (2010).

Boneh D, X Boyen and H Shacham, 'Short Group Signatures', in: *Advances in Cryptology - CRYPTO 2004, 24th Annual International Cryptology Conference, Proceedings* (Springer 2004) 41.

Camenisch J and A Lysyanskaya, 'An Efficient System for Non-transferable Anonymous Credentials with Optional Anonymity Revocation' in: *Advances in Cryptology* — EUROCRYPT (Springer 2001) 93.

Cavoukian A, *Privacy by Design – The 7 Foundational Principles*, https://www.ipc.on.ca/wp-content/uploads/Resources/7foundationalprinciples.pdf.

Chaum D, 'Security Without Identification: Transaction Systems to Make Big Brother Obsolete', *Communications of the ACM* (1985) 28(10) 1030–1044.

Cramer R, I Bjerre Damgård and J Buus Nielsen, *Secure Multiparty Computation and Secret Sharing* (Cambridge University Press 2015).

Dingledine R, N Mathewson and P F Syverson, 'Tor: The Second-Generation Onion Router' in *Proceedings of the 13th USENIX Security Symposium*, 2004.

Dwork C, 'Differential Privacy', *Proceedings of the 33rd International Conference on Automata, Languages and Programming Part II* (Springer 2006).

Finster S and I Baumgart, 'Privacy-Aware Smart Metering: A Survey' *IEEE Communications Surveys & Tutorials* (2014) 16(3) 1732.

Future Privacy Forum, *Workshop on Privacy Engineering Research*, https://fpf.org/2017/08/30/privacy-engineering-research-gdpr-trans-atlantic-initiative/

Gomez M, F Sorge, C Petrlic, R Ugus, O Westhoff D and G Martinez Perez, 'Privacy Enhanced Architecture for Smart Metering' *International Journal of Information Security* (2013) 12(2) 67.

Gürses S, C Troncoso and C Diaz, 'Engineering Privacy by Design Reloaded', *Amsterdam Privacy Conference, Amsterdam 2015*, https://software.imdea.org/~carmela.troncoso/papers/Gurses-APC15.pdf.

Heurix J, P Zimmermann, T Neubauer and S Fenz, 'A Taxonomy for Privacy Enhancing Technologies' *Computers & Security* (2015) 53 1.

Hoepman J-H, 'Privacy Design Strategies' in: N Cuppens-Boulahia, F Cuppens, S Jajodia, A El Kalam and T Sans (eds), *ICT Systems Security and Privacy Protection*, volume 428 of IFIP Advances in Information and Communication Technology, (Springer 2014) 446.

ISO/IEC 29100:2011 Information technology – Security techniques – Privacy framework, https://www.iso.org/standard/45123.html

Rivest Adi Shamir R and Y Tauman, 'How to Leak a Secret', in: *Proceedings of the 7th International Conference on the Theory and Application of Cryptology and Information* Security: Advances in Cryptology (ASIACRYPT '01) Colin Boyd (Ed.) (Springer 2001) 552.

Rost M and K Bock, *Privacy by Design and the New Data Protection Goals*, http://www.datenschutzgeschichte.de/pub/privacy/BockRost_PbD_DPG_en_v1f.pdf.

Sweeney L, 'K-anonymity: A Model for Protecting Privacy', *International Journal of Uncertainty, Fuzziness and Knowledge-Based Systems* (2002) 10(5) 557.

The Madrid Privacy Declaration of the 31st annual meeting of the International Conference of Privacy and Data Protection Commissioners from 3rd November 2009 recommended "comprehensive research into the adequacy of techniques that deidentify data to determine whether in practice such methods safeguard privacy and anonymity". http://thepublicvoice.org/TheMadridPrivacyDeclaration.pdf.

Van Rest J, D Boonstra, M Everts, M van Rijn and R van Paassen, 'Designing Privacy-by-Design', in: Bart Preneel and Demosthenes Ikonomou (eds) *Privacy Technologies and Policy. APF 2012. Lecture Notes in Computer Science*, vol 8319. Springer, Berlin, Heidelberg.

Van Rossum H, H Gardeniers, J J Borking, A Cavoukian, J Brans, N Muttupulle and N Magistrale, *Privacy-enhancing Technologies: The Path to Anonymity* (Den Haag 1995).

X, *The Standard Data Protection Model—A method for Data Protection advising and controlling on the basis of uniform protection goals*, Version 2.0b (English version), 2021, https://www.datenschutz-mv.de/static/DS/Dateien/Datenschutzmodell/SDM-Methode_V20b_EN.pdf

Zarsky T, 'Incompatible: The GDPR in the Age of Big Data', *Seton Hall Law Review* (2017) 47 42.

11. Privacy, data protection, and security studies

Matthias Leese

I. INTRODUCTION

The connection between privacy, data protection, and the study of security is not quite an obvious one. The field of security studies has classically been concerned with 'international security', or what could be called security between states in the international system. The field has thereby preeminently been dealing with issues such as warfare and the military (and on the flipside questions of peace and mediation, the non-proliferation of nuclear weapons, etc.), as well as foreign policy, broadly conceived. Thus, why should security scholars pay attention to privacy and data protection? Over the past decades, in a mutually constitutive relationship, security threats, security politics, and academic ways to study security have undergone far-reaching transformations.[1] The security agenda today includes the likes of international terrorism, global criminal networks, irregular migration, as well as domestic issues such as urban security or infrastructure protection. In the wake of these developments, the sites, tools, and practices of security have changed and have brought new questions to the fore.

The production of security has become increasingly predicated upon the collection and analysis of (digital) data (e.g., communications data, mobility data, or CCTV footage). Subsequently, questions surrounding the collection, retention, and use of data have become relevant in security contexts. As security practices have taken a turn towards the digital and today to a large extent present themselves as data-driven and algorithmically supported attempts to generate knowledge about threats, questions of privacy and data protection have become pertinent for a discipline that used to be firmly grounded in International Relations (IR) theory. Moreover, as parts of the security studies community have taken a 'critical' turn, scholars have started to increasingly turn their analyses to the potential negative ramifications of security politics and practices – a scope that strongly intersects with the concepts of privacy and data protection, as they are set to protect the individual from intrusions into their private (data) sphere.[2]

However, against the backdrop of this protective role, the problem of 'securitization' (the power of security discourses to override other norms due to arguments of survival and urgency) poses serious challenges to privacy and data protection, as security concerns can easily be considered as outweighing privacy and data protection. This conflict becomes aggravated by the notion of 'Big Data', as security practices increasingly rely on the theory-less, algorithmically powered analysis of large amounts of data. In this logic, every bit of information could turn out to be security-relevant in analyses at a later point in time and/or in conjunction with

[1] Barry Buzan and Lene Hansen, *The Evolution of International Security Studies* (Cambridge University Press 2009).

[2] Privacy is here defined as the abstract philosophical concept that deals with the protection of an individual's private sphere, whereas data protection is the tangible legal concept that regulates the collection, retention, exchange, and processing of personal data.

other data – even though this could not be known at the time of data collection. Therefore, in extension of the securitization argument that privacy and data protection could be overridden by security concerns in the first place, security professionals and policymakers often argue that data should preemptively be collected and stored – something which strongly clashes with the aims of privacy and data protection.

This chapter starts by discussing the concept of security and the field of security studies and traces its development from the narrowly confined origins in IR towards a multi-disciplinary field that has incorporated perspectives from adjacent disciplines such as sociology, surveillance studies, legal studies, cultural studies, and technical fields. The identification of new security issues, new sites of security production, and new security practices thereby lays the foundation for a review of new questions for security studies vis-à-vis privacy and data protection in the ensuing section, outlining the role of a privacy/data protection perspective for the (critical) study of security and its larger political, social, and economic ramifications. The last section will engage the challenges posed to privacy and data protection by securitization processes, particularly against the backdrop of a Big Data perspective on the analysis of security-relevant data.

II. SECURITY AND SECURITY STUDIES

Whereas 'security' as a societal issue used to be studied as part of political science or history, after the end of the Second World War the discipline of security studies emerged as a distinct academic field of research against the backdrop of the Cold War period and the specific threats it presented. Since their early Cold War days, security studies have however undergone a series of topical and conceptual transformations that have, among other, put questions of privacy and data protection on the agenda.[3] This section briefly retraces those transformations in terms of new security *issues*, new *sites* of security, and new security *practices*, and thereby shows why and how privacy and data protection questions have gradually become relevant for security scholars.

After 1945, a distinctive body of literature started to evolve around the notion of security. In contrast to earlier work on security-related questions, this literature did not exclusively focus on questions of defence and military strategy, but conceptualized security as a broader set of political issues that notably included diplomatic and foreign policy issues between the West and the East. As early as 1952, Arnold Wolfers, in a seminal article on national security, wrote that 'the term "security" covers a range of goals so wide that highly divergent policies can be interpreted as policies of security',[4] and highlighted the multiple meanings and political appropriations of the concept of security. While still very much focused on the state as the referent object of security, Wolfers thus set the stage for the study of security as a phenomenon that potentially included a wide variety of topics around the broad notions of national security and foreign policy.

---

[3] For an overview of the development of the field, see Buzan and Hansen (n 1); Gabi Schlag, Julian Junk and Christopher Daase (eds), *Transformations of Security Studies: Dialogues, Diversity and Discipline* (Routledge 2016).

[4] Arnold Wolfers, 'National Security' as an Ambiguous Symbol' (1952) 67 *Political Science Quarterly* 481–484.

The early stages of security studies must thereby be understood as largely dominated by the backdrop of the Cold War, and concentrated on a quite narrow set of questions that directly derived from the confrontational set-up between the West and the East. Preeminent security issues throughout most of the Cold War period consisted of matters of nuclear weaponry and deterrence, as well as the military-strategic challenges that the state of the world presented. An opening of the security studies agenda occurred only when the nuclear relationship between the USA and the Soviet Union had become consolidated and relatively stable in the 1970s. The lack of an immediate threat of nuclear escalation opened up the space for other security issues to be included in the political and academic agenda, such as for instance environmental questions and economic matters. Over the following two decades, this process of opening up continued and more novel issues started to draw the attention of security policymakers and scholars, such as for instance water and food security, and the concepts of human security and societal security that put the individual/society instead of the state at the centre stage of security.

This 'widening' (meaning the consideration of security threats other than warfare, such as, e.g., environmental pollution or poverty) and 'deepening' (meaning the consideration of other referent objects of security than the state, such as, e.g., society or the individual) of the academic agenda was however not welcomed by everyone. Conservative security scholars insisted that the field should not lose its focus and intellectual coherence, and should keep on engaging military and strategic questions rather than turning to issues that would belong in other academic disciplines. Stephen Walt has in this vein prominently argued that security studies should be confined to 'the study of the threat, use, and control of military force'.[5]

On the other side of the spectrum, parts of the security studies community however felt an increasing discontent with such a narrow analytical scope. After 1990, particularly European security scholars considered traditionalist accounts of the nation-state and military aspects as unfit to cope with the new challenges of the post-Cold War world. Subsequently, in addition to the incorporation of security issues other than the state and the military, parts of the field took a turn towards new theoretical and methodological currents such as poststructuralism, constructivism, post-colonialism, or feminism. This turn effectively caused a fork in the disciplinary evolution of security studies, branching off a 'critical security studies' agenda that, inspired by reflexive elements of new theoretical and methodological influences from beyond IR, started to challenge the concept of security in the first place, and re-engaged its role within society through social theory, philosophy, sociology, and other adjacent disciplines.

Keith Krause and Michael Williams' 1997 edited volume *Critical Security Studies: Concepts and Cases*[6] marked an important step towards this new academic agenda that refused to take assumptions about the meaning and means of security for granted, and instead posed

---

[5] Stephen M Walt, 'The Renaissance of Security Studies' (1991) 35 *International Studies Quarterly* 211–212.

[6] Keith Krause and Michael C Williams (eds), *Critical Security Studies: Concepts and Cases* (Routledge 1997); for other overviews of the field see c.a.s.e. collective, 'Critical Approaches to Security in Europe: A Networked Manifesto' (2006) 37 *Secur Dialogue* 443; David Mutimer, Kyle Grayson and J Marshall Beier, 'Critical Studies on Security: An Introduction' (2013) 1 *Critical Studies on Security* 1; Columba Peoples and Nick Vaughan-Williams, *Critical Security Studies: An Introduction* (Routledge 2010); Mark B Salter and Can E Mutlu (eds), *Research Methods in Critical Security Studies: An Introduction* (Routledge 2013); Claudia Aradau and others (eds), *Critical Security Methods: New Frameworks for Analysis* (Routledge 2015).

questions such as: Who does security? For whom? On behalf of whom? How is security produced? Which tools and practices are used? And which side-effects are produced by these practices? Analysing security through such a set of questions foregrounds the social construction of security problems, the (re-)production of power and authority through 'doing security', the involved actors and their stakes, as well as the value of security vis-à-vis other values. While critical security studies must not be mistaken for a coherent endeavour with a clear-cut research agenda, there is a certain consensus that scholars should, as Columba Peoples and Nick Vaughan-Williams write, be 'constantly involved in judgments about what security means, and in deciding and discriminating what the objects and objectives of security studies should be'.[7]

While this turn towards reflexivity vis-à-vis the concept of security and its implications was a first key step to bring questions of privacy and data protection to the fore, another major factor was the insight that the traditional categories of international security and domestic security (or, in other terms: external and internal security) could no longer be meaningfully maintained.[8] Contemporary security threats such as terrorism, international crime networks, trafficking, illegal migration, or cyber-attacks do not stop at national borders. On the contrary, these security issues are as much international as they are domestic in terms of the potential damage that they unfold, and most notably in terms of the ways to fight them.

In light of this cross-border nature of many of today's security threats, security professionals and policymakers have turned their attention to new sites of inquiry and new practices of security production. Pertinent questions in contemporary security practices are: Who or what could become a threat? Where and when could harm unfold? And how can knowledge be created about the identities and intentions of those who pose a threat to security? The answers to these questions can, so the assumption, be found in data. Data in this view present a unique window into the activities of individuals that can subsequently be used to identify suspicious behaviour, possibly indicating the intention to inflict harm on society. Once suspects would be identified, preventive security measures could then cancel out threats, and therefore maintain security. In other words: data are seen as a way to get a glimpse of the future in order to cancel that future out.[9]

International flows of mobility have in this vein become a key site for the identification of potential future threats. Be it humans, goods and services, or personal communications – objects that travel leave behind a data trail that can, so the logic goes, be analysed in order to find out who might be a terrorist, which routes illegal migrants are pursuing on their ways across borders, or at which port contraband or drug shipments are bound to arrive. The transportation and communication hubs of our times have thus in a parallel fashion emerged as security hubs where data are collected at scale. The revelations about governmental surveillance and data collection programs made by Edward Snowden have illustrated such practices quite aptly.[10] The harvested data are then subsequently turned into information about the

[7] Peoples and Vaughan-Williams, ibid.

[8] Didier Bigo, 'When Two Become One: Internal and External Securitisations in Europe' in Morten Kelstrup and Michael C. Williams (eds), *International Relations Theory and the Politics of European Integration* (Routledge 2000).

[9] Ben Anderson, 'Preemption, Precaution, Preparedness: Anticipatory Action and Future Geographies' (2010) 34 *Progress in Human Geography* 777.

[10] Zygmunt Bauman and others, 'After Snowden: Rethinking the Impact of Surveillance' (2014) 8 *International Political Sociology* 121; David Murakami Wood and Steve Wright, 'Editorial: Before and After Snowden' (2015) 13 *Surveillance & Society* 132.

future, predominantly in the form of risk assessments that indicate the potential realization of security threats.

The increasing digitization of our everyday lives and the production of data with many of our daily actions, in conjunction with increasing storage capacity and computational power, has thus empowered new security practices that are largely predicated upon the (algorithmic) analysis of data. The next section will explore some of these practices and security scholars' engagements with them in more depth, and sketch out the ways in which questions of privacy and data protection have become important in the academic analyses of security. To summarize thus far: we have retraced how the field of security studies has evolved from a narrow political science/IR focus on the security of states in the international system, into a multi-disciplinary and critical agenda that has produced a vibrant literature that engages data-driven security practices. As, by way of these data-driven practices, security is now (potentially) at all times deeply enmeshed in our everyday lives, privacy and data protection have in this literature increasingly been turned into pertinent topics – and notably into arguments against all-encompassing security measures.

III. NEW QUESTIONS FOR SECURITY STUDIES: PRIVACY AND DATA PROTECTION

If a critical contemporary research agenda on security incorporates questions about the political, social, and economic ramifications of security practices, this entails potential impacts on protective concepts and legal tools such as privacy and data protection. There is a wide variety of research into more general matters of societal transformations brought about by the introduction of (highly automated and partly autonomous) algorithmic exploitation of large-scale datasets in many organizational, administrative, and economic contexts (see, e.g., the *Information, Communication & Society* special issue on 'The social power of algorithms'[11] or the *European Journal of Social Theory* special issue on 'Politics and the digital'[12]). Yet much of this work does not explicitly engage algorithmic and data-driven security practices, and therefore provides little contextual sensitivity for the study of security. Understanding the particular security logics, questions, and institutions within which analyses of data are embedded is however paramount for an understanding how data-driven security practices unfold specific effects and impact other social issues and values. Thus, while many of the social theoretical, philosophical, and cultural accounts of new forms of government with and through the use of data are highly valuable and pertinent for the study of security, they fall short of engaging the specific relation between data and security and its implications for privacy and data protection. In fact, there are comparatively few works that explicitly engage data-driven security practices vis-à-vis privacy and data protection. This section provides a brief overview of some of the pertinent analyses from the field of security studies against this backdrop, and sketches out the prevalent lines of inquiry that scholars have pursued.

---

[11] David Beer, 'The Social Power of Algorithms' (2017) 20 *Information, Communication & Society* 1.

[12] Mareile Kaufmann and Julien Jeandesboz, 'Politics and 'the Digital': From Singularity to Specificity' (2017) 20 *European Journal of Social Theory* 309.

It should be noted here that a good deal of security studies work on questions of privacy and data protection is not necessarily to be found in dedicated security studies journals. There are special issues (*Security Dialogue* 2017 on 'Securing with algorithms'[13]) and debate sections (*International Political Sociology* 2014 forum on 'The politics of privacy in the age of preemptive security'[14]), but studies are also spread across outlets in neighbouring disciplines (see for instance the *Surveillance & Society* 2011 debate 'In defence of privacy'[15]). This is partly due to the fact that more traditional security studies journals are still not open to those kinds of inquiries, and partly due to the fact that the intersection of security, privacy, and data protection is genuinely cross-disciplinary in its essence and thus refuses to be confined within a single academic field. In the following, the contribution of security scholars to questions of privacy and data protection will be structured along the lines of conceptual issues (risk, uncertainty, and the production of knowledge), the relationship between security and privacy/data protection, and suggestions to reconcile the supposedly conflicting notions.

Mostly in the aftermath of 9/11 and the ensuing political shifts towards data collection and analysis for security purposes, security scholars have turned increasing attention to notions of surveillance and risk. Louise Amoore and Marieke de Goede in this sense speak of 'dataveillance'[16] as a new and encompassing form of surveillance that is predicated upon the large-scale harvesting of data about individuals in contexts such as financial transactions (the risk of terrorism financing), border crossing points (the risk of terrorists and other dangerous individuals entering a country), distinct forms of mobility (the risk of threats traveling from A to B), as well as biometrics (the idea of identifying risky individuals through unique bodily features). The collection and processing of data, so they argue, empowers security agencies to produce custom-tailored risk assessments in their fight against global terrorism, thereby turning individuals into computable and manageable commodities that can be treated differently according to their risk status – and all this within a logic of prevention/preemption that mandates security action before harm could eventually unfold.[17]

In close conjunction with this body of work, Claudia Aradau and Rens van Munster have shown how the idea of risk as a rational and computable unit becomes overstretched against the essential unpredictability of human behaviour, and particularly terrorism.[18] Building on Ulrich Beck's thesis of the risk society,[19] they argue that the political primacy of security has introduced risk as a new status quo. In other words, data-driven security practices suggest that we are all constantly at risk, and the mode of producing security that is required in such a world

[13] Louise Amoore and Rita Raley, 'Securing With Algorithms: Knowledge, Decision, Sovereignty' (2017) 48 *Secur Dialogue* 3.

[14] Marieke de Goede, 'The Politics of Privacy in the Age of Preemptive Security' (2014) 8 *International Political Sociology* 100.

[15] Colin J Bennett, 'In Defence of Privacy: The Concept and the Regime' (2011) 8 *Surveillance & Society* 485.

[16] Louise Amoore and Marieke de Goede, 'Governance, Risk and Dataveillance in the War on Terror' (2005) 43 *Crime, Law and Social Change* 149.

[17] See also Louise Amoore and Marieke de Goede (eds), *Risk and the War on Terror* (Routledge 2008).

[18] Claudia Aradau and Rens van Munster, 'Governing Terrorism Through Risk: Taking Precautions, (Un)Knowing the Future' (2007) 13 *European Journal of International Relations* 89; see also Claudia Aradau, Luis Lobo-Guerrero and Rens Van Munster, 'Security, Technologies of Risk, and the Political: Guest Editors' Introduction' (2008) 39 *Secur Dialogue* 147.

[19] Ulrich Beck, *World Risk Society* (Polity Press 1999).

dominated by risk is one that operates *through* this risk. Only constant assessments of risk for any given individual would, so their interpretation of the practices of the war on terror, ensure that security agencies could be adequately equipped for their tasks. In this sense, more data would mean more knowledge, which in turn could be turned into more security.

What these seminal accounts of risk against the backdrop of both the war on terror and new technologies have in common is their emphasis on digital data. In contemporary security practices, so they argue, data are the fuel that keeps the machinery of risk assessment running, and such risk assessments could then in turn be used to cancel out harm. This importance of data for security purposes has become reinforced and aggravated by the arrival of the notion of 'Big Data'. Understood as a way to algorithmically analyse vast datasets in a theory-less fashion, the promise of Big Data practices is to discover new patterns that had hitherto been unknown and unsuspected,[20] and thereby to add a genuinely new form of knowledge that might just be the decisive factor that is needed in the struggle against an unknown/hardly knowable future. The narrative of Big Data thereby closely speaks to the 'unknown unknowns' in security, as identified by former US secretary of defense Donald Rumsfeld. If the production of security means to preempt all kinds of conceivable threats, then this list would need to, so the assumption put forward by Rumsfeld, include inconceivable ones as well. Large-scale databases, coupled with sophisticated, largely automated algorithmic modes of analysis are thereby widely considered as a viable way to render even unknown unknowns knowable, and therefore eventually actionable and preventable.

Security scholars engaging security practices inspired by Big Data logics have pointed to the severe challenges that large-scale explorative data processing poses. Amoore, for example, speaks of an 'algorithmic war' that infiltrates mundane spaces such as public transportation or border sites with categories of self/other, here/there, safe/risky, and normal/suspicious in the name of the production of security.[21] For her, the implications of algorithmically calculated associations between people, objects, and places not only introduce a notion of permanent preemption into our banal, everyday activities, but she further argues that data-driven security practices produce 'data derivatives' that, irrespective of the quality of the underlying data, actively imagine a set of potential futures that would need to be acted upon.[22] Notably, for her, the notion of the derivative means that there need not be a congruency between a 'real' individual, their representation through potentially fragmented data, and the risk assessments and ensuing security actions that emerge along such data-driven security practices.

In a similar vein, I have elsewhere argued that profiling for security purposes undergoes deep-seated transformations through Big Data-inspired practices. Predicated upon data-driven, pattern-based categorizations that sort travellers and subsequently expose them to differentiated forms of surveillance and control, the produced categories/profiles might not correspond with real-live categories, might be unstable and short-lived due to live updates of databases, and thus pose major challenges for anti-discrimination legislation and data protection.[23] Aradau,

---

[20] Chris Anderson, 'The End of Theory: The Data Deluge Makes the Scientific Method Obsolete' (2008) *Wired*.

[21] Louise Amoore, 'Algorithmic War: Everyday Geographies of the War on Terror' (2009) 41 *Antipode* 49.

[22] Louise Amoore, 'Data Derivatives: On the Emergence of a Security Risk Calculus for Our Times' (2011) 28 *Theory, Culture & Society* 24.

[23] Matthias Leese, 'The New Profiling: Algorithms, Black Boxes, and the Failure of Anti-discriminatory Safeguards in the European Union' (2014) 45 *Secur Dialogue* 494.

in her analysis of the potential glitches and shortfalls of Big Data security analytics, similarly foregrounds that the significance of errors and clues can easily vanish in the complexity and opacity of the algorithmic methods of large-scale data exploitation.[24] Taken together, these accounts highlight not only challenges for the individual in terms of identity and subjectivity, but also in terms of the ethical and political responsibility and accountability of data-driven security practices.[25] The ensuing question for critical security scholars is: how can one react to these problems both in terms of the ways to study security and in terms of mediating the potential negative effects of data-driven security practices? Aradau and Tobias Blanke suggest in this sense that security scholars should pay closer attention to the debates on algorithms, data mining, and knowledge production in the technical disciplines in order to produce a more fine-grained understanding of the practices of a presupposed 'Big Data-security assemblage' in which humans cooperate with machines in order to identify potential security threats.[26]

Another way to engage data-driven security practices, and specifically their potential negative ramifications, is through the concepts of privacy and data protection themselves. Set out to protect the individual from unjustified intrusions into their (digital) private and intimate sphere, privacy and data protection regularly serve as anchor points for critical public debates about security practices – especially when it is not clear what kinds of data are being used and how they are processed, shared, and stored.[27] Against this backdrop, there is a debate whether the rather abstract and multi-faceted idea of privacy[28] might have become effectively undermined in an era that produces digital personal data on an unprecedented scale. Rocco Bellanova claims in this regard that while 'privacy may be dead, [..] data protection is alive and kicking'[29] and can serve as a legal reference point that determines whether data practices in security contexts are commensurate with the data protection framework. For him, governing through data (and subsequently risk, in the vein of Aradau and van Munster) implies to govern digital data in the first place, and data protection would thus present a fit lever for regulation.

Others, such as Valsamis Mitsilegas, highlight the ongoing value of the concept of privacy not only as reference point for critical debate and public inquiry, but also as a juridical and political concept to challenge the potentially all-encompassing and large-scale nature of data-driven security practices.[30] What should be noted here is that privacy is not a fixed concept, but a fluid notion that is subject to changes over time and cultural contexts. Amoore reminds us in this sense that it might be more appropriate to think about privacy as a context-specific

---

24 Claudia Aradau, 'The Signature of Security: Big Data, Anticipation, Surveillance' (2015) *Radical Philosophy* 21.

25 Amoore and Raley (n 13); Claudia Aradau and Tobias Blanke, 'Politics of Prediction: Security and the Time/Space of Governmentality in the Age of Big Data' (2017) 20 *European Journal of Social Theory* 373.

26 Claudia Aradau and Tobias Blanke, 'The (Big) Data-Security Assemblage: Knowledge and Critique' (2015) *Big Data & Society* 1.

27 de Goede (n 14).

28 Michael Friedewald and others, 'Privacy, Data Protection and Emerging Sciences and Technologies: Towards a Common Framework' (2010) 23 *Innovation: The European Journal of Social Science Research* 61.

29 Rocco Bellanova, 'Digital, Politics, and Algorithms: Governing Digital Data Through the Lens of Data Protection' (2017) 20 *European Journal of Social Theory* 329 1; see also Rocco Bellanova, 'Data Protection, with Love' (2014) 8 *International Political Sociology* 112.

30 Valsamis Mitsilegas, 'The Value of Privacy in an Era of Security: Embedding Constitutional Limits on Preemptive Surveillance' (2014) 8 *International Political Sociology* 104.

concept that hinges on how data are assembled and processed for security purposes.[31] Quirine Eijkman adds to these considerations that the enactment of privacy and data protection should analytically be traced to the street level, where security officers produce data about threats and deploy the knowledge about future threats calculated by algorithmic tools.[32] In a similar vein, Johann Čas and his colleagues point out that citizens' perspectives on surveillance and privacy vis-à-vis security should not easily be dismissed, but that they should be taken into account for policy-making, as, after all, citizens are the ones who are subject to data-driven security practices.[33]

IV. THE CHALLENGE OF SECURITIZATION

In many political and popular accounts, the relationship between privacy/data protection and security is portrayed as a trade-off model, implicating that some form of balance between the protection of individual data and the operational requirements of security agencies could be established. Security scholars have largely deemed such a conceptualization inadequate and empirically untenable, as both the notions of privacy and data protection, as well as the manifold data-driven security practices would be far too complex to be forced into a simplistic equation. Mark Neocleous even goes as far as to calling the very idea of any kind of balance a myth.[34] Building on the works of Michel Foucault, he instead argues that liberal politics fundamentally operates through ways of providing security, thus replacing an interpretation of liberty *vs.* security with one of liberty *as* security. Whereas for Neocleous, his analysis eventually leads him to a radical critique of the notion of liberal notion of security itself, others have critically engaged the presupposed trade-off model between privacy and security in more practical terms.

Elsewhere I have in this sense criticized that the tension between privacy/data protection and security is increasingly supposed to be eased through technological solutions that become built into security technologies themselves (e.g., through privacy-by-design approaches). Such privacy-protecting measures present however merely a 'technological fix for a technological fix' and do not address the problems posed by data-driven security practices in the first place, but merely remedy their negative impacts.[35] Govert Valkenburg, while being equally critical about the possibility of 'balancing', points out however that thinking about privacy, data protection, and security in terms of a balancing metaphor could nonetheless yield value as a heuristic device that could help to identify difficulties in the application of security technol-

31 Louise Amoore, 'Security and the Claim to Privacy' (2014) 8 *International Political Sociology* 108.

32 Quirine Eijkman, 'Digital Security Governance and Risk Anticipation: What About the Role of Security Officials in Privacy Protection?' (2014) 8 *International Political Sociology* 116.

33 Johann Čas and others, 'Introduction: Surveillance, Privacy and Security' in Michael Friedewald and others (eds), *Surveillance, Privacy and Security: Citizens' Perspectives* (Routledge 2017).

34 Mark Neocleous, 'Security, Liberty and the Myth of Balance: Towards a Critique of Security Politics' (2007) 6 *Contemporary Political Theory* 131.

35 Matthias Leese, 'Privacy and Security – On the Evolution of a European Conflict' in Serge Gutwirth, Ronald Leenes and Paul De Hert (eds), *Reforming European Data Protection Law* (Springer 2015).

ogies.[36] Moreover, so his argument, the simplicity of the image of balancing could help to put questions of privacy and data protection on the public agenda.

Daniel Solove, acknowledging the need to engage with popular debates and arguments about the relationship between security and privacy, criticizes the 'all-or-nothing propositions' often encountered in these debates, and contests that, given sensitive forms of regulation that meaningfully engage with both concepts, privacy and security need not stand in a mutually exclusive relationship in the first place.[37] Finally, Charles Raab proposes to read privacy itself as instrumental to security, as it could 'involve protective, defensive and risk-averse measures in the service of privacy, autonomy, dignity, and sociality'.[38] Notably, for him, privacy is as much a collective interest as 'national security' or 'societal security,' thus aligning the concepts from an analytical angle – only that threats to privacy need not be identical to those mobilized with regard to national security, and might even come from government itself.

Even despite the criticized under-complexity of a presupposed trade-off model, the idea to 'sacrifice' personal data to 'enhance' security has been quite persistent politically. This persistence is partly due to the ways in which security is often presented as paramount in the first place, and partly due to the persuasive power that security unfolds against the backdrop of threatening situations. 'Security' can in this sense be used as an argument to legitimize measures to counter threats. Ole Wæver in this regard speaks of processes of 'securitization', meaning that security is politically presented as a question of bare survival against an imminent threat. Subsequently, such a threat would need to be tackled with swift and decisive action, even if this would mean to apply exceptional means that would in other situations not be considered as adequate or morally acceptable.[39] As Barry Buzan, Wæver, and Jaap de Wilde write, 'the invocation of security has been the key to legitimizing the use of force, but more generally it has opened the way for the state to mobilize, or to take special powers, to handle existential threats'.[40] Within processes of securitization, normal democratic procedures for policy-making could thus effectively become side-tracked, as arguments of urgency and the exceptionality of threat situations would request immediate action to be undertaken in order to ensure survival.

Such prioritization of security-as-survival poses considerable challenges for privacy and data protection. Security scholars have largely described tightened regulations and protocols, as well as the implementation of new security technologies in the fight against terrorism after 9/11 as results of securitization processes. Particularly in the US, but also in Europe, security policies and resulting practices have been passed without adequate parliamentary or public debate. Examples for this are the above-mentioned governmental data-harvesting programmes revealed by Edward Snowden, increased surveillance competencies, or data retention laws that

---

36 Govert Valkenburg, 'Privacy versus Security: Problems and Possibilities for the Trade-Off Model' in Serge Gutwirth, Ronald Leenes and Paul De Hert (eds), *Reforming European Data Protection Law* (Springer 2015).

37 Daniel J Solove, *Nothing to Hide: The False Tradeoff Between Privacy and Security* (Yale University Press 2011).

38 Charles D Raab, 'Privacy as a Security Value' in Dag Wiese Schartum, Lee A Bygrave and Anne Gunn Berge Bekken (eds), *Jon Bing: En Hyllest / A Tribute* (Glydendal 2014) 55.

39 Ole Wæver, 'Securitization and Desecuritization' in Ronnie D Lipschutz (ed), *On Security* (Columbia University Press 1995); see also Barry Buzan, Ole Wæver and Jaap de Wilde, *Security: A New Framework for Analysis* (Rienner 1998).

40 Buzan, Wæver and de Wilde, ibid.

oblige telecommunication providers to store their customers' communication data and make them accessible for law enforcement agencies. Privacy and data protection and the values that they represent (the protection of the individuals' sphere of privacy and intimacy) thereby enter into an open conflict with the value of security. Security experts (professional practitioners as well as politicians) regularly put forward the presupposed necessity to violate privacy and data protection for the sake of the 'greater good' of security/survival, thus claiming the need to collect, store, and share as much information as possible to ensure constant input for algorithmic, data-driven security measures that perpetuate risk analysis in a world that is constantly 'at risk'.

While the concept of securitization as proposed by Wæver and his colleagues focuses on the discursive practices of 'speaking' security, others such as Didier Bigo have claimed that processes of securitization not only occur against the backdrop of exceptional threats and the debates that they spark, but that securitization is produced and reproduced in a much more banal, everyday fashion through the practices of security professionals.[41] Through their professional networks, so the argument goes, they could effectively put the need to collect, analyse, and share data among them on the political agenda and reinforce security discourses even beneath the level of public debate. Torin Monahan has in this vein shown how security agencies side-track privacy and data protection regulations and 'fuse' data in ways that go largely unnoticed.[42]

Data-driven security practices, aggravated by the promise of the Big Data narrative that if only enough data is at disposal new knowledge will sooner or later be extracted from such data, thus further and further colonize aspects of social life that leave collectable traces of data. The ability to combine and re-combine even fragmented data with other data opens up endless possibilities to build and continuously update large databases, or to pair genuine 'security data' with commercial or administrative data. For Jef Huysmans, securitization thus entails 'instances of the technologically mediated spread of surveillance and the folding of securitizing into everyday life'[43] that build on 'little security nothings' (for instance footage recorded by CCTV footage, the routine collection of cellphone location data, or commercial travel data collected by carrier companies such as PNR datasets). These little nothings, while in themselves not being noteworthy or 'dangerous', might unfold analytical power only after they have been combined with other data and repurposed for the search for terrorists, illegal migrants, or other security threats.

The issue from a perspective of privacy and data protection here is the problematization of their efficacy in a world where security is presented as paramount. In commercial contexts, data protection for example provides comparably clear-cut and enforceable principles such as purpose limitation, the right to access, the right to rectification, the right to compensation, or

---

[41] Didier Bigo, 'Security and Immigration: Toward a Critique of the Governmentality of Unease' (2002) 27 *Alternatives: Global, Local, Political* 63; Didier Bigo, 'Detention of Foreigners, States of Exception, and the Social Practices of Control of the Banopticon' in Prem Kumar Rajaram and Carl Grundy-Warr (eds), *Borderscapes Hidden Geographies and Politics at Territory's Edge* (University of Minnesota Press 2007).

[42] Torin Monahan, 'The Future of Security? Surveillance Operations at Homeland Security Fusion Centers' (2011) 37 *Social Justice* 84; Torin Monahan and Priscilla M. Regan, 'Zones of Opacity: Data Fusion in Post-9/11 Security Organizations' (2012) 27 *Canadian Journal of Law and Society* 301.

[43] Jef Huysmans, 'What's in an Act? On Security Speech Acts and Little Security Nothings' (2011) 42 *Secur Dialogue* 371–372.

the right to judicial redress. Such legal tools, however, become undermined by securitization processes in which arguments of survival, urgency, and not least the need for secrecy in the fight against terrorists and criminals are considered to trump doubts about the infringement of privacy and data protection.

V. CONCLUSION

This does however not mean that privacy and data protection would be a lost cause vis-à-vis security. On the contrary, even though the protection of personal data might have become a lot more challenging against the backdrop of data-driven security practices and the ensuing desire to accumulate as much data about populations as possible, the field of security studies itself can provide valuable support here. As discussed above, critical security scholars have increasingly started to question and challenge security practices considering the social and societal consequences that emerge from them. In this sense, the literature discussed throughout the preceding sections empirically and conceptually engages algorithmic, data-driven security practices and exposes them to much-needed critique and debate. This can be done through technically informed analyses that lay bare how precisely data are collected, processed, and used for computational risk models. It can be done through an engagement of the discourses and practices put forward by policymakers and security professionals. And it can be done through the rendering visible of the production of security to the public, thus providing the anchors for public debate that de Goede speaks of.[44]

Most notably, in this regard, security studies' engagement with privacy and data protection highlights the ethical responsibilities that come with advanced computational methods in a world where our actions increasingly happen in an entirely networked, online fashion – or at least leave digital traces that make us involuntarily subject to security practices that are not little security 'nothings', but eventually turn out to become security 'somethings' as they reveal who we talk to, where we are, what we consume, and what secrets we might want to keep to ourselves. Critical security scholars have repeatedly highlighted the need for reflexivity, including the appeal to call out security practices that are ethically questionable.[45] Here, the agendas of privacy, data protection, and security studies align in their desire to be protective of both collective and individual values – and the relationship between them becomes more obvious than suggested by our initial intuition.

Considering security scholars' engagements with privacy and data protection outlined here, and more specifically vis-à-vis the challenges that privacy and data protection face against the backdrop of security discourses, future research should take into consideration at least two major issues. First, it is apparent that more technical know-how among social scientists is needed to understand the precise workings of algorithmic data analysis. This is not an easy task, and it will require true interdisciplinarity not only among the social sciences, but with computer scientists and engineers. Aradau and Blanke have provided a first valuable venture

---

[44] de Goede (n 14).

[45] Christopher S Browning and Matt McDonald, 'The Future of Critical Security Studies: Ethics and the Politics of Security' (2013) 19 *European Journal of International Relations* 235; c.a.s.e. collective (n 6).

in this direction.[46] Second, and in close conjunction, empirically detailed and in-depth research will be paramount to be able to carefully contextualize data-driven security practices. If we seek to produce robust political and ethical evaluations of the impacts that such practices unfold, they must be analytically embedded within the organizational processes, historical (dis-)continuities, and discourses that surround them.

ACKNOWLEDGMENTS

Much appreciation goes to Myriam Dunn Cavelty and Rocco Bellanova for their critical and helpful comments on earlier versions of this chapter.

REFERENCES

Amoore L, 'Algorithmic War: Everyday Geographies of the War on Terror' (2009) 41 *Antipode* 49.
Amoore L, 'Data Derivatives: On the Emergence of a Security Risk Calculus for Our Times' (2011) 28 *Theory, Culture & Society* 24.
Amoore L, 'Security and the Claim to Privacy' (2014) 8 *International Political Sociology* 108.
Amoore L and de Goede M, 'Governance, Risk and Dataveillance in the War on Terror' (2005) 43 *Crime, Law and Social Change* 149.
Amoore L and de Goede M (eds), *Risk and the War on Terror* (Routledge 2008).
Amoore L and Raley R, 'Securing With Algorithms: Knowledge, Decision, Sovereignty' (2017) 48 *Secur Dialogue* 3.
Anderson B, 'Preemption, Precaution, Preparedness: Anticipatory Action and Future Geographies' (2010) 34 *Progress in Human Geography* 777.
Anderson C, 'The End of Theory: The Data Deluge Makes the Scientific Method Obsolete' (2008) *Wired.*
Aradau C, 'The Signature of Security: Big Data, Anticipation, Surveillance' (2015) *Radical Philosophy* 21.
Aradau C and Blanke T, 'The (Big) Data-Security Assemblage: Knowledge and Critique' (2015) *Big Data & Society* 1.
Aradau C and Blanke T, 'Politics of Prediction: Security and the Time/Space of Governmentality in the Age of Big Data' (2017) 20 *European Journal of Social Theory* 373.
Aradau C and others (eds), *Critical Security Methods: New Frameworks for Analysis* (Routledge 2015).
Aradau C, Lobo-Guerrero L and Van Munster R, 'Security, Technologies of Risk, and the Political: Guest Editors' Introduction' (2008) 39 *Secur Dialogue* 147.
Aradau C and van Munster R, 'Governing Terrorism Through Risk: Taking Precautions, (Un)Knowing the Future' (2007) 13 *European Journal of International Relations* 89.
Bauman Z and others, 'After Snowden: Rethinking the Impact of Surveillance' (2014) 8 *International Political Sociology* 121.
Beck U, *World Risk Society* (Polity Press 1999).
Beer D, 'The Social Power of Algorithms' (2017) 20 *Information, Communication & Society* 1.
Bellanova R, 'Data Protection, with Love' (2014) 8 *International Political Sociology* 112.
Bellanova R, 'Digital, Politics, and Algorithms: Governing Digital Data Through the Lens of Data Protection' (2017) 20 *European Journal of Social Theory* 329.
Bennett C J, 'In Defence of Privacy: The Concept and the Regime' (2011) 8 *Surveillance & Society* 485.
Bigo D, 'Detention of Foreigners, States of Exception, and the Social Practices of Control of the Banopticon' in Rajaram PK and Grundy-Warr C (eds), *Borderscapes Hidden Geographies and Politics at Territory's Edge* (University of Minnesota Press 2007).

[46] Aradau and Blanke (n 26).

Bigo D, 'Security and Immigration: Toward a Critique of the Governmentality of Unease' (2002) 27 *Alternatives: Global, Local, Political* 63.
Bigo D, 'When Two Become One: Internal and External Securitisations in Europe' in Kelstrup M and Williams MC (eds), *International Relations Theory and the Politics of European Integration* (Routledge 2000).
Browning C S and McDonald M, 'The Future of Critical Security Studies: Ethics and the Politics of Security' (2013) 19 *European Journal of International Relations* 235.
Buzan B and Hansen L, *The Evolution of International Security Studies* (Cambridge University Press 2009).
Buzan B, Wæver O and de Wilde J, *Security: A New Framework for Analysis* (Rienner 1998).
c.a.s.e. collective, 'Critical Approaches to Security in Europe: A Networked Manifesto' (2006) 37 *Secur Dialogue* 443.
Čas J and others, 'Introduction: Surveillance, Privacy and Security' in Friedewald M and others (eds), *Surveillance, Privacy and Security: Citizens' Perspectives* (Routledge 2017).
de Goede M, 'The Politics of Privacy in the Age of Preemptive Security' (2014) 8 *International Political Sociology* 100.
Eijkman Q, 'Digital Security Governance and Risk Anticipation: What About the Role of Security Officials in Privacy Protection?' (2014) 8 *International Political Sociology* 116.
Friedewald M and others, 'Privacy, Data Protection and Emerging Sciences and Technologies: Towards a Common Framework' (2010) 23 *Innovation: The European Journal of Social Science Research* 61.
Huysmans J, 'What's in an Act? On Security Speech Acts and Little Security Nothings' (2011) 42 *Secur Dialogue* 371.
Kaufmann M and Jeandesboz J, 'Politics and 'the Digital': From Singularity to Specificity' (2017) 20 *European Journal of Social Theory* 309.
Krause K and Williams M C (eds), *Critical Security Studies: Concepts and Cases* (Routledge 1997).
Leese M, 'The New Profiling: Algorithms, Black Boxes, and the Failure of Anti-discriminatory Safeguards in the European Union' (2014) 45 *Secur Dialogue* 494.
Leese M, 'Privacy and Security – On the Evolution of a European Conflict' in Gutwirth S, Leenes R and De Hert P (eds), *Reforming European Data Protection Law* (Springer 2015).
Mitsilegas V, 'The Value of Privacy in an Era of Security: Embedding Constitutional Limits on Preemptive Surveillance' (2014) 8 *International Political Sociology* 104.
Monahan T, 'The Future of Security? Surveillance Operations at Homeland Security Fusion Centers' (2011) 37 *Social Justice* 84.
Monahan T and Regan P M, 'Zones of Opacity: Data Fusion in Post-9/11 Security Organizations' (2012) 27 *Canadian Journal of Law and Society* 301.
Murakami Wood D and Wright S, 'Editorial: Before and After Snowden' (2015) 13 *Surveillance & Society* 132.
Mutimer D, Grayson K and Beier JM, 'Critical Studies on Security: An Introduction' (2013) 1 *Critical Studies on Security* 1.
Neocleous M, 'Security, Liberty and the Myth of Balance: Towards a Critique of Security Politics' (2007) 6 *Contemporary Political Theory* 131.
Peoples C and Vaughan-Williams N, *Critical Security Studies: An Introduction* (Routledge 2010).
Raab C D, 'Privacy as a Security Value' in Wiese Schartum D, Bygrave LA and Berge Bekken AG (eds), *Jon Bing: En Hyllest / A Tribute* (Glydendal 2014).
Salter M B and Mutlu C E (eds), *Research Methods in Critical Security Studies: An Introduction* (Routledge 2013).
Schlag G, Junk J and Daase C (eds), *Transformations of Security Studies: Dialogues, Diversity and Discipline* (Routledge 2016).
Solove D J, *Nothing to Hide: The False Tradeoff Between Privacy and Security* (Yale University Press 2011).
Valkenburg G, 'Privacy versus Security: Problems and Possibilities for the Trade-Off Model' in Gutwirth S, Leenes R and De Hert P (eds), *Reforming European Data Protection Law* (Springer 2015).
Wæver O, 'Securitization and Desecuritization' in Lipschutz RD (ed), *On Security* (Columbia University Press 1995).
Walt S M, 'The Renaissance of Security Studies' (1991) 35 *International Studies Quarterly* 211.

Wolfers A, '"National Security" as an Ambiguous Symbol' (1952) 67 *Political Science Quarterly* 481.

12. Data protection and consumer protection: The empowerment of the citizen-consumer

Damian Clifford

I. INTRODUCTION

The alignment of the data protection and consumer protection policy agendas is being increasingly discussed in academic literature,[1] policy making[2] and enforcement circles.[3] Although much of this movement towards an increased recognition of the overlaps and complementary functions of these two respective policy agendas has been limited to abstract pontifications as to the overall benefit for citizen-consumers, recent legislative changes and proposals are increasingly manifesting a more practical shift towards 'aligned' protection. But what does this mean in practice? It is undoubtedly clear that the data and consumer protection policy agendas share common ground, but one must wonder whether the alignment of these respective policy agendas also gives rise to problems. Although a complete examination of the potential issues is outside the scope of this chapter, the purpose of the analysis is to present some insights into the key legislative developments and overarching theoretical challenges. To achieve this goal the analysis will focus on the General Data Protection Regulation (GDPR)[4] and the specific reference to the Unfair Terms Directive (UCT Directive)[5] in Recital 42 GDPR regarding the use of 'pre-formulated declarations' of data subject consent. In essence, the analysis of pre-formulated declarations and the relevant data protection and consumer protection frameworks will thus act as a litmus test of the difficulties associated with alignment more generally.

---

[1] Natali Helberger, Frederik J Zuiderveen Borgesius and Agustin Reyna, 'The Perfect Match? A Closer Look at the Relationship between EU Consumer Law and Data Protection Law' (2017) 54 *Common Market Law Review* 1427; Dan Jerker B Svantesson, 'Enter the Quagmire – the Complicated Relationship between Data Protection Law and Consumer Protection Law' [2017] *Computer Law & Security* Review <http://linkinghub.elsevier.com/retrieve/pii/S0267364917302558> accessed 15 November 2017; Peter Rott, 'Data Protection Law as Consumer Law–How Consumer Organisations Can Contribute to the Enforcement of Data Protection Law' (2017) *6 Journal of European Consumer and Market Law* 113; Hans Schulte-Nölke, 'The Brave New World of EU Consumer Law–Without Consumers, or Even Without Law?' (2015) 4(4) *Journal of European Consumer and Market Law* 135.

[2] EDPS, 'Privacy and Competitiveness in the Age of Big Data: The Interplay between Data Protection, Competition Law and Consumer Protection in the Digital Economy' (European Data Protection Supervisor 2014) Preliminary Opinion of the European Data Protection Supervisor https://secure.edps.europa.eu/EDPSWEB/webdav/site/mySite/shared/Documents/Consultation/Opinions/2014/14-03-26_competitition_law_big_data_EN.pdf accessed October 2017.

[3] See: Nicolo Zingales, 'Between a Rock and Two Hard Places: WhatsApp at the Crossroad of Competition, Data Protection and Consumer Law' (2017) 33 *Computer Law & Security Review* 553.

[4] Regulation (EU) 2016/679 of the European Parliament and of the Council of 27 April 2016 on the protection of natural persons with regard to the processing of personal data and on the free movement of such data, and repealing Directive 95/46/EC (General Data Protection Regulation) OJ L 119, 1–88.

[5] Council Directive 93/13/EEC of 5 April 1993 on unfair terms in consumer contracts (OJ L 95, 29).

In this vein, the chapter aims to point towards the key challenges associated with the future plotting of the steps required to navigate this alignment quagmire. In this vein, the chapter relies on a descriptive and evaluative analysis of the EU data and consumer protection frameworks and aims to provide normative insights into the potential challenges. The legal instruments have been selected based on their substantive and material scope. The first section of the chapter briefly introduces the motivations for alignment by first summarising some of the problems associated with the functioning of the data protection framework before then exploring the potential role(s) for consumer protection. The second section of the chapter explores the explicit reference to the UCT Directive in Recital 42 GDPR. Finally, the last section of the chapter contextualises the difficulties discussed through the lens of pre-formulated declarations of data subject consent in order to point towards the more abstract legal difficulties. In particular, this will focus on the consequences of recognising the existence of a consumer contract when personal data is provided by a consumer and by questioning the role of the respective fairness principles in the GDPR and the UCT Directive vis-à-vis the legislative aims and primary law foundations of the respective secondary frameworks.

II. MOTIVATIONS FOR ALIGNMENT – THE BOLSTERING OF DECISION-MAKING CAPACITY

The introduction of the Lisbon Treaty was a watershed moment for both data and consumer protection in the EU. The common thread for both policy areas was the designation of binding force on the Charter of Fundamental Rights of the European Union.[6] Through this development data protection was recognised in the Treaties (Art 16 TFEU) and as a fundamental right (Art 8 Charter) in addition to the separate right to privacy (Art 7 Charter) (see notably chapter 1 in this book). Consumer protection was recognised as a principle (Art 38 Charter). The distinction between data protection as a right and consumer protection as a principle is significant. Article 52(1) of the Charter stipulates that any limitation on the exercise of rights and freedoms is required to be 'provided for by law and respect the essence of those rights and freedoms'. In contrast, principles, as per Article 52(5) Charter 'may be implemented by legislative and executive acts taken by institutions, bodies, offices and agencies of the Union, and by acts of Member States when they are implementing Union Law'. Moreover, Article 52(5) Charter goes on to further stipulate that principles are only 'judicially cognisable' in the interpretation of these acts. In short therefore, rights and principles are weighted differently in terms of their significance from a legislative perspective. Despite not being afforded the status of a right, however, Benöhr contends that the consumer protection agenda may be furthered by a broad range of Charter rights, including for instance the right to data protection.[7] This argument appears to be consistent with the aim of integrating consumer interests in all relevant

[6] Although the Charter was first drafted in 2000 it failed to gain binding status until 2009 with the adoption of the Lisbon Treaty. There had been a previously attempt with the failed Constitutional Treaty. However, there was some criticism of packaging of the Charter with the Treaty as some felt that it was being afforded a status that had not been conceived of at the time of drafting. Indeed at the time of writing there were significant differences in opinion regarding the role and scope of the Charter, for an overview see: Grainne De Búrca, 'The Drafting of the European Union Charter of Fundamental Rights' (2001) 26 *European Law Review* 1.

[7] Iris Benöhr, *EU Consumer Law and Human Rights* (OUP Oxford 2013) 59–60.

policies and the goal of targeting a more systematic approach for the protection of consumers as expressed in the European Consumer Agenda in 2012.[8] As such, it is arguable that the adoption of the Charter has breathed new life into consumer protection policy[9] as arguably manifested in the recent legislative changes and proposals.

As described in chapters 1 and 4, the data protection framework essentially targets the asymmetric data subject-controller relationship *via* the reliance on key principles, requirements and rights as manifested in the GDPR. In response to the technological developments, ubiquitous computing and the so-called 'datafication' of everything,[10] the EU legislator has reformed the data protection framework and explicitly introduced the principles of accountability and transparency, data protection by design and by default and has adopted a risk-based approach in the GDPR. In addition to these developments however, there have been increasing calls for the alignment of the consumer protection and data protection policy agendas in order to bolster citizen-consumer 'control' over personal data in light of pervasive collection.[11] As has been outlined elsewhere in this handbook (see chapter 1), data protection aims to rebalance the inherent asymmetries through the application of notions such as informed data subject consent and data subject rights to provide protections, empower individuals and enhance decision-making capacity. In the information society services (ISS) context, through the application of such data subject orientated protections or 'micro-rights', individuals are positioned as the key actors and are empowered to make decisions regarding their personal data.[12]

As mentioned above, these protections are supplemented by *inter alia* key principles (i.e. data minimisation, purpose limitation, data accuracy, accountability and data security) a risk-based approach, data protection impact assessments and data protection by default and design. Although practically speaking one may certainly question whether data subjects are always the key actors in all contexts, in the commercial B2C ISS setting consent is often the only relevant condition for the processing of personal data (see section III). Accordingly, in such circumstance the data protection framework places the control over one's personal data at the heart of individual empowerment and, in order to operationalise control, mobilises protections or 'environmental variables' comprised of technological and organisational safeguards to ensure a secure personal data processing environment.[13] It could be thus argued that

---

8 European Commission, 'Communication from the Commission to the European Parliament, the Council, the Economic and Social Committee and the Committee of the Regions a European Consumer Agenda – Boosting Confidence and Growth, COM(2012) 225.'

9 'European Commission, REFIT Fitness Check of Consumer Law' (December 2015) http://ec.europa.eu/smart-regulation/roadmaps/docs/2016_just_023_evaluation_consumer_law_en.pdf accessed 20 December 2017.

10 See: Viktor Mayer-Schonberger and Kenneth Cukier, *Big Data: A Revolution That Will Transform How We Live, Work and Think* (Houghton Mifflin Harcourt 2013).

11 In line with these developments one can also refer more generally to the recent European Parliament motion for a resolution on fundamental rights implications of big data: privacy, data protection, non-discrimination, security and law-enforcement see: 'Committee on Civil Liberties, Justice and Home Affairs, Ana Gomes (Rapporteur), Report on Fundamental Rights Implications of Big Data: Privacy, Data Protection, Nondiscrimination, Security and Law-Enforcement (2016/2225(INI)) (20.02.2017)' http://www.europarl.europa.eu/sides/getDoc.do?pubRef=-//EP//NONSGML+REPORT+A8-2017-0044+0+DOC+PDF+V0//EN accessed 20 December 2017.

12 Christophe Lazaro and Daniel Le Métayer, 'Control over Personal Data: True Remedy or Fairytale?' (2015) 12 SCRIPTed http://script-ed.org/?p=1927 accessed 7 November 2015.

13 Ibid.

the mobilisation of protections and the risk-based approach enshrined in the GDPR illustrate a more collective view of control as they aim to provide a secure environment for the processing of personal data.[14]

Despite the fact that this dual-role understanding of control is well established in the framework,[15] it has been suggested repeatedly that the framework's ongoing legitimacy is under strain.[16] In particular, it has been argued that data gathering in the 'big data' environment appears to be directly in contradiction with the data minimisation and purpose limitation principles given that data are often collected in an unrestricted manner for unspecified purposes and then mined for useful commercial applications.[17] This has led authors to highlight the potential for function creep.[18] Aside from the difficulties associated with the practical application of/respect for the purpose limitation principle, it should also be noted that there is a clear difficulty applying the data protection framework to profiling. More specifically, the connection between the processing risk and the notion of personal data is unclear given that data protection is focused on processing risks and not the substantial parts of profiling applications.[19] In simple terms, the GDPR instead merely provides that data subjects have the right not to be subject to an automated individual decision (i.e., rather than specifically regulating the subject matter of such decisions see Article 22 GDPR).[20] As will be discussed below, this arguably strengthens the call for a more holistic approach towards the protection of citizen-consumers and thus the alignment of the data protection and consumer protection policy agendas.

Aside from these more strictly technology driven difficulties, it should also be noted that the effectiveness of the dualist notion of control has also been repeatedly challenged given the asymmetric data subject-controller relationship. This arguably diminishes the legitimacy of data subject participation, presents barriers to the application of the accountability principle and also has a specific impact on data subject's bargaining power and decision-making capacity.[21] In commenting on the effects of this asymmetric relationship, Mantelero has observed that 'the self-determination of the single individual is inadequate and insufficient to create

---

[14] Ibid.

[15] Orla Lynskey, *The Foundations of EU Data Protection Law* (First, Oxford University Press 2016) 258–262.

[16] For a recent discussion here see: Tal Z Zarsky, 'Incompatible: The GDPR in the Age of Big Data' (2017) 47 *Seton Hall Law Review* 2. But also for instance Bert-Jaap Koops, 'The Trouble with European Data Protection Law' (2014) 4 *International Data Privacy Law* 250.

[17] Valerie Verdoodt, Damian Clifford and Eva Lievens, 'Toying with Children's Emotions, the New Game in Town? The Legality of Advergames in the EU' (2016) 32 *Computer Law & Security Review* 599, 608.

[18] Michael Curry, David Phillips and Priscilla Regan, 'Emergency Response Systems and the Creeping Legibility of People and Places' (2004) 20 *Information Society* 357, 362: Function creep relates to a situation 'when a system developed for a particular purpose comes to be used for, or to provide the underpinnings for other systems that are used for, different purposes'. Bert-Jaap Koops, 'On Decision Transparency, or How to Enhance Data Protection after the Computational Turn' in Mireille Hildebrandt and Katja de Vries (eds), *Privacy, Due Process and the Computational Turn: The Philosophy of Law meets the Philosophy of Technology* (Routledge 2013) https://vokaturi.com/ accessed 30 August 2017.

[19] Koops (n 18).

[20] Ibid.

[21] Orla Lynskey, 'Deconstructing Data Protection: The "Added-Value" of a Right to Data Protection in the EU Legal Order' (2014) 63 *International & Comparative Law Quarterly* 569.

an effective and conscious market activity concerning personal data'.[22] This is illustrative of Koops' argument that in a practical sense data subject involvement often has limited effect due to their ignorance regarding the extent of data gathering and processing operations.[23] Therefore, despite the balancing aims of the GDPR, asymmetries in bargaining and informational power render the reliance on data subject empowerment questionable, or at least open to criticism, due to the fact that such asymmetries undercut the value of accountability because of the role played by the data subject in operationalising this principle.[24] These concerns are further associated with (or arguably multiplied by) the rationality-based assumption imbued in the notion of data subject control. As noted by Lazaro and Le Métayer control 'is strongly associated with the conventional figure of the "rational and autonomous agent", capable of deliberating about personal goals, controlling the course of the events and acting under the direction of such deliberation'.[25] Behavioural science research has aimed to systematically illustrate the flawed reliance on the rationality of individual decision makers and thus explored the notion of bounded rationality and the inherent cognitive biases.[26] In a data protection context this has manifested itself in discussions regarding information overload (i.e., the failure of privacy policies to inform data subjects due to sheer volume of text often presented in complex legalese), the multiplicity of requests for consent and the 'stickiness' of defaults.[27] Such research seemingly further reduces the value of data subject participation.[28]

With these criticisms in mind, the need to align data and consumer protection in order to further empower the data subject is being increasingly recognised.[29] This reflects the desire for more holistic responses to the challenges posed by the emergence of new technologies as individual autonomy in the mediated environment is affected both in terms of the data and consumer protection safeguards. However, the precise overlaps and subtle distinctions between these respective policy agendas are far from clear. In addition, the technological developments combined with the emergence of the mediated environment render protections reliant on indi-

---

[22] Alessandro Mantelero, 'Competitive Value of Data Protection: The Impact of Data Protection Regulation on Online Behaviour' (2013) 3 *International Data Privacy Law* 229.

[23] Koops (n 18).

[24] According to the EDPS, the notion of accountability could be made more effective. This would involve a shift in the attribution of responsibility from the consumers to policy makers, self-regulatory mechanisms and/or businesses. EDPS (n 2).

[25] Lazaro and Le Métayer (n 12). The authors further note that this notion is both '*individualist*' given the emphasis on individual sovereignty and also '*active*' in that control implies effective participation of the data subject and the liberty to alienate their personal data provided that such '*alienation is informed and voluntary*'.

[26] Cass R Sunstein and Richard H Thaler, 'Libertarian Paternalism Is Not an Oxymoron' (2003) *The University of Chicago Law Review* 1159; Christine Jolls, Cass R Sunstein and Richard H Thaler, 'A Behavioral Approach to Law and Economics' (1998) 50 *Stanford Law Review* 1471; Cass Robert Sunstein, 'Fifty Shades of Manipulation' https://dash.harvard.edu/handle/1/16149947 accessed 31 May 2017.

[27] Lauren E Willis, 'Why Not Privacy by Default?' (2014) 29 *Berkeley Technology Law Journal* 61.

[28] Damian Clifford, 'EU Data Protection Law and Targeted Advertising: Consent and the Cookie Monster-Tracking the Crumbs of Online User Behaviour' (2014) 5 *Journal of Intellectual Property, Information Technology and Electronic Commerce Law* 194. The readiness of data subjects to consent to the surrender their personal data without being aware of the specific purpose indicated (or indeed of the data gathering in the first place) is a good illustration of this point.

[29] EDPS (n 2).

vidual rationality increasingly out-of-sync with reality. With this in mind, consumer protection is aligning with the data protection framework in two areas, namely:

1. As a supplement to data protection (i.e. or alternative route) for the protection of data subjects-consumers vis-à-vis personal data gathering practices; and
2. The protection of the consumer in relation to potentially harmful commercial practices that rely on personalisation and which may have an impact on the autonomy and consumer choice and hence its role as a toolbox to mobilise the protection of fundamental rights *ex post*.

It should be understood that both are complementary and aim to improve the decision-making capacity of consumers by addressing the power and information asymmetries evident in the digital economy. However, the purpose of this chapter is to explore the first of these areas. Indeed, as noted by Helberger *et al.*, '[c]onsumer law could thus be an important instrument to assess the fairness of terms and conditions regarding personal data, and the fairness of the conditions under which consumers agree to the processing of personal data in a commercial relationship'.[30] In this regard it is important to note that there has been an increasing number of enforcement actions being taken by national consumer protection authorities regarding the fairness of privacy policies and the legitimacy of data collection practices.[31] Nevertheless, the precise nature of the overlap with data protection and privacy is far from clear and hence, the analysis now turns to a more detailed examination of the GDPR and the specific reference to the UCT Directive.

III. PRE-FORMULATED DECLARATIONS OF DATA SUBJECT CONSENT AND RECITAL 42 GDPR

As described elsewhere in this book, the processing of personal data requires controllers to satisfy one of the conditions for lawful processing contained in Article 6(1) GDPR. For our current purposes it is sufficient to clarify that in a commercial setting (and for commercial purposes) consent (Art 6(1)(a) GDPR), contract (Art 6(1)(b) GDPR) and legitimate interests (Art 6(1)(f) GDPR) are specifically relevant. Moreover, in the context of the provision of ISS it has been repeatedly stated by the Article 29 Working Party that where large amounts of personal data are processed, consent will often be the only available condition.[32] As will be remembered from Chapter 1, in order for consent to be valid it must be 'freely given, specific, informed and unambiguous' as per the definition of consent provided in Article 4(11) GDPR. To comply with these requirements, controllers often rely on so-called privacy policies in order to specify the purposes, interests, and personal data collected to comply with *inter alia* the principles for

---

[30] Helberger, Zuiderveen Borgesius and Reyna (n 1) 1451.

[31] See: ibid., 1452–1453; Zingales (n 3).

[32] See: Article 29 Working Party, 'Opinion 02/2010 on Online Behavioural Advertising' (Article 29 Working Party 2010) WP 171 29 http://ec.europa.eu/justice/policies/privacy/docs/wpdocs/2010/wp171_en.pdf accessed 3 November 2012; Article 29 Working Party, 'Opinion 06/2014 on the Notion of Legitimate Interests of the Data Controller under Article 7 of Directive 95/46/EC' (European Commission 2014) Opinion WP 217 http://ec.europa.eu/justice/data-protection/article-29/documentation/opinion-recommendation/files/2014/wp217_en.pdf accessed 10 September 2014.

lawful processing contained in Article 5 GDPR and the other transparency principle inspired requirements evident throughout the Regulation.

Privacy policies are the norm due to practical realities. Controllers are required to inform data subjects and the scale of data processing operations necessitates the pre-formulation of detailed information. However, due to the difficulties associated with the reliance on the data subject's capacity to make informed decisions (as described above in section II), the legislator has introduced a series of changes bolstering data subject consent in the GDPR, most visibly *via* Article 7 GDPR. Aside from these steps, which relate predominantly to the more effective protection of the data subject through the further specification of the conditions for valid consent, reliance on the accountability principle and more generally the modifications implemented vis-à-vis enforcement, in Recital 42 GDPR reference is made to the UCT Directive regarding the use of pre-formulated declarations of data subject consent. Recital 42 GDPR stipulates the sole mentioning of pre-formulated declarations of consent, with the Articles of the GDPR providing for no specific delineation between boilerplate and individually negotiated declarations of consent or indeed privacy policies. Recital 42 GDPR states that:

> [w]here processing is based on the data subject's consent, the controller should be able to demonstrate that the data subject has given consent to the processing operation. In particular in the context of a written declaration on another matter, safeguards should ensure that the data subject is aware of the fact that and the extent to which consent is given. In accordance with Council Directive 93/13/EEC a declaration of consent pre-formulated by the controller should be provided in an intelligible and easily accessible form, using clear and plain language <u>and</u> [author's emphasis] it should not contain unfair terms. For consent to be informed, the data subject should be aware at least of the identity of the controller and the purposes of the processing for which the personal data are intended. Consent should not be regarded as freely given if the data subject has no genuine or free choice or is unable to refuse or withdraw consent without detriment.

From this Recital the requirements for pre-formulated declarations of consent are hence further specified with reference to the UCT Directive (i.e., Directive 93/13/EEC). It is also interesting to note that Recital 42 GDPR appears to differentiate the requirement for pre-formulated declarations to 'be provided in an intelligible and easily accessible form, using clear and plain language' from the obligation that such declarations 'should not contain unfair terms'.

The specification in Recital 42 that pre-formulated declarations should be provided 'in an intelligible and easily accessible form, using clear and plain language' repeats the terminology used in Article 7(2) GDPR and Article 12 GDPR (with some minor differences, see below), thereby reflecting the operation of the transparency principle. However, the terminology also appears to reflect the formal fairness element contained in the UCT Directive with Article 5 UCT Directive providing that '[i]n the case of contracts where all or certain terms offered to the consumer are in writing, these terms must always be drafted in plain, intelligible language'. There is therefore a clear overlap here given the repetition of both the 'plain' and 'intelligible' qualifiers. In its assessment of Article 5 UCT Directive in the *Kásler* case,[33] the Court of Justice found that the meaning of 'plain and intelligible' is not limited to grammatical intelligibility but instead should be understood in a broad manner to allow the consumer 'to evaluate, on

[33] Case C-26/13, *Árpád Kásler, Hajnalka Káslerné Rábai v OTP Jelzálogbank* Zrt, ECLI:EU:C:2014:282.

the basis of clear, intelligible criteria, the economic consequences for which derive from it'.[34] Plainness therefore appears to relate more to the legal effect of a term including that the effect of such a term should not put the seller or supplier in an advantageous position. Intelligibility on the other hand seems to incorporate a linguistic element in that the seller or supplier is required to ensure the intelligibility of a term for the consumer acting with reasonable care.[35]

Aside from the overlaps in terminology however, there are two interesting points of contrast with the provisions in the GDPR that must be highlighted. First, in contrast to Recital 42 GDPR and Articles 7(2) and 12 GDPR, Article 5 UCT Directive does not mention the 'easily accessible form' criterion and, although the case law appears to incorporate the requirement for 'clear criteria', this is inferred from the provision rather than being expressly included, in contrast to the GDPR. Hence, there seems to be a further specification of 'plain and intelligible' in the GDPR. This is further highlighted in the specific requirements relating to the provision of transparent information contained in Article 12 GDPR which also inserts 'concise' and 'transparent' as specific requirements and provides that:

> [t]he controller shall take appropriate measures to provide any information referred to in Articles 13 and 14 and any communication under Articles 15 to 22 and 34 relating to processing to the data subject in a concise, transparent, intelligible and easily accessible form, using clear and plain language, in particular for any information addressed specifically to a child. The information shall be provided in writing, or by other means, including, where appropriate, by electronic means. When requested by the data subject, the information may be provided orally, provided that the identity of the data subject is proven by other means.

This provision is indicative of the key role played by the transparency principle in the GDPR. Moreover, in contrast to the UCT Directive it also shows 'the cradle to the grave' nature of the GDPR as the transparency principle clearly applies in both an *ex ante* (in terms of *inter alia* purpose limitation and informed consent) and *ex post* sense vis-à-vis the application of data subject rights. Second, although less obvious than the insertion of additional terms, it is also important to highlight the role played by the accountability principle in the GDPR and thus the burden on controllers to ensure that the data subject is informed. In this regard, one can refer for instance to the requirement in Article 7(1) GDPR which stipulates that controllers must be able to demonstrate that the data subject has consented thereby seemingly creating a burden of proof for controllers vis-à-vis the validity of data subject consent.[36] This obligation seems connected to the accountability principle in Article 5(2) and also arguably manifests itself in the operation of the fairness principle in terms of a burden of care on controllers to take the interests of data subjects into account, in line with the fair balancing exercises inherent to the operation of the Regulation.[37] The heightened requirements in the GDPR are also manifested by the reference to the potential use of icons in the operation of the information provision requirements (See Art 12(7) GDPR and Recital 60 GDPR) which acts as a further practical

---

[34] Ibid., para. 75.

[35] Hans-W Micklitz, 'Unfair Terms in Consumer Contracts' in Norbert Reich and others (eds), *European Consumer Law* (2nd edn, Intersentia 2014) 142–145.

[36] See: Damian Clifford and Jef Ausloos, 'Data Protection and the Role of Fairness' [2018] *Yearbook of European Law* 1; Opinion of Advocate General Szpunar, delivered on 4 March 2020, Case C-61/19 *Orange România SA v Autoritatea Naţională de Supraveghere a Prelucrării Datelor cu Caracter Personal (ANSPDCP),* ECLI:EU:C:2020:158 19.

[37] Clifford and Ausloos (n 36).

illustration of the GDPR's greater specification of the intelligibility criterion contained in the UCT Directive.

As mentioned above, in addition to these transparency-based requirements, Recital 42 GDPR also refers to the obligation for pre-formulated declarations to 'not contain unfair terms'. The inclusion of this specification also seemingly inserts a reference to the substantive fairness element in the UCT Directive. The substantive fairness element contained in Article 3(1) UCT Directive states that 'if, contrary to the requirement of good faith, it causes a significant imbalance in the parties' rights and obligations arising under the contract, to the detriment of the consumer'. Hence, 'good faith' and 'significant imbalance' are the two key criteria in the assessment of the substantive fairness of terms. There has been intense academic debate as to the precise meaning of these terms given the potential openness of the tests[38] (i.e., it is hard to imagine a situation where there is no imbalance between a consumer and a seller or supplier) and the fact that the notion of good faith was alien to the common law tradition.[39] In recent years, preliminary reference rulings from the Court of Justice have provided a greater degree of clarity in terms of the meaning of the 'good faith and 'significant imbalance' criteria. For instance, in the *Aziz* case the Court of Justice found that when assessing whether there is a 'significant imbalance' the national court should consider the rules that would apply in the absence of a contractual agreement.[40] In determining when such an imbalance arises contrary to the 'good faith requirement' the Court of Justice found that Recital 16 UCT Directive[41] should be taken into account and therefore, 'whether the seller or supplier, dealing fairly and equitably with the consumer, could reasonably assume that the consumer would have agreed to such a term in individual contract negotiations' taking the particular circumstances of the case into account.[42] As such, in addition to the requirement for fair and equitable treatment, Recital 16 UCT Directive indicates that the assessment of good faith also obliges the consideration of:

- The bargaining power (including specific consumer vulnerabilities[43]);
- Whether the consumer was induced to accept the term; and also,

---

[38] Peter Rott, 'Unfair Contract Terms' in Christian Twigg-Flesner (ed), *Research Handbook on EU Consumer and Contract Law* (Edward Elgar Publishing 2016) 299 http://www.elgaronline.com/view/9781782547365.xml accessed 20 December 2017.

[39] Mary Donnelly and Fidelma White, *Consumer Law: Rights and Regulation* (Thomson Round Hall 2014) 248. Stephen Weatherill, *EU Consumer Law and Policy* (Edward Elgar 2005) 122.

[40] Case C-415/11, *Mohamed Aziz v Caixa d'Estalvis de Catalunya, Tarragona i Manresa (Catalunyacaixa),* ECLI:EU:C:2013:164.

[41] Recital 16 UCT Directive states that:

> Whereas the assessment, according to the general criteria chosen, of the unfair character of terms, in particular in sale or supply activities of a public nature providing collective services which take account of solidarity among users, must be supplemented by a means of making an overall evaluation of the different interests involved; whereas this constitutes the requirement of good faith; whereas, in making an assessment of good faith, particular regard shall be had to the strength of the bargaining positions of the parties, whether the consumer had an inducement to agree to the term and whether the goods or services were sold or supplied to the special order of the consumer; whereas the requirement of good faith may be satisfied by the seller or supplier where he deals fairly and equitably with the other party whose legitimate interests he has to take into account.

[42] Case C-415/11, *Mohamed Aziz v Caixa d'Estalvis de Catalunya, Tarragona i Manresa (Catalunyacaixa),* (n 40), para 69.

[43] Peter Rott (n 38) 301.

- Whether the goods and services were being sold or supplied by the 'special order' of the consumer.

The Court of Justice has also subsequently found that a 'significant imbalance' does not have to relate to an economic disparity but may instead be a consequence of a 'sufficiently serious impairment of the legal situation in which that consumer, as a party to the contract, is placed, vis-à-vis a restriction of rights or a constraint on the exercise of such rights'.[44]

In this regard one can also refer to Article 4(1) UCT Directive which highlights the importance of the individual circumstances of each case and stipulates that:

> ... the unfairness of a contractual term shall be assessed, taking into account the nature of the goods or services for which the contract was concluded and by referring, at the time of conclusion of the contract, to all the circumstances attending the conclusion of the contract and to all the other terms of the contract or of another contract on which it is dependent.

With this in mind, it should be noted that as the Court of Justice does not normally have access to the full facts of the case[45] (thereby reflecting the division of competence), the national Courts play an important role as the evaluators of the fairness of a specific term in the given circumstances. In this vein, it is also significant to highlight the role played by the grey-list of clauses that may be unfair contained in Annex 1 UCT Directive. Although the Court of Justice has found on several occasions that the adoption of the list is dependent on the Member States and that there is no presumption of unfairness unless otherwise provided by Member State law, as per the *Invitel* judgement it remains a key element through which the national court can base its assessment.[46] Importantly, this potential for disparity is furthered by Article 4(2) UCT Directive which stipulates that an:

> [a]ssessment of the unfair nature of the terms shall relate neither to the definition of the main subject matter of the contract nor to the adequacy of the price and remuneration, on the one hand, as against the services or goods supplies [sic] in exchange, on the other, in so far as these terms are in plain intelligible language.

This provision thereby exempts 'core terms' from the application of substantive fairness element unless otherwise provided by national law (i.e., the UCT Directive is a minimum harmonisation instrument) and importantly excludes the control of the fairness of the 'price'. The divergences in application allowed for by the minimum harmonisation UCT Directive would therefore seemingly run contrary to the maximum harmonisation approach espoused in the GDPR. As such, it is important to note that the Article 4(2) UCT Directive effectively restricts the application of the substantive fairness element to the more peripheral contractual aspects provided such terms respect the formal fairness element and are thus provided in 'plain intelligible language'. But what are the effects of this limitation on the scope of the application of the substantive fairness element when the UCT Directive is applied to pre-formulated declarations of data subject consent? Are personal data to be considered the 'price'?

---

[44] Case C-226/12, *Constructora Principado SA v José Ignacio Menéndez Álvarez*, ECLI:EU:C:2014:10.

[45] Peter Rott (n 38) 300.

[46] Case C-472/10, *Nemzeti Fogyasztóvédelmi Hatóság v Invitel Távközlési Zrt*, ECLI:EU:C:2012:242.

IV. CONTRACT AND CONSENT AND SEPARATING THE DIFFERING FORMS OF (UN)FAIRNESS

Even outside the context of the processing of personal data for commercial purposes, it should be noted that the issue of what comes within the scope of the notion of 'price' is one that is rife with controversy requiring one to look to national interpretations in order to gather context dependant insights.[47] Positioning personal data as a 'price' would exempt it from the scope of application of the substantive fairness element (unless otherwise provided by national law) and thus, the positioning of personal data as a price is of significant importance vis-à-vis the operation of the UCT Directive. Although the Court of Justice has found that the UCT Directive applies even when no monetary price is paid,[48] determining what will be classified as a price in the ISS B2C context is of clear importance as such services are often positioned as 'free' thereby raising concerns at least in common law countries as to whether such pre-formulated declarations of consent would be understood as part of a contract or merely a mere licence. This points to the fact that in order to assess the validity of the contract formation one is required to refer to the national level. Hence, although the Directive can certainly apply to contracts for 'free' services this is only the case where there is a valid contract under national law or alternatively where the scope of the Directive has been expanded in the national implementation to apply to notices such as in the UK.[49] It should be noted, however, that irrespective of this need to have regard to the distinctions between the rules regarding common and civil law contract formation, consumer protection authorities are increasingly positioning personal data as the price or 'counter-performance'.

An interesting example here is the fall-out from the Facebook/WhatsApp merger and the actions taken by the Italian competition and consumer protection authority (the AGCM).[50] As background to the AGCM rulings, despite public assurances that WhatsApp would not change how they used personal data,[51] within two years of the European Commission's merger approval the company introduced an update to WhatsApp's privacy policy, which allowed Facebook

---

[47] One can refer to the example of financial services here see: Peter Rott (n 38) 293.

[48] See: Case C-74/15, *Dumitru Tarcău, Ileana Tarcău v Banca Comercială Intesa Sanpaolo România SA and Others*, ECLI:EU:C:2015:772 772.

[49] Indeed, in this regard one can point towards the failed attempts to harmonise this contract law formation and the jettisoning of large parts of Directive 2011/83/EU of the European Parliament and of the Council of 25 October 2011 on consumer rights, amending Council Directive 93/13/EEC and Directive 1999/44/EC of the European Parliament and of the Council and repealing Council Directive 85/577/EEC and Directive 97/7/EC of the European Parliament and of the Council Text with EEA relevance OJ L 304, 64–88. during the negotiations Benöhr (n 7) 31–33. and the failure to adopt the proposed Regulation of the European Parliament and of the Council on a Common European Sales Law (known as the Optional Instrument). The optional instrument was designed to provide an optional alternative to national laws but failed to be adopted. Indeed, it recognised the validity of 'contracts for the supply of digital content whether or not supplied on a tangible medium which can be stored, processed or accessed, and re-used by the user, irrespective of whether the digital content is supplied in exchange for the payment of a price' (see Art 5(b) Optional Instrument proposal). Proposal for a Regulation of the European Parliament and of the Council on a Common European Sales Law {SEC(2011) 1165 final} {SEC(2011)1166 final}.

[50] A number of national consumer and data protection authorities have started investigations against Facebook. For an overview of these various national cases, see Zingales (n 3) 2–3.

[51] Jessica Guynn, 'Privacy Groups Urge FTC to Probe Facebook's Deal to Buy WhatsApp' *Los Angeles Times* (6 March 2014) http://www.latimes.com/business/technology/la-fi-tn-privacy-groups-urge-ftc-to-probe-facebooks-whatsapp-deal-20140306-story.html accessed 19 December 2017.

to use data from WhatsApp to better target advertisements on Facebook and Instagram.[52] This led to actions by both consumer and data protection authorities.[53] The AGCM launched two investigations one of which assessed the validity of the consumer's consent to the policy change under the Italian transposition of the Unfair Commercial Practices (UCP) Directive[54] and the other which examined the unfairness of the terms of the privacy policy itself under the transposition of the UCT Directive. In rejecting WhatsApp's line of argumentation, the authority found that consumer protection and competition law and indeed, the company itself all recognise the economic value of the data and thus refused to accept that personal data could not be construed as counter-performance.[55] This decision was subsequently partially upheld by the Administrative Court in Lazio (Tribunale Amministrativo Regionale).[56] However, it is important to note that this approach is not universally accepted across all the Member States. An interesting point of contrast here is a decision by the Berlin Regional Court.[57] More specifically although the German courts have accepted that data protection issues do come within the scope of consumer protection, the Berlin Regional Court found that this does not prevent *Facebook* from positioning itself as a 'free' service thus reflecting the court's refusal to recognise personal data as a price.[58] This case therefore illustrates an interesting distinction and the fact that EU consumer protection is thus clearly linked to contract and that contract is strongly linked to national traditions.[59]

Hence, recognising personal data as counter-performance is far from uncontroversial. The uncertainty caused by this debate has been manifested directly in the discussions regarding the recently adopted Directive on Contracts for the Supply of Digital Content (Digital Content Directive) which, in the original Commission proposal, positioned personal data as

---

[52] 'Looking Ahead for WhatsApp' (*WhatsApp.com*) https://blog.whatsapp.com/10000627/Looking-ahead-for-WhatsApp?l=en accessed 19 December 2017.

[53] Zingales (n 3).

[54] Directive 2005/29/EC concerning unfair business-to-consumer commercial practices in the internal market and amending Council Directive 84/450/EEC, Directives 97/7/EC, 98/27/EC and 2002/65/EC of the European Parliament and of the Council and Regulation (EC) No 2006/2004 of the European Parliament and of the Council ('Unfair Commercial Practices Directive') 2005 22.

[55] Zingales (n 3). In essence, WhatsApp had claimed (with reference to the EDPS opinion) that personal data could not be construed as counter-performance. However, the AGCM found, with reference to the recent common position on the application of consumer protection in the context of social media, that consumer protection and competition law and indeed, the company itself, all recognise the economic value of the data.

[56] Agnieszka Jabłonowska, 'Recent Developments in European Consumer Law: Data Protection (Violations) by Default: Stakeholder Views and New Developments in Enforcement' (*Recent developments in European Consumer Law*, 2 February 2020) https://recent-ecl.blogspot.com/2020/02/data-protection-violations-by-default.html accessed 10 March 2020.

[57] *verbraucherzentrale bundesverband (vzbv) e.v v Facebook* [2018] Landgericht Berlin (Berlin Regional Court) Case no. 16 O 341/15. See press release by *vzby*, 'Facebook Verstößt Gegen Deutsches Datenschutzrecht | VZBV' https://www.vzbv.de/pressemitteilung/facebook-verstoesst-gegen-deutsches-datenschutzrecht accessed 16 February 2018.

[58] The Court thus ruled that the UCP Directive required the payment of a tangible price and thus concluded that by describing itself as 'free', *Facebook* does not fall foul of the requirement to identify commercial practices (see point 20 of Annex 1 UCP Directive) as contracts for such services do not involve the payment of a tangible 'price'.

[59] Inge Graef, Damian Clifford and Peggy Valcke, 'Fairness and Enforcement: Bridging Competition, Data Protection, and Consumer Law' (2018) 8 *International Data Privacy Law* 200, 209.

'counter-performance'.[60] Although the adopted version excludes the term counter-performance, the Directive still recognises that the framework's protections apply where a trader supplies a digital service/content, and the consumer 'provides or undertakes to provide personal data'.[61] As such, the Directive aims *inter alia* to extend the protections provided to consumers by affording concrete consumer rights and remedies where the consumer consents to personal data being provided,[62] and access to a digital service or digital content is granted.[63]

Article 3(1) Digital Content Directive creates a clear delineation between contracts supplied for a price versus those created where the consumer provides personal data through some very careful wording. This drafting appears to be an attempt to incorporate the concerns associated with recognising personal data as counter-performance to be bargained. Here reference can also be made to Recital 13 Digital Content Directive which states *inter alia* that:

> [w]hile fully recognising that the protection of personal data is a fundamental right and therefore personal data cannot be considered as a commodity, this Directive should ensure that consumers are in the context of such business models entitled to contractual remedies.

---

60 In particular, in a critical report on the proposal, the EDPS outlined three specific concerns associated with the use of the term. First, the proposal failed to define counter-performance and the use of one simple catch-all term appears to oversimplify a variety of business models and data usages. Second, linking the active provision of data with the paying of a monetary price is misleading as consumers are often unaware of what they are giving away when it comes to data and this is not helped by the use of 'vague and elastic terms' to describe the use of the collected data. And finally, third data and money are clearly not identical as providing personal data does not deprive an individual of using this same data repeatedly and this complicates matters when it comes to restitution. European Data Protection Supervisor, 'Opinion on the Proposal for a Directive on Certain Aspects Concerning Contracts for the Supply of Digital Content' (EDPS 2017) Opinion 4/2017 https://edps.europa.eu/sites/edp/files/publication/17-03-14_opinion_digital_content_en_0.pdf accessed 11 April 2019.

61 According to Art 1 Digital Content Directive, the instrument aims to 'lay down common rules on certain requirements concerning contracts between traders and consumers for the supply of digital content or a digital service'. More specifically, this provision goes on to note that the Directive aims in particular to establish rules on (1) conformity of digital content/service with the contract; (2) remedies in case of the lack of such conformity or a failure to supply and the modalities for the exercise of those remedies and; (3) modification and termination of such contracts.

62 Indeed, it is the consent of the 'consumer-data subject' to the processing of personal that will – provided the other requirements contained in the Digital Content Directive (Compromise) are met – give rise to a consumer contract. This is manifested in two ways. First, the use of the phrasing 'the consumer provides or undertakes to provide personal data' which seemingly excludes processing based on Art 6(1)(f) GDPR (legitimate interest) from triggering a contract and second, the apparent exclusion of other 'necessary' processing. More specifically, as alluded to in Art 3(1) Digital Content Directive (Compromise) the Directive does not apply where the processing of personal data is exclusively required to supply the digital content or service or to comply with a legal obligation provided 'the trader does not process this data for any other purpose.' This specification therefore, excludes processing based on Art 6(1)(b) GDPR and Art 6(1)(c) GDPR from the scope of protection.

63 This is significant as currently at the EU level an infringement of the data protection framework may mean little in terms of consequences for a service contract. See: Helberger, Zuiderveen Borgesius and Reyna (n 1) 1440. Indeed as noted by Helberger et al.:

> [a clear] benefit of extending the scope of consumer law to data-related issues lies in giving consumers concrete rights against sellers if information obligations are violated. If a data controller breaches data protection law's information obligations, the processing may become unlawful. That unlawfulness, however, says little about the consequences for a possible contractual relationship between seller and consumer.

The Directive sits a bit oddly therefore, in that although it does provide protection where personal data are provided, it also explicitly states that personal data cannot be treated as a commodity. The uncertainty is further compounded here when one considers Article 3(9) which states that the Directive does not affect Member State law regarding the 'formation, validity, nullity or effects of contracts'. As noted by Mak, a significant doctrinal question therefore, relates to how this provision of personal data will give rise to a contract in national law.[64] Despite the fact that the commercialisation of personal data is a market reality, recognising the existence of a contractual relationship where personal data are provided for access to so-called 'free services' can be viewed as sitting a little oddly with the fundamental values underpinning data protection and privacy law. Indeed, the changes introduced by the GDPR may in fact be interpreted as prohibiting the formation of a contract obliging the provision of personal data beyond that which is necessary for the performance of the contract.[65]

More specifically, the positioning of the consent to the provision of personal data as giving rise to a consumer contract raises challenges regarding the compatibility of this business practice with Article 7 GDPR. Article 7 is a key innovation of the Regulation and can be understood as a legislative manifestation of the desire to bolster consent and render it more meaningful in practice. In short therefore, the introduction of Article 7 is best understood as a response to these concerns, which were previously hashed out in the analyses of the effectives of the former Data Protection Directive 95/46/EC and the *lex specialis* 'cookies' provisions in the ePrivacy Directive (see below).[66] However, Article 7 has its own ambiguities with the crux of the current discussion relating to the legality of rendering access to a service 'conditional' upon the individual's consent to the processing of personal data. To clarify, the debate swings on the interpretation of Article 7(4) GDPR. This provision states that:

> when assessing whether consent is *freely given, utmost account shall be taken of whether*, *inter alia*, the performance of a contract, *including the provision of a service*, is *conditional on consent* to the processing of personal data that is *not necessary for the performance of that contract.* [emphasis added]

This separation between the processing of personal data 'necessary for the performance of a contract' and consent is further evident in the non-binding Recital 43 GDPR. This states that where, 'the performance of a contract, including the provision of a service, is dependent on… consent despite such consent not being necessary for such performance', there is a presumption that consent is not freely given.[67] Interpreting Article 7(4) GDPR as delegitimising rendering access to services conditional on consent is clearly controversial given that consumers are often confronted with take-it-or-leave-it offers. Nevertheless, such an interpretation also raises clear questions regarding the complex overlaps between the Regulation and Digital Content Directive.

---

[64] Vanessa Mak, 'Contract and Consumer Law' in Vanessa Mak and others (eds), *Research Handbook in Data Science and Law* (Edward Elgar Publishing 2018) 33–34.

[65] This is in contrast to the old Directive 95/46/EC. For a discussion on the same topic through the lens of the then in force Directive see: Carmen Langhanke and Martin Schmidt-Kessel, 'Consumer Data as Consideration' (2015) 4 *Journal of European Consumer and Market Law* 218.

[66] For more see: Clifford (n 28).

[67] *Opinion on the Proposal for a Directive on Certain Aspects, supra* note at 18.

Regarding the legitimacy of 'take-it-or-leave-it' offers, one can also refer to the ongoing reform of the ePrivacy framework and the discussion regarding the legitimacy of so-called 'cookie walls' (i.e., landing pages giving users a binary option to consent to the use of cookies or to just leave the site without access to the content and or services).[68] Interestingly, however, Recital 14 Digital Content Directive states *inter alia* that the Directive should, not apply where the trader only collects metadata except where this situation is considered a contract under national law. This specification of the Directive's scope therefore, seemingly draws an odd distinction from a privacy and data protection perspective between different types of personal data. More specifically, 'metadata [...] concerning the consumer's device or the browsing history' such as IP addresses and cookies are both generally construed as personal data with the processing of such information for online behavioural advertising seemingly requiring the consent of the data subject.[69] Indeed, even excluding the potential for the applicability of other conditions for lawful processing in the B2C information society services context, (1) it is only the consent of the data subject which triggers the contractual protections provided in the adopted compromise Directive and; (2) as per the requirements in Article 5(3) of the ePrivacy Directive, consent is required to access/store information on a consumer's device.[70] It is therefore difficult from a data protection and privacy perspective to comprehend the delineation of such metadata from the scope of protection of the Directive. Such a delineation belies the fact that the metadata and the data triggering the application of the protections in the Directive both come within the scope of personal data in the GDPR and that it may often be the same consent that will be used to legitimise the provision of both. Accordingly, it is difficult to imagine how this could be justified and in particular, for example, how cookie banners can effectively be treated differently within the application of the Digital Content Directive even if this also raises complex questions regarding the application of national contract law rules relating to contract formation.[71] There is clearly a lot of uncertainty here and it is somewhat unclear why contractual protections should not be afforded to services only collecting metadata. This is particularly the case when one considers that it is this same metadata that is used to profile individuals and track them across the internet and thus, such an approach seems to miss the fact that it is largely this type of personal data which often poses a problem.

It therefore remains to be seen how this exclusion from the scope of Digital Content Directive and the GDPR's consent provisions will be interpreted in practice. Indeed, much will depend on how far consent will stretch but also how processing that is necessary for the performance of a contract/provision of a service will be delineated from additional activities

---

[68] See: Frederik J Zuiderveen Borgesius and others, 'Tracking Walls, Take-It-Or-Leave-It Choices, the GDPR, and the EPrivacy Regulation' (2017) 3 *European Data Protection Law Review* 353.

[69] See: Article 29 Working Party, 'Opinion on Online Behavioural Advertising' (n 32).

[70] More specifically, although in the context of IP addresses for instance, conditions such as, contract (Art 6(1)(b) GDPR) and legitimate interest (Art 6(1)(f) GDPR) as confirmed in the *Breyer* case), may be deemed appropriate the *lex specialis* rules in the ePrivacy Directive are clear. The specific exclusion of IP addresses is also interesting given the CJEU judgement which found dynamic IP addresses to be personal data see: Case C-582/14, *Breyer*, ECLI: EU:C:2016:779; Frederik J Zuiderveen Borgesius, 'The Breyer Case of the Court of Justice of the European Union: IP Addresses and the Personal Data Definition' (2017) 3 *European Data Protection Law Review* 130.

[71] For a similar discussion of these issues see: Romain Robert and Lara Smit, 'The Proposal for a Directive on Digital Content: A Complex Relationship with Data Protection Law' [2018] ERA Forum http://link.springer.com/10.1007/s12027-018-0506-7 accessed 6 July 2018.

requiring consent (as provided by Art 7(4) GDPR). This debate will run to the core of the operation of the UCT Directive in the context of pre-formulated declarations of data subject consent. As highlighted above, in this vein it is important to reiterate that consumer protection authorities are increasingly recognising personal data as counter-performance in practice and therefore as a core term within the meaning of UCT Directive. Moreover, the ambiguous overlaps between consent and contract are further compounded when one considers Article 7(2) GDPR. This provision requires consent to be presented 'in a manner which is clearly distinguishable from the other matters' and therefore, this provision creates some doubt as to the positioning of consent in relation to the UCT Directive. In particular, one must wonder whether consent to a pre-formulated declaration can actually be understood as a contract in its own right, given its required separation from the provision of a service contract. In other words, can consent to a pre-formulated declaration effectively act as a trigger for the formation of a B2C consumer contract? In answering this complex question, it is important to remember that it remains uncertain as to whether the separation of consent and contract in Article 7(4) GDPR is merely indicative of a scenario in which the 'freely given' stipulation may be violated and hence whether it in fact gives rise to a rebuttable presumption and does not entirely delegitimise rendering access to a service conditional upon the provision of personal data – an interpretation advocated by AG Szpunar in his opinion in the Plant 49 case.[72]

Despite the Article 29 Working Party's strict interpretation of these provisions therefore, this remains a matter for the Court of Justice to decide and it is arguable that privacy policies in addition to terms of use could be presented as the provisions of the contract with the declaration of consent being a separate (and indeed revocable) but connected part of the same overarching contractual agreement, despite the presumption and associated burden of proof.[73] In this vein, personal data does not necessarily have to constitute a price but its protection may be encompassed within the contractual agreement as both explicit (i.e., what the controller promises) and implied (legal obligations stemming from the GDPR) terms.[74] Currently interpreting where personal data fits is a matter for national law on contract formation and this requires more detailed analysis in future research. Importantly, such an interpretation does not render contract and consent synonymous as contract law assumes the autonomous decision-making capacity of individuals whereas consent in data protection aims to bolster the decision-making capacity of the data subject and contract is restricted to what is necessary for the performance of the contract. Hence, although the contract formation may require the voluntary assent of the parties, consent in the GDPR cannot be reduced to a form of contract given that it may not

---

[72] Opinion of Advocate General Szpunar delivered on 21 March 2019 in Case C-673/17 *Planet49 GmbH v Bundesverband der Verbraucherzentralen und Verbraucherverbände – Verbraucherzentrale Bundesverband eV*, ECLI:EU:C:2019:246.

[73] See: Damian Clifford, Inge Graef and Peggy Valcke, 'Pre-Formulated Declarations of Data Subject Consent—Citizen-Consumer Empowerment and the Alignment of Data, Consumer and Competition Law Protections' (2019) 20 *German Law Journal* 679.

[74] But what else then could be classified as the price? On the other hand, the viewing of advertisements (whether in addition to the provision of user generated content or not) can be regarded as the price for the purposes of Art 4(2) UCT Directive. From a competition law perspective, reference can be made here to the positioning of attention as a parameter on the basis of which market players compete in multi-sided markets where 'online attention rivals provide products and features to obtain the attention of consumers and sell some of that attention, through other products and services, to merchants, developers, and others who value it'. David S Evans, 'Attention Rivalry among Online Platforms' (2013) 9 *Journal of Competition Law and Economics* 313, 313.

be always 'freely given, specific, informed and unambiguous' for it to be considered a B2C contract. This is indicative of the fact that the UCT Directive focuses on the fairness of the terms themselves and explicitly excludes the analysis of the contract formation.

As a consequence, the precise overlaps between consumer and data protection are also unclear vis-à-vis the operation of the respective fairness principles and this is manifested in the uncertainties as to the precise relationship between the GDPR and the UCT Directive despite the specific cross-reference in Recital 42 GDPR. Additionally it should also be noted that divergences in terms of the foundations of the respective frameworks also have a potential impact in relation to the distinction between the role of rights and freedoms in contrast with consumer protection as a principle in Article 38 of the Charter. More specifically and as described elsewhere, the GDPR establishes a complex web of fairness check and balances incorporating both fair balancing and procedural fairness elements in order to respect the essence of the right to data protection in particular and rights and freedoms in general in line with Article 52(1) of the Charter.[75] In short, in order to comply with the necessity and proportionality requirements in Article 52(1) of the Charter, the GDPR creates *ex ante* and *ex post* fair balancing tests supplemented by a burden of care on controllers in line with the accountability principle which goes far beyond the transparency orientated protections provided for in the UCT Directive. The struggle associated with the interpretation of the precise contours of the relationship between the GDPR and the UCT Directive is illustrative of the inherent difficulties related to the alignment of the respective policy agendas and thus the bringing together of a fundamental rights orientated framework with the economically orientated objectives of the UCT Directive.

Interestingly, in its application of the UCT Directive in the Facebook/WhatsApp case, the AGCM focused on the choice of jurisdiction clause, the selection of official language, the limitations of liability and the right to terminate/rescind the contract or unilaterally interrupt the service. These are the more traditional concerns dealt with under unfair terms legislation however, it is notable that the issues regarding the failure to provide accurate information on the types of data being collected, the recipients and the specific purposes were not discussed.[76] This provides a contrast with the collaborative action taken by the Article 29 Working Party.[77] As such, the substantive divergences in the respective enforcement actions taken by data protection and consumer protection authorities, as contextualised above *via* a more detailed analysis of the substantive provisions of the UCT Directive, illustrate a clear delineation in the substantive application of the respective fairness assessments. Given the differences therefore,

---

[75] See: Clifford and Ausloos (n 36).

[76] 'Exchange of Personal Data with Facebook and Oppressive Clauses, Double Antitrust Investigation on WhatsApp' http://www.agcm.it/en/newsroom/press-releases/2358-exchange-of-personal-data-with-facebook-and-oppressive-clauses,-double-antitrust-investigation-on-whatsapp.html accessed 20 December 2017.

[77] In support of this contrast one can also refer to the recent common position taken by national consumer protection agencies through the Consumer Protection Collaboration Network in relation to the terms of service of social networking sites which clearly focused on similar issues (i.e., such as clauses relating to jurisdiction, the identification of commercial communications, the waiving of liability, the removal of content and unilateral rights to change, determine the scope and terminate agreements). See: EU Consumer Protection Agencies and European Commission (DG Justice), 'Common Position of National Authorities within the CPC Network Concerning the Protection of Consumers on Social Networks' http://europa.eu/rapid/press-release_IP-17-631_en.htm and Zingales (n 3).

one must question the precise relationship between the GDPR and the UCT Directive and thus the precise meaning of the cross-reference in Recital 42 GDPR.

It is argued here that a finding of a violation of consumer law would more readily result in the availability of supplementary citizen-consumer enforcement mechanisms rather than the further specification of the data protection framework, as any breach of the GDPR stipulated in a written declaration will not be binding in line with Article 7(2) GDPR (see Chapter 1). However, this is certainly not a straightforward matter. In commenting on this relationship Svantesson opines that the Recital perhaps indicates that the GDPR 'can be seen to provide *lex specialis* rules in giving guidance on how the unfairness rules provided under [the UCT Directive] applies [*sic*] in the data protection setting'.[78] Nevertheless, although at first glance there appears to be merit to this observation, the application of the substantive fairness element (i.e., as illustrated by the recent enforcement actions) places such an interpretation in doubt and therefore, it is alternatively suggested here that Recital 42 GDPR should in fact be viewed as providing for parallel but substantively distinct fairness assessments. The merit of this alternative interpretation is furthered when one takes a closer look at the normative foundation of the respective frameworks which is reflected in their relationship with the Charter of Fundamental Rights in particular. That being said, given that this discussion has focused on the fairness of terms a more detailed analysis of the data protection consumer protection relationship is merited vis-à-vis the operation of the 'freely given' criterion for valid consent and its relationship with and the operation of the Unfair Commercial Practices Directive.[79]

V. CONCLUSION

The analysis in this chapter has illustrated that there is a complex relationship between the respective data protection and consumer protection policy agendas. Through an examination of the protections for pre-formulated declarations of data subject consent, the analysis has aimed to point towards the fundamental challenges at the core of this debate. More specifically, the positioning of personal data as a counter-performance or a 'core term' and hence, the alignment of a fundamental rights orientated approach with economically focused protections are illustrative of a clear divide in thinking. That being said, there seems to be a definite move towards the alignment of the respective policy agendas despite the clear divergences in the positioning of personal data. Although it is arguable that the alignment of protections could afford citizen-consumers with more robust enforcement tools, such a development should not be sought at the expense of the protections afforded in the GDPR. In this vein, and as described above, the Digital Content Directive and the proposed ePrivacy Regulation appear to present some interpretative tests of the finalised GDPR. The alignment of the respective data protection and consumer protection frameworks raises a series of complex questions which go to the (contrasting) cores of the application of the respective frameworks. That being said, the need for some form of price inherently relates to the failed attempts to harmonise the law relating to

---

[78] Svantesson (n 1).

[79] See: 'WhatsApp Fined for 3 Million Euro for Having Forced Its Users to Share Their Personal Data with Facebook' http://en.agcm.it/en/media/detail?id=a6c51399-33ee-45c2-9019-8f4a3ae09aa1 accessed 20 December 2017 and Zingales (n 3).

the formation of contracts at the EU level and thus points to the continuing importance of the national contract law rules relating to formation.

This also raises clear challenges in relation to the operation of the protections afforded in the GDPR. Hence, there are several key issues which need to be ironed out. It is therefore certainly questionable whether the more recent legislative moves are a regulatory panacea to the difficulties being experienced by individuals navigating the online marketplace or instead a rather rushed attempt by the European legislator to revitalise the market integration objective. However, it is now for the Court of Justice to figure this out. In conclusion, case law developments should be closely watched.

REFERENCES

AGCM 'WhatsApp Fined for 3 Million Euro for Having Forced Its Users to Share Their Personal Data with Facebook' http://en.agcm.it/en/media/detail?id=a6c51399-33ee-45c2-9019-8f4a3ae09aa1 accessed 20 March 2020.

AGCM Exchange of Personal Data with Facebook and Oppressive Clauses, Double Antitrust Investigation on WhatsApp' https://en.agcm.it/en/media/detail?id=57b69a37-5e59-4143-b7db-e54b816acc6e accessed 20 March 2020.

Benöhr I *EU Consumer Law and Human Rights* (OUP Oxford 2013) 59.

Clifford D 'EU Data Protection Law and Targeted Advertising: Consent and the Cookie Monster-Tracking the Crumbs of Online User Behaviour' (2014) 5 *Journal of Intellectual Property, Information Technology and Electronic Commerce Law*.

Clifford D and J Ausloos 'Data Protection and the Role of Fairness' (2018) 37 *Yearbook of European Law* 130.

Clifford D, Graef I and P Valcke 'Pre-Formulated Declarations of Data Subject Consent—Citizen-Consumer Empowerment and the Alignment of Data, Consumer and Competition Law Protections' (2019) 20 *German Law Journal* 679.

Curry M, Phillips D and P Regan 'Emergency Response Systems and the Creeping Legibility of People and Places' (2004) 20(5) *Information Society* 357.

De Búrca G 'The Drafting of the European Union Charter of Fundamental Rights' (2001) 26(2) *European Law Review* 126.

Donnelly M and F White *Consumer Law: Rights and Regulation* (Thomson Round Hall 2014) 248.

Evans D S 'Attention Rivalry among Online Platforms' (2013) 9 *Journal of Competition Law and Economics* 313.

Graef I, Clifford D and P Valcke 'Fairness and Enforcement: Bridging Competition, Data Protection, and Consumer Law' (2018) 8(3) *International Data Privacy Law* 200.

Guynn J 'Privacy Groups Urge FTC to Probe Facebook's Deal to Buy WhatsApp' *Los Angeles Times* (6 March 2014) http://www.latimes.com/business/technology/la-fi-tn-privacy-groups-urge-ftc-to-probe-facebooks-whatsapp-deal-20140306-story.html accessed 19 March 2020.

Helberger N, Zuiderveen Borgesius F J and A Reyna 'The Perfect Match? A Closer Look at the Relationship between EU Consumer Law and Data Protection Law' (2017) 54 *Common Market Law Review* 1427.

Jabłonowska A 'Recent Developments in European Consumer Law: Data Protection (Violations) by Default: Stakeholder Views and New Developments in Enforcement' (*Recent developments in European Consumer Law Blog*, 2 February 2020) https://recent-ecl.blogspot.com/2020/02/data-protection-violations-by-default.html accessed 10 March 2020.

Jolls C, Sunstein CR and R H Thaler 'A Behavioral Approach to Law and Economics' (1998) 50 *Stanford Law Review* 1471.

Koops B-J 'The Trouble with European Data Protection Law' (2014) 4(4) *International Data Privacy Law* 250.

Koops B-J 'On Decision Transparency, or How to Enhance Data Protection after the Computational Turn' 196-220 in Hildebrandt M and K de Vries (eds), *Privacy, due process and the computational turn: the philosophy of law meets the philosophy of technology* (Routledge 2013).
Langhanke C and M Schmidt-Kessel 'Consumer Data as Consideration' (2015) 4 *Journal of European Consumer and Market Law* 218.
Lazaro C and D Le Métayer, 'Control over Personal Data: True Remedy or Fairytale?' (2015) 12 SCRIPTed http://script-ed.org/?p=1927 accessed 7 November 2019.
Lynskey O 'Deconstructing Data Protection: The "Added-Value" Of A Right To Data Protection In The EU Legal Order' (2014) 63 *International & Comparative Law Quarterly* 569.
Lynskey O *The Foundations of EU Data Protection Law* (First, Oxford University Press 2016) 258.
Mak V 'Contract and Consumer Law' in Vanessa Mak and others (eds), *Research Handbook in Data Science and Law* (Edward Elgar Publishing 2018) 33.
Mantelero A 'Competitive Value of Data Protection: The Impact of Data Protection Regulation on Online Behaviour' (2013) 3 *International Data Privacy Law* 229.
Mayer-Schonberger V and K Cukier *Big Data: A Revolution That Will Transform How We Live, Work and Think* (Houghton Mifflin Harcourt 2013).
Micklitz H-W 'Unfair Terms in Consumer Contracts' in N Reich and others (eds), *European Consumer Law* (2nd edition, Intersentia 2014) 142.
Robert R and L Smit 'The Proposal for a Directive on Digital Content: A Complex Relationship with Data Protection Law' (2018) ERA Forum 19, 159.
Rott P 'Data Protection Law as Consumer Law–How Consumer Organisations Can Contribute to the Enforcement of Data Protection Law' (2017) 6 *Journal of European Consumer and Market Law* 113.
Rott P 'Unfair Contract Terms' in C Twigg-Flesner (ed), *Research Handbook on EU Consumer and Contract Law* (Edward Elgar Publishing 2016).
Schulte-Nölke H 'The Brave New World of EU Consumer Law–Without Consumers, or Even Without Law?' (2015) 4(4) *Journal of European Consumer and Market Law* 135.
Sunstein C R 'Fifty Shades of Manipulation' (2016) SSRN, https://papers.ssrn.com/sol3/papers.cfm?abstract_id=2565892 accessed 10 March 2020.
Sunstein C R and R H Thaler, 'Libertarian Paternalism Is Not an Oxymoron' (2003) 70(4) *The University of Chicago Law Review* 1159.
Svantesson D J B 'Enter the Quagmire – the Complicated Relationship between Data Protection Law and Consumer Protection Law' (2017) 34(1) *Computer Law & Security Review* 25.
Verdoodt V, Clifford D and E Lievens 'Toying with Children's Emotions, the New Game in Town? The Legality of Advergames in the EU' (2016) 32(4) *Computer Law & Security Review* 599.
WhatsApp 'Looking Ahead for WhatsApp' (*WhatsApp.com*) https://blog.whatsapp.com/10000627/Looking-ahead-for-WhatsApp?l=en accessed 19 March 2020.
Weatherill S *EU Consumer Law and Policy* (Edward Elgar 2005).
Willis L E 'Why Not Privacy by Default?' (2014) 29(1) *Berkeley Technology Law Journal* 61.
Zarsky T 'Incompatible: The GDPR in the Age of Big Data' (2017) 47(4) *Seton Hall Law Review* 995.
Zingales N 'Between a Rock and Two Hard Places: WhatsApp at the Crossroad of Competition, Data Protection and Consumer Law' (2017) 33(4) *Computer Law & Security Review* 553.
Zuiderveen Borgesius F J 'The Breyer Case of the Court of Justice of the European Union: IP Addresses and the Personal Data Definition' (2017) 3(1) *European Data Protection Law Review* 130.
Zuiderveen Borgesius F J, Kruikemeier S, Boerman S and N Helberger 'Tracking Walls, Take-It-Or-Leave-It Choices, the GDPR, and the EPrivacy Regulation' (2017) 3(3) *European Data Protection Law Review* 353.

13. Data protection and competition law: The dawn of 'uberprotection'

Gabriela Zanfir-Fortuna[1] *and Sînziana Ianc*[2]

I. INTRODUCTION

It was a long and convoluted road, but data protection law and competition law are now crossing paths in meaningful ways in the EU legal framework and policymaking. They both aim to provide a meaningful layer of protection to individuals as market participants whose personal data feed unexplored competition parameters, as well as new, significant and profitable markets.

The assessment that best reflects the starting point of this convoluted path is the *obiter dictum* finding of the Court of Justice of the European Union (CJEU) in the 2006 *Asnef-Equifax*[3] judgment. The case referred to a potentially noncompetitive agreement between financial institutions to create a common database with debtors' credit history. The CJEU found that all concerns regarding the sensitivity of the personal data made available for this register are to be dealt exclusively with by data protection law, and they are not something that competition law should be affected by or concerned with.[4]

Roughly at the same time, the European Commission, in its role as EU Competition authority, completely ignored any personal data protection implications when assessing the *TomTom/TeleAtlas*[5] merger, in the markets of satellite maps and navigation systems. In a concomitant case where access to personal data was too significant to be fully ignored – that is, the *Google/DoubleClick*[6] merger in the markets of online advertising with its inherent issues of data transfers, the European Commission took the CJEU's approach, delineating its assessment to specifically exclude matters of data protection. However, just like in the *Asnef-Equifax* case, the adjudicators found it worthwhile to specifically exclude data protection from the scope of their analysis: this means that data protection questions were, naturally, expected to arise.

With the 'digital economy' starting to take shape and increasingly better understood,[7] as the role of personal data as facilitator for the exponential growth of this type of economy

---

1 The views expressed are those of the author alone.

2 The views expressed are those of the author alone.

3 Case C-238/05 *Asnef-Equifax et al v. Asociación de Usuarios de Servicios Bancarios*, EU:C:2006:734.

4 *Asnef-Equifax*, para 63.

5 European Commission, Case No COMP/M.4854 – *TomTom/Tele Atlas*.

6 European Commission, Case No COMP/M.4731 – *Google/DoubleClick*.

7 See Organisation for Economic Cooperation and Development ('OECD') DAF/COMP(2012)22 *The Digital Economy* (Report, 2012) http://www.oecd.org/daf/competition/The-Digital-Economy-2012.pdf accessed 9 August 2018.

was starting to be defined,[8] it became clear that data protection law and competition law naturally intersect and affect each other. It was just difficult to grasp exactly how. In a second phase of the evolution of data protection and competition law towards meaningful interplay and enhanced protection of the person as market participant to the digital economy, the European Commission dealt with two major cases, concerning the acquisition of WhatsApp by Facebook,[9] first, and that of LinkedIn by Microsoft, second.[10] In both cases, concluded in 2014 and 2016 respectively, the European Commission found the acquisitions compatible with the internal market. But a shift in the way the Commission incorporated data protection law in its assessments of competitive parameters was immediately apparent. In the *Facebook/WhatsApp* decision, indeed, the Commission maintained that any privacy related concerns fall outside the scope of the competition law analysis. However, the Commission started referring on substance to data protection requirements as part of its analysis. For instance, when analysing the impact of the merger in the online advertising market, the Commission took into account that the merged entity would be allowed to introduce targeted advertising on WhatsApp only if the latter would explicitly change its privacy policy.[11] Elements of data protection law assessment were more numerous, even if still ancillary, in the *Microsoft/LinkedIn* decision. The main aspect explored by the Commission was that data protection rules would reduce the anticompetitive effect of the merger, by limiting the way the two undertakings will have access to each other's personal data holdings post-merger.[12]

Facebook's announcement in early 2014 that it intended to acquire WhatsApp prompted more attention to the crossroads of data protection and competition law from Data Protection Authorities (DPAs) in the EU, with the European Data Protection Supervisor (EDPS) leading the way in policymaking.[13] National Competition Authorities (CAs) also started to look into 'some of the key issues and parameters that may need to be considered when assessing the interplay between data, market power and competition law'.[14] In a 2016 joint report, the French CA and the German Federal Cartel Office (FCO) recognized that amassed personal data is a game changing parameter of market behaviour in the digital economy, noting that should be taken into account when identifying and sanctioning anticompetitive behaviour. As for the interplay with data protection law, the two CAs started to depart from the tone set by the CJEU a decade earlier in *Asnef-Equifax,* declaring: 'Even if data protection and competition laws serve different goals, privacy issues cannot be excluded from consideration under competition law simply by virtue of their nature.'[15]

---

[8] See World Economic Forum, *Personal Data: The Emergence of a New Asset Class* (Report, 2011) http://www3.weforum.org/docs/WEF_ITTC_PersonalDataNewAsset_Report_2011.pdf accessed 9 August 2018.

[9] European Commission, Case No COMP/M.7217 - *Facebook/WhatsApp.*

[10] European Commission, Case M.8124 – *Microsoft/LinkedIn.*

[11] *Facebook/WhatsApp*, para 173.

[12] *Microsoft/LinkedIn*, paras 177, 179, 255 and 375.

[13] See EDPS, *Privacy and competitiveness in the age of Big Data: The interplay between data protection, competition law and consumer protection in the Digital Economy*, (Preliminary Opinion, March 2014) and Opinion 7/2015, *Meeting the Challenges of Big Data. A call for transparency, user control, data protection by design and accountability* (19 November 2015).

[14] Autorité de la Concurrence and Bundeskartellamt, *Competition Law and Data* Report (10 May 2016), 4.

[15] Ibid., 23.

All these steps, one by one, announced the dawn of an enhanced protection of individuals as data subjects and consumers in the digital economy through intertwined means of data protection law and competition law. We propose calling this development 'Uberprotection'. The German FCO announced at the beginning of 2019 the conclusion of its investigation into Facebook, finding that 'the extent to which Facebook collects, merges and uses data in user accounts constitutes an abuse of a dominant position'.[16] To reach this conclusion, the FCO explicitly relied on EU data protection law 'as a standard for examining exploitative abuse', and it said it cooperated with data protection authorities.[17] The FCO decision was challenged in court and is currently the subject of a reference for a preliminary ruling to the CJEU.[18]

The French CA published at the beginning of 2018 its conclusions after conducting a sector investigation into the online advertising market, highlighting the 'important role' that data protection provisions will play in the competitive functioning of this sector.[19] Moreover, the accumulation of personal data by dominant companies, especially when they provide online intermediary services, entered the realm of legislation. Amendments to the German antitrust law tailored to address this scenario entered into force in 2021.[20] Additionally, a legislative proposal published by the European Commission at the end of 2020 for the Digital Markets Act[21] puts forward a series of *ex ante* measures, including a prohibition for core platform services, or 'gatekeepers', to combine personal data from different sources in the absence of valid user consent under data protection law.

After introducing key concepts of competition law that are relevant for understanding how these two fields of law interact, this chapter continues by looking closer into each of the three stages identified in the evolution of the interplay between data protection and competition law from the point of view of enforcement: a first stage of the parallel pathways for the two fields of law, a second stage of acknowledging that the two fields interact and that they cannot remain in silos, and a third stage, which announces the beginning of a new era, ensuring ramped up protection of the individual as data subject and participant to the digital economy, as well as of an integrated, efficient and competitive digital market, before reaching conclusions.

---

[16] See Bundeskartellamt, *Press Release: Bundeskartellamt prohibits Facebook from combining user data from different sources* (17 February 2019), available at https://www.bundeskartellamt.de/SharedDocs/Meldung/EN/Pressemitteilungen/2019/07_02_2019_Facebook.html accessed 21 July 2021.

[17] Ibid.

[18] M. Steiert, *German Federal Cartel Office Against Facebook: Now the European Court of Justice Will Decide*, Bird & Bird blog (May 2021), available at https://www.twobirds.com/en/news/articles/2021/germany/german-federal-cartel-office-against-facebook-now-the-european-court-of-justice-will-decide accessed on 21 July 2021.

[19] Autorité de la concurrence, *Avis n° 18-A-03 portant sur l'exploitation des données dans le secteur de la publicité sur internet* (6 March 2018), 102.

[20] D. Seeliger, K. Gurer, D. de Crozals, T. Hainze, *The revolutionary reform of German competition law – leading the pack on digital enforcement and other stories*, Linklaters (20 January 2021), available at https://www.linklaters.com/en-us/insights/blogs/linkingcompetition/2021/january/the-revolutionary-reform-of-german-competition-law accessed on 21 July 2021.

[21] Proposal for a Regulation of the European Parliament and of the Council on contestable and fair markets in the digital sector (Digital Markets Act) COM/2020/842 final (15 December 2020).

II. KEY CONCEPTS OF COMPETITION LAW TO UNDERSTAND ITS INTERPLAY WITH DATA PROTECTION LAW

Notwithstanding some nuanced differences, the key concepts of competition law show fundamental similarities in the jurisdictions around the world. The common understanding of competition is that efficient competition between market players will result in lower prices, better goods and services and a wider choice for customers. In order to achieve this as far as possible, most competition laws around the world articulate their key prohibitions in similar terms.

Under the notion of anti-competitive agreements (cf. Art. 101 TFEU), agreements between competitors to fix prices, share markets or otherwise restrict competition and its benefits to consumers are prohibited. Undertakings are supposed to compete with each other, and not to aggregate their market power.

Another key notion is the unilateral abuse of a dominant position (cf. Art. 102 TFEU). Dominance is defined in the case law of the CJEU as 'a position of economic strength enjoyed by an undertaking which enables it to prevent effective competition being maintained on the relevant market by giving it the power to behave to an appreciable extent independently of its competitors, customers and ultimately of its consumers'.[22] While achieving and maintaining a dominant market position through endogenous efforts is not prohibited as such, a dominant undertaking 'has a special responsibility not to allow its conduct to impair undistorted competition'.[23] Abuses can be exploitative, earning an unjustifiably high profit at the expense of customers, or exclusionary, aimed at excluding competitors from the market by means other than competitive efficiency (e.g., by refusing to supply competitors with necessary input on upstream markets or by unjustifiably lowering prices).

Finally, another important notion are mergers that are harmful to competition, cf. Regulation 139/2004.[24] Instead of not competing by forming a cartel, undertakings could decide to aggregate market power by forming a single economic entity. This is why many (but not all) jurisdictions have a merger control system in place, enabling authorities to investigate mergers that can be harmful to the competitive process by combining too much market power.

Given the increasing role that data, including personal data, have for a successful presence on the market, and considering that data protection law in the EU applies whenever personal data are processed (that is, used in any way), it was only a matter of time before data protection law and competition law would start to interact in one way or another.

---

[22] Case 27/76, *United Brands v. Commission*, EU:C:1978:22, para 65.

[23] Case 322/81, *NV Nederlandsche Banden Industrie Michelin v Commission*, EU:C:1983:313, para 57.

[24] Council Regulation (EC) No 139/2004 of 20 January 2004 on the control of concentrations between undertakings, OJ L 24, 29.1.2004, p. 1–22.

III. FIRST STAGE: PARALLEL PATHWAYS

III.1 Isolationism as Starting Point

To understand the evolution of the interplay between competition law and data protection law in the EU, one should start from a finding of the CJEU from 2006 in *Asnef-Equifax*, a case that concerned a potential anticompetitive agreement between competing financial institutions to create a common credit history register of their customers: 'any possible issues relating to the sensitivity of personal data are not, as such, a matter for competition law, they may be resolved on the basis of the relevant provisions governing data protection'.[25] The lawfulness of the processing of personal data that was expected to be made available by the financial institutions acting as controllers was not taken at all into account by the Court. This prudent stance needs to be assessed against the procedural and jurisdictional framework of the judgment, which was issued following a reference for a preliminary ruling concerning exclusively the interpretation of the then Article 81 EC prohibiting anti-competitive agreements.

Nevertheless, the Advocate General, freer and more comprehensive in its non-binding statements, had been more nuanced. After stating in his Opinion that the sensitivity of data is not a matter of competition law, he had nevertheless added that:

> it is clear that there must be some way of informing the borrowers concerned of what data are recorded and of granting them the right to check the data concerning them or have them corrected where necessary. It appears that this point is settled, regard being had to the relevant Spanish legislation and also to clause 9 of the rules governing the register.[26]

The Advocate General had sensed that looking at the lawfulness and fairness of the processing of personal data subject to the agreement may be relevant in some way for the assessment of the case. But he did not include such analysis in the competition law assessment *per se*, framing it instead as a parallel issue.

Soon after the mentioned finding of the CJEU, the European Commission had several opportunities to apply this approach in merger control investigations concerning undertakings engaged in data intensive activities. In this sense, the *TeleAtlas/TomTom* vertical merger in the digital maps databases market was considered to raise 'serious doubts as to its compatibility with the common market' and prompted an in-depth, so-called 'Phase II' investigation, according to Article 6(1)(c) of the EU Merger Regulation. Pre-merger, TomTom integrated navigable digital databases it purchased from Tele Atlas into its own navigation software.[27] To provide navigation, the digital map database must be combined with a system for instant geographic positioning, primarily using Global Positioning System technology.[28] The parties argued that post-merger the significant amount of feedback data from TomTom's large customer base would improve Tele Atlas' map.[29] The European Commission did not make any determination as to whether some or all of the feedback data is personal data and did not

---

25 *Asnef-Equifax*, para 63.

26 Opinion of Advocate General Geelhoed in Case C-238/05 *Asnef-Equifax et al v. Asociación de Usuarios de Servicios Bancarios*, para 56.

27 *TeleAtlas/TomTom*, para 15.

28 Ibid., para 19.

29 Ibid., para 246.

mention at all whether data protection law would be relevant, even in a parallel assessment. This restrictive position must be, yet again, understood from a jurisdictional perspective. In principle, the merger control procedure only encompasses the assessment of the transaction under the EU Merger Regulation, i.e., the question of whether it would 'significantly impede effective competition in the common market or in a substantial part of it, in particular as a result of the creation or strengthening of a dominant position', cf. Article 2(1) and (2) and Article 8 of the EU Merger Regulation. Even the assessment under Article 101 TFEU is limited and explicitly provided for in the EU Merger Regulation.[30] Against this background, the cautious approach taken by the European Commission not to include data protection considerations in its assessment could be understood more like a political, rather than a legal stance. Including broad data protection considerations without an apparent reason to do so would have been a bold move that would have triggered judicial annulment actions, endangering the finalization of a long (approx. nine months) and burdensome investigation.

Nevertheless, although it did not include data protection in its assessment as such, the European Commission recognised the relevance of data as a competition parameter. For example, the Commission defined a narrow product market for digital maps, acknowledging data as a differentiating factor between digital maps, and maps more broadly.

III.2 First Big Question: the Google/DoubleClick Case

By contrast, the European Commission expressly placed data protection and competition law on parallel pathways in its clearance decision of the acquisition of DoubleClick by Google, affecting the markets for online advertising space, for the intermediation in online advertising and the provision of online display ad serving technology.[31] The Commission's Decision stated that it 'refers exclusively to the appraisal of this operation with Community rules on competition' and that it is 'without prejudice to the obligations imposed onto the parties by Community legislation in relation to the protection of individuals and the protection of privacy with regard to the processing of personal data'.[32]

However, just like the Advocate General in the *Asnef-Equifax* case, the Commission sensed that processing of personal data was somehow relevant for the Decision in this particular case. The Commission was well aware of the fact that 'internet service providers can track all of the online behavior of their users, following them to every website they visit' and that 'particularly large internet service providers could thus try to team up with advertisement companies to make use of this data under the restrictions imposed by privacy rules, but they could also try to use this data with their customers' consent, for instance in exchange for lower prices'.[33] However, it structured this analysis only with regard to the determination of the network effects deriving from DoubleClick's use of information about consumer behaviour collected through ad serving. A network effect occurs when the value of a good or service will increase the more people use it. For example, the more users a social network has, the more people

---

[30] Similarly, in State Aid proceedings, the Commission will only assess a measure under Arts 107 and 108 TFEU exceptionally under other legal provisions if these provisions are 'indissolubly linked' to the measure, cf. SA. 49275 *Novo Banco*, para 311 et seq.

[31] European Commission, Case No COMP/M.4731 – *Google/DoubleClick* (2008).

[32] Ibid., para 368.

[33] Ibid., para 271.

a user will be able to connect to, making the respective social network even more popular, and thus attracting new users and ensuring that current users will not leave the network. Network effects can be suitable to consolidate market power and to raise barriers to market entry, as new market actors would not be enabled to enhance the value of their product.

The determining factor in noting the lack of a network effect of the merger both on the advertisers' and publishers' sides was the fact that DoubleClick was 'contractually prohibited' to use the data it had collected in the past 'to offer better targeting to new advertiser customers'.[34] It could only do so to improve the service to the advertiser whose ads were served when the data was first recorded.[35] It is interesting how the European Commission considered the contractual confidentiality obligation an important factor in determining the inexistence of a network effect. Given that customers of DoubleClick do not allow 'their data' to be shared with or used 'for the benefit of [advertisers' and publishers'] rivals', 'any value to them from enhanced ad serving performance would be outweighed by the actual or perceived advantages that such data sharing would confer upon their competitors'.[36]

Thus, the European Commission noted that 'if DoubleClick did not agree to, or violated, the confidentiality provisions upon which its customers insist, there would be alternative ad serving providers to which these customers could and would switch'.[37] While the Commission concluded that the undertakings had an incentive to adhere to the contractual provisions on confidentiality, however it did not address how or whether confidentiality was *de facto* ensured. Moreover, it did not even construe it as constituting confidentiality of communications of the users for whom the ads will be displayed. There was no consideration given to the fact that DoubleClick customers' data used to offer better targeted ads would have likely contained, or even equated to, personal data. It is worthwhile noting, though, that the current Article 5(3) of Directive 2002/58/EC[38] (the 'ePrivacy Directive') was not yet adopted at the time the Commission made these determinations. However, the general Data Protection Directive[39] was in force.

The *Google/DoubleClick* merger was cleared also by the Federal Trade Commission (FTC) in the US. The FTC stated it did consider consumer privacy issues in its analysis: 'we investigated the possibility that this transaction could adversely affect non-price attributes of competition, such as consumer-privacy. ... We have ... concluded that privacy considerations, as such, do not provide a basis to challenge this transaction'.[40] However, one Commissioner published a detailed dissenting statement that shows the extent of the debate in the US on the

---

[34] Ibid., paras 183 and 184.

[35] Ibid., para 183.

[36] Ibid., para 277.

[37] Ibid., para 277.

[38] Directive 2002/58/EC of the European Parliament and of the Council of 12 July 2002 concerning the processing of personal data and the protection of privacy in the electronic communications sector (Directive on privacy and electronic communications), OJ L 201, 31/07/2002 P. 0037–0047. Art. 5(3) of the Directive was amended in 2009 changing the notice and consent requirements for placing cookies or similar technologies on devices.

[39] Directive 95/46/EC of the European Parliament and of the Council of 24 October 1995 on the protection of individuals with regard to the processing of personal data and on the free movement of such data, OJ L 281, 23/11/1995 P. 0031–0050.

[40] Statement of the Federal Trade Commission concerning Google/DoubleClick, FTC File No. 071-0170, 2.

relevance of privacy for antitrust preceding this decision of the FTC,[41] as well as the difficulties of merger control investigations, a sheer predictive exercise. In brief, Commissioner Pamela Jones Harbour dissented on the ground that she makes:

> alternate predictions about where this market is heading, and the transformative role the combined Google/DoubleClick will play if the proposed acquisition is consummated. If the Commission closes its investigation at this time, without imposing any conditions on the merger, neither the competition nor the privacy interests of consumers will have been adequately addressed.[42]

III.3 Incognito Data Protection Law Considerations

Following *Google/DoubleClick*, in another decision concerning a data intensive market, the European Commission made a *de facto* data protection law determination, without acknowledging it as such and without referring to any of the legal obligations stemming from data protection law. This happened in *Telefonica UK/Vodafone UK/Everything Everywhere*,[43] a decision on the creation of a joint venture offering various 'mobile commerce' services in the UK.[44] When assessing whether the concentration would raise horizontal competition concerns in the market for the provision of data analytics services in respect of online and offline advertising and transactions, the Commission found that 'historically, MNOs'[45] terms and conditions have only allowed the MNOs to send their own offers to their customers. Therefore, the Notifying Parties will have to build a largely new base of opt-in users for the purpose of data analytics and for JV Co's[46] advertising activity ... Obtaining opt-ins outside the framework of new contracts requires a campaign and positive responses (opt-ins) as a result of such campaigns'.[47] These conclusions were not a matter of 'history' or of 'terms and conditions', but rather a consequence of the general Data Protection Directive and, as the case may be, of the ePrivacy Directive. And the determination addressed fundamental data protection law issues: lawful grounds for processing and purpose limitation as a factor determining market behaviour.

When looking specifically at profiling for advertising purposes (calling it 'targeted advertising'), the European Commission mentioned that 'customers generally tend to give their personal data to many market players, which gather and market it. Therefore, this type of data

---

[41] See Peter Swire, 'Protecting Consumers: Privacy matters in antitrust analysis', a testimony submitted to the FTC Behavioural Advertising Town hall and published by Center for American Progress (2007) https://www.americanprogress.org/issues/economy/news/2007/10/19/3564/protecting-consumers-privacy-matters-in-antitrust-analysis/ accessed 9 August 2018. Swire argued that privacy harms can reduce consumer welfare, which is a principal goal of modern antitrust analysis and that privacy harms can lead to a reduction in the quality of a good or service, which is a standard category of harm that results from market power. Hence, it is a normal part of antitrust to assess such harms and aim to minimize them.

[42] Dissenting Statement of Commissioner Pamela Jones Harbour in the matter of Google/DoubleClick F.T.C. File No. 071-0170.

[43] European Commission, Decision in Case No COMP/M.6314 – *Telefónica UK/Vodafone UK/Everything Everywhere/JV*.

[44] Ibid., para 1.

[45] Mobile Network Operators.

[46] Joint Venture.

[47] *Telefonica/Vodafone*, para 542.

is generally understood to be a commodity'.[48] The Decision goes into sufficient detail to take into account real time geo-targeting, as well as the use of social media profiles or browser histories. It concludes that:

> on all possible sub-markets, the JV Co would indeed be able to collect a broad range of consumer information, which will be very valuable for its (mobile) data analytics services and advertising services. However, many other strong and established players are also able to offer comparable solutions to the JV Co.[49]

The Commission gave the green light to this joint venture.

The French CA brought privacy concerns raised by behavioural targeting into its first analysis of the online advertising market from 2010, only to point out that it is not up to it:

> to examine matters related to the privacy of web users; such matters are dealt with by the [CNIL] and by courts of law... the risks of invasion of privacy, if treated seriously by the authorities in charge of data protection and the competent courts, can have serious implications for the online searched-based ads market.[50]

These cases show that for some time competition law and data protection law were considered as being parallel issues. This was either stated as such in competition investigations, following the CJEU's approach in *Asnef-Equifax*, or was implied by ignoring data protection law in assessments that would have benefitted from an informed data protection analysis.

IV. SECOND STAGE: THERE IS SOMETHING ABOUT DATA PROTECTION AND COMPETITION LAW

IV.1 The Beginning of a Serious Interdisciplinary Conversation

The Treaty of Lisbon, in force since December 2009, amended Article 16 of the TFEU to introduce an explicit right of everyone 'to the protection of personal data concerning them'. Concurrently, the EU Charter of Fundamental Rights explicitly 'reaffirmed' (according to its Preamble) and codified the EU Fundamental Rights as they resulted *inter alia* from the constitutional traditions of the Member States and the case law of the CJEU. Adopted in 2000, it started to have full legal effect after the entry into force of the Lisbon Treaty. The Charter, which binds all EU institutions and Member State institutions when they are applying EU law,[51] articulates the right to the protection of personal data in its Article 8, while also specifying its limits.

This legal articulation was accompanied by factual and economic developments, i.e., the increasing relevance of amassing personal data for the profitability and the development of

---

[48] Ibid., para 543.

[49] Ibid., para 557.

[50] Autorité de la concurrence, *Opinion No 10-A-29 of 14 December 2010 on the competitive operation of online advertising* (2010), para 295.

[51] Cf. for the application of competition law by NCAs Art. 3 (1) Council Regulation (EC) No 1/2003 of 16 December 2002 on the implementation of the rules on competition laid down in Art. 81 and Art. 82 of the Treaty, OJ L 001, 04 January 2003 P. 0001–0025.

products and services of big tech companies and the announcement of impactful acquisitions in the market.[52] In this context, the EDPS became the first voice of the EU administration formally asking for increased dialogue between DPAs, CAs and Consumer Protection Authorities (CPAs). In a Preliminary Opinion published in 2014, the EDPS highlighted the role of personal data as 'the fuel of the digital economy',[53] and explained why data protection law, competition law and consumer protection law are all relevant for consumer welfare in the digital economy. The 2014 Preliminary Opinion identified a palette of interferences of these three fields of law, looking particularly at defining markets for services paid for with personal data, measuring the digital market power by the control of personal data, and appraising mergers while considering the risks to consumers and the role of consumer welfare, as well as how the growth of a vibrant market for privacy-enhancing services can be encouraged by strengthening informed consumer choice.

For instance, the EDPS argued that 'if market power in the digital economy can be measured according to control of commercialisable personal information, then merger decisions could in turn take account of the market effects of combining these capabilities'.[54] The policy recommendations for steps to be taken in the near future were on point: 'effective guidance on the application of privacy, competition and consumer protection rules for online services, in particular those promoted as free services', 'cooperation between authorities in investigation and enforcement', and 'a review of competition legislation for the 21st century digital markets'.[55]

The Competition and Markets Authority (CMA) in the UK followed by publishing a comprehensive report on the commercial use of consumer data,[56] where privacy and data protection analyses played a prominent role. Among other topics, the CMA brought into the debate the idea of competition in data protection.[57] It showed that the market can help achieve the protection of 'essential rights such as privacy' where 'regulations encourage competition and choice, allowing a "race to the top" by firms to offer consumers better services'.[58]

Another strong signal that data protection law had become relevant for competition assessments was given by the German and French CAs in their Joint Report on Competition Law and Data published in 2016. One of the practical contributions of the Report was the mapping of data related to anticompetitive conducts. Three main areas of concern were highlighted: mergers and acquisitions, exclusionary conducts and price discrimination.

With regard to mergers and acquisitions, the Joint Report made the point that a merger between an established undertaking and an innovative newcomer could be problematic in data-related markets, since it could result in differentiated data access and increase the

---

[52] At the beginning of 2014, Facebook announced that it intends to acquire WhatsApp. This was the most visible example of a trend. The OECD reported that in sectors related to data, "*the number of mergers and acquisitions (M&A) has increased rapidly from 55 deals in 2008 to almost 164 deals in 2012*". See OECD, *Data Driven Innovation. Big Data for Growth and Wellbeing,* 2015, p. 94.

[53] EDPS, *Privacy and competitiveness in the age of big data* (2014), p. 8.

[54] Ibid, p. 29.

[55] Ibid, p. 37-38.

[56] Competition and Markets Authority, *The commercial use of consumer data*, June 2015 ('CMA Report'), https://assets.publishing.service.gov.uk/government/uploads/system/uploads/attachment_data/file/435817/The_commercial_use_of_consumer_data.pdf accessed 9 August 2018.

[57] For a deeper analysis of competition in data protection, see Francesco Costa-Cabral, Orla Lynskey, 'Family Ties: The Intersection Between Data Protection and Competition Law' (2017) 54 *CMLR* 11–50.

[58] CMA Report, 8.

concentration of data related to this market if the newcomer has access to a large database.[59] Usually, this type of acquisition would not raise competition concerns given the newcomer's low market shares or even the lack of any horizontal overlap. The authorities also argued that a merger of two companies which already hold strong market positions in separate upstream or downstream markets could foreclose these markets for new competitors.[60] Finally, such mergers could also yield efficiencies gains which would have to be compared to the risks they entail for competition.[61] This analysis not only highlights the importance of access to data as a competitive parameter, but also confirms data's role as a criterion in assessing and confirming market power, even if, as such, an undertaking does not have a high turnover or market shares.

From the point of view of exclusionary conducts, the Joint Report highlighted that 'conducts depriving some competitors from access to data could also weaken competition and even lead to exclusion of competitors in different situations'.[62] Refusal of access to data can be anticompetitive if the data are an essential facility to the activity of the undertaking asking for access, if it is discriminatory, or if it is the result of exclusivity provisions with third-party providers or foreclosing opportunities for rivals to procure similar data by making it harder for consumers to adopt their technologies or platforms.[63] Another exclusionary conduct can result from a company developing or increasing its market power on another market in an anti-competitive way.[64]

Using data as a vehicle for price discrimination is another concern. If a company has market power, it can use data to set different prices for the different customer groups it has identified thanks to the data collected.[65] The issue of price discrimination is complex, since it can have both positive and negative effects on consumer welfare, depending on what end of the deal consumers get, but also on competition generally.

This entire analysis focused on data and how it restricts or enables competition. But what is the role of data protection law in looking at these issues? Even though they stated that privacy concerns are not, in and of themselves, within the scope of intervention of competition authorities,[66] the two CAs did identify how data protection issues may affect competition. Decisions taken regarding the collection and use of personal data 'can have, in parallel, implications on economic and competition dimensions'.[67] The way in which personal data is being processed 'could be considered from a competition standpoint whenever these policies are liable to affect competition, notably when they are implemented by a dominant undertaking for which data serves as a main input of its products or services'.[68]

---

59 *Competition Law and Data* Report (2016), p. 16.
60 Ibid., 16.
61 Ibid., 16. See also Inge Graef, 'Data as Essential Facility. Competition and Innovation on Online Platforms, PhD thesis, KU Leuven Centre for IT & IP Law (2016), p. 308–309.
62 *Competition Law and Data* Report (2016) p. 17.
63 Ibid., 17–19. See also A.P. Grunes and Maurice E. Stucke, *No Mistake About it: The Important Role of Antitrust in the Era of Big Data*, University of Tennessee Legal Studies Research Paper No. 269, 2015, 3.
64 Ibid., 20. See also Competition and Markets Authority, *The Commercial Use of Consumer Data*, 2015, p. 90.
65 *Competition Law and Data* Report (2016), 21.
66 Ibid., 22.
67 Ibid.
68 Ibid.

The Organization for Economic Cooperation and Development (OECD) joined the chorus of organizations that acknowledged the role of privacy for competitive behaviour in the data centric economy. In a 2016 Report it explained that 'the consideration of privacy as a relevant parameter of non-price competition would have significant implications for merger review and ultimately affect the decision to clear or block a merger'.[69] The OECD also pointed out that the consequence of this would be that competition authorities could decide to prevent the acquisition of the few companies in the market providing services with a greater extent of privacy protection.[70]

While the interplay of competition law and data protection law in the data centric economy was being analysed more and more seriously in reports and white papers of relevant institutions, some actual cases provided the opportunity to apply these new theories in practice. The extent to which they integrated privacy or data protection considerations was however not yet consistent with thought leadership in this area.

IV.2 The Catalyst: the *Facebook/WhatsApp* Case

The acquisition of WhatsApp by Facebook was cleared both by the Federal Trade Commission in the US[71] and by the European Commission in the EU.[72] Privacy turned out to be a relevant non-price competitive element: while Facebook offered a free texting application and accessed user data to target them with ads, WhatsApp charged a modest fee and promised not to use user data.[73] The European Commission analysed the merger on three markets: consumer communication services, social networking services and online advertising services. The European Commission clarified that for the purposes of the decision at hand it 'analyzed potential data concentration only to the extent that it is likely to strengthen Facebook's position in the online advertising market or in any sub-segments thereof' and that 'any privacy-related concerns flowing from the increased concentration of data within the control of Facebook as a result of the Transaction do not fall within the scope of the EU competition law rules but within the scope of the EU data protection rules'.[74] However, even if formally it took the 'parallel pathways' approach, the European Commission did make a few determinations on substance related to privacy.

In particular, it addressed the issue of the opportunity the merger creates for Facebook to access personal data of WhatsApp users in order to deliver targeted advertising on and outside WhatsApp. For the first time, the European Commission briefly analysed the impact of the merger not only on the advertising side, but also from the perspective of the consumers enjoy-

---

[69] OECD, *Big Data: Bringing Competition Policy to the Digital Era* (2016), para 59 ('OECD Report'), https://one.oecd.org/document/DAF/COMP(2016)14/en/pdf accessed 9 August 2018.

[70] Ibid.

[71] Letter from Jessica Rich, Dir., Bureau of Consumer Protection, FTC, to Erin Egan, Chief Privacy Officer, Facebook, Inc., and Anne Hoge, Gen. Counsel, WhatsApp Inc. (20 April 2014) http://www.ftc.gov/system/files/documents/public_statements/297701/140410facebookwhatappltr.pdf accessed 9 August 2010. In this letter, Facebook was warned that it could not use the data collected by WhatsApp without obtaining the explicit consent of users first.

[72] *Facebook/WhatsApp*.

[73] This precise parameter prompted the Commission to consider that the two were not close competitors regarding communication services.

[74] *Facebook/WhatsApp*, para 164.

ing free services in exchange for their data. The Commission acknowledged that accessing the personal data of WhatsApp users would be possible 'subject to WhatsApp changing its privacy policy'.[75] It further linked the issue to WhatsApp's 'no ads' strategy, arguing that such a development would 'prompt certain users who feel that the ads disrupt their experience to switch to competing apps free of ads'.[76] Finally, the Commission suggested that introducing targeted ads would likely mean abandoning end-to-end encryption and this would 'create dissatisfaction among the increasing number of users who significantly value privacy and security' and would reduce Facebook's incentive to do so.[77] In the same paragraph where it made the previous findings, the European Commission even acknowledged that 'privacy concerns have prompted a high number of German users to switch from WhatsApp to Threema in the 24 hours following the announcement of Facebook's acquisition of WhatsApp'.[78] Even though it was aware of the importance placed by WhatsApp's users on privacy, the Commission did not use privacy as a parameter to make any other further assessments.

Noting that Facebook had informed the European Commission that there were major obstacles for it to access the personal data of WhatsApp users and use the data for advertising,[79] the Commission articulated, for the first time and timidly, a theory of harm based on the accumulation of personal data. It pointed out that 'even if the merged entity were to start collecting and using data from WhatsApp users, the Transaction would only raise competition concerns if the concentration of data within Facebook's control were to allow it to strengthen its position in advertising'.[80]

The European Commission was criticized for the approach it took, some arguing that it should have investigated the possibility that WhatsApp's data protection conditions would be degraded post-merger and that it should have evaluated the privacy risks associated with the potential data concentration.[81] The EDPS was prompted to call for coherent enforcement of fundamental rights: 'in the case of future mergers of a similar nature, individuals might benefit from a more coherent response from competition, consumer and data protection authorities. Supervisory authorities must be fully equipped to anticipate and to prevent both behaviour and concentrations that could be harmful for the individual'.[82]

European Commission officials defended their approach, noting that the merger control clearance was granted only under the EU Merger Regulation and in line with the judgment of the CJEU in *Asnef-Equifax*.[83] One step forward, two back. Nonetheless, they argued that privacy is 'one of many parameters of competition between consumer communications apps,

---

[75] Ibid., para 173.

[76] Ibid., para 174.

[77] Ibid., para 174.

[78] Ibid., para 174.

[79] Ibid., para 185.

[80] Ibid., para 187.

[81] See Costa-Cabral and Lynskey (2017), p. 38 and Lisa Kimmel, Janis Kestenbaum, 'What's Up with WhatsApp? A Transatlantic View on Privacy and Merger Enforcement in Digital Markets' (2014) *Antitrust* p. 52.

[82] EDPS, Opinion 8/2016 on *Coherent enforcement of fundamental rights in the age of big data,* 23 September 2016, 10.

[83] Eleonora Ocello, Cristina Sjödin and Anatoly Subočs, 'What's Up with Merger Control in the Digital Sector? Lessons from the Facebook/WhatsApp EU merger case', Competition merger brief (2015) No 1, 2 – 7, http://ec.europa.eu/competition/publications/cmb/2015/cmb2015_001_en.pdf accessed 9 August 2018.

the others being price, reliability of the service, functionalities offered, size of the underlying network, trendiness, etc.', and they concluded that the majority of the communication apps did not actually compete on privacy features.[84]

Nevertheless, this European Commission decision had a further collateral impact, leading to the recognition of the economic value of the access to customer data. This transaction involved indeed the acquisition for a high price of a company with virtually no monetary turnover. Given the lack of 'actual' monetary turnover, the transaction was notifiable in just a small number of jurisdictions,[85] notwithstanding the significant value of the transaction and its potential impact on competitive dynamics. This realization led to legislative changes in various jurisdictions in order to properly 'monetize' the access to customer data, triggering merger filing requirements.[86]

The Commission's merger control clearance was not the last chapter in the Facebook/WhatsApp merger. Three years later, the Consumer Protection Authority in Italy fined WhatsApp with 3 million euros for *de facto* forcing users of its service 'to accept in full the new Terms of Use, and specifically the provision to share their personal data with Facebook, by inducing them to believe that without granting such consent they would not have been able to use the service anymore'.[87] It must be noted that as such, this was not a competition law related fine. The sanction was imposed for bypassing user consent and not for competition restriction.

After the European Commission fined Facebook 110 million euros for providing misleading information during the merger assessment with regard to its access to WhatsApp user data,[88] the Article 29 Working Party created a taskforce to work with WhatsApp for 'a clear, comprehensive resolution' and to ensure that 'the pause in data sharing for the purpose of improving Facebook products and enhancing targeted advertising on Facebook continues until such time as the matter is resolved to the satisfaction of data protection authorities'.[89]

IV.3 Officially Importing Data Protection Law Lexicon: The *Microsoft/LinkedIn* Case

A case where the European Commission signalled a more mature acknowledgement of data protection law considerations into competition law adjudication was the acquisition of LinkedIn by Microsoft. Here, however, the considerations were not stemming from a concern towards the privacy of users or the protection of their personal data, or from competition in

---

[84] Ocello et al, 6.

[85] *Facebook/WhatsApp*, para 10.

[86] See: https://www.bundeskartellamt.de/SharedDocs/Meldung/EN/Pressemitteilungen/2018/14_05_2018_TAW.html?nn=3591568 accessed 9 August 2018 and Ocello et al 2.

[87] Autorità Garante de la Concorrenza e del Mercato, *WhatsApp fined for 3 million euro for having forced its users to share their personal data with Facebook*, (Press Release, 12 May 2017) http://www.agcm.it/en/newsroom/press-releases/2380-whatsapp-fined-for-3-million-euro-for-having-forced-its-users-to-share-their-personal-data-with-facebook.html accessed 9 August 2018.

[88] European Commission, *Commission fines Facebook 110 million euro for providing misleading information about WhatsApp takeover,* (Press Release, 18 May 2017) http://europa.eu/rapid/press-release_IP-17-1369_en.htm accessed 9 August 2018.

[89] Article 29 Working Party Letter to Jan Koum (24 October 2017) https://ec.europa.eu/newsroom/just/document.cfm?doc_id=47964 accessed 9 August 2018.

data protection. Rather, the Commission relied on data protection law to assume that the personal data held by the two companies will not be combined. 'Any such data combination could only be implemented by the merged entity to the extent it is allowed by applicable data protection rules,'[90] the European Commission stated, adding that 'today, Microsoft and LinkedIn are subject to relevant national data protection rules with respect to the collection, processing, storage and usage of personal data, which, subject to certain exceptions, limit their ability to process the dataset they maintain'.[91] The Decision even refers to the GDPR, which had just been adopted but was not yet applicable at the time the Commission made its assessment, announcing that the GDPR:

> may further limit Microsoft's ability to have access and to process its users' personal data in the future since the new rules will strengthen the existing rights and empowering individuals with more control over their personal data (i.e. easier access to personal data; right to data portability etc.).[92]

Nevertheless, the European Commission also looked into the possibility that data protection legislation would not ultimately preclude Microsoft to access the personal data of LinkedIn following the merger. Two ways were identified for the merger to raise horizontal issues: (1) the combination of the two datasets post-merger would increase the merged entity's market power in a hypothetical market for the supply of this data or increase barriers to entry/expansion in the market for actual or potential competitors, which need this data to operate on the market; and (2) if pre-merger the two companies were competing with each other on the basis of the data they controlled and this competition would be eliminated by the merger.[93] The Commission considered that in the case at hand neither of the conditions was applicable.[94] Even if the references to data protection law were detailed, they did not touch on the point of 'competition in data protection'.

This second stage of development is characterized by the beginning of an understanding of how data protection law may in fact be relevant for competition law adjudication, and by significant exploration of the intersection of the two fields by both CAs and DPAs as policymakers. This step led to the third stage of interaction, characterized by the first signs of concrete action to afford coordinated protection to persons as both data subjects and market participants and by the declared realization that access to personal data and the control of the technological tools to exploit them are a determining competitive advantage.

---

90 *Microsoft/LinkedIn*, para 177.
91 Ibid., para 177.
92 Ibid., para 178.
93 Ibid., para 179.
94 Ibid., paras 180-181.

V. THIRD STAGE: THE DAWN OF UBERPROTECTION

V.1 Germany: The First Big Data-protection-law-centric Competition Decision

In March 2016,[95] the German FCO initiated an investigation against Facebook. The FCO explained that Facebook was 'possibly' dominant on the market for social networks and that its use of terms and conditions in violation of data protection rules could amount to an exploitative abuse of customers. The President of the FCO clarified that given the crucial importance of user data for advertising driven internet services like Facebook, it had to be ensured that 'consumers are sufficiently informed about the type and extent of data collected'. The FCO clearly stated that the infringement of data protection rules can amount to an abuse of dominance. Furthermore, the FCO explicitly stated that it would conduct the proceedings in close cooperation with the 'competent data protection agencies'.

In its preliminary assessment published in December 2017,[96] the FCO confirmed that Facebook is dominant on the German market for social networks. It also found that it 'is abusing its dominant position by making use of its social network conditional on its being allowed to limitlessly amass every kind of data generated by using third-party websites and merge it with the user's Facebook account'.[97] The FCO assessed that this collection and use of personal data 'violates data protection provisions to the disadvantage of its users', amounting to unfair (abusive) terms on conditions of a dominant company. The FCO explained that:

> the collection and processing of data is an entrepreneurial activity that has great relevance for the competitive performance of a company. (…) Monitoring the data processing activities of dominant companies is therefore an essential task of the competition authority which cannot be fulfilled by a data protection authority. In its assessment of whether the company's terms and conditions on data processing are unfair, the competition authority does, however, take account of the legal principles of data protection laws.

The pathways finally crossed, and compliance with data protection has become a criterion for the legal assessment of market behaviour.

In February 2019, the FCO confirmed this preliminary assessment in its final decision, which prohibited Facebook:

> from making the use of the Facebook social network by private users residing in Germany, who also use its corporate services WhatsApp, Oculus, Masquerade and Instagram, conditional on the collection of user and device-related data by Facebook and combining that information with the Facebook.com user accounts without the users' consent.[98]

---

[95] Bundeskartellamt, *Bundeskartellamt initiates proceedings against Facebook, on suspicion of having abused its market power by infringing data protection rules* (2 March 2016) https://www.bundeskartellamt.de/SharedDocs/Meldung/EN/Pressemitteilungen/2016/02_03_2016_Facebook.html?nn=3591568 accessed 9 August 2018.

[96] Bundeskartellamt, *Background information on the Facebook Proceedings* (19 December 2017) https://www.bundeskartellamt.de/SharedDocs/Publikation/EN/Diskussions_Hintergrundpapiere/2017/Hintergrundpapier_Facebook.pdf?__blob=publicationFile&v=6 accessed 9 August 2018.

[97] Bundeskartellamt, *Preliminary assessment in Facebook proceeding: Facebook's collection and use of data from third-party sources is abusive* (Press Release, 19 December 2017).

[98] Bundeskartellamt, *Case Summary: Facebook, Exploitative business terms pursuant to Section 19(1) GWB for inadequate data processing* (6 February 2019), available at https://www.bundeskartellamt

The FCO decision was appealed by the company, and the Düsseldorf Higher Regional Court suspended the order until it decides on the appeal. This decision was further challenged by the FCO at the German Federal Court of Justice, which annulled the Düsseldorf judgment, maintaining that there is an abuse of a dominant position in this case.[99] The case went back to the court in Düsseldorf to be decided on merit, but that court decided to hold proceedings and to send questions for a preliminary ruling to the CJEU to clarify the extent to which compliance with data protection law can be considered a parameter in competition adjudication.

V.2 France: Data Protection Rules Recognized as Significantly Influencing the Economic Regulation of the Online Advertising Sector

In this context, the French CA published revealing conclusions on its sector inquiry into online advertising two months before the GDPR became applicable.[100] Remarking that the sector experienced a rapid growth in the past ten years, the French CA recognized that online advertising is characterized by a proliferation of new players whose services are based, to varying degrees, on 'the massive exploitation of data warehouses related to individuals, thanks to new computing capabilities'.[101] At the same time, the authority acknowledged that 'the fundamental driver of the growth of this sector is the effectiveness of the targeting promised by the new forms of advertising, which, according to its promoters, would allow a higher efficiency than those of other advertising services in terms of return on investment'.[102] However, the CA also observed that not all players on the market benefit from the overall growth of this sector, with companies that have access to vast sets of high-quality personal data being advantaged.[103] In the view of the CA, this confirms that 'access to personal data in large numbers and with high added value, as well as the control of the technological tools making it possible to use and to valorize them are from now on determining competitive advantages'.[104]

The CA also noted that data protection rules will continue to play an important role in the competitive functioning of the sector, and that they will thus have 'a significant influence on the economic regulation of the online advertising sector'.[105] In fact, the CA dedicates a lot of attention to the draft ePrivacy Regulation[106] proposed by the European Commission. Article 8 of the draft regulation as proposed by the Commission requires any party who places cookies[107] or similar technology on devices of end users to obtain consent before placing them.

.de/SharedDocs/Entscheidung/EN/Fallberichte/Missbrauchsaufsicht/2019/B6-22-16.pdf?__blob=publicationFile&v=4 accessed 23 July 2021.

[99] Bundesgerichtshof, KVR 69/19, Decision of 23 June 2023.

[100] Autorité de la Concurrence, Avis no 18-A-03 portant sur l'exploitation des donnees dans le secteur de la publicite sur internet, 6 March 2018 (Online Advertising sector inquiry 2018).

[101] Ibid., 4 (unofficial translation).

[102] Ibid.

[103] Ibid., 11 (unofficial translation).

[104] Ibid.

[105] Ibid., 102 (unofficial translation).

[106] Proposal for a Regulation of the European Parliament and of the Council concerning the respect for private life and the protection of personal data in electronic communications and repealing Directive 2002/58/EC (Regulation on Privacy and Electronic Communications), Brussels 10.1.2017, COM(2017) 10 final.

[107] Cookies are short text files that are placed on devices after a website or application is accessed, being able to track online activity and communicate that data to first parties (entities that directly

Only very few exceptions apply from this rule of previous consent, i.e., when the cookies are necessary for the functionality of webpages or other services. The French CA warns that the draft regulation potentially introduces distortions of competition. According to the French CA, the draft Regulation would disfavour market actors that gather data by placing first- and third-party cookies[108] without having a direct relationship with a user, while favouring platforms that gather data from their logged in users, having obtained consent during registration for the service and perceived as generally allowing collection of personal data in return of the service performed.[109] This evaluation of the draft ePrivacy Regulation provisions is however premature, and does not take into account all requirements of valid consent as mandated by the GDPR:[110] Article 7(4) of the GDPR indeed 'seeks to ensure that the purpose of personal data processing is not disguised nor bundled with the provision of a contract of a service for which these personal data are not necessary'.[111]

Be that as it may, even though at first glance the stance of the CA seems to disregard privacy concerns in order to preclude preferential treatment on the market, the CA ends up proposing a privacy enhancing solution that would protect both effective competition and users' privacy: the obligation to obtain consent for tracking online behaviour for advertising purposes should be spelled out as applying to all entities involved in user tracking, including platforms that require log in. 'Failing that', it notes, 'the publishers themselves would probably be convinced to turn to logged environments, which would paradoxically go against the desire for anonymity sought by Internet users'.[112] In reality, the draft ePrivacy Regulation – which was still under debate more than four years after the proposal was published, seems to require just that, when read together with the valid consent requirements of the GDPR. All in all, the development is remarkable: a competition authority, by its own motion, has analysed draft legislation regulating privacy protections to draw conclusions and propose recommendations related to maintaining effective competition and at the same time ensuring user privacy.

V.3 The Digital Clearinghouse Functioning

Data Protection Authorities continue to make their voices heard, as the EDPS' initiative for a Digital Clearinghouse came to fruition. In a 2016 Opinion, the EDPS called for coherent enforcement of fundamental rights in the age of big data, and, more specifically, for the creation of a Digital Clearinghouse (DCH).[113] This Clearinghouse was conceived as a voluntary network of contact points in regulatory authorities at national and EU level who are respon-

---

place the cookie) and/or third parties (entities whose cookies are placed via third-party websites or applications).

[108] First-party cookies are placed on devices by the entity running the website or application placing the cookies, while third-party cookies are placed on devices by third parties other than the entity running the website or application, for purposes such as advertising or analytics.

[109] Autorité de la Concurrence, Online Advertising sector inquiry 2018, 112 (unofficial translation).

[110] Consent under the ePrivacy framework is to be understood as defined in the General Data Protection Regulation, according to Art. 9 of the proposed ePrivacy Regulation. Therefore, the definition of and the conditions for consent provided for in Art. 4(11) and Art. 7 of the GDPR apply.

[111] Article 29 Working Party/European Data Protection Board, *Guidelines on consent under Regulation 2016/*679, (10 April 2018), 8.

[112] Autorité de la Concurrence, Online Advertising sector inquiry 2018, 113 (unofficial translation).

[113] EDPS, Opinion 8/2016 on *Coherent enforcement of fundamental rights in the age of big data* (23 September 2016).

sible for regulation of the digital sector. This might also include authorities such as those in the telecommunications area who supervise the implementation of rules on confidentiality of communications.[114] The DCH was also endorsed by the European Parliament in a Resolution on fundamental rights implications of big data, adopted in 2017.[115] The first meeting of the DCH took place in May 2017. Since then, it has met twice per year. Participants to the DCH are representatives of competition authorities, data protection authorities and consumer protection authorities from all over the world, not only from the EU.[116] The purpose of these meetings is to, inter alia, allow for an informal exchange on best practices and experiences as well as on common public policy issues such as data portability and unfair terms and conditions, to inform on interrelated legislative developments and to explore ways for better cooperation between the various types of authorities.[117]

The Irish Data Protection Commissioner highlighted in her Annual Report for 2017 that coherence between data protection, competition and consumer law 'will be necessary to deliver a fair deal to service users. One hand cannot approve a merger without conditions while the other hand effectively has to try and block it after the fact by preventing data-sharing between the two'.[118] In the UK, the CMA and the Information Commissioner's Office (ICO) published a Joint Statement in May 2021 on Competition and Data Protection in Digital Markets, where they analysed the synergies and tensions between the two fields of law and committed to work together to promote regulatory coherence.[119]

Graef et al. explore all facets of the idea that 'fairness' is the common thread that bridges competition, data protection and consumer law,[120] paying attention to a topic that has been on the mind of the EU Commissioner for Competition Margrethe Vestager for some years now.[121] It can reasonably be expected that ensuring fairness as differently understood within the three fields of law will play a role in future enforcement cases.

As platforms are relying more and more on algorithmic decision-making, the main point of concern shifts from behavioural targeting to bias and harms created by algorithmic

---

[114] Ibid., p. 15.

[115] European Parliament resolution of 14 March 2017 on fundamental rights implications of big data: privacy, data protection, non-discrimination, security and law enforcement.

[116] For instance, the US Federal Trade Commission and the Privacy Commissioner of Hong Kong participated to the meetings; see Statement from the third meeting of the Digital Clearinghouse, available at https://edps.europa.eu/sites/edp/files/publication/18-06-22_third_meeting_digital_clearinghouse_statement_en.pdf accessed 9 August 2018.

[117] Giovanni Buttarelli, 'The Clearinghouse Gets to Work' (29 May 2017) https://edps.europa.eu/press-publications/press-news/blog/digital-clearinghouse-gets-work_en accessed 9 August 2018.

[118] Data Protection Commissioner, Annual Report 2017 (27 February 2018) https://www.dataprotection.ie/docimages/documents/DPC%20Annual%20Report%202017.pdf accessed 9 August 2018), 9.

[119] CMA and ICO, *Competition and Data Protection in Digital Markets: A joint statement between the CMA and the ICO*, (19 May 2021).

[120] Inge Graef, Damian Clifford and Peggy Valcke, 'Fairness and Enforcement: Bridging Competition, Data Protection and Consumer Law', forthcoming in IDPL (2018) (available at https://papers.ssrn.com/sol3/papers.cfm?abstract_id=3216198, accessed 9 August 2018).

[121] See Lewis Crofts and Mathew Newman, *Vestager's "fairness" mantra rattles through EU competition law,* MLex, 15 November 2016. Buttarelli also mentioned in his recount of the Digital Clearinhouse meeting in September 2016 that 'Commissioner Vestager identified fairness as the uniting thread in the enforcement of competition, consumer and data protection rule', see https://edps.europa.eu/press-publications/press-news/blog/big-data-rights-lets-get-together_en accessed 9 August 2018.

decision-making which relies on personal data. Hildebrandt is already looking beyond the intersection of the three fields of law and argues that, even together with tort law, they cannot contribute to the effective contestability of algorithmic decision-making by themselves.[122] To solve this, she proposes the recognition of primitives of legal protection that 'should offer protection at the gateways of the data-driven ecosystem, preventing a host of problems that must otherwise be solved at other levels, where the cost of both compliance and enforcement would be much higher'.[123] She identifies these primitives as *data minimization* – the principle according to which only that personal data necessary to achieve the purpose for which it is collected or processed must be used; *purpose limitation*[124] – the principle according to which personal data must be processed only for specified, explicit and legitimate purposes and not further processed in a manner that is incompatible with those purposes;[125] and *justification of automated decisions*[126] – a principle that requires those engaging in some types of automated decision-making to provide information about the logic involved in that process.

V.4 Defining 'Uberprotection'

Commissioner Vestager pointed out in one of her speeches how the current industrial revolution of digitalization changes 'the very nature of human relationships' and that 'we need to have the strength in our democracies to shape the rules, so that this revolution is serving us as citizens and so that we keep building up societies', adding that 'This is why we want privacy, platform to business relationships to be fair and transparent'.[127] The Digital Markets Act legislative proposal of the European Commission aims to address some of these challenges. According to its Explanatory Memorandum, 'unfair practices and lack of contestability lead to inefficient outcomes in the digital sector in terms of higher prices, lower quality, as well as less choice and innovation to the detriment of European consumers'. The DMA proposes a series of positive obligations and prohibited *ex ante* practices for dominant intermediary online platforms, the so-called 'gatekeepers'. For example, they would be prohibited from combining personal data from different sources in the absence of valid consent, or from preventing users from un-installing any pre-installed software or app if they wish so.

Across the Atlantic, a very similar debate is taking place. The US President published in July 2021 a sweeping Executive Order dedicated to Competition policy,[128] with an agenda for a 'whole of government' approach to enforcement of antitrust laws. The overarching theme of the Order is a concern with large platforms and the accumulation of data as an aspect of

---

[122] Mireille Hildebrandt, 'Primitives of Legal Protection in the Era of Data-Driven Platforms', 2 *Geo. L. Tech. Rev.* 252 (2018), 252.
[123] Ibid., 267.
[124] Art. 5(1)(c) GDPR.
[125] Art. 5(1)(b) GDPR.
[126] Art. 13(2)(f) GDPR and Art. 14(2)(g) GDPR.
[127] Margrethe Vestager, Ditchley Foundation Annual Lecture (7 July 2018) https://ec.europa.eu/commission/commissioners/2014-2019/vestager/announcements/playing-rules-globalised-world_en accessed 9 August 2018.
[128] White House, *Executive Order on Promoting Competition in the American Economy* (9 July 2021).

market dominance.[129] The order calls on the FTC to engage in specific rulemaking to address this issue. The FTC has been preparing for a while to act in this area, after holding in the past years a series of public hearings on whether 'broad-based changes in the economy, evolving business practices, new technologies, or international developments might require adjustments to competition and consumer protection enforcement law, enforcement priorities, and policy'.[130] One of the tracks explored by the FTC dealt with 'the intersection between privacy, big data and competition'.

We call this stage of development of the intersection between data protection law and competition law, with a flavour of consumer law, the dawn of 'Uberprotection'. By 'Uberprotection' we understand the protection of the rights of individuals and their welfare as data subjects, participants to the market and consumers, afforded by concerted enforcement and facilitated by coherent policymaking of competition authorities, data protection authorities and consumer protection authorities. There are already manifestations in practice where:

- data protection law concerns are taken into account in competition adjudication;
- the different types of authorities started to talk to each other and coordinate the way they look at the common issues posed by access to data, including personal data, and market dominant positions, as well as mergers; concrete steps are taken to officially reshape competition law enforcement.

However, it is important to note that this is indeed only the beginning of this type of comprehensive protection in the EU legal framework. It remains to be seen how the identified initial manifestations will play out and whether they will effectively ensure there are no holes in this 'umbrella'-type of protection.

VI. CONCLUSION

This chapter proposed a survey analysis of competition adjudication cases at EU level and at national level within Member States of the EU in order to identify possible trends or shifts in enforcement and policymaking with regard to data protection and privacy law issues as relevant factors for the assessment of anticompetitive behaviour. By analysing the decisions of CAs and their public statements or opinions relevant for policymaking, we were able to identify three stages of the intersection between data protection law and competition law.

The first stage is characterized by a kind of isolationism – well-established competition law parameters are to be applied to competition law adjudication and whatever issues related to privacy or data protection arise, those are to be treated separately and, in any case, not included in competition adjudication decisions. This approach did not survive for long, when it became obvious that data, and especially personal data, are an asset for market players, and, sometimes, are the determining asset for an acquisition. This realization defines the second

[129] S. Gray, G. Zanfir-Fortuna, *What the Biden Executive Order Means for Data Protection*, Future of Privacy Forum (16 July 2021), available at https://fpf.org/blog/what-the-biden-executive-order-means-for-data-protection/ accessed 23 July 2021.

[130] Federal Trade Commission, *FTC Announces Hearings on Competition and Consumer Protection in the 21st Century*, (Press Release, 20 June 2018) https://www.ftc.gov/news-events/press-releases/2018/06/ftc-announces-hearings-competition-consumer-protection-21st accessed 9 August 2018.

stage of development that we identified. Step by step, data protection language started to creep into competition investigations, even though assessments on substance were scarce. Most importantly, this stage is characterized by an impressive body of policy reports and opinions from both CAs and DPAs. All these reports and opinions pushed for recognizing the need to better understand and apply the intersection between data protection law and competition law, to which eventually consumer protection law was added.

Finally, the last stage is the result of a transition from policy declarations to action: enforcement cases, legislation action and executive action. The CFO's abuse of dominance investigation against Facebook is perhaps the most representative manifestation of this new stage. That case, along with the recent legislative changes in Germany and the legislative proposal of the Digital Markets Act at EU level, show how privacy and data protection concerns started to matter in competition investigations and policy. It is also important to mention that this fundamental shift is not only playing out in the EU, with the US taking serious action in the same direction. Developments in Japan[131] and Australia[132] in the past years are also relevant.

We think that the near future will bring more and more this 'Uberprotection' in action, at least in the EU. It remains to be seen whether other jurisdictions will follow suit. However, probably this is not going to be the last stage of development of the intersection between competition law and data protection law, which right now is focused on privacy concerns. As it is already clear in the EU legal framework, data protection rules cover more than just privacy.[133] It is likely that soon other concerns will permeate competition adjudication, and especially in relation with monopolies and dominant positions. As D'Cunha observed, four years after the EDPS has launched the idea of cooperation among competition law authorities, consumer protection authorities and data protection authorities, 'the debate on privacy and competition has broadened and deepened beyond notions of commercial fairness to questions of the longer-term sustainability of societal cohesion and democracy in the digital age'.[134] His observation is echoed across the Atlantic in Stucke's description of 'data-opolies' and their general effects on society:

> They can affect not only our wallets but our privacy, autonomy, democracy, and well-being. … Antitrust enforcement, while a necessary tool to prevent data-opolies and deter their abuses, is not sufficient. Antitrust enforcers must coordinate with privacy and consumer protection officials to ensure that the conditions for effective privacy competition are in place.[135]

---

[131] Y. Sagara, *Big Data Protection under Unfair Competition Prevention Act just started in Japan,* (8 July 2019), available at https://www.nakapat.gr.jp/en/legal_updates_eng/big-data-protection-under-unfair-competition-prevention-act-has-just-started-in-japan/ accessed 23 July 2021.

[132] Australian Competition and Consumer Commission, *Digital Platforms Inquiry. Final Report*, (June 2019), available at https://www.accc.gov.au/system/files/Digital%20platforms%20inquiry%20-%20final%20report.pdf accessed 23 July 2021.

[133] See EU Fundamental Rights Agency, Council of Europe and EDPS *Handbook on European Data Protection Law*, 2018 edition, p. 18 et seq.

[134] Christian D'Cunha, 'Best of frenemies? Reflections on privacy and competition four years after the EDPS Preliminary Opinion', 8(3) *IDPL*, 253–257, (2018).

[135] Maurice E. Stucke, 'Should We be Concerned about Data-opolies?', 2 *Geo. L. Tech. Rev.* 275, 323 (2018).

BIBLIOGRAPHY

Articles

Costa-Cabral, F., Lynskey, O., 'Family Ties: The Intersection Between Data Protection and Competition Law', 54 *CMLR* 11–50 (2017).
D'Cunha, C., 'Best of frenemies? Reflections on privacy and competition four years after the EDPS Preliminary Opinion', 8(3) *IDPL* 253–257 (2018).
Graef, I., Clifford, D., Valcke, P., 'Fairness and Enforcement: Bridging Competition, Data Protection and Consumer Law', forthcoming in *IDPL* (2018).
Gray, S., Zanfir-Fortuna, G., 'What the Biden Executive Order Means for Data Protection' Future of Privacy Forum Blog (2021).
Grunes, A.P. and Stucke, M.E., 'No Mistake about it: The Important Role of Antitrust in the Era of Big Data', University of Tennessee Legal Studies Research Paper No. 269 (2015).
Hildebrandt, M., 'Primitives of Legal Protection in the Era of Data-Driven Platforms', 2 *Geo. L. Tech. Rev*. 252 (2018).
Kimmel, L., Kestenbaum, J., 'What's Up with WhatsApp? A Transatlantic View on Privacy and Merger Enforcement in Digital Markets', Antitrust (2014).
Kuner, C. et al, 'When Two Worlds Collide: The Interface Between Competition Law and Data Protection, 4(4) *IDPL* (2014).
Ocello, E., Sjödin, C., and Subočs, A., 'What's Up with Merger Control in the Digital Sector? Lessons from the Facebook/WhatsApp EU Merger Case', in Competition Merger Brief, Issue 1 (2015).
Sagara, Y., 'Big Data Protection under Unfair Competition Prevention Act just started in Japan', Nakapat Blog, (2019).
Stucke, M.E., 'Should We be Concerned about Data-opolies?' 2 *Geo. L. Tech. Rev*. 275, 323 (2018).
Swire, P., *Protection Consumers: Privacy matters in antitrust analysis*, a testimony submitted to the FTC Behavioural Advertising Town hall and published by Center for American Progress, 19 October 2007.

Volumes

EU Fundamental Rights Agency, Council of Europe and EDPS *Handbook on European Data Protection Law*, 2018.
Graef, I. *Data as Essential Facility. Competition and Innovation on Online Platforms*, PhD thesis, KU Leuven Centre for IT & IP Law, Academic year 2015–2016.
OECD, *Data Driven Innovation. Big Data for Growth and Wellbeing,* 2015.

Cases

CJEU, Judgment in Case 27/76, *United Brands v. Commission*, , EU:C:1978:22.
CJEU, Judgment in Case 322/81, *NV Nederlandsche Banden Industrie Michelin v Commission*, EU:C:1983:313.
CJEU, Judgment in Case C-238/05 *Asnef-Equifax et al v. Asociación de Usuarios de Servicios Bancarios*, EU:C:2006:734.
Dissenting Statement of Commissioner Pamela Jones Harbour in the matter of Google/DoubleClick F.T.C. File No. 071-0170.
European Commission, Case M.8124 – *Microsoft/LinkedIn*.
European Commission, Case No COMP/M.4731 – *Google/DoubleClick*.
European Commission, Case No COMP/M.4854 – *TomTom/Tele Atlas*.
European Commission, Case No COMP/M.6314 – *Telefónica UK/Vodafone UK/Everything Everywhere/JV*.
European Commission, Case No COMP/M.7217 – *Facebook/Whatsapp*.
Opinion of Advocate General Geelhoed in Case C-238/05 *Asnef-Equifax et al v. Asociación de Usuarios de Servicios Bancarios*

Reports

Autorité de la concurrence and Bundeskartellamt, *Competition Law and Data* Report, 10 May 2016.
Autorité de la concurrence, *Avis n° 18-A-03 portant sur l'exploitation des données dans le secteur de la publicité sur internet*, 6 March 2018.
Autorité de la concurrence, *Opinion No 10-A-29 of 14 December 2010 on the competitive operation of online advertising*, 2010.
Australian Competition and Consumer Commission, *Digital Platforms Inquiry. Final Report*, June 2019.
Bundeskartellamt, *Case Summary: Facebook, Exploitative business terms pursuant to Section 19(1) GWB for inadequate data processing*, 6 February 2019.
Competition and Markets Authority (CMA), *The commercial use of consumer data*, June 2015.
CMA and ICO, *Competition and Data Protection in Digital Markets: A joint statement between the CMA and the ICO*, 19 May 2021.
Data Protection Commissioner of Ireland, Annual Report 2017, 27 February 2018.
EDPS, Opinion 7/2015, *Meeting the Challenges of Big Data. A call for transparency, user control, data protection by design and accountability*, 19 November 2015.
EDPS, Opinion 8/2016 on *Coherent enforcement of fundamental rights in the age of big data*, 23 September 2016.
EDPS, Preliminary Opinion on *Privacy and competitiveness in the age of Big Data: The interplay between data protection, competition law and consumer protection in the Digital Economy*, March 2014.
OECD, *Big Data: Bringing Competition Policy to the Digital Era*, 2016.
OECD, DAF/COMP(2012)22 *The Digital Economy* Report, 2012.
OECD, *Data Driven Innovation. Big Data for Growth and Wellbeing*, 2015.
World Economic Forum, *Personal Data: The Emergence of a New Asset Class* Report, 2011.

PART III

HOT TOPICS IN PRIVACY AND DATA PROTECTION

14. Privacy, data protection and the role of European Courts: Towards judicialisation and constitutionalisation of European privacy and data protection framework

Maja Brkan[1]

I. INTRODUCTION

Privacy and data protection are fields which have been, in recent years, subject to extensive 'judicialisation'[2] within Europe. Almost dormant for decades and for many years marked by underdeveloped EU legal regulation,[3] these areas have been put to the forefront of the legal and political fundamental rights discourse through flourishing jurisprudence of the highest European courts, notably the Court of Justice of the EU (CJEU) and the European Court of Human Rights (ECtHR). The annulment of the Data Retention Directive,[4] the confirmation of the right to erasure – usually designated as 'the right to be forgotten'[5] – and the invalidation of the Adequacy Decisions on the Safe Harbour Agreement[6] and on the Privacy Shield[7] have marked an era characterised by a high level of data and privacy protection in Europe that might have repercussions also on the global levels of protection. The significant impact of the courts on shaping the landscape of privacy and data protection has become even more challenging through the entry into force of the General Data Protection Regulation (GDPR)[8] and through the increased use and processing of big data, which triggers a greater legal complexity of protection than individual data.

---

[1] This chapter expresses personal views of the author and does not in any way reflect the views of the institution where she is employed.

[2] For the use of this term see, e.g., Ran Hirschl, 'The Judicialization of Politics' in Gregory A Caldeira, R Daniel Kelemen, and Keith E Whittington (eds), *The Oxford Handbook of Law and Politics* (OUP 2009).

[3] Directive 95/46/EC of the European Parliament and of the Council of 24 October 1995 on the protection of individuals with regard to the processing of personal data and on the free movement of such data [1995] OJ L 281/31.

[4] Directive 2006/24/EC of the European Parliament and of the Council of 15 March 2006 on the retention of data generated or processed in connection with the provision of publicly available electronic communications services or of public communications networks and amending Directive 2002/58/EC [2006] OJ L 105/54.

[5] Case C-131/12 *Google Spain and Google* ECLI:EU:C:2014:317.

[6] Case C-362/14 *Schrems* ECLI:EU:C:2015:650.

[7] Case C-311/18 *Facebook Ireland and Schrems* ECLI:EU:C:2020:559.

[8] Regulation (EU) 2016/679 of the European Parliament and of the Council of 27 April 2016 on the protection of natural persons with regard to the processing of personal data and on the free movement of such data, and repealing Directive 95/46/EC (General Data Protection Regulation), OJ L 119/1.

This chapter refrains from the daunting task of distinguishing the right to privacy and the right to protection of personal data, notably given the inconsistencies in the examined jurisprudence. While neither all of the EU Member States' constitutions nor the European Convention on Human Rights (ECHR) in its Article 8 consider data protection as a separate fundamental right, the Charter of Fundamental Rights of the EU (Charter or CFR) recognises the two rights as distinct under its Articles 7 and 8. Differently, the ECtHR considers data protection as a part of the fundamental right to privacy, also in the light of Convention No. 108, which protects the 'right to privacy, with regard to automatic processing of personal data'.[9] For the purposes of this chapter, the use of the terms 'privacy' and 'data protection' will follow the terminology used by different courts, without referring to a conceptual distinction between them.[10]

This chapter seeks to explore the impact that the European courts have on the application and interpretation of privacy and data protection rules and argues that these courts are the key players in setting rather high the bar of protection of the two rights in the ever more dynamic data protection and privacy landscape. In the first part, it discusses the role of the national courts of EU Member States in the fields of privacy and data protection (section II), and proceeds with examining the role of the CJEU in this field (section III). In the subsequent section, the impact of the ECtHR on privacy and data protection is analysed (section IV). In concluding remarks (section V), the chapter highlights the main findings of the analysis and points out the future challenges that these courts will need to face.

II. THE ROLE OF THE EU MEMBER STATES' COURTS

While this chapter focuses on the analysis of the role of the highest European courts for the European privacy and data protection landscape, it also seeks to offer examples portraying the role of the Member States' courts in these fields. This chapter puts forward different categories of litigation where Member States' courts play an important role, supported by examples from national case law. The choice of case law is not purported to be a systematic overview of national cases, but rather serves as an illustration of different types of functions that the

---

[9] Art 1 of the Convention No. 108 for the Protection of Individuals with regard to Automatic Processing of Personal Data, Council of Europe, Strasbourg, 28 January 1981, available on https://rm.coe.int/CoERMPublicCommonSearchServices/DisplayDCTMContent?documentId=0900001680078b37 accessed 27 October 2021.

[10] On the conceptual distinction between the two fundamental rights, see, e.g., Orla Lynskey, *The Foundations of EU Data Protection Law* (Oxford 2015), 91 et seq.; Maria Tzanou, 'Data Protection as a Fundamental Right Next to Privacy? 'Reconstructing' a not so new right', 3 *International Data Privacy Law* (2013) 2, 88–99; Gloria González Fuster, *The Emergence of Personal Data Protection as a Fundamental Right of the EU* (Springer 2014), 268 et seq.; Aidan Forde, The Conceptual Relationship between Privacy and Data Protection, 1 *Cambridge L. Rev.* (2016), 135–149. As argued elsewhere, the Luxembourg jurisprudence varies from cases distinguishing between the two rights to cases where this distinction is blurred or where the right to data protection is seen merely as a subset of the right to privacy. See Maja Brkan, 'The Court of Justice of the EU, privacy and data protection: Judge-made law as a leitmotif in fundamental rights protection' in Maja Brkan and Evangelia Psychogiopoulou (eds), *Courts, Privacy and Data Protection in the Digital Environment* (Edward Elgar 2017) 13–17. It is probable that this distinction will become more pronounced with the GDPR which builds only upon the fundamental right to data protection and not to the right to privacy, without however explaining the relationship between the two rights.

national courts have in the judicial pyramid related to privacy and data protection. Indeed, analysing the impact of the courts on privacy and data protection is impossible without situating these courts into a broader multi-level structure of fundamental rights and judicial protection. Just as the European sources for the protection of fundamental rights to privacy and personal data are multi-layered – encompassing EU Member States' constitutions, the CFR and the ECHR – so is the accompanying judicial apparatus for the safeguarding and enforcement of those rights. It should not be forgotten that the base of this apparatus features the courts of the Member States, where litigation is nascent and to which data subjects have recourse in case of breach of their rights to privacy and data protection.

The most obvious source that the Member States' courts use to adjudicate privacy and data protection disputes is EU secondary legislation. However, on the constitutional level, the national courts are faced with a multitude of legal sources: not only their national constitutions, protecting privacy and (or) personal data, but also the Charter and the ECHR. Their task of simultaneous application of several fundamental rights sources is slightly facilitated by the fact that the Charter applies whenever the Member States are 'implementing Union law' as results from the interpretation of Article 51(1) CFR in *Åkerberg Fransson.*[11] In practice this means that the application of national transposition measures of the (old) Directive 95/46 triggered also the application of the Charter. When it comes to the GDPR, national courts have to apply this legal source directly, thus opening the way for further application of the Charter. However, it is unclear whether the adoption of additional national measures explicitly authorised by the GDPR, such as acceptance of more specific provisions on processing[12] or allowing for the possibility of automated decision-making,[13] will equally fall under 'implementation' of EU law, triggering the application of the Union's fundamental rights instrument. It is submitted that this should be the case, since the same privacy and data protection standards should be applicable for the whole body of law protecting these two societal values.

From the perspective of protection of the two rights, when adjudicating in cases concerning data protection and privacy, national courts have a threefold function. First, when judging in such cases, these courts serve as a forum for an independent (private or public) enforcement of data protection rights and, in this role, complement the functions of Member States' supervisory authorities. Before the applicability of the GDPR, the role of the national courts in the field of private enforcement depended to a great extent on whether national procedural law allowed for an action that could bring together claims of different claimants.[14] While the Directive 95/46 allowed for a judicial remedy to be brought by 'every person' whose rights were breached, it did not contain a specific provision on the grouping of those claims, thus leaving data subjects without a strong incentive to bring such claims. The CJEU case law

---

[11] Case C-617/10 *Åkerberg Fransson* ECLI:EU:C:2013:105, paras 12–14.

[12] Art 6(2) GDPR.

[13] Art 22(2)(b) GDPR.

[14] For example, Austrian law allows for a collective action (*Sammelklage*) and the Belgian law allows for different types of collective redress. See, e.g., the decision of the Belgian court in the *Test-Achat* case where the court answered negatively the question of whether a company can have access to identification information of a person posting a comment on the forum of the Belgian consumer organisation. See Liège Court of Appeals, 22 October 2009, (2010) 38 R.D.T.I. 95, confirmed by Belgian Court of Cassation, no C.10.0153.F, 16 June 2011. For further analysis, see Paul De Hert, 'Courts, Privacy and Data Protection in Belgium: Fundamental rights that might as well be struck from the Constitution' in Brkan and Psychogiopoulou (n 10) 76–77.

clarifies that such grouping of claims before national courts is equally not possible under the Regulation No 44/2001,[15] the EU's private international law measure.[16] The GDPR modifies this and consequently strengthens the role of the Member States' courts in data protection litigation. Besides continuing the legacy of Directive 95/46 and offering each data subject the right to an effective judicial remedy to enforce his or her rights stemming from its provisions,[17] the GDPR also provides for a possibility of representative claims brought by a non-profit body, organisation or association, through which these bodies would exercise the data subject's right to an effective judicial remedy.[18] It could be expected that, through massive litigation relying on this provision, Member State courts could potentially become the centre of data protection litigation and thus bear an increasing responsibility in this domain, notably because representative claims will encompass the exercise of the right of data subjects to receive compensation for damage caused by data protection breaches.[19] While the GDPR gives the data subject the right to give a mandate to a representative body to enforce his or her claims, Member States can take a further step and allow for such claims before the courts also without a specific mandate by the data subject.[20]

Moreover, according to the GDPR, the jurisdictions of courts and supervisory authorities are not mutually exclusive as the data subject has 'the right to an effective judicial remedy' that can be exercised 'without prejudice to any available administrative or non-judicial remedy'.[21] With regard to private enforcement, it is to be noted that the GDPR expressly provides for the possibility of data subjects to request material and non-material damage from the controller or processor causing this damage (Art 82(1)), giving jurisdiction to adjudicate on these claims either to courts of the Member State of the establishment of the controller or, alternatively, to the courts of the Member State of data subject's habitual residence, except if a controller is a public authority (Art 79(2)). The complementary nature of claims before the courts or supervisory authorities is aimed at effective enforcement of the rights to privacy and data protection from the viewpoint of data subjects.

Second, national courts also exercise control over decisions of national supervisory authorities and have, in that capacity, a more reactive and monitoring role, ensuring not only the accuracy of such decisions, but also, to the extent possible, unity on legal issues in national practice on privacy and data protection. Examples of cases issued under Article 28 of Directive 95/46, the provision that gave data subjects a simple right to appeal the decision of a national supervisory authority, can be found in national case law. Cases falling under the courts' monitoring power over supervisory authorities are, for example, national Finnish proceedings in the *Satamedia* case where the national courts were asked to check the accuracy of the national authority's refusal to issue a decision on sharing of tax data (court action filed by the

---

[15] Council Regulation (EC) No 44/2001 of 22 December 2000 on jurisdiction and the recognition and enforcement of judgments in civil and commercial matters (OJ 2001 L 12, p. 1).

[16] Case C-498/16, *Schrems* ECLI:EU:C:2018:37, paras 42–49.

[17] Art 79 GDPR.

[18] Art 80 GDPR. This provision expressly refers to the exercise of the right to an effective judicial remedy in Art 79 GDPR.

[19] Art 80(1) GDPR.

[20] Art 80(2) GDPR.

[21] Art 79(1) GDPR.

Finnish Data Protection Ombudsman),[22] or, comparably, national proceedings in the *Schrems* case where the Irish High Court was asked to assess the legality of the Irish Data Protection Commissioner's rejection of Schrems' complaint (court action filed by the data subject).[23]

In this capacity, national courts acted as a judicial instance having the competence to control, monitor and alter the decision of a national supervisory authority, taking from the latter the authority of a final decision in the case. This power of control over administrative decisions is expressly foreseen also in the GDPR. The GDPR gives both the data subject and the data controller[24] an express right 'to an effective judicial remedy against a legally binding decision of a supervisory authority'.[25] Not only are the data subjects and controllers legally empowered to challenge the decisions of supervisory authorities, but also their lack of reaction within the prescribed time-limits.[26] The national courts are therefore endowed with a powerful position of control over the decisions of national supervisory authorities and can have an important impact on the development, interpretation and enforcement of data protection law.

Third, the courts in EU Member States can also represent a forum for raising the issue of validity of EU acts. This role of the courts is not privacy-specific. An example are the national proceedings in the *Facebook Ireland and Schrems* case,[27] brought by the Irish Data Protection Commissioner, concerning the validity of the Commission Decision on standard contractual clauses[28] and the Commission Decision on the adequacy of the EU-US Privacy Shield.[29] Within such proceedings, the national courts are obliged to refer the preliminary question on validity of an EU act to the CJEU, in accordance with the *Foto Frost*[30] doctrine.[31] Therefore, the national proceedings giving rise to such a preliminary reference are complementary to the direct actions for annulment pursuant to Article 263 TFEU,[32] and the fields of privacy and data protection are no exception in this regard.[33]

While ordinary national courts usually deal with adjudication of cases, the higher national courts (constitutional and supreme courts) have two additional functions. On the one hand, they represent a forum and a source for a potential policy change in privacy and data protection.

---

[22] See the Finnish Supreme Administrative Court, judgment KHO 2009:82: *Tietosuojavaltuutettu v Satakunnan Markkinapörssi Oy ja Satamedia Oy,* 23 September 2009 and the CJEU case C-73/07 *Satakunnan Markkinapörssi and Satamedia.*

[23] Case C-362/14 *Schrems*, paras 28–30.

[24] The exact wording of Art 78(1) reads that this right appertains to 'each natural or legal person'.

[25] Art 78(1) GDPR.

[26] Art 78(2) GDPR.

[27] Case C-311/18 *Facebook Ireland and Schrems*.

[28] Commission Decision 2010/87/EU of 5 February 2010 on standard contractual clauses for the transfer of personal data to processors established in third countries under Directive 95/46, OJ L 39/5, as amended by Commission Implementing Decision (EU) 2016/2297 of 16 December 2016, OJ L 344/100.

[29] Commission Implementing Decision (EU) 2016/1250 of 12 July 2016 pursuant to Directive 95/46 on the adequacy of the protection provided by the EU-US Privacy Shield, OJ L 207/1.

[30] Case 314/85 *Foto-Frost* ECLI:EU:C:1987:452.

[31] For an early comment on the *Foto-Frost* case, see, e.g., Gerhard Bebr, 'The Reinforcement of the Constitutional Review of Community Acts Under Article 177 EEC Treaty (Case 314/85 and 133 to 136/85)' (1988), 25(4) *Common Market Law Review* 667–691.

[32] On differences between preliminary reference on validity and an action for annulment see, e.g., Koen Lenaerts, Ignace Maselis, Kathleen Gutman, *EU Procedural Law* (Oxford 2014), 468–469.

[33] A further question, which exceeds the scope of this chapter, is whether the role of the national courts regarding the validity of EU acts and related preliminary reference procedures could depend on the national rules of standing that might or might not allow direct validity actions on the national level.

On the other hand, they are active interlocutors in judicial dialogue with other, non-national, courts. The question of judicial dialogue in the multi-level judicial structure is further discussed in the next part of this chapter. It is to be added, however, that the judicial dialogue does not only take place between the highest national and European courts, but is supposed to be exercised also among ordinary courts themselves. The current GDPR expressly encourages such judicial dialogue by prescribing, in its Article 81, that a Member State court should contact a court in another Member State in order to verify whether the latter is adjudicating in proceedings 'concerning the same subject matter as regards processing by the same controller or processor'. If there are parallel proceedings before courts in different Member States, the court that was not first seized may either suspend its proceedings[34] or even decline jurisdiction if it is a court of first instance.[35] Putting this provision in practice will require active communication between Member States' courts, most likely through judicial networks,[36] which will enable these courts to be updated about the existence and parties to the claim.

III. THE ROLE OF THE CJEU IN PRIVACY AND DATA PROTECTION

III.1 Multi-level Judicial Protection and Judicial Dialogue between the CJEU and National Courts

Within the multi-layered European judicial apparatus, attached to the multi-level sources of fundamental rights protection, the CJEU, when deciding in constitutionally relevant cases involving fundamental rights to privacy and data protection as guaranteed in Articles 7 and 8 CFR, exercises its role as guardian of high-level protection of these fundamental rights. In data privacy litigation, the CJEU has affirmed time and again not only the constitutional importance of the fundamental rights to privacy and data protection, but also the need to strengthen the protection of these rights either through the interpretation of secondary legislation in conformity with these rights[37] or through the assessment of compatibility of EU measures with these rights and hence the validity of the former.[38] Regardless of the procedural venue chosen by the parties or national courts – be it a preliminary reference procedure on interpretation or on validity of EU norms or a direct action for annulment of EU secondary legislation – the CJEU has consistently maintained a high standard of fundamental rights protection of European data subjects.

---

[34] Art 81(2) GDPR.

[35] Art 81(3) GDPR.

[36] More generally on dialogues within European judicial networks see Monica Claes and Maartje de Visser, 'Are You Networked Yet? On Dialogues in European Judicial Networks' (2012) 8(2) *Utrecht Law Review* 100–114.

[37] Joined Cases C-465/00, C-138/01 and C-139/01 *Österreichischer Rundfunk and others* ECLI:EU:C:2003:294, para 68; Case C-131/12 *Google Spain and Google*, para 68; Joined Cases C-141/12 and C-372/12 *YS and others* ECLI:EU:C:2014:2081, para 54; Case C-212/13 *Ryneš* ECLI:EU:C:2014:2428, para 29: Case C-398/15 *Manni* ECLI:EU:C:2017:197, para 39.

[38] Joined Cases C-92/09 and C-93/09 *Volker und Markus Schecke and Eifert* ECLI:EU:C:2010:662; Case C-293/12 and C-594/12 *Digital Rights Ireland and Seitlinger and Others* ECLI:EU:C:2014:238; Case C-362/14 *Schrems*; Case C-311/18 *Facebook Ireland and Schrems*.

The CJEU is thus an important driver of a policy reform which is often exercised in partnership with the (highest) national courts that refer questions for preliminary ruling to the CJEU. An example of such partnership with the CJEU is the controversial litigation on data retention laws in several Member States taking place, among others, in Austria, Bulgaria, Czech Republic, Cyprus, Germany, Ireland and Romania[39] that ultimately led to the annulment of the Data Retention Directive by the CJEU[40] instigated by preliminary references from Irish and Austrian courts. This pan-European litigation, loaded with strategic intent of the claimants focusing on invalidation of the said directive, had a significant impact not only on EU policy makers,[41] but also on national authorities and controllers who remained unsure as to how to apply national data retention laws.[42] The recent Grand Chamber judgments in *La Quadrature du Net and Others*[43] and *Prokuratuur*[44] brought some clarity in this regard.

Moreover, the data retention legislation illustrates well the reach and importance of judicial dialogue between European courts, notably between the highest national judicial authorities and the CJEU.[45] For example, in the aftermath of the judgment of the CJEU annulling the Data Retention Directive, the Belgian Constitutional Court annulled the Belgian Act on Electronic Communications;[46] the Constitutional Law Committee of the Finnish Parliament significantly revised the Finnish Information Society Code insofar as it was related to data retention[47] and the Slovak Constitutional Court invalidated pertinent data retention provisions of Slovak acts transposing the Data Retention Directive.[48] There are other courts that however did not take part in this dialogue by not responding to the invalidation of the Data Retention Directive by the CJEU, such as for example the Italian judiciary.[49] Moreover, the Swedish and the UK courts in *Tele2 Sverige AB and Watson et al.* asked for guidance as to how to apply the national

---

[39] For an overview, see Eleni Kosta, 'The Way to Luxembourg: National Court Decisions on the Compatibility of the Data Retention Directive with the Rights to Privacy and Data Protection' (2013) 10(3) *SCRIPTed* 339–363.

[40] Joined Cases C-293/12 and C-594/12 *Digital Rights Ireland* and *Seitlinger and Others*.

[41] After the invalidation of the Data Retention Directive by the CJEU, the Commission announced that it will not take initiative for new legislation on data retention, but rather monitor developments at national level; after a period of reflection, discussions on a more targeted approach to data retention emerged; see, e.g., European Parliament document 'Data Retention for the Purposes of Prevention, Investigation and Prosecution of Crime' https://www.europarl.europa.eu/legislative-train/theme-area-of-justice-and-fundamental-rights/file-data-retention-directive accessed 28 October 2021.

[42] See Joined Cases C-203/15 and C-698/15 *Tele2 Sverige AB and Watson et al.* ECLI:EU:C:2016:970.

[43] Joined Cases C-511/18, C-512/18 and C-520/18 *La Quadrature du Net and Others* ECLI:EU:C:2020:791.

[44] Case C-746/18 *Prokuratuur* ECLI:EU:C:2021:152.

[45] On judicial dialogues, see Anthony Arnull, 'Judicial Dialogue in the European Union' in Julie Dickson and Pavlos Eleftheriadis, *Philosophical Foundations of European Union Law* (Oxford 2012) 109–133; Claes and Visser (n 36), 100–114; Anne-Marie Slaughter, 'Judicial Globalization' (2000) 40 *Virginia Journal of International Law* 1103–1124; Elaine Mak, *Judicial Decision-Making in a Globalised World: A Comparative Analysis of the Changing Practices of Western Highest Courts* (Hart 2013); Michal Bobek, *Comparative Reasoning in European Supreme Courts* (OUP 2013).

[46] Belgian Constitutional Court, judgment No. 84/2015, 11 June 2015.

[47] See Opinion 18/2002 of the Constitutional Law Committee of the Finnish Parliament.

[48] Judgment of Slovak Constitutional Court, PL. ÚS 10/2014, 29 April 2015.

[49] Claudio Di Cocco and Giovanni Sartor, 'Courts, privacy and data protection in Italy: Implied constitutional rights' in Maja Brkan and Evangelia Psychogiopoulou (eds), *Courts, Privacy and Data Protection in the Digital Environment* (Edward Elgar 2017) 158.

legislation that remained in force after the annulment of the contested directive.[50] Similarly, in the abovementioned cases *La Quadrature du Net and Others*,[51] the French Council of State and the Belgian Constitutional Court asked for further clarifications regarding data retention in the electronic communications sector, and in the case *Prokuratuur*,[52] the Estonian Supreme Court posed questions for preliminary ruling regarding comparable national legislation. Therefore, the data retention saga is a salient example of an ongoing dialogue between the national highest courts themselves, between these courts and the CJEU and even between the CJEU and the ECtHR. While for example the ECtHR referred to *Digital Rights Ireland and Seitlinger*[53] in its judgment in *Szabó and Vissy*,[54] the CJEU in the former judgment equally invoked ECtHR jurisprudence,[55] therefore working towards a dialogue between the two courts. We address the issue of dialogue between the CJEU and the ECtHR in the next part of this chapter.

III.2 Constitutionalisation of Privacy and Data Protection

The trend of permanent reinforcing of protection of privacy and personal data that can be recognised in numerous CJEU cases, for example *Digital Rights Ireland*,[56] *Schrems*[57] and *Google Spain*,[58] is persisting also in its recent judgments, such as *Tele2 Sverige and Watson*,[59]

---

[50] See Joined Cases C-203/15 and C-698/15 *Tele2 Sverige AB and Watson et al.* The Irish High Court delivered its judgment following the CJEU's judgment on 3 October 2017, https://dataprotection.ie/documents/judgements/DPCvFBSchrems.pdf accessed 28 October 2021. Another preliminary reference from a Greek court was referred to the CJEU, but was withdrawn after the *Tele2 and Watson* judgment; see order in Case C-475/16, *Criminal proceedings against K.*, ECLI:EU:C:2017:630.

[51] Case C-511/18 *La Quadrature du Net and Others.*

[52] Case C-746/18 *Prokuratuur.*

[53] Joined Cases C-293/12 and C-594/12 *Digital Rights Ireland and Seitlinger and Others.*

[54] *Szabó and Vissy v Hungary* App no 37138/14 (ECtHR, 12 January 2016), paras 68 and 70. See Evangelia Psychogiopoulou, 'The European Court of Human Rights, privacy and data protection in the digital era' in Brkan and Psychogiopoulou (n 10), 62.

[55] *Digital Rights Ireland*, paras 35, 47, 54–55. The CJEU referred, among others, to judgments in *Leander v Sweden* App no 9248/81 (ECtHR, 26 March 1987), para 48; *Rotaru v Romania* App no 28341/95 (ECtHR, 4 May 2000), para 46; and *S. and Marper v the UK* App nos 30562/04 and 30566/04 (ECtHR, 4 December 2008), para 102.

[56] Joined Cases C-293/12 and C-594/12 *Digital Rights Ireland.* On the constitutional significance of this judgment, see Orla Lynskey, 'The Data Retention Directive is incompatible with the rights to privacy and data protection and is invalid in its entirety: Digital Rights Ireland' (2014) 51(6) *Common Market Law Review* 1789–1811.

[57] Case C-362/14 *Schrems.* For a commentary, see, e.g., Loïc Azoulai and Marijn van der Sluis, 'Institutionalizing Personal Data Protection in Times of Global Institutional Distrust: Schrems' (2016) 53(5) *Common Market Law Review* 1343–1371.

[58] Case C-131/12 *Google Spain and Google.* Hijmans stresses that *Google Spain* fits within the 'general tendency…to attach great importance to the effective protection of fundamental rights'; Hielke Hijmans, 'Evidence of Effective Data Protection: Case C-131/12 Google v. Agencia Española de Protectión de Datos (AEPD) and Mario Costeja Gonzalez, Judgment of 13 May 2014' (2014) 21(3) *Maastricht Journal of European and Comparative Law* 556. For an analysis of an (international) constitutional impact of the *Google Spain* case, see Krystyna Kowalik-Bańczyk, 'International Constitutionalisation of Protection of Privacy on the Internet: The Google Case Example', in Andrzej Jakubowski and Karolina Wierczyńska, *Fragmentation vs the Constitutionalisation of International Law: A Practical Inquiry* (Routledge 2016), 106-117.

[59] Joined Cases C-203/15 and C-698/15 *Tele2 Sverige AB and Watson et al.* For a commentary, see, e.g., Aqilah Sandhu, 'Die Tele2-Entscheidung des EuGH zur Vorratsdatenspeicherung in den

Breyer,[60] *Nowak*,[61] as well as *Facebook Ireland and Schrems*.[62] Regardless of whether the fundamental rights are used as a benchmark to assess compatibility of EU secondary legislation, such as in *Digital Rights Ireland, Schrems* or *Facebook Ireland and Schrems*, whether they serve as values competing with other interests as in *Google Spain* or whether they impact the scope of national legislation through conform interpretation as in *Tele2 Sverige and Watson*, *La Quadrature du Net and Others* or *Prokuratuur*, these cases, through a strong fundamental rights discourse, strengthen the value of privacy and data protection as fundamental rights within the EU.[63] Furthermore, in *Breyer*, the main question brought to the attention of the CJEU was whether a dynamic IP address constitutes personal data within the meaning of EU secondary legislation on data protection.[64] Even though in its judgment the CJEU did not expressly consider the fundamental rights argument, it is submitted that the decision nevertheless had an impact on the scope of application of the fundamental right of data protection. Indeed, as Muir correctly argues, EU secondary legislation on data protection 'gives specific expression' to data protection as a fundamental right,[65] meaning that the CJEU's interpretation of the scope of application of EU secondary legislation in *Breyer*, that is, the inclusion of a dynamic IP address within the notion of personal data, influences also the scope of the corresponding fundamental right to data protection. Similarly, in *Nowak*, the broadening of the scope of the notion of 'personal data' to exam answers and examiner's comments[66] impacts the scope of application of this fundamental right. The academic literature widely recognises the trend of constitutionalisation of EU data protection and privacy regime.[67]

Mitgliedstaaten und ihre Auswirkungen auf die Rechtslage in Deutschland und in der Europäischen Union' (2017) *Europarecht* 453-469; Will R Mbioh, 'Post-och Telestyrelsen and Watson and the Investigatory Powers Act 2016' (2017) 3 *European Data Protection Law Review* 273–282; Xavier Tracol, 'The Judgment of the Grand Chamber dated 21 December 2016 in the Two Joint Tele2 Sverige and Watson Cases: The need for a harmonised legal framework on the retention of data at EU level' (2017) *Computer Law Review International* 1–12.

[60] Case C-582/14 *Breyer* ECLI:EU:C:2016:779.

[61] Case C-434/16 *Nowak* ECLI:EU:C:2017:994.

[62] Case C-311/18 *Facebook Ireland and Schrems*.

[63] Fabbrini points out, with regard to *Digital Rights Ireland* case, that the Court's decision enshrines 'the idea that core constitutional protections of privacy rights must be strengthened...in an era of increasing digitalization'; Federico Fabbrini, 'Human Rights in the Digital Age: The European Court of Justice Ruling in the Data Retention Case and Its Lessons for Privacy and Surveillance in the United States' (2015) 28 *Harv. Hum. Rts. J.* 65, 67. Hijmans points out that the Court 'plays a key role in the interpretation of the rights to privacy and data protection'; Hielke Hijmans, *The European Union as Guardian of Internet Privacy: The Story of Art 16 TFEU* (Springer 2016), 196. Kuner states that the Court, in *Google Spain*, 'concentrated on affirming the fundamental right to data protection'; Christopher Kuner, 'Google Spain in the EU and International Context' (2015) 22(1) *Maastricht Journal of European and Comparative Law* 163. Tzanou considers that the 'judgments in *Digital Rights Ireland, Google Spain* and *Schrems* demonstrate that the Court's data protection jurisprudence has reached its maturity'; Maria Tzanou, *The Fundamental Right to Data Protection: Normative Value in the Context of Counter-Terrorism Surveillance* (Hart 2017), 62. For the analysis of the gradual use of data protection and privacy as fundamental rights by the CJEU, see González Fuster (n 10), 234 et seq.

[64] *Breyer*, para 31.

[65] Elise Muir, 'The Fundamental Rights Implications of EU Legislation: Some Constitutional Challenges' (2014) 51 *Common Market Law Review* 226.

[66] *Nowak*, para 62.

[67] On constitutionalisation of data protection and privacy see Joseph A Cannataci and Jeanne Pia Mifsud-Bonnici, 'Data Protection Comes of Age: The Data Protection Clauses in the European

However, the trend of constitutionalisation of these fields does not stem merely from the CJEU guaranteeing an ever enhanced level of protection of privacy and personal data as fundamental rights, but also from the interpretation of certain concepts, such as the notion of essence of fundamental rights from Article 52(1) CFR, bearing an importance for the general fundamental rights doctrine. Even though there was a general agreement among the drafters of the Charter on including the notion of essence into its text,[68] the exact meaning of this concept was far from clear and it was precisely data privacy litigation that gave the CJEU an opportunity for its interpretation and clarification. While the CJEU examined whether there has been a breach of essence of the fundamental right to privacy already in *Digital Rights Ireland,*[69] the Court did not find a breach of its essence since the contested Data Retention Directive did not permit anyone to obtain information on the *content* of electronic communication.[70] This reasoning was confirmed in *Tele2 Sverige*, a continuation of the data retention saga where the CJEU concluded that national legislation allowing for an indiscriminate retention of traffic and location data and the access of the competent national authorities to the retained data is precluded by EU law.[71] As previously, a breach of essence was not found regarding both fundamental rights to privacy and data protection.[72]

Differently, in *Schrems*,[73] the first case where a breach of the essence of the fundamental right to privacy and of the fundamental right to effective judicial protection was found, the controllers had general access to the *content* of electronic communication of data subjects.[74] This led the Irish High Court in *Facebook Ireland and Schrems* to include the question on the notion of essence in its reference for a preliminary ruling and to specifically ask the CJEU whether the level of data protection offered by the US through the Privacy Shield respects the essence of the fundamental right to an effective remedy enshrined in Article 47 of the Charter.[75] The CJEU followed its decision from the first *Schrems*[76] case and similarly ruled that a complete absence of legal remedies, not giving an individual any possibility to request access, rectification or erasure of data 'does not respect the essence of the fundamental right to effective judicial protection' from Article 47 of the Charter.[77]

Constitutional Treaty' (2005) 14 *Information and Communications Technology Law* 1, 5–15; Paul De Hert and Serge Gutwirth, 'Data Protection in the Case Law of Strasbourg and Luxemburg: Constitutionalisation in Action', in Serge Gutwirth et al., *Reinventing Data Protection?* (Springer 2009), 3–44; Nadezhda Purtova, *Property Rights in Personal Data: A European perspective* (BOXPress 2011), 214–215. From a comparative perspective, for constitutionalisation of privacy in English law, see, e.g., Alison L Young, 'The Human Rights Act 1998, Horizontality and the Constitutionalisation of Private Law' in Katja S Ziegler and Peter Huber, *Current Problems in the Protection of Human Rights: Perspectives from Germany and the UK* (Hart 2013), 82 et seq.

[68] Jürgen Meyer (ed), *Charta der Grundrechte der Europäischen Union* (Nomos 2011) 670; Oliver Dörr, Rainer Grote, Thilo Marauhn (eds), *EMRK/GG: Konkordanzkommentar zum europäischen und deutschen Grundrechtsschutz* (Mohr Siebeck 2006) 370.

[69] Joined Cases C-293/12 and C-594/12 *Digital Rights Ireland.*

[70] Ibid., para 39.

[71] Case C-203/15 *Tele2 Sverige*, para 134.

[72] Ibid., para 101.

[73] Case C-362/14 *Schrems*.

[74] Ibid., para 94.

[75] Case C-311/18 *Facebook Ireland and Schrems*, para 68.

[76] *Schrems,* para 59.

[77] Case C-311/18 *Facebook Ireland and Schrems*, para 187.

In consequence, the CJEU through its case law enshrining the notion of essence undoubtedly contributed to the interpretation of this notion and hence to the general fundamental rights doctrine in the EU.[78] The Court seemed to have confirmed that every fundamental right possesses an inalienable core which can, under no circumstances, be restricted or infringed.[79] Therefore, the Court seems to have, at least implicitly, distinguished between the breach of essence of a fundamental right (which cannot be justified), and an ordinary or particularly serious breach (for which justifications are possible).[80]

Moreover, voices have been expressed in the academic debate that the CJEU, when performing the balancing exercise between data privacy and other fundamental rights or interests, in its zealous efforts to ensure a high level of privacy and data protection, gave in a principled way more weight to these two fundamental rights in comparison to other fundamental rights and interests.[81] Even though this view is not shared by all scholars,[82] it should be pointed out that, in *Google Spain*,[83] the CJEU ruled that the fundamental rights to privacy and data protection 'override, as a rule' the economic interests of the controller and the freedom of information of the general public.[84] While it can indeed be argued that the CJEU created a hierarchy between different rights and interests, the Court also pointed out that, before a definitive conclusion on whether privacy and data protection prevail, 'the role played by the data subject in public life'

---

[78] On the analysis of the notion of essence relating to data protection and privacy, see Tuomas Ojanen, 'Making the Essence of Fundamental Rights Real: The Court of Justice of the European Union Clarifies the Structure of Fundamental Rights under the Charter: ECJ 6 October 2015, Case C-362/14, Maximillian Schrems v Data Protection Commissioner' (2016) 12(2) *European Constitutional Law Review* 326; Tzanou (n 63), 95–96. More generally, see Von Bogdandy et al., 'Reverse Solange–Protecting the essence of fundamental rights against EU Member States' (2012) 49 *CML Rev* 489–519; Maja Brkan, 'The Concept of Essence of Fundamental Rights in the EU Legal Order: Peeling the Onion to its Core' (2018) 14(2) *European Constitutional Law Review* 332.

[79] Some authors refer to that as an 'extreme infringement' of a fundamental right; see Julian Rivers, 'Proportionality and Variable Intensity of Review' (2006) 65(1) *The Cambridge Law Journal* 184.

[80] Regarding the conceptual distinction between the breach of essence and (particularly serious) breach of a fundamental rights, see Brkan (n 78).

[81] See, in this sense, Eleni Frantziou, 'Further Developments in the Right to be Forgotten: The European Court of Justice's Judgment in Case C-131/12, Google Spain, SL, Google Inc v Agencia Espanola de Proteccion de Datos' (2014) 14(4) *Human Rights Law Review* 766; Édouard Cruysmans and Alain Strowel, 'Un droit à l'oubli face aux moteurs de recherche: droit applicable et responsabilité pour le référencement de données "inadéquates, non pertinentes ou excessives"' (2014) *Journal des tribunaux* 459; Steve Peers, 'The CJEU's Google Spain judgment: failing to balance privacy and freedom of expression' (EU Law Analysis, 13 May 2014), http://eulawanalysis.blogspot.nl/2014/05/the-cjeus-google-spain-judgment-failing.html accessed 28 October 2021; Stefan Kulk and Frederik Zuiderveen Borgesius, 'Google Spain v. González: Did the Court Forget About Freedom of Expression?' (2014) 3 *European Journal of Risk Regulation*; Bilyana Petkova, 'Towards an Internal Hierarchy of Values in the EU Legal Order: Balancing the Freedom of Speech and Data Privacy' (2016) 23(3) *Maastricht Journal of European and Comparative Law* 421; Maja Brkan, 'The Unstoppable Expansion of EU Fundamental Right to Data Protection: Little Shop of Horrors?' (2016) 23(5) *Maastricht Journal of European and Comparative Law* 825–827.

[82] For example, Pau De Hert and Vagelis Papakonstantinou, 'Google Spain: Addressing Critiques and Misunderstandings One Year Later' (2015) 22(4) *Maastricht Journal of European and Comparative Law* 633, consider that the Court simply applied the principle of proportionality in the framework of which the Court 'balanced the potential consequences of this type of processing for individuals' rights against the search engines' financial interests and decided in favour of the former'.

[83] Case C-131/12 *Google Spain and Google*.

[84] Ibid., paras 97 and 99.

should be taken into account, notably if it justifies the 'interest of the general public' in having 'access to the information in question'.[85] The argument of hierarchy between different rights and interests is therefore potentially weakened by the obligation of taking into account these additional factors that seem to prevent privacy to prevail automatically. In balancing between sensitive data published online and freedom of information of internet users, the CJEU seems to have adopted a slightly more nuanced approach. In the case *GC and Others (De-referencing of sensitive data)*,[86] the CJEU ruled that websites containing sensitive data may be included among the search results only if that information is 'strictly necessary for protecting the freedom of information of internet users potentially interested in accessing that web page'.[87] The standard of 'strict necessity' seems to suggest that the balancing should be performed, but that the scale is slightly tilted towards data protection.

However, in *Manni*,[88] the CJEU does not seem to follow the reasoning of a prevailing privacy. Mr Manni requested deletion of information on insolvency of his company from the companies register, raising the questions whether an individual should be able to make such a request and whether the authority in charge of the register should, on a case-by-case basis, limit access to the contested data.[89] The CJEU pointed out that the balancing has to take into account 'the data subject's particular situation'[90] and that a limited access to these data is possible only on the basis of an objective and exceptional[91] justification. Indeed, the legal and factual circumstances in *Manni* differ considerably from the ones in *Google Spain* in that the controller is a public authority vested with official powers of keeping the register and that the contested data appears in such public register.[92] Nevertheless, *Manni* demonstrates that such disparate circumstances may alter the outcome of a balancing exercise and hence confirms that the hypothesis of pre-established ranking of values should not necessarily be endorsed.

Furthermore, in the case *Google (Territorial scope of de-referencing)*,[93] the CJEU seems to take a more cautious approach towards ensuring a high level of data protection by not endorsing the request for global de-referencing on all versions of the Google search engine.[94] Rather, according to the Court, that obligation extends to the versions of a search engine appertaining to all Member States.[95] The Court therefore seems to have shown a certain degree of sensitivity towards a broad criticism of its earlier *Google Spain* decision, which led, in the view of

---

85 Ibid., para 99.

86 Case C-136/17 *GC and Others (De-referencing of sensitive data)* ECLI:EU:C:2019:773.

87 Ibid., para 68.

88 Case C-398/15 *Manni*.

89 Ibid., para 30. On the case and more generally data in public registers see Stefan Kulk and Frederik Zuiderveen Borgesius, 'Privacy, Freedom of Expression and the Right to Be Forgotten in Europe', in Evan Selinger, Jules Polonetsky, Omer Tene (eds), *The Cambridge Handbook of Consumer Privacy* (Cambridge 2018), 315 et seq.

90 *Manni*, para 47.

91 *Manni*, paras 47, 60, 63, 64.

92 See also in this sense Eike Michael Frenzel, 'Facilitating the Flow of Public Information: The CJEU in Favour of Distinctive Rule/Exception Regulations in Member States Journal Article' (2017) 3(2) *European Data Protection Law Review* 286.

93 C-507/17 *Google (Territorial scope of de-referencing)* ECLI:EU:C:2019:772.

94 Ibid., paras 53–65.

95 Ibid., para 73.

many authors, to fears about potential internet censorship.[96] Yet, the case *Google (Territorial scope of de-referencing)* expressly allows a national supervisory or judicial authority to order global de-referencing should the circumstances so require.[97] In that sense, the Court allows for a higher level of protection of fundamental rights in accordance with Article 53 of the Charter and its *Melloni*[98] jurisprudence.[99]

From the constitutional perspective, cases that ought to be mentioned are also those confirming the necessity of conform interpretation of national legislation and EU secondary data protection legislation with fundamental rights. The importance of such conform interpretation of national legislation was pointed out for example in *Lindqvist* where a private individual posted online private information about her colleagues.[100] Deciding that such activity constitutes processing of personal data and pointing out that the EU secondary legislation does not bring about a conflict with freedom of expression or other rights, the CJEU urged the national court to interpret national legislation implementing the EU legislation in a way 'to ensure a fair balance between the rights and interests in question, including the fundamental rights'.[101] In other cases, such as *Österreichischer Rundfunk*[102] and *YS*,[103] the Luxembourg court pointed out the importance of interpretation of the EU secondary legislation with fundamental rights. For example, in *Österreichischer Rundfunk*, where the CJEU dealt with the question of whether this legislation stands in a way of a national rule requiring national bodies to collect data on their employees if their income exceeds a certain threshold, this Court not only provided for a fully-fledged analysis of interference with fundamental right to privacy, but also pointed out the need of interpretation of EU legislation with fundamental rights.[104]

In other cases, namely *Ryneš*,[105] *Schecke*[106] and *IPI*,[107] the CJEU established a broad application of secondary rules on data protection due to restrictive interpretation of exceptions. Obviously, not all cases relevant for the field of data protection are of constitutional relevance, such as the second *Schrems* case on the question of determination of (civil) jurisdiction in data protection related cases,[108] or the *Tele2 (Netherlands)* case allowing telecom companies

---

[96] The academic sources containing such criticism are too numerous to be cited exhaustively. See, e.g., Tika Lubis, 'The Ruling of Google Spain Case: 'The Right to Be Forgotten' or 'The Right to Censorship'?' (November 25, 2015), available at https://ssrn.com/abstract=2872874 or http://dx.doi.org/10.2139/ssrn.2872874 accessed 28 October 2021; Joseph Jones, 'Control-alter-delete: the "right to be forgotten"' (2014) *European Intellectual Property Review* 599–600. Compare Irma Spahiu, 'Case Note: Google Spain and Google' (2015) 21(4) *European Public Law* 696, 700, 701. *Contra* Jef Ausloos, *The Right to Erasure in EU Data Protection Law* (Oxford 2020), 400, who argues that the claims of censorship 'seem absurdly overblown'.

[97] *Google (Territorial scope of de-referencing)*, para 72.

[98] Case C-399/11 *Melloni* EU:C:2013:107, para 60.

[99] *Google (Territorial scope of de-referencing)*, para 72.

[100] Case C-101/01 *Lindqvist* ECLI:EU:C:2003:596.

[101] Ibid., paras 87, 90.

[102] Joined Cases C-465/00, C-138/01 and C-139/01 *Österreichischer Rundfunk and others* ECLI:EU:C:2003:294.

[103] Joined Cases C-141/12 and C-372/12 *YS and others* ECLI:EU:C:2014:2081.

[104] *Österreichischer Rundfunk*, para 68.

[105] Case C-212/13 *Ryneš* ECLI:EU:C:2014:2428.

[106] Joined Cases C-92/09 and C-93/09 *Volker und Markus Schecke and Eifert* ECLI:EU:C:2010:662.

[107] Case C-473/12 *IPI* ECLI:EU:C:2013:715.

[108] C-498/16 *Schrems*.

to publish users' personal data in a second directory where the user gave consent for inclusion in the first directory, even though data is transferred from one to another EU Member State.[109]

IV. THE ROLE OF THE ECTHR IN PRIVACY AND DATA PROTECTION

In its abundant jurisprudence on privacy, including data protection, the ECtHR, on the one hand, acts as an interpretative authority, filling the notions from Article 8 ECHR with meaning and, on the other hand, as a judicial body facing the increasingly complex interferences with privacy, driven by the development of new technologies. When it comes to the interplay and distinction between privacy and data protection, the ECtHR follows the well-established structure of legal sources within the Council of Europe, which considers the right to data protection as a subset of the right to privacy. Relying on Article 8 ECHR (right to respect for private and family life) that lacks a reference to data protection, and on the Convention No. 108 for the Protection of Individuals with regard to Automatic Processing of Personal Data that includes the protection of personal data within the protection of privacy,[110] the ECtHR subsequently analyses all data protection cases under the auspices of Article 8 ECHR. This approach, which could be explained by historical reasons of lesser data protection concerns at the time when the Convention was drafted and the lack of political readiness to later modify the Convention to that effect, distinguishes itself from the Charter's outlook that protects the two fundamental rights separately. For that reason, this part of the chapter will predominantly use the terminology referring to the right to privacy.

IV.1 Compliance Requirements with Article 8 ECHR

Article 8 ECHR gives a rather clear guidance as to when an interference with the right for private life is allowed.[111] As spelt out in case law, the second paragraph of this provision allows for an interference 'only if it is in accordance with the law, pursues one or more of the legitimate aims referred to in [this] paragraph ... and is necessary in a democratic society in order to achieve the aim or aims'.[112] The jurisprudence of the ECtHR clearly demonstrates that the requirements for compatibility with Article 8 ECHR are cumulative as this court can, for example, omit the analysis of the 'quality of law' and substitute it with the analysis of proportionality[113] or, inversely, find a violation of this provision already after establishing that the national legislation does not meet the condition of 'in accordance with the law'.[114] *Leander v*

---

[109] Case C-536/15 *Tele2 (Netherlands) and Others* ECLI:EU:C:2017:214.

[110] The Convention protects, in its Art 1, the 'right to privacy, with regard to automatic processing of personal data' and designates it as 'data protection'.

[111] For an extensive analysis of ECtHR cases on privacy and data protection, see Evangelia Psychogiopoulou, 'The European Court of Human Rights, Privacy and Data Protection in the Digital Era' in Brkan and Psychogiopoulou (n 10), 62.

[112] *Liberty and Others v UK* App no 58243/00 (ECtHR, 1 July 2008), para 58; *Weber and Saravia v Germany* App no 54934/00 (ECtHR, 29 June 2006), para 80.

[113] *S. and Marper v UK* App nos 30562/04 and 30566/04 (ECtHR, 4 December 2008), para 125.

[114] *M.M. v the UK* App no 24029/07 (ECtHR, 13 November 2012), para 207.

Sweden, one of the cases where the ECtHR devoted equal attention to all three components and found no violation of Article 8, equally reveals the cumulative nature of these components.[115]

The analysis by the ECtHR of the first requirement, obliging an interference with the right to privacy to be 'in accordance with the law', shows this court as a meticulous judicial institution developing rather precise criteria of compatibility with the right to privacy. From *Liberty and Others v UK*, a case where the interception of communication by British authorities was found to violate Article 8 ECHR due to insufficient clarity of domestic legislation, it can be understood that an allowed interference has to have 'some basis in domestic law' which is 'compatible with the rule of law and accessible to the person concerned, who must, moreover, be able to foresee its consequences for him'.[116] Foreseeability aims to prevent arbitrariness of authorities exercising surveillance and requires the law to provide for minimum safeguards for preventing an abuse of power, as clarified in *Weber and Saravia v Germany*.[117] Minimum safeguards, for example those regarding secret surveillance through telephone tapping, are defined in a rather detailed manner, ranging from determination, by the law, of the nature of offences giving rise to interception and a limit on the duration of telephone tapping to the procedure for data processing, safeguards for data sharing and circumstances, in which recordings may or must be erased.[118]

The Court exercises close scrutiny notably towards the requirement of guarantees of preventing arbitrariness and risk of abuse, at stake particularly in cases of secret surveillance, as can be discerned from *Zakharov v Russia*,[119] *Szabó and Vissy v Hungary*[120] and other cases.[121] In *Zakharov*, scrutinising the Russian legislation allowing for secret surveillance of any Russian mobile phone user, the ECtHR found a violation of Article 8 ECHR as the law did not clearly define the circumstances for instituting and terminating the surveillance measures, the conditions for storing data and effective remedies.[122] Similarly, in *Szabó and Vissy*, the violation of Article 8 ECHR was found due to the lack of safeguards that would be 'sufficiently precise, effective and comprehensive on the ordering, execution and potential redressing of such measures'.[123]

Moreover, in the recent cases *Big Brother Watch v UK*[124] and *Centrum för rättvisa v Sweden*,[125] the Strasbourg Court specified the standards to assess the lawfulness of secret surveillance programmes that entail bulk interception of communications and intelligence sharing. These standards merge the requirements of 'quality of law' and 'necessity' and comprise eight criteria focusing on grounds, procedures and safeguards in case of bulk intercep-

---

[115] *Leander v Sweden* App no 9248/81 (ECtHR, 26 March 1987), paras 52–67.
[116] *Liberty*, para 59.
[117] *Weber and Saravia v Germany* App no 54934/00 (ECtHR, 29 June 2006).
[118] Ibid., para 95.
[119] *Zakharov v Russia* App no 47143/06 (ECtHR, 4 December 2015).
[120] *Szabó and Vissy v Hungary* App no 37138/14 (ECtHR, 12 January 2016).
[121] See, e.g., *Association "21 December 1989" and Others v Romania* App nos 33810/07 and 18817/08 (ECtHR, 24 May 2011).
[122] *Zakharov*, para 302.
[123] *Szabó and Vissy*, para 89.
[124] *Big Brother Watch and Others v UK* App nos 58170/13, 62322/14 and 24960/15 (ECtHR, 25 May 2021).
[125] *Centrum för rättvisa v Sweden* App no 35252/08 (ECtHR, 25 May 2021).

tion.[126] A meticulous analysis of the UK and Swedish regimes led the ECtHR to conclude that they do not comply with these standards,[127] although the judicial decisions were not without critical comments.[128]

The requirement of national legislation to be 'in accordance with the law' is not subject to rigorous examination only regarding matters of surveillance, but also in cases on retention of data by public authorities, as in *Rotaru v Romania*.[129] In *Rotaru*, where the national authorities kept allegedly incorrect information about the applicant, imprisoned during the communist regime, the Romanian law did not meet that requirement as it lacked to define, in particular, the time limit for keeping the information, the persons authorised to access data and necessary procedures for the use of data.[130] Thus, by continuously reaffirming its position that uncontrolled mass surveillance and blanket retention of data not subjected to safeguards do not meet the standards guaranteed by Article 8 ECHR, the ECtHR also voiced a policy stance towards these issues. As a firm guarantor of high standard of privacy protection, the ECtHR can be paralleled with the CJEU, which equally maintains such a high standard on the EU level.

The second requirement of compliance with Article 8 ECHR is for the interference to pursue one or more of the legitimate aims listed in the article. According to the blackletter of its second paragraph, potential competing interests are 'the interests of national security, public safety or the economic well-being of the country,... the prevention of disorder or

---

[126] *Big Brother Watch*, para 361; *Centrum för rättvisa*, para 275; which lay down the following criteria:

> the grounds on which bulk interception may be authorised; the circumstances in which an individual's communications may be intercepted; the procedure to be followed for granting authorisation; the procedures to be followed for selecting, examining and using intercept material; the precautions to be taken when communicating the material to other parties; the limits on the duration of interception, the storage of intercept material and the circumstances in which such material must be erased and destroyed; the procedures and modalities for supervision by an independent authority of compliance with the above safeguards and its powers to address non-compliance; the procedures for independent ex post facto review of such compliance and the powers vested in the competent body in addressing instances of non-compliance.

[127] In *Big Brother Watch*, the UK regime did not comply with Art 8 ECHR due to 'the absence of independent authorization' of the bulk interception regime; the failure to include the categories of selectors in the application for a warrant; and the failure to subject selectors linked to an individual to prior internal authorisation' (para 425). In *Centrum för rättvisa*, the ECtHR found non-compliance of the Swedish regime with Art 8 due to 'the absence of a clear rule on destroying intercepted material which does not contain personal data'; non-consideration of 'the privacy interests of individuals' when transferring data to foreign intelligence agencies; and 'the absence of an effective ex post facto review' (para 369).

[128] For the first critical reflections, see for example Juraj Sajfert, 'The Big Brother Watch and Centrum för Rättvisa judgments of the Grand Chamber of the European Court of Human Rights – the Altamont of privacy?' (*European Law Blog*, 8 June 2021) https://europeanlawblog.eu/2021/06/08/big-brother-watch-and-centrum-for-rattvisa-judgments-of-the-grand-chamber-of-the-european-court-of-human-rights-altamont-of-privacy accessed 28 October 2021; Marko Milanovic, 'The Grand Normalization of Mass Surveillance: ECtHR Grand Chamber Judgments in Big Brother Watch and Centrum för rättvisa' (EJIL: Talk!, 26 May 2021) https://www.ejiltalk.org/the-grand-normalization-of-mass-surveillance-ecthr-grand-chamber-judgments-in-big-brother-watch-and-centrum-for-rattvisa accessed 28 October 2021; Nora Ni Loideain, 'Not So Grand: The Big Brother Watch ECtHR Grand Chamber judgment' (Information Law and Policy Centre, 28 May 2021) https://infolawcentre.blogs.sas.ac.uk/2021/05/28/not-so-grand-the-big-brother-watch-ecthr-grand-chamber-judgment accessed 28 October 2021.

[129] *Rotaru v Romania* App no 28341/95 (ECtHR, 4 May 2000).

[130] Ibid., para 57 et seq.

crime, ... the protection of health or morals, or ... the protection of the rights and freedoms of others'. Balancing between different interests comes to the spotlight in particular regarding potential conflicts between Article 8 and Article 10 (freedom of expression) ECHR that put to the forefront notably difficulties of a suitable equilibrium of public access to private data. Methodologically, the cases can reach the ECtHR either though an alleged violation of privacy, such as *Węgrzynowski and Smolczewski v Poland*,[131] or through a purported encroachment on freedom of speech, as in *Delfi v Estonia*.[132] Differently than the CJEU in *Google Spain*, the ECtHR in its standing case law expressly points out that the two fundamental rights 'as a matter of principle... deserve equal respect', thus leaving the applicants with a free hand as to whether to lodge the case under one or the other provision.[133]

In *Delfi*, the liability of a professional portal for users' defamatory comments on an article published on the portal did not infringe its freedom of speech since the EctHR gave express preference to the right to reputation which is protected under Article 8 ECHR as a constitutive part of the right to private life.[134] Differently, in *Węgrzynowski and Smolczewski*, the balance was in turn tilted towards the freedom of expression under Article 10 ECHR, in circumstances where two Polish lawyers alleged an infringement of their right to privacy by a national courts' refusal to order a removal of a defamatory article from a newspaper's online archive. By way of an epic reasoning that judicial authorities should not be 'rewriting history by ordering the removal...of publications' that were previously judicially found defamatory, the EctHR not only turned its back on internet censorship, but also sought to find a midway solution by allowing for a rectifying notice to be published with the defamatory news content.[135] The case could be paralleled with the CJEU's *Google Spain*, where the CJEU granted the data subject the right to request a deletion of a link from an index of a search engine upon simple request. Even though it might appear that the two courts reached an opposite conclusion in a similar set of facts, the outcome of the two cases is only seemingly contradictory since, in essence, both rulings confirm the right of the initial publisher to preserve the contested publication in the newspaper archive. Indeed, differently from ECtHR in *Węgrzynowski and Smolczewski*, the CJEU in *Google Spain* adjudicated solely on the rights and obligations of a *search engine* and not of the initial news publisher themselves.

The third component of the ECtHR's examination of compliance with Article 8 ECHR obliges the court to verify whether the interference is 'necessary in a democratic society in order to achieve the aim' pursued, in other words, whether the interference complies with the principle of proportionality. More precisely, an interference is necessary in a democratic society if it 'answers a pressing social need' and 'if the reasons adduced by the national authorities to justify it are relevant and sufficient'.[136] In the seminal case tackling the issue of proportionality in the framework of data retention, *S. and Marper v UK*, the ECtHR found a violation of Article 8 ECHR due to an indeterminate retention of data subjects' fingerprints, cell samples and DNA profiles despite the lack of a conviction in criminal proceedings against them. The

---

[131] *Węgrzynowski and Smolczewski v Poland* App no 33846/07 (ECHR, 16 July 2013).

[132] *Delfi v Estonia* App no 64569/09 (ECHR, 16 June 2015).

[133] Ibid., para 139; *Axel Springer AG v Germany* Ap no 39954/08 (ECtHR, 7 February 2012), para 87; *Von Hannover v Germany (no. 2)* App nos 40660/08 and 60641/08 (ECtHR, 7 February 2012), para 106.

[134] *Delfi*, para 137.

[135] *Węgrzynowski and Smolczewski*, para 67.

[136] *Marper*, para 101.

ECtHR, after a careful analysis of domestic legislation, affirmed that a blanket, indiscriminate and indefinite retention of data does not strike a fair balance between the competing public and private interests, that is, the interest of detection and prevention of crime on the one hand and the right to privacy on the other hand.[137] Similar disproportionate retention of data was found also in *M.K. v France*[138] and *Brunet v France*[139] where personal data was retained in the fingerprints database after discontinuance or acquittal of criminal proceedings against the applicant. To the contrary, in *B.B. v France*,[140] *Gardel v France*[141] and *M.B. v France*,[142] the retention of data of offenders sentenced for rape of minors for a maximum period of 30 years was considered proportionate with the aim of protection of public order and prevention of criminal offences, in particular because the applicants had the right to request the deletion of data after that time period.[143] As explained above, in cases of the assessment of lawfulness of secret surveillance programmes that entail bulk interception of communications, the ECtHR relies on a specific multi-step test, developed in *Big Brother Watch v UK*[144] and *Centrum för rättvisa v Sweden*.[145] This test merges the requirements of 'quality of law' and 'necessity' and takes into account the grounds, procedures and safeguards for such bulk interception.[146]

IV.2 ECtHR v CJEU: Judicial Dialogue or Monologue?

The jurisdiction that the highest European courts exercise in the privacy and data protection fundamental rights landscape is embedded in a complex web of multi-layered sources for protection of these rights. Differently from the ECtHR, which relies solely on the ECHR when scrutinising the law and practice of States parties to the ECHR, the CJEU is bound to joggle with both Charter and the ECHR considering that, as stipulated in Article 52(3) CFR, 'the meaning and scope' of Charter rights corresponding to ECHR rights 'shall be the same as those laid down by the said Convention'. This provision allows the CJEU to guarantee also a higher level of protection of Charter rights.

Nonetheless, the ECtHR's venues of reasoning periodically stumble upon EU law. An exemplary case in this regard is the ECtHR judgment in *Satakunnan Markkinapörssi Oy and Satamedia Oy v Finland*,[147] decided after the CJEU issued a prior judgment on the EU level[148] following a request for a preliminary ruling by the Finnish Supreme Administrative Court. Satakunnan Markkinapörssi and Satamedia are Finnish companies that published, in a newspaper, information regarding the taxable income and assets of approximately 1.2 million natural persons. Having received the published data in an electronic form from the first company,

---

[137] Ibid., para 125.

[138] *M.K. v France* App no 19522/09 (ECtHR, 18 April 2013).

[139] *Brunet v France* App no 21010/10 (ECtHR, 18 September 2014).

[140] *B.B. v France* App no 5335/06 (ECtHR, 17 December 2009).

[141] *Gardel v France* App no 16428/05 (ECtHR, 17 December 2009).

[142] *M.B. v France* App no 22115/06 (ECtHR, 17 December 2009).

[143] *B.B. v France*, paras 58, 62, 67, 70; *Gardel v France*, paras 59, 63, 68, 71; *M.B. v France*, paras 50, 54, 59, 62.

[144] *Big Brother Watch and Others v UK.*

[145] *Centrum för rättvisa v Sweden.*

[146] *Big Brother Watch*, para 361; *Centrum för rättvisa*, para 275.

[147] *Satakunnan Markkinapörssi Oy and Satamedia Oy v Finland* App no 931/13 (ECtHR, 21 July 2015).

[148] Case C-73/07 *Satakunnan Markkinapörssi and Satamedia* ECLI:EU:C:2008:727.

Satamedia established, in cooperation with a telephone operator, a system whereby taxation information could be requested by way of a simple text message.[149] The obvious balance to be struck in these factual circumstances was thus the one between the right to privacy and freedom of expression, and in particular the journalistic aspect of the latter. In a rather scarce and open-ended reasoning, the CJEU refrained from striking that balance, leaving the task to the national court all the while giving it a vague guidance as to how to approach the question of this challenging equilibrium. In view of the CJEU, the contested activities of Finnish companies could be seen as having constituted processing of personal data carried out 'solely for journalistic purposes', but only *if* 'the sole object of those activities was the disclosure to the public of information, opinions or ideas' which was to be determined by the national court.[150]

The reasoning of the judgment, affirming in the same breath the necessity of a broad interpretation of journalism as part of freedom of expression and the need for application of journalistic derogations from the right to privacy only if strictly necessary,[151] reveals not only the struggle of the CJEU related to weighing of the two rights, but also the general tension of their juxtaposition. Faced with this (lack of) guidance, the Finnish Supreme Administrative Court, estimating that the publication of the entire database could not be considered as journalistic activity since the public interest did not justify the *extent* to which personal data were published,[152] proved itself a pro-privacy oriented judicial body that is willing to enter the nuances regarding the scope of journalistic exception. However, this decision was to the dissatisfaction of the two publishing companies having brought the matter before the ECtHR.

The ECtHR judgment in *Satamedia*, finding no violation of freedom of expression (Art 10 ECHR) and hence letting the right to privacy (Art 8 ECHR) prevail, draws the contours of intricate relationships between ECtHR, on the one hand, and the CJEU and the national courts on the other. With regard to the latter, it is to be noted that the ECtHR explicitly confirms the position and agrees with the reasoning of the Finnish national court. In fact, declaring the reasoning of this court 'acceptable' and 'convincing', it recalls that it would need 'strong reasons to substitute its own view for that of the domestic courts'.[153] This approach exemplifies the reluctance of the ECtHR to enter into overt conflicts with the (highest) national courts, based on the presumption of correctness of the balancing exercise by those courts. When it comes to the relationship and an opportunity for a dialogue with the CJEU, the ECtHR in *Satamedia* remains startlingly silent. Apart from referring to the CJEU's *Satamedia* judgment and summarising its reasoning,[154] the ECtHR gives no explicit indication as to whether or not it agrees with this reasoning and the CJEU's guidance given to the national court. Indeed, it could be argued that the ECtHR nevertheless implicitly approves of its Luxembourg counterparts' interpretative approach given that the latter's interpretation is channelled into the decision of the national court – which the ECtHR finds convincing. However, such a view requires some reading between the lines, since the decision of the CJEU gave the national court a nearly free hand in respect of the outcome of balancing between the two competing fundamental rights. Anyhow, until (and if ever) the EU becomes a party to the Convention, the ECtHR will be, for-

---

149 For the factual background see ECtHR *Satamedia*, paras 5–24; CJEU *Satamedia*, paras 25–32.
150 CJEU *Satamedia*, para 62.
151 Ibid., para 56.
152 ECtHR *Satamedia*, para 17.
153 Ibid., para 72.
154 Ibid., para 69.

mally speaking, unwilling to see the CJEU as a 'domestic court' whose view the ECtHR is not willing to substitute.[155] The long-awaited ECtHR *Satamedia* judgment of the Grand Chamber unsurprisingly confirms the reasoning of the previous judgment of the Fourth Section and comes to the conclusion that the right to privacy in this set of facts prevails over the right to freedom of expression and information.[156]

Furthermore, examples of cases where the ECtHR judgments do make reference to the CJEU jurisprudence are *Zakharov v Russia*, *Szabó and Vissy v Hungary*, *Delfi v Estonia*, *Big Brother Watch v UK* and *Centrum för rättvisa v Sweden*. In *Zakharov*, the reference to the CJEU's *Digital Rights Ireland and Seitlinger* case appears merely in the framework of relevant legal sources and not in the reasoning itself, which seems a logical consequence of the circumstance that the case was lodged against Russia and not against an EU Member State.[157] Similarly, in *Big Brother Watch* and *Centrum för rättvisa*, a number of CJEU cases, including *Digital Rights Ireland and Seitlinger*, *Tele2 Sverige*, *Schrems* and *La Quadrature du Net* are included mostly in the legal framework[158] and partially in parties' observations[159] and a separate opinion,[160] however, not in the reasoning of the ECtHR itself. This indicates that the ECtHR is somewhat reluctant to draw inspiration from the CJEU case law, perhaps precisely because – as the Norwegian Government argued before the ECtHR – many of the States that are parties to the ECHR are not also EU Member States.[161]

Differently, in *Szabó and Vissy*, after making a reference to *Digital Rights Ireland and Seitlinger* under sources of international law,[162] the ECtHR rather interestingly treats the CJEU as if it was an *amicus curiae* expressing views notably on the issue of safeguards in mass surveillance. In this sense, the ECtHR takes into account 'the observations made' by the CJEU on the 'importance of adequate legislation of sufficient safeguards' in technically advanced surveillance[163] and it 'considers [it] convenient to endorse' the position of the CJEU

[155] The accession of the EU to the ECHR came to a halt after the CJEU's Opinion 2/13 ECLI:EU:C:2014:2454. For a commentary see Bruno de Witte and Šejla Imamović, 'Opinion 2/13 on Accession to the ECHR: Defending the EU Legal Order Against a Foreign Human Rights Court' (2015) 40(5) *European Law Review* 683; Johan Callewaert, Bruno de Witte, Marc Joseph Bossuyt, Emmanuelle Bribosia, Christophe Hillion, Martin Kuijer, Šejla Imamovic, Jörg Polakiewicz and Monica Claes, 'The EU Fundamental Rights Landscape after Opinion 2/13 (June 22, 2016)' Maastricht Faculty of Law Working Paper No. 2016/3 https://ssrn.com/abstract=2799100 accessed 28 October 2021.

[156] *Satakunnan Markkinapörssi Oy and Satamedia Oy v. Finland* App no 931/13 (ECtHR, 27 June 2017). For a commentary, see Magdalena Jozwiak, 'The Scale Matters: The ECtHR Grand Chamber Finds That Prohibition of Mass Publication of 'Raw' Taxation Data Does Not Infringe Right to Freedom of Expression' (2018) 4(1) *European Data Protection Law Review* 127–134.

[157] *Zakharov,* para 147.

[158] For more precise references, see *Big Brother Watch*, paras 209–241; *Centrum för rättvisa,* paras 98–130.

[159] *Big Brother Watch*, para 302 (submissions of French Government) and para 310 (submissions of Norwegian Government); *Centrum för rättvisa*, para 235 (submissions of Norwegian Government).

[160] Partly concurring and partly dissenting opinion of Judge Pinto De Albuquerque in *Big Brother Watch*, paras 9, 11, 12, 14 and 59.

[161] Ibid., Norwegian Government invited the ECtHR to *not* rely on criteria developed by CJEU in its jurisprudence, notably because nineteen Contracting States of Council of Europe are not EU Member States.

[162] *Szabó and Vissy*, para 23.

[163] Ibid., para 68.

that requires 'secret surveillance measures to answer to strict necessity'.[164] Even though the Strasbourg Court considers the views of the Luxembourg Court together with the opinions of the United Nations Special Rapporteur, the former court's reasoning is still inspired by and built upon the CJEU's positions. The ECtHR therefore seems to enter into a dialogue whereby it not only recognises the CJEU's formal authority, but also approves of its assessment on the merits in *Digital Rights Ireland and Seitlinger*.

Moreover, in *Delfi v Estonia*, several CJEU cases are referred to in the section on legal sources or observations of the parties,[165] while merely *Google Spain* is invoked in the ECtHR's reasoning on the merits. The reference to *Google Spain* is made in the context of considerations as to whether the liability of the *authors* of defamatory comments on the Delfi news portal would be a viable alternative to the liability of the news portal itself.[166] The Strasbourg Court, rightly recognising that the speed of dissemination of information over the internet and its persistence on this medium magnifies the negative consequences of defamatory comments, gives credit to *Google Spain* where the CJEU tackled the question 'of the availability on the Internet of information seriously interfering with a person's private life over an extended period of time'.[167] Interestingly, by adding that its Luxembourg counterpart ruled 'that the individual's fundamental rights, as a rule, overrode the economic interests of the search engine operator and the interests of other internet users', the Strasbourg Court seems to concur with this reasoning that can be, as analysed above, potentially problematic from the perspective of balancing of different rights and interests. Even though in *Delfi* the CJEU is not treated as a quasi *amicus curiae*, both in this case and in *Szabó and Vissy* the CJEU plays a role of a judicial authority whose decisions merit having an informative and perhaps even an advisory function for the ECtHR.

In its reasoning in selected cases, the EctHR thus shows a certain openness towards conducting a dialogue with the Luxembourg Court. Unfortunately, this openness is confined to a limited number of judgments and is not systematic even in instances where such a dialogue would have been expected, such as in *Węgrzynowski and Smolczewski*, where a reference to *Google Spain* would have been suitable. Yet, such absence of dialogue could be explained by the circumstance that *Węgrzynowski and Smolczewski* opened the question of removal of information from the newspaper archive and not from an index of a search engine and that the reasoning of the CJEU in *Google Spain* could not, in any way, strengthen the argumentation of the ECtHR. Finally, the judgments in the post-Snowden mass surveillance cases *Big Brother Watch and Others v UK*[168] and *Centrum för rättvisa v Sweden*,[169] also show the reluctance of the ECtHR to draw inspiration from the CJEU's case law on that matter.

The CJEU, for its part, equally engages in a dialogue with the Strasbourg Court, albeit not systematically in all privacy and data protection related cases. Prior to the Charter acquiring legally binding force, and due to the lack of its own jurisprudence in this field, this court had

---

[164] Ibid., para 73.

[165] More precisely, the cases referred to are Joined Cases C- to C- *Google France and Google* ECLI:EU:C:2010:159; Case C- *L'Oréal and Others* ECLI:EU:C:2011:474; Case C- *Scarlet Extended* ECLI:EU:C:2011:771; Case C- *SABAM* ECLI:EU:C:2012:85; Case C- *Google Spain and Google*; and Case C- *Papasavvas* ECLI:EU:C:2014:2209. See *Delfi*, paras 43, 52–57, 85.

[166] *Delfi*, para 147.

[167] Ibid.

[168] *Big Brother Watch and Others v UK.*

[169] *Centrum för rättvisa v Sweden.*

recourse to the ECtHR case law, for example in *Österreichischer Rundfunk and others,* to determine whether there was an interference with private life and whether the interference was justified.[170] Other earlier cases, such as *Lindqvist*[171] and *Promusicae,*[172] only make reference to Articles 10 and 8 ECHR respectively,[173] but do not invoke the corresponding Strasbourg jurisprudence.

Differently, *Digital Rights Ireland and Seitlinger* as well as *Tele2 Sverige and Watson* are the seminal examples of judgments where the CJEU took the ECtHR jurisprudence into account when deciding on the merits of the case. In *Digital Rights Ireland*, the CJEU heavily relied on the ECtHR case law in order to establish the existence of an interference with fundamental rights to privacy and data protection, interference that was not only found due to the retention of data itself, but also due to the *access* of national authorities to this data as in *Leander v Sweden, Rotaru v Romania* and *Weber and Saravia v Germany*.[174] Moreover, in the framework of the proportionality analysis of this interference, the CJEU, while invoking the ECtHR jurisprudence by analogy, stressed the importance of minimum safeguards that is even greater if data is processed automatically and if 'there is a significant risk of unlawful access to those data'.[175] Furthermore, from a viewpoint of the assessment of national laws on data retention, the *Tele2 Sverige and Watson* case equally relies on the Strasbourg jurisprudence.[176] Finally, the CJEU in *La Quadrature du Net and Others*[177] strongly relies on ECtHR case law, not only to establish the interference with the fundamental rights to privacy and data protection through indiscriminate retention of traffic and location data,[178] but, more importantly, to establish positive obligations[179] of Member States to protect private and family life[180] and to adopt rules to facilitate effective combating of criminal offences.[181]

These cases demonstrate that the CJEU looks to its Strasbourg counterpart when it is necessary to strengthen its reasoning on issues where its own case law is lacking and thus applies the ECtHR jurisprudence to fill in the missing pieces of the argumentation jigsaw. As a matter of fact, given that the Charter requires parallel interpretation with ECHR rights, and that the meaning of the latter rights is filled by the Strasbourg case law which becomes an intrinsic part of those rights, it can be argued that the CJEU has no choice but to observe the Strasbourg jurisprudence.

---

170 Joined Cases C-465/00, C-138/01 and C-139/01 *Österreichischer Rundfunk and others* ECLI:EU:C:2003:294, paras 73, 77.

171 Case C-101/01 *Lindqvist* ECLI:EU:C:2003:596.

172 Case C-275/06 *Promusicae* ECLI:EU:C:2008:54.

173 *Lindqvist*, para 72, 90; *Promusicae*, para 64.

174 *Digital Rights Ireland and Seitlinger*, para 35.

175 Ibid., paras 54–55.

176 *Tele2 Sverige and Watson*, paras 119–120. One of the preliminary questions in that case was also the question whether the CJEU's interpretation of Arts 7 and 8 CFR expanded the protection under Art 8 ECHR, but that question was declared inadmissible as having a hypothetical character; *Tele2 Sverige and Watson*, paras 126–133.

177 Joined cases C-511/18, C-512/18 and C-520/18 *La Quadrature du Net and Others*.

178 Ibid., paras 115–116.

179 More extensively on positive obligations in the EU legal order, see in particular Malu Beijer, *The Limits of Fundamental Rights Protection by the EU: The Scope for the Development of Positive Obligations* (Intersentia 2017).

180 *La Quadrature du Net and Others*, para 126.

181 Ibid., paras 126, 145.

The CJEU makes use of both the Charter and the ECHR which represents, within the EU, only a minimum standard of fundamental rights protection. Indeed, as stipulated in Article 52(3) CFR, the circumstance that the 'meaning and scope' of Charter rights 'shall be the same' as those in the ECHR does not prevent the possibility of the EU to guarantee, through more extensive interpretation, a higher level of protection. To the knowledge of the author, the CJEU in its jurisprudence on data protection and privacy has so far not *formally* relied on the possibility of enhancing the Convention's standard of protection. Rather, the Luxembourg Court aligns its level of protection and the reasoning on merits to the one of the Strasbourg Court[182] as in *Digital Rights Ireland and Seitlinger* as well as in *Tele2 Sverige and Watson*. Nevertheless, cases such as *Google Spain* show that the CJEU does not refrain from putting a benchmark of privacy and data protection very high, perhaps even higher than the ECtHR, and to maintain positions that are independent from the latter.

For its part, the ECtHR, building its jurisprudence upon Article 8 ECHR, does not formally rely on Luxembourg jurisprudence, but at the same time also refrains from issuing judgments that would overtly create tension between the two courts. In this regard, the ECtHR implicitly or explicitly follows its *Bosphorus*[183] presumption that was further developed in *Michaud*[184] and *Avotiņš*.[185] Nevertheless, it is somewhat surprising that the Strasbourg Court in *Big Brother Watch and Others v UK* and *Centrum för rättvisa v Sweden* did not at least position the analysis in its judgments in relation to comparable CJEU cases, especially since it cited CJEU case law in the legal framework section. Moreover, the scrutiny of the ECtHR might be somewhat challenged after the entry into force of the GDPR. The GDPR unifies the legislation on the level of the EU and is directly applicable in the EU Member States; hence, it could be the subject of review by the ECtHR in a framework of an application lodged against an EU Member State. Once (and if) the EU accedes to the ECHR,[186] there will be even more room for such direct scrutiny of EU data protection legislation. Finally, given the ever-increasing global nature of privacy and data protection disputes, the judgments by European courts in these domains are expected to attract attention also of non-European courts and authorities.

V. CONCLUSION

As the present chapter demonstrates, European courts have an unprecedented impact on the shaping of data protection and privacy rules and on the direction in which the current European data protection and privacy regime develops. As the European citizens litigate in national judicial fora, the courts of the Member States represent the first drivers of potential policy reforms, not only for national data protection and privacy provisions, but also for the European ones through preliminary ruling procedures. This chapter reveals that the EU national courts have various roles when it comes to privacy and data protection. Besides complementing the

---

[182] At the same time, the CJEU does not hesitate to point out that the Convention does not constitute 'a legal instrument which has been formally incorporated into EU law'; see Case C-311/18 *Facebook Ireland and Schrems*, para 98.

[183] *Bosphorus Hava Yolları Turizm ve Ticaret Anonim Şirketi v Ireland* App no 45036/98 (ECtHR, 30 June 2005).

[184] *Michaud v France* App no 12323/11 (ECtHR, 6 December 2012).

[185] *Avotiņš v Latvia* App no 17502/07 (ECtHR, 23 May 2016).

[186] As mentioned above, the accession is currently put on hold due to the CJEU's Opinion 2/13.

national supervisory authorities in enforcing data protection and privacy rights and verifying the accuracy of their decisions, national courts also build a culture of dialogue with the CJEU and the ECtHR. Not only can they engage in a dialogue with the CJEU through the preliminary reference mechanism, but their voice is also respected by the ECtHR, which stresses that it would need 'strong reasons to substitute its own view for that of the domestic courts'.[187]

Concerned with the fundamental rights protection of EU citizens, the CJEU on its part uses its judicial powers to increase the level of data and privacy protection, sometimes even beyond the one envisaged by the legislator. The ECtHR, in its jurisprudence, partially seems to follow a comparable approach, in particular in its earlier data retention cases such as *Marper*, *M.K.* and *Brunet*. Yet, it is debatable whether this holds true also for the more recent *Big Brother Watch* and *Centrum för rättvisa* cases. In his partly concurring and partly dissenting opinion in the *Big Brother Watch* case, Judge Pinto De Albuquerque picturesquely compares the Luxembourg Court to 'the lighthouse for privacy rights in Europe' and opines that the Strasbourg Court 'lags behind' in this respect. In any event, the cross-referencing of case law between the ECtHR and the CJEU shows that both courts are avoiding potential jurisprudential conflicts in the field of privacy and data protection.

Given the rich jurisprudence of the CJEU in the recent years, the impact of its judgments can be estimated as having the broadest range among the three categories of courts. The impact of activist CJEU can be detected on several levels. The most notable impact of the CJEU is the influence on the European legislator, both regarding the drafting of new legislation and modifying current legislative acts. As an illustration of this legislative impact, the CJEU influenced the way certain GDPR provisions were drafted, the most obvious example being the insertion of the right to erasure into the GDPR text,[188] following the *Google Spain* judgment.[189] Invalidation of the Data Retention Directive in *Digital Rights Ireland* equally falls within this category of impact, currently left without a follow-up at EU legislative level. Institutionally, the CJEU in this role acts as a 'corrector' of EU legislation and a guarantor of fundamental rights of the EU citizens. It has become almost a truism that the European data protection and privacy landscape would have developed in a very different direction had the Court not persistently pushed for a strong protection, setting high legal standards.

Furthermore, the jurisprudence of the CJEU has not only impacted the EU legislature, but has also an influence on the EU executive with regard to (re)negotiation of international agreements. International agreements are not immune to the CJEU's scrutiny and it is arguable whether this Court sometimes steps out of the shoes of the judicial authority almost into the shoes of a legislative authority, as in *Opinion 1/15* on EU-Canada PNR agreement.[190] Indeed, in its judgment, the Court almost shaped the content of negotiating mandate to the EU negotiator, specifying very precisely which elements the new agreement has to contain to be compliant with Articles 7 and 8 of the Charter.[191] An earlier PNR case on transfer of PNR data

---

[187] ECtHR *Satamedia*, para 72.

[188] Art 17 GDPR.

[189] The GDPR for example also expressly refers to case law of the CJEU regarding the interpretation of the concept of damage. See Recital 146 GDPR.

[190] *Opinion 1/15* ECLI:EU:C:2017:592.

[191] The reactions of the doctrine on detailed instructions of the Court vary. Docksey, e.g., notes that the Court 'indicated in some detail how the Agreement would have to be amended'; see Christopher Docksey, 'Opinion 1/15: Privacy and security, finding the balance' (2017) 24(6) *Maastricht Journal of European and Comparative* Law 769. Hijmans is more critical, claiming that 'the opinion positions

to the USA equally led to a renegotiation of the PNR agreement,[192] albeit with less impact of the Court on the actual content of the agreement.

As the highest adjudicator on privacy and data protection within the EU, the CJEU therefore pushes for policy reforms and forces the policy-makers to reconsider their choices. A typical example in this regard are the two *Schrems* cases which led to a cascade effect of initial annulment of the adequacy decision on Safe Harbour,[193] renegotiation and the birth of Privacy Shield and subsequent annulment of the adequacy decision on Privacy Shield.[194] The CJEU can even be perceived as an actor in international arena, having an important political impact and being crucial in determination of the future transatlantic privacy and data protection arrangements. Consequently, the CJEU has an influence on international relations of the EU with third countries. From that perspective, the CJEU significantly shapes the EU's external relations policy regarding privacy and data protection.

Linked to that is the impact of the CJEU case law beyond the EU borders, both on third countries as well as on foreign controllers. On the one hand, as determined by the Court in *Schrems*, the third countries to which data can be transferred due to an adequacy decision, have to abide by data protection standards that are 'essentially equivalent'[195] to those in the EU; it seems that the Court thereby *de facto* pushes for compliance of third country controllers with the level of data protection guaranteed within the EU. This impact is even more apparent after the *Facebook Ireland and Schrems* case.[196]

On the other hand, the case law of the CJEU also impacts foreign controllers, notably by providing a broad territorial scope of data protection legislation.[197] In *Google Spain*, the CJEU ruled in favour of a 'particularly broad territorial scope' of Directive 95/46[198] by including within its scope of application also Google's European subsidiary which did not process data, but was established in Europe for promoting and selling advertising space on the search engine.[199] Consequently, Google's main establishment, located outside Europe and responsible for the processing of data, had to comply with the EU data protection standards for such processing. However, this broad territorial scope was somewhat limited in *Google (Territorial*

---

the CJEU as a sort of co-legislator'; Hielke Hijmans, 'PNR Agreement EU-Canada Scrutinised: CJEU Gives Very Precise Guidance to Negotiators' (2017) 3 *European Data Protection Law Review* 410. Compare also Arianna Vedaschi and Chiara Graziani, 'PNR Agreements Between Fundamental Rights and National Security: Opinion 1/15' (European Law Blog, 23 January 2018) http://europeanlawblog.eu/2018/01/23/pnr-agreements-between-fundamental-rights-and-national-security-opinion-115 accessed 28 October 2021.

[192] Joined Cases C-317/04 and C-318/04 *European Parliament v Council and Commission* ECLI:EU:C:2006:346.

[193] Case C-362/14 *Schrems*.

[194] Case C-311/18 *Facebook Ireland and Schrems*.

[195] *Schrems*, paras 73, 74, 96.

[196] Case C-311/18 *Facebook Ireland and Schrems*.

[197] For a more general analysis of the broad scope of EU data protection laws see Dan Jerker B Svantesson, 'The Extraterritoriality of EU Data Privacy Law – its Theoretical Justification and its Practical Effect on U.S. Businesses' (2013) 50(1) *Stanford Journal of International Law* 53–117.

[198] *Google Spain*, para 54. The broad applicability of the EU data protection regime was further confirmed by the Court in its *Weltimmo* judgment. C-230/14, *Weltimmo*, ECLI:EU:C:2015:639.

[199] *Google Spain*, para 60. In the aftermath of Google Spain, the Article 29 Working Party updated its Opinion on applicable law; see Update of Opinion 8/2010 on applicable law in light of the CJEU judgement in *Google Spain*, adopted on 16 December 2015, 176/16/EN.

scope of de-referencing),[200] where the CJEU decided that the EU legislation on data protection does not require de-referencing on all domain names of a search engine.[201] What challenges lie ahead of the European judiciary with regard to the privacy and data protection standards? The ECtHR might have to take a clearer stance on how to position the CJEU case law in its own jurisprudence when deciding cases regarding similar issues.

The national courts and the CJEU are, on their part, busy with the application and interpretation of the GDPR. As an example, with regard to the territorial scope, the GDPR poses new interpretative challenges for the European judiciary by partially introducing new rules on territorial scope. [202] In particular, the standard of 'offering of goods or services…in the Union' is expected to have important consequences on controllers established anywhere in the world, orientating their sales towards the EU. In this regard, the crucial interpretative task of the CJEU will be to fill the notions of 'offering' and 'in the Union' with the meaning that will either further expand or reasonably limit this broad criterion. The CJEU will therefore have a pivotal function in determining as to whether the European data protection standards will have a global impact also in the future. The final answers to these interpretative questions will be given by the CJEU which is expected not only to give the GDPR a broad territorial scope of application, but also to continue its strong pro-data protection stance when interpreting other GDPR provisions.

REFERENCES

Arnull A, 'Judicial Dialogue in the European Union' in J Dickson and P Eleftheriadis (eds. *Philosophical Foundations of European Union Law* (Oxford University Press 2012).

Ausloos J, *The Right to Erasure in EU Data Protection Law* (Oxford 2020).

Azoulai L and M van der Sluis, 'Institutionalizing Personal Data Protection in Times of Global Institutional Distrust: Schrems' (2016) 53(5) *Common Market Law Review* 1343.

Bebr G, 'The Reinforcement of the Constitutional Review of Community Acts Under Article 177 EEC Treaty (Case 314/85 and 133 to 136/85)' (1988) 25(4) *Common Market Law Review* 667.

Beijer M, *The Limits of Fundamental Rights Protection by the EU: The Scope for the Development of Positive Obligations* (Intersentia 2017).

Bobek M, *Comparative Reasoning in European Supreme Courts* (OUP 2013).

Bodoni S, 'If Trump Spoils Privacy Pact, We'll Pull It, EU Official Warns' (Bloomberg News, 2 March 2017) https://www.bloomberg.com/news/articles/2017-03-02/if-trump-spoils-privacy-pact-we-ll-pull-it-eu-official-warns.

Brkan M, 'The Concept of Essence of Fundamental Rights in the EU Legal Order: Peeling the Onion to its Core' (2018) 14(2) *European Constitutional Law Review* 332.

Brkan M, 'The Court of Justice of the EU, privacy and data protection: Judge-made law as a leitmotif in fundamental rights protection' in M Brkan and E Psychogiopoulou (eds), *Courts, Privacy and Data Protection in the Digital Environment* (Edward Elgar 2017).

---

[200] C-507/17 *Google (Territorial scope of de-referencing)*.

[201] Ibid., paras 53-65.

[202] Apart from keeping the current criterion of 'context of the activities of an establishment of a controller' (Art 3(1) GDPR), the Regulation also applies in cases of 'offering of goods or services' to data subjects in the Union (Art 3(2)(a) GDPR) and to the 'monitoring of their behaviour' within the Union (Art 3(2)(b) GDPR). For an analysis, see, e.g., Paul De Hert and Michal Czerniawski, 'Expanding the European Data Protection Scope Beyond Territory: Article 3 of the General Data Protection Regulation in its wider context' (2016) 6(3) *International Data Privacy Law* 230–243.

Brkan M, 'The Unstoppable Expansion of EU Fundamental Right to Data Protection: Little Shop of Horrors?' (2016) 23(5) *Maastricht Journal of European and Comparative Law* 812.
Callewaert J, B de Witte, M J Bossuyt, E Bribosia, C Hillion, M Kuijer, Š Imamovic, J Polakiewicz and M Claes, 'The EU Fundamental Rights Landscape after Opinion 2/13 (June 22, 2016)' (Maastricht Faculty of Law Working Paper No. 2016/3) https://ssrn.com/abstract=2799100.
Cannataci J A and J P Mifsud-Bonnici, 'Data Protection Comes of Age: The Data Protection Clauses in the European Constitutional Treaty' (2005) 14(1) *Information & Communications Technology Law* 5.
Claes M and M de Visser, 'Are You Networked Yet? On Dialogues in European Judicial Networks' (2012) 8(2) *Utrecht Law Review* 100.
Cruysmans E and A Strowel, 'Un droit à l'oubli face aux moteurs de recherche: droit applicable et responsabilité pour le référencement de données "inadéquates, non pertinentes ou excessives"' (2014) *Journal des tribunaux* 459.
De Hert P and M Czerniawski, 'Expanding the European Data Protection Scope Beyond Territory: Article 3 of the General Data Protection Regulation in its Wider Context' (2016) 6(3) *International Data Privacy Law* 230.
De Hert P and S Gutwirth, 'Data Protection in the Case Law of Strasbourg and Luxemburg: Constitutionalisation in Action' in S Gutwirth et al., *Reinventing Data Protection?* (Springer 2009).
De Hert P and V Papakonstantinou, 'Google Spain: Addressing Critiques and Misunderstandings One Year Later' (2015) 22(4) *Maastricht Journal of European and Comparative Law* 633.
De Hert P, 'Courts, Privacy and Data Protection in Belgium: Fundamental Rights that Might as Well be Struck from the Constitution' in M Brkan and E Psychogiopoulou (eds), *Courts, Privacy and Data Protection in the Digital Environment* (Edward Elgar 2017).
De Witte B and Š Imamović, 'Opinion 2/13 on Accession to the ECHR: Defending the EU Legal Order Against a Foreign Human Rights Court' (2015) 40(5) *European Law Review* 683.
Di Cocco C and G Sartor, 'Courts, Privacy and Data Protection in Italy: Implied Constitutional Rights' in M Brkan and E Psychogiopoulou (eds) *Courts, Privacy and Data Protection in the Digital Environment* (Edward Elgar 2017) 138–161.
Docksey C, 'Opinion 1/15: Privacy and Security, Finding the Balance' (2017) 24(6) *Maastricht Journal of European and Comparative Law* 769.
Dörr O, R Grote and T Marauhn (eds), *EMRK/GG: Konkordanzkommentar zum europäischen und deutschen Grundrechtsschutz* (Mohr Siebeck 2006).
EDPS Opinion 4/2016 on the EU-U.S. Privacy Shield draft adequacy decision, available at https://edps.europa.eu/sites/edp/files/publication/16-05-30_privacy_shield_en.pdf.
European Commission 'Report from the Commission to the European Parliament and the Council on the first annual review of the functioning of the EU–U.S. Privacy Shield', COM(2017) 611.
Fabbrini F, 'Human Rights in the Digital Age: The European Court of Justice Ruling in the Data Retention Case and Its Lessons for Privacy and Surveillance in the United States' (2015) 28 *Harvard Human Rights Journal* 65.
Forde A, 'The Conceptual Relationship between Privacy and Data Protection' (2016) 1 *Cambridge Law Review* 135.
Frantziou E, 'Further Developments in the Right to be Forgotten: The European Court of Justice's Judgment in Case C-131/12, Google Spain, SL, Google Inc v Agencia Espanola de Proteccion de Datos' (2014) 14(4) *Human Rights Law Review* 766.
Frenzel EM, 'Facilitating the Flow of Public Information: The CJEU in Favour of Distinctive Rule/Exception Regulations in Member States Journal Article' (2017) 3(2) *European Data Protection Law Review* 286.
González Fuster G, *The Emergence of Personal Data Protection as a Fundamental Right of the EU* (Springer 2014).
Hijmans H, 'Evidence of Effective Data Protection: Case C-131/12 Google v. Agencia Española de Protectión de Datos (AEPD) and Mario Costeja Gonzalez, Judgment of 13 May 2014' (2014) 21(3) *Maastricht Journal of European and Comparative Law* 556.
Hijmans H, 'PNR Agreement EU-Canada Scrutinised: CJEU Gives Very Precise Guidance to Negotiators' (2017) 3 *European Data Protection Law Review*.
Hijmans, H, *The European Union as Guardian of Internet Privacy: The Story of Art 16 TFEU* (Springer 2016).

Hirschl R, 'The Judicialization of Politics' in GA Caldeira, RD Kelemen, and KE Whittington (eds), *The Oxford Handbook of Law and Politics* (OUP 2009).
Jones J, 'Control-alter-delete: the "right to be forgotten"' (2014) *European Intellectual Property Review* 599.
Jozwiak M, 'The Scale Matters: The ECtHR Grand Chamber Finds That Prohibition of Mass Publication of 'Raw' Taxation Data Does Not Infringe Right to Freedom of Expression' (2018) 4(1) *European Data Protection Law Review* 127.
Kosta E, 'The Way to Luxembourg: National Court Decisions on the Compatibility of the Data Retention Directive with the Rights to Privacy and Data Protection' (2013) 10(3) SCRIPTed 339.
Kowalik-Bańczyk K, 'International Constitutionalisation of Protection of Privacy on the Internet: the Google Case Example' in A Jakubowski and K Wierczyńska, *Fragmentation vs the Constitutionalisation of International Law: A Practical Inquiry* (Routledge 2016).
Kulk S and F Zuiderveen Borgesius, 'Google Spain v. González: Did the Court Forget About Freedom of Expression?'(2014) 5(3) *European Journal of Risk Regulation* 389.
Kulk S and F Zuiderveen Borgesius, 'Privacy, Freedom of Expression and the Right to Be Forgotten in Europe' in E Selinger Polonetsky J and O Tene (eds), *The Cambridge Handbook of Consumer Privacy* (Cambridge 2018).
Kuner C, 'Google Spain in the EU and International Context' (2015) 22(1) *Maastricht Journal of European and Comparative Law* 163.
Lenaerts K, I Maselis and K Gutman, *EU Procedural Law* (Oxford 2014).
Lynskey O, 'The Data Retention Directive is incompatible with the rights to privacy and data protection and is invalid in its entirety: Digital Rights Ireland' (2014) 51(6) *Common Market Law Review* 1789.
Lynskey O, *The Foundations of EU Data Protection Law* (Oxford 2015).
Mak E, *Judicial Decision-Making in a Globalised World: A Comparative Analysis of the Changing Practices of Western Highest Courts* (Hart 2013).
Mbioh WR, 'Post-och Telestyrelsen and Watson and the Investigatory Powers Act 2016' (2017) 3 *European Data Protection Law Review* 273.
Meyer J (ed), *Charta der Grundrechte der Europäischen Union* (Nomos 2011).
Milanovic M, 'The Grand Normalization of Mass Surveillance: ECtHR Grand Chamber Judgments in Big Brother Watch and Centrum för rättvisa' (EJIL:Talk!, 26 May 2021) https://www.ejiltalk.org/the-grand-normalization-of-mass-surveillance-ecthr-grand-chamber-judgments-in-big-brother-watch-and-centrum-for-rattvisa.
Muir E, 'The Fundamental Rights Implications of EU Legislation: Some Constitutional Challenges' (2014) 51 *Common Market Law Review* 226.
Ni Loideain N, 'Not So Grand: The Big Brother Watch ECtHR Grand Chamber judgment' (Information Law and Policy Centre, 28 May 2021) https://infolawcentre.blogs.sas.ac.uk/2021/05/28/not-so-grand-the-big-brother-watch-ecthr-grand-chamber-judgment.
Ojanen T, 'Making the Essence of Fundamental Rights Real: The Court of Justice of the European Union Clarifies the Structure of Fundamental Rights under the Charter: ECJ 6 October 2015, Case C-362/14 Schrems M v Data Protection Commissioner' (2016) 12(2) *European Constitutional Law Review* 326.
Peers S, 'The CJEU's Google Spain judgment: failing to balance privacy and freedom of expression' (EU Law Analysis blog, 13 May 2014) http://eulawanalysis.blogspot.nl/2014/05/the-cjeus-google-spain-judgment-failing.html.
Petkova B, 'Towards an Internal Hierarchy of Values in the EU Legal Order: Balancing the Freedom of Speech and Data Privacy' (2016) 23(3) *Maastricht Journal of European and Comparative Law* 421.
Psychogiopoulou E, 'The European Court of Human Rights, Privacy and Data Protection in the Digital Era' in M Brkan and E Psychogiopoulou (eds) *Courts, Privacy and Data Protection in the Digital Environment* (Edward Elgar 2017).
Purtova N, *Property Rights in Personal Data: A European Perspective* (BOXPress 2011).
Rivers J, 'Proportionality and Variable Intensity of Review' (2006) 65(1) *The Cambridge Law Journal* 184.
Sajfert J, 'The Big Brother Watch and Centrum för Rättvisa judgments of the Grand Chamber of the European Court of Human Rights – the Altamont of privacy?' (*European Law Blog*, 8 June 2021) https://europeanlawblog.eu/2021/06/08/big-brother-watch-and-centrum-for-rattvisa-judgments-of-the-grand-chamber-of-the-european-court-of-human-rights-altamont-of-privacy.

Sandhu A, 'Die Tele2-Entscheidung des EuGH zur Vorratsdatenspeicherung in den Mitgliedstaaten und ihre Auswirkungen auf die Rechtslage in Deutschland und in der Europäischen Union' (2017) *Europarecht* 453–469.
Slaughter A-M, 'Judicial Globalization' (2000) 40 *Virginia Journal of International Law* 1103.
Spahiu I, 'Case Note: Google Spain and Google' (2015) 21(4) *European Public Law* 696.
Svantesson D J B, 'The Extraterritoriality of EU Data Privacy Law - Its Theoretical Justification and its Practical Effect on U.S. Businesses' (2013) 50(1) *Stanford Journal of International Law* 53.
Tracol X, 'The Judgment of the Grand Chamber dated 21 December 2016 in the two joint Tele2 Sverige and Watson cases: The need for a harmonised legal framework on the retention of data at EU level' (2017) *Computer Law & Security Review* 1.
Tzanou M, 'Data protection as a fundamental right next to privacy? "Reconstructing" a not so new right' (2013) 3(2) *International Data Privacy Law* 88.
Tzanou M, *The Fundamental Right to Data Protection: Normative Value in the Context of Counter-Terrorism Surveillance* (Hart 2017).
Vedaschi A and C Graziani, 'PNR Agreements Between Fundamental Rights and National Security: Opinion 1/15' (European Law Blog, 23 January 2018) http://europeanlawblog.eu/2018/01/23/pnr-agreements-between-fundamental-rights-and-national-security-opinion-115/.
Von Bogdandy A et al., 'Reverse Solange–Protecting the Essence of Fundamental Rights Against EU Member States' (2012) 49 *Common Market Law Review* 489.
Young A L, 'The Human Rights Act 1998, Horizontality and the Constitutionalisation of Private Law' in KS Ziegler and P Huber, *Current Problems in the Protection of Human Rights: Perspectives from Germany and the UK* (Hart 2013).

15. Surveillance at the borders: Travellers and their data protection rights[1]

Diana Dimitrova

I. INTRODUCTION

In the past years, people travelling to and from different parts of the world have been subject to more intensive identity checks, as well as to more sophisticated risk assessment measures. Profiling can start already *before* travellers reach an external border, for example with risk assessment in the framework of the Passenger Name Record (PNR). The checks continue *during the actual crossing*, e.g. through biometric identity checks and recording entry and exit details, especially of foreign nationals. And the data may be processed further *after the border has been crossed*, e.g. it could be re-used for law enforcement purposes and for monitoring the legality of people's stay in a foreign country.

The present chapter will examine the issue of surveillance at the borders, taking as starting point recent EU border control trends. In legal terms, in the EU 'border surveillance' refers to surveillance between border crossing points (BCPs) and of BCPs outside the working hours,[2] that is, it does not directly refer to checks on travellers. Therefore, this chapter will employ a different definition of surveillance, borrowed from Lyon, Marx and Gandy. They define surveillance as any data processing in order to influence or manage the data subjects, for instance to classify and sort them. Surveillance, they argue, is daily and routine, invisible and pre-emptive.[3]

Adapted to the border context, surveillance could refer to the collection of personal data by private and public authorities, e.g., by airlines or visa-issuing authorities; to the invisible flow of data from one entity to another one, e.g., from airlines to law-enforcement authorities and within them; to the building of individual profiles in order to assign travelling people to different risk categories and/or nationalities, to registered or non-registered travellers, etc. Most importantly, data and the created profiles are used to take decisions, for instance as to whether to grant someone a visa or not, to carry out deeper border checks, whether to detain someone, to admit a certain traveller into a certain country, etc. While the surveillance may not be daily or even routine for every traveller, the impact that it has on (also potential) travellers

---

1 The present chapter is based on research performed in the framework of the author's doctoral dissertation 'Data Subject Rights: The Rights to Access and Rectification in the Area of Freedom, Security and Justice' defended at the Vrije Universiteit Brussel, 2021.

2 Regulation (EU) 2016/399 of the European Parliament and of the Council of 9 March 2016 on a Union Code on the rules governing the movement of persons across borders (Schengen Borders Code) (2016) OJ L77/1, (Schengen Borders Code), art 2 (12).

3 The definitions of Lyon, Marx and Gandy are quoted by Colin J. Bennett, 'What Happens when you Book an Airline Ticket? The Collection and Processing of Passenger Data Post-9/11,' in Elia Zureik and Mark B. Salter (eds), *Global Surveillance and Policing: Borders, Security, Identity* (Willan Publishing 2005), p. 132.

is still significant, as decisions to refuse entry, to apprehend people at borders, to track their movements, etc., have a huge impact on their movements.

This situation gives rise to the question of how the main data protection principles are challenged by the new trends in border surveillance in the EU. The question is especially important as privacy and data protection are recognized fundamental rights in the EU legal order.[4]

To answer the question, first the global trends on border management will be presented in order to provide context to the discussion (section II). Secondly, we discuss the existing legal framework applicable to border control in the EU (section III). We will then present the main data processing operations to which travellers travelling to and from the EU are subject – from before they embark on the journey, until after the time they have crossed the border (section IV). The new EU interoperability framework will be presented, especially in terms of the changes it will bring about for the management of traveller data (section V).

These new initiatives are subsequently analysed from a data protection point (sections VI and VII). Our discussion will focus mainly on the impact of EU policy making on the main data protection principles (section VI) and on the safeguards for travellers trying to exercise their data subject rights (section VII). A final section will wrap up the discussion and conclude (section VIII).

II. GLOBAL BORDER CONTROL TRENDS: DIGITAL BORDERS, BIOMETRICS, BIG DATA AND INTEROPERABILITY

Travelling across international borders is not a new phenomenon. Neither is identifying travellers at borders and controlling their entries and exits, which has traditionally been an essential part of State's responsibilities. In the past decades, however, border control policies and processes globally have been changing tremendously, leading to the creation of what some call a 'new border architecture'.[5] Information technology and the fear of terrorism have been identified as the main drivers behind the said changes, and technology marks the major transformation in border management.[6]

As a result, borders are becoming digital.[7] New technologies are hailed and marketed as smarter technologies,[8] which is also seen in the name of programmes such as the EU Smart Borders Package (SBP).[9] With the help of these technologies authorities seek to sort legal from

---

[4] Charter of Fundamental Rights of the European Union (2012) OJ C326/391 (CFREU), arts 7 and 8.

[5] Demetrios G. Papademetriou and Elizabeth Collett, 'A New Architecture for Border Management,' (2011) Migration Policy Institute, p. 1.

[6] Dennis Broeders, 'The New Digital Borders of Europe: EU Databases and the Surveillance of Irregular Migrants,' (2007) 22(1), *International Sociology*, 71, 78. Papademetriou and Collett (n. 5) 14.

[7] Broeders (n. 6) 73.

[8] Elspeth Guild and Sergio Carrera, 'EU Borders and Their Controls: Preventing unwanted movement of people in Europe,' (2013) 6 (14) CEPS Essay, p. 4.

[9] European Commission, DG Migration and Home Affairs, *Smart Borders*, https://ec.europa.eu/home-affairs/what-we-do/policies/borders-and-visas/smart-borders_en accessed 03 January 2020.

the illegal travellers,[10] and the risky from the trusted.[11] This sorting is presented as a datified activity,[12] since it relies on the processing of vast amounts of personal data – both alphanumeric and biometric.

One hallmark of these information technologies is the growing reliance on biometric identifiers, such as facial images, fingerprints and iris scans, which are classified as sensitive data in the EU data protection framework.[13] They allow new modes of traveller identity verification and/or identification, e.g., through technologies deployed for Automated Border Control (ABC).

New databases containing such biometric identifiers, such as Registered Traveller Programme (RTP) databases, designed especially but not exclusively for Third Country Nationals (TCNs), allow authorities to create claims to someone's identity, alternative to official identity documents.[14] Thus, these traveller databases signify a shift towards identification through individual characteristics rather than nationality.[15] Further, biometric identities are accepted as a symbol of secure identities. Nations which do not issue biometric identities rank lower in the hierarchy of nations. Thus, the significance of biometric identification goes beyond that of individual identification at borders.[16] For example, the EU has granted visa waivers on condition TCNs hold biometric passports.[17]

Therefore, biometric based RTPs are part of the general trend of moving away from country-centric to person-centric border control.[18] RTPs are different from other border control measures in that they are voluntary programmes and the data collection is visible. In this way the registered traveller exchanges their data for a low-risk status and lighter border checks. It is thus a 'self-governance' tool and a valuable source for more hard facts about the passenger.[19]

---

[10] Broeders (n. 6) 71.

[11] Dennis Broeders, Erik Schrijvers, Bart van der Sloot, Rosamunde van Brakel, Josta de Hoog, Ernst Hirsch Ballin, 'Big Data and Security Policies: Towards a Framework for Regulating the Phases of Analytics and Use of Big Data,' (2017) 33 *Computer Law & Security Review*, 3019, 311.

[12] Ibid.

[13] Regulation (EU) 2016/679 of the European Parliament and of the Council of 27 April 2016 on the protection of natural persons with regard to the processing of personal data and on the free movement of such data, and repealing Directive 95/46/EC (General Data Protection Regulation), (2016) OJ L119/1, (GDPR), articles 4 (14) and 9.

[14] Guild and Carrera (n. 8) 8.

[15] Papademetriou and Collett (n. 5), 3–6.

[16] Benjamin J. Muller, 'Borders, Bodies and Biometrics: Towards Identity Management,' in Elia Zureik and Mark B. Salter (eds), *Global Surveillance and Policing: Borders, Security, Identity* (Willan Publishing 2005), p. 93.

[17] Jennifer Rankin, 'European Commission Faces Challenge to Grant Visa-free Travel to Turks,' *The Guardian* (Brussels, 4 May 2016) https://www.theguardian.com/world/2016/may/04/european-commission-urges-eu-backing-for-visa-free-travel-for-turks-ankara, accessed 27 December 2019.

[18] Guild and Carrera (n. 8) 7.

[19] Matthias Leese, 'Blurring the Dimensions of Privacy? Law Enforcement and Trusted Traveller Programmes,' (2013) 29 *Computer Law & Security Review,* 480, 486–7. Also compare the RTP to PNR, whereby the PNR consists of data provided by passengers when booking a plane ticket and whose accuracy cannot be verified at booking.

Currently several EU Member States and some third countries, such as Canada,[20] USA,[21] Japan[22] and Hong Kong[23] operate such programmes.

In addition, governments have been investing in large-scale information systems, both centralized and de-centralized, in an effort to collect and store more personal data of travelling people. This allows for sophisticated analysis to be performed on the data and for the tracking of travellers' movements. Examples from the EU are the already existing SIS II, VIS, Eurodac, PNR and the soon-to-be built Entry-Exit System (EES) and European Travel Information and Authorisation System (ETIAS). These databases will be further discussed below. Briefly, they target especially TCNs by enabling the tracking of their movements and imposing stricter entry requirements. Such trends have led some to refer to Europe as 'Fortress Europe' or 'Panoptycon Europe'.[24]

The described collection and sophisticated analysis of personal data have enabled governmental authorities to engage increasingly in traveller profiling, risk analysis and predictive data-mining, in a fashion of 'intelligence-led' policing.[25] This amassing and analysis of data in security domains is paving the way for big data analytics in the security and immigration sectors.[26] Traveller profiling is enabled by the data sharing framework between them and private actors, for instance in PNR where airline companies send detailed information on passengers to specially designated law enforcement units. Thus, private data collection has been playing a bigger role in security, supplementing government sources.[27]

Traveller profiling is also enabled by the data sharing collaboration between the border control and law enforcement authorities, blurring the lines between the two.[28] This development also occurs outside Europe. In the US, for instance, the FBI and CIA have been free to access immigration data.[29] This phenomenon of entanglement of law enforcement and

---

[20] CATSA, 'Trusted Travellers,' http://www.catsa.gc.ca/node/11 accessed 28 October 2021.

[21] Several programmes, amongst which Global Entry, available both for US citizens and a selected number of Third Countries: U.S. Customs and Border Protection, 'Eligibility for Global Entry,' 01 May 2017, https://www.cbp.gov/travel/trusted-traveler-programs/global-entry/eligibility accessed 28 October 2021 and U.S. Customs and Border Protection, 'Global Entry,' 03 July 2017 https://www.cbp.gov/travel/trusted-traveler-programs/global-entry accessed 28 October 2021.

[22] Immigration Bureau of Japan, 'Outline of the Trusted Traveller Programme,' (2016) http://www.immi-moj.go.jp/ttp2/en/outline/index.html accessed 28 October 2021.

[23] Immigration Department, The Government of the Hong Kong Special Administrative Region, 'e-Channel Services for Frequent Visitors,'11 January 2017, http://www.immd.gov.hk/eng/services/echannel_visitors.html accessed 28 October 2021.

[24] Broeders (n. 6) 74.

[25] Julien Jeandesboz, 'Reinforcing the Surveillance of EU Borders: The Future Development of FRONTEX and EUROSUR,' (2008) 11 Challenge Liberty and Security, p. 4; Didier Bigo, Sergio Carrera, Ben Hayes, Nichola Hernanz and Julien Jeandesboz, 'Justice and Home Affairs Databases and a Smart Borders System at the EU External Borders: An Evaluation of Current and Forthcoming Proposals,' (2012) 52 CEPS Paper in Liberty and Security in Europe, p. 2 and 3. Louise Amoore, 'Biometric Borders: Governing Mobilities in the War on Terror,' (2006) 25 *Political Geography* 336, 337.

[26] Broeders, Schrijvers, van der Sloot, van Brakel, de Hoog, Hirsch Ballin (n. 11) 315.

[27] Leese (n. 19) 487; Broeders, Schrijvers, van der Sloot, van Brakel, de Hoog, Hirsch Ballin (n. 11) 313.

[28] Bigo, Carrera, Hayes, Hernanz and Jeandesboz (n. 25) 1.

[29] Spencer Woodman, 'Palantir Enables Immigration Agents to Access Information from the CIA,' *The Intercept* (17.03.2017) https://theintercept.com/2017/03/17/palantir-enables-immigration-agents-to-access-information-from-the-cia/, accessed 15 December 2019.

immigration has been termed as 'crimmigration'.[30] A further step is the new EU framework on interoperability between the different Area of Freedom, Security and Justice (AFSJ) databases, which are normally used for different purposes.[31] Such 'information management' is characterized by information sharing by default, availability and interoperability.[32] It confirms the trend that border control extends within the borders, merging border control and internal control, which is made possible by the databases set up for multiple purposes.[33]

Data from social media and the information stored on travellers' mobile devices is also being caught in the border surveillance net(work). For example, in the USA the Electronic System for Travel Authorisation (ESTA) applicants are asked to provide details about their social networks. This means that the US authorities would be able to glean not only additional private information about the applicants, but also personal information about their social contacts.[34] Even if US-bound travellers decide not reveal this information, their electronic devices might still be seized at the border and under pressure their owners might be compelled to reveal their passwords.[35] This is not foreign to Europe. Recently in London a traveller was charged under the British Terrorism Act for refusing to provide the password to his mobile devices, where not only his information is stored, but also that of his clients, who are trying to prove their torture cases in which the US might be involved.[36]

III. THE EU LEGAL FRAMEWORK ON BORDER CHECKS

III.1 The Operational Texts: the Schengen Framework

We will now turn to the existing EU legal framework on border checks to look at the applicable legal instruments and main policies related to border control. This overview will provide

---

[30] Katja Franko Aas, ''Crimmigrant' Bodies and Bona Fide Travelers: Surveillance, Citizenship and Global Governance,' (2011) 15 (3) *Theoretical Criminology* 331.

[31] Regulation (EU) 2019/818 of the European Parliament and of the Council of 20 May 2019 on establishing a framework for interoperability between EU information systems in the field of police and judicial cooperation, asylum and migration and amending Regulations (EU) 2018/1726, (EU) 2018/1862 and (EU) 2019/816, (2019) OJ L135/85; Regulation (EU) 2019/817 of the European Parliament and of the Council of 20 May 2019 on establishing a framework for interoperability between EU information systems in the field of borders and visa and amending Regulations (EC) No 767/2008, (EU) 2016/399, (EU) 2017/2226, (EU) 2018/1240, (EU) 2018/1726 and (EU) 2018/1861 of the European Parliament and of the Council and Council Decisions 2004/512/EC and 2008/633/JHA, (2019) OJ L135/27 (Interoperability Regulations).

[32] Bigo, Carrera, Hayes, Hernanz and Jeandesboz (n. 25) 1 and 2.

[33] Ibid., 1 and 2. Broeders (n. 6) 72 and 87.

[34] The US Department of Homeland Security, 'Privacy Impact Assessment Update for the Electronic System for Travel Authorization (ESTA), DHS/CBP/PIA-007(g),' 1 September 2016, https://www.dhs.gov/sites/default/files/publications/privacy-pia-cbp-esta-september2016.pdf accessed 28 October 2021.

[35] Cora Currier, 'Lawmakers Move to Stop Warrantless Cellphone Searches at the U.S. Border,' *The Intercept*, (04 April 2017) https://theintercept.com/2017/04/04/lawmakers-move-to-stop-warrantless-cell-phone-searches-at-the-u-s-border/ accessed 28 October 2021.

[36] Ewen MacAskill, 'Cage Director Charged under Terrorism Act after Failing to Hand Over Passwords,' *The Guardian*, (17 May 2017) https://www.theguardian.com/uk-news/2017/may/17/cage-campaign-group-director-muhammed-rabbani-charged-under-terrorism-act, accessed 12 December 2019.

the background for our overview of specific surveillance measures and checks applied to travellers.

In EU law terms, border control consists of (1) border checks on persons and their means of transportation, especially to check whether persons fulfil the entry requirements, and (2) border surveillance of and between border crossing points.[37] The purposes of border control are to 'help combat illegal immigration and trafficking in human beings and to prevent any threat to the Member States' internal security, public policy, public health and international relations'.[38] In addition, border control includes 'an analysis of the risks for internal security and of the threats that may affect the security of external borders'.[39]

In the EU, border controls are just one aspect of the broader, already mentioned, concept of the AFSJ. The idea behind this concept is the abolition of border checks within the Schengen area, while at the same time establishing a common external border control, asylum and migration policy, accompanied by measures for police and judicial cooperation in order to guarantee the security within the area.[40] Policy making around the AFSJ embarked outside the then European Community/Union framework with the Schengen Agreement, in 1982, and the Convention Implementing the Schengen Agreement, in 1985.[41] Both Schengen texts (international conventions concluded between 'some' European states) were strictly speaking not part of EU law, but were evidently of interest to the EU (then European Community). The Amsterdam Treaty consequently integrated these border control mechanisms into the EU framework, in the previous first pillar, and police and judicial cooperation in the more intergovernmental ex-third pillar.[42] The Lisbon Treaty 'shifted' all the AFSJ policies to the former 'first pillar,' so they would be part of the unionized policies and no longer a part of the intergovernmental structures of the EU. The analysis further below will demonstrate how the AFSJ policies interact with each other, especially how border control is becoming more and more intertwined with internal security and police and judicial cooperation policies.

The rules on border checks on persons are further regulated in detail in secondary law, namely in the regulation called the Schengen Borders Code (SBC). The SBC prescribes the steps that have to be followed by border guards at the border. Not every traveller is subject to the same checks. This depends on whether the traveller is broadly speaking a citizen enjoying the Union right to free movement[43] or a TCN. In addition to the Schengen Borders Code, the legal instruments regulating the usage of the AFSJ background information systems, as well as regulatory instruments on travel documents and free movement provisions,[44] provide

---

[37] Schengen Borders Code, art 2 (10), (11) and (12).

[38] Ibid., recital 6.

[39] Ibid., recital 8.

[40] Consolidated Version of the Treaty on the Functioning of the European Union (2012) OJ C326/47, (hereinafter 'TFEU'), art 67. Emphasis added.

[41] Broeders (n. 6) 77.

[42] Francesca Ferraro, 'Schengen Governance after the Lisbon Treaty,' (2013) 120358REV1 European Parliament, Library Briefing, https://www.europarl.europa.eu/RegData/bibliotheque/briefing/2013/130358/LDM_BRI(2013)130358_REV1_EN.pdf accessed 28 October 2021, p. 1; Sarah Wolff, 'EU Integrated Border Management beyond Lisbon: Contrasting Policies and Practice,' *CESP*, 23 https://www.clingendael.nl/sites/default/files/20100900_cesp_chapter_wolff.pdf accessed 28 October 2021.

[43] I.e. Citizens of the EU/EEA/CH and some of their family members who are TCNs.

[44] E.g. Council Regulation (EC) No 2252/2004 of 13 December 2004 on standards for security features and biometrics in passports and travel documents issued by Member States (2004) OJ L385/1

further regulatory requirements on border checks. An overview of the information systems is provided at the end of this section.

The legal instruments establishing and regulating the powers of several EU bodies and agencies are also part of the legal landscape of border surveillance and control. These agencies are beginning to play an increasing role in the risk assessment of travellers. The main ones are the European Border and Coast Guard Agency, which, together with the Member State authorities responsible for border management and returns of TCNs, form the European Border and Coast Guard (EBCG).[45] The EBCG Agency (known also as FRONTEX), together with the Member States, is responsible for the implementation of the European integrated border management (EIBM).[46] In addition, Europol – the EU's law enforcement agency which supports Member States' law enforcement cooperation – also plays a part in traveller checks and risk assessment. EASO – the EU Asylum Support Office – supports the Member States' asylum authorities, but does not have executive powers.[47] Finally, when it comes to the EU large-scale information systems, which are explicitly mentioned as an element of the state-of-the art technologies whose development and usage is encouraged in the EIBM,[48] eu-LISA is responsible for their operational management but also for the set-up of new databases, such as the EES and ETIAS.[49]

III.2 The Data Protection Framework for Border Controls

The processing of personal data, whether in the framework of large-scale information systems or not, is essential for border checks. Thus, another key element of the regulatory framework is data protection provisions. On a primary law level, Article 7 of the Charter of Fundamental Rights of the EU (CFREU) and Articles 8 CFREU and Article 16 TFEU on the fundamental rights to privacy and data protection are applicable to Member State authorities when carrying out border checks. In addition, Article 8 of the European Convention on Human Rights on the right to private life is applicable, too. On a secondary law level, the applicable data protection regime is rather complex. The General Data Protection Regulation (GDPR), replacing Directive 95/46/EC, is applicable to the processing of data for administrative purposes, for instance to check whether a certain travel document is still valid or when processing visa applications of TCNs.[50]

(e-Passport Regulation) and Directive 2004/38/EC of the European Parliament and of the Council of 29 April 2004 on the right of citizens of the Union and their family members to move and reside freely within the territory of the Member States amending Regulation (EEC) No 1612/68 and repealing Directives 64/221/EEC, 68/360/EEC, 72/194/EEC, 73/148/EEC, 75/34/EEC, 75/35/EEC, 90/364/EEC, 90/365/EEC and 93/96/EEC (2004) OJ L158/77.

[45] Regulation (EU) 2019/1896 of the European Parliament and of the Council of 13 November 2019 on the European Border and Coast Guard and repealing Regulations (EU) No 1052/2013 and (EU) 2016/1624 (2019) OJ L295/1 (EBCG Regulation), art 4.

[46] EBCG Regulation, art 7.

[47] https://easo.europa.eu/about-us accessed 28 October 2021.

[48] EBCG Regulation, art 3(j).

[49] https://www.eulisa.europa.eu/About-Us/Who-We-Are accessed 28 October 2021.

[50] E.g. Regulation (EC) No 767/2008 of the European Parliament and of the Council of 9 July 2008 concerning the Visa Information System (VIS) and the exchange of data between Member States on short-stay visas (VIS Regulation) (2008) OJ L218/60, recital 17; e-Passport Regulation, recital 8.

However, border checks and border control also aim to prevent threats such as security threats to the Member States. To that end, for example, national, international (Interpol) and European (SIS II) databases on wanted criminals or suspects, and stolen objects, may be consulted, or risk analysis under the PNR system can performed.[51] Such processing of personal data falls outside the scope of the GDPR and is regulated by the new Directive on Data Protection in the law enforcement sector (Directive 2016/680).[52]

This distinction in data protection regimes has historical roots and remained even after the entry into force of the Lisbon Treaty. This is because the Lisbon Treaty retained certain special provisions for judicial and police cooperation in criminal matters due to the 'specific nature of these fields'.[53] The EU institutions/bodies/agencies add a further level of complication since they are subject to a different data protection regime. Some bodies, e.g., the EBCG Agency, are subject to the data protection regime of Regulation 2018/1725, a data protection instrument which applies to most EU institutions, agencies and bodies.[54] However, ex-third pillar bodies such as Europol have their own data protection rules enshrined in their respective legal frameworks and, at present, are not subject to Regulation 2018/1725. However, in the future they will be subject to Chapter IX of it, which resembles the provisions of Directive 2016/680.[55] Thus, it is already evident that the protection of personal data in the border control context is rather complex and that the regulatory framework is fragmented.

Before moving on to presenting the border checks in more detail, Table 15.1 shows the main EU databases used when checking travelling people is presented.

---

[51] See Table 15.1 below.

[52] E.g., compare Regulation (EC) No 1987/2006 of the European Parliament and of the Council on the establishment, operation and use of the second generation Schengen Information System (SIS II) (2006) OJ L381/4, recital 21; Directive (EU) 2016/681 of the European Parliament and of the Council of 27 April 2016 on the use of passenger name record (PNR) data for the prevention, detection, investigation and prosecution of terrorist offences and serious crime (2016) OJ L119/132 (EU PNR Directive), recital 27; Directive (EU) 2016/680 of the European Parliament and of the Council of 27 April 2016 on the protection of natural persons with regard to the processing of personal data by competent authorities for the purposes of the prevention, investigation, detection or prosecution of criminal offences or the execution of criminal penalties, and on the free movement of such data, and repealing Council Framework Decision 2008/977/JHA (2016) OJ L119/89, (Directive 2016/680) art 1.

[53] Declaration (No. 21) to the TFEU on the protection of personal data in the fields of judicial cooperation in criminal matters and police cooperation (2016) OJ C202/345.

[54] Regulation (EU) 2018/1725 of the European Parliament and of the Council of 23 October 2018 on the protection of natural persons with regard to the processing of personal data by the Union institutions, bodies, offices and agencies and on the free movement of such data, and repealing Regulation (EC) No 45/2001 and Decision No 1247/2002/EC (2018) OJ L295/39 (Regulation 2018/1725).

[55] Shara Monteleone, 'Briefing – EU Legislation in Progress. Rules for EU institutions' processing of personal data,' (2018) European Parliamentary Research Service; Chapter IX Regulation 2018/1725; See also the proposed amendments to the Europol legal basis which clearly intends to make Regulation 2018/1725 applicable to Europol: European Commission, Proposal for a Regulation of the European Parliament and of the Council amending Regulation (EU) 2016/794, as regards Europol's cooperation with private parties, the processing of personal data by Europol in support of criminal investigations, and Europol's role on research and innovation' COM (2020) 796 final, 09 December 2020.

Table 15.1 EU databases related to checks on travelling people in the EU

Info System Features	Schengen Information System[1]	VIS[2]	EURODAC	EU PNR[3] – decentralized	API/Nominal Lists (NL) – decentralized	Entry-Exit System[4] (In development)	ETIAS (In development)[5]
Personal and material scope	Alerts on Third Country Nationals (TCNs) against whom there are entry bans. Alerts on persons and objects for the purpose of police and judicial cooperation in criminal matters, e.g. criminals, witnesses, missing persons, individuals subject to discreet surveillance; stolen identity documents, banknotes, vehicles. TCNs subject to return decisions (SIS III) Unknown wanted persons (SIS III)	TCNs who are applying for a short-stay Schengen visa, who have been granted such a visa, whose visa has been refused, revoked, cancelled or extended.	Current[6] and Proposed Amendment (P.Am.)[7] TCNs or stateless persons who apply for international protection (refugees, asylum seekers). TCNS or stateless persons who are apprehended for having irregularly crossed the EU external borders or having been found as illegally staying in a MS. P.Am. – individuals subject to return decisions.	Any air passenger flying in and out of the EU. Possibility to include intra-EU flights.	API: All passengers travelling by airplane.[8] NL: Cruise ship passengers.[9]	Short-stay TCNs (both visa exempt and requiring visa). TCNs whose entry has been refused.	Visa-exempt TCNs who are short-stayers.

Info System Features	Schengen Information System[1]	VIS[2]	EURODAC	EU PNR[3] – decentralized	API/Nominal Lists (NL) – decentralized	Entry-Exit System[4] (In development)	ETIAS (In development)[5]
Personal data	R: Alphanumeric data, e.g. names, nationality, sex, date and place of birth, nationality, permanent physical characteristics. Also photographs and fingerprints. Doc number and date of issue (in cases of misused identity). Type of offence and data on objects, e.g. on identity papers and vehicle identification, European Arrest Warrant (criminal cooperation). SIS III: also palm prints and identity document details/ copies, DNA, facial images, national registration number.	Alphanumeric data: e.g. name, application and visa sticker number, travel document number, issuing authority and expiration date, nationality, date of birth. Biometric data: 10 fingerprints and facial image.[10]	In the Central System: fingerprints, sex, EU MS of origin, MS reference number, date of fingerprinting and transmitting the data to the EURODAC central server and further metadata (asylum seekers and apprehended as illegally crossing a border). Those apprehended as illegally residing in a MS shall not have their fingerprint data stored in the Central System. P. Am. – name(s), age, date of birth, nationality, identity documents, as well as a facial image. Also, data of illegally residing TCNs to be stored in the Central System. Fingerprinting of children as of 6 years of age, not 14.	18 categories of data, taken from the booking details, e.g. names, travel document number, expiration date, issuing authority, sex, date of birth, nationality, payment details, seating, dietary requirements, contact information, travel itinerary, status (e.g. checked-in), any changes to the above information. (Annex I)	API: Alphanumeric data, e.g. names, travel document number and type, date of birth, nationality, Member States of entry, embarkation port, departure and arrival times. NL: API + ports of embarkation and disembarkation.	TCNs with visas: names, DoB, nationality/ies, sex, type, number three letter code of issuing country of the travel documents; expiry date of travel document; facial image. At entry – date and time, BCP, visa number and issuing state, type of visa, last day of authorized stay, expiry date of visa. At exit – date and time, BCP, visa data update if necessary; participation in national facilitation programme. Visa-exempt TCNs: same as above, but excludes visa data; includes fingerprints (12y+); participation in national facilitation programme.	Names, date of birth, sex, place and country of birth, nationalities, first names of parents, travel document details, residential address, email address, phone number, level of education, job group, Member State and possibly address of first intended stay, for minors – details about parents, if applicable – details of the organisation submitting the application on behalf of the applicant, if applicable – details about being a family member of EU/EEA/CH, whether the applicant has been convicted of any of the predefined criminal offences, or been subject to return decisions or decisions requiring him to leave a Member State of the EU or a list of Third Countries, whether they have been in a conflict zone within the previous 20 years and where, and the IP address from which the application was submitted. ETIAS watchlist: surname (at birth) and other names, date of birth, travel document details, home address, email and phone number, IP address, name, e-mail address, mailing address, phone number of a firm or organisation; possibly first names, sex, nationality, country and place of birth.

Info System Features	Schengen Information System[1]	VIS[2]	EURODAC	EU PNR[3] – decentralized	API/Nominal Lists (NL) – decentralized	Entry-Exit System[4] (In development)	ETIAS (In development)[5]
Purpose	Ensure public security and public policy, apply the free movement of persons provisions, including border control. Refuse entry or stay in Schengen MS (Art. 31 (1)). Reacting to the different alerts. Carry out return (SIS III)	Implement the common visa policy, facilitate border checks, identify persons who do not fulfil the entry and stay requirements, facilitate the asylum application, prevent threats to MS internal security. Contribute to the prevention, detection or investigation of terrorist offences and other serious offences.	Apply the Dublin Convention, e.g. identify the Member State responsible for examining the application for international protection (Article. Law-enforcement purposes. Member States may use the data they collect for EURODAC for own purposes. P.Am. – Wider immigration purposes, e.g. return, not only asylum purposes.	Preventing, detecting, investigating and prosecuting terrorist offences and serious crime.	API: Advance checks to improve border control and fight against illegal immigration. Possibility to use the data for law-enforcement purposes.	Recording the entry and exit details of the concerned TCNs, calculation of authorized stay, generation of alerts when authorized stay expires, recording the refusal of entry; prevention, detection and investigation of serious crime and terrorism. Enhance efficiency of border checks, help identify TCNs who do not satisfy the conditions for entering and residing in the EU, help identify overstayers, check refusals of stay electronically, enable automation of border checks, grant visa authorities access on the lawful use of previous visas, inform TCNs of the duration of their authorized stay, gather statistics, combat identity fraud and the misuse of travel documents.	High level security by a thorough security risk assessment, prevention of illegal migration, public health, enhance effectiveness of border checks, prevention, detection and investigation of serious crime and terrorism, support the objectives of SIS.

Info System Features	Schengen Information System[1]	VIS[2]	EURODAC	EU PNR[3] – decentralized	API/Nominal Lists (NL) – decentralized	Entry-Exit System[4] (In development)	ETIAS (In development)[5]
Access rights	Border control, visa and immigration authorities, authorities responsible for police and customs checks within the Member States, national judicial authorities. Vehicle registration authorities.[11] Europol – alerts for arrest, discreet or specific checks, objects for seizure or use as evidence in criminal proceedings. Eurojust – alerts on persons for arrest, missing persons, witnesses, objects. Broader access to Europol and Eurojust, EBCG and its teams, e.g. return alerts (SIS III).	Visa, asylum and border control authorities, authorities may carry out checks on the territory of Member States to check whether individuals fulfil the requirements on entry into, stay and residence in the Member States.[12]	Immigration authorities, Member State law-enforcement authorities and Europol. P.Am. – eu-LISA to process real personal data for testing purposes and to receive information on false hits.	Member State Passenger Information Units (PIUs).	Border control authorities Possibility also for law-enforcement authorities (API)	Border, immigration, visa authorities; Member States' designated law-enforcement authorities and Europol.	ETIAS Central Unit; Member State national Units for ETIAS, border guards (only to check the status of a n authorization and flags), carriers (only to status of authorization), immigration authorities; Europol: in cases of hits against Europol data and access to the ETIAS watchlist; Member State law enforcement authorities.

Info System Features	Schengen Information System[1]	VIS[2]	EURODAC	EU PNR[3] – decentralized	API/Nominal Lists (NL) – decentralized	Entry-Exit System[4] (In development)	ETIAS (In development)[5]
Search options/ Data	1:n searches with alphanumeric data (name and data of birth).[13] 1:1 verifications with biometric data.[14] 1:1 verification of biometric data. 1:n fingerprint searches, 1:n facial image searches for consistency purposes with the EES (SIS III).	At the border: 1:n searches with the visa sticker number, 1:1 verification of fingerprints. Possibility to perform 1:n searches with the fingerprints for identification purposes at the border, inside Member States and for asylum application examination.	1:n searches of the applicants for international protection and those apprehended as illegally staying with the fingerprints stored in the Central System. Comparison of fingerprints for LEA purposes. P.Am. – searches with facial images in combination with fingerprints. Allows searches with facial images and fingerprints of all three categories of individuals against all the stored data.	Comparing the PNR data against law enforcement information systems.	Not specified.	At the border – alphanumeric 1:n search at each entry and exit; TCNs with visas are searched against VIS directly from the EES; when file found – 1:1 facial verification against facial images stored in EES or 1:1 finger verification against EES (visa exempt) or against VIS (TCNs with visa). If no file found, verification fails or there are doubts about the traveller's identity, 1:n biometric identification against EES. For visa-holding TCNs – also 1:n identification in VIS. If no file found on visa exempt TCNs, 1:n identification against VIS. Visa authorities: 1:n searches with alphanumeric data, visa number, fingerprints and/or facial image. National facilitation programme: 1:n alphanumeric and/or biometric searches. Checks within MS territory: 1:n alphanumeric search + 1:1 biometric verification. If verification fails, no record in EES found or doubts on identity, 1:n biometric identification.	In the application stage – submitted data automatically checked against information systems, e.g. SIS II, VIS, EES, Eurodac, Interpol and Europol, ETIAS screening rules, ETIAS watchlist. Manual verification of hits. By carriers: 1:n search with the Machine Readable Zone of the travel document and Member State of entry. At the border: 1:n search with the Machine Readable Zone of the travel document. Immigration authorities: 1:n search with names, nationality, date/place/country of birth, travel document details, sex, first name of parents. LEA access: 1:n search with a pre-defined set of alphanumeric data.

Notes:

1. **SIS II (still applicable)**: Regulation (EC) No 1987/20061 of the European Parliament and of the Council on the establishment, operation and use of the second generation Schengen Information System (SIS II) (2006) OJ L381/4; Council Decision 2007/533/JHA on the establishment, operation and use of the second generation Schengen Information System (SIS II) (2007) OJ L205/63. **SIS III (not yet applicable)**: Regulation (EU) 2018/1862 of the European Parliament and of the Council of 28 November

2018 on the establishment, operation and use of the Schengen Information System (SIS) in the field of police cooperation and judicial cooperation in criminal matters, amending and repealing Council Decision 2007/533/JHA, and repealing Regulation (EC) No 1986/2006 of the European Parliament and of the Council and Commission Decision 2010/261/EU (2018) OJ L312/56; Regulation (EU) 2018/1861 of the European Parliament and of the Council of 28 November 2018 on the establishment, operation and use of the Schengen Information System (SIS) in the field of border checks, and amending the Convention implementing the Schengen Agreement, and amending and repealing Regulation (EC) No 1987/2006 (2018) OJ L312/14; Regulation (EU) 2018/1860 of the European Parliament and of the Council of 28 November 2018 on the use of the Schengen Information System for the return of illegally staying third-country nationals (2018) OJ L312/1.

[2.] VIS Regulation (n. 49).

[3.] EU PNR Directive (n. 51).

[4.] Regulation (EU) 2017/2226 of the European Union and of the Council of 30 November 2017 establishing an Entry/Exit System (EES) to register entry and exit data and refusal of entry data of third-country nationals crossing the external borders of the Member States and determining the conditions for access to the EES for law-enforcement purposes, and amending the Convention implementing the Schengen Agreement and Regulations (EC) No 767/2008 and (EU) No 1077/2011 (2017) OJ L327/20 (EES Regulation).

[5.] Regulation (EU) 2018/1240 of the European Parliament and of the Council of 12 September 2018 establishing a European Travel Information and Authorisation System (ETIAS) and amending Regulations (EU) No 1077/2011, (EU) No 515/2014, (EU) 2016/399, (EU) 2016/1624 and (EU) 2017/2226 (2018) OJ L236/1 (ETIAS Regulation).

[6.] Regulation (EU) No 603/2013 of the European Parliament and of the Council of 26 June 2013 on the establishment of 'Eurodac' for the comparison of fingerprints for the effective application of Regulation (EU) No 604/2013 establishing the criteria and mechanisms for determining the Member State responsible for examining an application for international protection lodged in one of the Member States by a third-country national or a stateless person and on requests for the comparison with Eurodac data by Member States' law enforcement authorities and Europol for law enforcement purposes, and amending Regulation (EU) No 1077/2011 establishing a European Agency for the operational management of large-scale IT systems in the area of freedom, security and justice (recast) (2013) OJ L180/1.

[7.] Proposal for a Regulation of the European Parliament and of the Council on the establishment of 'Eurodac' for the comparison of fingerprints for the effective application of [Regulation (EU) No 604/2013 establishing the criteria and mechanisms for determining the Member State responsible for examining an application for international protection lodged in one of the Member States by a third-country national or a stateless person], for identifying an illegally staying third-country national or stateless person and on requests for the comparison with Eurodac data by Member States' law enforcement authorities and Europol for law enforcement purposes (recast), Brussels, COM(2016) 272 final, 4.5.2016.

[8.] Council Directive 2004/82/EC of 29 April 2004 on the obligation of carriers to communicate passenger data (2004) OJ L261/24 (API Directive).

[9.] Annex VI, Chapter III, Schengen Borders Code (2016) OJ L77/1.

[10.] VIS Regulation, article 9 (4); Regulation (EC) No 810/2009 of the European Parliament and of the Council of 13 July 2009 establishing a Community Code on Visas (2009) OJ L243/1, art (1) and (2).

[11.] Regulation (EC) No 1986/2006 of the European Parliament and of the Council of 20 December 2006 regarding access to the second generation Schengen Information System (SIS II) by the services in the Member States responsible for issuing vehicle registration certificates (2006) OJ L381/1.

[12.] Council Decision 2008/633/JHA of 23 June 2008 concerning access for consultation of the Visa Information System (VIS) by designated authorities of Member States and by Europol for the purposes of the prevention, detection and investigation of terrorist offences and of other serious criminal offences (2008) OJ L218/129.

[13.] Costica Dumbrava, 'Revision of the Schengen Information System for border checks,' European Parliamentary Research Service, Briefing: EU Legislation in Progress (2017) http://www.europarl.europa.eu/RegData/etudes/BRIE/2017/599341/EPRS_BRI(2017)599341_EN.pdf, accessed 10 December 2019.

[14.] 'Second generation Schengen Information System (SIS II) – former 1st pillar regulation,' (2010) Eurlex, http://eur-lex.europa.eu/legal-content/en/TXT/?uri=URISERV: l14544, accessed 15 November 2019.

IV. PROCESSING OF TRAVELLER DATA: IDENTIFICATION, ELIGIBILITY AND RISK ASSESSMENT

This section will walk the reader though the steps concerning traveller identification and risk assessment, paying special attention to data collection and further processing.

IV.1 Travellers' Data are Collected and Analysed Before Starting the Journey

In the first place, before travellers set out on a journey to or from a Schengen border, they have to possess a valid travel document. For EU citizens and citizens of the European Economic Area (EEA) and Switzerland this could be either an ID card or a passport, whereas TCNs always need to present a passport. When applying for a passport, the EU/EEA/Swiss citizens have to provide two of their fingerprints and a facial image, which are stored on the chip of the passport, in addition to alphanumeric data such as name, date of birth, nationality, etc.[56] As of August 2021, the ID cards of EU citizens issued by their Member State of nationality and the residence documents issued to EU citizens and their family members when exercising their right to free movement would also have to contain a chip storing a facial image and two fingerprints next to the alphanumeric data.[57]

Additionally, the TCNs who are under a visa obligation have to apply for a visa, undergoing a risk and eligibility assessment, and have their alphanumeric and biometric data recorded in the Visa Information System (VIS).[58]

As to the visa-exempt TCNs who would visit the EU on a short stay, in the future they will need to apply for an electronic authorization in the framework of the Electronic Travel Information and Authorisation System (ETIAS), the purpose of which is to fill a perceived information gap about these travellers.[59] The data submitted in ETIAS, which do not include biometric data, will be checked not only against the existing EU large databases, e.g., SIS, but also against specially pre-established screening rules which are explicitly referred to as 'an algorithm enabling profiling' within the meaning of the GDPR.[60] Whereas a member of a national authority will always have to verify hits and take manually a decision to grant or refuse a travel authorization,[61] the process leading to such a decision is largely influenced by algorithms.

Another interesting upcoming feature is the ETIAS watchlist, a newly established database with names of persons suspected of terrorism or other serious crimes. It will be fed by Member

---

[56] Regulation (EC) No 444/2009 of the European Parliament and of the Council of 28 May 2009 amending Council Regulation (EC) No 2252/2004 on standards for security features and biometrics in passports and travel documents issued by Member States (2009) OJ L142/1.

[57] Regulation (EU) 2019/1157 of the European Parliament and of the Council of 20 June 2019 on strengthening the security of identity cards of Union citizens and of residence documents issued to Union citizens and their family members exercising their right of free movement (2019) OJ L188/67, art 3 (5).

[58] See VIS Regulation.

[59] Explanatory Memorandum, Proposal for a Regulation of the European Parliament and of the Council establishing a European Travel Information and Authorization System (ETIAS) and amending Regulations (EU) 515/2014, (EU) 2016/399, (EU) 2016/794 and (EU) 2016/1624, COM (2016) 731 final, Brussels, 16.11.2016, 20.

[60] ETIAS Regulation, art 33.

[61] ETIAS Regulation, art 26.

State law enforcement authorities and Europol, and it will be consulted when ETIAS applications are examined.[62] This means that Europol will influence who may enter the EU.

Furthermore, under ETIAS the background information systems will be consulted not only during the application process, but also routinely, i.e., not only the applications but also the granted authorizations will be checked. A match could conditionally lead to revoking the already granted travel authorization.[63] Therefore, the monitoring of travellers' eligibility to enter the EU would be continuous, i.e., not only at the time of the application and the actual border crossing.

Another pre-border data collection and risk assessment operation occurs in the framework of RTPs or as far as TCNs travelling to and from the EU are concerned – national facilitation programme. Pursuant to these programmes, travellers may apply for membership by providing their biometric data and go through a pre-screening process, including about whether they pose a security threat by verifying whether alerts on them exist in the SIS II.[64] Once 'cleared', the travellers are treated as *bona fide* and would benefit from lighter checks at the borders.[65] Border guards may still deny them entry in accordance with the applicable border control law if they detect irregularities.

Finally, before air passengers start their trip to or from the EU, their API and PNR data are supposed to be sent to border control or law-enforcement authorities of the concerned EU Member State of destination which operate such programmes, respectively.[66] On the basis of the PNR data, pre-checks will be carried out and the passengers will be profiled against pre-established profiles and risk criteria.[67] This is to assess the risk they pose to the EU Member States. This means that all air passengers will soon undergo an assessment for potential involvement in serious crime and terrorism. In addition, the EU is exploring the opportunity for expanding the PNR measures beyond air traffic.[68] A similar pre-check is supposed to take place in the framework of maritime travel. To that end, the nominal lists of cruise ship passengers are also sent to the border guard authorities.[69]

IV.2 Data are Collected and Further Processed at the Border

The data collection and further processing continues when travellers arrive at the border. There, they are checked according to the process prescribed in the Schengen Borders Code

---

62 ETIAS Regulation, art 34.

63 ETIAS Regulation, art 41.

64 Regulation (EU) 2017/2225 of the European Parliament and of the Council of 30 November 2017 amending Regulation (EU) 2016/399 as regards the use of the Entry/Exit System (2017) OJ L327/1 Regulation 2017/2225, article 8d; EES Regulation, art 25.

65 Regulation 2017/2225, art 8d (2).

66 EU PNR Directive, art 8 and API Directive, art 3.

67 EU PNR Directive.

68 Council of the European Union, *Widening the scope of passenger name record (PNR) data legislation to transport forms other than air traffic - An impact assessment - Draft Council Conclusions* (Document number 12649/19); See also 'Belgian Act on Passenger Name Records published,' Stibbe/Lexology (Belgium, 24 February 2017) http://www.lexology.com/library/detail.aspx?g=bff6b66b-0f27-415d-8ba2-217732b836f5 accessed 29 October 2019.

69 Annex VI Schengen Borders Code.

(SBC), especially in Article 8 of the SBC.[70] The SBC distinguishes between EU citizens and TCNs. Thus, it provides for different checks on those who enjoy the Union right to free movement (URFM), i.e., EU citizens, citizens of the EEA and Switzerland (CH), as well as certain of their TCN family members, and the other category of travellers, which consists of the remaining TCNs.

According to Article 8(2) SBC, with regards to all categories of travellers, in the course of the border check border guards should establish the traveller's identity on the basis of the travel document (TD) presented. A TD inspection includes examining whether:

1. A certain traveller is the rightful holder of the travel document;[71]
2. The TD is lost, stolen, invalidated or misappropriated via a search in EU background databases such as SIS II, Interpol and relevant national databases;
3. The TD is authentic, i.e., inspecting the TD for signs of falsification and counterfeiting;
4. The TD is valid by looking at its validity/expiry date.

For EU/EEA/CH travellers if there are doubts about the authenticity of the travel document or the identity of its holder, the border guard should verify the biometric identifiers stored on the chip by matching them against the live biometrics presented (1:1 match).[72] Although this possibility existed already under Regulation 2252/2004, there was previously no such obligation under the SBC.[73] This is an example of the creeping-in of biometric data into the identity check on a broader category of travellers.

Until April 2017 border guards were supposed to check on a non-systematic basis whether a URFM traveller presents a 'genuine, present and sufficiently serious' threat to public policy, internal security, health and international relations of the Member States.[74] This is performed by searching the alerts on persons in the SIS II or relevant national databases. However, with the latest amendments to the SBC, this check became systematic and the requirement on 'genuine, present and sufficiently serious' has been dropped.[75] Thus, the level of threat which could impede the free movement of URFM citizens has been lowered. A possible consequence could be that also background databases which are consulted for the purposes of such checks are being fed with more trivial alerts on persons.

This type of a check was always supposed to be systematic for TCNs not enjoying the URFM. They have also been subject to additional checks. Thus, short-stay visa holders have to have their fingerprint(s) verified (1:1) against the VIS to verify the identity of the visa-holder

---

[70] Schengen Borders Code, art 8(1). The SBC applies to all EU Member States except the UK and Ireland and it applies also the Switzerland, Norway, Liechtenstein and Iceland.

[71] This is based on the presumption that the travel document represents a traveller's true identity, see more in Edgar A. and Whitley and Bronwen Manby, 'Questions of Legal Identity in the Post-2015 Development Agenda,' (2015) LSE Human Rights.

[72] Regulation (EU) 2017/458 of the European Parliament and of the Council of 15 March 2017 amending Regulation (EU) 2016/399 as regards the reinforcement of checks against relevant databases at external borders (2017) OJ L74/1, new art 8 (2).

[73] See Footnote 76 in Chapter 6 'Other Border Measures' in Steve Peers, Elspeth Guild and Jonathan Tomkin (eds) *EU Immigration and Asylum Law (Text and Commentary): Second Revised Edition. Volume 1: Visas and Border Controls*, (Martinus Nijhoff Publishers 2012), 215.

[74] Schengen Borders Code before the March 2017 amendment, art 8 (2).

[75] Regulation (EU) 2017/458, new art 8 (2) (a).

and the authenticity of the visa.[76] As to residence permit holders, they possess electronic cards which contain chips with biometric data, namely two fingerprints and a photo, similar to the EU/EEA/CH passports. While there is no obligation to verify the biometrics, legally there is a possibility to perform a match to verify the identity of the residence permit holder and the authenticity of the residence permit.[77]

An additional check is whether a visa-free TCNS possesses an ETIAS and whether travellers, independent of their nationality, are a member of a registered traveller or national facilitation programme.[78] Then, all short-stay visitors are supposed to be enrolled at the border in the soon-to-be-established Entry/Exit System (EES), including their alphanumeric and biometric data and their entry and exit date, time and place. The EES would monitor whether the travellers have exited the EU until the last day of their authorized stay. In case of overstay, the system would automatically generate an alert. Whether they have been enrolled and have a history of overstay will be also checked at entry and exit against the EES (see Table 15.1 above).

The above discussion has so far focused on the profiling and checks mainly of regular travellers. However, asylum seekers, stateless persons and those illegally entering the EU and illegally residing in it are also part of the EU's digital landscape. Although their data is not collected for border control purposes, but rather for asylum ones, it is nevertheless often the case that the data collection takes place around border areas. The dedicated information system is called EURODAC,[79] which currently contains the fingerprints of asylum seekers and those illegally crossing the EU external borders. In the future it is planned to add the fingerprints of those apprehended as illegally residing and to add alphanumeric data and facial images to the fingerprints, as well as introduce screening rules for the different categories of irregular migrants.[80] The proposed amendments, some of which date from as far back as 2016 and the newer ones – from 2020 – indicate the difficulty of tracing the different proposed amendments which are being negotiated in parallel and overlap in certain aspects.

Finally, it is worth mentioning Eurosur. Eurosur is not a border control measure, but rather a border and pre-border surveillance measure.[81] This means that it could be used to surveil both the border areas as well as to maintain a common pre-frontier intelligence picture.[82] Eurosur

---

[76] Schengen Borders Code, art 8 (3) (b) j VIS Regulation, art 18.

[77] Council Regulation (EC) No 380/2008 of 18 April 2008 amending Regulation (EC) No 1030/2002 laying down a uniform format for residence permits for third-country nationals (2008) OJ L115/1, amended art 4.

[78] Regulation (EU) 2017/2225, art 8d.

[79] See Table 15.1 above.

[80] European Commission, 'Amended proposal for a Regulation of the European Parliament and of the Council on the establishment of 'Eurodac' for the comparison of biometric data for the effective application of Regulation (EU) XXX/XXX [Regulation on Asylum and Migration Management] and of Regulation (EU) XXX/XXX [Resettlement Regulation], for identifying an illegally staying third-country national or stateless person and on requests for the comparison with Eurodac data by Member States' law enforcement authorities and Europol for law enforcement purposes and amending Regulations (EU) 2018/1240 and (EU) 2019/818' COM (2020) 614 final; European Commission, 'Proposal for a Regulation of the European Parliament and of the Council introducing a screening of third country nationals at the external borders and amending Regulations (EC) No 767/2008, (EU) 2017/2226, (EU) 2018/1240 and (EU) 2019/817' COM (2020) 612 final.

[81] EBCG Regulation, art 18.

[82] Ibid., arts 18 and 19.

provides a common framework for information exchange and cooperation between the EU Member States, more precisely their National Coordination Centres (NCCs), and Frontex in order to increase their situation awareness and reaction capabilities at external borders. This is to help them fight serious cross-border crime, illegal immigration and protect and save the lives of migrants.[83]

In the framework of Eurosur personal data may be processed by the NCCs and by Frontex, e.g., in the framework of situational pictures[84] and when Frontex provides fusion services such as 'media monitoring, open source intelligence and analysis of internet activities'.[85] However, the exchange of personal data within Eurosur and its processing in the framework of the national and European common situational picture is supposed to be the exception. It is exceptionally allowed as concerns ship and aircraft identification numbers. However, personal data may be processed also for other purposes, as long as these fall within the designated purposes of Eurosur, which are quite broad.[86] The Eurosur Regulation does not regulate the processing of personal data on a national level, beyond specifying that it should be compliant with the GDPR and Directive 2016/680. It also does not help clarify when a certain processing falls under the GDPR and when – under Directive 2016/680.[87]

IV.3 Travellers' Data are Processed after they have Crossed the Border

The data collected and processed in the border and pre-border context is very often processed also after travellers have crossed the border and exited the country. This is the case with all the databases presented above. The data are further processed mainly for law enforcement and broader immigration purposes. This has been made legally possible by granting access to the Member State competent authorities and Europol to the databases. This happened either by granting this access after the system was established (VIS and EURODAC), it was built-in from the outset into the more recent databases (EES and ETIAS) or the information system pursued mainly law enforcement purposes (SIS, PNR).

The obvious trend has been to grant law enforcement access to the data from the outset and to expand the purposes and scope of this access. For example, the PNR scheme, which is *per se* a law enforcement and not a border control tool, by setting the broader objective of fighting serious crime, has justified storing and processing the data of passengers after they have crossed the border.[88]

Another example is ETIAS, which has as one of its purposes to support several of the SIS II/III objectives.[89] This will be achieved by notifying the Member State which entered an SIS alert on certain categories of individuals in case an ETIAS applicant's data produces a hit with one or more of the alerts. Thus, ETIAS would serve also law enforcement purposes even when it is not consulted by a law enforcement authority in the framework of a specific investigation. This is a difference to the regime on law enforcement access to VIS and EURODAC or the

---

[83] Ibid., art 19.

[84] Ibid., arts 24–26.

[85] Ibid., art. 28 (2) (h).

[86] Ibid., art 89 (2) and 89 (3).

[87] Ibid., art. 89.

[88] By analogy Case *Opinion 1/15 of the Court (Grand Chamber)* (2017), ECLI:EU:C:2017:592, paras 204–206.

[89] ETIAS Regulation, art 23.

other provisions on law enforcement access to ETIAS, pursuant to which a law enforcement authority should request access to the data of particular individuals and first obtain the approval by an independent verification authority.

The collected data are re-purposed not only for law enforcement purposes, but also for broader migration purposes. For example, the EES biometrics would be used also to identify individuals who are suspected of illegally residing in a Member State.[90] This enables the authorities to exercise more intense internal control and identify individuals regardless of the fact whether they possess identity documents or not. It also shows the links with EURODAC, which would most likely register those apprehended as illegally residing, e.g., after overstaying their legal stay. The increasing role of law enforcement and immigration authorities in border control matters demonstrates that measures related to border control are integrated more intensely in the other policies as part of the more intrusive security measures.

Finally, another opportunity for control beyond borders comes from EU identity documents, especially the EU passports which contain a chip with biometric data. The justification for the EU biometric passport was preventing forgery and identity theft in the framework of border crossings.[91] However, some Member State authorities have been reportedly storing the biometric data on national databases for their own purposes. Thus, the enforcement of border control regulations has been used as a justification for this data collection well beyond the context of border checks, which the CJEU did not reverse when it had the opportunity to do so.[92]

V. INTEROPERABILITY OF AFSJ DATABASES

As already evident from the overview of the individual EU information systems, they contain similar sets of data, stored however on different databases for different purposes. This fragmentation was considered to be a weakness, making it difficult to find information available on the same individual. Interoperability between the databases was seen as a solution. In a relatively short period of time the EU legislature managed to adopt in 2019 two Regulations which will enable the communication between the EES, VIS, ETIAS, Eurodac, SIS II/III, and the European Criminal Records Information System for TCNs (ECRIS – TCN)[93] and partially also Interpol and Europol data.[94] Since the PNR system is not a centralized system, it is at the moment not planned to be included in the interoperability framework.

More precisely, interoperability would consist of:

---

[90] EES Regulation, art 26.

[91] Case C-291/12 *Schwarz v Stadt Bochum* (2013), ECLI:EU:C:2013:670.

[92] Joined cases C-446/12 to C-449/12 *Willems* (2015) paras 18–20 and 53, ECLI:EU:C:2015:238.

[93] ECRIS-TCN would be an instrument mainly for judicial cooperation in criminal matters, helping one EU Member State find whether and which other Member State(s) have issued a final criminal conviction against a TCN. Similar to the other AFSJ databases, the system would contain alphanumeric data, facial and fingerprint images. Although it is not an instrument for border control, because of which it is not discussed in the present chapter, the fact that it would be interoperable with the other databases, signals again the intertwinement of border and immigration control, security and judicial cooperation. See Regulation (EU) 2019/816 of the European Parliament and of the Council of 17 April 2019 establishing a centralised system for the identification of Member States holding conviction information on third-country nationals and stateless persons (ECRIS-TCN) to supplement the European Criminal Records Information System and amending Regulation (EU) 2018/1726 (2019) OJ L135/1.

[94] Interoperability Regulation, art 1, 3 and 6.

- European Search Portal (ESP), which would allow the simultaneous searches of the different AFSJ systems, plus Interpol and Europol data. The searches could be performed both with alphanumeric and biometric data. The search would operate on a hit/no-hit basis, displaying the information systems in which data on a certain individual are recorded.[95]
- shared Biometric Matching Service (sBMS), which would store the templates of the biometric data and thus provide a common storage platform for the biometric databases, allowing the simultaneous searches with biometric data in the different databases.[96]
- Common Identity Repository (CIR), which would be shared by the different AFSJ databases and would store the alphanumerical and biometric identity data from each system. Still, the data would continue to belong to the original system where they were recorded. For technical reasons, SIS II would not be part of the CIR.[97]
- Multiple-Identity Detector (MID), which would create and store links between data in the different interoperable systems included in CIR and SIS II to detect multiple identities. Where the information systems contain biometric data, the search in CIR and SIS II would be performed with biometric data.[98]

It is evident that interoperability will not simply allow the exchange of information between the underlying databases. It will also create new ones: e.g., the MID is *per se* a new database. In addition, the CIR may also be searched by law enforcement officials within the Member State territories in order to identify persons or for criminal law purposes, e.g., to investigate or prevent crimes.[99] Thus, interoperability will make law enforcement access to information easier.[100] This is also because if earlier, e.g., in the framework of EES, ETIAS, EURODAC and VIS, law enforcement authorities would need an authorization by a verification authority in order to access data on these databases, now via the ESP they would be allowed to check whether data on certain individuals is stored on one of the databases and know on which one it is stored. This can already reveal information on the individual.

Typically the discussion on interoperability has focused on its implications for the AFSJ databases. However, it is noteworthy that interoperability is part of other trends related to information management and automation of border control processes. In recent years travellers, especially EU/EEA/CH citizens and certain TCNs, started being able to use gates and kiosks for automated border control (ABC). ABC allows passengers to scan their travel document at a dedicated reader at an e-Gate or kiosk. This extracts the necessary personal data and perform the legally required checks, e.g., verify the document's validity and authenticity and run the necessary searches in background databases. In parallel, biometric data are used to verify the identity of the traveller. While ABC seems to 'only' automate already existing

[95] Ibid., Chapter II.

[96] Ibid., Chapter III.

[97] Since SIS contains (partial) national copies. See Chapter IV Interoperability Regulations.

[98] Interoperability Regulations, Chapter V.

[99] Ibid., arts 20 and 22.

[100] See also a data protection critique on how the Interoperability Regulations would make law enforcement access easier via the verification procedures in the framework of the MID, Diana Dimitrova and Teresa Quintel, 'Technological Experimentation Without Adequate Safeguards? Interoperable EU Databases and Access to the Multiple Identity Detector by SIRENE Bureaux', in Dara Hallinan, Ronald Leenes, Paul De Hert (eds), *Data Protection and Privacy. Data Protection and Artificial Intelligence* (Hart Publishing, 2021), 217–253.

processes, it makes it mandatory for each user to provide their biometric data.[101] This in turn creates the *technical* possibility for the processing of biometric data against the growing number of background databases, possibly also against the sBMS. This is also alluded to in the new SIS III framework. For example, Article 43 (4) of Regulation 2018/1862 provides for the possibility for using facial images and fingerprints for identification purposes 'in the context of regular border crossing points'. It remains to be seen whether this will materialize. In any case, the implications of the interoperability framework and SIS III are numerous and will continue being 'discovered' and assessed in the course of time.

VI. EU BORDER CONTROL CHALLENGES THE MAIN EU DATA PROTECTION PRINCIPLES

The outlined technological innovations are often presented as purely technical measures, for instance the EES.[102] However, they have an impact on travellers' fundamental rights. Therefore, calls have been made that new programmes and technologies have to operate within the limits of the applicable legal framework, e.g., the applicable data protection framework, noting that even if something would be technically feasible, it does not mean in itself that it should be pursued unconditionally.[103] Civil society, academia and advisory groups and others, such as the Article 29 Working Party, the European Data Protection Supervisor (EDPS), CEPS and the Meijers Committee, have raised concerns about the deepening and broadening of the surveillance measures imposed on travelling people. They all in one way or another argue that the different border surveillance measures, sometimes referred to as 'dataveillance,'[104] pose severe challenges to the main EU data protection principles.

A complete data protection and privacy assessment of the above-discussed initiatives is close to impossible, since some of the individual information systems and the interoperability concept and components are not yet developed, while existing systems such as EURODAC are being revised.[105] These dynamic developments happening in parallel are not easy to follow and mapping their potential impact on fundamental rights such as privacy and data protection is challenging, especially as regards the principles of necessity and proportionality. This is, however, an essential element in examining the compliance of certain measures with fundamental rights, notably privacy and data protection.

[101] Frontex 'Best Practice Operational Guidelines for Automated Border Control (ABC) Systems,' (2015) Warsaw.

[102] Ben Hayes and Mathias Vermeulen, 'Borderline: The EU's New Birder Surveillance Initiatives: Assessing the Costs and Fundamental Rights Implications of EUROSUR and the "Smart Borders" Proposals,' *Study by the Heinrich Böll Stiftung* (2012), 12.

[103] Papademetriou and Collett (n. 5) 14–15.

[104] Louise Amoore and Marieke de Goede, 'Governance, Risk and Dataveillance in the war on Terror,' (2005) 43 (2) *Crime, Law and Social Change* 149.

[105] European Data Protection Supervisor, 'Opinion 4/2018 on the Proposals for two Regulations establishing a framework for interoperability between EU large-scale information systems,' (Brussels, 2018), p.9, para 22; European Union Agency for Fundamental Rights, 'Interoperability and fundamental rights implications, FRA Opinion 1/2018,' 12.

In that respect some argue that the feasibility, effectiveness and need for the high level of intrusion of the different programmes have not been convincingly proven.[106] For example, no convincing evidence that on national and international level the EES is effective and efficient was presented when the EU EES was proposed.[107] Further, subjecting all travellers to the expanding risk profiling under PNR is said to create a 'regime of suspicion',[108] which creates proportionality problems. On that note some claim that risk analysis via profiling is not an effective tool in preventing terrorist attacks by finding the needle in the haystack. While pattern recognition works well for offences that show a fixed and repeated pattern, this is not the case with terrorist attacks.[109] Thus, e.g., PNR leads to a massive collection of data which is not necessary for immigration purposes.[110]

It is noted here that one of the contentious topics in EU law is the strict necessity and proportionality of surveillance measures. While the CJEU argued in *Digital Rights Ireland* and *Tele2* that access by law enforcement authorities to the data of persons against whom there is no suspicion of being involved in criminal activities is not proportionate,[111] the same Court accepted in its Canada PNR Opinion that identifying risky passengers by performing risk analysis on all passengers as provided for in the EU-Canada PNR Agreement does not go beyond what is strictly necessary.[112] However, the legal challenges concerning PNR schemes are not over – recently the Belgian Constitutional Court referred a set of questions for preliminary ruling to the CJEU, including the question of whether the systematic processing of PNR data of all air passengers is compatible with the fundamental rights to privacy and data protection.[113] Thus, the debate on that topic is continuing.

Necessity and proportionality are seen as problematic also in the case of biometrics. The new EU Data Protection framework classifies biometrics as sensitive data when they are used to uniquely identify or confirm the identity of natural persons, e.g. as is the case with facial image and dactyloscopic data.[114] While the GDPR puts higher requirements on the legality of biometric data processing,[115] this has not stopped the EU from initiating new databases with biometric identifiers, e.g., the EES, or lowering the age of the persons to be fingerprinted as in the new EURODAC Proposal or extending the biometric identifiers to palm prints and DNA as

---

[106] Julien Jeandesboz, Didier Bigo, Ben Hayes, Stephanie Simon, 'The Commission's Legislative Proposals on Smart Borders: Their Feasibility and Costs', (2013) European Parliament, Policy Department C: Citizens' Rights and Constitutional Affairs study; Hayes and Vermeulen (n. 102) 9.

[107] Hayes and Vermeulen (n. 102) 9.

[108] Franziska Boehm, 'European Flight Passenger Under General Suspicion – The Envisaged Model of Analysing Flight Passenger Data,' in Serge Gutwirth, Ronald Leenes, Paul De Hert, Yves Poullet (eds.) *Privacy and Data Protection, An Element of Choice* (Springer 2011), 171–199.

[109] Broeders, Schrijvers, van der Sloot, van Brakel, de Hoog, Hirsch Ballin (n. 11) 313.

[110] European Data Protection Supervisor, "Opinion 5/2015 Second Opinion on the Proposal for a Directive of the European Parliament and of the Council on the use of Passenger Name Record data for the prevention, detection, investigation and prosecution of terrorist offences and serious crime," (Brussels, 2015).

[111] Case C-293/12 *Digital Rights Ireland* and 594/12 *Seitlinger and Others* (2014) ECLI:EU:C:2014:238; Cases C-203/15 and C-698/15, *Tele2 Sverige AB v Postoch telestyrelsen and Secretary of State for the Home Department v Watson, Brice, Lewis* (2016) ECLI:EU:C:2016:970.

[112] Canada PNR Opinion, paras 186–189.

[113] Belgian Constitutional Court, Press release on judgment 135/2019, 17 October 2019.

[114] GDPR, art 4 (14); Directive 2016/680, art 3 (13).

[115] GDPR, art 9; Directive 2016/680, art 10.

in SIS III. The motivation for the usage of biometric data both for 1:1 identity verification and 1:n identification against a high number of entries in large-scale systems such as EES seems to be easily accepted by the law-makers. It thus seems unlikely that the trend of large-scale deployment of biometrics will be reversed.[116]

The following paragraphs will discuss the challenges which the border control measures pose to the EU principles of data protection and to the data protection safeguards and subjective rights of travellers. The data protection principles to be discussed are the same for the GDPR, Directive 2016/680 and Regulation 2018/1725, although references below will be made to the respective articles in the GDPR. As to the safeguards, the significant differences between the different instruments will be pointed out. We will first show how the EU border control measures discussed so far challenge the very foundational principles of data protection law. In a next section we will focus on the difficulties of persons to exercise their data subject rights.

First of all, concerns have been raised with regards to the *purpose limitation principle*.[117] The purpose limitation principle in Article 5 (1) (b) GDPR is challenged both by allowing Member State LEAs and Europol (more extended), quicker and easier access to travellers' data and allowing immigration authorities to use law-enforcement databases for traveller screening. This is going to be exacerbated by implementing elements of interoperability between the AFSJ databases, making the exchange of data much quicker and easier, enabling their further processing. It is argued by the FRA that interoperability would in certain cases allow officials to access more data than currently allowed under the regulations on large-scale databases, e.g., border officials to access ECRIS-TCN when verifying links between data in the different databases in the framework of MID.[118] Function creep is also inherent in Big Data analytics,[119] which is the direction in which the risk analysis of travellers is taking, e.g., PNR and ETIAS.

Furthermore, the *data accuracy principle* in Article 5 (1) (d) GDPR is at stake. This is especially the case with biometrics, whose matching *per se* cannot be 100 per cent correct. This is particularly the case when biometrics are used for 1:n identification purposes as compared to a 1:1 verification. Problems might emerge if quality of enrolment when done at borders is poor (e.g., EES enrolment), which is likely if the enrolment is done under time pressure and border guards lack proper biometric skills.[120] In *Schwarz* the CJEU swiftly did away with the argument that fingerprint matching (1:1) is not 100 per cent precise by simply acknowledging this fact and discarding it as not decisive in allowing biometric technologies for identity verification.[121] However, when it comes to 1:n biometric identification in large-scale databases, e.g., EES and SIS III, this issue becomes especially essential for the proper functioning of the

---

[116] This confirms the argument that past policy options in the AFSJ are irreversible, see Bigo, Carrera, Hayes, Hernanz and Jeandesboz (n. 25) 4.

[117] European Data Protection Supervisor, 'Opinion of the European Data Protection Supervisor on the Communication from the Commission to the European Parliament and the Council entitled 'Strengthening law enforcement cooperation in the EU: the European Information Exchange Model (EIXM),' (Brussels, 2013), paras 15, 16, 28.

[118] FRA Opinion on interoperability (n. 117) 39.

[119] David Lyon, *Surveillance Studies: An Overview* (Cambridge: Polity Press 2007) 52.

[120] See discussion in Diana Dimitrova, 'The "Smartification" of EU Borders: When "Smart" Technology Does Not Come with "Smart" Safeguards,' CiTiP Working Paper 28/2016. Available at SSRN: http://ssrn.com/abstract=2800115, June 2016 accessed 29 October 2021.

[121] *Schwarz*, para 43.

system. In addition, in an interoperability environment once data are recorded incorrectly in one information system, they can be incorrectly transferred in another one or wrong decisions could be directly made about travellers.[122] A recent study by the Fundamental Rights Agency (FRA) revealed that there are many concerns about the quality of the data, both alphanumeric and biometric, as enrolled in the existing EU large-scale information systems. Sometimes it is the accuracy of the data, e.g., wrong spelling, low fingerprint quality or false match, which is problematic, and sometimes there are administrative mistakes, e.g., attaching someone's biometric data to the alphanumeric data of other people.[123] Thus, travellers might be inconvenienced since the accuracy of the data, especially biometric data, and the quality of the decisions based on them, is not 100 per cent accurate.[124] The accuracy of decision-making and decisions is another problematic area. The reason is that these could generate false acceptances and false negatives or produce statistical discrimination.[125]

The new trends in border surveillance pose a problem also for the *data minimization principle* in Article 5(1)(c) GDPR. The logic of the data minimization principle is to allow the processing of only the minimum data in order to fulfil the pre-defined legitimate purposes. However, the logic of the ambition to assess the different risk factors of each traveller more thoroughly has led to more and more data being at the disposal of the immigration, border control and law-enforcement authorities, e.g., information about seating on an airplane in the framework of PNR. Thus, especially risk assessment technologies by design operate on the basis of data maximization.[126]

The *storage periods* of such data open up the opportunities for more historical datamining and complete profiling and raise issues as to the storage limitation principle in Article 5 (1) (e) GDPR and proportionality.[127] For example, in the CJEU Opinion on the EU-Canada PNR Agreement, the Court pointed out that the storage of PNR data of all passengers after they have left Canada cannot be justified, as such passengers normally can no longer pose a threat. Exceptions could exist if suspicions about particular passengers have been identified and data needs to be stored longer to investigate organized crime, but data of all passengers is not strictly necessary.[128] However, the EU PNR Directive still allows for a six-month storage period of all data in identified form and four and a half years in de-personalized form which allows the re-identification of the data under certain conditions.[129] These long storage periods

---

[122] Franziska Boehm, *Information Sharing and Data Protection in the Area of Freedom, Security and Justice: Towards Harmonized Data Protection Principles for Information Exchange at EU level* (Springer 2012), 10–11.

[123] European Union Agency for Fundamental Rights, 'Under watchful eyes: biometrics, EU IT systems and fundamental rights,' (2018), Section 5.

[124] Council of Europe, 'Progress report on the application of the principles of Convention 108 to the collection and processing of biometric data (2005),' p. 86 ff.

[125] Bigo, Carrera, Hayes, Hernanz and Jeandesboz (n. 25).

[126] Fanny Coudert, 'The Europol Regulation and Purpose Limitation: From the "Silo-Based Approach" to … What Exactly?' (2017) 3 *EDPL* 320.

[127] Article 29 Working Party, "Opinion 05/2013 on Smart Borders," (2013) 00952/13/EN, WP206, p.11; Julien Jeandesboz, Jorrit Rijpma, Didier Bigo, 'Smart Borders Revisited: An Assessment of the Commission's revised Smart Borders proposal: Study for the LIBE Committee,' (2016) European Parliament, GD for Internal Policies, Policy Department Citizens' Rights and Constitutional Affairs, p. 10.

[128] Opinion 1/15 of the Court (2017), paras 204–206.

[129] EU PNR Regulation, art 12 (1) and (2).

are partially the result of the broader and broadening purposes for which the systems have been designed. For example, if the EES had been designed as a purely border control measure, its justified storage periods might have been shorter. However, broader migration purposes, e.g., to monitor the history of overstay of individual travellers, lead also to longer storage periods.

Last but not least, the complexity of the systems hampers not only the data protection and fundamental rights assessment of the new technologies. The new technologies raise the question of whether even the officials supposed to operate them understand how they operate and how certain outcomes have been reached, e.g., why a certain individual was classified as a risk. Thus, can the officials challenge the technologies? Can they account for the decisions they take based on the new technologies? Briefly put, accountability is a major problem in systems of automated decision-making, raising the question whether even the responsible authorities can review the decisions taken or influenced by algorithms.[130] On the other hand, machine decisions could be controlled by humans,[131] which casts doubt on their neutrality.

VII. DATA SUBJECTS' RIGHTS ARE DIFFICULT TO EXERCISE

A key question in the data protection analysis of border control trends is whether the data protection framework and practical arrangements allow for the robust safeguards for travellers, such as an adequate framework for the exercise of their data protection rights. The EU legal framework on data protection gives every data subject, in this case every traveller, the right to be informed about the processing of their personal data, to access their personal data, to have it rectified, erased or have its processing restricted, to object to the processing of their personal data and the right not to be subject to automated individual decision-making such as profiling. None of these rights is absolute, and they may be restricted under certain conditions, for instance if disclosing information that someone is subject to secret surveillance would jeopardize the investigations against them.[132]

In this context, two major problems emerge: first, the patchwork of data protection regimes, which could create inconsistencies in the exercise of data protection rights, and, second, practical problems which impede the exercise of these rights.

As discussed above, the data protection framework for border control is fragmented and complex. Whereas the different data protection instruments are based on the same principles and contain similar provisions, some significant differences remain. For example, under Directive 2016/680 the data subjects do not have the right to object to the processing of their data. Furthermore, the right not to be subjected to automated decisions is much more limited, and fewer safeguards apply in these cases, such as the right to contest the decision.[133] On that note, in academia and in practice there is no agreement on what exactly an automated decision is, that is, how involved should an officer be in order for a decision to be considered

[130] High-level expert group on information systems and interoperability, 'Report - Second meeting - 20 September 2016,' European Commission, DG Migration and Home Affairs.

[131] Mathias Vermeulen and Rocco Bellanova, 'European "Smart" Surveillance: What's at Stake for Data Protection, Privacy and Non-discrimination,' (2012) 4 *Security and Human Rights*, 308 and 311.

[132] See CFREU, art 8; Chapter III GDPR and Directive 2016/680. The GDPR also provides for a right to data portability. However, this paper does not discuss whether this right might be applicable in the border control context, e.g., in the framework of voluntary national facilitation programmes.

[133] Compare GDPR, art 22 and Directive 2016/680, art 11.

as not having been taken automatically.[134] The differences in the data protection framework are especially problematic when the same set of data are re-used for different purposes – such as migration and law enforcement – and their usage could be subject to the GDPR and the Directive 2016/680.

For instance, the right to rectification of incorrect or incomplete data under Article 16 GDPR does not regulate the case in which the data subject and the data controller disagree on whether the data is accurate or not. Such a situation is called *non liquet*. Article 18 GDPR allows for the restriction of processing of the data only as long as the claimed inaccuracy of the data is being examined. By contrast, Article 16 (3) (a) Directive 2016/680 explicitly provides for the long-term restriction of the processing of the data where neither its accuracy nor inaccuracy can be ascertained.[135] Especially in an interoperability environment where all identity data is going to be stored on the CIR and accessed by different authorities for different purposes, it is not clear how the controller(s) should react to a *non liquet* situation. Thus, the fragmentation of data protection regimes could leave a traveller in a situation of legal vacuum. On a related note, the right to restriction of the processing of the data is not provided in all proposed or existing legal instruments on the EU IT databases.[136]

Beyond the issues related to the imperfections of the legal framework, practical problems emerge. The key to exercising one's rights is having information about the fact that someone's data are being processed and that every traveller has the above-mentioned data protection rights in an understandable and transparent manner. However, many travellers are not sufficiently aware of this and solutions to this problem are sought for. The growing number of purposes for the processing of the data, the multiple instances at which the data is collected for one trip, e.g., through ETIAS, PNR and EES, the complexity of the data protection operations, and the growing time pressure to which border guards and immigration authorities are subject, make it difficult for the data subjects to be properly informed.[137]

Procedural problems are also not rare, e.g., with regards to the right to access, rectification, deletion and restriction of the processing of the data. Pursuant to a FRA study, despite the fact that the right of access exists, there have been very few applications for access to one's own data and to having the data rectified or deleted. This could be due to the low awareness, numerous administrative obstacles, and the lack of enough specialized lawyers.[138] More specifically as regards biometric matching, data subjects and their legal defendants might have technical difficulties disputing the correctness of a biometric match as they might not have the technical skills to dispute a system match or the confirmation of this match by the authorities.[139]

Pursuant to a detailed study concerning the rights of data subjects in the Schengen Information System, especially with regards to the cross-border cooperation between Member State executive and judicial authorities, this cooperation is not always smooth and efficient in responding to data subjects' request for exercising their data and enforcing decisions in other

---

[134] Article 29 Working Party, "Guidelines on Automated individual decision-making and Profiling for the purposes of Regulation 2016/679," (2018) 17/EN, WP251rev.01.

[135] Enrico Peuker, Europäische Datenschutzgrundverordnung: Handkommentar, Sydow (ed), (Nomos 2017), 476.

[136] FRA Study on large-scale information systems (n. 117) 103.

[137] Ibid., Section 1.

[138] Ibid., Section 6.

[139] Ibid., pp. 76 and 102.

Member States.[140] This issue is especially important in the context of EU-wide databases and in the interoperability context. Last but not least, the issue of exercise of data subjects' rights links to one of the fundamental concepts of EU data protection law, namely that of the controller, who is responsible for compliance with the data protection requirements and for responding to data subject requests. In the context of large-scale systems and in the interoperability landscape it is not always clear which the responsible authority is. Sometimes responding to a request might require cooperation between these, which as concluded by Brouwer, is not always smooth.[141]

VIII. CONCLUSION: NEW EU BORDER CONTROL FRAMEWORK NEEDS CRITICAL RE-THINKING AND MORE SAFEGUARDS

The present chapter has demonstrated that the EU is not isolated from the trend of blurring the lines between migration, internal security and the fight against serious crime and terrorism. This trend is being especially reinforced by the new framework of interoperability between the AFSJ databases.[142] Technically, this enables the intensified monitoring of travelling people for a variety of purposes by different Member State authorities and the 'compilation' of data from different sources, allowing a broad overview of the track records of individuals.

Furthermore, while the current border control framework affects the TCNs more than the EU/EEA/CH citizens, one begins to see the synchronisation between the surveillance measures on EU/EEA/CH and TCNs.[143] For example, in *Schwarz* the CJEU found the purpose of issuing biometric passports of EU citizens legitimate partially because TCN visa-holders have their fingerprints processed for border control purposes and security features of EU documents should not lag behind in order to prevent document falsification and fraudulent use.[144] It remains to be seen whether and which synchronisation measures could develop in the future and what role interoperability could play in this process.

Going back to the definition of the purposes of border control as per the Schengen Border Code, it is acknowledged that the assessment of security and illegal immigration risks are amongst the legitimate objectives of border control, and that the responsible authorities should be given the adequate resources to perform their duties. However, as much as technologies might help gather more information about travellers and perform complex analysis of this data, the new technologies are problematic from a data protection point of view.

On one hand, the new technological developments and initiatives are being developed in parallel, and change very dynamically, which makes their data protection and privacy assessments difficult, especially the assessment of the necessity and proportionality of the different initiatives, which are key principles under EU data protection law. This is further problematic

---

[140] Evelien Brouwer, *Digital Borders and Real Rights. Effective Remedies for Third-Country Nationals in the Schengen Information System* (Martinus Nijhoff Publishers 2008).

[141] Brouwer (n. 140).

[142] European Data Protection Supervisor, Opinion on Interoperability (n. 117) p. 9, para 20.

[143] Essential differences remain: EU do not have periods of stay monitored, no stamps, interview or travel approvals, e.g., visa or another form of authorisation.

[144] *Schwarz*, par. 19.

as without a proper assessment, one cannot define sufficient data protection safeguards for travellers, and such safeguards could be further weakened by the fragmentation of the EU data protection framework. Irrespective of this fragmentation, as evident from the discussion above, the new trends challenge the main EU data protection principles.

On the other hand, whereas the technologies are spreading and affecting more and more travellers, it is questioned whether traveller awareness and safeguards for travellers are at a par with this technological expansion. This poses a problem for the exercise of the travellers' data protection rights and being able to challenge decisions and biometric matches. It is acknowledged that the data subject rights play a role in ensuring the legality of data processing and thus for holding data controllers accountable for the data they process and the decisions they adopt on the basis of this data.

Last but not least, the recent border control measures do not always have as primary or sometimes even secondary focus another important border control purpose, namely preventing trafficking in human beings. It is questionable how the above technologies can identify potential victims of trafficking in human beings since their primary focus is on illegal migrants and potential serious offenders.

BIBLIOGRAPHY

Academic sources

Aas K.F., '"Crimmigrant" Bodies and Bona Fide Travelers: Surveillance, Citizenship and Global Governance,' (2011) 15(3) *Theoretical Criminology* 331.

Amoore L., 'Biometric Borders: Governing Mobilities in the War on Terror,' (2006) 25 *Political Geography* 336.

Amoore L. and M. de Goede, 'Governance, Risk and Dataveillance in the War on Terror,' (2005) 43(2) *Crime, Law and Social Change*.

Bigo D., S. Carrera, B. Hayes, N. Hernanz and J. Jeandesboz, 'Justice and Home Affairs Databases and a Smart Borders System at the EU External Borders: An Evaluation of Current and Forthcoming Proposals,' (2012) 52 CEPS Paper in Liberty and Security in Europe.

Bennett C.J., 'What Happens when you Book an Airline Ticket? The Collection and Processing of Passenger Data Post-9/11,' in Elia Zureik and Mark B. Salter (eds), *Global Surveillance and Policing: Borders, Security, Identity* (Willan Publishing 2005).

Boehm F., 'European Flight Passenger Under General Suspicion – The Envisaged Model of Analysing Flight Passenger Data', in Serge Gutwirth, Ronald Leenes, Paul De Hert, Yves Poullet (eds.) *Privacy and Data Protection, An Element of Choice* (Springer 2011), 171–199.

Boehm F., *Information Sharing and Data Protection in the Area of Freedom, Security and Justice: Towards Harmonized Data Protection Principles for Information Exchange at EU level* (Springer 2012).

Broeders D., 'The New Digital Borders of Europe: EU Databases and the Surveillance of Irregular Migrants,' (2007) 22(1) *International Sociology* 71.

Broeders D., E. Schrijvers, B. van der Sloot, R. van Brakel, J. de Hoog, E. Hirsch Ballin, 'Big Data and Security Policies: Towards a Framework for Regulating the Phases of Analytics and Use of Big Data,' (2017) 33 *Computer Law & Security Review* 319.

Brouwer E., 'Ignoring Dissent and Legality: The EU's proposal to share the personal information of all passengers', Centre for European Policy Studies, June 2011.

Brouwer E., *Digital Borders and Real Rights. Effective Remedies for Third-Country Nationals in the Schengen Information System* (Martinus Nijhoff Publishers 2008).

Dimitrova D., 'Data Protection at the Schengen Borders after Paris,' (2016) LSE Media Policy Blog.

Dimitrova D., 'Connecting the Dots in the Area of Freedom, Security and Justice (AFSJ) – Part I' (2017) KU Leuven CiTiP Blog https://www.law.kuleuven.be/citip/blog/connecting-the-dots-in-the-area-of-freedom-security-and-justice-afsj-part-i/.

Dimitrova D., 'Connecting the Dots in the Area of Freedom, Security and Justice (AFSJ) – Part II' (2017) KU Leuven CiTiP Blog https://www.law.kuleuven.be/citip/blog/connecting-the-dots-in-the-area-of-freedom-security-and-justice-afsj-part-ii/.

Dimitrova D., 'The "Smartification" of EU Borders: When "Smart" Technology Does Not Come with "Smart" Safeguards', *CiTiP Working Paper* 28/2016. Available at SSRN: http://ssrn.com/abstract=2800115, June 2016.

Dimitrova D. and T. Quintel, 'Technological Experimentation Without Adequate Safeguards? Interoperable EU Databases and Access to the Multiple Identity Detector by SIRENE Bureaux', Dara Hallinan, Ronald Leenes, Paul De Hert (eds), *Data Protection and Privacy. Data Protection and Artificial Intelligence* (Hart Publishing 2021).

Coudert F., 'The Europol Regulation and Purpose Limitation: From the Silo-Based Approach to … What Exactly?' (2017) 3 *EDPL*.

Ferraro F., 'Schengen Governance after the Lisbon Treaty,' (2013) 120358REV1 European Parliament, Library Briefing, https://www.europarl.europa.eu/RegData/bibliotheque/briefing/2013/130358/LDM_BRI(2013)130358_REV1_EN.pdf.

Guild E. and S. Carrera, 'EU Borders and Their Controls: Preventing unwanted movement of people in Europe,' (2013) 6 (14) CEPS Essay.

Hayes B. and M. Vermeulen, 'Borderline: The EU's New Birder Surveillance Initiatives: Assessing the Costs and Fundamental Rights Implications of EUROSUR and the "Smart Borders" Proposals,' *Study by the Heinrich Böll Stiftung* (2012), 12.

Jeandesboz J., 'Reinforcing the Surveillance of EU Borders: The Future Development of FRONTEX and EUROSUR,' (2008) 11 *Challenge Liberty and Security*.

Jeandesboz J., D. Bigo, B. Hayes and S. Simon, "The Commission's Legislative Proposals on Smart Borders: Their Feasibility and Costs' (2013) European Parliament, Policy Department C: Citizens' Rights and Constitutional Affairs study.

Jeandesboz J., J. Rijpma, D. Bigo, 'Smart Borders Revisited: An Assessment of the Commission's revised Smart Borders proposal: Study for the LIBE Committee,' (2016) European Parliament, GD for Internal Policies, Policy Department Citizens' Rights and Constitutional Affairs.

Leese M., 'Blurring the Dimensions of Privacy? Law Enforcement and Trusted Traveller Programmes,' (2013) 29 *Computer Law & Security Review* 480.

Lynskey O., 'Tele2 Sverige AB and Watson et al: Continuity and Radical Change', European Law Blog, 12 January 2017, http://europeanlawblog.eu/2017/01/12/tele2-sverige-ab-and-watson-et-al-continuity-and-radical-change/.

Lyon D., *Surveillance Studies: An Overview* (Cambridge: Polity Press 2007).

Monteleone S, 'Briefing – EU Legislation in Progress. Rules for EU institutions' processing of personal data' (2018) European Parliamentary Research Service.

Muller B.J., 'Borders, Bodies and Biometrics: Towards Identity Management,' in Elia Zureik and Mark B. Salter (eds), *Global Surveillance and Policing: Borders, Security, Identity* (Willan Publishing 2005).

Papademetriou D.G. and El. Collett, 'A New Architecture for Border Management,' (2011) Migration Policy Institute.

Peers S., E. Guild and J. Tomkin (eds) *EU Immigration and Asylum Law (Text and Commentary): Second Revised Edition. Volume 1: Visas and Border Controls*, (Martinus Nijhoff Publishers 2012).

Peuker E. 'Europäische Datenschutzgrundverordnung: Handkommentar' Sydow (ed), (Nomos 2017).

Vermeulen M. and R. Bellanova, 'European "Smart" Surveillance: What's at Stake for Data Protection, Privacy and Non-discrimination' (2012) *4 Security and Human Rights*

Edgar A. Whitley and B. Manby, 'Questions of Legal Identity in the Post-2015 development agenda,' (2015) *LSE Human Rights*.

Wolff S., 'EU Integrated Border Management beyond Lisbon: Contrasting Policies and Practice,' *CESP*, 23 https://www.clingendael.nl/sites/default/files/20100900_cesp_chapter_wolff.pdf.

Opinions, reports and others

Arrêté du 20 mai 2011 modifiant l'arrêté du 25 octobre 2010 pris pour l'application du décret n° 2010-1274 du 25 octobre 2010 portant création d'un traitement automatisé de données à caractère personnel dénommé PARAFE; http://www.legifrance.gouv.fr/affichTexte.do;jsessionid=D6DECDC0BBA2B9213EC9DA5FB36AEC7C.tpdjo14v_1?cidTexte=JORFTEXT000024113938&dateTexte=&oldAction=rechJO&categorieLien=id.

Article 29 Working Party, 'Opinion 4/2007 on the concept of personal data,' (2007) 01248/07/EN, WP 136.

Article 29 Working Party, 'Opinion 05/2013 on Smart Borders,' (2013) 00952/13/EN, WP206.

Article 29 Working Party, 'Guidelines on Automated individual decision-making and Profiling for the purposes of Regulation 2016/679,' (2018) 17/EN, WP251rev.01.

Belgian Act on Passenger Name Records published, 24 February 2017, http://www.lexology.com/library/detail.aspx?g=bff6b66b-0f27-415d-8ba2-217732b836f5.

Belgian Constitutional Court, Press release on judgment 135/2019, 17 October 2019.

Council of the European Union, *Widening the scope of passenger name record (PNR) data legislation to transport forms other than air traffic - An impact assessment - Draft Council Conclusions* (Document number 12649/19).

Commission Staff Working Document, Impact Assessment, Impact Assessment Report on the establishment of an EU Entry Exit System, SWD (2016) 115 final, 6.4.2016.

Communication from the Commission to the European Parliament and the Council, "Stronger and Smarter Information Systems for Borders and Security," COM (2016) 205 final, 6.4.2016.

Cora Currier, 'Lawmakers move to stop warrantless cellphone searches at the U.S. Border,' *The Intercept*, 04 April 2017, https://theintercept.com/2017/04/04/lawmakers-move-to-stop-warrantless-cell-phone-searches-at-the-u-s-border/.

Costica Dumbrava, 'Revision of the Schengen Information System for border checks,' European Parliamentary Research Service, Briefing: EU Legislation in Progress (2017) http://www.europarl.europa.eu/RegData/etudes/BRIE/2017/599341/EPRS_BRI(2017)599341_EN.pdf.

Council of Europe, 'Progress report on the application of the principles of Convention 108 to the collection and processing of biometric data (2005)' (2005).

Décret n° 2010-1274 du 25 octobre 2010 portant création d'un traitement automatisé de données à caractère personnel dénommé PARAFE http://www.legifrance.gouv.fr/affichTexte.do;jsessionid=?cidTexte=JORFTEXT000022959780&dateTexte=&oldAction=rechJO&categorieLien=id.

European Commission, DG Migration and Home Affairs, 'High-level expert group on information systems and interoperability. Second meeting – 20 September 2016. Report.'

European Commission, 'Feasibility Study for a European Travel Information and Authorization System (ETIAS): Final Report,' (2016) PwC.

European Commission, 'Security Union: Commission welcomes political agreement on the European Travel Information and Authorisation System (ETIAS) for a stronger and more secure Union,' (Brussels, 2018) http://europa.eu/rapid/press-release_STATEMENT-18-3527_en.htm.

European Commission, *Smart Borders': Enhancing mobility and security*, 28.02.2013, http://europa.eu/rapid/press-release_IP-13-162_en.htm.

European Commission and PwC, 'Technical Study on the Smart Borders, Final Report,' (2014).

Eu-Lisa, 'Conference Report, eu-LISA International Conference. The future tested: Towards a Smart Borders Reality,' (Tallinn, 2015).

European Commission, DG Migration and Home Affairs, *Smart Borders*, https://ec.europa.eu/home-affairs/what-we-do/policies/borders-and-visas/smart-borders_en accessed 03 January 2020.

European Commission, 'Final report by the High Level Expert Group on Information Systems and Interoperability (HLEG), May 2017,' found in Council of the European Union Document 8434/17, (Brussels, 2017).

European Commission, *Annex to the Commission Recommendation adopting the Practical Handbook for implementing and managing the European Border Surveillance System (Eurosur Handbook),* C(2015) 9206 final.

European Data Protection Supervisor, 'Opinion of the European Data Protection Supervisor on the Communication from the Commission to the European Parliament and the Council entitled

"Strengthening law enforcement cooperation in the EU: the European Information Exchange Model (EIXM)," (Brussels, 2013).
European Data Protection Supervisor, 'Opinion of the European Data Protection Supervisor on the Proposals for a Regulation establishing an Entry/Exit System (EES) and a Regulation establishing a Registered Traveller Programme (RTP),' (Brussels 2013).
European Data Protection Supervisor, "Opinion 5/2015 Second Opinion on the Proposal for a Directive of the European Parliament and of the Council on the use of Passenger Name Record data for the prevention, detection, investigation and prosecution of terrorist offences and serious crime," (Brussels, 2015).
European Data Protection Supervisor, 'Opinion 06/2016. EDPS Opinion on the Second EU Smart Borders Package. Recommendations on the revised Proposal to establish and Entry/Exit System,' (Brussels, 2016).European Data Protection Supervisor, 'Opinion 4/2018 on the Proposals for two Regulations establishing a framework for interoperability between EU large-scale information systems,' (Brussels, 2018).
Eu-Lisa, 'Smart Borders Pilot Project. Report on the technical conclusions of the Pilot,' (2015) 1.
Eu-Lisa, 'Smart Borders Pilot Project. Technical Report Annexes,' (2015) 2.
FRONTEX, 'Best Practice Operational Guidelines for Automated Border Control (ABC) Systems,' (Warsaw, 2015).
European Union Agency for Fundamental Rights, 'Interoperability and fundamental rights implications, FRA Opinion 1/2018.
European Union Agency for Fundamental Rights, 'Under watchful eyes: biometrics, EU IT systems and fundamental rights,' (2018).
Ewen MacAskill, 'Cage Director Charged under Terrorism Act after Failing to hand over passwords,' *The Guardian*, 17 May 2017, https://www.theguardian.com/uk-news/2017/may/17/cage-campaign-group-director-muhammed-rabbani-charged-under-terrorism-act.
Final Report of the High Level Expert Group on Information Systems and Interoperability, May 2017 in Council of the European Union Doc. Nr. 8434/17, 08.05.2017, Brussels.
High-level expert group on information systems and interoperability, 'Report - Second meeting - 20 September 2016,' European Commission, DG Migration and Home Affairs.
Immigration Bureau of Japan, 'Outline of the Trusted Traveller Programme,' 2016 http://www.immi-moj.go.jp/ttp2/en/outline/index.html.
Immigration Department, The Government of the Hong Kong Special Administrative Region, 'e-Channel Services for Frequent Visitors,' 11 January 2017, http://www.immd.gov.hk/eng/services/echannel_visitors.html.
Jennifer Rankin, 'European Commission Faces Challenge to Grant Visa-Free Travel to Turks,' *The Guardian* (Brussels, 4 May 2016) https://www.theguardian.com/world/2016/may/04/european-commission-urges-eu-backing-for-visa-free-travel-for-turks-ankara.
On Privium (the Netherlands): http://www.schiphol.nl/Travellers/AtSchiphol/Privium.htm
U.S. Customs and Border Protection, "Eligibility for Global Entry," 01.05.2017, https://www.cbp.gov/travel/trusted-traveler-programs/global-entry/eligibility.
Parafe (France) 'You do not have a French biometric passport,' Ministry of the Interior, 2012, http://www.parafe.gouv.fr/en/category/vous-ne-possedez-pas-de-passeport-biometrique/.
'Second generation Schengen Information System (SIS II) – former 1st pillar regulation,' (2010) Eurlex, http://eur-lex.europa.eu/legal-content/en/TXT/?uri=URISERV:l14544, accessed 15 November 2019.
Spencer Woodman, 'Palantir Enables Immigration Agents to Access Information from the CIA,' *The Intercept* (17.03.2017) https://theintercept.com/2017/03/17/palantir-enables-immigration-agents-to-access-information-from-the-cia/.
'Strengthening law enforcement cooperation in the EU: the European Information Exchange Model (EIXM),' (Brussels, 2013).
US Customs and Border Protection, "Global Entry," 03.07.2017 https://www.cbp.gov/travel/trusted-traveler-programs/global-entry.
US Department of Homeland Security, 'Privacy Impact Assessment Update for the Electronic System for Travel Authorization (ESTA), DHS/CBP/PIA-007(g),' (2016), https://www.dhs.gov/sites/default/files/publications/privacy-pia-cbp-esta-september2016.pdf.

16. Big data and data protection[1]

Alessandro Mantelero

I. THE LOGIC OF BIG DATA APPLICATIONS AND THE PRINCIPLES OF DATA PROTECTION

Data protection regulations have their social roots in the societal consequences of the computer revolution of the late 50s, when the migration from dusty paper archives to computer memories permitted, for the first time, the aggregation of information about every citizen that was previously spread over different archives.[2] In this sense, data protection was the response by legislators to the growing concern of citizens about the risk of computer-based social control by governments[3] and large corporations.[4]

As a consequence, the notion of data protection was originally based on the idea of control over information[5] and the first data protection regulations gave individuals a sort of counter-control over collected data.[6] They pursue this goal by increasing the level of transparency about data processing and safeguarding the right to access to information.

Mandatory notification of new databases, registration, licensing procedures and independent authorities were the fundamental elements of these regulations. Another key component was the right to access, which allows citizens to ask data owners about the manner in which information is being used and, consequently, about the exercise of power over information. Finally, the entire picture was completed by the creation of ad hoc public authorities to safeguard and enforce citizens' rights.

In this model there was no space for individual consent, since the collection of information was mainly made by public entities for purposes related to public interests and mandatory. At

---

[1] This chapter was last revised in March 2020 and reflects the analysis of the existing legal framework at that time. For a further analysis, see Alessandro Mantelero, *Beyond Data. Human Rights, Ethical and Social Impact Assessment in AI* (Springer 2022).

[2] *See* Secretary's Advisory Committee on Automated Personal Data Systems, 'Records, Computers and the Rights of Citizens' (1973) http://epic.org/privacy/hew1973report/ accessed 27 March 2017.

[3] Arthur R. Miller, *The Assault on Privacy Computers, Data Banks, Dossiers* (University of Michigan Press 1971) 54–67; Viktor Mayer-Schönberger, 'Generational Development of Data Protection in Europe?' in Philip E. Agre and Marc Rotenberg (eds), *Technology and Privacy: The New Landscape* (MIT Press 1997) 221–225. *See also* Gloria González Fuster, *The Emergence of Personal Data Protection as a Fundamental Right of the EU* (Springer International Publishing 2014) 28–36.

[4] *See* Colin J. Bennett, *Regulating Privacy: Data Protection and Public Policy in Europe and the United States* (Cornell University Press 1992) 29–33, 47; Myron Brenton, *The Privacy Invaders* (Coward-McCann 1964); Vance Packard, *The Naked Society* (David McKay 1964). *See also* Secretary's Advisory Committee on Automated Personal Data Systems (n 2) and Lee A. Bygrave, *Data Protection Law. Approaching Its Rationale, Logic and Limits* (Kluwer Law International 2002), 107–112.

[5] *See* Alan F. Westin, *Privacy and Freedom* (Atheneum 1970), 7; Daniel J. Solove, *Understanding Privacy* (Harvard University Press 2008) 24-29.

[6] See Secretary's Advisory Committee on Automated Personal Data Systems (n 2). *See also* Viktor Mayer-Schönberger, (n 3) 223.

the same time, personal information did not have an economic value for private companies: data about clients and suppliers were mainly used for operational functions regarding the execution of company activities. Finally, only a select number of technicians were able to use the new computer mainframes. For this reason, it did not make sense to give citizens the freedom to choose, since they were unable to understand the way in which their data was processed.

This scenario changed in the mid-80s, when in many cases the big mainframe computers were superseded by personal computers, at a relatively low cost. Consequently, the computational capacity was no longer an exclusive privilege of governments and big companies, but became accessible to many entities and consumers.

This period witnessed another transformation involving direct marketing: new forms of marketing based on customer profiling and extensive data collection took place; information was no longer collected to support supply chains, logistics and orders, but to target products at specific users. As a result, the data subject became the focus of the process and personal information acquired an economic and business value.

These changes in the technological and business frameworks led legislators to face new demands from society, since citizens wanted to have the chance to negotiate their personal data and gain something in return. Although the new generations of the European data protection laws placed personal information within the context of fundamental rights,[7] the main goal of these regulations was to pursue economic interests related to the free flow of personal data,[8] even though the European approach was, and remains, less market-oriented than other legal systems.

Both the theoretical model of fundamental rights, based on self-determination, and the rising data-driven economy highlighted the importance of users' consent in consumer data processing. Consent does not only represent an expression of choice with regard to the use of personality rights by third parties, but is also an instrument to negotiate the economic value of personal information. Moreover, effective self-determination in data processing, both in terms of protection and economic exploitation of personality rights, cannot be obtained without adequate and prior notice. For this reason, the 'notice and consent' model[9] added a new layer to the previous paradigm based on transparency and access.

---

[7] *See* Council of Europe, Convention for the Protection of Individuals with regard to Automatic Processing of Personal Data, opened for signature on 28 January 1981 and entered into force on 1 October 1985 http://conventions.coe.int/Treaty/Commun/QueVoulezVous.asp?NT=108&CL=ENG (accessed February 27, 2017); OECD, Annex to the Recommendation of the Council of 23rd September 1980: Guidelines on the Protection of Privacy and Transborder Flows of Personal Data http://www.oecd.org/internet/ieconomy/oecdguidelinesontheprotectionofprivacyandtransborderflowsofpersonaldata.htm#preface (accessed February 27, 2017). *See also* González Fuster (n 3), 163–205 and 253–272; Maria Tzanou, 'Data Protection as a Fundamental Right Next to Privacy? "Reconstructing" a not so new Right' (2013) 3 (2) *IDPL* 88–99; Stefano Rodotà, 'Data Protection as a Fundamental Right' in Serge Gutwirth, Yves Poullet, Paul De Hert, Cécile de Terwangne and Sjaak Nouwt (eds), *Reinventing Data Protection?* (Springer, 2009) 77–82.

[8] Directive 95/46/EC of the European Parliament and of the Council of 24 October 1995 on the protection of individuals with regard to the processing of personal data and on the free movement of such data [1995] OJ L281/31. *See also* Yves Poullet, 'EU Data Protection Policy. The Directive 95/46/EC: Ten Years After' (2006) 22 (3) CLSR 206; Spiros Simitis, 'From the Market to the Polis: The EU Directive on the Protection of Personal Data' (1995) 80 *Iowa L Rev* 445.

[9] *See* Arts 2 (h), 7 (a) and 10, Directive 95/46/EC.

During the 80s and 90s, data analysis increased in quality, but its level of complexity was still limited. Consequently, consumers were able to understand the general correlation between data collection and the related purposes of data processing (e.g., profiling users, offering customized services or goods). At that time, informed consent and self-determination were largely used as synonyms, but this changed with the advent of big data analytics. In many respects, the new big data environment resembles the origins of data processing, when, in the mainframe era, technologies were held by few entities and data processing was too complex to be understood by data subjects. Big data analytics make it possible to infer predictive information from large amounts of data in order to acquire further knowledge about individuals and groups, which may not necessarily be related to the initial purposes of data collection.[10] Analytics group people together by their qualitative attributes and habits (e.g., 'working-class mom' or 'metro parents'[11]) and predict the future behaviour of these groups of individuals.[12]

In these cases, predictions based on correlations[13] do not only affect individuals, who may behave differently from the rest of the group to which have been assigned, but also affect the whole group and set it apart from the rest of society. Moreover, users are often unaware of these forms of data analysis and of the impact that some information may have on their membership of one or another group created by analytics. Finally, decision-makers use the outcomes generated by big data analytics to take decisions that affect individuals and groups, without allowing them any participation in the process, which remains primarily based on obscure data management and frequently takes place in situations of imbalance between data gatherers and data subjects.

All these different aspects should lead regulators to reflect on elements of the traditional model of personal information protection.[14] First, the use of personal information and big data

---

[10] *See* David Bollier, 'The Promise and Perils of Big Data' (Aspen Institute, Communications and Society Program 2010) http://www.aspeninstitute.org/sites/default/files/content/docs/pubs/The_Promise_and_Peril_of_Big_Data.pdf accessed 27 February 2017. *See also* Pertti Ahonen, 'Institutionalizing Big Data Methods in Social and Political Research' (2015) *Big Data & Society* 1–12 http://bds.sagepub.com/content/2/2/2053951715591224 accessed 21 July 2016. Since, in terms of data protection, the main issues regarding big data do not concern their volume, velocity, and variety, but the analysis of the data using software to extract new and predictive knowledge for decision-making purposes, the present contribution focuses on big data analytics.

[11] These are the categories used by US data brokers to define specific segments of population based on models of predictive behaviour. *See* Federal Trade Commission, 'Data Brokers: A Call for Transparency and Accountability' (2014), 20 and Appendix B https://www.ftc.gov/system/files/documents/reports/data-brokers-call-transparency-accountability-report-federal-trade-commission-may-2014/140527databrokerreport.pdf accessed 27 February 2016.

[12] *See* Alessandro Mantelero, 'Personal Data for Decisional Purposes in the Age of Analytics: From an Individual to a Collective Dimension of Data Protection' (2016) 32 (2) *CLSR* 238–255; Linnet Taylor, Luciano Floridi, Bart van der Sloot (eds), *Group Privacy: New Challenges of Data Technologies* (Springer International Publishing 2017).

[13] *See* Bollier (n 10). *See also* Mireille Hildebrandt, 'Profiling: From Data to Knowledge. The Challenges of a Crucial Technology' (2006) 30(9) Datenschutz und Datensicherheit 548.

[14] *See also* Fred H. Cate and Viktor Mayer-Schönberger, 'Data Use and Impact. Global Workshop' (The Center for Information Policy Research and The Center for Applied Cybersecurity Research, Indiana University 2013) http://cacr.iu.edu/sites/cacr.iu.edu/files/Use_Workshop_Report.pdf accessed 27 February 2017; Alessandro Mantelero, 'The Future of Consumer Data Protection in the E.U. Rethinking the "notice and consent" Paradigm in the New Era of Predictive Analytics' (2014) 30 (6) *CLSR* 643–660.

analytics to support decisions goes beyond the boundaries of the individual dimension and assumes a collective dimension, with potentially harmful consequences for some groups.[15] In this sense, prejudice can result not only from the well-known privacy-related risks (e.g., illegitimate use of personal information, data security), but also from discriminatory and invasive forms of data processing.[16]

Second, the use of big data analytics not only impacts on the nature of the protected interests, but also on the traditional manner of data processing and, therefore, affects data protection regulation. In this sense, the 'transformative' use[17] of data often makes it difficult or impossible to put in place the purpose limitation principle as happened prior to the advent of big data and, as a consequence, to provide a proper notice about data processing.

Since big data applications collect a large amount of information from different sources and analyse it to identify new trends and correlations in datasets, data can be processed to pursue purposes not adequately specified in advance – related to the correlations found in the datasets – and potentially different from the purposes of the initial collection. This contrasts with the notion of 'explicit' and 'specified' purposes defined at the moment of data collection, which represents a constitutive element of data protection regulation.[18]

II. THE EUROPEAN UNION APPROACH IN REGULATING BIG DATA

At a global level, the EU model is probably the most successful regulation in the field of data protection, in terms of influence on third countries' regulations.[19] Nevertheless, different regulatory approaches are supported by other countries and at international level (APEC, Council of Europe, OECD). Hence, the EU data protection reform could be placed in the

---

[15] *See also* Kate Crawford, Gustavo Faleiros, Amy Luers, Patrick Meier, Claudia Perlich and Jer Thorp, 'Big Data, Communities and Ethical Resilience: A Framework for Action' (2013) 6–7 http://www.rockefellerfoundation.org/app/uploads/71b4c457-cdb7-47ec-81a9-a617c956e6af.pdf accessed 5 April 2017; danah boyd, Karen Levy, Alice Marwick, 'The Networked Nature of Algorithmic Discrimination', in Seeta Peña Gangadharan, Virginia Eubanks and Solon Barocas, *Data and Discrimination: Collective Essays* (Open Technology Institute and New America 2014) 56 http://www.newamerica.org/downloads/OTI-Data-an-Discrimination-FINAL-small.pdf accessed 14 April 2017.

[16] *See also* The White House, Executive Office of the President, 'Big Data: Seizing Opportunities, Preserving Values' (2014) https://obamawhitehouse.archives.gov/sites/default/files/docs/big_data_privacy_report_5.1.14_final_print.pdf accessed 4 March 2017. *See also* Tal Z. Zarsky, 'Transparent Predictions' (2013) 4 *U Ill L Rev* 1503, 1560–1563; Anton H. Vedder, 'Privatization, Information Technology and Privacy: Reconsidering the Social Responsibilities of Private Organizations' in Geoff Moore (ed), *Business Ethics: Principles and Practice* (Business Education Publishers 1997) 215–226.

[17] *See* Omer Tene and Jules Polonetsky, 'Privacy in the Age of Big Data: A Time for Big Decisions' (2012) *Stan L Rev Online* 64.

[18] *See* Art 5.4.b of the Draft Modernised Convention 108.

[19] *See* Graham Greenleaf, 'Global Data Privacy Laws 2017: 120 National Data Privacy Laws, Including Indonesia and Turkey' (2017) 145 *PL&B Intl Rep* 10–13; Graham Greenleaf, 'Global Data Privacy Laws 2015: 109 Countries, with European Laws now in a Minority' (2015) 133 *PL&B Intl Rep* 14–17; Graham Greenleaf, 'The Influence of European Data Privacy Standards Outside Europe: Implications for Globalization of Convention 108' (2012) 2 (2) *International Data Privacy Law* 68–92. *See also* Paul De Hert and Vagelis Papakonstantinou, 'The New General Data Protection Regulation: Still a Sound System for the Protection of Individuals?' (2016) 32 (2) *CLSR* 194.

broader context of a global 'competition' over the international regulation of data protection, which involves different economic areas and organizations. From this perspective, the new Regulation (EU) 2016/679 (hereinafter GDPR) can be seen as an attempt to reinforce the EU's leadership in setting a future global regulatory standard in data protection.

The EU's intention to retain its prominent role in the international scenario, established with Directive 95/46/EC,[20] may be one of the reasons that induced the EU legislator to remain on the path defined in 1995, without reconsidering the main pillars of its model. Another reason can be found in the legislative process used to build a uniform EU data protection framework: Directive 95/46/EC created a convergence which it intends to reinforce with the GDPR in a manner which is necessarily consistent with the founding principles defined in the Directive. Nevertheless, the challenges of big data analytics scarcely seem to be addressed within the framework designed in the 90s.

Despite this decision of the EU legislator to maintain the regulatory paradigm as framed in 1995, in the GDPR there are specific provisions which, although not directly focused on big data, may be applied to this context. In this sense, the progressive shift of the regulatory focus from individual self-determination to forms of accountability based on risk-assessment[21] reduces the difficulties in regulating big data since the adoption of a risk-based approach may offer a partial remedy to the potential negative outcomes of the use of big data analytics.

---

[20] *See* above fn. 8. *See also* Anu Bradford, 'The Brussels Effect' (2015) 107 *Nw U L Rev* 1–67 http://scholarlycommons.law.northwestern.edu/nulr/vol107/iss1/1 accessed 4 March 2017.

[21] *See* Article 29 Data protection Working Party, 'Guidelines on Data Protection Impact Assessment (DPIA) and determining whether processing is 'likely to result in a high risk' for the purposes of Regulation 2016/679' (2017) http://ec.europa.eu/newsroom/document.cfm?doc_id=44137 accessed 13 April 2017. *See also* CNIL, 'Privacy Impact Assessment (PIA). Methodology (how to carry out a PIA)' (2015) https://www.cnil.fr/sites/default/files/typo/document/CNIL-PIA-1-Methodology.pdf accessed 25 February 2017; CNIL, 'Privacy Impact Assessment (PIA). Tools (templates and knowledge bases)' (2015) <https://www.cnil.fr/sites/default/files/typo/document/CNIL-PIA-2-Tools.pdf accessed 25 February 2017; CNIL, 'Measures for the privacy risk treatment' (2012) https://www.cnil.fr/sites/default/files/typo/document/CNIL-PIA-3-GoodPractices.pdf accessed 25 February 2017; Article 29 Data Protection Working Party, 'Statement on the role of a risk-based approach in data protection legal frameworks' (2014) http://ec.europa.eu/justice/data-protection/article-29/documentation/opinion-recommendation/files/2014/wp218_en.pdf accessed 27 February 2017; Article 29 Data Protection Working Party, 'Opinion 07/2013 on the Data Protection Impact Assessment Template for Smart Grid and Smart Metering Systems ('DPIA Template') prepared by Expert Group 2 of the Commission's Smart Grid Task Force' (2013) http://ec.europa.eu/justice/dataprotection/article-29/documentation/opinion-ecommendation/files/2013/wp209_en.pdf accessed 27 February 2017; Article 29 Data Protection Working Party, 'Opinion 9/2011 on the revised Industry Proposal for a Privacy and Data Protection Impact Assessment Framework for RFID Applications' (2011) http://ec.europa.eu/justice/policies/privacy/docs/wpdocs/2011/wp180_en.pdf accessed 27 February 2017; Trilateral Research & Consulting, 'Privacy impact assessment and risk management. Report for the Information Commissioner's Office prepared by Trilateral Research & Consulting' (2013) https://ico.org.uk/media/1042196/trilateral-full-report.pdf accessed 25 February 2017. *See also* Charles Raab and David Wright, 'Surveillance: Extending the Limits of Privacy Impact Assessment' in David Wright and Paul De Hert (eds), *Privacy Impact Assessment* (Springer 2012) 363–383; Anton Vedder and Laurens Naudts, 'Accountability for the use of algorithms in a big data environment' (2017) 31 (29) *International Review of Law, Computers & Technology* 206–224.

The main limit of these provisions is the existing relationship between risk assessment and the purposes of data processing.[22] As a consequence, the criticisms that characterize the application of the purpose limitation principle in the big data context also affect risk assessment. Indeed, any assessment is related to the use of data for a specific purpose and, according to the GDPR, data processing purposes should be 'specific, explicit and legitimate', and defined at the moment of data collection.[23] However, this is not consistent with the transformative use of data by private and public bodies through big data analytics. A further limit concerns the nature of the risk-assessment required by the Regulation. In this regard, the notion of risk adopted in the new Regulation focuses on 'material or non-material damages' that prejudice the 'rights and freedoms of natural persons',[24] in line with the rights-based approach to risk management of the EU data protection regulation.[25] According to this approach, when a risk of prejudice exists and cannot be mitigated or excluded, data processing becomes unlawful, despite the presence of any legitimate grounds, such as the data subject's consent. Thus Recital no. 75 of the Regulation provides a long list of cases where data processing is considered unlawful.

It should be pointed out that this recital does not limit these hypotheses to the security of data processing, but also takes into account the risk of discrimination and 'any other significant economic or social disadvantage'. This notion of risk impact, which is echoed in Article 35 of the Regulation, represents an important step in the direction of an impact assessment of data processing that is no longer primarily focused on data security[26] but evolves into a more robust and broader assessment of the different implications of data use.[27]

Attention to the economic and social implications of data use assumes significant relevance in the big data context, where analytics become part of decision-making processes and may have negative impacts on individuals, in terms of discrimination[28] rather than in terms of data

---

[22] *See* Art 35 (1) of the GDPR:

> Where a type of processing in particular using new technologies, and taking into account the nature, scope, context and purposes of the processing, is likely to result in a high risk to the rights and freedoms of natural persons") and 35(7)(b) ("[The assessment shall contain at least] an assessment of the necessity and proportionality of the processing operations in relation to the purposes.

[23] *See* Art 5(1)(b) of the GDPR.

[24] *See* Recital no. 75 of the GDPR.

[25] While according to the risk/benefit approach, the assessment should be based on the comparison between the importance of benefits and the sum of all risks, without any distinction regarding the nature of risks and benefits, the right-based approach focuses on rights protection and not on a general trade-off between risks and benefits. On the different classifications of risks related to privacy and data protection, *see also* David Wright and Charles Raab, 'Privacy Principles, Risks and Harms' (2014) 28(3) *International Review of Law, Computers & Technology* 277–298.

[26] *See* Art 32 of the GDPR.

[27] *See also* Article 29 Data Protection Working Party, 'Guidelines on Data Protection Impact Assessment (DPIA) and determining whether processing is 'likely to result in a high risk' for the purposes of Regulation 2016/679' (2017) 15 ('the reference to "the rights and freedoms" of the data subjects primarily concerns the right to privacy but may also involve other fundamental rights such as freedom of speech, freedom of thought, freedom of movement, prohibition of discrimination, right to liberty, conscience and religion'); Article 29 Data protection Working Party, 'Statement on the role of a risk-based approach in data protection legal frameworks' (2014) http://ec.europa.eu/justice/data-protection/article-29/documentation/opinion-recommendation/files/2014/wp218_en.pdf accessed 28 October 2021 .

[28] *See* The White House, Executive Office of the President, 'Big Data: A Report on Algorithmic Systems, Opportunity, and Civil Rights' (2016) https://obamawhitehouse.archives.gov/sites/default/files/microsites/ostp/2016_0504_data_discrimination.pdf accessed 4 March 2017. *See also* European Data Protection Supervisor, 'Opinion 7/2015. Meeting the challenges of big data. A call for transpar-

security.[29] However, the provisions of the Regulation do not offer an adequate framework for the assessment of this kind of negative outcome.

The risk-mitigation approach adopted by the Regulation still seems far from the idea of a privacy, ethical and social impact assessment,[30] which is a multiple and participative risk-assessment process where the potential negative outcomes of data processing are not only measured in terms of information protection, but also encompass the societal consequences of data uses and their impact on the application of ethical values.

The lack of this broader perspective represents a limit, since the use of big data analytics in decision-making processes raises important questions regarding the values that should drive the future algorithmic society. Moreover, the increasing importance of the collective dimension of data use should lead rule-makers to reflect on the role that the different social stakeholders can play in assessing the societal impacts of data use.[31]

Apart from risk assessment, there are provisions in the GDPR concerning other aspects that are important in processing personal information by means of analytics. One of these aspects regards the transformative use of data in analysis based on correlations. Article 5.1.b of the GDPR is relevant on this point, since it admits that data collected can be processed for further purposes, if these purposes are not incompatible with the purposes for which the personal data were initially collected. To decide whether there is compatibility between the purposes, Recital no. 50 and Article 6.4 consider:

(a) any link between the purposes for which the personal data have been collected and the purposes of the intended further processing;
(b) the context in which the personal data have been collected, in particular regarding the relationship between data subjects and the controller;[32]
(c) the nature of the personal data, in particular whether special categories of personal data are processed, pursuant to Article 9, or whether personal data related to criminal convictions and offences are processed, pursuant to Article 10;
(d) the possible consequences of the intended further processing for data subjects;
(e) the existence of appropriate safeguards.

This notion of compatibility necessarily limits the application of these provisions to cases in which big data analytics are used for purposes that are not too far from the initial one. For this

---

ency, user control, data protection by design and accountability' (2015) https://secure.edps.europa.eu/EDPSWEB/webdav/site/mySite/shared/Documents/Consultation/Opinions/2015/15-11-19_Big_Data_EN.pdf accessed 12 February 2017.

[29] *See also*, more recently, European Parliament, 'European Parliament resolution of 14 March 2017 on fundamental rights implications of big data: privacy, data protection, non-discrimination, security and law-enforcement (2016/2225(INI))' (2017) http://www.europarl.europa.eu/sides/getDoc.do?pubRef=-//EP//TEXT+TA+P8-TA-2017-0076+0+DOC+XML+V0//EN&language=EN accessed 16 March 2017.

[30] With regard to the ethical assessment in research and innovation, *see* Clare Shelley-Egan et al., 'SATORI Deliverable D2.1 Report (handbook) of participatory processes' (2014) http://satoriproject.eu/work_packages/dialogue-and-participation/ accessed 15 February 2017, 42–44.

[31] *See* Mantelero (n 12).

[32] *See also* Recital no. 50:

In order to ascertain whether a purpose of further processing is compatible with the purpose for which the personal data are initially collected, the controller [...] should take into account, inter alia [...] the context in which the personal data have been collected, in particular the reasonable expectations of data subjects based on their relationship with the controller as to their further use; the nature of the personal data.

reason, Article 5.1.b of the GDPR represents only a partial solution to the issues concerning data processing in the big data context, where the potential outcome of data analysis, in terms of results and rising correlations, is often largely unpredictable. This does not rule out the possibility of a potential application of these provisions in specific, narrow focus, uses of analytics, due to the use of broad notions such as the 'reasonable expectations of data subjects' and the 'consequences of the intended further processing for data subjects'.[33]

Moreover, Article 5 should be complemented by the subsequent Article 13.3, which states that:

> where the controller intends to further process the personal data for a purpose other than that for which the personal data were collected, the controller shall provide the data subject prior to that further processing with information on that other purpose and with any relevant further information as referred to in paragraph 2.

This provision reduces the chance of further personal information processing for new purposes in the big data context, because it creates an obligation that is unlikely to be fulfilled in the presence of massive data collections and ongoing detection of new correlations, as frequently happens in big data applications.

Another solution that partially addresses the issues of the transformative use of personal data in the big data context relies on the second part of Article 5.1.b, which allows further processing of data for statistical purposes. As observed by legal scholars,[34] this statistical exception can be applied to a limited range of cases, since 'processing of personal data for statistical purposes may only result in aggregate data which cannot be re-applied to individuals'.[35] However, many big data applications either apply the results of predictive aggregate analysis to specific individuals singled out from the crowd of each cluster of people or focus on individual profiling. For these reasons, the statistical exception has necessarily a limited application. Finally, this analysis should consider the safeguards that may be provided to data subjects in the context of big data processing. Although the technologically neutral approach adopted in the GDPR excludes specific safeguards concerning big data applications, some provisions on transparency and automated decision-making may play a role in this regard.

Transparency of algorithms[36] is crucial to safeguard data subjects' self-determination in the context of analytics. At the same time, transparency is not a new issue[37] (although this is a debated topic after the adoption of the GDPR[38]) and represents only a part of the solution

---

[33] The reference to the 'consequences of the intended further processing for data subjects' is important in terms of shifting the assessment from the compatibility between purposes to the compatibility between risks associated to data use. Although this change of perspective is still marginalized in the Regulation, it may represent the most adequate manner to address the challenges of big data analytics. *See also* below section III.1.

[34] *See* Viktor Mayer-Schönberger and Yann Padova, 'Regime Change? Enabling Big Data through Europe's Data Protection Regulation' (2016) XVII *Colum. Sci. & Tech. L. Rev.* 315, 327.

[35] *See* European Parliament (n 29).

[36] *See* Jenna Burrell, 'How the Machine 'thinks': Understanding Opacity in Machine Learning Algorithms' (2016) 3(1) Big Data & Society https://doi.org/10.1177/2053951715622512 accessed 03 March 2018.

[37] *See* e.g., ibid.

[38] *See* e.g. Francesca Rossi, 'Artificial Intelligence: Potential Benefits d Ethical Considerations' (European Parliament: Policy Department C: Citizens' Rights and Constitutional Affairs 2016)

to address the challenges of big data.[39] In the big data context, the notion of transparency has different meanings. It may consist in the mere disclosure about the use of analytics, in the description of their logic or in the access to the structure of the algorithms used for analytics and – when applicable – to the datasets used to train these algorithms.

Although awareness is important for a public scrutiny of automated decision-making models, a generic information on the use of analytics weakly contributes to tackle the risks of unfair or illegitimate data use. On the contrary, the access to the structure of algorithms makes it possible to assess potential biases, but IP protection and competition issues may limit this access. Moreover, in some cases, transparency may also be in conflict with the performance of the tasks carried out by public bodies (e.g., predictive policing systems).

For these reasons, the solution focused on the disclosure of the logic of algorithms may be the most appropriate. In this sense, the GDPR focuses on 'the logic involved' in data processing and 'the envisaged consequences'.[40] Nonetheless, these definitions can be interpreted in a restrictive or in an extensive manner.[41] Providing information about the nature of input data and expected output,[42] disclosing the variables of algorithms and their weight, and providing access to the architecture of analytics are different possible interpretations.

Moreover, complex models of analysis (e.g., *deep-learning*) challenge this notion of transparency, in terms of explanation of the logic of algorithms[43] and of the decisions adopted using analytics.[44] Finally, the dynamic nature of analytics may contrast with a static idea of transparency.[45]

Briefing PE 571.380 http://www.europarl.europa.eu/RegData/etudes/BRIE/2016/571380/IPOL_BRI(2016)571380_EN.pdf accessed 03 March 2018; Sandra Wachter, Brent Mittelstadt and Luciano Floridi, 'Why a Right to Explanation of Automated Decision-making does not Exist in the General Data Protection Regulation' (2017) 7(2) *International Data Privacy Law* 76–99; Andrew D. Selbst and Julia Powles, 'Meaningful Information and the Right to Explanation' (2017) 7(4) *International Data Privacy Law* 233–242; Lilian Edwards and Michael Vale, 'Slave to the Algorithm? Why a "Right to an Explanation" Is Probably Not the Remedy You Are Looking For' (2017) 16(1) *Duke Law and Technology Review* 18–84.

39 Transparency does not necessarily increase data subjects' safeguards or induce data controllers to adopt data protection-oriented solutions. However, it increases the level of awareness and facilitates data subjects' and data protection authorities' actions against unlawful data processing.

40 *See* Recital no. 63 and Arts 13, 14 and 15 of the GDPR.

41 *See* the narrow interpretation suggested by the Article 29 Data Protection Working Party, 'Guidelines on Automated individual decision-making and Profiling for the purposes of Regulation 2016/679', 2018, 25–26.

42 This information may be provided through learning by use models, giving data subjects the chance to test analytics with different input values. Nevertheless, also in this case there is a risk of a misleading identification of the relevant input; *see* Nicholas Diakopoulps, *Algorithmic Accountability Reporting: on the Investigation of Black Boxes* (Tow Center for Digital Journalism 2013) 18.

43 *See* Bryce Goodman and Seth Flaxman, 'EU Regulations on Algorithmic Decision-Making and a "right to Explanation"' (2016) [2016] arXiv:1606.08813 [cs, stat] http://arxiv.org/abs/1606.08813 accessed 03 March 2019.

44 In these cases, it may be impossible providing an explanation of the reason for the decision suggested by the algorithm; *see* Burrell (n 36) at fn. 18.

45 In light of the above, transparency may be less effective than expected or must assume different forms, such as third-party audits or use of algorithms to repetitively test a given analytics and detect potential bias.

Against this background, a set of articles in the GDPR has been used by legal scholars to frame the so-called right to explanation.[46] The first articles to be taken into account are Articles 13.2.f and 14.2.g, which state that, in case of automated decision-making, 'meaningful information about the logic involved, as well as the significance and the envisaged consequences of such processing' must be provided to data subjects. These articles concern information provided to data subjects at the moment of data collection or within a reasonable period (Recital 61). In this sense, they necessarily concern the logic and consequences of data processing in general and not with regard to a specific adopted decision, except in cases of analytics based on deterministic models. On the contrary, the similar wording in Article 15.1.h does not exclude an *ex post* explanation of a specific decision, since it concerns the right of access, which can be exercised by data subjects even after the adoption of any decisions concerning them.[47]

The focus on transparency in these three articles is different from the approach adopted in Article 22.3 and Recital 71. Recital 71 concerns the right 'to obtain an explanation of the decision reached after such assessment and to challenge the decision'. Here the assessment is the one carried out by a human decision-maker when a data subject has exercised 'the right to obtain human intervention' (Art 22.3). This is not a general right to explanation concerning analytics, like in the provisions mentioned above. In this case, the explanation concerns the specific decision taken by the human decision-maker whose intervention has been obtained.

In this sense, Article 22 provides a specific remedy in the case of automated decision-making, which is not based on the idea of transparency but on human intervention in the automated decision process.[48] In this regard, the first observation to make concerns the field of application of this article: only a limited number of applications based on big data are full automated decision-making processes. In many cases, big data analytics are decision-support tools. But, the results of algorithms benefit from the allure of mathematical objectivity, which combined with the complexity of data management and the subordinate position of the decision-makers in the organization, make it difficult for a human decision-maker to take a decision different to the one suggested by the algorithm.[49]

When an automated decision-making process exists, the GDPR only recognizes the data subject's 'right to obtain human intervention on the part of the controller, to express his or her point of view and to contest the decision', except in cases in which the automated decision-making processes are authorized by law, which provides 'suitable measures to safeguard the data subject's rights and freedoms and legitimate interests'. The aim of this provision is to guarantee human intervention in automated decision-making processes but suffers from the same limitations mentioned above with regard to decision-support tools.

In this sense, the crucial aspects of the use of personal information in decision-making seem to be the advisability of using data-driven systems for specific purposes and the values that should motivate these systems. This also in light of the right 'not to be subject to a decision based solely on automated processing' which is recognized by Article 22.2, although this right can be easily derogated on the basis of contractual purposes or consent[50] which substantially

---

[46] *See* above fn. 38.
[47] *See also* Selbst and Powles (n 38) 239; *contra* Wachter, Mittelstadt and Floridi (n 38) 78, 83–84.
[48] *See also* Edwards and Vale (n 38).
[49] *See also* below section III.1.
[50] *See* Art 22.2.a and 22.2.c of the GDPR.

reduces the efficacy of this safeguard, given the well-known weaknesses surrounding the data subject's consent in terms of self-determination.[51]

In conclusion, the different provisions of the new Regulation do not provide a general and systematic answer to the very real conflict between the purpose specification principle and the peculiar nature of data processing based on analytics. Nor do they offer remedies that address the issues arising from the increasingly extensive application of analytics to decision-making processes. The GDPR only provides partial solutions. In this sense, the GDPR 'can be seen as a stepping stone, pointing towards the need to evolve data protection beyond the old paradigm, yet not fully committed to doing so'.[52]

More recently, in the context of the EU regulatory framework, the European Parliament has adopted a specific resolution on big data, focusing on the fundamental rights implications of big data (hereinafter the Resolution).[53] This Resolution has various element in common with the Guidelines on Big Data adopted in January 2017 by the Council of Europe,[54] starting from the focus on big data analytics rather than merely the extensive collection of data characterized by volume, variety and velocity.

As in the Guidelines of the Council of Europe, the European Parliament points out the 'legal, social and ethical implications' of data use, the risk of discrimination of the use of analytics for decision-making purposes,[55] and the blurring of the distinction between personal and non-personal data[56] and between sensitive and non-sensitive data.[57] Analogies are also present with regard to the possible remedies, where the Resolution mentions the role of education and digital literacy[58] and the assessment of the risk of re-identification of anonymous data.[59]

On the other hand, the Resolution does have a broader scope than the Guidelines of the Council of Europe, since it also concerns the activities of the intelligence services and the media,[60] and takes into account encryption,[61] ISP liability[62] and law enforcement.[63] Finally, the Resolution reaffirms the principles and provisions of the GDPR with regard to transparency, accountability,[64] data protection by design and by default, anonymization, impact assessments and use of data for scientific purposes.[65] Despite the analogies with the provisions of the GDPR and the Guidelines of the Council of Europe, the Resolution differs from both of them,

---

[51] Edwards and Vale (n 38) 46 also highlight the uncertainty of the notion of decision based solely on automated processing, provided by Art 22, when it is used in the context of algorithm-based systems.

[52] *See* Mayer-Schönberger Padova (n 33) 332.

[53] European Parliament (n 29).

[54] *See* below section III.1.

[55] *See* letter M and no. 2, 5, 19–22 and 31 of the Resolution.

[56] *See* letter J of the Resolution.

[57] *See* no. 3 of the Resolution. *See also* De Hert and Papakonstantinou (n 19) 183.

[58] *See* no. 4 of the Resolution.

[59] *See* no. 7 of the Resolution. *See also* Arvind Narayanan, Joanna Huey and Edward W. Felten, 'A Precautionary Approach to Big Data Privacy' in Serge Gutwirth, Ronald Leenes, Paul De Hert (eds), *Data Protection on the Move: Current Developments in ICT and Privacy/Data Protection* (Springer Netherlands 2016) 357–385.

[60] *See* no. 13 of the Resolution.

[61] *See* no. 16 of the Resolution.

[62] *See* no. 18 of the Resolution.

[63] *See* no. 25–32 of the Resolution.

[64] *See* letter N of the Resolution.

[65] *See* no. 11, 17, 23, 24 of the Resolution.

since it is less focused on the regulatory perspective and its purpose is primarily political. In this sense, consistent with its nature as a recommendation, the Resolution is more an overview of the various issues regarding big data applications and of possible general remedies, than an attempt to provide specific solutions.[66]

III. REGULATING BIG DATA BEYOND THE EU BORDERS

Looking at the regulatory initiatives in the field of big data beyond EU borders, there are only a limited number of proposals. This is probably due to the fact that the adoption of basic data protection regulation is still ongoing in many countries[67] and the lack or paucity of such regulations means that there is little focus on new and challenging issues such as those arising from big data applications. From this perspective, it is no wonder that the main non-EU initiatives have been adopted by the Council of Europe – which has a broader territorial scope than the EU, but remains an international body mainly situated in European legal culture – and by the United States, which have played a central role in the debate on privacy-related issues, since its origins.

Comparing the approaches adopted by the EU and the Council of Europe, the GDPR still primarily protects personal data by means of individual rights and an assessment of the social and ethical consequences of data use is still not developed. On the other hand, the Guidelines on big data adopted by the Council of Europe[68] take into account both the individual and collective dimensions of data protection. In this sense they develop a model for the ethical and social impact assessment of data uses.[69] Moreover, the Guidelines reveal an awareness of

---

[66] *See*, for instance, no. 9 of the Resolution, which points out the importance of a 'closer collaboration among regulators of conduct in the digital environment, so as to strengthen the synergies between regulatory frameworks for consumers and competition and data protection authorities', calls for adequate funding and staffing of such authorities and explicitly refers to the proposal of the EDPS to establish a Digital Clearing House among the different authorities. *See* European Data Protection Supervisor, 'Opinion 8/2016. EDPS Opinion on coherent enforcement of fundamental rights in the age of big data' (2016) 3, 15.

[67] *See* Greenleaf (2017 and 2015) (n 19).

[68] *See* 'Guidelines on the protection of individuals with regard to the processing of personal data in a world of Big Data' (hereinafter Guidelines). The final version of the Guidelines was adopted on January 23. The Guidelines were approved by the 50 voting members of the Council, with the abstention of Denmark, Liechtenstein and Luxembourg, while Germany and Ireland objected. The Guidelines are available at https://rm.coe.int/CoERMPublicCommonSearchServices/DisplayDCTMContent?documentId=09000016806ebe7a accessed 4 February 2017. The author of this chapter had the privilege to be appointed as consultant expert in drafting the text of the guidelines and to follow the discussion of the proposal by the representatives of the Parties to Convention 108 in the Bureau of the Consultative Committee of Convention 108 and the Plenary Meeting.

[69] For a literature review on the ethical impact assessment, *see* Rasmus Øjvind Nielsen, Agata M. Gurzawska and Philip Bray, 'Principles and Approaches in Ethics Assessment. Ethical Impact Assessment and Conventional Impact Assessment. Annex 1.a Ethical Assessment of Research and Innovation: A Comparative Analysis of Practices and Institutions in the EU and selected other countries. Project Stakeholders Acting Together on the Ethical Impact Assessment of Research and Innovation – SATORI. Deliverable 1.1' (2015) http://satoriproject.eu/work_packages/comparative-analysis-of-ethics-assessment-practices/ accessed 15 February 2017.

the limits affecting the data subject's consent and encourage a participatory model[70] of risk assessment.

In this regard, the principle-based approach of the Convention 108 and the broad nature of the principles makes it possible to give a specific interpretation of them in the big data context. The Guidelines thus benefit from a greater margin of manoeuvre in implementing the provisions originally established in 1981, adopting more innovative solutions than the GDPR.

With regard to US initiatives on big data, they have not yet reached the stage of the EU and Council of Europe instruments, but they do represent an interesting step forward in the ongoing US debate on the protection of citizens and consumer rights with regard to the new data processing technologies. Moreover, the proposal of a Consumer Privacy Bill of Rights[71] represents a change in the US approach to data protection, since it suggests adopting a uniform minimum standard at federal level. Unfortunately, it is hard to see these efforts having any outcome under the new US administration, though society and business players show an increasing interest in the protection of personal information and in having a clear and homogenous regulatory framework.

III.1 The Guidelines of the Council of Europe: Towards a Different Approach

The Guidelines on the Protection of Individuals with Regard to the Processing of Personal Data in a World of Big Data, adopted in January 2017 by the Consultative Committee of Convention 108, are the first guidelines on data protection provided by an international body which specifically address the issues concerning big data applications. These Guidelines are not legally binding, but practical and operative instructions to the Parties to the Convention to facilitate the application of the principles of the Convention in the specific context of big data applications.[72] They are therefore primarily addressed to data controllers and data processors.[73]

The Guidelines try to address the limits of the purpose limitation principle and the notice and consent model mentioned in the previous sections. To achieve this, they provide an interpretation of the principles of Convention 108 that takes into account 'the given social and technological context' and 'a lack of knowledge on the part of individuals' with regard to big data applications.[74]

---

[70] *See also* Shelley-Egan et al. (n 30).

[71] *See* The White House, Administration Discussion Draft: Consumer Privacy Bill of Rights Act 2015 https://obamawhitehouse.archives.gov/sites/default/files/omb/legislative/letters/cpbr-act-of-2015-discussion-draft.pdf accessed 25 June 2017. *See also* Center for Democracy & Technology, 'Analysis of the Consumer Privacy Bill of Rights Act (2015) https://cdt.org/insight/analysis-of-the-consumer-privacy-bill-of-rights-act/ accessed 1 July 2017.

[72] *See* Guidelines, Section II (Scope):

> The present Guidelines recommend measures that Parties, controllers and processors should take to prevent the potential negative impact of the use of Big Data on human dignity, human rights, and fundamental individual and collective freedoms, in particular with regard to personal data protection.

[73] Given the broad range of application of big data analytics, the Guidelines are necessarily general and may be complemented by sector-specific guidance. *See* Guidelines, Section II (Scope).

[74] *See* Guidelines, Section I (Introduction). *See also* Section II:

> Given the nature of Big Data, the application of some of the traditional principles of data processing (e.g. minimization principle, purpose specification, meaningful consent, etc.) may be challeng-

Placing the safeguard of the individual's 'right to control his or her personal data and the processing of such data'[75] in the context of big data uses, the Guidelines consider the notion of control not as circumscribed to individual control (as in the 'notice and consent' model). Instead, they adopt a broader idea, according to which 'individual control evolves in a more complex process of multiple-impact assessment of the risks related to the use of data'[76]. This perspective led the Council of Europe to go beyond the individual dimension of data protection and investigate aspects that concern relations among individuals and society at large. In light of this, potential prejudices are not restricted to well-known privacy-related risks (e.g., illegitimate use of personal information, data security) but also include other prejudices that may concern the conflict with ethical and social values.[77] However, the assessment concerning the impact of the use of data on ethical and social values is more complicated than the traditional data protection assessment. Moreover, while individual rights concerning data processing are generally recognized by different national regulations and international conventions, and data security and data management best practices are commonly adopted by data controllers, the values that should underpin the use of data are more indefinite and context-based. This makes it more complicated to identify a benchmark for these values that can be used in the ethical and social risk assessment.[78]

Although the Guidelines recognize these difficulties, they do not shrink from proposing some practical steps to identify these values. They define an architecture based on three layers. The first general level is represented by the 'common guiding ethical values' of international charters of human rights and fundamental freedoms. The second layer takes into account the context-dependent nature of the social and ethical assessment and focuses on the values and social interests of given communities. Finally, the third layer consists in a more specific set of ethical values provided by ethics committees and focused on a given use of data.[79]

---

ing in this technological scenario. These guidelines therefore suggest a tailored application of the principles of the Convention 108, to make them more effective in practice in the Big Data context.

[75] *See* Preamble of the Draft modernized Convention for the Protection of Individuals with Regard to the Processing of Personal Data:

> Considering that it is necessary to secure the human dignity and protection of the human rights and fundamental freedoms of every individual and [...] personal autonomy based on a person's right to control of his or her personal data and the processing of such [personal] data.

[76] *See* Guidelines, Section I (Introduction).

[77] *See* above fn. 16.

[78] *See* Guidelines, Section IV, para 1.1: 'controllers and processors should adequately take into account the likely impact of the intended Big Data processing and its broader ethical and social implications' and para 1.2 'Personal data processing should not be in conflict with the ethical values commonly accepted in the relevant community or communities'.

[79] *See also* Omer Tene and Jules Polonetsky, 'Beyond IRBs: Ethical Guidelines for Data Research' (2016) 72 *Was. & Lee L Rev Online* 458–471; Urs Gasser, Alexandra Wood, David R. O'Brien, Effy Vayena & Micah Altman, 'Towards a New Ethical and Regulatory Framework for Big Data Research' (2016) 72 *Was. & Lee L Rev* 420, 432–441; Ryan Calo, 'Consumer Subject Review Boards: A Thought Experiment' (2013) 66 *Stan L Rev Online* 97–102 http://www.stanfordlawreview.org/online/privacy-and-big-data/consumer-subject-review-boards accessed 15 February 2017; European Data Protection Supervisor, 'Opinion 7/2015. Meeting the challenges of big data A call for transparency, user control, data protection by design and accountability' (n 28).

These values are used to put in place a risk assessment that encompasses a broader range of interests.[80] In this vein, the Guidelines also require data controllers to adopt 'preventive policies' in order to adequately address and mitigate the potential risks related to the use of big data analytics.[81]

The attention to the social and ethical dimensions of data processing sheds light on the collective dimension of data processing[82] and, in this sense, the Guidelines encourage an approach that gives voice to the different groups of persons potentially affected by a given use of data.[83] Unlike the GDPR, the results of the risk assessment of data uses are public and this provides data subjects with a better understanding of the purposes of data processing, increasing their awareness about their choices concerning personal information.[84]

The minor provisions of the Guidelines concern the notice that should be given to data subjects, which should be comprehensive of the outcome of the assessment process and 'might also be provided by means of an interface which simulates the effects of the use of data and its potential impact on the data subject, in a learn-from-experience approach'.[85] Moreover, when the data subject's consent is required, it cannot be considered freely given when 'there is a clear imbalance of power between the data subject and the Data Controllers or Data Processors, which affects the data subject's decisions with regard to the processing.[86]

Finally, the Guidelines devote a section to the role of human intervention in big data-supported decisions,[87] reaffirming that the use of big data 'should preserve the autonomy of human intervention in the decision-making process'. In this light, where decisions based on big data might affect individual rights significantly or produce legal effects, a human decision-maker should, upon request of the data subject, 'provide her or him with the reasoning underlying the processing, including the consequences for the data subject of this reasoning'. In the same vein, the autonomy of decision-makers should be preserved and, on the basis of 'reasonable arguments', they should be allowed the freedom not to rely on the result of the recommendations provided using big data.

---

[80] Given the complexity of this assessment, the Guidelines require that the risk-assessment 'should be carried out by persons with adequate professional qualifications and knowledge to evaluate the different impacts, including the legal, social, ethical and technical dimensions'.

[81] *See* Guidelines, Section IV, para 2.2. This provision is consistent with Art 8bis (2) of the Draft modernised Convention for the Protection of Individuals with Regard to the Processing of Personal Data, which focuses both on risk analysis and the design of data processing 'in such a manner as to prevent or minimise the risk of interference with [...] rights and fundamental freedoms'.

[82] *See* above fn. 12.

[83] *See* Guidelines, Section IV, para 2.7 ('With regard to the use of Big Data which may affect fundamental rights, the Parties should encourage the involvement of the different stakeholders (e.g. individuals or groups potentially affected by the use of Big Data) in this assessment process and in the design of data processing').

[84] *See* Guidelines, Section IV, paras 3.2 and 3.3. According to the suggestion of legal scholars, the assessment results should be made publicly available 'without prejudice to secrecy safeguarded by law'. In the presence of such secrecy, data controllers 'shall provide any sensitive information in a separate annex to the risk-assessment report'. Although this annex is not public, it may be accessed by Supervisory Authorities. *See* Mantelero (n 14) 655 and David Wright, 'A Framework for the Ethical Impact Assessment of Information Technology' (2011) 13(3) *Ethics Inf Technol* 222.

[85] *See* Guidelines, Section IV, para 5.1.

[86] *See* Guidelines, Section IV, para 5.3. In these cases, data controller "should demonstrate that this imbalance does not exist or does not affect the consent given by the data subject".

[87] *See* Guidelines, Section IV, para 7.

III.2 The US Initiatives

Whereas in Europe the initiatives concerning big data focus on the possible regulatory responses, in the form of general data protection laws, in other countries the debate remains mainly at a theoretical level, with proposals that are mainly in the field of soft law. In this scenario, the most significant initiative is represented by the various documents adopted by US government bodies,[88] which have notably led to the Consumer Privacy Bill of Rights proposed by the Obama administration[89] and, within the specific field of big data, in the Podesta Report.[90] These documents are here briefly discussed since, although they represent a valuable initiative adopted by the Obama administration to improve data protection, there is not any expectation that it will be endorsed by the present US administration.

The Podesta Report identifies five areas of concern in terms of benefits and harms of big data:

1. Preserving Privacy Values: Maintaining our privacy values by protecting personal information in the marketplace, both in the United States and through interoperable global privacy frameworks;
2. Educating Robustly and Responsibly [...];
3. Big Data and Discrimination: Preventing new modes of discrimination that some uses of big data may enable;
4. Law Enforcement and Security [...]; and
5. Data as a Public Resource.

The report outlines specific policy recommendations to address these issues: the first is the adoption of the proposed Consumer Privacy Bill of Rights, followed by other regulatory initiatives including the adoption of a national data breach bill and provisions to safeguard students' data processed for educational purposes.

Although these initiatives had a limited outcome under the Obama administration and the Consumer Privacy Bill of Rights remained a mere proposal,[91] they are significant for two reasons. First, from a European perspective, the social context of the US shed light on the risk of discrimination as one of the most relevant potential negative outcomes of decision-making

---

[88] *See* The White House, Executive Office of the President (n 16); The White House, Executive Office of the President (n 28); The White House, 'A Consumer Data Privacy in a Networked World: A Framework for Protecting Privacy and Promoting Innovation in the Global Digital Economy' (2012) http://www.whitehouse.gov/sites/default/files/privacy-final.pdf accessed 25 June 2014; the file is no longer available in the original address, but the document was published in (2012) 4 (2) *Journal of Privacy and Confidentiality* 95, 136–138 http://repository.cmu.edu/cgi/viewcontent.cgi?article=1096&context=jpc accessed 6 March 2017; Executive Office of the President, President's Council of Advisors on Science and Technology, 'Big Data and Privacy: A Technological Perspective' (2014) https://bigdatawg.nist.gov/pdf/pcast_big_data_and_privacy_-_may_2014.pdf accessed 6 May 2017; The White House, 'Big Data: Seizing Opportunities and Preserving Values: Interim Progress Report' (2015) https://obamawhitehouse.archives.gov/sites/default/files/docs/20150204_Big_Data_Seizing_Opportunities_Preserving_Values_Memo.pdf accessed 6 May 2017. *See also* Federal Trade Commission (n 11).

[89] *See* The White House (n 71), *see also* The White House (n 89) 47–48. This bill, which is based on the Fair Information Practice Principles, recognize the following rights to consumers: individual control over their personal data, transparency, respect for context, data security, access and accuracy, focused collection, accountability.

[90] *See* The White House, Executive Office of the President (n 16).

[91] *See* The White House (n 72).

processes based on big data analytics.[92] At that time, this aspect was largely underestimated in Europe and the documents adopted in the US stimulated the debate on it. Second, with regard to the US, the issues concerning big data contributed to a broader reflection on the possibility of adopting a general legal framework on data protection at federal level, with a focus on privacy risks. Although the current US administration seems less inclined in this direction, the debate about big data in general, as well as about specific applications in the field of intelligence and law enforcement, has induced civil society and corporations to demand a higher protection for personal information.

IV. FROM BIG DATA TO AI

The most recent development of the European debate on large-scale data applications reflects the technological evolution and the new wave of AI systems that has characterised the last few years. Although "algorithms and artificial intelligence have come to represent new mythologies of our time",[93] the focus of the ongoing regulatory initiatives is on the existing and near-term applications of AI, leaving aside the big questions surrounding human-like AI.[94]

The major threats relating to AI concern the sets of values and principles underpinning AI development, mainly in the area of decision support and decision-making systems, given their impact on individuals and society. The growing adoption of AI-based solutions characterised by complexity and, in many cases, opacity in data processing is challenging and progressively eroding the traditional cornerstone of data protection represented by individual self-determination. Moreover, data overload, the complexity of data processing and an extreme data-centred logic could undermine the democratic use of data, supplanting the freedoms and self-determination of individuals and groups with a kind of data dictatorship[95] imposed by data scientists insensitive to societal issues.

To prevent the adverse consequences of AI outweighing its benefits,[96] European regulators have stressed the centrality of the human being in technology development. Nevethless, the early stage of this debate on AI regulation has been marked by two different approaches: that adopted by the European Union focused mainly on ethics, and another taken by the Council of Europe centred on legally binding and non-binding instruments.

---

[92] *See also* The White House, Executive Office of the President (n 16).

[93] CNIL, How Can Humans Keep the Upper Hand? The Ethical Matters Raised by Algorithms and Artificial Intelligence. Report on the Public Debate Led by the French Data Protection Authority (CNIL) as Part of the Ethical Discussion Assignment Set by the Digital Republic Bill, 2017 <https://www.cnil.fr/sites/default/files/atoms/files/cnil_rapport_ai_gb_web.pdf> accessed 10 March 2020.

[94] *See* Nick Bostrom, *Superintelligence paths, dangers, strategies* (Oxford University Press 2016) and Raymond Kurzweil, *The singularity is near: when humans transcend biology* (Duckworth, 2016).

[95] *See* Cathy O'Neil, *Weapons of math destruction* (Penguin Books, 2017).

[96] *See* World Economic Forum, How to Prevent Discriminatory Outcomes in Machine Learning, 2018 <http://www3.weforum.org/docs/WEF_40065_White_Paper_How_to_Prevent_Discriminatory_Outcomes_in_Machine_Learning.pdf> accessed 10 March 2020.

Whereas the European Commission[97], and the EDPS[98], has emphasised the importance of ethics in addressing the societal challenges of AI, the Council of Europe has focused its initiatives[99] on a regulatory approach, including the adoption of soft-law instruments to enact the principles enshrined in the existing binding instruments.[100]

However, the European Commission's ethical emphasis has proved contradictory, due to the overlapping in guiding principles between ethics and existing legally binding provisions, including fundamental rights. The proposed ethical guidelines for trustworthy AI[101] are a mix of ethical and legal requirements, which can create confusion among adopters regarding what is required by law and what is an expression of a non-binding ethics-oriented approach. Moreover, the lack of a clear ethical framework (Western moral principles alone contain several different ethical approaches) and the necessarily context-based nature of ethical principles make it difficult to build a strong overall framework for AI development in Europe.

Against this background, the new European Commission has recently decided to reconsider its ethics-centred focus and shift towards a new approach clearly based on binding regulatory instruments and a review of the existing legal framework.[102] Both the Council of Europe and the European Union recognise that data protection can be a stepping stone towards a different data society, where AI development ceases to be driven purely by economic interest or dehumanising algorithmic efficiency.

The future of data-centric AI should therefore look to the principles of Convention 108+, further contextualised in the AI Guidelines,[103] and to the GDPR as a starting point for broader

---

[97] *See* High-Level Expert Group on Artificial Intelligence, Ethics Guidelines for Trustworthy AI, Brussels, 2019 <https://ec.europa.eu/futurium/en/ai-alliance-consultation> accessed 10 March 2020.

[98] *See* EDPS Ethics Advisory Group, Towards a Digital Ethics, Brussels, 2018, https://edps.europa.eu/sites/edp/files/publication/18-01-25_eag_report_en.pdf.

[99] *See* <https://www.coe.int/en/web/artificial-intelligence/home> accessed 10 March 2020.

[100] *See* Consultative Committee of the Convention for the Protection of Individuals with Regard to Automatic Processing of Personal Data (Convention 108), Guidelines on Artificial Intelligence and Data Protection, Strasbourg, 25 January 2019; CEPEJ. 2019. European Ethical Charter on the use of artificial intelligence (AI) in judicial systems and their environment <https://www.coe.int/en/web/cepej/cepej-european-ethical-charter-on-the-use-of-artificial-intelligence-ai-in-judicial-systems-and-their-environment> accessed 10 March 2020. *See also* Alessandro Mantelero, Artificial Intelligence and Data Protection: Challenges and Possible Remedies, Council of Europe, 2019 <https://rm.coe.int/artificial-intelligence-and-data-protection-challenges-and-possible-re/168091f8a6> accessed 10 March 2020; Council of Europe-Committee of experts on internet intermediaries (MSI-NET), Study on the Human Rights Dimensions of Automated Data Processing Techniques (in Particular Algorithms) and Possible Regulatory Implications, Council of Europe, 2018 <https://rm.coe.int/algorithms-and-human-rights-en-rev/16807956b5> accessed 10 March 2020; Frederik Zuiderveen Borgesius, Discrimination, Artificial Intelligence, and Algorithmic Decision-Making, Council of Europe, 2018 <https://rm.coe.int/discrimination-artificial-intelligence-and-algorithmic-decision-making/1680925d73> accessed 10 March 2020.

[101] *See* fn. 94.

[102] *See* European Commission, White Paper on Artificial Intelligence - A European approach to excellence and trust, COM(2020) 65 final, 2020, 10 ("A solid European regulatory framework for trustworthy AI will protect all European citizens and help create a frictionless internal market for the further development and uptake of AI as well as strengthening Europe's industrial basis in AI").

[103] *See* Consultative Committee of the Convention for the Protection of Individuals with Regard to Automatic Processing of personal data (Convention 108), Guidelines on Artificial Intelligence and Data Protection, T-PD(2019)01, 2019 <https://rm.coe.int/guidelines-on-artificial-intelligence-and-data-protection/168091f9d8> accessed 10 March 2020. *See also* the related preliminary studies: Alessandro

regulation based on a review of the existing legal framework[104] focusing on the following key concepts:

- Proportionality: the development of AI should be inspired by the proportionality principle and efficiency should not override the rights and freedoms of individuals. Individuals have the right not to be subordinated to automated AI systems and legislators should curb AI applications to safeguard individual and societal interests.
- Responsible innovation: responsibility is not mere accountability but requires AI developers and decision-makers to act in a socially responsible manner. This also entails the creation of specific bodies to support and monitor their actions.
- Risk management: accountable AI means assessing the potentially adverse consequences of AI applications, and taking appropriate steps to prevent or mitigate such consequences. The notion of risk therefore plays a central role in the future regulation of AI. The Council of Europe seems to be more oriented in this regard towards open procedures for risk assessment, centred on the impacts on human rights and freedoms, while the European Commission has suggested a more formalised approach. The EU's first response is to outline a model largely based on two cumulative criteria: high-risk sectors and significant risk of AI use in specific sectors.[105] However, this model seems to underestimate the difficulty of considering individual sectors in the context of AI, which is frequently cross-sectoral.
- Participation and the collective dimension: the impact of AI systems should be seen not only from an individual perspective, but also from the perspective of society as a whole. Participatory forms of risk assessment are therefore essential to give voice to citizens and adequately consider the collective dimension[106] of AI applications. At the same time, citizens' participation should not be exploited as a way to reduce decision-makers' responsibility.
- Transparency: despite the current limitations affecting the transparency of AI, it can help to ensure effective citizen participation and reach a more accurate assessment of the consequences of AI applications.

Finally, it is worth noting that this new regulatory wave has also affected the US, as a result of a number of highly controversial cases and various different factors: the growing power of

---

Mantelero, Artificial Intelligence and Data Protection: Challenges and Possible Remedies. Report on Artificial Intelligence, Consultative Committee of the Convention for the Protection of Individuals with Regard to Automatic Processing of personal data, T-PD(2018)09Rev, Strasbourg, 2019, <https://rm.coe.int/artificial-intelligence-and-data-protection-challenges-and-possible-re/168091f8a6> accessed 10 March 2020.

[104] On 11 September 2019, the Committee of Ministers of the Council of Europe set up an Ad Hoc Committee on Artificial Intelligence – CAHAI, which will examine the feasibility and potential elements on the basis of broad multi-stakeholder consultations, of a legal framework for the development, design and application of artificial intelligence, based on Council of Europe's standards on human rights, democracy and the rule of law <https://www.coe.int/en/web/artificial-intelligence/cahai> accessed 10 March 2020. *See also* European Commission (n 99) 10, fn. 95 ("there is a need to examine whether current legislation is able to address the risks of AI and can be effectively enforced, whether adaptations of the legislation are needed, or whether new legislation is needed [...] Any changes should be limited to clearly identified problems for which feasible solutions exist").

[105] The model can be complemented by voluntary labelling schemes for no-high risk applications.

[106] *See also* Mantelero (n 12).

digital platforms, the even more pervasive use of predictive analytics, the increasing number of large-scale data breaches, and the biased nature of several algorithm-based solutions.

The initial response to these challenges and concerns have been several regulatory initiatives focused on data protection at state level,[107] such as the California Consumer Privacy Act,[108] and at the federal level[109] which also led the US legislator to reconsider the sector-specific approach adopted over the years. Here, targeted proposals have concerned Big Data analytics and AI more broadly. This was the case of several proposals on AI-based facial recognition systems and algorithms in general,[110] and some hard-law[111] and soft-law[112] instruments with a specific AI focus.

Although it is as yet hard to foresee the future direction of this changing scenario and differences still remain between the approaches adopted on the two sides of the Atlantic, the common challenges of Big Data and AI are fostering a higher level of compatibility between different regulatory models, focusing on risk management, accountability and safeguards on individual rights and freedoms in technology development.

V. CONCLUSIONS

This chapter discussed the regulatory challenges arising from the adoption of the Big Data paradigm in data processing, where the use of analytics in decision-making processes and the focus on group profiling tend to take us beyond the confines of the individual dimension towards the collective dimension of data protection.

From a regulatory and global perspective, the most recent initiatives and policy recommendations have shed light on the existing tension between the traditional approach to data protection and the way Big Data analytics and AI are used to shape our data-driven society.

At this stage of the debate, the responses provided by the European Union with the GDPR seem to offer partial remedies to the challenges of these technologies, but which go beyond the data protection context. A more articulated response to the various issues posed by datafication and predictive tools, with respect to the collective dimension of data protection and the limits of the data subject's self-determination, were provided by the Council of Europe in its guidelines on Big Data and AI.

The biggest initiatives in the global debate are coming from Europe, despite some valuable contributions from the US. However, the regulatory and policy documents adopted are only

---

[107] *See* Mitchell Noordyke, US State Comprehensive Privacy Law Comparison, 2020 <https://iapp.org/resources/article/state-comparison-table/> accessed 10 March 2020.

[108] California Consumer Privacy Act of 2018 ('CCPA').

[109] *See e.g.* Senate Bill ('SB') S.3300 which was introduced on 13 February 2020 to establish a Federal data protection agency ('DPA') and for other purposes ('the Bill'). This is the latest of several relevant proposals that have been introduced and debated in U.S. Congress in the past year.

[110] *See e.g.* the California's AB 2269 on automated decision systems, the California's Assembly Bill ('AB') 2261 on facial recognition technology, and the Illinois' Bill HB2557 (Artificial Intelligence Video Interview Act).

[111] *See e.g.* the Algorithmic Accountability Act of 2019 proposed by Senators Cory Booker (D-NJ) and Ron Wyden (D-OR).

[112] *See e.g.* the Universal Guidelines for Artificial Intelligence proposed by The Public Voice <https://thepublicvoice.org/ai-universal-guidelines/>.

a first step towards a new paradigm in data protection and there is still a long way to go to before we arrive at new frameworks that properly address the challenges of our algorithmic society. The ongoing European regulatory process both in the EU and the Council of Europe is expected to make a significant contribution to the AI question by broadening the scope of data regulation, including a variety of issues beyond data protection, such as antidiscrimination, freedom of expression and democratic participation.

REFERENCES

Ahonen P., 'Institutionalizing Big Data Methods in Social and Political Research' (2015) *Big Data & Society* 1.

Bennett C.J., Regulating Privacy: Data Protection and Public Policy in Europe and the United States (Cornell University Press 1992).

Bollier D., 'The Promise and Perils of Big Data' (Aspen Institute, Communications and Society Program 2010). http://www.aspeninstitute.org/sites/default/files/content/docs/pubs/The_Promise_and_Peril_of_Big_Data.pdf accessed 27 February 2017.

Bostrom N. *Superintelligence paths, dangers, strategies* (Oxford University Press 2016).

Boyd D., K. Levy and A. Marwick, 'The Networked Nature of Algorithmic Discrimination', in S. Peña Gangadharan, V. Eubanks and S. Barocas, *Data and Discrimination: Collective Essays* (Open Technology Institute and New America 2014) 56 http://www.newamerica.org/downloads/OTI-Data-an-Discrimination-FINAL-small.pdf accessed 14 April 2017.

Bradford A., 'The Brussels Effect' (2015) 107 *Northwestern University Law Review* 1 http://scholarlycommons.law.northwestern.edu/nulr/vol107/iss1/1 accessed 4 March 2017.

Brenton M., *The Privacy Invaders* (Coward-McCann 1964).

Burrell J., 'How the Machine 'thinks': Understanding Opacity in Machine Learning algorithms' (2016) 3(1) *Big Data & Society*.

Bygrave L.A., Data Protection Law. Approaching Its Rationale, Logic and Limits (Kluwer Law International 2002).

Calo R., 'Consumer Subject Review Boards: A Thought Experiment' (2013) 66 *Stan L Rev* Online 97 http://www.stanfordlawreview.org/online/privacy-and-big-data/consumer-subject-review-boards accessed 15 February 2017.

Cate F.H. and V. Mayer-Schönberger 'Data Use and Impact. Global Workshop' (The Center for Information Policy Research and The Center for Applied Cybersecurity Research, Indiana University 2013) http://cacr.iu.edu/sites/cacr.iu.edu/files/Use_Workshop_Report.pdf accessed 27 February 2017.

CNIL, How Can Humans Keep the Upper Hand? The Ethical Matters Raised by Algorithms and Artificial Intelligence. Report on the Public Debate Led by the French Data Protection Authority (CNIL) as Part of the Ethical Discussion Assignment Set by the Digital Republic Bill, 2017 https://www.cnil.fr/sites/default/files/atoms/files/cnil_rapport_ai_gb_web.pdf, accessed 10 March 2020.

Crawford K., G. Faleiros, A. Luers, P. Meier, C. Perlich and J. Thorp, 'Big Data, Communities and Ethical Resilience: A Framework for Action' (2013) 6–7 http://www.rockefellerfoundation.org/app/uploads/71b4c457-cdb7-47ec-81a9-a617c956e6af.pdf accessed 5 April 2017.

De Hert P and V Papakonstantinou, 'The new General Data Protection Regulation: Still a sound system for the protection of individuals? (2016) 32 (2) *Computer Law Security Review* 194.

Diakopoulps N., Algorithmic Accountability Reporting: on the Investigation of Black Boxes (Tow Center for Digital Journalism 2013) 18.

Edwards L. and M. Vale, 'Slave to the Algorithm? Why a "Right to an Explanation" Is Probably Not the Remedy You Are Looking For' (2017) 16(1) *Duke Law and Technology Review* 18.

European Data Protection Supervisor, 'Opinion 7/2015. Meeting the challenges of big data A call for transparency, user control, data protection by design and accountability' (2015) 16 https://edps.europa.eu/sites/edp/files/publication/15-11-19_big_data_en.pdf accessed 23 March 2017.

European Data Protection Supervisor (EDPS) Ethics Advisory Group, Towards a Digital Ethics, Brussels, 2018, https://edps.europa.eu/sites/edp/files/publication/18-01-25_eag_report_en.pdf. *See* https://www.coe.int/en/web/artificial-intelligence/home, accessed 10 March 2020.
Federal Trade Commission, 'Data Brokers: A Call for Transparency and Accountability' (2014), 20 and Appendix B https://www.ftc.gov/system/files/documents/reports/data-brokers-call-transparency-accountability-report-federal-trade-commission-may-2014/140527databrokerreport.pdf accessed 27 February 2016.
Gasser U., A. Wood. D.R. O'Brien, E. Vayena and M. Altman, 'Towards a New Ethical and Regulatory Framework for Big Data Research' (2016) 72 *Was. & Lee L Rev* 420, 432.
González Fuster G., The Emergence of Personal Data Protection as a Fundamental Right of the EU (Springer International Publishing 2014).
Goodman B. and S. Flaxman, 'EU Regulations on Algorithmic Decision-Making and a "right to Explanation"' (2016) [2016] arXiv:1606.08813 [cs, stat] http://arxiv.org/abs/1606.08813 accessed 03 March 2018.
Greenleaf G., 'Global Data Privacy Laws 2015: 109 Countries, with European Laws Now in a Minority' (2015) 133 *Privacy Laws & Business International Report* 14.
Greenleaf G., 'Global Data Privacy Laws 2017: 120 National Data Privacy Laws, Including Indonesia and Turkey' (2017) 145 *Privacy Laws & Business International Report* 10.
Greenleaf G., 'The Influence of European Data Privacy Standards Outside Europe: Implications for Globalization of Convention 108' (2012) 2 (2) *International Data Privacy Law* 68.
Hildebrandt M., 'Profiling: From Data to Knowledge. The Challenges of a Crucial Technology' (2006) 30(9) Datenschutz und Datensicherheit 548.
Kurzell R., *The singularity is near: when humans transcended biology* (Duckworth, 2016).
Mantelero A., 'The Future of Consumer Data Protection in the E.U. Rethinking the "notice and consent" Paradigm in the New Era of Predictive Analytics' (2014) 30(6) *Computer Law Security Review* 643.
Mantelero A.,'Personal Data for Decisional Purposes in the Age of Analytics: From an Individual to a Collective Dimension of Data Protection' (2016) 32 (2) *Computer Law Security Review* 238.
Mantelero A., Artificial Intelligence and Data Protection: Challenges and Possible Remedies. Report on Artificial Intelligence, Consultative Committee of the Convention for the Protection of Individuals with Regard to Automatic Processing of personal data, T-PD(2018)09Rev, Strasbourg, 2019, https://rm.coe.int/artificial-intelligence-and-data-protection-challenges-and-possible-re/168091f8a6, accessed 10 March 2020.
Mayer-Schönberger and Yann Padova, 'Regime Change? Enabling Big Data through Europe's Data Protection Regulation' (2016) XVII *Colum. Sci. & Tech. L. Rev*. 315, 327.
Mayer-Schönberger V, 'Generational Development of Data Protection in Europe?' in P.E. Agre and M. Rotenberg (eds), *Technology and Privacy: The New Landscape* (MIT Press 1997).
Miller A.R., *The Assault on Privacy Computers, Data Banks, Dossiers* (University of Michigan Press 1971).
Narayanan A., J. Huey and E.W. Felten, 'A Precautionary Approach to Big Data Privacy' in Serge Gutwirth, Ronald Leenes, Paul De Hert (eds), *Data Protection on the Move: Current Developments in ICT and Privacy/Data Protection* (Springer Netherlands 2016) 357.
Noordayke M. US State Comprehensive Privacy Law Comparison, 2020 https://iapp.org/resources/article/state-comparison-table/ accessed 10 March 2020.
O'Neil C., *Weapons of math destruction* (Penguin Books, 2017).
Øjvind Nielsen R., A.M. Gurzawska and P. Bray, 'Principles and Approaches in Ethics Assessment. Ethical Impact Assessment and Conventional Impact Assessment. Annex 1.a Ethical Assessment of Research and Innovation: A Comparative Analysis of Practices and Institutions in the EU and selected other countries. Project Stakeholders Acting Together on the Ethical Impact Assessment of Research and Innovation – SATORI. Deliverable 1.1' (2015) http://satoriproject.eu/work_packages/comparative-analysis-of-ethics-assessment-practices/ accessed 15 February 2017.
Packard V., *The Naked Society* (David McKay 1964).
Poullet Y., 'EU Data Protection Policy. The Directive 95/46/EC: Ten Years After' (2006) 22 (3) *CLSR* 206.
Raab C. and D. Wright, 'Surveillance: Extending the Limits of Privacy Impact Assessment' in D Wright and P De Hert (eds), *Privacy Impact Assessment* (Springer 2012) 363.

Rodotà S., 'Data Protection as a Fundamental Right' in S. Gutwirth, Y. Poullet, P. De Hert, C. de Terwangne and S. Nouwt (eds), *Reinventing Data Protection?* (Springer, 2009).
Rossi F., 'Artificial Intelligence: Potential Benefits d Ethical Considerations' (European Parliament: Policy Department C: Citizens' Rights and Constitutional Affairs 2016) Briefing PE 571.380. http://www.europarl.europa.eu/RegData/etudes/BRIE/2016/571380/IPOL_BRI(2016)571380_EN.pdf accessed 03 March 2018.
Secretary's Advisory Committee on Automated Personal Data Systems, 'Records, Computers and the Rights of Citizens' (1973) http://epic.org/privacy/hew1973report/ accessed 27 March 2017.
Selbst A.D. and J. Powles, 'Meaningful Information and the Right to Explanation' (2017) 7(4) *International Data Privacy Law* 233.
Shelley-Egan C. et al., 'SATORI Deliverable D2.1 Report (handbook) of participatory processes' (2014) http://satoriproject.eu/work_packages/dialogue-and-participation/ accessed 15 February 2017, 42–44.
Simitis S., 'From the Market to the Polis: The EU Directive on the Protection of Personal Data' (1995) 80 *Iowa L Rev* 445.
Solove D.J., *Understanding Privacy* (Harvard University Press 2008).
Taylor L, Floridi L, van der Sloot B (eds), *Group Privacy: New Challenges of Data Technologies* (Springer 2017).
Tene O. and J. Polonetsky, 'Beyond IRBs: Ethical Guidelines for Data Research' (2016) 72 *Was. & Lee L Rev Online* 458.
Tene O. and J. Polonetsky, 'Privacy in the Age of Big Data: A Time for Big Decisions' (2012) *Stanford Law Review Online* 64.
Trilateral Research & Consulting, 'Privacy impact assessment and risk management. Report for the Information Commissioner's Office prepared by Trilateral Research & Consulting' (2013) https://ico.org.uk/media/1042196/trilateral-full-report.pdf accessed 25 February 2017.
Tzanou M., 'Data Protection as a Fundamental Right Next to Privacy? "Reconstructing" a not so new Right' (2013) 3(2) *International Data Protection Law.*
Vedder A. and L. Naudts, 'Accountability for the Use of Algorithms in a Big Data Environment' (2017) 31 (29) *International Review of Law, Computers & Technology* 206.
Vedder A.H., 'Privatization, Information Technology and Privacy: Reconsidering the Social Responsibilities of Private Organizations' in Geoff Moore (ed), *Business Ethics: Principles and Practice* (Business Education Publishers 1997) 215.
Wachter S., B. Mittelstadt and L. Floridi, 'Why a Right to Explanation of Automated Decision-making does not Exist in the General Data Protection Regulation' (2017) 7(2) *International Data Privacy Law* 76–99.
Westin A.F., *Privacy and Freedom* (Atheneum 1970).
Wright D., 'A Framework for the Ethical Impact Assessment of Information Technology' (2011) 13(3) *Ethics in Information Technology* 222.
Wright D. and C. Raab, 'Privacy Principles, Risks and Harms' (2014) 28(3) *International Review of Law, Computers & Technology* 277.
Zarsky T.Z., 'Transparent Predictions' (2013) 4 *University of Illinois Law Review* 1503, 1560.
Zuiderveen Borgesius F., Discrimination, Artificial Intelligence, and Algorithmic Decision-Making, Council of Europe, 2018 https://rm.coe.int/discrimination-artificial-intelligence-and-algorithmic-decision-making/1680925d73 accessed 10 March 2020.

17. Data protection and children's online privacy

Valerie Steeves and Milda Mačėnaitė

I. INTRODUCTION

On 17 October, 2008, the 30th International Conference of Data Protection and Privacy Commissioners issued a resolution on children's online privacy (Strasbourg Resolution), raising specific concerns about the 'vast amounts of personal information' that are being collected from and about children in networked environments.[1] Together, the Commissioners called for legislation to limit the collection, use and disclosure of children's information, especially in the context of micro-targeting and behavioural advertising. They also urged organizations to develop plain language privacy policies and user agreements to facilitate the consent process, and supported the creation of educational resources to help young people access 'a safe online environment respectful of their privacy'.[2]

The Resolution suggests that children's online privacy is a special case, for three inter-related reasons. First, children are more vulnerable than adults to pressures to disclose information about themselves simply because they are young; in the Commissioners' words, they often 'lack the experience, technical knowledge and tools to mitigate [the privacy] risks'[3] they encounter as they blog, text, share photos, play games and interact online. Second, the creation of a permanent digital record may be more harmful to children than it is to adults. Not only are children more likely to make missteps because of their relative immaturity, those missteps may be especially difficult or embarrassing to explain when individuals are publicly called to account for them as adults in the future. Accordingly, the protection of children's privacy requires that there be 'no lasting ... record of content created by children on the Internet which challenges their dignity, security and privacy or otherwise renders them vulnerable now or at a later stage in their lives'.[4] Third, children's privacy is contextualized by the United Nations Convention on the Rights of the Child[5] (CRC) which calls upon states to 'respect and ensure the rights of children, including the right to the protection of their privacy'.[6]

---

1 30th International Conference of Data Protection and Privacy Commissioners, 'Resolution on Children's Online Privacy' (Strasbourg, 17 October 2008) para 2.

2 Ibid., para 12. See also 38th International Conference of Data Protection and Privacy Commissioners, 'Resolution for the Adoption of an International Competency Framework on Privacy Education' (Marrakesh, 18 October 2016).

3 Ibid., para 5.

4 Ibid., para 8.

5 United Nations General Assembly, *Convention on the Rights of the Child*, 20 November 1989, United Nations, Treaty Series, 1577. The Convention has been ratified by every state in the world except the United States of America.

6 Ibid., paras 6–7.

The CRC is of particular note. Although privacy rights are included in general human rights instruments,[7] the CRC imposes additional obligations on states with respect to children. Under its provisions, children are entitled to 'special care and assistance'[8] because of their status as children, and the standard to be applied when drafting legislation affecting children's rights is in the 'best interests of the child'. [9] Legislators must accordingly ensure that regulations are crafted in ways that promote children's well-being.[10] CRC rights are also governed by the '3 Ps': provision; protection; and participation.[11] Provisions that protect children from inappropriate information practices[12] are simply one part of meeting the obligations on states pursuant to the CRC. States are also required to provide children with an appropriate media environment[13] and ensure that young people are able to participate in decisions that affect them in that environment.[14] At the same time, their evolving maturity also means that parents are expected to play a key role in children's decision-making.[15]

This chapter examines the ways in which key jurisdictions have responded to the special privacy needs of children. In particular, we map the emergence of children's privacy as a trade issue in the United States, and outline the provisions of the Children's Online Privacy Protection Act. We contrast the child-specific approach taken in the US with the application of general private-sector data protection principles to children's privacy issues in Canada and Australia. We then explore the transition in the EU from general protection to child-specific provisions, and the ways in which the European commitment to privacy as both a human right and a child's right have shaped existing regulations as well as the newly enacted General Data Protection Regulation.

II. THE EMERGENCE OF CHILDREN'S ONLINE PRIVACY AS A TRADE ISSUE IN THE UNITED STATES, CANADA AND AUSTRALIA

When data protection regulation was first enacted in Europe and North America in the 1970s, there was no mention of children or children's privacy in spite of the fact that both private and public sector organizations were collecting information from children at the time. For example, children's attendance in school and visits to hospitals generated a plethora of records that literally followed the child from cradle to grave, and marketing tactics like warranty registration cards and magazine subscriptions collected demographic details that could be linked to

---

7 See, for e.g., art 12 of the *Universal Declaration of Human Rights*, 10 December 1948, United Nations General Assembly, Resolution 217A.

8 CRC (n 5), Preamble.

9 Ibid., art 3(1).

10 Ibid., art 3(2).

11 Ann Quennerstedt, 'Children, But Not Really Humans? Critical Reflections on the Hampering Effect of the "3 p's"' (2010) 18 *IJCR* 619.

12 CRC (n 5), arts 16–17.

13 Ibid., art 17. See also Valerie Steeves, (2017). 'Snoops, Bullies and Hucksters: What Rights Do Young People Have in a Networked Environment?' in N.A. Jennings and S.R. Mazzarella (eds.), *20 Questions about Youth and Media*, (2nd ed., New York: Peter Lang).

14 Ibid., arts 17, 31.

15 Ibid., art 5.

children's interests in toys, games, popular culture and fashion. Over the years, access rights to information held by the public sector were given to children and/or their parents in particular contexts, particularly education and health, but it was generally assumed that the burgeoning market in young people's information would be governed by general data protection legislation enacted within a particular jurisdiction.

The advent of the World Wide Web in the 1990s significantly changed the landscape, as website operators developed online playgrounds designed both to attract children and to encourage them to disclose their personal information for commercial purposes.[16] The first jurisdiction to respond to this as a distinct privacy issue was the US which passed the Children's Online Privacy Protection Act[17] (COPPA) in 1998.

COPPA is child-specific data protection legislation that requires parental consent for the collection, use and disclosure of personal information of children under 13 years of age.[18] It is commercial legislation,[19] akin to other forms of consumer protection, and as such is administered by the Federal Trade Commission (FTC). Its provisions require website operators and other online services (including mobile apps and connected toys) to publish privacy notices that provide children and their parents with information about their information practices,[20] and to obtain parental consent[21] to the collection, use and disclosure terms that are set out in the privacy notice. Parents also have the right to access their children's personal information,[22] and services are required to take steps to protect the information's confidentiality, security and integrity.[23] As such, the focus of the legislation is on parents' rights as opposed to children's rights: in the words of the FTC website, the 'primary goal of COPPA is to place parents in control over what information is collected from their young children online'.[24]

---

16 Valerie Steeves, 'It's Not Child's Play: The Online Invasion of Children's Privacy' (2006) 3 *UOLTJ* 169; Sara M. Grimes and Leslie Regan Shade, 'Neopian Economics of Play: Children's Cyberpets and Online Communities as Immersive Advertising in Neopets.com' (2005) *1 International Journal of Media & Cultural Politics* 181; Kathryn Montgomery, *Generation Digital: Politics, Commerce, and Childhood in the Age of the Internet* (2007) MIT Press; Kathryn Montgomery, 'Youth and Surveillance in the Facebook Era: Policy Interventions and Social Implications' (2015) 39 *Telecommunications Policy* 771.

17 15 U.S.C. §§ 6501–6506.

18 Under COPPA, children 13 and over can consent on their own behalf.

19 In the words of former Federal Trade Commission Chairman Jon Leibowitz:

> Let's be clear about one thing: under this rule, advertisers and even ad networks can continue to advertise, even on sites directed to children. Business models that depend on advertising will continue to thrive. The only limit we place is on behavioral advertising, and in this regard our rule is simple: until and unless you get parental consent, you may not track children to build massive profiles for behavioral advertising purposes. Period.

Quoted in Katy Vachman, 'FTC restricts behavioural targeting of kids: New rules go into effect next July' (Ad Week, 19 December 2012) http://www.adweek.com/digital/ftc-restricts-behavioral-targeting-kids-146108/ accessed 10 January 2019.

20 United States Electronic Code of Federal Regulations, Title 16 Chapter 1, Subchapter C, Part 312, as per 6502 (b)(1)(A).

21 Ibid., Part 312.5.

22 6502 (b)(1)(B).

23 6502 (b)(1)(D).

24 Federal Trade Commission, 'Complying with COPPA: Frequently asked questions' (20 March 2015) https://www.ftc.gov/tips-advice/business-center/guidance/complying-coppa-frequently-asked-questions accessed 10 January 2019.

To satisfy this goal, COPPA has developed nuanced risk-based requirements for parental consent. Where a service uses children's data for internal purposes, it has to employ a lighter consent mechanism, such as the sending of an email to the parent and taking an additional confirming step after receiving the parent's response (the 'email plus' method). The highest risk services are those that disclose personal data to third parties, use behavioural advertising and enable children to publicly post information. These services must comply with the most rigid consent mechanisms, such as parents filling in and returning consent forms by mail, fax or scan, the provision of a credit card number, contacting the service provider via a toll-free number or video conference, and the verification of an official identification document.

Under the legislation, trusted third-party verification services can be developed and used, to minimize the amount of personal data the service has to process itself. Several technologies have been proposed by American corporations in this respect. Examples include the use of a knowledge-based authentication method (a way to verify the identity of a user by asking a series of challenge questions, typically that rely on so-called 'out-of-wallet' information[25]) or the use of a 'face match to verified photo identification' method[26] to verify that the person providing consent for a child is in fact the child's parent. Codes of conduct can also be proposed by industry setting out how parental consent is to be obtained.[27]

COPPA has had a significant impact on practices outside the US. Part of this reflects the popularity of American sites with non-American children, but many services targeted at children rely on the bright age-line approach and only require parental consent for children under 13 even when their domestic legislation is not age-specific.[28] In addition, the commercial imperatives behind COPPA have shaped non-American approaches.

Canada and Australia are good examples of this dynamic. Both Canada and Australia have comprehensive personal data protection schemes in place, which are a combination of federal and state/provincial and territorial Acts. In Canada, public sector collection is governed by first-generation data protection legislation that was enacted in the 1980s. The federal government only turned its mind to private sector legislation when the EU changed its regulations in 1995 to restrict cross-border flows of information to jurisdictions without adequate levels of protections.[29] Because of this, private sector data protection regulation was cast as a commercial issue and a necessary step in building consumer confidence in the emerging information

[25] Federal Trade Commission, 'Imperium, LLC Proposed Verifiable Parental Consent Method Application (FTC Matter No. P135419)' (23 December 2013) https://www.ftc.gov/sites/default/files/attachments/press-releases/ftc-grants-approval-new-coppa-verifiable-parental-consent-method/131223imperiumcoppa-app.pdf accessed 10 January 2019.

[26] Federal Trade Commission, 'Commission Letter Approving Application Filed by Jest8 Limited (Trading As Riyo) For Approval of A Proposed Verifiable Parental Consent Method Under the Children's Online Privacy Protection Rule' (19 November 2015) https://www.ftc.gov/public-statements/2015/11/commission-letter-approving-application-filed-jest8-limited-trading-riyo accessed 10 January 2019.

[27] Art 40(2)(g).

[28] Valerie Steeves, 'Terra Cognita: Surveillance of Young People's Favourite Websites' in Tonya Rooney and Emmeline Taylor (eds), *Surveillance Futures: Social and Ethical Implications of New Technologies of and Children and Young People* (Routledge 2016).

[29] Directive 95/46/EC of the European Parliament and of the Council of 24 October 1995 on the protection of individuals with regard to the processing of personal data and on the free movement of such data [1995] *OJ L 281, 31-50.*

economy.[30] The resulting federal legislation, the Personal Information and Protection of Electronic Documents Act[31] (PIPEDA), applies across the country unless substantially similar legislation is passed to govern private sector collection of personal information within the provinces or territories. In like vein, the main piece of legislation in Australia, the Federal Privacy Act[32] 1988, incorporating the Australian Privacy Principles, is applicable to the federal public sector agencies as well as credit reporting organisations and the private sector.

Despite the extensive coverage of these specific and comprehensive schemes, both frameworks neither explicitly acknowledge children as data subjects nor refer to a specific age threshold after which children can give consent to their personal data processing. Enforcement of the general rules that apply to everyone is complicated by the fact that children do not have the legal status to make decisions about their information until they reach the age of majority or are recognized in law as mature minors. Because of this vacuum, COPPA has in practice set the de facto standard for networked services as most non-American services aimed at children tend to ask for parental consent for children under 13.[33]

At the same time, both the Canadian and Australian privacy commissioners have been actively engaged with children's privacy issues. The Canadian Commissioner took the lead role in creating the Strasbourg Resolution, and her findings in complaints against Facebook[34] in 2009 and Nexopia[35] in 2013 were important landmarks in using general data protection principles to restrain the collection of children's information on social media sites. The Australian Commissioner has also exercised his jurisdiction against children's services[36] and, in explicitly addressing his regulatory choices, has followed an articulated line of thinking about the regulation of children's consent.

The first Australian discussions about the need to address children's privacy took place at the time of passage of the Privacy Amendment (Private Sector) Act 2000 (Cth), shortly after the adoption of COPPA in the US. Initially, there was an identical, yet unsuccessful, effort to introduce an amendment that would require commercial service providers to obtain the consent of a child's parent before collecting, using or disclosing personal information of

---

[30] Industry Canada and Department of Justice, *Building Canada's Information Economy and Society: The Protection of Personal Information* (White Paper, C (2nd series), 1998)

[31] Personal Information Protection and Electronic Documents Act, SC 2000, c 5.

[32] The Privacy Act was last amended by the Privacy Amendment (Enhancing Privacy Protection) Act 2012, which came into force on 12 March 2014.

[33] See, e.g., Steeves, 'Terra Cognita: Surveillance of Young People's Favourite Websites' (n 28).

[34] Privacy Commissioner of Canada Investigation, 'Report of Findings into the Complaint Filed by the Canadian Internet Policy and Public Interest Clinic (CIPPIC) against Facebook Inc. Under the *Personal Information Protection and Electronic Documents Act*' PIPEDA Report of Findings #2009-008.

[35] Privacy Commissioner of Canada Investigation, 'Social networking site for youth, Nexopia, breached Canadian privacy law' PIPEDA Report of Findings #2012-001.

[36] See, e.g., Office of the Australian Information Commissioner (OAIC),'Proposed changes to Facebook Data Use Policy and Statement of Rights and Responsibilities – OAIC letter to Facebook' (12 September 2013) https://www.oaic.gov.au/media-and-speeches/statements/changes-to-facebooks-statement-of-rights-and-responsibilities-and-data-use-policy#proposed-changes-to-facebook-data-use-policy-and-statement-of-rights-and-responsibilities-oaic-letter-to-facebook accessed 10 January 2019; Statements on Facebook and Cambridge Analytica, 'Investigation into Facebook opened' (5 April 2018) https://www.oaic.gov.au/media-and-speeches/statements/facebook-and-cambridge-analytica#investigation-into-facebook-opened accessed 10 January 2019.

a child aged 13 or under.[37] The issue remained on the political agenda. In 2001, a consultative group on children's privacy was established by the Attorney-General's Department, but again no tangible outcome was achieved.[38]

Some years later, the issue was again picked up by the Australian Law Reform Commission (ALRC) which in 2008 investigated the extent to which the Privacy Act 1988 provides effective protection for individuals, including children and young people, and recommended reforms.[39] In a nutshell, the ALRC recommended a model for consent that combines individual assessment and a minimum age of presumption of capacity. Recognizing that 'individual assessment is the fairest and most appropriate way to determine if an individual under the age of 18 has the capacity to make a decision', [40] the ALRC concluded that such an assessment is not always practicable and reasonable, for example due to the online nature of the interaction or inadequate training of an organization's staff. Therefore, the ALRC recommended a combined model to consent, which was later embraced by the Commissioner in his non-binding guidelines.[41] In line with the ALRC view, the guidelines of the Commissioner state that organizations should consider in each case whether an individual child has capacity, i.e., sufficient understanding and maturity, to give consent, to make a request or exercise a right of access under the Privacy Act or whether a parent or guardian has to consent on behalf of a child.[42] Where such an assessment on a case-by-case basis is not reasonable or practicable, a general presumption exists that a person 15 and older has capacity to consent, unless any reasons suggest otherwise.[43]

III. THE EUROPEAN UNION AND THE HUMAN RIGHTS APPROACH TO CHILDREN'S ONLINE PRIVACY

Private sector regulation of privacy in the EU has been contextualized by strong protections for privacy as a human right in EU law.[44] The growing importance of children's rights in all policies and measures affecting children, including the digital environment, has been affirmed in many strategic EU policy documents.[45] The EU commitment to safeguard children's

---

[37] Commonwealth of Australia, *Parliamentary Debates,* Senate, 30 November 2006, 20302 (N Bolkus). The amendment was supported by the Australian Democrats: *Commonwealth of Australia*, Parliamentary Debates, Senate, 29 November 2000, 20162 (N Stott Despoja), 20165.

[38] D Williams (Attorney-General), 'First Meeting of Consultative Group on Children's Privacy' (Press Release, 4 June 2001). Cited in Australian Law Reform Commission, *Australian Privacy Law and Practice* (Report 108, Vol 3, 2008) 2254.

[39] Australian Law Reform Commission, *Australian Privacy Law and Practice* (Report 108, Vol 3, 2008).

[40] Office of the Australian Information Commissioner, *Australian Privacy Principles Guidelines: Privacy Act 1988* (31 March 2015) 12–13.

[41] Ibid.

[42] Ibid.

[43] Ibid.

[44] Besides a right to private life enshrined in art 7, the Charter of Fundamental Rights of the European Union ([2000] OJ C364/1) recognises the protection of personal data as a separate right under its art 8.

[45] Commission (EC), 'European Strategy for a Better Internet for Children' (Communication) COM/2012/0196 final, 2 May 2012; Commission (EC), 'An EU Agenda for the Rights of the Child' (Communication) COM/2011/0060 final, 15 February 2011.

rights to protection and care has been explicitly enshrined in the Charter of Fundamental Rights.[46] Although early iterations of privacy laws have been universal in application, recently a child-specific perspective in the context of online privacy has been increasingly embraced by policy makers not only in the EU but also on a broader regional and international level.[47]

The normative reasons to treat children differently to adults in data protection law include the need to respect the specific catalogue of the child rights, in particular the best interest of the child, their evolving capacity, and participation,[48] and to avoid conflicts between adults and child rights.[49] The practical reasons to design a child-tailored data protection regime relate to more recently collected empirical data vis-à-vis the risks for children and excessive and complex children's data collection practices online, all witnessing against the age-blind approach to children's privacy in the online context. A growing body of social science research on children's online behaviour demonstrated the need to account for particular characteristics and potential vulnerabilities of children as internet users and to address the potentially more serious impact of harm on them. The developmental science added further claims that children, particularly adolescents, are potentially more risk-prone and impulsive, i.e., the behavioural features suggesting them being in a different position than adults when making long-term decisions and acting on their own behalf.[50] Also, academics have established the link between developmental needs and interest, such as identity formation, developing one's agency and establishing autonomy, and creating peer relations and online privacy behaviour of adolescents.[51] Consequently, it has been claimed that the online data-gathering techniques are often tailored to satisfy adolescents' needs and to exploit vulnerabilities, all fears that have raised concerns among academics and policy makers.[52] In sum, the specific developmental features and needs might influence children's online behaviour and increase the possibility of online victimisation among peers, as well as the possibility of commercial personal data exploitation, to a level higher than that of cases involving adults.

---

[46] Charter of Fundamental Rights of the European Union [2000] OJ C364/1, art 24

[47] Council of Europe, Strategy for the Rights of the Child 2016-2021 (March 2016); UN Committee on the Rights of the Child, 'Digital media and children's rights' (report of the 2014 Day of General Discussion, May 2015); UNICEF, 'Privacy, protection of personal information and reputation rights' (discussion paper, 2017); UK Children's Commissioner, 'Growing Up Digital: A report of the Growing Up Digital Taskforce' (January 2017); UK House of Lords Committee on Communications, 'Growing up with the internet' (2nd Report of Session 2016–17, March 2017).

[48] Simone van der Hof, 'I Agree, or Do I: A Rights-Based Analysis of the Law on Children's Consent in the Digital World' (2017) 34(2) *Wis. Int'l L.J.* 409. Eva Lievens, 'Children's Rights and Media: Imperfect But Inspirational', in Eva Brems, Wouter Vandenhole and Ellen Desmet (eds), *Children's Rights Law in the Global Human Rights Landscape: Isolation, Inspiration, Integration?* (Routledge 2017). Sonia Livingstone, 'Children: A Special Case for Privacy?' (2008) 46(2) *Intermedia* 18.

[49] Kirsty Hughes, 'The Child's Right to Privacy and Article 8 European Convention on Human Rights' in Michael Freeman (ed), *Current Legal Issues: Law and Childhood Studies, Vol. 14* (OUP 2012).

[50] Cheryl B. Preston and Brandon T. Crowther, "Legal Osmosis: The Role of Brain Science in Protecting Adolescents (2014*) Hofstra Law Review* 447.

[51] Jochen Peter and Patti M. Valkenburg, 'Adolescents' Online Privacy: Toward a Developmental Perspective' in Sabine Trepte and Leonard Reinecke (eds), *Privacy Online: Perspectives on Privacy and Self-Disclosure in the Social Web* (Springer 2011). Wouter M.P. Steijn and Anton Vedder, 'Privacy under Construction: A Developmental Perspective on Privacy Perception' (2015) 40(4) *Science, Technology, & Human Values* 615.

[52] Montgomery, 'Youth and surveillance in the Facebook era' (n 16).

Since 1995, in the EU children have been covered by the age-generic data protection provisions of Directive 95/46/EC[53] placing them in one single group of data subjects together with adults. In line with the universal human rights perspective, the Directive 95/46/EC was in essence designed to protect all the natural persons whose data is processed by organizations or institutions (data controllers) established or using data processing means in the EU, despite the age, nationality, or the place of residence of these persons.[54] The lack of harmonized legal provisions governing children's personal data in the EU opened the door for individual countries to regulate the matter as they deemed necessary, resulting in an uneven and diverging European regulatory picture.

Some countries chose to add more specifics on minors' consent in their national data protection laws. Hungary, the Netherlands and Spain introduced exact age thresholds for consent to personal data processing.[55] The Spanish Personal Data Protection Law added some additional protections: it prohibited the collection of data from minors regarding members of their family, such as their profession or financial information, without the consent of these family members.[56] The sole exception was data regarding the child's identity and address for the purpose of obtaining parental consent.

Some countries remained silent on the age threshold for consent in data protection law and in practice relied on other branches of law, especially contract law provisions establishing when a person becomes fully competent to acquire and assume rights and obligations. If children could carry out basic legal acts without the consent of their representatives in civil law, such as conclude small, daily transactions, they were also allowed to consent to some basic personal data processing operations.[57] In contrast, the majority of the EU countries tried to assess the concrete situation on a case-by-case basis applying the general criteria of the child's best interest, level of moral and psychological development, and capacity to understand the consequences of giving consent as well as other specific circumstances (such as the age of the child, the purpose of data processing, and the type of personal data involved).[58] Although such an evaluation is both context-specific and child-specific, data protection authorities typically developed assumption-based exemplar age thresholds for consent.

For example, the United Kingdom's Information Commissioner (ICO) indicated that 'assessing understanding, rather than merely determining age, is the key to ensuring that per-

---

[53] Directive 95/46/EC of the European Parliament and of the Council of 24 October 1995 on the protection of individuals with regard to the processing of personal data and on the free movement of such data [1995] *OJ L 281, 31-50.*

[54] Ibid., art 4.

[55] Parental consent was required for the processing of personal data of children under the age of 14 in Spain (art 13 of the Spanish Royal Decree 1720/2007 of 21 December) and 16 in the Netherlands (art 5 of the Dutch Personal Data Protection Act [25 892] of 23 November 1999) and Hungary (s 6[3] of the Hungarian Act CXII of 2011 on the Right of Informational Self-Determination and on Freedom of Information).

[56] In many other EU countries even without explicit provisions no collection of data on family would be allowed from a minor as this under the general data protection principles would be considered excessive in relation to the purpose and unfair.

[57] See, e.g., Czech Republic and Portugal, *Global Privacy and Information Management Handbook* (Baker McKenzie, 2017).

[58] Article 29 Working Party, *Opinion 2/2009 on the protection of children's personal data (General Guidelines and the special case of schools)* (WP 160, 11 February 2009).

sonal data about children is collected and used fairly'.[59] However, when services were directed at children, the UK ICO required services to obtain parental consent for children under the age of 12. In Belgium, the data protection authority acknowledged the gradual development of minors and the need for more independence with growth, but advised services to get parental consent when a child is not mature enough to be able to understand the implications of the giving of consent.[60] Yet, it stated that parental consent should be required for the collection of sensitive data from children under 16, and in all cases when data processing was not in the interest of the child.[61]

Other countries have increasingly provided specific rights to enable children and their parents to access and erase their personal data. The UK Data Protection Act included a special section on the exercise of data protection rights in Scotland and established a presumption that a person of 12 years of age or more is of sufficient age and maturity to understand and exercise these rights.[62] In 2016, France introduced the right to be forgotten for minors allowing to erase their online personal data through an accelerated procedure.[63] France also made it possible for minors of 15 years or older to exercise their rights of access, rectification and opposition and to refuse to allow their parents to be informed and have access to their personal data.[64] Finally, some countries provided specific safeguards in data protection law against the dissemination of personal data related to children in judicial non-criminal proceedings and press coverage, explicitly stating that the child's right to privacy takes precedence over both freedom of expression and freedom of the press.[65]

The diversity of national approaches across the EU resulted in a lack of clarity regarding the interpretation of data protection requirements in relation to children. Services collecting children's information often faced legal uncertainty and were subjected to diverging legal rules. The question 'at what age can children consent to have their personal data processed' even became ironically known as 'the million euro question' among European privacy experts.[66]

It should be noted, that the lack of specific data protection provisions for children in the rest of the European countries was to a limited extent compensated by legally non-binding guidelines. Some data protection authorities issued comprehensive advice on the protection of children's online privacy.[67] Other authorities partially covered the topic when raising awareness among children and parents through leaflets, articles and opinions, and specific awareness

---

[59] UK Information Commissioner's Office, *Personal information online* (Code of Practice, 2010).

[60] Belgian Privacy Commission, *Advice No. 38/2002 of 16 September 2002 concerning the protection of the private life of minors on the Internet* (2002).

[61] Ibid.

[62] UK Data Protection Act 1998, s 66.

[63] Law no. 2016-1321 of October 7, 2016 for a Digital Republic ("French Digital Law"), art 40, art 58.

[64] Ibid.

[65] Italian Data Protection Code (Legislative Decree no. 196 of 30 June 2003) s 50 and 52.5. Code of Practice Concerning the Processing of Personal Data in the Exercise of Journalistic Activities [1998] OJ 179, s 7.

[66] Giovanni Buttarelli, 'The Children Faced with the Information Society' (Speech, 1st Euro-Ibero American Data Protection Seminar 'On Protection of Minors', Data Protection, Cartagena de Indias, 26 May 2009).

[67] Belgian Privacy Commission, *Advice No. 38/2002 of 16 September 2002 concerning the protection of the private life of minors on the Internet* (2002). Dutch Data Protection Authority, *Guidelines for the publication of personal data on the internet* (2007).

raising websites. At the EU level, the Article 29 Working Party, an independent advisory body made up of the representatives from all the EU data protection authorities (DPAs), adopted an opinion dedicated to children's personal data with a particular focus on schools.[68] The Working Party emphasized the child rights perspective, examining the main principles embedded in the CRC (such as the best interest of the child, protection and care, participation and evolving maturity) in the context of data protection.[69] It also focused on how the general principles of data protection (e.g., data quality, fairness, legitimacy, proportionality, retention, and data subject rights) apply to the field of education.[70] It took a flexible approach to the question of consent; rather than setting precise age limits for parental consent, it underlined the importance of taking the maturity of a child and complexity of the data processing at hand into account.[71] In addition, in several other subject-specific opinions, the Working Party made it clear that children's personal data should be processed with more protection and care than that of adults.[72]

IV. THE EUROPEAN UNION GENERAL DATA PROTECTION REGULATION

The EU General Data Protection Regulation[73] (GDPR) has significantly changed the *status quo* and addressed specific needs of children as data subjects. It explicitly recognized that children deserve more protection than adults, especially online, as 'they may be less aware of risks, consequences, safeguards and their rights in relation to the processing of personal data' (Recital 38). Such specific protection is afforded through a two-tiered protection regime.[74] The first tier of the regime is composed of general, age-generic GDPR provisions which are specifically relevant to children and their online activities: the right to erasure; the right to data portability; obligations of data protection by design and by default; data protection impact assessments; requirements for awareness raising; and the provision of transparent information. The second tier refers to two provisions specifically applying to children as data subjects: restrictions on the profiling and marketing activities of data controllers, especially the prohibition of automated decisions that produce legal effects or similarly significantly affect the child (Recitals 38 and 71 GDPR) and the parental consent requirement (art 8).

The latter is the most significant, albeit controversial, child-specific provision in the GDPR. It imposes specific conditions for a child's consent in relation to online services. Where the

---

68 Article 29 Working Party, *Opinion 2/2009 on the protection of children's personal data (General Guidelines and the special case of schools)* (WP 160, 11 February 2009).

69 Ibid.

70 Ibid.

71 Ibid.

72 Article 29 Working Party, *Opinion 02/2013 on apps on smart devices* (WP 202, 27 February 2013), *Opinion 2/2010 on online behavioural advertising* (WP 171, 22 June 2010).

73 Regulation (EU) 2016/679 of the European Parliament and of the Council of 27 April 2016 on the protection of natural persons with regard to the processing of personal data and on the free movement of such data, and repealing Directive 95/46/EC (General Data Protection Regulation) (2016) *OJ L 119*, 1–88.

74 Milda Mačėnaitė, 'From Universal Towards Child-specific Protection of the Right to Privacy Online: Dilemmas in the EU General Data Protection Regulation' (2017) 19(5) *New Media & Society* 765.

child is below the age of 16, personal data collection and further processing is only lawful 'if and to the extent that consent is given or authorised by the holder of parental responsibility over the child' (art 8(1) GDPR). The age limit of 16 has not, however, become a uniform standard for digital consent in Europe, as the GDPR has afforded a margin of manoeuvre for individual EU Member States to lower the age to 13 in their national data protection laws. Many Member States have selected different age thresholds within the 13–16 range,[75] undermining the much-expected harmonization effect of the GDPR and maintaining significant challenges for companies that provide cross-border services.

The process of adopting Article 8 has been long, inconsistent and not grounded in evidence. The initial effort to closely mimic the US COPPA standards was unexpectedly challenged by calls for different age limits without any clear justification.[76] Even more controversially, the EU missed an opportunity to re-affirm its commitment to protect the rights of the child online in a systematic manner in other relevant regulations, e.g., the draft ePrivacy Regulation,[77] a *lex specialis* to the GDPR, neither addresses the distinction between adults and children as data subjects nor refers to the specific consent requirements.

At the same time, by explicitly acknowledging children as special data subjects and providing them with a wider set of rights, the GDPR sets a benchmark in Europe and beyond. Yet, at the current stage many questions still need to be clarified to ensure that its provisions, in particular Article 8, are clear and fully operationalized in practice. For example, although the GDPR requires parental consent under the specific age when data controllers provide information society services directly to children, the exact scope of this provision is still questionable. Although free commercial services are covered by the parental consent requirement, it is debatable whether online services for children provided by non-profit or educational organisations or certain online services that entail substantial offline components constitute an information society service.[78] In addition, it is still unclear to what extent online services created for adults but used by children are covered by the GDPR.[79] Cases brought before data

---

[75] The age thresholds indicated in national laws are the following: 13 in Belgium, Denmark, Estonia, Finland, Latvia, Poland, Portugal, Spain, Sweden, UK; 14 in Austria, Bulgaria, Cyprus; 15 in Czech Republic, France, Greece, Slovenia, and 16 in Croatia, Germany, Hungary, Ireland, Italy, Lithuania, Luxembourg, Malta, Romania, Slovakia, the Netherlands. Please note that the chapter was drafted in 2018 and it does not take into account the latest legislative developments and guidelines adopted by the EU member states.

[76] Milda Mačėnaitė and Eleni Kosta, 'Consent of Minors to their Online Personal Data Processing in the EU: Following in US Footsteps?' (2017) 26(2) *Information and Communications Technology Law* 146.

[77] Proposal for a Regulation of the European Parliament and of the Council concerning the respect for private life and the protection of personal data in electronic communications and repealing Directive 2002/58/EC (Regulation on Privacy and Electronic Communications) [2017] 2017/0003 (COD).

[78] Information society services are defined as services that are 'normally offered for remuneration, at a distance, by electronic means, and at the individual request of a recipient of services'. Directive (EU) 2015/1535 of the European Parliament and of the Council of 9 September 2015 laying down a procedure for the provision of information in the field of technical regulations and of rules on Information Society services (Text with EEA relevance) [2015] OJ L 241, 1, art 1.1(b).

[79] According to the Article 29 Working Party, in order to avoid the application of the parental consent requirement, an information society service provider should "make(s) it clear to potential users that it is only offering its service to persons aged 18 or over, and this is not undermined by other evidence (such as the content of the site or marketing plans)". *Guidelines on Consent under Regulation 2016/679* (WP 259, 10 April 2018) 25.

protection authorities and courts will show how easy it will be to prove that the services are directed *de facto* to children and which of the factual evidence (e.g., the subject matter, the use of animated characters, advertising) will be given weight in the assessment. This clarification will be important in terms of actual protection as the terms of use of services often clearly exclude users below a certain age from the use of services but such users are present there in substantive numbers.

The GDPR also does not set out practical ways to obtain parental consent or to verify that a particular individual has a right to consent on child's behalf. The Article 29 Working Party has recommended a proportionate approach to data collection when obtaining and verifying consent, according to the principle of data minimisation.[80] However, it is still unclear whether and when parental consent verification can be based on a simple email exchange between a service provider and a parent and when the service provider requires additional proof. The Article 29 Working Party seems to accept in principle that in some cases an email to a parent would suffice to acquire parental consent, but the concrete application of this method alone in practice needs to be carefully assessed in specific cases. According to the Article 29 Working Party:

> What is reasonable efforts, when verifying that a person providing consent on behalf of a child is a holder of parental responsibility, may depend upon the risks inherent in the processing as well as the available technology. In low-risk cases, verification of parental responsibility via email may be sufficient. Conversely, in high-risk cases, it may be appropriate to ask for more proof, so that the controller is able to verify and retain the information pursuant to Article 7(1) GDPR.[81]

In this regard, EU data controllers could look to the nuanced risk-based requirements for parental consent that have been developed under COPPA in the US.

Although the GDPR does not explicitly refer to the obligation to verify the age of the child, it is implicitly required in some cases. For example, if a child consents without being old enough to do so, the data processing would be considered unlawful in this case.[82] Therefore, according to the Article 29 Working Party '(w)hen providing information society services to children on the basis of consent, controllers will be expected to make reasonable efforts to verify that the user is over the age of digital consent, and these measures should be proportionate to the nature and risks of the processing activities'.[83] If the child indicates that he or she is below the age of consent, the controller can accept this statement on face value but must then take steps to obtain parental consent, including steps to verify that the person consenting is the person with parental authority over the child.[84] In both cases, verification should not involve disproportionate data processing, but it is yet to be seen if data controllers will favour the least intrusive age verification methods, such as anonymous credentials and attributes, over more data-intensive options.

In keeping with the child's need for both protection and participation, Recital 30 of the GDPR states that consent by a parent or guardian is not required in the context of preventive

---

[80] Article 29 Working Party, *Guidelines on Consent under Regulation 2016/679* (WP 259, 10 April 2018).

[81] Ibid., 25–26.

[82] Ibid.

[83] Ibid, 25.

[84] Ibid.

or counselling services offered directly to a child. The rationale for such an exemption is the understanding that children may need to access certain services designed to help them and parental consent could create a barrier to such access. For example, online helplines for victims of sexual abuse would be able to obtain counselling if their parents are closely linked to the problem. In practical terms this exception means that the data controllers operating helplines or providing other preventive or counselling services online to a child (e.g., an online chat service to report abuse or violence) should not require prior parental consent from children.

V. CONCLUSION

Certainly, as a growing number of online services collect and monetize children's data, it is difficult to ensure that young people understand how information about them is being collected, used and disclosed. Bright line age restrictions underscore how problematic it is to place the burden of managing the risks on the shoulders of young children. However parental consent requirements are not a complete corrective, especially when viewed through the lens of the CRC. Many scholars are concerned that the various consent rules fail to fully take the best interests of children and their need for autonomy into account, either because they focus too much on protection or on the needs of online commerce.[85] It has also been suggested that strict parental consent requirement can negatively impact children's rights to freedom of expression and access to information.[86]

The Australian combined model, has an advantage of being both flexible and able to account for the developing cognitive capacity, autonomy and participation of children, but at the same time to remain operational in practice.[87] At a first glance, it seems to stand in stark contrast to the regulatory model introduced by the COPPA in the US or the GDPR in the EU, both of which entirely exclude the individual assessment element and rely on a bright line rule, presuming that from a certain age all children are able to provide their consent. However, when applied in practice both the Australian and the European models are likely to lead to a similar, if not an identical, outcome. The EU parental consent requirement applies only in the context of the information society services, i.e., to the online environment, where individual assessment is hardly possible. The GDPR does not exclude the individual assessment possibility when personal data of children is processed offline, which is not explicitly addressed in its text. Before the GDPR, EU data protection authorities have previously emphasized the importance of a case-by-case assessment when asking for consent from minors.[88] Yet, discretion to assess the actual capacity of each child or each age group is an attractive option from a child rights perspective, which is difficult to implement in law as opposed to non-binding

[85] Mačėnaitė (n 74) van der Hof (n 48). Valerie Verdoodt and Eva Lievens, 'Targeting Children with Personalised Advertising: How to Reconcile the (Best) Interests of Children and Advertisers' in Gert Vermeulen and Eva Lievens (eds) *Data Protection and Privacy under Pressure: Transatlantic Tensions, EU Surveillance and Big Data* (Maklu-Publishers 2017).

[86] Mačėnaitė, ibid.

[87] As the ALRC noted 'it provides certainty and enables practical operation in those situations where individual assessment is not reasonable or practicable'. Australian Law Reform Commission, *Australian Privacy Law and Practice* (Report 108, Vol 3, 2008) 2287.

[88] Article 29 Working Party, *Opinion 2/2009 on the protection of children's personal data (General Guidelines and the special case of schools)* (WP 160, 11 February 2009).

guidelines, which needs to set clear and precise standards and obligations for data controllers who risk being imposed huge fines for non-compliance like in the GDPR and COPPA.

In an attempt to balance the competing pressures of online commerce and child rights, many data protection regimes also impose a social responsibility on online services directed towards children; certainly, early efforts at legislation such as COPPA called for transparent privacy policies written in plain language to better support informed consent. The EU has equally emphasized transparency and accountability of data controllers and the role of codes of conduct in its GDPR. However, studies indicate that privacy statements are often written in language well above young people's reading abilities,[89] and that compliance rates with the legislation are low.[90] In light of this, privacy by design and data protection impact assessments could significantly strengthen protection of children's personal data.[91]

It is also important to take the needs and perspectives of young people into account. Multiple research projects report that the mere fact that young people disclose information about themselves online does not mean that they have abandoned their interest in privacy.[92] Emerging work also suggests that they use different devices for different things, relying on texting, instant messaging and ephemeral technologies like SnapChat for more personal and intimate interactions;[93] however, the information infrastructures that govern the collection, use and disclosure of information on those platforms mirrors the structures on more 'public' platforms like Instagram and Twitter. This means that, even when young people put up barriers between their intended audiences in an attempt to protect their privacy, the information they share is collected, collated and used to shape their online behaviours and sense of self.[94]

But perhaps the most important way to evaluate the effectiveness of current approaches to protecting children's online privacy is to ask whether or not it limits the collection of children's data in the first place. A study of the top 50 websites visited by Canadian children suggests that commercial collection by these services is rampant: 96 per cent of them used an average of five trackers to continually collect data from children and, although 80 per cent had privacy settings, only 12 per cent were set to private by default.[95] This suggests that data

---

[89] Anca Micheti, Jacquelyn Burkell and Valerie Steeves, 'Fixing Broken Doors: Strategies for Drafting Privacy Policies Young People Can Understand' (2010) 30(2) *Bulletin of Science, Technology & Society* 130.

[90] For example, a recent study in the US reports that the majority of over 5,000 popular children's apps are potentially in violation of COPPA: Irwin Reyes, Primal Wijesekera, Joel Readon, Amit Elaxai Bar On, Abbas Razaghpanah, Narseo Vallina-Rodriguez and Serge Egelman, 'Won't Somebody Think of the Children?: Examining COPPA Compliance at Scale' (2018) 3 *Proceedings on Privacy Enhancing Technologies* 63.

[91] Simone van der Hof and Eva Lievens, 'The Importance of Privacy by Design and Data Protection Impact Assessments in Strengthening Protection of Children's Personal Data Under the GDPR' (2018) 23(1) *Communications Law* 33.

[92] Valerie Steeves, 'Privacy, Sociality and the Failure of Regulation: Lessons Learned from Young Canadians' Online Experiences' in Beate Roessler and Dorota Mokrosinska (eds), *Social Dimensions of Privacy: Interdisciplinary Perspectives* (Cambridge University Press 2015); Alice E. Marwick and danah boyd, 'Networked Privacy: How Teenagers Negotiate Context in Social Media' (2015) 16 *New Media and Society* 1051.

[93] Matthew Johnson, Valerie Steeves, Leslie Shade and Grace Foran, *To Share or Not to Share: How Teens Make Privacy Decisions about Photos on Social Media* (Ottawa: MediaSmarts 2017).

[94] Ibid.

[95] Steeves, 'Terra Cognita: Surveillance of Young People's Favourite Websites' in Tonya Rooney and Emmeline Taylor (n 28). See also Irwin Reyes et al., 'Won't Somebody Think of the Children?:

protection authorities have more work to do to ensure that regulatory frameworks provide the kinds of privacy protections children deserve.

REFERENCES

Primary sources: Regulation and policy documents

30th International Conference of Data Protection and Privacy Commissioners, 'Resolution on Children's Online Privacy' (Strasbourg, 17 October 2008) para 2.
38th International Conference of Data Protection and Privacy Commissioners, 'Resolution for the Adoption of an International Competency Framework on Privacy Education' (Marrakesh, 18 October 2016).
Article 29 Working Party, *Guidelines on Consent under Regulation 2016/679* (WP 259, 10 April 2018).
Article 29 Working Party, *Opinion 02/2013 on apps on smart devices* (WP 202, 27 February 2013).
Article 29 Working Party, *Opinion 2/2010 on online behavioural advertising* (WP 171, 22 June 2010).
Article 29 Working Party, *Opinion 2/2009 on the protection of children's personal data (General Guidelines and the special case of schools)* (WP 160, 11 February 2009).
Article 7, the Charter of Fundamental Rights of the European Union ([2000] OJ C364/1)
Australian Law Reform Commission, *Australian Privacy Law and Practice* (Report 108, Vol 3, 2008) 2287.
Belgian Privacy Commission, *Advice No. 38/2002 of 16 September 2002 concerning the protection of the private life of minors on the Internet* (2002).
Charter of Fundamental Rights of the European Union [2000] OJ C364/1, art. 24.
Commission (EC), 'European Strategy for a Better Internet for Children' (Communication) COM/2012/0196 final, 2 May 2012.
Commission (EC), 'An EU Agenda for the Rights of the Child' (Communication) COM/2011/0060 final, 15 February 2011.
Commonwealth of Australia, *Parliamentary Debates,* Senate, 30 November 2006, 20302 (N Bolkus). The amendment was supported by the Australian Democrats: *Commonwealth of Australia*, Parliamentary Debates, Senate, 29 November 2000, 20162 (N Stott Despoja), 20165.
Council of Europe, Strategy for the Rights of the Child 2016–2021 (March 2016).
Federal Trade Commission, 'Complying with COPPA: Frequently asked questions' (20 March 2015) https://www.ftc.gov/tips-advice/business-center/guidance/complying-coppa-frequently-asked-questions accessed 10 January 2019.
Global Privacy Enforcement Network, '2015 GPEN Sweep – Children's Privacy' (Final results, 2015).
Italian Data Protection Code (Legislative Decree no. 196 of 30 June 2003) section 50 and 52.5. Code of Practice Concerning the Processing of Personal Data in the Exercise of Journalistic Activities [1998] OJ 179, section 7.
Law no. 2016-1321 of October 7, 2016 for a Digital Republic ('French Digital Law'), art 40, art 58.
Office of the Australian Information Commissioner (OAIC),'Proposed changes to Facebook Data Use Policy and Statement of Rights and Responsibilities - OAIC letter to Facebook' (12 September 2013) https://www.oaic.gov.au/media-and-speeches/statements/changes-to-facebooks-statement-of-rights-and-responsibilities-and-data-use-policy#proposed-changes-to-facebook-data-use-policy-and-statement-of-rights-and-responsibilities-oaic-letter-to-facebook; Statements on Facebook and Cambridge Analytica, 'Investigation into Facebook opened' (5 April 2018) https://www.oaic.gov.au/media-and-speeches/statements/facebook-and-cambridge-analytica#investigation-into-facebook-opened accessed 10 January 2019.

Examining COPPA Compliance at Scale' (2018) 3 *Proceedings on Privacy Enhancing Technologies* 63 and Global Privacy Enforcement Network, '2015 GPEN Sweep – Children's Privacy' (Final results, 2015).

Office of the Australian Information Commissioner, *Australian Privacy Principles Guidelines*: *Privacy Act 1988* (31 March 2015) 12–13.
Privacy Commissioner of Canada Investigation, 'Report of Findings into the Complaint Filed by the Canadian Internet Policy and Public Interest Clinic (CIPPIC) against Facebook Inc. Under the *Personal Information Protection and Electronic Documents Act*' PIPEDA Report of Findings #2009-008.
Privacy Commissioner of Canada Investigation, 'Social networking site for youth, Nexopia, breached Canadian privacy law' PIPEDA Report of Findings #2012-001.
Proposal for a Regulation of the European Parliament and of the Council concerning the respect for private life and the protection of personal data in electronic communications and repealing Directive 2002/58/EC (Regulation on Privacy and Electronic Communications) [2017] 2017/0003 (COD).
Regulation (EU) 2016/679 of the European Parliament and of the Council of 27 April 2016 on the protection of natural persons with regard to the processing of personal data and on the free movement of such data, and repealing Directive 95/46/EC (General Data Protection Regulation) (2016) *OJ L 119*, 1–88.
UK Children's Commissioner, 'Growing Up Digital: A report of the Growing Up Digital Taskforce' (January 2017).
UK Data Protection Act 1998, section 66.
UK House of Lords Committee on Communications, 'Growing up with the internet' (2nd Report of Session 2016–17, March 2017).
UK Information Commissioner's Office, *Personal information online* (Code of Practice, 2010).
UN Committee on the Rights of the Child, 'Digital media and children's rights' (report of the 2014 Day of General Discussion, May 2015).
UNICEF, 'Privacy, protection of personal information and reputation rights' (discussion paper, 2017).
United States Electronic Code of Federal Regulations, Title 16 Chapter 1, Subchapter C, Part 312, as per 6502 (b)(1)(A).
Williams D (Attorney-General), 'First Meeting of Consultative Group on Children's Privacy' (Press Release, 4 June 2001). Cited in Australian Law Reform Commission, *Australian Privacy Law and Practice* (Report 108, Vol 3, 2008) 2254.

Secondary literature

Baker McKenzie, *Global Privacy and Information Management Handbook* (Baker McKenzie, 2017).
Grimes S.M. and L. Regan Shade, 'Neopian Economics of Play: Children's Cyberpets and Online Communities as Immersive Advertising in Neopets.com' (2005) 1 *International Journal of Media & Cultural Politics* 181.
Hughes K. 'The Child's Right to Privacy and Article 8 European Convention on Human Rights' in Michael Freeman (eds), *Current Legal Issues: Law and Childhood Studies, Vol. 14* (OUP 2012).
Johnson M., V. Steeves, L. Shade and G. Foran, *To Share or Not to Share: How Teens Make Privacy Decisions about Photos on Social Media* (Ottawa: MediaSmarts 2017).
Lievens E. 'Children's Rights and Media: Imperfect But Inspirational', in E. Brems, W. Vandenhole and E. Desmet (eds), *Children's Rights Law in the Global Human Rights Landscape: Isolation, Inspiration, Integration?* (Routledge 2017).
Livingstone S. 'Children: A Special Case for Privacy?' (2008) 46(2) *Intermedia* 18.
Mačėnaitė M. and E. Kosta, 'Consent of Minors to their Online Personal Data Processing in the EU: Following in US Footsteps?' (2017) 26(2) *Information and Communications Technology Law* 146.
Mačėnaitė M. 'From Universal Towards Child-specific Protection of the Right To Privacy Online: Dilemmas in the EU General Data Protection Regulation' (2017) 19(5) *New Media & Society* 765.
Marwick A.E. and d. boyd, 'Networked privacy: How teenagers negotiate context in social media' (2015) 16 *New Media and Society* 1051.
Micheti A, J. Burkell and V Steeves, 'Fixing Broken Doors: Strategies for Drafting Privacy Policies Young People Can Understand' (2010) 30(2) *Bulletin of Science, Technology & Society* 130.
Montgomery K. *Generation Digital: Politics, Commerce, and Childhood in the Age of the Internet* (2007 MIT Press).
Montgomery K. 'Youth and Surveillance in the Facebook Era: Policy Interventions and Social Implications' (2015) 39 *Telecommunications Policy* 771.

Peter J. and P.M. Valkenburg, 'Adolescents' Online Privacy: Toward a Developmental Perspective' in Sabine Trepte and Leonard Reinecke (eds), *Privacy Online: Perspectives on Privacy and Self-Disclosure in the Social Web* (Springer 2011).
Preston C.B. and B.T. Crowther, 'Legal Osmosis: The Role of Brain Science in Protecting Adolescents' (2014) *Hofstra Law Review* 447.
Quennerstedt A. 'Children, But Not Really Humans? Critical Reflections on the Hampering Effect of the "3 p's"' (2010) 18 *IJCR* 619.
Reyes, I., P. Wijesekera, J. Readon, A. Elaxai Bar On, a. Razaghpanah, N. Vallina-Rodriguez and S Egelman, 'Won't Somebody Think of the Children?: Examining COPPA Compliance at Scale' (2018) 3 *Proceedings on Privacy Enhancing Technologies* 63.
Steeves V. 'It's Not Child's Play: The Online Invasion of Children's Privacy' (2006) 3 *UOLTJ* 169.
Steeves V. 'Privacy, Sociality and the Failure of Regulation: Lessons Learned from Young Canadians' Online Experiences' in B Roessler and D Mokrosinska (eds), *Social Dimensions of Privacy: Interdisciplinary Perspectives* (Cambridge University Press 2015).
Steeves V. 'Terra Cognita: Surveillance of Young People's Favourite Websites' in Tonya Rooney and Emmeline Taylor (eds), *Surveillance Futures: Social and Ethical Implications of New Technologies of and Children and Young People* (Routledge 2016).
Steeves V., 'Snoops, Bullies and Hucksters: What Rights Do Young People Have in a Networked Environment?' in N.A. Jennings and S.R. Mazzarella (eds.), *20 Questions About Youth and Media* (2nd edn, 2017 New York: Peter Lang).
Steijn W.M.P. and A. Vedder, 'Privacy under Construction: A Developmental Perspective on Privacy Perception' (2015) 40(4) *Science, Technology, & Human Values* 615.
Vachman K. 'FTC restricts behavioural targeting of kids: New rules go into effect next July' (Ad Week,19 December 2012) http://www.adweek.com/digital/ftc-restricts-behavioral-targeting-kids-146108/ accessed 10 January 2019.
Van der Hof S. 'I Agree, or Do I: A Rights-Based Analysis of the Law on Children's Consent in the Digital World' (2017) 34(2) *Wis. Int'l L.J.* 409.
Van der Hof S. and E. Lievens, 'The Importance of Privacy by Design and Data Protection Impact Assessments in Strengthening Protection of Children's Personal Data Under the GDPR' (2018) 23(1) *Communications Law* 33.
Verdoodt V. and E. Lievens, 'Targeting Children with Personalised Advertising: How to Reconcile the (Best) Interests of Children and Advertisers in Gert Vermeulen and Eva Lievens (eds) *Data Protection and Privacy under Pressure: Transatlantic Tensions, EU Surveillance and Big Data* (Maklu-Publishers 2017).

18. Biometric data processing: Is the legislator keeping up or just keeping up appearances?

Els J. Kindt

I. INTRODUCTION

The high-tech measurement of unique characteristics of the human body is in the 21st century no longer fiction. Biometric information embedded in ID documents is automatically compared in fractions of seconds by e-gates, biometric technology is used at the company entrance and biometric data processing is finding its way in online payment authorization systems 'by a blink of the iris'. All these applications promise more security but also convenience. Biometric technology is highly interesting because of its exceptional benefit of allowing the identification or verification of individuals by comparison with reference data. Experts and scholars have however also pointed to the awkward marriage between 'public' biometric characteristics which can easily be captured and its use for security finalities. Besides a promising future in security and convenience applications, and in a soon to come Internet-of-Things environment, the technology is also deployed by law enforcement authorities and by governments for monitoring public audiences. Surveillance cameras are increasingly replaced by 'intelligent' models capturing and processing humans' features of for example faces and voice, but also of movements, behaviour and emotions. In order to secure a bright and fair future use of biometric technology, a debate is needed to know how and to what extent biometric data processing is useful, acceptable, or necessary in society.

Biometric data processing is however complex, allowing for a large variety of uses, and until recently only a few seemed to pose the right questions and to grasp how to deal with the challenges posed by this new technology. In this chapter, we first discuss the values and freedoms from a European perspective which are at stake when biometric data are processed and some major themes. In Section II, we present the new EU privacy and data protection legal framework which regulates biometric data and question whether this solves the pending issues. We further point in Section III to the need of applying upon any assessment of biometric data a double framework of fundamental rights on one hand and of data protection legislation on the other. We finally touch upon how the courts cope with the availability of biometric data, emerging new legislation and see for the ways forward.[1] The General Data Protection Regulation (EU) 2016/679 (the 'GDPR') defines biometric data and expects a lot of the accountability and the responsibility imposed upon biometric application controllers, by requiring an impact assessment if 'high risks to the rights and freedoms of natural persons' are 'likely to occur', and further requires that privacy and data protection apply by design and by

[1] Ethical and societal aspects are not the subject of this contribution. About the ethical aspects, see e.g., Irma Van der Ploeg, 'Biometrics and the Body as Information: Normative Issues in the Socio-technical Coding of the Body' in David Lyon (ed.), *Surveillance as Social Sorting: Privacy, Risk and Automated Discrimination* (New York, Routledge, 2002), 57–73.

default.[2] In this contribution, we wonder whether this approach of the legislator is adequate to resolve the numerous issues raised by biometric technologies and argue – for some time – that there is a need for adequate and specific legislation.[3]

We briefly analyse in this chapter risks, legislation, findings of courts, studies and literature. We need in-depth discussions and analyses of the many benefits as well as of the several risks when relying on biometric technologies. Such threats relate to the functioning of the technology, such as inaccuracies, but also to its (mis)use and vulnerability due to for example spoofing and manipulation attacks, while these threats evolve constantly. A public debate about biometric data processing took off recently in the context of 'live' facial recognition tested in several countries.[4] An exhaustive discussion of all issues of (hard and soft) biometric data processing is unfortunately not possible within the scope of this chapter and we recommend to consult additional studies, reports and literature, some herein referenced, for a correct understanding of the many legal, ethical and societal issues.

II. VALUES, FREEDOMS AND FUNDAMENTAL RIGHTS IN DEMOCRATIC SOCIETIES

The impact, the advantages and the threats of collecting, using, reproducing and transferring *unique* characteristics of humans in automated applications, for individuals and the society, have been studied for some time.[5] While biometric technologies offer many advantages,

---

[2] The General Data Protection Regulation (EU) 2016/679 replaces the Directive 95/46/EC imposing since 1995 minimum harmonization requirements for national data protection laws in the European Union. These laws emerged about 50 years ago because of the profound concern for data collection about citizens and the processing by mainframe computers owned by governments and large companies. This Directive needed an update due to new technologies and practices.

[3] See also Els Kindt, *Privacy and Data Protection Issues of Biometric Applications. A Comparative Legal Analysis* (Springer 2013) Chap. 9, 831–907 ('Kindt, Biometric Applications 2013').

[4] See e.g., in the UK, Pete Fussey and Daragh Murray, *Independent Report on the London Metropolitan Police Service's Trial of Live Facial Recognition Technology*, The Human Rights, Big Data and Technology Project, July 2019. Facial recognition was also tested in Nice, France, in 2019 during carnival: see, S. Mayhew, 'Facial recognition software tested during Carnival in Nice', 24.2.2019, available at https://www.biometricupdate.com/201902/facial-recognition-software-tested-during-carnival-in-nice accessed 30 October 2021; for the US, see Clare Garvie, Alvaro Bedoya and Jonathan Frankle, *The Perpetual Line-up. Unregulated Police Recognition in America,* 18.10.2016, 119 p., Georgetown Law. Center on Privacy & Technology, available at https://www.perpetuallineup.org/ accessed 30 October 2021 ('Garvie e.a., The perpetual line-up, 2016.')

[5] See, e.g., European Commission and the Institute of Prospective Technological Studies, *Biometrics at the Frontiers: Assessing the Impact on* Society, Seville, European Commission, DG JRC, January 2005, 144 p. ('EU Commission and IPTS, Biometrics at the Frontiers, 2005'); Consultative Committee of the Convention for the Protection of Individuals with regards to Automatic Processing of Personal Data [CETS No. 108] (T-PD), *Progress report on the application of the principles of convention 108 to the collection and processing of biometric data*, Strasbourg, Council of Europe, CM(2005)43, March 2005 ('Council of Europe, Progress report, 2005'), and the updated *Progress Report* of 2013, T-PD(2013)06, https://rm.coe.int/progress-report-on-the-application-of-the-principles-of-convention-108/1680744d81 accessed 30 October 2021; P. Rotter (ed.), 'Large-scale Biometrics Deployment in Europe: Identifying Challenges and Threats', JRC Scientific and Technical Reports, European Commission JRC – IPTS, Seville, 2008, 135; Els Kindt and Lorenz Müller (eds.), *D3.10. Biometrics in Identity Management*, December 2007, Frankfurt, Fidis, 130 p., available at www.fidis.net accessed 30 October 2021; Kindt,

important concerns from an ethical, societal and human rights point of view were identified and still hold. European courts including the European Court of Human Rights (ECtHR), have qualified the (compulsory) capture and storage of biometric information in databases as an interference with the right to respect for private live.[6] In the meantime, behavioural biometric data processing, categorization and emotion capture are on the rise as well. We discuss hereunder briefly some of these rights as important freedoms and values for society with the aim to demonstrate the threats posed by this new technology.[7] The reference framework is the fundamental rights protection offered by the European Convention on Human Rights of 1950 and the EU Charter legally binding as of 1 December 2009. Interference with these rights is only permitted in case of a legitimate aim or objective of general recognized interest, in respect of 'the essence' of the fundamental rights at stake, with a law as basis and upon the condition of necessity and proportionality (see for these requirements Section III below).

II.1 Freedom of Movement – Freedom of Assembly and of Association – Freedom of Expression

Unlimited biometric data collection combined with surveillance (see below) has a freezing ('chilling') effect on democratic values and fundamental rights, including the freedom of movement and the freedom of assembly and of association.[8] The exercise of related other fundamental and civil rights, including the right to express one's opinion freely and to participate in protest marches, are also at risk.[9] The use and technical limitations of biometric technology at (automated) borders, such as e-gates, create particular risks as well, including for human treatment, the right of free movement (within the Union) and the right to asylum.[10]

Biometric Applications 2013, Chap. 4, 275–402, where both the advantages and risks are discussed and classified depending on the nature, the architecture and the use of biometric data. These studies need to be complemented with the many additional recent studies on new biometric developments and use.

[6] See ECtHR, *S. and Marper* 2008, § 86; ECtHR, *M.K. v France* 2013, § 26; ECtHR, *Gaughran v. The United Kingdom* 2020, §70.

[7] For each specific biometric system deployment, varying fundamental rights and freedoms may be at stake and need to be carefully identified, e.g., for the fundamental rights concerns when law enforcement deploys 'live' facial recognition, see Fundamental Rights Agency, *Facial recognition technology: fundamental rights considerations in law enforcement*, 27 November 2019, 36 p., available at https://fra.europa.eu/en/news/2019/facial-recognition-technology-fundamental-rights-considerations-law-enforcement accessed 30 October 2021.

[8] Art. 45 EU Charter and Art. 12 EU Charter. Also freedom of religion could be hampered.

[9] See Art. 11 EU Charter. The taking and retention of 'anonymous' photographs and other identifying information of participants at a protest by the police was the subject of ECtHR, *Friedl v Austria,* no. 28/1994/475/556. It was back in 1995 decided to be no interference with the right to respect for private life. With present biometric comparison technologies and the existence of databases, courts nowadays are likely to come to other conclusions. See and compare with e.g., ECtHR, *Aycaguer v France*, no 8806/12, 22.6.2017 ('ECtHR, Aycaguer 2017') in which the ECtHR concluded that convicting a participant in a protest organized by an agricultural trade union for refusing to provide a biological sample for DNA profiling and inclusion in the national database infringed Art. 8 ECHR.

[10] See Arts 4 and 18 EU Charter. About the large EU IT systems and fundamental rights, see Fundamental Rights Agency, *Under Watchful Eyes: Biometrics, EU IT Systems and Fundamental Rights, 2018,* 133 p.

II.2 Equal Treatment, Algorithmic Inequalities and Intransparencies

Biometric applications could in many ways instigate discriminatory effects. Inherently relying on bodily characteristics, varying in ethnic origin and in colour, age and gender, the processing of such information shows varying accuracy rates which could easily lead to intentional or unintentional discriminatory practices without objective justification and leading to stigmatization. This has been demonstrated in several studies and reports.[11] The reason is the nature of the data, but also the (limited) data sets on which the algorithms have been trained and the (big) data sets used. Algorithmic inequalities, discrepancies and intransparancies are hence major issues which need to be addressed for biometric systems as well.

II.3 Omnipresent Surveillance, from Early Childhood?

Intelligent cameras equipped with voice, face and other biometric characteristic recognition functionalities are becoming an integral part of the security policy and strategy in many countries, in cities and at public events. This surveillance cameras network combined with widely collected and available biometric data makes that such 'data are retained and subsequently used without (...) being informed' which (soon) is 'likely to generate in the minds of the persons concerned the feeling that their private lives are the subject of constant surveillance'.[12] The Court of Justice pointed to this risk in the context of the blanket retention of electronic communication data in 2014, but this applies all the more when massive amounts of biometric data are collected by modernized surveillance camera infrastructures in the Member States allowing for comparison with previously registered biometric information. Systems for suspect recognition are known to have been deployed since about two decades. While the ECtHR acknowledged that governments may turn to cutting-edge technologies in specific circumstances, any such government and legislation should provide safeguards to avoid broad secret surveillance activities, abuse and provide judicial control checks.[13] This threat obviously increases in a 'big data' use context. This is all the more problematic if such surveillance becomes a given from early childhood, which is well under way with the increasing number of biometric applications in schools, risking transforming behaviour indefinitely.[14] Moreover, individuals are treated as

---

[11] See e.g., Joy Buolamwini and Timnit Gebru, *Gender Shades: Intersectional Accuracy Disparities in Commercial Gender Classification*, 2018, 15 p. MIT Media Lab, Algorithmic Justice League Project, available at http://proceedings.mlr.press/v81/buolamwini18a/buolamwini18a.pdf accessed 30 October 2021, demonstrating gender and racial biases in commercial face recognition systems sold by Microsoft, IBM and Megvii, whereby e.g., the accuracy in gender classification for darker females reached between 65.3 and 79.2 per cent while between 99.2 and 100 per cent for lighter males; see also e.g., Garvie e.a., The perpetual line-up, 2016, 53–60, the report explains how the face recognition used by police will disproportionately affect African Americans.

[12] See ECJ, joined cases C-293-12 and C-594/12, *Digital Rights Ireland v Minister for Communications* e.a., 8.04.2014, §37.

[13] ECtHR, app. n° 37138/14, *Szabó and Vissy v Hungary*, 12.1.2016.

[14] Surveillance, such as designed by Bentham's panopticon, is believed to or will make that individuals behave better. About the surveillance risks, see also Juliet Lodge, *Quantum Surveillance and "Shared Secrets". A biometric step too far?* (2010) CEPS 2010; Steven Graham and David Wood, 'Digitizing surveillance: categorization, space, inequality' in *Critical Social Policy* 23:2, 2003, pp. 227-248, available at http://journals.sagepub.com/doi/pdf/10.1177/0261018303023002006 ('Graham and Wood, Digitizing surveillance, 2003'). In France, the regulator repeated by a decision of 17 October 2019 that facial rec-

suspects which is against the right to the presumption of innocence. A US scholar rightfully stated that when a school requires *from children* to provide fingerprints, palm prints or iris scans in order to attend school, such collection and disclosure is no less compulsory than when police authorities detain *suspects* for fingerprinting and identification.[15]

Along the surveillance risks, the 'right to anonymity', online but also offline, for example in public places, risks being discarded.[16] While discussion could remain as to whether such 'anonymity right' exists, the risks of omnipresent identification everywhere by anyone all the time has been considered important enough to agree already in 2011 upon good practices for the use of face recognition technologies in the US.[17] In the recent years, regulatory legislation and legislation imposing bans or moratoria are emerging, especially in the US.

II.4 Effects on Principles of Justice: Right of Due Process and Right to a Remedy – Presumption of Innocence

Biometric technology requires a full assessment of all its risks for important principles of justice as well. The right to effective remedies and a fair trial, especially if rights and freedoms are violated, and of the presumption of innocence are cornerstones of democratic societies.[18] This should not be troubled by the reign of any technology. Biometric decision mechanisms are of a high complexity and very technical, while being not transparent and leading to results (e.g., refusal to enter the territory) which may be very hard – as a human – to understand and/or to contest and to remedy.[19] In addition, biometric technology is mistakenly (ab)used if deployed in such way that all individuals are treated as suspects, rather than being presumed innocent until the contrary is proven. At the same time, the technology is also prone to abuse, such as spoofing or morphing.[20] Such misuse needs to be detected in order to be able to safely rely on the technology.

---

ognition for security and convenience reasons at school entrances is not proportionate. See https://www.cnil.fr/fr/biometrie accessed 30 October 2021.

[15] Stefan P Schropp, 'Biometric Data Collection and RFID Tracking in Schools: A Reasoned Approach to Reasonable Expectations of Privacy' (2016) 94 *N.C.L. Review* 1068, 1085.

[16] About this risk, see also Kindt, Biometric Applications 2013, Chap. 4, 295-319. See also BBC reporter Sudworth in December 2017, identified in public space by the CCTV surveillance system and stopped in seven minutes by the police in China, available at BBC News at https://www.bbc.com/news/av/world-asia-china-42248056/in-your-face-china-s-all-seeing-state accessed 30 October 2021.

[17] See the Federal Trade Commission 2011 Consent Order to Facebook, threatened by recent business practices changes by Facebook. See also EPIC's complaint to the FTC and request for investigation, 6.4.2018, available at https://epic.org/privacy/facebook/FTC-Facebook-FR-Complaint-04062018.pdf accessed 30 October 2021. In November 2021, Facebook announced that it will no longer use facial recognition software on its platforms.

[18] See also Arts 47 and 48 EU Charter.

[19] This happened to Brandon Mayfield, who was arrested and wrongly accused by the FBI of involvement in the 2004 Madrid train bombing attack due to reliance on digital images of partial latent fingerprints.

[20] Spoofing refers to presenting a false probe, e.g., a gummy finger, to a biometric system, e.g., to pass a control under another identity. About the progress in detecting this, see Sébastian Marcel, Mark Nixon, Julien Fierrez and Nicholas Evans (eds), *Handbook of Biometric Anti-Spoofing – Presentation Attack Detection, Second edition,* Advances in Computer Vision and Pattern Recognition, Springer 2018. Morphing is a recent phenomenon where characteristics of several individuals are merged in one biomet-

II.5 Respect for Private Life and the Right to Data Protection

Privacy and data protection rights have been at the forefront of debates about the risks of the capture, retention and use of biometric data[21] while individuals should be able to control their identities.[22] (Re-)identification and tracking, the use as unique identifiers for linking information contained in databases, but also (racial) profiling, 'singling out' and the risk of 'function creep'[23] are amongst the most important risks. One of the first national court case on facial recognition and biometric identification by law enforcement took place in the UK. In this case the court found on appeal that the system tested by the South Wales police interfered with the right to respect for privacy and lacked a sufficient legal framework.[24] Because of the wide variety of uses of biometric data, the purpose limitation principle, explicitly stated in Article 8 of the EU Charter as one of the elements of the fundamental right to data protection, is crucial while being under much (political) pressure. But risks of inaccuracies are also a problem and require appropriate guarantees. Another major issue is that biometric characteristics cannot be revoked or changed by individuals (e.g., as compared to passwords).[25]

Several authors have also pointed to the possible disclosure of medical information for almost all traits.[26] This remains a problem both under data protection as for privacy reasons.

---

ric image, allowing several individuals to e.g., travel under the same biometric (morphed) characteristics embedded in an ePassport.

[21] See also in particular: Article 29 Data Protection Working Party, *Working Document on Biometrics*, WP 80, 1 August 2003, 11; Article 29 Data Protection Working Party, *Opinion 3/2011 on developments in biometric technologies,* WP193, 27 April 2012, 34; and Article 29 Data Protection Working Party, *Opinion 02/2012 on facial recognition in online and mobile services*, WP192, 22 March 2012, 9. The fundamental rights of privacy and data protection are also closely related to the right to autonomy.

[22] See also the Electronic Privacy Information Center, stating that 'controlling one's identity requires the choice to remain anonymous': Electronic Privacy Information Center, *Comments of the Electronic Privacy Information Center to the Federal Trade Commission. Face Facts: A Forum on Facial Recognition*, project number P115406, 31 January 2012, 24 p. ('EPIC, Comments to the FTC. Face Facts, 2012'), available at http://epic.org/privacy/face recognition/EPIC-Face-Facts-Comments.pdf accessed 30 October 2021.

[23] Function creep refers to the gradual shifting and widening of the use of a technology or of a system beyond the original purpose. This is problematic for many (large-scale) systems. Eurodac, e.g., which collects and stores all ten fingerprints of every asylum applicant and alien apprehended for irregular border crossing or found illegally present in an EU Member State originally for helping and identifying asylum seekers for designating the responsible Member State under the 1999 Dublin Convention, has later been made accessible to law enforcement authorities. The largest biometric database, Aadhaar in India, set up for providing all Indians with an identity, has been criticized in this context as well. For a critical review of the Aadhaar project, and the role of regulation, see N. Ranganathan, 'The Economy (and Regulatory Practice) that Biometrics Inspires: A Study of the Aadhaar Project' in A. Kak (ed.) *Regulating Biometrics. Global Approaches and Urgent Questions*, AINow Institute, New York University, New York, September 1, 2020, pp. 52–61, available at https://ainowinstitute.org/regulatingbiometrics.pdf accessed 30 October 2021.

[24] [2020] EWCA Civ 1058.

[25] This also puts the right to physical integrity at risk, when individuals change their characteristics, e.g., fingerprints to pass border controls.

[26] See, e.g., Emilio Mordini and Holly Ashton, 'Chapter 12 The Transparent Body: Medical Information, Physical Privacy and Respect for Body Integrity', in Emilio Mordini and Dimitros Tzovaras (eds), *Second Generation Biometrics: The Ethical, Legal and Social Context,* Dordrecht, Springer, 2012,

If the data are stored, they can be re-used and analysed, also for inferring medical information or weaknesses.

II.6 The Reading and Disclosure of Human Characteristics and Human Dignity – Right to Integrity

Last, but not least, human dignity prevails as one of the premium and utmost important fundamental rights. Using human bodies as part of, and as a chain in, an information system is a reminder of malpractices of dictatorial regimes in recent history, aided by IT specialists.[27] This right to protection of human dignity and the other (fundamental) right to develop freely one's personality form the basis of the concept of informational self-determination, developed by the German Constitutional Court in its milestone decision of 1983. It argued that *data collection and use in the computer era* have a threatening aspect in *that individual behaviour could be mapped* and individuals have no idea what data is collected or how it is used.[28] This reasoning is in our view all the more valid for the need of maintaining *control over unique identifying irrevocable human characteristics*, which one cannot hide, and any other bodily characteristics, including emotions.[29] *The ever-evolving technology also leads to more* biometric characteristics being deployable, from a distance, and collected unnoticed, while a certain degree of uniqueness will in most cases allow to trace the data back to particular persons, but in such way that the humans become the object of an ever further invasive technology, which endangers human dignity.[30] *Compulsory* or *unnoticed* biometric disclosure flirts with this human dignity principle. Moreover, one shall not take it for granted that everyone is fit for being 'read out' by the system or agrees with such submission.

III. OTHER LEGAL NORMS

In addition to the rights and freedoms set out in the European Convention on Human Rights and in the EU Charter, more specific legislation applies to biometric data processing in the EU. We focus in this chapter primarily on Regulation 2016/679, which sets in the Union the general legal data protection framework save for specific processing activities, such as by law enforcement authorities, which is governed by the Directive 2016/680.[31]

---

(257) 262 ('Mordini and Tzovaras, Second Generation Biometrics 2012); Kindt, Biometric Applications 2013, Chap. 4, 324–335.

27 Human dignity is taken over in the Charter of Fundamental Rights of the EU ('EU Charter') and must at all times be fully respected and protected (see Art. 1).

28 BVerfG, 15.12.1983, BVerfGE 65, 1 ('Volkszählung'). The court hereby invalidated the Census Act.

29 About facial emotion detection, see EDPS, TechDispatch 1/2021 – Facial Emotion Recognition, 26.5.2021, available at https://edps.europa.eu/data-protection/our-work/publications/techdispatch/techdispatch-12021-facial-emotion-recognition_en accessed 30 October 2021.

30 More human characteristic than initially expected seem to have this certain degree of uniqueness allowing identification or at least recognition – e.g., heart rhythm patterns, which can be detected and captured unnoticed from a distance, e.g., by ECGs, are a new means of biometric recognition.

31 Directive (EU) 2016/680 imposes harmonized national law for personal data processing activities by law enforcement authorities. See Directive (EU) 2016/680 of the European Parliament and of the Council of 27 April 2016 on the protection of natural persons with regard to the processing of personal

III.1 The Privacy and Data Protection Legal Framework from the Early Eighties until Regulation (EU) 2016/679

When the Council of Europe adopted the first binding data protection legislation in 1981 by opening up Convention No 108 for signature and ratification and the EU issued the Directive 95/46/EC about 15 years later, based upon this Convention, biometric data processing was not at all an issue for the legislator. Biometric technology remained at that time almost exclusively in the military and intelligence services domain and was deployed for a handful specific and limited applications. Treaties, EU directives and data protection legislation adopted by Member States therefore mentioned nor explicitly regulated biometric data processing activities in that period.

This changed however after the 9/11 events of 2001 in the US. From that point on, a variety of stakeholders defended the overall utility of biometric data for increasing security and the use of biometric data was advanced as 'a technology standard' for establishing and verifying the identity of persons, such as for border control.[32] The EU followed the US government's requirements on biometric data from *third country nationals* entering the territory by adopting the Regulation (EC) No 2252/2004 (the 'ePassport Regulation') in 2004. This Regulation required from EU Member States to include biometric data, in particular the facial image and two (index) fingerprints into the electronic storage medium of passports and travel documents issued to *EU citizens*.[33] From then on, the deployment of biometric data spread out fast in EU Member States in the public and private sector while there was in general no or very limited guidance in the legislation or by data protection authorities.[34]

---

data by competent authorities for the purposes of the prevention, investigation, detection or prosecution of criminal offences or the execution of criminal penalties, and on the free movement of such data, and repealing Council Framework Decision 2008/977/JHA, *O.J.* L 119, 4.05.2016, pp. 89-131, available at http://eur-lex.europa.eu/legal-content/EN/TXT/PDF/?uri=OJ:L:2016:119:FULL&from=NL ('Directive (EU) 2016/680') accessed 30 October 2021.

[32] See the US Patriot Act, H.R. 3162, section 403(c). The US Visit (Entry-Exit) program was set up shortly thereafter, collecting at the border – since 2008 all ten (10) – fingerprints and the digital facial image of US visitors under the Visa Waiver Program. The International Civil Aviation Organization (ICAO) had shortly before, in 1999, selected the facial image as the globally interoperable 'biometric' for Machine Readable Travel Documents, in particular the ePassport. It is interesting to note that fingerprints were for ICAO only an optional trait. About this important step, see M. Stanton, 'ICAO and the Biometric RFID Passport: History and Analysis' in C.J. Bennett and D. Lyon (eds), *Playing the Identity Card: Surveillance, Security and Identification in Global Perspective* (London, Routledge 2008), 253–267; see also Martin Meints and Marit Hansen (eds.), *D.3.6 Study on ID Documents* (Frankfurt, Fidis 2006), available at www.fidis.net accessed 30 October 2021.

[33] Council Regulation (EC) No 2252/2004 of 13 December 2004 on standards for security features and biometrics in passports and travel documents issued by Member States, *O.J.* L 385, 29 December 2004, pp. 1–6. This EU Regulation was pushed through because of the 2002 US Enhanced Border Security and Visa Entry Reform Act, mandating to include biometric data in the passports of Visa Waiver Program travelers (H.R. 3525, section 303); see also G. Hornung, 'The European Regulation on Biometric Passports: Legislative Procedures, Political Interactions, Legal Framework and Technical Safeguards' (2007) 4(3) *SCRIPTed*.

[34] See Els Kindt and Lorenz Müller (eds.), *D13.4. The Privacy Legal Framework for Biometrics* (Frankfurt, Fidis 2009), 134 available at http://www.fidis.net/fileadmin/fidis/deliverables/new_deliverables3/fidis_ deliverable13_4_v_1.1.pdf accessed 30 October 2021.

France, however, was an important exception. Based on the parliamentary Report Cabal of 2003, the general data protection act No 78-17 of 1978 was modified in 2004, requiring prior authorization of the French data protection authority, the CNIL, when using biometric data for the control of the identity and, if operated for the government, a decree.[35] The CNIL has consequently developed a very detailed jurisprudence, assessing in a detailed manner the risks of biometric data processing, providing detailed guidance and limiting authorizations for biometric applications.[36] The CNIL hereby specified detailed technical and processing criteria and maintained the view that centralized biometric data requires 'a major stake which surpasses the strict interests of the organization', hereby especially warning for the central storage of biometric data, in particular as an instrument of law enforcement ('*un outil de police judiciaire*').[37] Other data protection authorities issued later opinions and guidelines as well imposing the proportionate use of biometric data, emphasizing *inter alia* the importance of the privacy-friendly *local storage* of the data, for example on a card.[38] Finally, Member States joining the EU in 2004 started to explicitly mention biometric data in their data protection legislation. More recently, and since the GDPR, SAs also started to impose fines.[39]

But this did not solve all issues. Discussions remained for example as to whether and as of when biometric data were personal data.[40] The nature, the content and the format of biometric data are however not decisive for the qualification of biometric data as personal data. To the extent that the information 'relates to' an individual who is 'identified or identifiable', taking into account 'all the means likely reasonably to be used' by the controller or any third party,

---

[35] As of the GDPR, the Act No 78-17 of 1978 requires that if a biometric processing necessary for the_identification or verification of the identity of individuals is operated for the government, *an authorization by decree* by the *Conseil d'Etat* after an opinion of the CNIL is needed (art 27.I 2° - ('State biometrics')) safe for those cases mentioned in art 27.II where an order or decision of the organising authority is sufficient.

[36] For an interesting overview, see C. Gayrel, 'The principle of Proportionality Applied to Biometrics in France: Review of Ten Years of CNIL's Deliberations' (2016) *CLSR* 2016, 450 ('Gayrel, Proportionalité in ten years of CNIL's deliberations, 2016'). The French law also provides for so-called 'Unique Authorizations' ('*décisions uniques*'), whereby the CNIL sets pre-conditions for biometric data use in particular domains, upon which controllers can self-certify that they meet such conditions. In that case, no distinct authorization is needed anymore. About France, see also Kindt, Biometric Applications 2013, Chap. 5, 517–550. The CNIL has in the meantime reviewed some of its views and discarded, e.g., the distinction between characteristics that were deemed to leave traces and those which do not.

[37] See also Kindt, Biometric Applications 2013, Chapt. 5, 525, § 433.

[38] See, e.g., the Belgian supervisory authority and its Advice 17/2008 (in French or Dutch); see also the guidelines of the Italian authority of 2005 and 2014, in particular the General Application Order of 12 November 2014, available at https://www.garanteprivacy.it/en/home/docweb/-/docweb-display/docweb/3590114 accessed 30 October 2021.

[39] See, e.g., the Swedish SA, fining in 2019 a school which used facial recognition and the Dutch SA (Autoriteit Persoonsgegevens), imposing in 2019 a fine of 725,000 euros for unlawful fingerprinting of employees for access control, available at https://autoriteitpersoonsgegevens.nl/nl/nieuws/boete-voor-bedrijf-voor-verwerken-vingerafdrukken-werknemers (in Dutch) accessed 30 October 2021.

[40] Some scholars defended earlier the point of view that biometric templates stored on a chip card held by the data subject for 'offline verification' were not to be considered personal data. This was rejected by the Article 29 Working Party in its Working Document on Biometrics of 2003 (p. 5) by stating that 'measures of biometric identification or their digital translation in a template form "are" in most cases (…) personal data', while at the same time also leaving in a footnote the possibility open that templates are not (always) personal data.

biometric information will be personal data.[41] Biometric data will in most applications refer to individuals as, after all, most systems endeavour precisely to link the biometric information to a particular person, whether identified or not, such as to authenticate the claim of someone to have access rights. But even categorization based upon bodily characteristics, such as gender, may lead to 'singling out' individuals and consequences for them. Another question was whether biometric data should be considered 'sensitive data'.[42] Because of the complex technical features, transformations and deployment of biometric systems, many discussions confused the minds and most importantly, remained unsolved. Moreover, the outcome of the assessments of the legality and the proportionality of biometric systems, sometimes for same or similar applications, was far from harmonized either, being influenced by diverging legal traditions, and therefore legal uncertainty reigned.[43]

In the meantime, citizens contested the collection of biometric data for identity and travel documents in national courts, such as in the Netherlands, Germany, France and Belgium. In *Schwarz* and in *Willems*, two cases ending up before the European Court of Justice (the 'ECJ'), individuals refused to have their biometric data recorded for obtaining an ePassport or an identity card because of the lack of guarantees for re-use and claimed that their fundamental rights were not respected. In *Schwarz,* the ECJ stated that the use and storage of biometric data *on the chip* of the ePassport for *verifying* the authenticity of the document or the identity of the holder *met the conditions for limitations* to the fundamental right to data protection.[44] The ECJ missed another chance in *Willems* by not pronouncing clearly the need for legal protection when governments are collecting and storing biometric data.[45] At the same time, the Court pointed to the need of 'examination by the national courts of the compatibility of all national measures relating to the use and storage of biometric data with their national law and, if appropriate, with the European Convention on the Protection of Human Rights and Fundamental Freedoms (...)'.[46] The need for a check with the fundamental rights upon biometric data use is in our view hence clear and confirmed by the ECJ. The ECJ however at the same time *leaves much discretion to the Member States* to review and decide as to when and under which conditions

---

[41] The fact that captured biometric samples have been manipulated and transformed in one or more numerical representations of the characteristic shall not determine whether the information is personal data or not.

[42] About this issue and the qualification of biometric data as personal data, see Kindt, Biometric Applications 2013, Chapt. 3, 89 *et seq.* and Chapt. 4, 319–335.

[43] For the review of the difficulty and the different outcomes of the assessments according to supervisory authority guidelines in that period, see Kindt, Biometric Applications 2013, Chapt. 5, 499–568.

[44] ECJ, C-291/12, *Schwarz v Bochum*, 17.10.2013 ('ECJ, Schwarz 2013'), §58. The Court limited itself by stating that the ePassport Regulation does not provide a legal basis for centralized storage (§61). Although this judgment could be supported to the extent that Regulation No 2252/2004 indeed only mandates the local storage of biometric data under the control of the individual and its use for verification purposes, the Court left Member States to act at their discretion when they seize this opportunity of collection for the ePassport to keep, store, organize and proclaim other uses of the data once collected, while at the same time acknowledging the 'risk that, once fingerprints have been taken pursuant to that provision, the – extremely high quality – data will be stored, perhaps centrally, and used for purposes other than those provided for by that regulation'.

[45] ECJ, C- 446/12 to C-449-12, *Willems e.a. v Burgemeester van Nuth* e.a., 16.4.2015, p. 5 ('ECJ, Willems 2015'). The ECJ stated that the ePassport Regulation does not require Member States to guarantee in their legislation that the data hence collected will not be stored, processed and used for other purposes. The court followed herein a strict legalistic approach.

[46] Ibid., p. 5.

biometric data may be stored. This seems a quite important (political) issue on which Member States may differ.

III.2 The General Data Protection Regulation (EU) 2016/679 and Directive (EU) 2016/680: First and Specific References to Biometric Data

The era when biometric data processing was not specifically regulated – except for large-scale EU systems – now seems past time with the adoption of the GDPR as a framework legislation. We hereunder briefly review and assess whether the legislator in the Union keeps up with the challenges of the 21st century and the increasing spread and uses of biometric data in the private and public sector.

A new definition

The GDPR, as well as the Directive (EU) 2016/680, now contain a definition of biometric data. Biometric data is defined as data that 'result from specific technical processing' 'relating to the physical, physiological or behavioural characteristics of a natural person', 'which allow or confirm the unique identification of that natural person'. Facial images and dactyloscopic data (fingerprints) are further given as examples in the same definition.[47] On the basis of this definition, it seems that the concept of biometric data is narrowed down to biometric processing or the actual use of 'biometric data' being the result of a particular technical operation. The mere collecting and storing of *images* of the face, fingerprint or iris for example *seems* by the legislator hence not considered as biometric data or processing biometric data.[48] Facial images only become biometric data under the GDPR and the Directive (EU) 2016/680 if they are used in a biometric comparison, and more precisely, if they are 'personal data resulting from specific technical processing'. This reduction to a technical concept is important to note, while not being in line with a general understanding of biometric data, such as for example as defined in regulation for the Union's large-scale information systems or the ISO Harmonized Biometric Vocabulary by the stakeholders, considering images of unique human characteristics to fall under the definition of biometric data.[49]

Inclusion of specific processing of 'biometric data' in the list of 'sensitive data'

The Regulation (EU) 2016/679 further added biometric data to the list of 'sensitive' data in Article 9(1) GDPR not as defined but as a processing operation, more specifically 'biometric data *processed for the purpose* of *uniquely identifying* a natural person'. The Directive (EU)

---

[47] Art. 4(14) GDPR and Art. 3(13) Directive (EU) 2016/680. For a critical assessment of the changes introduced into the definition, see Catherine A. Jasserand, 'Avoiding Terminological Confusion Between the Notions of 'Biometrics' and 'Biometric Data': An Investigation into the Meanings of the Terms from a European Data Protection and a Scientific Perspective' (2016) *International Data Protection Law* 63–76 and also Catherine A. Jasserand 'Legal Nature of Biometric Data: From 'Generic' Personal Data to Sensitive Data' (2016) *European Data Protection Law* 297–311.

[48] This seems implied in the reading and as explained in Recital 51 of the GDPR.

[49] See e.g., the European Entry-Exit System ('EES'), where biometric data is defined as including images: '"biometric data" means fingerprint data and facial image' (Regulation 2017/2226, Art. 3.1 (18)). See the adopted ISO Harmonized Biometric Vocabulary ISO/IEC 2382-37:2012, term. 37.03.06 (biometric data), which was taken over in the update of 2017.

2016/680 equally includes in a same way biometric data in the list of special categories.[50] As a result, the processing of biometric data for the purpose of uniquely identifying a natural person, is under the GDPR *forbidden* as a general principle. It is however unclear if the objective of the processing for *identification rather than verification* purposes is important or not. And there is more. As Member States seemingly could not agree on further harmonization, Article 9.4 GDPR states that they may maintain or introduce further conditions, including limitations, with regard to the processing of biometric data (sic). The GDPR will hence not be the only source of specific regulation of biometric data in the Union, notwithstanding its harmonization ambitions. National laws will be equally important which will complicate further development and use of biometric solutions and threaten legal certainty.

In other words, Article 9(1) GDPR refers to *the use* of the biometric data, in particular the processing for a particular purpose, but this is not at all clear. Some may argue that the processing of biometric data *tout court* (whether for identification or verification) is forbidden, save the exemptions of Article 9(2) GDPR. If not, the inclusion of biometric data in this list of 'sensitive data' of Article 9(1) GDPR reflects a quite subjective approach. In such approach, the 'use' is the determining factor, rather than – in an objective approach – the 'fitness' of biometric data for a particular use. A major question hence remains whether this wording of Article 9(1) GDPR *aims to make a distinction between the use of biometric data for its identification functionality and the verification use*. If this were the case, the local storage and use of biometric data solely for verification, may not fall in this list of special categories and hence not fall under the prohibition of Article 9(1) GDPR, save exceptions.[51] It further does not solve the earlier discussion as to whether biometric images and data could presumably reveal information relating to race or ethnic origin and relating to health. National courts have previously taken the position that facial images are 'sensitive'.[52] This was also a concern by some supervisory authorities. This is not addressed by the GDPR. Finally, defining biometric data as 'sensitive' if used for purposes of identification, may address the risks of identification and maybe tracking, but does not take the many other risks to values and rights as listed above into account, such as if emotion recognition technology would be used to screen candidates in a job interview. It should therefore be further evaluated whether this Article 9 GDPR reaches its objectives of providing data protection to individuals upon the processing of their bodily data. Furthermore, supervisory authorities of particular countries, such as in France, also continue to provide authorizations and guidelines, continuing hereby their own views and tradition.[53]

---

[50] Compare however with Art. 6 on the processing of sensitive data in the modernized Convention 108+ and the Explanatory Report available at https://rm.coe.int/convention-108-convention-for-the-protection-of-individuals-with-regar/16808b36f1 accessed 30 October 2021; see also Consultative Committee of the Convention for the Protection of Individuals with regard to automatic processing of personal Data, Progress Report on the Application of the Principles of Convention 108 to the Collection and Processing of Biometric Data, T-PD(2013)06, 20.9.2013.

[51] See also Els Kindt, 'Having Yes, Using No? About the New Legal Regime for Biometric Data' (2018) *CLSR* 523–538, available at http://authors.elsevier.com/sd/article/S0267364917303667 ('Kindt, Having yes, using no 2018').

[52] See, e.g., the Dutch Supreme Court: Hoge Raad, 23.3.2010, LJN BK6331.

[53] CNIL, *Délibération n°2016-187* of 30 June 2016 relating to the 'unique authorization' for access control to places, devices and computer applications in the workplace based on templates stored in a database (AU-053), 15 p., available at https://www.cnil.fr/sites/default/files/atoms/files/au-053.pdf accessed 30 October 2021.

Data Protection Impact Assessment (DPIA) required

Regulation (EU) 2016/679 further addresses biometric data by imposing accountability upon the controller and an obligation for a data protection impact assessment (DPIA) by Article 35.3(b) GDPR, *inter alia* when special categories of data are processed *on a large scale.*[54] Such assessment will also be required if biometric data are processed for uniquely identifying persons upon the *condition* that it is *on a large scale.*[55] However, Art. 35.1 GDPR is also likely to impose such DPIA as well, since biometric technology is new and because of the nature of biometric data. In case the DPIA indicates that the processing *would result in a high risk in the absence of or which the controller cannot mitigate by appropriate measures* 'in terms of available technology and costs of implementation',[56] hence when *residual risks remain high*[57] and the data controller cannot find sufficient measures to cope with them, prior consultation with the supervisory authority (SA) will be further needed. The SAs of *inter alia* France and the UK are further providing more guidance on how to conduct a DPIA,[58] also for biometric applications.[59]

One could think of measures and available technology to provide safeguards and to cope with particular risks, such as for example by using so-called 'protected templates' allowing for the transformation of the original biometric data into irreversible, unlinkable and revocable templates. This technique, which allows for the creation of *multiple* biometric identifiers *and pseudo identities*, meets various fundamental rights concerns discussed above, including the revocability of the identifiers, and preserves privacy and data protection rights of individuals in many aspects.[60] Implementing such technology, fit for most characteristics with increasingly good performance, also for central databases, is a good example of data protection by

---

54 See and compare with a similar but not the same obligation in Art. 27 Directive (EU) 2016/680. For guidance, also with regard to the concept of 'large scale', see Article 29 Data Protection Working Party, *Guidelines on Data Protection Impact Assessment (DPIA) and determining whether processing is 'likely to result in a high risk' for the purposes of Regulation 2016/679*, WP 248 rev.01, 4.10. 2017.

55 The European Data Protection Board requested in 2018, for consistency purposes, all Member States submitting their draft lists requiring a DPIA to add biometric data processing for uniquely identifying, if in combination with at least one other requirement, without prejudice to Art. 35(2) GDPR.

56 Recital 84 GDPR. See Art. 36 GDPR.

57 An example of an unacceptable high residual risk given by the Art. 29 WP is where 'the data subjects may encounter significant, or even irreversible, consequences, which they may not overcome, and/or when it seems obvious that the risk will occur.' In the biometric context, this could be where the data subject cannot change its biometric credentials in case of theft of its biometric identity details (WP 29 Guidelines on DPIA (WP248), p. 18).

58 See, e.g., France, where the CNIL published an update of its PIA Guides, 26.2.2018, available at https://www.cnil.fr/en/cnil-publishes-update-its-pia-guides accessed 30 October 2021. It includes besides explanation of the methodology and a template, also a software tool for conducting the DPIA.

59 See e.g., France, CNIL, *AU-053. Grille D'Analyse. Autorisation unique AU-053, Contrôle d'accès biométrique avec base centrale*, 27.9.2016, 11 p., available at https://www.cnil.fr/fr/biometrie-un-nouveau-cadre-pour-le-controle-dacces-biometrique-sur-les-lieux-de-travail accessed 30 October 2021.

60 For a description of the concept, see Jeroen Breebaart Christoph Busch, Justine Grave and Els Kindt, 'A Reference Architecture for Biometric Template Protection Based on Pseudo Identities', in Brömme, A. (ed.), *BioSig 2008. Proceedings of the Special Interest Group on Biometrics and Electronic Signatures* (Bonn, Gesellschaft für Informatik, 2008), pp. 25–37; see also Kindt, Biometric Applications 2013, Chap. 8, 794–806, the ISO standard ISO/IEC 24745:2011 in this regard and Christina-Angeliki Toli and B. Preneel (supervisor), *Secure and Privacy-Preserving Biometric Systems*, Ph.D, 2018, available at https://limo.libis.be/primo-explore/fulldisplay?docid=LIRIAS2313297&context=L&vid=Lirias&search_scope=Lirias&tab=default_tab&lang=en_US&fromSitemap=1 accessed 30 October 2021.

design. However, data controllers seem not to be much guided and more specific directions or requirements by the regulator in this regard would be very much welcomed and even necessary for a further general take up of the positive aspects of biometric technology, such as the ability to verify identities (as opposed to identify).

Evaluation

The *collection* of biometric *images* and the *central storage* of the data does not seem to be tackled by the recent EU framework legislation discussed above. The new definition of biometric data in the GDPR and the Directive (EU) 2016/680 is also debated. As explained, a database with images of face or fingerprints without biometric processing may well be *not* considered a database with biometric data and therefore also not be subject to the general prohibition or DPIA requirement as discussed above. One should understand however that it is precisely such database that is the pre-condition for and allows for biometric identification and which hence may pose a profound risk. This also applies when the data are 'public' or are harvested from the Internet.[61] In the last two decades, supervisory authorities have mainly considered databases as a risk for the fundamental rights and freedoms of the data subjects. Taking the 'fitness' of data to be used by automated means for identification or identity verification rather than any actual (future) use, could be a more defendable approach when developing a legal protective framework.[62] The legislator should also attach importance to the possibility of control by the data subject, for example, by requiring by default the local storage of 'biometric data', for example on a personal object or personal 'wallet', allowing to control one's biometric identity, save well defined exceptions. Once the data of such special nature are collected and centrally stored without many safeguards, it is far more difficult to control the further use and abuse of the collected 'biometric data'.

Furthermore, and based on the above, it seems that the European legislator and the courts so far *leave it to the Member States and to the controllers* to tackle and solve the biometric data protection issues. The GDPR imposes upon the controller herein an important responsibility. Because of the legal uncertainties and the possible different national legal traditions, laws and guidelines in the Member States, the DPIA obligation and a data protection by design and by default obligation for controllers, the present legal framework risks not only to not offer the required protection but also to impose important burdens and increased liability for the controllers and processors. The *GDPR does not seem to be able to tackle modern new technologies such as biometric systems and to provide legal certainty*. In conclusion, we are of the opinion that the issues and risks of processing biometric data are not sufficiently addressed by the GDPR. The question under which conditions the central storage of biometric data – which in principle allows for identification but also for 'function creep' and security risks – is proportionate or not, and identifying and other bodily information, including emotions, can be processed (or not) and which safeguards are needed, remains open.

Excellent research is further being done in various other research centres in the world improving the performances of these techniques for privacy and data protection by design and by default.

[61] Clearview 'harvested' 3 billion of these images and provided them to law enforcement. The German regulator now ordered Clearview to remove particular biometric data (see also below).

[62] This approach is e.g., taken in the California Consumer Protection Act of 2018 (Section 3(e) CCPA).

IV. DOUBLE FRAMEWORK AND DOUBLE NECESSITY AND PROPORTIONALITY TEST

We reiterate that the regulatory framework relevant to biometric data processing in the Union is not only about understanding the GDPR, but requires in addition the grasping of the fundamental rights of privacy[63] and data protection,[64] amongst others, and the interplay of the fundamental rights' principles (and strict conditions for any permitted interference further to Article 8 §2 ECHR and Article 52(1) EU Charter) with the prescriptive rules of the Directive 95/46/EC, now replaced by the GDPR.[65] For example, the ECtHR has stated in the – for biometric data milestone – decision *S. and Marper* that beyond a person's name, private life may include *other means of personal identification* and stated that not only the retention of DNA samples and profiles, but also the *retention of fingerprints*, taken in the context of criminal proceedings and *permanently recorded* in a nationwide database and regularly processed by automated means for criminal identification purposes *without consent and appropriate safeguards* constituted an interference with the right to respect for private life.[66] In several cases, courts have judged that the processing of various biometric characteristics posed in several circumstances risks or interferes with the rights to privacy and data protection, in particular where there is no fair balance between competing public and private interests.[67] Courts may rather easily accept a legitimate aim or objective of general recognized interest,[68] for an interference with these fundamental rights posed by the use of biometric technology, such as the aiding of the identification of future offenders,[69] the finding of suspects or protecting against the fraudulent use of passports and the illegal entry into the Union.[70] But the review of the compatibility with the

---

[63] The concept of privacy is a broad concept 'not susceptible to exhaustive definition' and shall be reviewed from case to case, also for biometric applications. See also above. 'Data privacy' has become part of Art. 8 ECHR and was much needed, as there is so far no distinct right on data protection under the European Convention on Human Rights of 1950. Non-respect of 'data privacy' is hence judged by the ECtHR under Art. 8 ECHR. See e.g., ECtHR, Aycaguer 2017.

[64] About both notions, see e.g., Gloria González Fuster, *The Emergence of Personal Data Protection as a Fundamental Right of the EU* (Springer, 2014), 274.

[65] See also Parliamentary Assembly of the Council of Europe, *The need for a global consideration of the human rights implications of biometrics*, Doc. 12522, 16.2.2011 available at http://assembly.coe.int/nw/xml/XRef/Xref-XML2HTML-en.asp?fileid=17968&lang=en accessed 30 October 2021 and EDPS, *Developing a 'toolkit' for assessing the necessity of measures that interfere with fundamental rights*, Background paper, 16.6.2016.

[66] ECtHR, *S. and Marper v the United Kingdom* [GC]GC, nos. 30562/04 and 30566/04, 4.12.2008, §66 and § 86 ('ECtHR, S. and Marper 2008'). See also and compare with ECtHR, *Gaughran v. The United Kingdom* 2020.

[67] For example, the systematic or permanent recording of voice, which by some is argued to be in the public domain, for further analysis by police in conjunction with other personal data is considered as amounting to interference in *P.G. and J.H. v the United Kingdom* (no 44787/98, 25.9.2001, §§ 59–60). This decision is also relevant in the present discussion about the use of face recognition by police (see *below*).

[68] Art. 52(1) EU Charter requires that the limitation shall 'genuinely' meet 'objectives of general interest recognized by the Union' or the need to protect the rights and freedoms of others, while the law needed shall at all times respect 'the essence' of the rights and freedoms at stake, i.e., shall respect the core of a right and cannot empty such right or freedom of all meaning.

[69] ECtHR, S. and Marper 2008, § 100.

[70] ECJ, Schwarz 2013, § 40 and § 47.

rule of law and of the *necessity in a democratic society,* i.e., that the measure answers a 'pressing social need' without any other alternative less infringing solution while being *relevant and sufficient*, and *effective* and *proportionate* (in that the measure is the least intruding and does not go beyond what is needed *to achieve the aim* by applying specific safeguards) has proven to be far more challenging.[71] One should further note that the ECJ requires 'strict necessity'. This check of biometric systems under the fundamental rights framework, in particular the necessity and proportionality test, is hence not easy to apply but remains the basic test to be made at all times when there is (a risk of) interference.

This fundamental rights' test is not to be confused with the other necessity and proportionality test and requirements set forth in the Directive 95/46/EC, presently the GDPR,[72] which *come in addition* once the necessity and proportionality test under the fundamental rights' framework has been made. Necessity has under this framework an own independent meaning and shall be interpreted and applied in a way which reflects the goal.[73] It should hence be clear that *just data protection legislation will not be sufficient to approach biometric data processing*. The national courts and SAs however have struggled with applying both frameworks to biometric data processing, especially in the era when the risks of biometric data processing under both fundamental rights and data protection were not yet fully acknowledged. The risk based approach in the GDPR now reinforces this idea of a proper assessment under the fundamental rights and freedoms. This is quite clear in the wording of for example Article 35 GDPR imposing a DPIA, as discussed above. This will hopefully put an end to the one-dimensional view that data protection legislation provides for the rules when interfering with the fundamental right to privacy (and data protection) and that when only applying such data protection legislation, this would meet fundamental rights concerns.

V. 'LEGAL POLITICS'

The difficulties in applying the double review of biometric applications under both the fundamental rights and data protection regime brings us to legal politics. There are some interesting observations when reviewing the developments in biometric use, politics and regulation since 2001 until now.

First, while the risks to the values and freedoms at stake when using high-tech biometric data processing are largely known, based upon various studies and (parliamentary) reports as mentioned above, including by the Council of Europe, at least for 'traditional' biometric data, a *general consensus* amongst Member States on how to deal with biometric data collection and use is *far from being reached.* This is also reflected in the provision on biometric data in the GDPR leaving the possibility for Member States to impose further conditions. Some countries are more 'sensitive' to the urgency to counter the risks and have already taken or will take

---

[71] ECtHR, S. and Marper 2008. About these criteria, see also Kindt, Biometric Applications 2013, Chapt. 5, 456–499.

[72] The data protection legislation proportionality requirements are set forth in the general principles of Art. 5 GDPR and the lawful processing requirements set forth in Art. 6 GDPR. About the need for this 'double proportionality test', see also Kindt, Biometric Applications 2013, Chap.6, 570–572.

[73] ECJ, C-524/06, *Huber v Germany* , 3.4.2008 ('Huber, 2008').

soon more specific legislative action, in particular outside the Union.[74] Some countries in the Union have also not awaited the initiatives of the EU Commission to further regulate, such as France by requiring a decree, an order or authorization by the SA or allowing '*règlements types*' developed by the SA, or the Netherlands, by allowing the use of biometric systems if necessary for authentication or security purposes. The patchwork of biometric regulations will hence remain, even with the GDPR, leaving room in the Union for country specific biometric legislation save appropriate initiatives of the Commission for a common regulation. For biometric data processing by competent authorities in the law enforcement sector, national laws implementing Directive 2016/680 will reign as well.

Secondly, the position of the courts as to the use of unique characteristics of citizens by governments and the State, while possible useful for security but permitting easily a slide toward surveillance, is also ambivalent. After the political choice of the Union to use the data in travel documents for border security and in its large-scale systems[75] for a variety of purposes, the ECJ is very prudent and *leaves it so far to the Member States* to decide for which period and how to store the data once collected pursuant to Regulation (EC) No 2252/2004. We refer hereby in particular to its decision in *Willems* 2015 discussed above.[76] The Court herein did not – rather surprisingly as compared to its (more recent) overall concern for effective protection of human rights – take the opportunity to clarify the complex issues of biometric data collection and use. As a result, and since there is not a political consensus as to the relevant importance of the interests at stake or as how to protect best these interests, the margin of appreciation of the Member States is wider[77] and States have more freedom to regulate in accordance with their own traditions, concerns and scale of values. This allows the judges to deploy varying proportionality criteria which is not without importance as biometric databases of all citizens may provide States a lot of power over such citizens.

Indeed, last, but not least, one of the main *questions as to* whether and under which conditions third parties but also governments are authorized to maintain *central databases* with unique characteristics of humans is not solved. As the Article 29 Working party already clearly pointed out in 2005 in the context of the implementation of the ePassport Regulation: 'Any central database would increase the risks of misuse and misappropriation. It would also intensify the dangers of abuse and function creep'.[78] This group of national supervisory authority

---

[74] This seems especially the case, e.g., in some States and cities in the US. This also includes moratorium bills for systems inferring emotions or a person's sentiment. See A. Kak, 'The State of Play and Open Questions for the Future' in A. Kak (ed.), *Regulating Biometrics. Global Approaches and Urgent Questions* (AINow Institute, New York University, New York, 2020), available at https://ainowinstitute.org/regulatingbiometrics.pdf accessed 30 October 2021 (Kak, State of Play, 2020).

[75] We refer to Eurodac, VIS, SIS II, ... to name a few, while more are coming into full operation soon, including the Entry-Exit system (see Regulation (EU) 2017/2226) for third-country nationals). See also the interoperability regulations (EU) 2019/817 and (EU) 2019/818 which provide for these EU large-scale information systems for several additional technical components and biometric functionalities aiming at reaching full interoperability based upon biometric identifiers.

[76] For a critical note about this decision, see Tijmen Wisman, 'Willems: Giving Member States the Prints and Data Protection the Finger' (2015) *European Data Protection Law Review* 245–248.

[77] This follows clearly from the case law. See on this aspect also Kindt, Biometric Applications 2013, Chap.5, 491–494.

[78] Article 29 Data Protection Working Party, *Opinion 3/2005 on Implementing the Council Regulation (EC) No 2252/2004 of 13 December 2004 on standards for security features and biometrics in passports and travel documents issued by Member States,* 30.9.2005, WP112, pp. 8–9. See also and

('SA') representatives, now the European Data Protection Board (EDPB), hereby expressed more than 12 years earlier *clear reservations about any centralized European or national database containing biometric data*. This issue is politically quite sensitive. In the UK, for example a previous attempt to build a biometric identity data base was in vain[79] as it was in the Netherlands.[80] A political and legal battle about the set up of a centralized biometric database of identity card and ePassports holders has been going on in France as well,[81] while in Israel a central biometric identity database could only be set up after several court proceedings, several modifications and with a number of safeguards.[82]

Governments are interested to establish not only registries with alphanumeric identity details of its citizens and others, but also databases with biometric identifiers linked to such identities. Such central databases risk however for allowing for much more than only identification or reliable ID documents, as they could also be re-used for crime investigations[83] but also for surveillance, which is by some defended for example in cases of public health emergencies, such as a pandemic, raising plenty of fundamental rights concerns. At the same time, such database could be useful when checking during pre-enrolment for avoiding that individuals – often with criminal intentions – obtain ID documents under different names or with forged or morphed images and hence adopt more than one identity. The *fair balancing of the interests*, of the governmental objectives and individual rights and freedoms alike, including the right to respect for privacy and data protection, shall be done very precisely, with appropriate safeguards if needed, in a democratic society, and *shall not be done purely formal*

---

compare with Huber 2008 in which the Court considered the centralized register for security, police services and crime investigation of foreign nationals only was not strictly necessary and discriminatory.

[79] See the UK Identity Cards Act 2006, which was repealed by the Identity Documents Act 2010 and whereby previously collected biometric data was all deleted.

[80] See also the critical report for the Netherlands: Max Snijder, *Het biometrisch paspoort in Nederland: crash of zachte landing*, WRR nr. 51, 2010, 159, https://library.oapen.org/handle/20.500.12657/33961 accessed 30 October 2021.

[81] See the project 'titres électroniques sécurisés' (TES) and the French law ('*décret*') of 28.10.2016 concerning the central biometric database of all French nationals. See also in Belgium the (negative) advises no 39/2017 and no 19/2018 of the Belgian supervisory authority in relation to the Bill relating to the prolonged retention of fingerprints collected for Belgian passports and travel documents to combat fraud. The Belgian constitutional court in its decision of 14 January 2021 upheld the relevant provision art. 27 of the law of 25 November 2018 mandating the integration of a digital image of two fingerprints in the Belgian eID card.

[82] For Israel, see the 5770-2009 Act, as amended. The central database aims to ensure reliable ID documents and to combat double enrolment (i.e., of the same individual obtaining various identities and plural ID documents). Safeguards include *inter alia* the *isolation* of the central biometric database, *separate* storage of the biometric data and the corresponding alphanumerical identity details, *two separate competent authorities* (Ministry of the Interior and the Biometric Database Authority) and the assignment of a number *other* than the national ID number (based upon presentation by Roy Friedman, Chief Executive Director, Identity and Biometric Applications Unit, Israel National Cyber Directorate, *National Approach for Identity*, 2018, Lausanne).

[83] For example, the use by the large-scale biometric databases in the Union of the Automated Fingerprint Identification System (AFIS system) used since long by police authorities, and more recently as central Biometric 'Matching' System (BMS) allows interoperability between such systems and points in this direction of reuse of these systems for law enforcement. See also Foegle, Jean-Phillipe, 'Sans doigt, ni loi : La CJUE donne son "feu vert" à la biosurveilance', *La Revue des droits de l'homme*, 2015, 22 p., available at https://revdh.revues.org/1394 accessed 30 October 2021 and in general Graham and Wood, Digitizing surveillance, 2003.

or theoretically.[84] Any such need to centralize biometric data, for example to detect double enrolment for combating identity theft, should hence be carefully assessed and it may well be that such centralization is not required.[85] Simple measures, such as for example requiring photographs to be taken by governmental services at enrolment for obtaining identity documents, are often useful to tackle complicated issues. While one cannot deny that identity theft is on the rise in recent years, both in the US and in the EU, and biometric identifiers have been pushed forward as a means to reveal misuse and to make identity theft more difficult, central databases kept by governments pose specific risks as well, especially if maintained by the government. Law enforcement authorities also increasingly rely on databases combining alphanumerical data with biometric data.[86] Databases in combination with face recognition overall could be used without knowledge of individuals who are screened on public place as all were suspects, both in Europe as in the US for example.[87] But central repositories in the private sector equally raise concern, as being *inter alia* an easy target for attacks and for risks of loss of anonymity, risks of function creep and access by law enforcement. Overall, whether the data are kept by government or private players, is no longer so important, as access to the collections of private entities will always remain a risk and be possible. Biometric data hereby play a crucial role, as a cross-over index or unique identifier for all these databases, permitting to link and make databases interoperable.[88] Misuse by biometric technology requires in most cases a (central) repository against which can be compared, and such *biometric repositories* risk to be established precisely by such third parties, such as social network services, employers, banks, sport clubs without safeguards for the rights and interests of the individuals. Biometric data, while fit for efficient procedures, convenience or for bringing more security under specific and strict conditions, hence also allow for mixed uses and re-purposing of data *if centrally stored without safeguards*, risking to bring society gradually closer to a policing and surveillance society.[89] Early 2020, there was a public outcry when it became known that multiple police

---

[84] ECtHR, *Bărbulescu v Romania*, No. 61496/08, 5.9.2017,§ 139.

[85] See Claude Castelluccia and Daniel Le Métayer, *Titres électroniques sécurisés : la centralisation des données biométriques est-elle vraiment inévitable ? Analyse comparative de quelques architectures,* Inria, 1.2.2017, 15 p. available at https://www.inria.fr/actualite/actualites-inria/titres-electroniques-securises-et-centralisation-des-donnees accessed 30 October 2021; see also Edgar Whitley and Gus Husein, 'Global Identity Policies and Technology. Do We Understand the Question?' (2011–2012) *Keesing Journal of Documents & Identities*, available at http://www.keesingjournalofdocuments.com/content /Identity_management/Keesing_Identity_Management_2012_Whitley_Hosein.pdf accessed 30 October 2021: Whitley and Hosein in our view correctly pointed out: 'Too often the complexity of implementing an identity policy is concealed through the undefined and indeterminate use of concepts including identification, biometrics, enrolment and verification. Despite commonly held beliefs, not all transactions require identification.'

[86] For example, the Schengen Information System (SIS) II.

[87] For reports on these widely used practices based on face recognition, see fn 4 *above.* Face recognition was also illegally used by the Belgian federal police at Brussels Airport in 2019 and before, as revealed in a report by the Belgian Supervisory authority for police information. These practices are also heavily debated in the UK: see, e.g., Gaetan Portal, *Police facial recognition system faces legal challenge,* 25.7.2018, available at https://www.bbc.co.uk/news/uk-44928792 accessed 30 October 2021.

[88] Paul De Hert and Annemarie Sprokkereef, 'Regulation for Biometrics as a Primary Key for Interoperability?' in Els Kindt and Lorenz Müller (eds), *D.3.10. Biometrics in identity management*, Frankfurt, FIDIS, 2007, pp. 47–55.

[89] This risk was also mentioned by Van der Ploeg a decade ago several times: '(…) the trend towards multi-modal and distant sensing indicates a decreasing sense of the necessity of actually asking people for

forces in the US and elsewhere were deploying face recognition tools with poor accuracy requirements and performance, while using and having the disposition of the facial images database of Clearview, a New York based facial recognition company, having scraped the Internet for such images of more than 3 billion users, allowing such forces to identify a huge number of individuals.[90] The unregulated use of face recognition by police both in Europe as in the US hence already clearly illustrates that governments are interested in using biometric data available everywhere and retained in central repositories, as well as the lack and urgent need for specific regulation, including of the underlying reference databases.

VI. NEED FOR LEGISLATION: BY THE NATIONAL LEGISLATOR OR ON EU LEVEL?

If a society decides that biometric data brings progress and is desirable, its use cannot be stopped.[91] Secure identification becomes very important in this automated, online and distant information society, let alone in the Internet-of-Things context soon to come, requiring constant interaction, also with humans, in which biometric data could add an additional factor of security but also of convenience and useability. At the same time, biometric data processing is invasive at least in that it by its present own definition allows to uniquely identify individuals and affects individuals, also when their behaviour is constantly monitored. If massive collection of such data is permitted, citizens risk to be at all times identifiable, traceable and monitored. This is the ultimate dream of governments in a dystopian society, wanting to control at all times the citizens, who never know when they are tracked and traced.[92] If biometric data processing is here to stay, appropriate legislation is needed. Some have argued that the traditional guardians in democracies, the parliaments, have already been too long absent when needed to scrutinizing government actions.[93] It is interesting to note that the regulation

their cooperation, and constitutes a good step towards involuntary, behind-their-back scrutiny and virtual bodily searches. (…); beyond the level of individual rights, it might affect the quality of democratic societies, and the power relations that constitute them' in Irma Van der Ploeg, 'Chapter 13. Security in the Danger Zone: Normative Issues of Next Generation Biometrics' in Mordini and DTzovaras, Second Generation Biometrics 2012, (287) 300.

[90] This practice led to reaction of regulators worldwide, including the Australian SA and the UK SA. For example, the Hamburg SA ordered Clearview to delete the biometric hash data after it received a complaint by an individual. See Hamburg SA, Consultation, 27.1.2021, available at https://noyb.eu/sites/default/files/2021-01/545_2020_Anh%C3%B6rung_CVAI_ENG_Redacted.PDF; see also C. Stupp, *Clearview AI Raises Disquiet at Privacy Regulators,* 4.2.2021, WSJPro.

[91] This also applies to soft and the so-called second-generation biometrics in all its kinds and uses. See on this subject the monograph Mordini and Tzovaras, Second Generation Biometrics 2012.

[92] See also and compare with the theories of the French social theorist M. Foucault, pointing to 'biopolitics' as techniques to manage and control entire populations and using the term 'biopower' as 'techniques for achieving the subjugations of bodies and the control of populations': Michel Foucault, *Naissance de la biopolitique, Cours au Collège de France (1978-79)* François Ewald, Alessandro Fontana and Michel Senellart (eds) (Seuil/Gallimard, 2004).

[93] See Juliet Lodge, 'The Dark Side of the Moon: Accountability, Ethics and New Biometrics', in Mordini and Tzovaras, Second Generation Biometrics 2012, (305) 309; see also e.g., Scottish Government, *Independent Advisory Group on the Use of Biometric Data in Scotland,* March 2018, 92 p. which clearly states the need for legislation for the retention of custody images by law enforcement. The early study EU Commission and IPTS, Biometrics a the Frontiers, 2005 as well as the group of data

of DNA has been confronted with similar delays and hesitations for regulation, while several risks were known. Biometric data, similar in some ways to other highly personal data, such as DNA, requires a profound reflection and legislation as it cannot be compared with any other 'ordinary' personal data.

We make hereunder some further observations.

First, in the last 15 years, data protection authorities and a few legislators in the Union grappled with the assessment and (refusal of) authorization of biometric data use.[94] One of the outcomes of our earlier comparative research was that the application of the proportionality principle by courts and authorities – while being very important – can be highly political and does not offer 'ready solutions' for biometric applications. This needs rather to be ensured and strengthened by legislation forbidding or allowing for such applications while imposing specific (minimum) safeguards.[95] This is also because of the – by case law imposed – positive obligations of Member States to protect individuals' fundamental rights and freedoms. For interfering applications, legislation is needed specifying the finality and the required safeguards.

The next question is for which legitimate aims could law authorize biometric data processing, including central storage? The GDPR allows for the processing of special categories of personal data, including the processing of biometric data for the purpose of 'uniquely identifying' in ten described exceptions to the general prohibition. In five of the ten exemptions of Article 9(2) GDPR, additional *Union or Member State law*, providing safeguards for the fundamental rights and interests of the individuals concerned, is needed. We here mention one important exemption ground of Article 9(2)(g) GDPR, i.e., *necessity* for reasons of *substantial public interest provided law is adopted* which shall be *proportionate* and *respect the essence* of the *right to data protection and shall provide suitable and specific safeguards for the fundamental rights and interests of the data subjects*. The French SA has pointed in the previous years to this exception ground for biometric applications for its authorizations.[96] One could think of the legislator considering adequate *border control* as a substantial public interest for collecting, storing and processing biometric data subject to precise safeguards. Also, its use for asylum application and migration purposes could be envisioned, although several problems remain here. But one shall keep asking if a law allowing biometric technology, such as face recognition, in public places collecting faces from all citizens, by governments, and even law enforcement, could ever be strictly necessary and proportionate while respecting the essence of fundamental rights. For the prevention, investigation, detection and prosecution of criminal offences, the basis is broader in that such is allowed for Member States (a) 'where strictly necessary, subject to appropriate safeguards' *and* in combination with (b) law, the

---

protection authorities in their Madrid Declaration of 2009 (available at https://thepublicvoice.org/madrid-declaration/ accessed 30 October 2021) also clearly identified already at that time the need for new legislation for biometric applications.

[94] For example, in France, C. Gayel Proportionalité in ten years of CNIL's deliberations, 2016.

[95] Kindt, Biometric Applications 2013, Chap. 9, 831 *et seq.*; Paul De Hert, 'Biometrics and the Challenge to Human Rights in Europe. Need for Regulation and Regulatory Distinctions' in Patrizio Campisi (ed.), *Security and Privacy in Biometrics* (Springer, 2013) 369–413.

[96] Note that contrary to Art. 8.4 of the Directive 95/46/EC, authorizations by decision of the supervisory authorities for the processing of 'sensitive' data for substantial public interest is no longer sufficient.

protection of a vital interest *or* if the data were manifestly made public.[97] For the 40th anniversary of the Convention 108, the Committee of the Convention issued Guidelines on Facial Recognition. These Guidelines *urge for appropriate domestic law*, for specific use and when strictly necessary and proportionate, specifying the specific purposes and legal basis, for all different phases, including the creation of databases, and adapted safeguards. [98] This should be compared with the approach in the US, where several cities and States already ban face recognition and awaited federal legislation rather tends to point in the direction of a ban of use by governments including police.[99] These Guidelines should also be compared with the proposed AI Act 2021, discussed below.

Secondly, the responsibility of the States to regulate the automated use of unique and other human characteristics cannot be underestimated. It is exemplary that the ECtHR has stated in particular that *the use of modern scientific techniques* in the criminal-justice system *could not be allowed at any cost and without carefully balancing* the potential benefits of the extensive use of such techniques against important private-life interests. Any State claiming a pioneer role in the development of new technologies bears special responsibility for 'striking the right balance'.[100] In striking such balance, safeguards and additional technology which may implement data protection by design and by default should be looked at. Not only the use of templates should be preferred, but also additional safeguards, including the use of so-called 'protected templates' as discussed above as well as other measures and guarantees.[101] But where Member States take initiatives or responsibility, this will be to the detriment of harmonization. Much is therefore expected of the European legislator and the European Data Protection Board in that regard. The EU Commission is sensible to the debate and stressed in its 2020 White Paper on artificial intelligence the need to respect fundamental rights when deploying remote biometric identification.[102] In its recent proposal for Regulation for AI ('Proposed AI Act 2021'), the Commission proposes to prohibit (only) 'real time' remote biometric identification in publicly accessible spaces *by law enforcement* except in three defined situations for substantial public interest, outweighing the fundamental rights risks. The proposal requires that such exceptions are based upon detailed *national legislation*, are subject to an express and specific *autorisa-*

---

[97] Art. 10 Directive (EU) 2016/680. Especially 'if the data were manifestly made public' might raise further discussion. See also EDPB, *Guidelines 3/2019 on Processing of Personal Data through Video Devices, on Video Surveillance,* January 29, 2020, which state in the context of the GDPR that merely 'entering into the range of the camera does not imply that the data subject intends to make public special categories of data relating to him or her' (p. 17).

[98] Consultative Committee of the Convention for the Protection of Individuals with regard to Automatic Processing of Personal Data, *Guidelines on Facial Recognition*, T-PD(2020)03rev4, 28.1.2021, 19.

[99] Kak, 'The State of Play', pp. 16–43.

[100] ECtHR, S. and Marper 2008, § 112.

[101] For examples of other data protection by design measures, in the context of border control, see e.g., Pagona Tsormpatzoudi, Diana Dimitrova, Jessica Schroers, and Els Kindt, 'Privacy by Design – The Case of Automated Border Control' in *Privacy and identity Management for the Future Internet in the Age of Globalisation,* Chapter 10, 2014, Berlin, Springer, also available at http://papers.ssrn.com/sol3/papers.cfm?abstract_id=2548516 accessed 30 October 2021.

[102] EU Commission, *White Paper on Artificial Intelligence: a European Approach to Excellence and Trust*, COM(2020)65final, February 19, 2020, pp. 21-22, available at https://ec.europa.eu/info/publications/white-paper-artificial-intelligence-european-approach-excellence-and-trust_en accessed 30 October 2021.

tion by a judicial authority or by an independent administrative authority of a Member State for allowing this on its territory and additional *safeguards*, including limitations in time and place, logging and human oversight.[103] However, 'post' remote biometric identification by law enforcement and 'real-time' remote biometric identification systems in publicly accessible spaces for purposes *other than by law enforcement*, including by competent authorities, is *not* covered by the prohibition in the proposed AI Act 2021. Cities, intending to use biometric identification, could still consider to do so, for example, based upon substantial public interest, such as public order or safety, subject to the (vague) GDPR requirements. The proposal at the same time considers the use of AI for emotion recognition and biometric categorization systems as AI systems with 'limited risks', which is in our view questionable.

Thirdly, and as stated above, it is clear that *general data protection legislation alone will not be sufficient* to approach biometric data processing. A fundamental rights assessment is key to any biometric data application. This comes in addition to the assessment under the data protection legislation. Controllers however are on their own when conducting a DPIA, albeit with the help of the data protection officer if any, in assessing the specific risks and in determining the possible safeguards. Such safeguards could *inter alia* include as mentioned the use of protected templates,[104] but also the decomposition of biometric images in separate databases and other differential privacy measures.[105] More (harmonized) guidelines and legislation – without being technology specific – in order to protect the values and rights of individuals on EU level would therefore be welcomed. The Proposed Artificial Intelligence Act 2021 currently suggests for the conformity assessment of remote biometric identification systems by a third party. Self-regulation, which emerged for example for face recognition by social networks after some public debate 'Face Facts' in the US, or when IBM and Microsoft decided in 2020 to stop selling facial recognition systems to law enforcement and Amazon placed a moratorium,[106] could be helpful as well. Also certification of certain biometric pro-

---

[103] EU Commission, *Proposal for a Regulation of the European Parliament and of the Council laying down Harmonised Rules on Artificial Intelligence (Artificial Intelligence Act) and Amending Certain Union Legislative Acts,* 2021/0106(COD), 21.4.2021, 108 p. and Annexes 1 to 9 (COM(2021)206 final, 21.4.2021, 17 p. ('Proposed AI Act 2021'). In the initial proposal, the three narrowly defined situations are for : (i) identification of potential victims of crime, including missing children; (ii) certain threats to the life or physical safety of natural persons or of a (*sic*)terrorist attack; and (iii) the detection, localisation, identification or prosecution of perpetrators or suspects of the criminal offences referred to in Council Framework Decision 2002/584/JHA38 (on Arrest Warrant) if those criminal offences are punishable in the Member State concerned by a custodial sentence or a detention order for a maximum period of at least three years and as defined in national legislation. For the reference databases, the proposal only requires that such should be 'appropriate' for each use case (cons.20, p. 22). The EDPB and EDPS at the same time plead for a full ban: see https://edpb.europa.eu/news/news/2021/edpb-edps-call-ban-use-ai-automated-recognition-human-features-publicly-accessible_en. An extensive analysis of the proposed AI Act 2021 is however out of the scope of this chapter.

[104] See Anil K Jain, 'Fingerprint Template Protection: From Theory to Practice' in P. Campisi (ed.), *Security and Privacy in Biometrics* (Springer, 2013), 187–214.

[105] See e.g., Arun Ross and Assem Othman, 'Visual Cryptography for Biometric Privacy', 2011, available at https://ieeexplore.ieee.org/document/5658142/ accessed 30 October 2021. About making sensitive information in biometric data neutral, see Assem Otham and Arun Ross, 'Privacy Of Facial Soft Biometrics: Suppressing Gender But Retaining Identity' in *Lecture Notes in Computer Science* (Springer, 2015), 682–696.

[106] Further to public pressure after the *Gender Shades* report as discussed *above* and George Floyd's murder, IBM announced it was to discontinue selling its face recognition system and Microsoft from

cesses under the GDPR or the proposed AI Act 2021 is worth considering and being further explored. Self-regulation however will not have the same effect as effective legislation.

Finally, it is of utmost important to keep in mind that the ECtHR has clearly stated that:

> (t)he *mere storing of data relating to the private life* of an individual *amounts to an interference* within the meaning of Article 8 of the European Convention on Human Rights, which guarantees the right to respect for private and family life, home and correspondence ... The *subsequent use of the stored information has no bearing on that finding*" (italics added).[107]

It is clear that this is all the more true for the retention of information relating to unique characteristics but also when recording behavioural and other biometric data or emotions.[108] Therefore, the new turn in the recent GDPR with regard to biometric data, in which collecting and storing images and 'biometric data' seems not so much considered a problem, but rather the use, the lack of clarity around the biometric 'prohibition' in the GDPR with many exceptions and the Directive (EU) 2016/680 allowing biometric data processing is all *problematic* and *additional specific legislation* is needed.[109]

VII. CONCLUSION

The key for biometric data processing regulation lays in the careful assessment of the compliance of the processing with *both* fundamental and privacy and data protection rights requirements. Any biometric data processing contains potential (high) risks to the rights of freedoms of individuals because of the 'unique' nature of some bodily data allowing to identify individuals, but also of other biometric data allowing to track and monitor, and the possibility to capture emotions. The risks should be fully taken into account, law adopted and appropriate safeguards designed. In case of risks, a double proportionality test is required as a minimum, as explained above. While a processing may be in compliance with data protection requirements as imposed by the GDPR, or legislation implementing Directive (EU) 2016/680, risks for fundamental rights, in particular but not only for privacy and data protection rights, may remain and should be assessed.

In addition, clarity and legal certainty with regard to the definition and concepts and the prohibition to process biometric data in Article 9 GDPR should be provided. The proposed AI Act 2021 makes a first attempt to address the most urgent question of remote biometric identification for law enforcement purposes, while not forbidding in principle biometric

---

selling to law enforcement until federal regulation. This was followed by Amazon announcing a one-year moratorium for police use of its best-selling system Rekognition, which was extended in 2021.

[107] ECtHR, S. and Marper 2008, § 67.

[108] Furthermore: "in determining whether the personal information retained by the authorities involves any ... private-life aspects ..., the Court will have due regard to the specific context in which the information at issue has been recorded and retained, the nature of the records, the way in which these records are used and processed and the results that may be obtained ..." (ECtHR, S. and Marper 2008, § 67).

[109] Kindt, Having yes, using no 2018. See also Els J. Kindt, 'A first Attempt at Regulating Biometric Data in the Union', in A. Kak (ed.), *Regulating Biometrics. Global Approaches and Urgent Questions* (AINow Institute, New York University, New York, September 1, 2020), pp. 62-69, available at https://ainowinstitute.org/regulatingbiometrics.pdf accessed 30 October 2021.

identification systems by public authorities and private parties in publicly accessible places. The proposal imposes detailed obligations for these high-risk AI systems, which include such other 'real time' and 'post' remote biometric identification systems, as well as for some other AI systems relying on biometric data, including emotions, such as for border control. Furthermore, the establishment of central biometric databases should in society be questioned and become the subject of legislative attention as well. To conclude, more guidance on biometric data processing is needed from the legislator, in particular under which conditions and safeguards biometric data may be captured, retained and processed and centralized biometric databases could be justified, legal, necessary and proportionate. While some will criticize the too detailed obligations in the proposed AI Act 2021 risking to kill AI initiatives, this attempt to regulate may be going in the right direction, while being subject of further debate.

ACKNOWLEDGEMENT

This chapter received partial funding by the Cybersecurity Initiative Flanders – Strategic Research Program (CIF).

REFERENCES

EU Commission, *White Paper on Artificial Intelligence: a European Approach to Excellence and Trust*, COM(2020)65final, February 19, 2020.

EU Commission, *Proposal for a Regulation of the European Parliament and of the Council laying down Harmonised Rules on Artificial Intelligence (Artificial Intelligence Act) and Amending Certain Union Legislative Acts,* 2021/0106(COD), 21.4.2021, 108 p. and Annexes 1 to 9 (COM(2021)206 final, 21.4.2021, 17.

Consultative Committee of the Convention for the Protection of Individuals with regard to Automatic Processing of Personal Data, *Guidelines on Facial Recognition*, T-PD(2020)03rev4, 28.1.2021, 19.

Article 29 Data Protection Working Party, *Guidelines on Data Protection Impact Assessment (DPIA) and determining whether processing is "likely to result in a high risk" for the purposes of Regulation 2016/679*, WP 248 rev.01, (4.10. 2017).

Article 29 Data Protection Working Party, Opinion 3/2005 on Implementing the Council Regulation (EC) No 2252/2004 of 13 December 2004 on standards for security features and biometrics in passports and travel documents issued by Member States (30.9.2005 WP112).

Breebaart J., C. Busch, J. Grave and E. Kindt, 'A Reference Architecture for Biometric Template Protection Based on Pseudo Identities', in A Brömme (ed.), *BioSig 2008. Proceedings of the Special Interest Group on Biometrics and Electronic Signatures* (Gesellschaft für Informatik 2008).

Buolamwini J. and T. Gebru, *Gender Shades: Intersectional Accuracy Disparities in Commercial Gender Classification*, 2018, 15, MIT Media Lab, Algorithmic Justice League Project, available at http://proceedings.mlr.press/v81/buolamwini18a/buolamwini18a.pdf.

Castelluccia C. and D. Le Métayer, *Titres électroniques sécurisés : la centralisation des données biométriques est-elle vraiment inévitable ? Analyse comparative de quelques architectures,* Inria (1.2.2017), https://www.inria.fr/actualite/actualites-inria/titres-electroniques-securises-et-centralisation-des-donnees.

CNIL, *AU-053. Grille D'Analyse. Autorisation unique AU-053*, *Contrôle d'accès biométrique avec base centrale* (27.9.2016) https://www.cnil.fr/fr/biometrie-un-nouveau-cadre-pour-le-controle-dacces-biometrique-sur-les-lieux-de-travail.

Consultative Committee of the Convention for the Protection of Individuals with regards to Automatic Processing of Personal Data [CETS No. 108] (T-PD), *Progress report on the application of the principles of convention 108 to the collection and processing of biometric data*, Strasbourg, Council

of Europe, CM(2005)43, March 2005 ('Council of Europe, Progress report, 2005'), https://wcd.coe.int/ViewDoc.jsp?Ref=CM(2005)43&Language= lanEnglish&Site=COE&BackColorInternet=DBDCF2&BackColorIntranet=FDC864&BackColorLogged=.
De Hert P. and A. Sprokkereef, 'Regulation for Biometrics as a Primary Key for Interoperability?' in E. Kindt and L. Müller (eds.), *D.3.10. Biometrics in Identity Management* (FIDIS, 2007).
De Hert P., 'Biometrics and the Challenge to Human Rights in Europe. Need for Regulation and Regulatory Distinctions' in P. Campisi (ed.) *Security and Privacy in Biometrics* (Springer 2013).
EDPS, *Developing a 'toolkit' for assessing the necessity of measures that interfere with fundamental rights,* Background paper, (16.6.2016).
EDPS, TechDispatch 1/2021 – *Facial Emotion Recognition*, 26.5.2021, available at https://edps.europa.eu/data-protection/our-work/publications/techdispatch/techdispatch-12021-facial-emotion-recognition_en.
EDPB, *Guidelines 3/2019 on Processing of Personal Data through Video Devices, on Video Surveillance,* January 29, 2020.
European Commission and the Institute of Prospective Technological Studies, *Biometrics at the Frontiers: Assessing the Impact on* Society, Seville, European Commission, DG JRC, (January 2005).
Foegle J.-Ph., 'Sans doigt, ni loi : La CJUE donne son "feu vert" à la biosurveilance', La Revue des droits de l'homme (online 28 juillet 2015) https://revdh.revues.org/1394.
Foucault M., *Naissance de la biopolitique, Cours au Collège de France (1978–79)* F. Ewald, A. Fontana and M. Senellart (eds) (Seuil/Gallimard 2004).
Fundamental Rights Agency, *Facial recognition technology: fundamental rights considerations in law enforcement*, 27 November 2019, 36.
Fundamental Rights Agency, *Under watchful eyes: biometrics, EU IT systems and fundamental rights* (2018).
Fussey, P. and D. Murray, 'Independent Report on the London Metropolitan Police Service's Trial of Live Facial Recognition Technology' The Human Rights, Big Data and Technology Project, July 2019.
Garvie C., A. Bedoya and J. Frankle, *The Perpetual Line-up. Unregulated Police Recognition in America,* (18.10.2016) Georgetown Law. Center on Privacy & Technology, https://www.perpetuallineup.org/ 53.
Gayrel C., 'The Principle of Proportionality Applied to Biometrics in France: Review of Ten Years of CNIL's Deliberations' (2016) *Computer Law and Security Review* 450, also available at https://doi.org/10.1016/j.clsr.2016.01.013.
González Fuster G., *The Emergence of Personal Data Protection as a Fundamental Right of the EU* (Springer 2014).
Graham S. and D. Wood, 'Digitizing Surveillance: Categorization, Space, Inequality' (2003) 23(2) *Critical Social Policy* 227.
Hornung G., 'The European Regulation on Biometric Passports: Legislative Procedures, Political Interactions, Legal Framework and Technical Safeguards' (2007) *SCRIPTed* 4(3).
Jain A.,'Fingerprint Template Protection: From Theory to Practice' in P Campisi (ed.), *Security and Privacy in Biometrics* (Springer 2013).
Jasserand C.A., 'Avoiding Terminological Confusion Between the Notions of 'Biometrics' and 'Biometric Data': An Investigation into the Meanings of the Terms from a European Data Protection and a Scientific Perspective' (2016) *International Data Protection Law* 63.
Jasserand C.A., 'Legal Nature of Biometric Data: From 'Generic' Personal Data to Sensitive Data' (2016) *European Data Protection Law* 297.
Kak A., 'The State of Play and Open Questions for the Future' in A. Kak (ed.), *Regulating Biometrics. Global Approaches and Urgent Questions* (AINow Institute, New York University, New York, September 1, 2020), available at https://ainowinstitute.org/regulatingbiometrics.pdf.
Kindt E. and L. Müller (eds.), *D13.4. The Privacy Legal Framework for Biometrics* FIDIS May 2009).
Kindt E. and L. Müller (eds.), *D3.10. Biometrics in Identity Management* (FIDIS 2007).
Kindt E., 'Having Yes, Using No? About the New Legal Regime for Biometric Data' (2018) *Computer Law and Security Review* 523.
Kindt E., *Privacy and Data Protection Issues of Biometric Applications. A Comparative Legal Analysis* (Springer 2013).

Kindt, E., 'A First Attempt at Regulating Biometric Data in the Union', in A. Kak (ed.), *Regulating Biometrics. Global Approaches and Urgent Questions*, AINow Institute, New York University, New York, September 1, 2020, pp. 62-69, available at https://ainowinstitute.org/regulatingbiometrics.pdf.
Lodge J., 'Quantum Surveillance and "Shared Secrets". A Biometric Step Too Far?' (2010) *CEPS* 43.
Lodge J., 'The Dark Side of the Moon: Accountability, Ethics and New Biometrics', in E Mordini and D Tzovaras (eds.) *Second Generation Biometrics* (Springer 2012).
Marcel S., M. Nixon, J. Fierrez and N. Evans (eds) *Handbook of Biometric Anti-Spoofing – Presentation Attack Detection*, 2nd edn, Advances in Computer Vision and Pattern Recognition (Springer 2018).
Meints M and M Hansen (eds.), *D.3.6 Study on ID Documents* (FIDIS 2006).
Mordini E. and H. Ashton, 'Chapter 12 The Transparent Body: Medical Information, Physical Privacy and Respect for Body Integrity', in E. Mordini and D. Tzovaras (eds.), *Second Generation Biometrics: The Ethical, Legal and Social Context* (Dordrecht, Springer 2012).
Otham A. and A. Ross, 'Privacy of Facial Soft Biometrics: Suppressing Gender but Retaining Identity' in Lecture Notes in Computer Science (Springer, 2015).
Parliamentary Assembly of the Council of Europe, *The need for a global consideration of the human rights implications of biometrics* (Doc. 12522, 16.2.2011) http://assembly.coe.int/nw/xml/XRef/Xref-XML2HTML-en.asp?fileid=17968&lang=en.
Portal G, *Police facial recognition system faces legal challenge* (25.7.2018) https://www.bbc.co.uk/news/uk-44928792.
Ross A. and A. Othman, 'Visual Cryptography for Biometric Privacy' (2011) 6(1) *IEEE Transactions on Information Forensics and Security* 70.
Rotter P. (ed.), 'Large-scale Biometrics Deployment in Europe: Identifying Challenges and Threats (2008) JRC Scientific and Technical Reports, European Commission JRC – IPTS, Seville.
Schropp S., 'Biometric Data Collection and RFID Tracking in Schools: A Reasoned Approach to Reasonable Expectations of Privacy' (2016) 94 *N.C.L. Review* 1068.
Scottish Government, *Independent Advisory Group on the Use of Biometric Data in Scotland* (March 2018).
Snijder M., *Het biometrisch paspoort in Nederland: crash of zachte landing* (2010) WRR 51.
Stanton M., 'ICAO and the Biometric RFID Passport: History and Analysis' in C.J. Bennett and D. Lyon (eds.), *Playing the Identity Card: Surveillance, Security and Identification in Global Perspective* (Routledge 2008).
Tsormpatzoudi P., D. Dimitrova, J. Schroers and E. Kindt, 'Privacy by Design – The Case of Automated Border Control' in Camenisch J., S. Fischer-Hübner and M. Hansen (eds.) *Privacy and identity Management for the Future Internet in the Age of Globalisation,* (Springer 2014).
Van der Ploeg I., 'Biometrics and the Body as Information: Normative Issues in the Socio-technical Coding of the Body' in D. Lyon (ed.), *Surveillance as Social Sorting: Privacy, Risk and Automated Discrimination* (Routledge, 2003).
Van der Ploeg I., 'Security in the Danger Zone: Normative Issues of Next Generation Biometrics' in E. Mordini and D. Tzovaras (eds.) *Second Generation Biometrics* (Springer 2012).
Whitley E. and G. Husein, 'Global Identity Policies and Technology. Do We Understand the Question?' (2011) *Keesing Journal of Documents & Identities*.
Wisman T., 'Willems: Giving Member States the Prints and Data Protection the Finger' (2015) *European Data Protection Law Review* 245.

19. Co-regulation and competitive advantage in the GDPR: Data protection certification mechanisms, codes of conduct and data protection-by-design

Maximilian von Grafenstein

I. INTRODUCTION

The European legislator has frequently stressed the competitive advantage that is provided in the General Data Protection Regulation (GDPR).[1] However, there is little scientific evidence as to whether this promise will come true or not. Focusing on data protection certification mechanisms, this chapter illustrates why the regulatory approach inherent in the GDPR has indeed the potential to provide its regulation addressees, that are, data controllers and processors, competitive advantage and even enhance data-driven innovation. Therefore, this chapter will first outline an approach that will help to conduct research on the effects of regulatory instruments on innovation. This perspective differentiates between two perspectives. In a first step, the approach assesses which regulatory instruments are best suited to protect the individuals against the risks caused by innovation. In a second step, the approach focuses on the question on how these risk protection instruments should be designed to not unnecessarily hamper innovation, or even enhance innovation. This two-level approach does not only help the legislator to draft laws that both effectively protect against risks *and* support innovators in their innovation processes, but the approach also helps interpret existing laws regarding both regulatory functions. In this regard, this chapter will first demonstrate that a co-regulation strategy is particularly suitable for reaching this aim, and secondly, that the GDPR can be interpreted in such a way that it does not only protect against data protection risks but, indeed, also provides for competitive advantages. This becomes clear, in general, when examining the effects of data protection certification mechanisms on a micro-, meso-, and macroeconomic level, if these mechanisms are used to specify and standardize, for example, the data protection- and security-by-design requirements (Arts 25 and 32 GDPR).

Following the proposed levels at which the competitive advantage can be achieved, conclusions can be drawn on the following aspects. First, the different economic effects of data protection certification mechanisms compared to codes of conduct (and to a limited extent also to binding corporate rules – in the following also referred to as 'BCR'). Secondly, the different incentives to specify and standardise the GDPR provisions that depend on the type of data con-

[1] See, instead of many other statements, the 'Statement by Vice President Neelie Kroes ,on the consequences of living in an age of total information' from the 4th of July 2013, (Sep. 30, 2017), http://europa.eu/rapid/press-release_MEMO-13-654_en.htm accessed Oct. 30, 2021; see also, the German discussion, e.g., Roßnagel (1997) DuD 505 (514); Helmut Bäumler, Albert von Mutis 'Datenschutz als Wettbewerbsvorteil' (1st edn, Vieweg+Teubner Verlag, 2002).

trollers and processors. Third, the appropriate level of protection signalled by data protection certification mechanisms and its interplay with the 'state of the art'-requirement. Fourthly, the suitable object of data protection certification mechanisms with respect to the ability of data subjects to assess the level of protection. Lastly, three selected key questions on how to cope with the complexity of such 'data protection markets', considering the perspective of certification bodies, data controllers as well as processors, and data subjects. On this basis, the chapter concludes by highlighting the need for empirical research to answer several remaining questions on the effectiveness of the discussed regulatory instruments from the point of view of regulating innovation.

II. REGULATING DATA-DRIVEN INNOVATION: STUCK IN A REGULATORY DILEMMA?

To answer the question under which conditions the GDPR can lead to a competitive advantage, this chapter builds on the research approach of regulating innovation. From the regulator's point of view, this approach raises two fundamental questions: First, which regulatory instruments protect best against the risks caused by innovation; and second, among those instruments, which hinder the innovation processes of the regulation addressees the least, or can even enhance innovation.[2] From this perspective, the law as such is not an inherent barrier to innovation, but rather a leveller of innovation.[3] In fact, under which conditions a law protects, effectively, individuals against risks caused by innovation and under which conditions this does not unnecessarily hinder innovation processes, or even enhances such processes, cannot be answered by legal research alone. Instead, in order to do research on the effects of regulatory instruments, it is necessary to build upon other (in particular, economic) research disciplines by using their concepts, theories and (in particular, empirical) research methodologies.[4] With these considerations in mind, the next few sections show why the upcoming GDPR provides a set of instruments that are, in principle, well-suited for the regulation of data-driven innovation, and could indeed provide a competitive advantage.

II.1 Knowledge Uncertainty as an Inherent Element of Innovation

The approach of regulating innovation understands knowledge uncertainties as an inherent element of innovation processes. Schumpeter was one of the first economists to recognize innovation as a key driver of social change. In doing so, he contradicted the prevailing view

---

[2] See Wolfgang Hoffmann-Riem, Innovationsoffenheit und Innovationsverantwortung durch Recht – Aufgaben rechtswissenschaftlicher Innovationsforschung (Openness toward Innovation and Responsibility for Innovation by means of Law), in: Archiv des öffentlichen Rechts 123 (4) 513–540 (1998).

[3] See Viktor Mayer-Schönberger, The Law as Stimulus: The Role of Law in Fostering Innovative Entrepreneurship, 6 (2) 159–169 (2010); Urs Gasser, Cloud Innovation and the Law: Issues, Approaches, and Interplay, No. 2014-7 19-20 https://papers.ssrn.com/sol3/papers.cfm?abstract_id=2410271 accessed Oct. 30, 2021.

[4] See Wolfgang Hoffmann-Riem, Saskia Fritzsche, Innovationsverantwortung - Zur Einleitung, 39, in: Martin Eifert, Wolfgng Hoffmann Riem (eds.), Innovations und Recht III - Innovationsverantwortung, 11–41, (Duncher & Humboldt, 1st ed., 2009).

on price competition as the primary economic force. Instead, Schumpeter identified 'the new consumers' goods, the new methods of production or transportation, the new markets, the new forms of industrial organization that capitalist enterprise creates' as the essential impulse 'that sets and keeps the capitalist engine in motion'.[5] Focusing on the 'entrepreneur' as the actor who brings such innovations to the market, Schumpeter stressed the 'function of entrepreneurs (...) to reform or revolutionize the pattern by exploiting an invention or, more generally, an untried technological possibility for producing a new commodity or producing an old one in a new way (...) and so on.'[6]

From such an understanding of *evolutionary* markets, the approach of regulating innovation takes it as a matter of fact that the regulator has limited knowledge about future events.[7] Focusing on risks, as one side of the 'innovation coin', there has been an intensive – and still ongoing – debate on how to define risks. Especially in the German environmental protection law debate, the discussion has focused, mainly in the 80s, on clarifying the different terms of 'risks' and 'dangers' that were, more and more, parallel used in laws. Pursuant to sociological approaches, the term 'risk' aims to make an incalculable danger calculable. Thus, the specific knowledge about the probability and severity of a 'danger' makes this danger a 'risk'.[8] In the German legal discussion, however, both terms have been actually used for nearly a century in the opposite sense: a 'danger' is referred to as the calculable threat, whereas 'risk' is used to refer to a situation where there is not enough knowledge about whether a certain action leads to harm for a specific object of protection.[9] However, this short summary of the discussion does not aim to decide in favour of the one or the other definition. Rather, the aim

---

[5] See Joseph Schumpeter, *Capitalism, Socialism and Democracy*, 82–83 (5th ed. 2003).

[6] See Schumpeter, ibid., p. 132.

[7] See Wolfgang Hoffmann-Riem, Saskia Fritzsche, (n 4), 259–262; Ivo Appelt, Aufgaben und Verfahren der Innovationsfolgenabschätzung (Tasks and Procedures of the Innovation Impact Assessment), in: Martin Eifert, Wolfgang Hoffmann-Riem, Innovation und Recht III – Innovationsverantwortung, 147–181 (149) (Mohr Siebeck, 1st ed., 2009); cf., regarding technology regulation, Charles D. Raab and Paul De Hert, Tools for Technology Regulation: Seeking Analytical Approaches Beyond Lessig and Hood, in: Roger Brownsword, Karen Yeung (eds.), *Regulating Technologies – Legal Futures, Regulatory Frames and Technological Fixes*, 263–285 (2008); concerning cyber regulation, Andrew Murray, Conceptualising the Post-Regulatory (Cyber)state, in: Roger Brownsword, Karen Yeung (eds.), ibid., 287–316 (2008); further developed: Andrew Murray, The Regulation of Cyberspace – Control in the Online Environment In: *Modern Law Review* 70, (5) 879–883 (2007); and with respect to regulation *per se*, Robert Baldwin, Martin Cave, Martin Lodge, *Understanding Regulation – Theory, Strategy and Practice*, (2nd ed.) (2013); Claudio Franzius, Modalitäten und Wirkungsfaktoren der Steuerung durch Recht (Modes and Impact Factors for the Control through Law), § 4, in: Wolfgang Hoffmann-Riem, Eberhard Schmidt-Aßmann, Andreas Voßkuhle (eds.), Grundlagen des Verwaltungsrechts – Band I "Methoden – Maßstäbe – Aufgaben – Organisation", (C.H. Beck, 2nd ed., 2012); see also Martin Eifert, Reguierungsstrategien (Regulation Strategies), in: ibid.

[8] See Liv Jaeckel, Gefahrenabwehrrecht und Risikodogmatik – Moderne Technologien im Spiegel des Verwaltungsrechts (Prevention of Danger through Law and Legal Conceptualization of Risk), 51–52, (Mohr Siebeck, 1st ed., 2010), by referring to Adalbert Evers, Helga Novotny, Umgang mit Unsicherheit, (Suhrkamp, 1st ed., 1987); cf. also Raphael Gellert, Data Protection: A Risk Regulation? Between the Risk Regulation of Everything and the Precautionary Alternative, 7-13, in: *International Data Privacy Law*, 5 (1), 3–19, (2015); referring to Patrick Peretti-Watel, La société du risque (Repères. La Découverte, 1st ed.2010); Olivier Borraz, Les politiques du risque (Presses de Sciences Po, 1st ed., 2008), Jenny Steele, *Risks and Legal Theory*, (Hart Publishing, 1st ed., 2004) 21, Jacqueline Peel, *Science and Risk Regulation in International Law*, 79-80 (Cambridge University Press, 2010).

[9] See Jaeckel, ibid., pp. 52 and 55–56.

is to demonstrate that the legal discussion has implicitly acknowledged that the regulator is confronted with different types of threats resulting from different types of knowledge uncertainties: on the one hand, there are situations where it is possible to say, with a certain degree of probability, that a certain action can lead to harm for a specific object of protection; on the other hand, there are situations in which there is not enough knowledge about such a linear causal-effect-relationship, but the mere possibility of harm is already sufficient to justify a (precautionary) protection.[10]

The same differentiation of knowledge uncertainties can be observed when the regulator's perspective is changed to the perspective of innovative entrepreneurs as the addressees of the regulation. Economists essentially conceptualize, an entrepreneurial process as a bundle of the following activities: locating business opportunities, accumulating resources, and building organizations to produce market products or services, while constantly interacting within the entrepreneurial environment.[11] What matters here is how economists look at the way entrepreneurs locate their business opportunities. In this regard, two main theories are relevant here: The Discovery Theory and the Creation Theory. The first theory says that an entrepreneur 'discovers' an already existing business opportunity, building on the situation where an entrepreneur has sufficient knowledge about a specific outcome of his or her actions. Such an entrepreneur cannot be completely sure about the outcome but he or she can at least expect it with some probability.[12] In contrast, the Creation Theory refers to a situation where an entrepreneur does not have enough knowledge of the likelihood of a particular outcome. In this case, economists stress that 'entrepreneurs maximize their probability of success by (1) engaging in iterative, incremental, and inductive decision-making, (2) developing very flexible and constantly adjusting business plans'[13] and generating 'resources that, from the point of view of potential competitors, are intractable (...) and causally ambiguous (...).'[14] This second theory is particularly relevant in innovative, highly dynamic, non-linear environments.[15]

So far, this section has shown that both the regulator and the regulation addressees face the same knowledge uncertainties in highly dynamic, innovative environments. Given the described knowledge uncertainties, the question arises as to which regulatory instruments are most suitable for an effective regulation.

---

[10] See Jaeckel, ibid., 69–81; cf. Luiz Costa, Privacy and the Precautionary Principle, 14-19, in: *Computer Law & Security Review*, 14–24 (2012).

[11] See, for instance, William B. Gartner, A Conceptual Framework for Describing the Phenomenon of New Venture Creation, p. 702, in: *The Academy of Management Review* 10 (4) 696–706 (1985).

[12] See Sharon Alvarez and Jay B Barney, Discovery and Creation: Alternative Theories of Entrepreneurial Action, 13 in: *Strategic Entrepreneurship Journal* 1 (1) 11–26 (2007).

[13] See Alvarez and Barney, ibid., p. 32.

[14] See Alvarez and Barney, ibid., pp. 36–37.

[15] See Alvarez and Barney, ibid., pp. 33–34, regarding the knowledge uncertainties, and regarding the non-linearity of innovative environments, Jan Fagerberg, Innovation: A Guide to the Literature, Box 1.3 "What innovation is not: the linear model", 11, in: Jan Fagerberg, David C. Mowery (eds.), *The Oxford Handbook of Innovation* (Oxford University Press, 2004).

II.2 Openness of Regulatory Instruments to Innovation (e.g., Legal Principles and Broad Legal Terms)

Legal scholars have long been debating the appropriate functions, modes, and strategies that could be considered for an effective regulation in complex, highly dynamic, innovative environments. Even if the debate does not always use the same terminology, the common starting point, as previously described, are the knowledge uncertainties of the actors involved in these environments.[16] As one of them, Eifert determines the regulatory strategies for the role a State plays within a regulatory complex field, differentiating between imperative law ('command and control', often also referred to as 'rules'), State-regulated self-regulation ('co-regulation', also described as 'principles' or 'standards'), and social self-regulation. Focusing on imperative law (command-and-control) and instruments of regulated self-regulation (co-regulation),[17] Eifert provides a useful summary of the advantages and disadvantages of these two types of regulation:

> A command-and-control regulation provides for a high degree of legal certainty given the clarity of the 'if-then'-rules and a more direct form of execution. However, this type of regulation can be inefficient because it does not take the specific circumstances of the regulation addressees and the constraints of their economic behaviour into account. The inflexibility of this type of regulation can severely restrict their room of action because they cannot react to and adapt to the dynamic changes in the environment when they want to meet the regulatory expectations. Therefore, the more knowledge the regulator has of the effectiveness and efficiency of its protection instruments, the more appropriate this type of regulation will be. On the other hand, if the regulator does not have sufficient knowledge, such as in complex, highly dynamic, innovative environments, this type of command-and-control regulation does not provide the most appropriate instruments.[18]

Regarding complex, dynamic, and innovative environments, Eifert instead emphasizes co-regulation as the more appropriate regulatory strategy. The main reason for this is that this strategy can build much better on the decentralized knowledge of private entities in order to react more specifically to the particularities of certain environments.[19] As mentioned above, in innovative environments, legislators lack sufficient knowledge to pinpoint the circumstances of the entrepreneurial activities and the impact of these activities on individuals. Precise (if-then) rules therefore carry the risk of over-regulation and of ineffectively addressing the actual threat. Therefore, the regulator may decide to establish legal principles and/or broad legal terms so that the regulation addressees have more room to find the best solution by them-

---

[16] Cf. Baldwin, Cave and Lodge (n 9); Raab and De Hert (n 7); Murray (n 7); Franzius (n 7).

[17] See Eifert (n 7), 13–15; focusing on privacy-related principles; Winston J. Maxwell, Principles-based Tegulation of Personal Data: The Case of 'fair processing', in: *International Data Privacy Law*, 205–216, 5 (3) (2015), referring to Julia Black, Forms and Paradoxes of Principles Based Regulation', in: *Capital Markets Law Journal*, 3 (4), 425–457 (2008); , Louis Kaplow, Rules Versus Standards: An Economic Analysis, in: *Duke L. J.* 42 (3) (1992); Richard A Posner, *Economic Analysis of Law*, 747 (Aspen/Wolters, 8th ed.).

[18] See Eifert, ibid., 25–26; cf, focusing on 'privacy seals': Rowena Rodrigues, David Wright, Kush Wadhwa, Developing a Privacy Seal Scheme (That Works), 109-110, in: *International Data Privacy Law*, 3 (2), 100–116 (2013).

[19] See Eifert, ibid., cip. 59; cf. Rowena Rodrigues, David Wright, Kush Wadhwa, ibid., 110–111.

selves to achieve the regulatory objective.[20] Since this strategy is based on the decentralized knowledge of all regulation addressees, it potentially increases the problem-solving skills in society. Since this strategy is based on the logic of entrepreneurial behaviour, its regulatory instruments are – at least in principle – also more effective.[21]

Keeping these different regulation strategies in mind, a closer look at the GDPR shows that the legislator has obviously opted, at least to a substantial extent, for a principle-based approach. This applies at least to the processing principles under Art. 5 GDPR, as well as the data protection and security-by-design requirements under Arts 25 and 32 GDPR. In doing so, the legislator has combined, with respect to Art. 5 and Art. 25 GDPR, two approaches with each other, the so-called rights-based approach (as enshrined in Art. 5 GDPR) and the so-called risk-based approach (as stated in Art. 25 GDPR). There are several commonalities and differences between the two approaches.[22] However, what is most relevant for this chapter, is how the legislator has combined the principles under Art. 5 GDPR, which are applicable to all kinds of processing of personal data, with the risk-based approach under Art. 25 GDPR that enables the regulation addressee to take the contextual particularities into account. Pursuant to Art. 25 GDPR, the data controller has to implement the principles listed in Art. 5 GDPR by taking, among other aspects, the 'risk', 'purpose' and 'context' of its processing into account. While all these legal principles and terms are rather broad and vague, the advantage of this combined approach is that the regulation addressees have both a normative direction and enough leeway to find solutions that best fit the regulatory goal, taking into account the specifics of their entrepreneurial processing context.[23]

II.3 Legal Uncertainty as a Hindering Factor for Innovation

One drawback of such broad and vague provisions is, in general, that the way a regulatory addressee applies the law may not be in line with the regulator's expectations.[24] There may be two different scenarios in this regard: In the first scenario, the regulation addressee really wants to meet the regulatory aim but does not succeed because he or she does not know what the regulator is explicitly expecting from them. In the second scenario, the addressee does not want to meet the regulator's expectations and uses the broadness and vagueness of the legal provisions as a loophole, abusing its advanced knowledge about its specific entrepreneurial circumstances to the detriment of the individuals concerned. This might be the case, for instance, if the regulator grants these entrepreneurs privileges because it believes that their

---

[20] Cf. Eifert, ibid., ci25–26; Franzius (n 7), 7, 17, 81–103; Raab and De Hert (n 7), 278; focusing on the technological neutrality of data protection law, Irene Kamara, Co-regulation in EU Personal Data Protection: The Case of Technical Standards and the Privacy By Design Standardisation 'Mandate', in *European Journal of Law and Technology*, 8 (1), 8-11, (2017).

[21] See Eifert, ibid., 59.

[22] Comparing both approaches in detail see: Raphael Gellert, We Have Always Managed Risks in Data Protection Law: Understanding the Similarities and Differences Between the Rights-Based and the Risk-Based Approaches to Data Protection, in: *European Data Protection Law Review* (EDPL), 4 (2), 481–492, (2016).

[23] See, in more detail, Max v. Grafenstein, *The Principle of Purpose Limitation in Data Protection Laws: The Risk-Based Approach, Legal Principles and Private Standards as Elements for Regulating Innovation*, in particular, pp. 508–590, (Mohr Siebeck,1st ed., 2018, to be published).

[24] See Eifert (n 7), 60; cf. Rodrigues, Wright, and Wadhwa (n 18), 110–111, focusing on self-regulation of 'privacy seals'.

solutions serve the persons concerned, but only serve their business interests.[25] In the first scenario, legal uncertainty negatively affects the innovative entrepreneurs, and in the second scenario, the individuals concerned.

This fact leads to a regulatory dilemma in innovative environments. On the one hand, if the regulator provides for specific rules, these rules run the risk of over-regulation and of not meeting the actual threat that is caused by innovation. On the other hand, if the regulator provides for broad legal terms and/or principles that are basically open toward innovation (because innovative entrepreneurs are able to adapt these legal requirements to the particularities of a specific case), this reduces legal certainty.

III. ESCAPING THE DILEMMA: CO-REGULATION AND SPECIFYING STANDARDS

To solve this conflict between legal principles and/or broad legal terms, which are open to innovation, and legal uncertainty, the regulator can add procedural instruments enabling the regulation addressees to increase legal certainty on their own. A prominent example are standards that are set up by private entities, by involving to some extent the regulator, that specify the law in regard to technical and organisational requirements.[26] Such a combination of legal principles or broad legal terms with procedural instruments is typical for a co-regulation strategy. With respect to the described knowledge uncertainties, such a strategy is particularly useful for assessing the risks caused by innovation because it enables the regulation addressees to take the particularities of their specific context into account, whether in relation to a particular product or service category, or a certain type of processing activity.[27] However, the next sections will focus on the other side of the 'innovation coin'. Thus, the question concerns the conditions under which these risk-protection instruments can not only be opened up for

---

[25] See Eifert, ibid., 60; see also Kamara (n 20), 4, referring, on the one hand, to Colin J. Bennett and Charles D. Raab *The Governance of Privacy: Policy Instruments in Global Perspective* 155, (MIT Press, updated paperback ed., 2006) and on the other hand, to Dennis D. Hirsch, In Search of the Holy Grail: Achieving Global Privacy Rules Through Sector-Based Codes of Conduct in*: Ohio St. LJ*, 74 (6), 1029 (1043), (2013).

[26] See, e.g., the International Organization for Standardization (ISO) and the International Electrotechnical Commission of Standardization (IEC) defining a 'standard' as a 'document, established by consensus and approved by a recognized body, that provides, for common and repeated use, rules, guidelines or characteristics for activities or their results, aimed at the achievement of the optimum degree of order in a given context', under http://www.iso.org/sites/ConsumersStandards/1_standards .html accessed Oct. 30, 2021, (re-called 20 January 2017); see for further definitions, Paul De Hert, Vagelis Papakonstantinou, Irene Kamara, The Cloud Computing Standard ISO/IEC 27018 Through the Lens of the EU Legislation On Data Protection, 18, in: *Computer Law & Security Review* 32 (1), 16–30.

[27] See Eifert (n 7), 59; see also von Grafenstein, Refining the Concept of the Right to Data Protection in Article 8 ECFR – Part I, II and III, EDPL 4/2020, 2/2021, 3/2021; cf. also Kamara (n 20), 13–14, who discusses the issue taking the example of the European Commission's privacy by design standardisation request with regard to European data protection law. However, this perspective is, in the view of the author of this contribution, not sufficiently context-specific to properly address the context-dependency of data protection risks; in contrast, see the considerations regarding the ISO Cloud Standard at De Hert, Papakonstantinou and Kamara (n 26), 27, which seems therefore to be a better example in this context.

innovation, but even enhance innovation and market competition.[28] In this regard, the first part focuses on the microeconomic level on how increasing legal certainty can have a positive effect on entrepreneurial activity. At the mesoeconomic level, the second section concentrates on the positive impacts of standards on the decisions of consumers or business customers purchasing innovative products or services. Finally, the third section gives an outlook on how this kind of regulation can have positive effects on the innovation capacity of a market as a whole.

III.1 Reducing the Complexity of an Entrepreneurial Process (Microeconomic Level)

To understand the effects of standards on the microeconomic level, one must first look more closely at the effects of legal certainty and uncertainty on entrepreneurial activity. Authors in the economic discipline see high legal certainty as an enhancing factor rather than a hindrance to doing business. The reason for this is that the law does not only limit the room for manoeuvre of an entrepreneur but also helps him or her to defend and enforce legal claims.[29] However, some studies show that legal certainty tends to help large enterprises rather than small- and medium-sized companies.[30] Levie and Autio explain this observation, bearing in mind that smaller companies usually have:

> disproportionately high compliance costs, because their small initial size makes it costly for them to maintain compliance functions internally. For industry incumbents, whose large size permits a greater degree of internal specialisation and the maintenance of a larger administrative function in absolute terms, compliance costs are less significant.[31]

However, the study by Levie and Autio also demonstrates that if the regulatory burden is low, companies (not just large but also small- and medium-sized companies) can benefit from a high level of legal certainty.[32] In this case, '[B]ureaucracy and red tape [do not] hamper entrepreneurial growth and divert scarce resources of potentially high-growth entrepreneurial firms away from their core business'.[33]

This last consideration leads to the reason why an increase of legal certainty can be a factor in enhancing innovation (given a low regulatory burden): Legal certainty can be an enhancing factor for entrepreneurial activity, because entrepreneurs generally prefer, given the high level of uncertainty they face during their innovation processes, to know exactly what the regulator

---

[28] Cf. with respect to the effects of technical standards on innovation, Knut Blind, The Impact of Standardization and Standards on Innovation, in: Manchester Institute of Innovation Research (ed.), *Compendium of Evidence on the Effectiveness of Innovation Policy Intervention*, (2013), available at http://www.innovation-policy.org.uk/compendium/section/Default.aspx?topicid=30 accessed Oct. 30, 2021.

[29] See, e.g., Chantal Hartog et al., Institutions and Entrepreneurship: The Role of the Rule of Law, 8. (7 January 2018), http://ondernemerschap.panteia.nl/main/publication/bestelnummer/h201003 accessed Oct. 30, 2021.

[30] See Hartog et al., ibid., p. 3.

[31] See Jonathan Levie, Erkko Autio, Regulatory Burden, Rule of Law, and Entry of Strategic Entrepreneurs: An International Panel Study, 1411 in: *Journal of Management Studies* 48 (6) 1392–1419 (2011).

[32] See Levie and Autio, ibid., pp. 1400–1401.

[33] See, ibid., p. 1411.

expects from them.[34] Mayer-Schönberger sums up this point of view by arguing that 'the role of the legal system in facilitating entrepreneurial activity is to reduce the uncertainties that entrepreneurs perceive'.[35] Mayer-Schönberger also draws several conclusions from this function of the law: Empirical studies show that individuals are more risk-averse, the higher the final payoff. Thus, he proposes, for example, to increase legal certainty when entrepreneurs face high profits or costs. Second, as individuals are more risk-averse when they evaluate profits and more risk-taking regarding eventual losses, Mayer-Schönberger suggests 'that lawmakers should focus on making legal rules more certain for financial benefits offered to entrepreneurs, like subsidies, rather than costs, like taxes'.[36]

From this perspective, the law does indeed not hinder innovation, but can rather serves as a business opportunity: Tied to the entrepreneurial Discovery Theory, the regulation strategy of 'command-and-control' provides entrepreneurs with precise criteria for applying the law. Entrepreneurs must 'discover' these criteria and organize their processes according to these criteria in a 'causal-linear' way. In highly dynamic, innovative environments, however, this regulatory strategy runs the risk of unnecessarily increasing bureaucracy and hindering entrepreneurial activity. Therefore, the regulator can also build on the logic of the Creation Theory by establishing legal principles and/or broad legal terms and, in addition, procedural mechanisms that allow entrepreneurs to specify these norms for themselves. As such procedural instruments, data protection certification mechanisms established under Arts 42 and 43 GDPR, as well as codes of conduct pursuant to Arts 40 and 41 GDPR, can be introduced because they enable data controllers and processors to specify and standardize the legal principles and broad legal terms, thus increasing legal certainty.[37] Entrepreneurs can use these mechanisms to ensure that the way they specify the legal principles and broad legal terms really meets the regulators' expectations. To summarize, this regulatory strategy is not only open to innovation but has also the potential to enhance entrepreneurial innovative capacities.

III.2 Signalling a Certain Level of Protection to Market Participants (Mesoeconomic Level)

Moreover, such a co-regulation strategy can also have positive effects on a mesoeconomic dimension. By laying down legal principles and broad legal terms, the regulator leaves data controllers and processors sufficient room for their specific application. This, in turn, leads to a variety of possible solutions.[38] From the point of view of New Institutional Economics,

---

[34] Cf. also Kloepfer, Law enables Technology – About an Underestimated Function of Environmental and Technology Law, in: *Natur und Recht* 417–418 (1997).

[35] See Mayer-Schönberger (n 3), 177–178.

[36] See ibid., 179–180.

[37] See, e.g., Stefan Heilmann and Wolfgang Schulz in: *Kommentar Datenschutz-Grundverordnung* (Sibylle Gierschmann, Katharina Schlender, Rainer Stentzel, Winfried Veil (eds), (Bundesanzeiger Verlag 2017), Art. 40 cip. 1 and Art. 42 cip. 2; however, see Eric Lachaud, The General Data Protection Regulation and the Rise of Certification as a Regulatory Instrument, in: *Computer Law and Security Review* (March 2017), who argues that the data protection certification mechanisms have to be categorised under a new category called 'monitored self-regulation'.

[38] See Gerhard Wegner, Nachhaltige Innovationsoffenheit dynamischer Märkte (Dynamic Markets and their Persistent Openness to Innovation), 74–75, in: Martin Eifert, Wolfgang Hoffmann-Riem (eds), Innovationsfördernde Regulierung – Innovation und Recht II, 71-91 (Duncker & Humblot, 1st ed. 2009).

Wegner demonstrates under which circumstances the regulator can enable such market creativity.[39] He explains that given the evolutionary nature of innovations, such market creativity depends on how quickly the entrepreneurs react to constant changes in their respective environments. From this economic point of view, the best that a regulator can actually do is to guarantee the existence of fair competition in the markets, as well as guaranteeing that the entrepreneurs participating in a market can make autonomous decisions. If, on the other hand, the legislator requires entrepreneurs to apply a regulatory objective in a specific way it minimizes their entrepreneurial capacity to innovate and, thus, the variety of possible solutions overall.[40] From this (economic) perspective, the regulation 'command-and-control' strategy (also) is, therefore, less able to uphold market creativity than a co-regulation strategy containing the provision of legal principles and broad legal terms.[41]

On this basis, consumers decide for or against certain products or services of specific qualities that determine the success of entrepreneurial, innovative activities. In terms of data protection law, this means that data subjects must be able to choose which product or service of certain 'data protection qualities' they prefer: Data subjects who prefer a lower data protection level (for instance, for a cheaper price) do not have to buy products or services with a higher protection level (hence, for a probably higher price).[42] A data controller can thus determine the quality of (data) protection of a specific product or service, whether with the involvement of the regulator (co-regulation) or without it (self-regulation). The standardization of such a product or service quality, for example, in the form of a certificate, then signals this level of protection to the data subject.[43]

There are also some pitfalls in this concept. One pitfall certainly is the risk of marginalising data subjects who cannot afford higher prices for better data protection quality (however, see the state of the art requirement in the next section, which counteracts this pitfall). Another pitfall is when the transaction costs of the consumers are too high to verify the 'data protection quality' of a certain product or service in question. This may be the case if there is no common scale that is necessary in order to compare the differences in quality. This can be particularly relevant with respect to the so-called risk-based approach.[44] The risk-based

---

[39] See Wegner, ibid., 73.

[40] See ibid., 74–80.

[41] Cf. already the regulatory perspective focusing on the regulator's knowledge deficiencies, above under point 'Knowledge uncertainty as an inherent element of innovation.'

[42] Cf. Wegner (n 38), 84–85; in contrast, many authors mainly consider the compliance function of Arts 42 and 43 GDPR (which was discussed in the previous section), e.g., ENISA, Recommendations on European Data Protection Certification, Version 1.0, 13, (November 2017); Rowena Rodrigues, David Barnard-Willsa, Paul De Hert and Vagelis Papakonstantinou, The Future of privacy certification in Europe: An Exploration of Options Under Article 42 of the GDPR, 249, in: *International Review of Law, Computers & Technology*, 30 (3), 248–270, (2016), available at: http://dx.doi.org/10.1080/13600869.2016.1189737 accessed Oct. 30, 2021; however, see Rodrigues, Wright, and Wadhwa (n 18), 105, who also considers, beside the compliance function, the additional goal 'to ensure a higher level of protection for individuals'.

[43] Cf. Wegner (n 38), 85–86; Roßnagel, Data protection in computerized everyday life, 195, (2007), http://library.fes.de/pdf-files/stabsabteilung/04548.pdf accessed Oct. 30, 2021; critical regarding such a competition amongst certification bodies, Rowena Rodrigues, David Barnard-Wills, Paul De Hert and Vagelis Papakonstantinou, ibid., p. 263.

[44] See von Grafenstein, Refining the Concept of the Right to Data Protection in Article 8 ECFR – Part I, II and III, EDPL 4/2020, 2/2021, 3/2021; see also the risk-based approach regarding Directive 95/46/EC, Article 29 Data Protection Working Party, Statement on the role of a risk-based approach

approach is an essential element, for example, of the data protection and security-by-design requirements under Arts 25 and 32 GDPR. The risk-based approach requires data controllers and partly processors to implement data protection measures according to the specific risks.[45] Consequently, the 'data protection quality' also depends on the risk measurement. So, if there is no common scale to measure data protection risks, it will not be possible for data subjects to compare products or services of different 'data protection quality'.[46] Another pitfall refers to the situation where the market for a certain product or service is so fragmented that the data subject loses the overview even if there was a common scale that makes a comparison of products possible.[47] This may be the case, for example, if there are too many data protection certificates on the market and the data subjects are overwhelmed by the variety. However, the guiding principle should be clear that a co-regulation strategy that provides controllers and processors with the ability to specify and standardize legal requirements can, at least in principle, strengthen the competition in a market and, consequently, market creativity because they can signal the data protection quality (of their specific product or service) to the data subject (i.e., consumer). Users of such a standard which signal a certain (data protection) quality of a specific product and/or service (for example, by using a data protection certification mechanism, pursuant to Art. 42 GDPR) can thus turn the room for manoeuvre that is laid out by law into a competitive advantage.

III.3 The 'State of the Art' as a Driver of Market Innovation (Macroeconomic Level)

Last but not least, there is another related factor that can enhance the innovative capacity of a market on the macroeconomic level. This factor does not result from the standardization *per se* of legal requirements, but rather from a particular element of the data protection and security-by-design requirements under Arts 25 and 32 GDPR. Both provisions require data

---

in data protection legal frameworks, 14/EN, WP 218, http://ec.europa.eu/justice/data-protection/article-29/documentation/opinion-recommendation/files/2014/wp218_en.pdf accessed Oct. 30, 2021, 30 May 2014; regarding the DPIA under Art. 35 GDPR, ibid., 17/EN WP 248 rev.01, Guidelines on Data Protection Impact Assessment (DPIA) and determining whether processing is 'likely to result in a high risk' for the purposes of Regulation 2016/679, ec.europa.eu/newsroom/document.cfm?doc_id=47711, (4 April 2017) accessed Oct. 30, 2021; Friedewald et al., Forum Privatheit, White Paper Datenschutz-Folgenabschätzung: http://www.forum-privatheit.de/forum-privatheit-de/publikationen-und-downloads/veroeffentlichungen-des-forums/themenpapiere-white-paper/Forum-Privatheit-WP-DSFA-3-Auflage-2017-11-29.pdf, (2017) accessed Oct. 30, 2021; see also the internet knowledge base of the CNIL https://www.cnil.fr/en/PIA-privacy-impact-assessment-en accessed Oct. 30, 2021.

[45] See Jana Moser, Art. 25, cip. 59 ff.; Johann Jergl, Art. 32, cip. 21 ff., in: Sibylle Gierschmann, Katharina Schlender, Rainer Stentzel, Winfried Veil, Kommentar Datenschutz-Grundverordnung (Bundesanzeiger Verlag, 1st ed, 2017); comprehensively, regarding the risk-based approach of the GDPR, Winfried Veil, ibid, Art. 24, cip. 78–190.

[46] In the opinion of the author of this contribution, the discussion on the data protection risk assessment methodology has not yet reached a level at which data subjects can reliably assess data protection risks and are able to compare, on that basis, different levels of data protection provided for by a certain processing operation. Given that data-driven products build on a whole bundle of processing operations, the data subjects are even less able to assess the level of protection of these products; however, see also von Grafenstein et al., Effective data protection by design through interdisciplinary research methods, under review at CLSR.

[47] See Wegner (n 38), 80–82; cf., Rodrigues, Barnard-Wills, De Hert, Papakonstantinou (n 42), 263.

controllers, and partly processors, to take the 'state of the art' into account when implementing appropriate technical and organisational measures to mitigate the risks caused by their data processing activities. Legal scholars determine the nature of this term (i.e., the 'state of the art') as an 'undetermined legal concept'.[48] To specify this legal concept, legal scholars in Germany refer to the same terms and related terms that are already used in other regimes, such as environmental and technology laws. In doing so, they define the term 'state of the art' as the 'best available technology' in the sense of proven most effective implementation.[49] The legal meaning of this term can be located between the following two related notions on a normative level: the 'generally accepted rules of technology' (in German: 'allgemein anerkannte Regeln der Technik') and the 'state of science and technology' (in German: 'Stand der Wissenschaft und Technik'). While the first notion provides for a lower level of protection, the second notion leads to a higher protection level than indicated by the term 'best available technology'. The reason for this is that the notion 'generally accepted rules of technology' only requires that a certain technology must be approved in practice and accepted amongst many experts. The technology does, therefore, not have to be the 'best' technology available. In contrast, the notion 'state of science and technology' requires, at least in principle, a higher level of protection since the obligation to use such a technology does not depend on its market availability.[50] This comparison may convey to the reader what it means when the term 'state of the art' is interpreted as 'best available technology'.

Regardless of the precise meaning, legal scholars agree on the dynamic function of this reference.[51] At first view, such a dynamic reference can serve as an innovation-enhancing factor on the market because it requires data controllers (and partly processors) to *constantly* adapt their protection measures to the 'state of the art', which can *constantly* evolve.[52] The state of the art-requirement also protects data subjects who cannot afford a higher data protection quality. The second view on behavioural dynamics, however, shows significant pitfalls of the regulatory concept behind such a dynamic reference.[53] In particular, the economist Gawel notes that this requirement actually deprives many regulation addressees of the incentive to innovate (i.e., to further develop the 'state of the art'). Following the logic of the market economy, the main reason for this is that entrepreneurs will only advance a certain state of the art if it helps them to position themselves on the market with a higher 'data protection quality' than their competitors do. However, as soon as all competitors are required to equally

---

48 See Art. 25 cip. 38-42.

49 Cf. Art. 3 Nr. 10 RL 2010/75/EU; see at Mario Martini, Integrierte Regelungsansätze im Immissionsschutzrecht, 210 and subs (C.H. Beck, 1st ed., 2000); Ulrich Baumgartner, Tina Gausling, Datenschutz durch Technikgestaltung und datenschutzfreundliche Voreinstellungen, in: ZD 2017, 308; see for empirical evidence of effectiveness, von Grafenstein et al., Effective data protection by design through empirical research methods, under review at CLSR.

50 Cf. Jarass, BImSchG, § 3, cip. 92–96.

51 See, instead of many other authors, Paal/Pauly, Datenschutz-Grundverordnung, DS-GVO Art. 32, cip. 56–59; in contrast, much less optimistic, see Lee A. Bygrave, Data Protection by Design and by Default: Deciphering the EU's Legislative Requirements, 117 et seq., in: *Oslo Law Review*, 4 (2), 105–120, (2017).

52 Cf. Paal/Pauly, Datenschutz-Grundverordnung, DS-GVO Art. 32, cip. 56-59.

53 See the summary at Eric Gawel, Technologieförderung durch 'Stand der Technik': Bilanz und Perspektiven, 216, in: Martin Eifert, Wolfgang Hoffmann-Riem (eds.), Innovationsfördernde Regulierung – Innovation und Recht II, 197-220, (Duncker & Humblot, 1st ed. 2009) 216; see, regarding further economic resistances, Bygrave (n 51), 119.

provide for this higher product or service quality, the innovator loses its competitive advantage and thus its business opportunity. The dynamic function of this reference thus leads to the situation where the innovator can no longer refinance development costs for its higher 'protection quality'. The result of this dynamic is that the 'state of the art' requirement provides an incentive for the addressees to hide. This is the case with respect to the two following aspects: what the *actual* risk is that they may discover according to the particularities of their specific context; and what the appropriate measures of protection are that could *be* available in order to mitigate these risks. This regulatory approach, therefore, often leads to the opposite of what the regulator wants to achieve. Instead of the fact that the regulation addressees innovate and, what is equally important, reveal the information about such an innovation to others, it leads to a so-called 'cartel of silence' because pushing a 'state of the art' means investing without return opportunities.[54]

Gawel stresses that there are only a few factors that can break such a 'cartel of silence' among the regulation addressees. The most important factor is a market participant that considers the further development of the 'state of the art' as its core business 'value proposition'. Unlike the other regulation addressees, these market participants do not directly target the data subjects, whether they are consumers or business customers of data-driven products or services, but to other regulation addressees who in turn target the data subjects.[55] In this case, these market participants can use the legal requirement referring to the 'state of the art' as a constantly renewed business opportunity because their business model relies on the legal obligation of the other regulation addressees: Each time these market participants push the 'state of the art', they put the other addressees under pressure to implement the newly developed and now appropriate protection instruments. Coming back to Arts 25 and 32 GDPR, if the 'state of the art'-requirement gets properly enforced,[56] this mechanism could well break the resistances of the 'normal' regulation addressees.

IV. IMPLICATIONS FOR THE INTERPRETATION OF THE GDPR

In legal literature, there is a lively discussion on the pros and cons of different options of how to implement the co-regulatory instruments established under the GDPR, especially the certification mechanisms of the data protection certification mechanisms of Arts 42 and 43.[57] This chapter does not aim to comment on all the questions that arose through the debate. Instead,

---

[54] See Gawel, ibid., 200–204.

[55] Cf. ibid., 204.

[56] For example by data protection authorities on the basis of Art. 83 sect. 4 lit. a GDPR, or even by a data controller (or processor) as the 'competitor' of the violating data controller (or processor) on the basis of §3a German Unfair Competition Act – see regarding the latter aspect, Gerald Spindler, Nationale Umsetzung der Datenschutzgrundverordnung im Bereich der Ko-Regulierung - Politikempfehlungen zur Schaffung rechtlicher Anreize für die Wirtschaft zur Entwicklung und Implementierung von Verhaltensregeln und Zertifizierungen, availabel under: https://sriw.de/images/pdf/2016-Gutachen-EU-DSGVO-SRIW---final_druck.pdf accessed Oct. 30, 2021, (2016), who considers that the German Unfair Competition Act can be at least applicable if a competitor infringes the GDPR.

[57] See, e.g., Rodrigues, Barnard-Wills, De Hert, Papakonstantinou (n 42); ENISA, Recommendations on European Data Protection Certification, Version 1.0, (November 2017).

the purpose of this analysis is to determine how these provisions can be interpreted for the political promise to be fulfilled that the GDPR provides a competitive advantage. Based on the previous structure, the next sections will first address certain aspects regarding the function of increasing legal certainty with respect to codes of conduct and data protection certification mechanisms (and, to a very limited extent, BCR). While data protection certification mechanisms refer to specific 'processing operations by controllers and processors' (Art. 42 sect. 1 sent. 1 GDPR), codes of conduct are more generally related to 'the specific features of the various processing sectors' (Art. 40 sect. 1 GDPR). Therefore, both mechanisms have different goals and can be used complementary to each other.[58] However, the following sections focus on specific questions with respect to data protection certification mechanisms. The last section will address issues of how to handle the complexity of this co-regulatory instrument.

IV.1 Legal Certainty Function

This section compares codes of conduct and data protection certification mechanisms (and, to a very limited extent, BCR) with respect to its effects on increasing legal certainty. In this regard, the section also discusses how exactly these instruments should specify the law, and finally, various incentives for data controllers and processors to use these mechanisms.

IV.1.1 Certification mechanisms and codes of conduct (as well as BCR)

Both codes of conduct and data protection certification mechanisms can reduce the complexity of entrepreneurial processes of the data controllers and processors by increasing legal certainty. In contrast, this function is limited with respect to BCR. In regards of codes of conduct and data protection certification mechanisms, this function is evident in several recitals. Recital 77 sent. 1 GDPR for example states:

> *Guidance* on the implementation of appropriate measures and *on the demonstration of compliance by the controller or the processor*, especially as regards the identification of the risk related to the processing, their assessment in terms of origin, nature, likelihood and severity, and the identification of best practices to mitigate the risk, *could be provided in particular by means of approved codes of conduct, approved certifications,* guidelines provided by the Board or indications provided by a data protection officer [emphasis added].

With respect to the legal effects of complying with a data protection certification mechanism or code of conduct, recital 81 sent. 2 GDPR also stresses that:

> The *adherence* of the processor *to an approved code of conduct or an approved certification* mechanism *may be used as an element to demonstrate compliance* with the obligations of the controller [emphasis added].

Both mechanisms, therefore, intend to increase legal certainty with respect to either specific processing operations or, more generally, processing sectors. This legal-certainty-increasing function becomes apparent in several provisions: Pursuant to Art. 24 sect. 3 GDPR, the appli-

---

[58] See Heilmann and Schulz (n 37), Art. 42 GDPR, cip. 10, in: Sybille Gierschmann, Katharina Schlender, Rainer Stentzel Winfried Veil, Kommentar Datenschutz-Grundverordnung, (Bundesanzeiger-Verlag, 1st ed., 2017).

cation of codes of conduct or certificates 'may be used as an element by which to demonstrate compliance with the obligations of the controller'; while only certificates can be used as an element to demonstrate compliance with the data protection-by-design requirement (Art. 25 sect. 3 GDPR), both certificates and codes of conduct can be used for demonstration purposes with respect to the security-by-design requirement (Art. 32 sect. 3 GDPR); both mechanisms can also help to demonstrate compliance with the necessary guarantees if personal data are processed on behalf of a controller or indirectly for another processor (Art. 28 sect. 5 GDPR); finally, certificates and codes of conduct can even help legitimise the transfer of personal data to a third country outside the EU (pursuant to Art. 46 sect. 2 lit. e and f GDPR). In all these cases, both mechanisms help to reduce the complexity of entrepreneurial data-driven processes. In contrast, the functions of BCR are limited, in this regard, to only one of these aspects, that is, legitimizing the transfer of personal data to a third country outside the EU (Art. 46 sect. 2 lit. b). In this contribution, however, BCR do not play a further role because of this limited functionality.

IV.1.2 Degree of granularity of codes of conduct and certificates

So far, one conclusion can be drawn from the common function of increasing legal certainty on the level of granularity that is required for the specification of a code of conduct or certification mechanism. Both mechanisms can serve as an incentive for data controllers and processors to comply with the law by allowing them to specify broad legal terms and legal principles, thereby increasing legal certainty. At the microeconomic level, increasing legal certainty can, therefore, enhance the entrepreneurial innovation processes, as data controllers (and in some cases processors) can use the adherence to data protection certification mechanisms or codes of conduct as a means of demonstrating compliance with multiple requirements (pertaining to the legal principles or broad legal terms). It must be stressed, however, that such a compliance function only works if the data protection certification mechanism or code of conduct indeed specifies the law, thus making it more specific.[59] For example, a data protection certification mechanism that specifies the data protection-by-design requirement for certain processing operations, must not simply repeat the legal text, in all its vagueness. Instead, such a data protection certification mechanism or a code of conduct may be more effective in exploiting the legal certainty increasing feature the more precisely it determines how this requirement is met with respect to specific processing activity. It is important to stress this aspect because previous examples have already shown that stakeholders who are involved in such a standardization process do not always make the law more specific.[60]

In summary, the adherence to a data protection certification mechanism or code of conduct can demonstrate compliance with legal requirements more effectively, the more precisely the certification mechanism or code of conduct determines such a requirement. Conversely, if

---

[59] Cf. Heilmann and Schulz (n 37), Art. 42, cip. 33, focusing on the control function; Matthias Bergt Art. 42 cip. 15, in: Jürgen Kühling, Benedikt Buchner, Datenschutz-Grundverordnung - Bundesdatenschutzgesetz (CH. Beck, 2nd ed., 2018).

[60] See, e.g., the code of conduct that was established in Germany by the Federal Insurance Industry Association (Gesamtverband der deutschen Versicherungswirtschaft e.V.), available under https://www.gdv.de/resource/blob/23938/8db1616525e9a97326e2f2303cf42bd5/download-code-of-conduct-data.pdf accessed Oct. 30, 2021, which was set up under the application of § 38a of the German Federal Data Protection Act (BDSG); in contrast, see the considerations regarding the ISO Cloud Standard at De Hert, Papakonstantinou and Kamara (n 26), 27, which seems therefore to be a better example.

a data protection certification mechanism or code of conduct (or parts of it) simply repeat the legal text, its compliance function is zero.

IV.1.3 Different incentives for different types of data controllers and processors

Another conclusion can be drawn regarding the incentives of data controllers and processors to reduce the complexity of their entrepreneurial processes.[61] If Mayer-Schönberger's conclusions are correct, the incentive to apply the law, given the opportunity to increase legal certainty, works best if data controllers (and partly, processors) face high benefits or costs. However, if they do not have much to lose or gain, the incentive will have less impact on an entrepreneur's decision to comply with data protection requirements. This means, for example, that a start-up at an early stage of its development, which still operates based on a low investment, will pay less attention to the possibility of increasing legal certainty. By contrast, the higher the investment or the chance of an economic breakthrough on the market, the more important the entrepreneurial opportunity to increase legal certainty becomes. To make sure that an enterprise that still makes little investment, has an incentive to increase legal certainty (i.e., complying with the law), the regulator, such as a data protection authority, can still focus on fines. Although a potential loss through fines may be less effective than a potential gain as an entrepreneurial incentive to comply with the law, it is not ineffective. In this respect, data controllers who follow an entrepreneurial approach can also use, their compliance to a data protection certification mechanism and/or code of conduct as an element in order to decrease the potential loss, i.e., a fine pursuant to Art. 83 sect. 2 lit. j GDPR.

IV.2 Signalling Function

This section discusses the effects of data protection certification mechanisms and codes of conduct on market competition with respect to their signalling function. Having first identified, in this regard, the main differences between certification mechanisms and codes of conduct, the following sections focus on certification mechanisms and discuss the level of protection that these mechanisms can signal on the market and the appropriate certification object.

IV.2.1 Differences between certification mechanisms and codes of conduct

In addition to the common function of increasing legal certainty, both mechanisms also show significant differences with respect to their effects on the mesoeconomic level. As explained earlier, standards can be used to signal to business customers and consumers the quality of certain data-driven products and services in terms of the level of data protection envisaged. Consumers and business customers can choose from a variety of products and/or services of different 'data protection qualities' belonging to the same category; this, in turn, offers data controllers (and in part processors) the business opportunity to provide consumers or business customers with higher quality products or services who prefer such products or services to offers that belong to the same category but are of lower quality. In this regard, legal principles and broad legal terms, as discussed previously, combined with standardisation procedures that

---

[61] See, in general, ENISA, ibid., p. 24, referring to Andrej Tomšič, Jelena Burnik, et al., 19, Consolidated report on enhancing confidence and acceptability of new certification measures, CRISP project, (2017).

enable data controllers to specify the regulatory expectations, have the effect that data protection law can create a competitive advantage.

However, as also shown above, this feature works only if different products or services belong to the same category but *can* have different data protection qualities. Only certificates can thus lead to such a competitive advantage at a mesoeconomic level, but not codes of conduct. The reason for this is that a code of conduct relates to a specific processing sector as a whole and, in principle, defines a common level of protection for all processing activities. As a result, all products and services in this sector provide the same level of protection. In contrast, certification mechanisms only apply to specific processing operations, not to one sector. As a result, products or services may belong to the same category but have different 'data protection qualities'. Unlike data protection certification mechanisms, codes of conduct do thus not give entrepreneurs the opportunity to offer higher quality products and/or services at a higher price, or of a lower quality and for a lower price.

IV.2.2 Level of protection signalled by data protection certification mechanisms

This difference between codes of conduct and data protection certification mechanisms leads us to the question whether it is, in fact, legally allowed that these certification mechanisms signal such a higher level of protection and, therefore, rely on criteria that are stricter than the level of protection provided for by law.

On the one hand, the wording of Art. 42 sect. 1 GDPR '(...) demonstrating compliance with this Regulation' seems to imply that data protection certification mechanisms should only demonstrate legal compliance but should not go beyond it by requiring from data controllers or processors a higher level of protection and signalling this to data subjects.[62] On the other hand, some legal scholars argue that the law should not be interpreted too narrowly as the possibility of offering data protection certification mechanisms in the market with an even higher level of protection than provided for by law could increase competition in the market.[63] As described above, offering various data-driven products or services of different 'data protection qualities' has indeed the potential to enhance competition on the market. In fact, the wording of the law does not even prohibit different levels of protection as long as each level offered is within the scope of the law and, thus complies with it. Recital 100 GDPR also tends in this direction. This recital states that data protection certification mechanisms allow 'data subjects to *quickly assess the level of data protection* of relevant products and services' [emphasis added]. Of course, this wording, on the one hand, could simply lead to a certification mechanism helping, in any case, to assess the level of protection *quickly*, if ultimately only the same level of protection exists. As mentioned earlier, the assessment made by data subjects is likely to be faster if they can refer to a certification mechanism than without having such a signal as a basis for

---

[62] See Patrick von Braunmühl, Art. 42, cip. 15 in Plath BDSG/DSGVO; Paal/Pauly, Paal, Art. 42, cip. 7; Gerrit Hornung, Korbinian Hartl, Datenschutz durch Marktanreize - auch in Europa? (Data Protection through Market Incentives – in Europe, too?), 224–225, In: ZD 4 (5) 219–225 (2014).

[63] See Heilmann and Schulz (n 37) Art. 42, cip. 34; Hornung and Hartl, ibid., 221; see also the argument at Eric Lachaud, Why the Certification Process Defined in the General Data Protection Regulation Cannot be Successful, 820, in: *Computer Law and Security Review*, 32 (6), 814–826 (2016), that if there was only one level of protection, the use of data protection certification mechanisms would conflict with Provision 10 in Table 1 of the Directive 2005/29/EC ('Unfair Commercial Practices Directive'), which considers as unfair 'Presenting rights given to consumers in law as a distinctive feature of the trader's offer.'

their purchasing decision. On the other hand, the wording makes more sense if several products of the same category offer different levels of protection. The reason for this is that the assessment of the actual level of protection by data subjects is, in fact, superfluous if there is only one level of protection, that is, the level of protection provided for by law. Therefore, it is more plausible to interpret the law in such a way that it allows for different levels of protection.

However, it should be emphasized that there are, in fact, not many cases where it makes sense to discuss this question of different levels of protection. The reason for this is that the category of an equal level of protection does not match with the characteristics of a legal principle or broad legal term. As explained above, both legal instruments provide for regulatory objectives and leave, as its main characteristic, data controllers and processors enough room to find different ways of achieving these aims. This essentially allows three different kinds of varieties: First, different types of protection measures that are applied with regard to different risks (e.g., on the one hand, special information against the risk of being manipulated by personalized marketing, and on the other hand, encryption measures against the different risk that communication will not remain confidential). Secondly, given one specific risk, there are several measures that ensure the same level of protection (such as a data protection authority or specialized private data broker, both acting on behalf of data subjects). Thirdly, a specific risk in which different types of measures result in different levels of protection (e.g., opt-in instead of opt-out mechanisms). It only actually makes sense to talk about different levels of protection in this last case.

Even if the same risk were present and data protection certification mechanisms could require a higher level of protection from the data controllers and/or processors and would be allowed to signal this to data subjects, the 'state of the art'-requirement further restricts these (potentially) competition-enhancing effects. The reason for this is that the data protection and security-by-design requirements oblige the regulation addressees to consider the 'state of the art' in any case, which means the most effective implementation. Thus, as far as data controllers or processors must apply the 'state of the art', there is actually no higher, i.e. more effective, level of protection that could be signalled by a data protection certification mechanism. This requirement thus deprives 'normal' regulation addressees who provide for a higher level of protection of their business opportunity because this higher level of protection constitutes the 'state of the art' that all other regulation addressees have to consider. Thus, these addressees cannot refinance their development costs because they cannot use their 'better' product as a unique selling point anymore. Only entities that see the development of the 'state of the art' as their core business value proposition can economically benefit from this requirement. They can use the requirement as an ever-renewing business opportunity: Each time they push the 'state of the art', they put the other regulation addressees under pressure to implement (and buy) these newly developed protection measures. Only these entities, therefore, will have an interest in signalling the higher level of protection of their new technical or organizational solution. However, in this regard, all data protection certification mechanisms must, or at least, should refer to the constantly evolving 'state of the art', and consequently, signal it. Because if they did not refer to the 'state of the art', they would not be able to demonstrate that the certified processing operation complies with the 'state of the art'-requirement under Arts 25 and 32 GDPR. As far as data controllers or processors have to apply the 'state of the art' and the certification mechanism refers to the 'state of the art'-requirement, these certification mechanisms can therefore not signal a higher level of protection.

Only if data controllers or processors do not have to apply the 'state of the art', a certification mechanism can require and signal a higher level of protection that constitutes a competitive advantage. According to Art. 25 and 32 GDPR, this is the case (i.e., data controllers and processors have not to apply the 'state of the art'), if the implementation costs outweigh the need for protection.[64]

IV.2.3 Suitable objects of data protection certification mechanisms

Another question that should be clarified refers to the object of data protection certification mechanisms, that is, asking what can or should be certified. This question arises given the divergent wording used within the law. On the one hand, Art. 42 sect. 1 sent. 1 GDPR refers to 'the establishment of data protection certification mechanisms and of data protection seals and marks, for the purpose of *demonstrating compliance with this Regulation of processing operations* [emphasis added] by controllers and processors.' On the other hand, Recital 100 GDPR highlights the function of data protection certification mechanisms 'allowing data subjects to quickly assess *the level of data protection of relevant products and services* [emphasis added]'.

Some authors advocate sticking with the original wording used within the law itself, so that the wording of Recital 100, which has only the function of an element for the interpretation of the law, is given little weight. von Braunmühl justifies this statement on the grounds, for example, that the certification of 'something' that complies with data protection laws can logically be related only to processing operations and not to products or services. The simple reason for this is that the material scope of data protection refers to the 'processing of personal data' and not to products or services.[65] Instead, other authors want that products and services also should be certifiable. These authors argue that consumers can understand which product and/or service has which kind of 'data protection quality' better when certifying the product or service as a whole. Similarly, the marketing of data-driven products and services of high 'data protection quality' can be more effective if the entire product or service is certified.[66]

Considering the above-described signalling function of certificates, the crucial aspect for a solution to this discussion is that certificates must not mislead consumers and/or business customers. Therefore, it is indeed correct to primarily refer to a specific 'processing operation' rather than a product or service that may rely on a whole system of processing operations.[67] A data protection certification mechanism must make it clear from the perspective of the data subjects and/or the business customer, whether this is a data controller or processor, to what exactly it refers to: Is it a single processing or a whole system of operations that could involve multiple data controllers and/or processors? In the end, an answer to this question also depends on the legal provision to which the data protection certification mechanism relates: If a data controller (or processor) can use such a mechanism in order to demonstrate compliance, for instance, with the data protection and security-by-design requirements under Arts 25 and 32

[64] This contribution does not further explore the precise meaning of the legal term 'costs of implementation' under Art. 25 sect. 1 and 32 sect. 1 GDPR; for the line of argumentation, it is sufficient to understand the consideration in general.

[65] See Patrick von Braunmühl, Art. 42 Rn. 7, in: Kai Uwe Plath, BDSG/DSGVO sowie den Datenschutzbestimmungen des TMG und TKG, (Otto Schmidt, 2nd ed., 2016).

[66] See Philip Laue, Judith Nink, Sascha Kremer, 264, Das neue Datenschutzrecht in der betrieblichen Praxis (Nomos, 1st ed., 2016); von Braunmühl, ibid.

[67] Cf. ENISA (n 42), 15, 22.

GDPR, the mechanism must make it clear what is actually considered to be compliant with the specific requirement. A certification mechanism must, therefore, clarify, in essence, (1) to which processing operation(s) it refers, (2) which risk this causes (that is, the likelihood and severity of the risk for the rights and freedoms of the data subjects) and (3) the implemented safeguards mitigating this risk. This means that a data protection certification mechanism can only refer to a product or service as a whole if the certification procedure addresses at least all processing operations on that the product or service relies on. If a certificate addresses only certain parts of the processing operations on which a product or service relies on, it must clarify these limitations.

This leads us to the main challenge that data protection certification mechanisms have to cope with. This challenge refers to the question of how such a certification mechanism should be designed so that data subjects are able 'to *quickly assess the level of data protection* of relevant products and services' [emphasis added].[68] A data protection certification mechanism must keep its promises. Conversely, if a data protection certification mechanism signals a different level of protection that is actually not present in that situation, this can lead to significant legal consequences: a data controller or processor may lose its certification (Art. 42 sect. 7 sent. 2 GDPR) or is subjected to another sanction mechanism (Art. 43 sect. 2 lit. d and e GDPR).[69] Moreover, this could happen because the certification body loses its accreditation (Art. 43 sect. 7 GDPR) or one or all of them receive a penalty or fine (Art. 83 sect. 4 lit. a and b GDPR).[70] The reason for these consequences could be that (1) the certification mechanism signals to cover more processing operations than it actually does, or (2) signals a lower or even another risk caused by the data processing or (3) signals more protection provided for by certain safeguards against a certain risk, but these do not work properly. In conclusion, the question of what a certification mechanism de facto signals depends on two aspects: On the one hand, an exact definition of the data processing and the level of data protection that the certification mechanism really covers. On the other hand, the specific way how both aspects (i.e., the processing and level of protection that is covered by the certification mechanism) is shown to data subjects so that they can actually understand it. While the first question may be answered by legal and technical experts, the second question may primarily be answered by user experience design. Such a combination of different disciplinary concepts makes it so difficult for the regulation addressees to meet the regulatory expectations.

IV.3 Coping with Complexity

The preceding considerations have shown how complex questions surrounding data protection certification mechanisms can become. This last section focuses on three particular aspects of the complexity taking the viewpoint of the following three stakeholders into account: Entities that issue data protection certification mechanisms, which means, certification bodies or data protection authorities (in the following also 'DPA'); data controllers and processors wishing to

---

[68] See Recital 100 GDPR.

[69] Heilmann and Schulz (n 37), Art. 42, cip. 39.

[70] The sending of false signals might also conflict with the prohibition of unfair commercial practices, e.g., because it is misleading, pursuant to Arts 5–7 of Directive 2005/29/EC ('Unfair Commercial Practices Directive'), Gerald Spindler considers, at least, that the German Unfair Competition Act can be principally applicable if a competitor infringes the GDPR, Spindler (n 56).

submit their data processing operations(s) to a certification mechanism; and data subjects who wish to estimate the level of protection of a certain processing operations (or products and/or services) by referring to a certain data protection certification mechanism.

IV.3.1 The monitoring of the 'state of the art' by certification bodies (or DPAs)

The first aspect to be discussed refers to the interplay between data protection certification mechanisms and the 'state of the art'-requirement under Arts 25 and 32 GDPR. As already emphasized before, all data protection certification mechanisms must or at least should refer to the constantly evolving 'state of the art', as otherwise, they could not be used to demonstrate that the certified processing operation complies with Arts 25 and/or 32 GDPR.

On the one hand, this does not mean that Arts 42 and 43 GDPR *require* the certification body or DPA to constantly monitor the 'state of the art'. Sect. 5 sent. 1 of Art. 42 GDPR merely states that a 'certification pursuant to this Article shall be issued by the certification bodies (...) or by the competent supervisory authority, on the basis of criteria approved by that competent supervisory authority' or by the European Data Protection Board. Correspondingly, sect. 7 sent. 2 requires a certificate to 'be withdrawn, as applicable, by the certification bodies (...) or by the competent supervisory authority where the requirements for the certification are not or are no longer met'. Thus, the obligation of the certification body or the DPA depends on the approved criteria: As long as the criteria do not refer to the 'state of the art'-requirement, the certification body (or DPA) does not have to assess, not even in the moment it issues the certificate, seal or mark, whether or not the data controller (or processor), who wants its data processing operation(s) to be certified, takes, sufficiently, the 'state of the art' into account. Similarly, at least in principle: as long as the criteria only require the data controller (or processor) to apply the 'state of the art' at the time the certificate is issued (but not longer), the certification body (or DPA) does not have to constantly monitor the evolvement of the 'state of the art' and assess whether the data controller (or processor) still takes the 'state of the art' sufficiently into account, even after the certificate was issued.

On the other hand, such a limited scope of a certification mechanism is in some way contrary at least to Art. 25 GDPR, according to which the data controller must comply with this provision 'both at the time of the determination of the means for processing and at the time of the processing itself'. In summary, therefore, it must be said that the certification mechanism loses, at least, its legal certainty increasing function, the more time has passed since the certificate was issued. In contrast, if a certification body (or data protection authority) wishes to offer a data protection certification mechanism that demonstrates compliance with the state of the art-requirement throughout the period in which the mechanism is used by a controller, this body must constantly monitor the 'state of the art' (and assess whether the controller applies the criteria or not). This task could become very complex if the market for technical and organisation data protection measures becomes dynamic. However, a certification body (or DPA) can perform this task much better than the typical data controller because the existence of data protection law (and its complexity) is, so to speak, the reason for its existence.

IV.3.2 Modularizing the scope of data protection certification mechanisms

Even if data controllers (and processors) can outsource the monitoring of the 'state of the art' to a certification body (or DPA), the procedure itself for receiving a data protection certificate, seal or mark can still be quite complex. This may cause a conflict with Art. 42 sect. 1 sent. 2 GDPR, which states that '[T]he specific needs of micro, small and medium-sized enterprises shall be taken into account.' The idea behind this provision is to organize the procedures related to a data protection certification mechanism in a way that makes it also affordable for micro-, small-, and medium-sized enterprises given their limited resources.[71] Therefore, the question arises how such procedures may be organized so that it does not divert too many 'scarce resources of potentially high-growth entrepreneurial firms away from their core business.'

To prevent such a situation, there are two main factors: the rigour of control mechanisms and the scope of the certificate. With respect to the first factor, the certification procedure becomes more complex the more stringent the certification body (or DPA) assesses whether the data controller or processor wishing to have their data processing operation(s) certified meets the certification criteria. In this regard, Art. 42 sect. 6 GDPR states that the controller or processor must provide the certification body or DPA 'with all information and access to its processing activities which are necessary to conduct the certification procedure'. As such, it makes sense to adapt the depth of the assessment to the data protection risk that is typically caused by the processing operation in question.[72] However, this chapter does not go into this question any further. In contrast, the following paragraphs will focus on the second factor, that is, the scope of the data protection certification mechanism.

As mentioned earlier, the scope of a data protection certification mechanisms depends essentially on the following aspects: First, if the certification mechanism covers only one single, several or all processing operations on which a product or service is build; second, if it covers all or only specific risks caused by such (a) processing operation(s). In this context, the risk-based approach again plays an important role.[73] Using the example of the German IT-Grundschutz model (that was developed and) is currently being modernized by the German Office for Information Security ('Bundesamt für Informationssicherheit'; in the following also 'BSI'), a data protection certification mechanism could be designed in such a way that it differentiates between context-specific risks. With respect to data protection risks, a certification mechanism could thus enable controllers and processors to first concentrate on the most relevant data protection risks (caused by one or several processing operations). Subsequently, they can then extend the scope and/or gradually increase the protection level.[74]

Such a risk-based, modular data protection certification mechanism requires a robust risk assessment methodology.[75] However, regardless of how such a robust methodology should be designed, the following examples are intended to illustrate how such a modular scheme could look like: The most important starting point of these considerations is that every data processing operation in data protection law is determined by the purpose of the operation and the technical and organisational means used to achieve this purpose. The purpose pursued

---

[71] See Laue, Nink and Kremer (n 66), 263 seq., referring to the European Parliament's draft of GDPR; see also Lachaud (n 37), p. 820, who emphasizes the potentially discriminatory effect in detriment of companies who cannot afford the costs for going through a certification process.

[72] Cf. Heilmann and Schulz (n 37), Art. 41, cip. 21, with respect to codes of conduct.

[73] See, in particular, Art. 24, 25 and 32 GDPR; Heilmann and Schulz, ibid., Art. 42, cip. 35.

[74] See Bundesamt für Informationssicherheit, Motivation und Ziele der Modernisierung des IT-Grundschutzes, available under. https://www.bsi.bund.de/DE/Themen/ITGrundschutz/IT-Grundschutz-Modernisierung/Motivation/itgrundschutz_motivation_node.html accessed Oct. 30, 2021, (re-called 3 October 2017).

[75] Cf. Gellert (n 22), 490–492; see von Grafenstein, Refining the Concept of the Right to Data Protection in Article 8 ECFR – Part I, II and III, EDPL 4/2020, 2/2021, 3/2021.

therefore is the primary starting point as in how far a controller causes as risk to the fundamental rights of data subject. Thus, the risks of data processing can be precisely determined by the purpose and the means.[76] In summary, it depends on the most relevant purpose and means causing a risk and the strategy regarding the controller's (or processor's) position in the market, which processing operation, i.e. which risk caused by the means and its purpose, is first certified, which processing operation comes next and so on. Such a modular data protection certification mechanism could at least reduce the efforts significantly when undergoing a certification process, significantly.

On the other hand, a modular certification mechanism that enables data controllers and processors to differentiate between the purposes, means and risks that a processing operation causes, further increases the complexity for the data subject. To avoid the situation where a data subject does not understand what type of risk was caused, for example, by a bundle of processing operations on which a data-driven product is built on, the data protection certification mechanism must clearly signal its scope. Here again, it will be a question for future research how such a modular scheme must be worked out in order to not deceive the data subjects. This question may specifically address the domain of user experience design. Another question is, in fact, whether it is (both technically and normatively) possible to separate different risks from each other. It may well be the case that one risk is extremely related to another so it cannot be mitigated separately. In such a case, it would probably be misleading for the data subject if a data protection certification mechanism relates to only one of the two risks. In that case, such a data protection certification mechanism had thus to relate to both risks and the corresponding level of protection.

IV.3.3 The degree of diversity of certificates offered on the market

From the point of view of data subjects, the complexity increases further if one considers that there is not only one certification body operating on the 'data protection market' but in principle an unlimited number of them. This can lead to the situation where data subjects (completely) lose the overview.[77] Then these mechanisms lose their function to effectively signal the level of protection of, let us say, a data-driven product that operates based on a bundle of processing operations to a data subject who wishes to purchase that product.

A solution to such market fragmentation is, of course, to centralize the offer. If fewer entities offer certificates on a 'data protection market', there is a smaller risk for the market to become too fragmented. For example, if only data protection authorities could offer data protection certification mechanisms,[78] the number of certification bodies in the European Single Market would (almost) equal the number of EU Member States.[79] One can also categorize the European Data Protection Seal as a similar mechanism, which may even add to the previous

---

[76] Grafenstein, HIIG Discussion Paper, Specific GDPR certification schemes as rule, general schemes (and criteria) as exception, accessed Dec. 8, 2021 under https://edpb.europa.eu/sites/default/files/webform/public_consultation_reply/Position%20Statement_HIIG-ECDF%20%28author_%20Grafenstein%29_0.pdf.

[77] See ENISA (n 42), 24; Rodrigues, Barnard-Wills, De Hert and Papakonstantinou (n 42), 257.

[78] However, see the risks of such a solution discussed at Rodrigues, Barnard-Wills, De Hert and Papakonstantinou, ibid., 262–263; see also ENISA, ibid., 25.

[79] However, in Germany, the market may remain rather fragmented in light of its federal structure, which leads to more than 16 data protection authorities, cf. Peter Schaar, Datenschutz und Föderalismus. Schöpferische Vielfalt oder Chaos, cip. 36–37, in: Ines Härtel, Handbuch des Föderalismus -

mechanism. Pursuant to Art. 42 sect. 5 GDPR, as mentioned before, a certification can only be issued by a certification body or a DPA based on criteria approved by that DPA or the European Data Protection Board; if the European Data Protection Board approves the criteria, sent. 2 regulates that 'this may result in a common certification, the European Data Protection Seal.' If this certification mechanism is established in a way that includes all other corresponding national mechanisms that could be operated by private certification bodies or DPAs, it will have a resounding, harmonizing, even homogenizing effect on the 'data protection market'.[80]

As already explained, however, such a solution based on the centralization of knowledge may conflict with the need for market creativity. Such market creativity is at least necessary when a central entity is unable to react quickly enough to the dynamics of innovative markets, which essentially means to collect the necessary knowledge about context-specific risks and the corresponding measures that can best mitigate those risks. From this perspective it can be better to allow a multitude of entities to act as scheme owners and/or certification bodies so that they can create a variety of data protection certification mechanisms that can cover the variety of context-specific risks. On the one hand, such a homogenizing, in other words, 'creativity-reducing' effect does not seem to be severe if a European Data Protection Seal addresses only specific data protection risks caused by certain processing operations. In this case, the market can still develop its creative dynamics by discovering new processing operations or new risks (which do not necessarily have to be caused by new operations but may also be caused by already well-known operations), and thus quickly find suitable solutions. Only if a European Data Protection Seal covered a wide range of processing operations and risks – providing for criteria on a rather abstract level – this would hamper the required market creativity. In this case, however, the criteria may not adequately specify the law, but functions at a similar abstract level such as the law itself.[81]

Besides the simple reduction of the certification mechanism, however, there are also 'softer' solutions.[82] Among them, a solution should be discussed quickly, as it addresses, in particular, the problem that data subjects may be unable to keep track of all the variety of certificates. DPAs could help data subjects to obtain and/or maintain an overview about certificates that best meet their specific needs by testing and ranking the quality of data protection certification mechanisms. In this case, DPAs do not only act as entities supervising the creation and control of the data protection certification mechanisms by private certification bodies, which are subject to their competencies. They can also compare data protection certification mechanisms across the European market.[83] In this regard, the registration and publication of data protection

Föderalismus als demokratische Rechtsordnung und Rechtskultur in Deutschland, Europa und der Welt. Band III - Entfaltungsbereiche des Föderalismus (Springer, 1st ed., 2012).

[80] Cf. Rodrigues, Barnard-Wills, De Hert and Papakonstantinou (n 42), 264, discussing the opposite constellation, that is, the negative effects, if there were a European privacy Seal that does not include any other seals operated by the DPA.

[81] Cf., e.g., the 'EuroPriSe Criteria for the certification of IT products and IT-based services', which do not make further differences between IT products and services, https://www.european-privacy-seal.eu/EPS-en/Criteria (3 March 2018); in contrast, see the considerations regarding the ISO Cloud Standard at de Hert, Papakonstantinou and Kamar (n 26), p. 27, which seems therefore to be a better example.

[82] See, e.g., Rodrigues, Barnard-Wills, De Hert and Papakonstantinou (n 42) 256 subseq., focusing on the available options of the European Commission to enhance the implementation of data protection certification mechanisms.

[83] Consumer protection agencies could take over such a function, as well, as long as the data-driven service being certified creates the overlap between data protection and consumer protection law, in other

certification mechanisms in the European Single Market, pursuant to Art. 42 sect. 8 GDPR, is an important step. In order to enable such a European-wide comparison, this provision should therefore be understood in a way that not only European Data Protection Seals have to be registered, but also national data protection certification mechanisms.[84] Through publicity the regulator can also learn which mechanisms work best in which context under which conditions, and frequently (re-)evaluate and (re-)adapt its regulatory instruments according to its regulatory objectives.[85]

Only if the regulator, for example, the European Data Protection Board concludes that these 'creativity-preserving' mechanisms do not give the data subjects the necessary overview, it should consider further steps, such as reducing the number of data protection certification mechanisms.

V. CONCLUSION

The preceding considerations addressed the question under which conditions the political promise that the GDPR gives its regulation addressees of a competitive advantage could apply in business practice. Integrating concepts of evolutionary market theories and entrepreneurship research to the equation, the regulator is, at least in principle, able to strengthen competition in the 'data protection market(s)'. In this regard, legal principles and broad legal terms such as the data protection and security-by-design requirements, combined with co-regulatory instruments, in particular, the data protection certification mechanisms and codes of conduct, can play a major role. The reason for this is that in innovative and dynamic environments, the regulator is hardly able to centralize the knowledge about context-specific risks and thus the necessary protection instruments. Legal principles and broad legal terms can therefore be appropriate regulatory instruments because they leave the regulation addresses enough room to explore, in accordance to their specific purpose(s) and means, the risks and thus the best solution to mitigate these risks. By using codes of conduct, and even more so, data protection certification mechanisms, data controllers and processors can turn the vagueness of the law into a competitive advantage. These effects can be demonstrated on three different levels:

At the microeconomic level, data controllers and partly processors, are able to increase legal certainty by specifying and standardising legal principles and broad legal terms through these co-regulatory instruments. The increase in legal certainty offers them a competitive advantage because it reduces the complexity of their entrepreneurial process. This function is inherent in both instruments, that are, codes of conduct and data protection certification mechanisms (and BCR, to a very limited extent). However, the previous analysis has shown that both instruments increase legal certainty, the more detailed they specify the law; if they merely repeat the wording of the law, their function in increasing legal certainty is zero. The incentive of data

words, in situations where data subjects are, simultaneously, consumers; cf., regarding the variety of questions on the interplay between data protection law, consumer protection law, and competition law, Preliminary Opinion of the European Data Protection Supervisor (EDPS), Privacy and competitiveness in the age of big data: The interplay between data protection, competition law and consumer protection in the Digital Economy, 26 (March 2014).

[84] Leaving open that question, ENISA (n 42), p. 27.

[85] Cf. Eifert (n 7), 60; Franzius (n 7), 81–103.

controllers and processors to use these legal instruments varies depending on what they lose or gain when they can demonstrate compliance with the law or, vice versa when it turns out that they violate the law. The higher the investments or the expected profits are, the more likely it is that they want to make sure that they are legally compliant. The question of how these positive and negative incentives (gaining trust of consumers or business customers versus receiving a fine) should be designed to make sure that the potential of the legal certainty increasing function is fully exploited, must also be researched empirically.

In contrast to codes of conduct, data protection certification mechanisms can also offer, at least in principle, a competitive advantage on a mesoeconomic level. The reason for this is that controllers and processors can: first, use the vagueness of legal requirements as a business opportunity to offer their consumers or business customers a higher level of protection than their competitors do (so that their customers and/or consumers pay a higher price or buy more products of this higher quality). Whether the GDPR allows such a competitive function or only aims for the compliance function (that is, to reduce legal certainty) is debated in legal literature. Regardless of the outcome of this debate, the previous analysis has shown that there are only a few cases where such a competitive function could become relevant. First, the question becomes only relevant if there is (1) a specific processing operation with (2) a specifically defined risk and (3) different safeguards lead, in fact, either to a higher or lower level of protection. Given the multitude of processing operations and different risks (whether the risks are truly different or just higher or lower) most data protection certification mechanisms do not signal a higher or lower level of protection but simply refer to another (incomparable) case. Secondly, even if two (or more) specific processing operations create the same risk and thus safeguards could provide a higher or lower level of protection (which could be signalled by a data protection certification mechanism), there is another legal mechanism that limits the potential competitive advantage of this situation. This legal mechanism is the 'state of the art'-requirement under Arts 25 and 32 GDPR, which obliges data controllers, and in some cases processors, to constantly consider the most effective (i.e. highest) level of protection offered on the market. Therefore, there is only little room for manoeuvre in which different levels of protection become relevant. Such a limitation on the variety of data protection certification mechanisms on the market might not be the worst result, as it is already difficult enough to signal a specific level of protection of a specific processing operation to the data subject, so that they understand it correctly. How this, in the end, should be done cannot only be answered by legal and technical expertise but additionally, through means of user experience design.

The 'state of the art'-requirement under Arts 25 and 32 GDPR is another factor that can boost innovation even at the macroeconomic level. This requirement can enhance innovation if specialised companies focus on developing the 'state of the art' and put it as their core value proposition for the other 'normal' regulation addressees. These specialized entities can use the requirement as a business opportunity that constantly renews itself because they constantly put pressure on other regulatory addressees to implement (and buy) the 'state of the art', which they themselves are pushing ahead time and again. If this mechanism creates a dynamic market for data protection-by-design solutions, it can get quite difficult for data controllers and processors to see what the 'state of the art' of a solution against a specific risk caused by a certain data processing operation currently is. In this regard, scheme owners and certification bodies (and DPA) can play an important role. If a certification mechanism offered by these bodies has to prove, pursuant to its criteria, compliance with the 'state of the art'-requirement, and possibly not only in the moment the certificate, seal or mark is issued but also throughout the period when it is in use, the body has to constantly monitor the market for the 'state of the art' and frequently re-assess whether the data controller still complies with it or not. Such a function of data protection certification mechanisms can be an important benefit and thus an incentive for data controllers to use these certification mechanisms because it significantly reduces the complexity to comply with the law.

However, this does not mean that the process through which data controllers and processors must go through to certify one or more of its processing operations is not complex. The legislator has clearly seen that the complexity of certification mechanisms can conflict with the needs of micro-, small- and medium-sized companies due to their limited resources. One way to reduce this complexity is to limit the scope of a data protection certification mechanism, in addition to financial aids or reducing the depth of how compliance with the criteria of such a mechanism is controlled. For example, if a data controller can choose a certification mechanism that addresses only a specific risk for a particular processing operation of which the controller thinks that its level of protection is most relevant to be signalled on the market, the procedural complexity is limited to this particular case. In contrast, the procedural complexity increases the more data processing operations and the more risks the certification mechanism aims to cover. To find a balance between scaling the mechanisms and reducing its complexity, the mechanisms could be modularized so that data controllers and processors could begin with one module that covers a specific risk of a particular operation, adding more modules step by step, expanding to further risks and further operations. How such a modularized mechanism must be designed so that data subjects can truly understand which risk of which processing operation the specified module of the data protection certification mechanism covers depends not only on legal and technical expertise but also on research in the field of user experience design.

Finally, from the point of view of data subjects, the degree of complexity of data protection certification mechanisms is also relevant. The previous considerations have shown that the market success of such mechanisms depends on whether data subjects can understand which mechanism signals which level of protection for which processing operation. For the data subjects, this is an already very complex issue, which is even more valid the more certification mechanisms are offered on the market. One solution to reducing this complexity is to reduce the number of certification mechanisms. In this respect, the European Data Protection Seal can be crucial, given that this mechanism harmonizes the criteria according to which national certification mechanisms are issued to data controllers and processors. However, this mechanism should not lead to the situation in which the market creativity loses its ability to react quickly and effectively to newly discovered risks or even unknown operations. This situation can be avoided if European Data Protection Seals are sufficiently specific, that is, are not based on abstract-general criteria, but refer to specific risks of certain processing operations. This indeed poses the same questions as before.

After all, these are just a few of the remaining questions; and even these few questions show that research into the impact of regulatory instruments on data-driven innovation and competitive advantage is a rather complex issue. The complexity requires the ability of a regulator to learn, and thus to frequently (re-)evaluate and (re-)adapt its regulatory instruments according to its goals.[86] If done well, this approach will at least increase the rationality of the

[86] Cf. Eifert, ibid., 60; Franzius, ibid., 81–103.

law, regardless of whether or not the political promise that the GDPR provides for competitive advantage becomes true.[87]

REFERENCES

Appelt, I, Aufgaben und Verfahren der Innovationsfolgenabschätzung (Tasks and Procedures of the Innovation Impact Assessment), in: Martin Eifert, Wolfgang Hoffmann-Riem, Innovation und Recht III – Innovationsverantwortung, 147–181 (Mohr Siebeck, 1st ed., 2009).

Article 29 Data Protection Working Party Guidelines on Data Protection Impact Assessment (DPIA) and determining whether processing is 'likely to result in a high risk' for the purposes of Regulation 2016/679, available under: ec.europa.eu/newsroom/document.cfm?doc_id=47711, (4 April 2017).

Article 29 Data Protection Working Party Statement on the role of a risk-based approach in data protection legal frameworks, 14/EN, WP 218, available at: http://ec.europa.eu/justice/data-protection/article-29/documentation/opinion-recommendation/files/2014/wp218_en.pdf, (30 May 2014).

Baldwin, R, M Cave and M Lodge, *Understanding Regulation – Theory, Strategy and Practice* (Oxford Press, 2nd ed., 2013).

Baumgartner, U and T Gausling, Datenschutz durch Technikgestaltung und datenschutzfreundliche Voreinstellungen, in: ZD 2017, 308.

Bennett, CJ and CD Raab, *The Governance of Privacy: Policy Instruments in Global Perspective* (MIT Press, updated paperback ed., 2006).

Bergt, M, Art. 42 cip. 15, in: Jürgen Kühling, Benedikt Buchner, Datenschutz-Grundverordnung - Bundesdatenschutzgesetz (CH. Beck, 2nd ed., 2018).

Black, J, Forms and Paradoxes of Principles Based Regulation, in: *Capital Markets Law Journal*, 3 (4), 425–457, (2008).

Blind, K, The Impact of Standardization and Standards on Innovation, in: Manchester Institute of Innovation Research (ed.), *Compendium of Evidence on the Effectiveness of Innovation Policy Intervention*, (2013), availabe at: http://www.innovationpolicy.org.uk/compendium/section/Default.aspx?topicid=30.

Borraz, O, Les politiques du risque (Presses de Sciences Po, 1st ed., 2008).

von Braunmühl, P, Art. 42, in: Kai Uwe Plath, BDSG/DSGVO sowie den Datenschutzbestimmungen des TMG und TKG, (Otto Schmidt, 2nd ed., 2016).

Bundesamt für Informationssicherheit (BfS) Motivation und Ziele der Modernisierung des IT-Grundschutzes, available under https://www.bsi.bund.de/DE/Themen/ITGrundschutz/IT-Grundschutz-Modernisierung/Motivation/itgrundschutz_motivation_node.html (accessed 3 October 2019).

Bygrave, LA, Data Protection by Design and by Default: Deciphering the EU's Legislative Requirements, in: *Oslo Law Review* 4 (2), 105–120, (2017).

Costa, L, Privacy and the Precautionary Principle, in: *Computer Law & Security Review*, 28 (1), 14–24, (2012).

De Hert, P, V Papakonstantinou and I Kamara, The Cloud Computing Standard ISO/IEC 27018 Through the Lens of the EU Legislation on Data Protection, in: *Computer Law & Security Review*, 32 (1), 16–30, (2016).

Eberhard Schmidt-Aßmann, Andreas Voßkuhle (eds.), Grundlagen des Verwaltungsrechts – Band I 'Methoden – Maßstäbe – Aufgaben – Organisation', (C.H. Beck, 2nd ed., 2012).

Eifert, M, Regulierungsstrategien (Regulation Strategies), in: Wolfgang Hoffmann-Riem.

EU Agency for Network and Information Security ENISA, Recommendations on European Data Protection Certification, Version 1.0, 13, (November 2019).

European Data Protection Supervisor (EDPS) Preliminary Opinion of the European Data Protection Supervisor (EDPS), Privacy and competitiveness in the age of big data: The interplay between data protection, competition law and consumer protection in the Digital Economy, (March 2014).

[87] Cf. Hoffmann-Riem and Fritzsche (n 6), 39.

Evers, A and H Nowotny, Umgang mit Unsicherheit (Suhrkamp, 1st ed., 1987).
Fagerberg, J, 'Innovation: A Guide to the Literature. What Innovation is Not: The Linear Model' in: J Fagerberg and D C Mowery (eds) *The Oxford Handbook of Innovation* (Oxford University Press, 1st ed., 2004).
Franzius, C, Modalitäten und Wirkungsfaktoren der Steuerung durch Recht (Modes and Impact Factors for the Control through Law), § 4, in: Wolfgang Hoffmann-Riem, Eberhard Schmidt-Aßmann, Andreas Voßkuhle (eds.), Grundlagen des Verwaltungsrechts – Band I 'Methoden – Maßstäbe – Aufgaben – Organisation', (C.H. Beck, 2nd ed., 2012).
Friedewald, M et al., Forum Privatheit, White Paper Datenschutz Folgenabschätzung., available under: http://www.forum-privatheit.de/forum-privatheit-de/publikationen-und-downloads/veroeffentlichungen-des-forums/themenpapiere-white-paper/Forum-Privatheit-WP-DSFA-3-Auflage-2017-11-29.pdf, (2017).
Gartner, W B A, Conceptual Framework for Describing the Phenomenon of New Venture Creation, in: *The Academy of Management Review* 10 (4) 696-706 (1985).
Gasser, U, Cloud Innovation and the Law: Issues, Approaches, and Interplay, No. 2014-7 19-20.
Gawel, E, Technologieförderung durch 'Stand der Technik': Bilanz und Perspektiven, in: Martin Eifert, Wolfgang Hoffmann-Riem (eds), Innovationsfördernde Regulierung – Innovation und Recht II, 197–220, (Duncker & Humblot, 1st ed. 2009).
Gellert, R, Data Protection: a Risk Regulation? Between the Risk Regulation of Everything and the Precautionary Alternative, in: *International Data Privacy Law*, 5 (1), 3–19, (2015).
Gellert, R, We Have Always Managed Risks in Data Protection Law: Understanding the Similarities and Differences Between the Rights-Based and the Risk-Based Approaches to Data Protection, in: *European Data Protection Law Review* (EDPL), 4 (2), 481–292, (2016).
Hartog, C, et al., *Institutions and Entrepreneurship: The Role of the Rule of Law*, 8. (7 January 2018), available under: http://ondernemerschap.panteia.nl/main/publication/bestelnummer/h201003.
Heilmann S and W Schulz, Art. 40 and Art. 42 in: *Kommentar Datenschutz-Grundverordnung* (Sibylle Gierschmann, Katharina Schlender, Rainer Stentzel, Winfried Veil (eds), (Bundesanzeiger Verlag 2017).
Hirsch, D D, In Search of the Holy Grail: Achieving Global Privacy Rules Through Sector-Based Codes of Conduct, in: *Ohio St. LJ*, 74 (6), 1029 subseq., (2013).
Hoffmann-Riem, W, Innovationsoffenheit und Innovationsverantwortung durch Recht – Aufgaben rechtswissenschaftlicher Innovationsforschung (Openness toward Innovation and Responsibility for Innovation by means of Law), in: Archiv des öffentlichen Rechts 123 (4) 513–540 (1998).
Hoffmann-Riem, W and S Fritzsche, Innovationsverantwortung - Zur Einleitung, 39, in: Martin E and W Hoffmann Riem (eds.), Innovations und Recht III - Innovationsverantwortung, 11–41, (Duncker & Humblot, 1st ed., 2009).
Hornung, G, and K Hartl, Datenschutz durch Marktanreize - auch in Europa? (Data Protection through Market Incentives – in Europe, too?), in: ZD 4 (5) 219-225 (2014).
Jaeckel, L, Gefahrenabwehrrecht und Risikodogmatik – Moderne Technologien im Spiegel des Verwaltungsrechts (Prevention of Danger through Law and Legal Conceptualization of Risk), 5–52, (Mohr Siebeck, 1st ed., 2010).
Jarass, HD, Bundes-Immissionsschutzgesetz, BImSchG (C.H. Beck, 12th ed., 2017).
Jergl, J, Art. 32, cip. 21 subseq., in: S Gierschmann, K Schlender, R Stentzel and W Veil, Kommentar Datenschutz-Grundverordnung (Bundesanzeiger Verlag, 1st ed, 2017).
Kamara, I, Co-regulation in EU Personal Data Protection: The Case of Technical Standards and the Privacy by Design Standardisation 'Mandate', in *European Journal of Law and Technology*, 8 (1), 8–11, (2017).
Kaplow, L. Rules Versus Standards: An Economic Analysis, in: *Duke L. J.*, 42 (3), (1992).
Kloepfer, M. Law Enables Technology – About an Underestimated Function of Environmental and Technology Law, in: *Natur und Recht* 417–418 (1997).
Kroes, N, Statement by Vice President Neelie Kroes ‚on the consequences of living in an age of total information´ from the 4th of July 2013, (Sep. 30, 2017), available under: http://europa.eu/rapid/press-release_MEMO-13-654_en.htm accessed 15 05 2020.
Lachaud, E, The General Data Protection Regulation and the Rise of Certification as a Regulatory Instrument, in: *Computer Law and Security Review* (March 2017).

Lachaud, E, Why the Certification Process Defined in the General Data Protection Regulation Cannot be Successful, 820, in: *Computer Law and Security Review,* 32 (6), 814–826 (2016).
Laue, P and S Nink, Das neue Datenschutzrecht in der betrieblichen Praxis (Nomos, 1st ed., 2016).
Levie, J and E Autio, Regulatory Burden, Rule of Law, and Entry of Strategic Entrepreneurs: An International Panel Study, 1411. in: *Journal of Management Studies*, 48 (6) 1392–1419 (2011).
Martini, M, Integrierte Regelungsansätze im Immissionsschutzrecht, (C.H. Beck, 1st ed., 2000).
Maxwell, W J, Principles-based Regulation of Personal Data: The Case of 'Fair Processing', in: *International Data Privacy Law*, 5 (3), 205–216, (2015).
Mayer-Schönberger, V, 'The Law as Stimulus: The Role of Law' in *Fostering Innovative Entrepreneurship*, 6 (2) 159–169 (2010).
Moser, J, Art. 25, cip. 59 subseq.; Art. 32, cip. 21 ff., in: Sibylle Gierschmann, Katharina Schlender, Rainer Stentzel, Winfried Veil, Kommentar Datenschutz-Grundverordnung, (Bundesanzeiger Verlag, 1st ed, 2017).
Murray A, Conceptualising the Post-Regulatory (Cyber)state, in: Roger Brownsword, Karen Yeung (eds.), ibid., 287–316 (2008).
Murray, A, The Regulation of Cyberspace – Control in the Online Environment In: *Modern Law Review*, 70, (5) 879–883 (2007).
Paal, B B and D A Pauly, Datenschutz-Grundverordnung, Bundesdatenschutzgesetz, DS-GVO - BDSG, (C.H. Beck, 2nd ed., 2018).
Peel, J, *Science and Risk Regulation in International Law* (Cambridge University Press, 1st ed., 2010).
Peretti-Watel, P, *La société du risque* (Repères. La Découverte, 1st ed., 2010).
Posner, R A, *Economic Analysis of Law* (Aspen/Wolters, 8th ed., 2010).
Raab, C D and P De Hert, Tools for Technology Regulation: Seeking Analytical Approaches Beyond Lessig and Hood, in: Roger Brownsword, Karen Yeung (eds.), *Regulating Technologies – Legal Futures, Regulatory Frames and Technological Fixes*, 263–285 (2008).
Rodrigues, R, D Wright and K Wadhwa, Developing a Privacy Seal Scheme (That Works), in: *International Data Privacy Law* 3 (2), 100–116 (2013).
Rodrigues, R, D Barnard-Wills, P De Hert and V Papakonstantinou, The Future of Privacy Certification in Europe: An Exploration of Options under Article 42 of the GDPR, 249, in: *International Review of Law, Computers & Technology* 30 (3), 248–270, (2016).
Roßnagel, A, Data Protection in Computerized Everyday Life, (2007), Gutachten im Auftrag der Friedrich-Ebert-Stiftung, available under: http://library.fes.de/pdf-files/stabsabteilung/04548.pdf accessed 12/12/2020.
Schaar, P, Datenschutz und Föderalismus. Schöpferische Vielfalt oder Chaos, in: Ines Härtel, Handbuch des Föderalismus - Föderalismus als demokratische Rechtsordnung und Rechtskultur in Deutschland, Europa und der Welt. Band III - Entfaltungsbereiche des Föderalismus (Springer, 1st ed., 2012).
Schumpeter, J, *Capitalism, Socialism and Democracy*, 82–83 (5th ed. 2003).
Spindler, G, Nationale Umsetzung der Datenschutzgrundverordnung im Bereich der Ko-Regulierung – Politikempfehlungen zur Schaffung rechtlicher Anreize für die Wirtschaft zur Entwicklung und Implementierung von Verhaltensregeln und Zertifizierungen, availabel under: https://sriw.de/images/pdf/2016-GutachenEU-DSGVO-SRIW---final_druck.pdf, (2016).
Steele, J, *Risks and Legal Theory* (Hart Publishing, 1st ed., 2004).
Tomšič, A, J Burnik et al. Consolidated Report on Enhancing Confidence and Acceptability of New Certification Measures., CRISP project, (2017).
v. Grafenstein, M, *The Principle of Purpose Limitation in Data Protection Laws: The Risk-Based Approach, Legal Principles and Private Standards as Elements for Regulating Innovation*, (Mohr Siebeck, 1st ed., 2018, to be published).
v. Grafenstein, M, *Refining the Concept of the Right to Data Protection in Article 8 ECFR – Part I: Finding an Appropriate Object and Concept of Protection by Re-Connecting Data Protection Law with Concepts of Risk Regulation*, 509 - 521 (EDPL 4/2020); ibid., *Part II: Controlling Risks Through (not to) Article 8 ECFR Against Other Fundamental Rights*, 190 - 205 (EDPL 2/2021); ibid., *Part III: Consequences for the interpretation of the GDPR (and the Lawmaker's Room for Manoeuvre)*, 373 - 387 (EDPL 3/2021).
v. Grafenstein, M, HIIG Discussion Paper, Specific GDPR certification schemes as rule, general schemes (and criteria) as exception, accessed Dec. 8, 2021 under https://edpb.europa.eu/sites/default/

files/webform/public_consultation_reply/Position%20Statement_HIIG-ECDF%20%28author_%20Grafenstein%29_0.pdf.
v. Grafenstein, M, Jakobi, T, Stevens, G, *Effective data protection by design through interdisciplinary research methods*, under review at CLSR.
Veil, W, Aart. 24, cip. 78-190, in: S Gierschmann, K Schlender, R Stentzel and W Veil, Kommentar Datenschutz-Grundverordnung (Bundesanzeiger Verlag, 1st ed, 2017).
Wegner, G, Nachhaltige Innovationsoffenheit dynamischer Märkte (Dynamic Markets and their Persistent Openness to Innovation), in: Martin Eifert, Wolfgang Hoffmann-Riem (eds.), Innovationsfördernde Regulierung – Innovation und Recht II, 71-91, (Duncker & Humblot, 1st ed. 2009).

20. Automated decision-making and data protection in Europe

Gianclaudio Malgieri

I. INTRODUCTION

Profiling algorithms and automated decision-making are a growing reality in the current data-driven society. Policymakers, scholars and commentators are more and more concerned with the risks of a black box society[1] in several fields: finance, insurance, housing, police investigations, e-commerce, work life, etc.

In general terms, a decision is a choice that one makes about something after considering several possibilities.[2] A decision has been defined also as any action upon resolution or more simply, in the AI sphere, an action taken after consideration of input information comprising the algorithmic output.[3] Decision-making can be, thus, a human-driven, automated or semi-automated process in which a specific decision is taken. Generally, this process starts from an analysis of (personal or non-personal) data and can be either intended to produce individual decisions or to produce general decisions (i.e., decisions who do not target a specifically identified individual, but, e.g., a general situation).

The EU General Data Protection Regulation (2016) has tried to provide a solution to the risks of automated decision-making through different tools, notably: (1) a right to receive/access meaningful information about the logic, significance and envisaged effects of automated decision making processes producing legal or similarly significant effects (Arts 13–15); and (2) the right not to be subject to such automated decision making with several safeguards and restrains for the limited cases in which automated decision making is permitted (Art 22).

Different scholars have discussed the exact scope of such provisions. The main issues of discussion have been the notion of 'decisions based solely on automated means' and what is

---

1 Frank Pasquale, *The Black Box Society: The Secret Algorithms That Control Money and Information* (Cambridge: Harvard Univ Pr, 2015); Virginia Eubanks, *Automating Inequality: How High-tech Tools Profile, Police, and Punish the Poor* (New York, NY: St Martins Pr, 2018); See also Joshua Kroll et al., 'Accountable Algorithms', *University of Pennsylvania Law Review* 165, no. 3 (1 January 2017): 633; Giovanni Comandè, 'Regulating Algorithms' Regulation? First Ethico-Legal Principles, Problems, and Opportunities of Algorithms', in *Transparent Data Mining for Big and Small Data*, ed. Tania Cerquitelli, Daniele Quercia, and Frank Pasquale, vol. 32, Studies in Big Data (Cham: Springer International Publishing, 2017), 169–206, https://doi.org/10.1007/978-3-319-54024-5_8 (last visited, 30 October 2021); Danielle Citron and Frank Pasquale, 'The Scored Society: Due Process for Automated Predictions', *Faculty Scholarship*, 1 January 2014, https://digitalcommons.law.umaryland.edu/fac_pubs/1431.

2 Cambridge Dictionary, 'Decision', https://dictionary.cambridge.org/dictionary/english/decision (last visited, 30 October 2021).

3 Information Commissioner's Officer, 'Explaining Decisions Made with AI' (ICO, 19 May 2021), 3, https://ico.org.uk/for-organisations/guide-to-data-protection/key-data-protection-themes/explaining-decisions-made-with-artificial-intelligence/ (last visited, 30 October 2021).

the minimum level of human involvement required to make decisions not solely automated; what does 'legal or similarly significant effect' mean, and which safeguards the data controller should implement (in particular if a right to explanation exists).

In this chapter we will show how the Article 29 Working Party – endorsing part of existing literature – supported a broad interpretation for the scope of Article 22, extending both the notion of 'solely automated' decisions and the scope of relevant 'effects'. Even though the right to individual explanation is not always applicable, it is always useful to enable other rights under Article 22 (e.g., right to contestation). In addition, according to the accountability principle (Art 5(2)) and the risk-based approach (Art 24), the data controller shall be required to implement a right to explanation at least for data processing putting at higher risks the rights and freedoms of data subjects.

Section II will describe the issue of human and machine biases in automated decisions, and section III will briefly mention the automated decisions regulations in EU law before the era of the GDPR (in particular, in the EU Data Protection Directive of 1995). Then, section IV will focus on the specific regulation of algorithmic decision-making within the GDPR (Arts 13–15 and Art 22). Consequently, section V will address possible interpretations of the GDPR provisions, mentioning the pertinent academic debate. In addition, section VI will discuss the specific safeguards that data controllers could take when performing automated decisions, in particular following the Article 29 Working Party Opinion interpretation of profiling and automated decisions regulation in the GDPR. Finally, section 7 will briefly touch upon automated decision-making regulation in the new version of Convention 108 of the Council of Europe.

II. AUTOMATED DECISION-MAKING AND THE ISSUE OF MACHINE AND HUMAN BIASES

Biases in algorithmic decisions are one of the most relevant issues within automated profiling:[4] automated decision-making processing may produce outputs representing a distorted, incomplete or misleading reality.[5] It has been argued that distortions and mistakes can manifest themselves in machine judgments in three ways: the data; the design of the algorithm; and the outcome.[6] The impact of these biases is often underestimated: there is a common idea that

[4] Julia Powles and Helen Nissenbaum, 'The Seductive Diversion of 'Solving' Bias in Artificial Intelligence', *Medium*, 7 December 2018, https://onezero.medium.com/the-seductive-diversion-of-solving-bias-in-artificial-intelligence-890df5e5ef53 (Last visited, August 2018).

[5] Ziad Obermeyer et al., 'Dissecting Racial Bias in an Algorithm Used to Manage the Health of Populations', *Science* 366, no. 6464 (25 October 2019): 447–53, https://doi.org/10.1126/science.aax2342.

[6] Solon Barocas and Andrew D. Selbst, 'Big Data's Disparate Impact', *California Law Review* 104 (2016): 680, https://doi.org/10.2139/ssrn.2477899; Kroll et al., 'Accountable Algorithms'; James Grimmelmann and Daniel Westreich, 'Incomprehensible Discrimination', *Cornell Law Faculty Publications*, 1 March 2017, https://scholarship.law.cornell.edu/facpub/1536.

machine rationality cannot be 'biased'.[7] Analogously, also data controllers may often ignore that an algorithm used in their decision-making processes have biases.[8]

As regards their source, machine biases can be classified into two different categories: 'cognitive biases' and 'statistical biases'.[9] Cognitive biases occur when errors in data collection lead to inaccurate depictions of reality due to conventional flaws in data collection like inaccurate methodologies.[10] The difficulty to translate the external reality in objective categories can lead to implicit biased data clustering when designing algorithms.[11] In other terms, these machine biases are due to 'biased inputs' or biased perception of reality of the algorithm designers (e.g., using categories that are irrelevant in a specific field).[12]

Statistical biases happen when the underlying subject matter draws on information that is also inextricably linked to structural discrimination,[13] and thus biases the data as a result.[14] In particular, poorly written algorithms interpreting vast data sets may exclude certain groups[15] and perpetuate existing inequality.[16] In other words, algorithms tend to find patterns and models through the statistical analysis of Big Data, but when in a certain field there is an imbalance (e.g., in terms of gender representation) the pattern is biased itself.[17]

---

[7] See, e.g., Kristina Hammond, '5 Unexpected Sources of Bias in Artificial Intelligence', *TechCrunch* (blog), accessed 27 May 2021, https://social.techcrunch.com/2016/12/10/5-unexpected-sources-of-bias-in-artificial-intelligence/; Tal Zarsky, 'Understanding Discrimination in the Scored Society', *Washington Law Review* 89, no. 4 (1 December 2014): 1375.

[8] Daniel McDuff, Roger Cheng, and Ashish Kapoor, 'Identifying Bias in AI Using Simulation', *ArXiv:1810.00471 [Cs, Stat]*, 30 September 2018, http://arxiv.org/abs/1810.00471.

[9] Kate Crawford and Meredith Whittaker, 'The AI Now Report – The Social and Economic Implications of Artificial IntelligenceTechnologies in the Near-Term', 2016, 6, https://ainowinstitute.org/AI_Now_2016_Report.pdf (Last visited, August 2018); For a taxonomy of machine bias see also Mireille Hildebrandt, 'The Issue of Bias: The Framing Powers of ML', in *Machine Learning and Society: Impact, Trust, Transparency*, ed. Marcello Pelillo (MIT Press, 2021).

[10] Hildebrandt, 'The Issue of Bias: The Framing Powers of ML'.

[11] Drew Roselli, Jeanna Matthews, and Nisha Talagala, 'Managing Bias in AI', in *Companion Proceedings of The 2019 World Wide Web Conference*, WWW '19 (New York, NY, USA: Association for Computing Machinery, 2019), 539–44, https://doi.org/10.1145/3308560.3317590.

[12] Tarleton Gillespie, 'The Relevance of Algorithms', in *Media Technologies*, ed. Tarleton Gillespie, Pablo J. Boczkowski, and Kirsten A. Foot (The MIT Press, 2014), 5, https://doi.org/10.7551/mitpress/9780262525374.003.0009 according to whom: 'Categorization is a powerful semantic and political intervention: what the categories are, what belongs in a category, and who decides how to implement these categories in practice, are all powerful assertions about how things are and are supposed to be'.

[13] Xavier Ferrer et al., 'Bias and Discrimination in AI: A Cross-Disciplinary Perspective', *ArXiv:2008.07309 [Cs]*, 11 August 2020, http://arxiv.org/abs/2008.07309.

[14] Gillespie, 'The Relevance of Algorithms', 3; Crawford and Whittaker, 'The AI Now Report - The Social and Economic Implications of Artificial IntelligenceTechnologies in the Near-Term', 6.

[15] Meredith Whittaker et al., 'Disability, Bias, and AI', 2019, 32.

[16] Danah Boyd, 'Networked Privacy', *Surveillance & Society* 10, no. 3/4 (22 December 2012): 348–50, https://doi.org/10.24908/ss.v10i3/4.4529.

[17] Crawford and Whittaker, 'The AI Now Report - The Social and Economic Implications of Artificial IntelligenceTechnologies in the Near-Term', 6 mentioning the case where data on job promotions (that are used to predict career success) was gathered from an industry that systematically promoted men instead of women.

III. AUTOMATED DECISION-MAKING BEFORE THE GDPR: THE DATA PROTECTION DIRECTIVE

Before the adoption of the GDPR, the Data Protection Directive (95/46/EC) also regulated algorithmic decision-making, in particular through right to access and right not to be subject to automated decisions.[18] Those provisions, however, were more general and less strict than actual Articles 15 and 22 of the GDPR.

In particular, Article 12 of the Data Protection Directive stated that Member States must:

> guarantee every data subject the right to obtain from the controller: (a) without constraint at reasonable intervals and without excessive delay or expense (…): *knowledge of the logic involved in any automatic processing of data concerning* him at least in the case of the automated decisions referred to in Article 15 (1).[19]

On the other hand, Article 15 of the Data Protection Directive regulated 'automated individual decision' as follows:

> (1) Member States shall grant the right to every person not to be subject to a decision which produces legal effects concerning him or significantly affects him and which is based solely on automated processing of data intended to evaluate certain personal aspects relating to him, such as his performance at work, creditworthiness, reliability, conduct, etc.
> (2) Subject to the other Articles of this Directive, Member States shall provide that a person may be subjected to a decision of the kind referred to in paragraph 1 if that decision:
> (a) is taken in the course of the entering into or performance of a contract, provided the request for the entering into or the performance of the contract, lodged by the data subject, has been satisfied or that there are suitable measures to safeguard his legitimate interests, such as arrangements allowing him to put his point of view; or
> (b) is authorized by a law which also lays down measures to safeguard the data subject's legitimate interests'.

In other words, Directive 95/46/EC defined automated decisions as decisions based solely on automated processing and producing *legal effects* or *significant effects*, in particular because intended to evaluate certain personal aspects relating to the subject (such as performance at work, creditworthiness, reliability, conduct, etc.).[20] In these cases, the Directive provided that data controllers had to disclose to the data subjects the 'logic involved' in that automated processing, and that 'every person' (not only 'data subjects') should have a right not to be subject to such automated decisions, unless taken within contractual or pre-contractual circumstances or authorized by a law with relevant safeguards for data subjects.

---

[18] Lee A Bygrave, 'Minding the Machine: Article 15 of the EC Data Protection Directive and Automated Profiling', *Computer Law & Security Review* 17, no. 1 (1 January 2001): 17–24, https://doi.org/10.1016/S0267-3649(01)00104-2.

[19] Emphasis added.

[20] Lee A Bygrave, 'Automated Profiling', 17.

IV. AUTOMATED DECISION-MAKING IN THE GDPR (ARTS 15 AND 22)

The GDPR tried to provide a solution to the risks of automated decision-making through different tools: a right to receive/access meaningful information about the logic, significance and envisaged effects of automated decision-making processes (cf. Arts 13(2)(f); 14(2)(g); and 15(1)(h)); the right not to be subject to automated decision making (Art 22) with several safeguards and restrains for the limited cases in which automated decision making is permitted.

Article 22(1) states as follows: 'the data subject shall have the right not to be subject to *a decision based solely on automated processing, including profiling, which produces legal effects concerning him or her or similarly significantly affects him or her*'. This right shall apply almost always in case of processing of sensitive data[21] (Art 22(4)). For the processing of other personal data, shall not apply in only three cases:

(a) if the decision 'is necessary for entering into, or performance of, a contract between the data subject and a data controller';
(b) 'is authorised by Union or Member State law to which the controller is subject and which also lays down *suitable measures to safeguard the data subject's rights and freedoms and legitimate interests*'; or
(c) 'is based on the data subject's explicit consent' (Art. 22(2)).

In cases (a) and (c), 'the data controller shall implement *suitable measures to safeguard the data subject's rights and freedoms and legitimate interests, at least the right to obtain human intervention on the part of the controller, to express his or her point of view and to contest the decision*' (Art. 22(4)). In addition, Recital 73 explains that such suitable safeguards 'should include specific information to the data subject and the right to obtain human intervention, to express his or her point of view, to *obtain an explanation* of the decision reached after such assessment and to challenge the decision'.

Therefore, in principle we can summarize that in case of a 'decision based solely on automated processing, including profiling, which produces legal effects concerning [subjects] or similarly significantly affects [them]', individuals have two different protections:

1. *The right to know the existence* of that processing and *meaningful information* about its *logic, significance and consequences.*
2. *The right not to be subject to that processing*, unless in specific cases (pre-contractual processing, explicit consent of data subjects) where other *appropriate safeguards* must be provided, such as (at least):
   i. *the right to obtain human intervention* from the controller;
   ii. *the right to express his or her point of view*;
   iii. *the right to contest the decision* (or 'challenge' it, as referred at recital 73);

[21] For sensitive data we refer to 'special categories of personal data' according to Art 9(1). This exemption does not apply in case of point (a) or (g) of Art 9(2) (i.e., sensitive data given with explicit consent of data subject or processing necessary for reason of substantial public interest) when 'suitable measures to safeguard the data subject's rights and freedoms and legitimate interests are in place'.

iv. eventually, the *right to 'obtain an explanation* of the decision reached after such assessment'. However, this right is not included in the body of article 22, but only in the explanatory recital 71.

In addition to the GDPR, other EU legal sources are also relevant for the regulation of automated decision-making, namely especially Article 11 of the Directive 2016/680 (Law Enforcement Directive) and Article 77 of the Regulation 2018/1725 for data protection for EU Institutions (EUDPR).[22] However, the scope of this chapter is limited to the GDPR, considering that those other legal texts have a more limited approach to the regulation of automated decision-making.

V. DEBATE AND INTERPRETATIONS

The interpretation of automated decision-making regulation in the GDPR has triggered a vivid debate in legal doctrine. In particular, there are three main views in the existing literature: (a) several scholars have interpreted this net of provisions as constituting a new right to algorithm explanation;[23] (b) other scholars have adopted a more sceptical approach, focusing on the limits and constraints of the GDPR provision,[24] concluding that the data subjects rights are more limited than expected, and that there is no right to explanation;[25] (c) finally, other scholars have preferred a contextual interpretation of Articles 13–15 and 22, suggesting that the scope of those provisions is not so limited, and that they actually can provide individuals with more transparency and accountability.[26]

This last view was confirmed by the Article 29 Working Party, which released guidelines on profiling and automated decision-making.[27] In these guidelines, the WP29 confirmed that

---

[22] 'Regulation (EU) 2018/1725 of the European Parliament and of the Council of 23 October 2018 on the Protection of Natural Persons with Regard to the Processing of Personal Data by the Union Institutions, Bodies, Offices and Agencies and on the Free Movement of Such Data, and Repealing Regulation (EC) No 45/2001 and Decision No 1247/2002/EC (Text with EEA Relevance.)', Pub. L. No. 32018R1725, 295 OJ L (2018), http://data.europa.eu/eli/reg/2018/1725/oj/eng.

[23] Bryce Goodman and Seth Flaxman, 'European Union Regulations on Algorithmic Decision-Making and a 'Right to Explanation'', *AI Magazine* 38, no. 3 (2 October 2017): 50–57, https://doi.org/10.1609/aimag.v38i3.2741.

[24] See, e.g., Lilian Edwards and Michael Veale, 'Slave to the Algorithm? Why a 'Right to an Explanation' Is Probably Not the Remedy You Are Looking For', *Duke Law & Technology Review* 16, no. 1 (4 December 2017): 18–84.

[25] Sandra Wachter, Brent Mittelstadt, and Luciano Floridi, 'Why a Right to Explanation of Automated Decision-Making Does Not Exist in the General Data Protection Regulation', *International Data Privacy Law* 7, no. 2 (1 May 2017): 76–99, https://doi.org/10.1093/idpl/ipx005.

[26] Andrew D. Selbst and Julia Powles, 'Meaningful Information and the Right to Explanation', *International Data Privacy Law* 7, no. 4 (1 November 2017): 233–42, https://doi.org/10.1093/idpl/ipx022; Gianclaudio Malgieri and Giovanni Comandé, 'Why a Right to Legibility of Automated Decision-Making Exists in the General Data Protection Regulation', *International Data Privacy Law* 7, no. 4 (1 November 2017): 243–65, https://doi.org/10.1093/idpl/ipx019; Margot Kaminski, 'The Right to Explanation, Explained', *Berkeley Technology Law Journal* 34, no. 1 (13 May 2019): 189, https://doi.org/10.15779/Z38TD9N83H.

[27] Article 29 Working Party, 'Guidelines on Automated Individual Decision-Making and Profiling for the Purposes of Regulation 2016/679', 3 October 2017.

the scope of Article 22 should be interpreted extensively: decisions based 'solely on automated means' must include any decision in which the human intervention is not meaningful.[28] Also the notion of 'legal effects or similarly significant effects' should be considered in a broad sense: even online marketing or price discrimination, at some conditions, could be considered as having significant effects relevant under Article 22.[29] Section VI (below) will come back to these guidelines, and in particular to their relevance for the discussion about the right to explanation.

Another relevant issue is the question of the suitable measures that should enable automated decision making in some cases. Indeed, since Article 22(2) allows automated decision-making under wide and general conditions (contract, explicit consent, EU or Member State law), the real challenge is to understand which safeguards (e.g., ex post explanation, ex ante information, right to contest, etc.) could protect and empower more data subjects in those possibly numerous cases.

Scholars have proposed six notable different ways for addressing the issue of suitable safeguards as indicated at Article 22(3). In particular:

- a model of counterfactual explanations, i.e., a duty to clarify for individuals targeted by automated decisions, amongst others, 'what would need to change in order to receive a desired result in the future, based on the current decision making model';[30]
- transparency and comprehensibility merged in the concept of '*legibility*', a term used by computer scientists[31] to indicate that individuals should be able to understand autonomously (readability) the importance and implications (comprehensibility) of algorithmic data processing;
- a more dynamic link between existing data protection rights (access, erasure, rectification, portability, etc.) in order to react to adverse effects of automated decisions;[32]
- a dualistic approach based on individual rights and on a multi-level design of algorithms (co-governance);[33]
- a practice of 'agonistic machine learning' as core to scientifically viable integration of data-driven applications into our environments while simultaneously bringing them under the rule of law;[34]
- a system of multi-layered explanations, based on Data Protection Impact Assessment.[35]

---

[28] Article 29 Working Party, 21.

[29] Ibid., 21–22.

[30] Sandra Wachter, Brent Mittelstadt, and Chris Russell, 'Counterfactual Explanations without Opening the Black Box: Automated Decisions and the GDPR', *Harvard Journal of Law & Technology*, 2018, http://arxiv.org/abs/1711.00399.

[31] Richard Mortier et al., 'Human-Data Interaction: The Human Face of the Data-Driven Society', *ArXiv:1412.6159 [Cs]*, 6 October 2014, 2, http://arxiv.org/abs/1412.6159; Malgieri and Comandé, 'Why a Right to Legibility of Automated Decision-Making Exists in the General Data Protection Regulation', 14.

[32] Edwards and Veale, 'Slave to the Algorithm?'

[33] Kaminski, 'The Right to Explanation, Explained'.

[34] Mireille Hildebrandt, 'Privacy as Protection of the Incomputable Self: From Agnostic to Agonistic Machine Learning', *Theoretical Inquiries in Law* 20, no. 1 (23 January 2019), https://www7.tau.ac.il/ojs/index.php/til/article/view/1622 (Last visited, August 2018).

[35] Margot Kaminski and Gianclaudio Malgieri, 'Multi-Layered Explanation from Algorithmic Impact Assessments in the GDPR', in *FAT 2020 Proceedings* (ACM publishing, 2020).

All these proposed solutions are extremely interesting and useful. They are all strongly interrelated to each other: agonistic machine learning is mainly based on participatory algorithmic design, where also individual rights play a fundamental role and counterfactual explanation might be a good practical solution.[36]

VI. 'SUITABLE SAFEGUARDS' FOR AUTOMATED DECISION-MAKING: THE 2017 WP29 GUIDELINES

One remaining problem is the exact interpretation of GDPR provisions and, in particular, the exact meaning of 'suitable measures to safeguard the data subject's rights and freedoms and legitimate interests' that should be taken when the automated decision-making is authorized by Union or Member State law (Article 22(2)(b)); or when the decision making is necessary for entering into, or performance of, a contract (22(1)(a)(or is based on the data subjects' explicit consent (22(1)(c)) according to Article 22(3).

The WP29, rephrasing Article 22(3) GDPR, mentioned some examples of suitable measures, i.e., 'a minimum a way for the data subject to obtain *human intervention*, *express their point of view*, and *contest the decision*'.[37] In particular, human intervention is considered a 'key element': it should be based on the assessment of all the relevant data, including any additional information provided by the data subject, and it should be carried out by someone with the appropriate authority and capability to change the decision.[38]

Recital 71 – as also the WP29 acknowledged – mentions other two relevant examples of 'suitable safeguards': the right to receive *specific information* and the right to obtain an *explanation* of the decision reached after such assessment and to *challenge the decision*. Actually, these three safeguards (right to information, right to explanation, right to challenge the decision) can all be inferred from other provisions in the GDPR. In particular, the reference to 'specific information' can be well inferred from Article 15(2)(h), that is, the right to receive 'meaningful information about the logic involved, as well as the significance and the envisaged consequences' of automated decision-making data processing: it is not clear whether '*specific*' information should refer to something more, but a contextual interpretation of 'meaningful information'[39] under Article 15(2)(h) seems a good safeguard, even though it should be clarified with more detail.

The right to 'challenge' an automated decision is another interesting safeguard:[40] it seems it might be inferred from the 'right to contest' at Article 22(3). In this sense, *challenging* the

---

[36] See, e.g., Hildebrandt, 'Privacy as Protection of the Incomputable Self', 31.

[37] Article 29 Working Party, 'Guidelines on Automated Individual Decision-Making and Profiling for the Purposes of Regulation 2016/679', 27.

[38] Ibid.

[39] Selbst and Powles, 'Meaningful Information and the Right to Explanation'; Malgieri and Comandé, 'Why a Right to Legibility of Automated Decision-Making Exists in the General Data Protection Regulation'.

[40] Kaminski, 'The Right to Explanation, Explained'.

decision and *contesting* the decision might be synonyms,[41] even though these two terms have different nuances.[42]

As for the right to explanation – the most controversial 'right' in this area – it is interesting how the WP29 justified the existence of this right as connected to the right to challenge the decision: 'the data subject will only be able to challenge a decision or express their view if they fully understand how it has been made and on what basis'.[43] This idea of 'full understanding' of the automated decision-making mechanism reminds of the idea of *legibility* that we have mentioned above.[44]

The WP29 highlighted also that effective safeguards should include also frequent assessments on the data sets they process to check for any bias (e.g., incorrect classifications, imprecise projections, negative impact on individuals), and develop ways to address any prejudicial elements, including any over-reliance on correlations.[45] Such assessments should be structured as regular reviews (e.g., systems of algorithms auditing) of the accuracy and relevance of automated decision-making, and should include procedures and measures that prevent errors, inaccuracies and discrimination based on sensitive data, on a cyclical basis (i.e., not only at the design stage, but also afterwards, and the outcome should feed back into the system design).[46]

In addition, the WP29 provided in an Annex a list of specific recommendations, also in terms of practical safeguards under Article 22(3) GDPR.[47] The list includes: regular quality assurance checks against discrimination and unfair treatment; algorithmic auditing (even with independent third-party auditing); contractual assurances for third-party algorithms; data minimization measures; anonymization/pseudonymization measures; ways to allow the data subject to express his or her point of view and contest the decision; a structured mechanism for human intervention in the automated decision-making process. Additional safeguards might be: certification mechanisms; codes of conduct; and ethical review boards.[48] Disappointingly, in the list of recommendations there is no reference to the three safeguards mentioned at Recital 71 (information, explanation, challenge of the decision). The asymmetry between the text of the WP29 guidelines and the annexed list of best practices is not the only problematic issue, however: several safeguards still need to be clarified in detail.

---

[41] See the word 'Contest' in Thesuarus.com, https://www.thesaurus.com/browse/contest?s=t (Last visited, 10 August 2018).

[42] The verb 'Challenge' in Oxford Dictionary is explained as: 'Dispute the truth or validity of'. The verb 'Contest' in Oxford Dictionary is explained as: 'Oppose (an action or theory) as mistaken or wrong' or 'Engage in dispute about', https://en.oxforddictionaries.com/definition/challenge (Last visited, 10 August 2018).

[43] Kaminski, 'The Right to Explanation, Explained'.

[44] See Malgieri and Comandé, 'Why a Right to Legibility of Automated Decision-Making Exists in the General Data Protection Regulation'.

[45] Article 29 Working Party, 'Guidelines on Automated Individual Decision-Making and Profiling for the Purposes of Regulation 2016/679', 28.

[46] Article 29 Working Party, 28; Alessandro Mantelero, 'AI and Big Data: A Blueprint for a Human Rights, Social and Ethical Impact Assessment', *Computer Law & Security Review* 34, no. 4 (1 August 2018): 754–72, https://doi.org/10.1016/j.clsr.2018.05.017.

[47] Article 29 Working Party, 'Guidelines on Automated Individual Decision-Making and Profiling for the Purposes of Regulation 2016/679', 32.

[48] Article 29 Working Party, 32; See, also, Lilian Edwards and Michael Veale, 'Enslaving the Algorithm: From a 'Right to an Explanation' to a 'Right to Better Decisions'?', *IEEE Security & Privacy* 16, no. 3 (2018): 46–54.

Notably, automated profiling producing legal or similarly significant effects is an explicit case of high-risk data processing for which a Data Protection Impact Assessment (DPIA) is mandatory (Art 35(1)). As many scholars have argued, the DPIA is an opportunity to detect and mitigate many of the automated decision-making risks for data subjects' rights and freedoms,[49] but also a way to empower individual rights in the automated decision-making systems (transparency rights and participatory rights) through a cyclic and comprehensive accountability mechanism.[50]

VII. AUTOMATED DECISION-MAKING AND THE COUNCIL OF EUROPE CONVENTION 108

Interestingly, also the Council of Europe Convention 108, as lastly revised,[51] has provided a specific case of explanation of automated decision-making. While the original version of Convention 108 had no mention to automated decisions,[52] the modernized version at Article 9(1), point (c) states as follows: '[every individual shall have the right] to obtain, on request, knowledge of the reasoning underlying data processing where the result of such processing are applied to him or her'.

Apparently, the scope of this right is wider than the GDPR provisions because it applies to any data processing (not only data processing involving automated decision-making), but the information that data controllers should disclose is apparently more specific ('reasoning underlying'). In other words, it seems to refer to specific explanations on decisions rationale, rather than general ex ante information on the data processing mechanism. This is in line with how several Member States in Europe (e.g., France, Hungary) have specified Article 22(3) GDPR safeguards in their national laws.[53] Interestingly, Article 9 of Convention 108 is also very similar to some extra-EU algorithmic regulations (see in particular, e.g., the new Brazilian Data Protection law).[54]

---

[49] Heleen L. Janssen, 'An Approach for a Fundamental Rights Impact Assessment to Automated Decision-Making', *International Data Privacy Law*, accessed 10 April 2020, https://doi.org/10.1093/idpl/ipz028; Mantelero, 'AI and Big Data'.

[50] Margot E Kaminski and Gianclaudio Malgieri, 'Algorithmic Impact Assessments under the GDPR: Producing Multi-Layered Explanations', *International Data Privacy Law*, no. ipaa020 (6 December 2020), https://doi.org/10.1093/idpl/ipaa020; Margot E. Kaminski and Gianclaudio Malgieri, 'Multi-Layered Explanations from Algorithmic Impact Assessments in the GDPR', in *Proceedings of the 2020 Conference on Fairness, Accountability, and Transparency*, FAT* '20 (Barcelona, Spain: Association for Computing Machinery, 2020), 68–79, https://doi.org/10.1145/3351095.3372875.

[51] 128th Session of the Committee of Ministers, (Elsinore, Denmark, 17-18 May 2018), Modernised Convention for the Protection of Individuals with Regard to the Processing of Personal Data, https://search.coe.int/cm/Pages/result_details.aspx?ObjectId=09000016807c65bf (Last visited, 10 August 2018).

[52] Convention for the Protection of Individuals with regard to Automatic Processing of Personal Data, Strasbourg, 28.I.1981.

[53] Gianclaudio Malgieri, 'Automated Decision-Making in the EU Member States: The Right to Explanation and Other 'Suitable Safeguards' in the National Legislations', *Computer Law & Security Review* 35, no. 5 (1 October 2019): 105327, https://doi.org/10.1016/j.clsr.2019.05.002.

[54] Law No. 13,709, of August 14, 2018 - Provides for the protection of personal data and changes Law No. 12,965, of April 23, 2014 (the 'Brazilian Internet Law'), Article 20, §1.

Considering how this new right to explanation in Modernized Convention 108 is regulated and how it is apparently broader than the GDPR transparency duties at Articles 13–15, one might wonder whether Member States (that are forced to implement every Council of Europe conventions in their own national legislation) will be obliged to extend the requirements of Articles 13–15 and 22(3) in their national laws, in order to be compliant with Convention 108, or whether the GDPR is already an adequate implementation of that Modernized Convention.

At the same time, there is no mention to the right to contestation, human involvement or to represent one's view. The reason why Modernized Convention 108 does not introduce these new rights, might be that the scope of this right to explanation at Article 9 is very broad: it encompasses any kind of data processing, either automated or not, and in any field, even in the criminal investigation field.[55]

VIII. THE REGULATION OF AUTOMATED DECISIONS IN THE EU PROPOSED AI ACT

In addition to the existing legal framework described above, the European Commission proposed in April 2021 a new Regulation on AI ('AI Act')[56] that would introduce many novelties and design rules of automated decision-making systems.[57] The proposed AI Act introduces a risk-based approach to AI-based products and services, with ambitious design rules and administrative burdens.[58]

The definition of 'AI systems' in the proposed Regulation does not exactly overlap with the aforementioned definition of automated decision-making: while the latter is limited to decisions made on personal data, based solely on automated means and producing legal or similarly significant effects;[59] the first is neither limited to personal data, nor it is based on solely automated means, nor it is restricted to AI systems producing certain relevant effects. On the contrary, AI systems refer to software (developed through machine learning, statistical approaches, etc.)[60] that 'can, for a given set of human-defined objectives, generate outputs such as content, predictions, recommendations, or decisions influencing the environments they interact with'.[61] In sum, the AI definition seems much broader than the automated

---

55 The GDPR material scope does not include also data processing regulated by criminal procedure law, see Article 2(2) point (d). Instead, Council of Europe Convention 108 has not such scope limitations.

56 European Commission, Proposal for a Regulation of the European Parliament and of the Council laying down harmonised rules on Artificial Intelligence (Artificial Intelligence Act) and amending certain Union legislative acts, Brussels, 21.4.2021 COM(2021) 206 final.

57 Lucilla Sioli and Roberto Viola, 'European Commission: "Here Lies the True Strength of Our AI Regulation"', *Agenda Digitale*, 30 April 2021, https://www.agendadigitale.eu/cultura-digitale/european-commission-here-lies-the-true-strength-of-our-ai-regulation/ (Last visited, August 2018).

58 Gianclaudio Malgieri, 'Réglementer l'intelligence artificielle : 'Le nouveau modèle s'appuie de plus en plus sur la responsabilisation des entreprises', *Le Monde.fr*, 13 May 2021, https://www.lemonde.fr/idees/article/2021/05/13/reglementer-l-intelligence-artificielle-le-nouveau-modele-s-appuie-de-plus-en-plus-sur-la-responsabilisation-des-entreprises_6080117_3232.html (Last visited, August 2018).

59 Michael Veale and Lilian Edwards, 'Clarity, Surprises, and Further Questions in the Article 29 Working Party Draft Guidance on Automated Decision-Making and Profiling', *Computer Law & Security Review* 34, no. 2 (1 April 2018): 398–404, https://doi.org/10.1016/j.clsr.2017.12.002.

60 See Annex I of the Proposed Regulation on AI.

61 Art 3(1) of the Proposed Regulation on AI.

decision-making definition in the GDPR for what concerns the input/output data (in the AI definition, data do not need to be 'personal'), the means (even semi-automated means are under the AI definition) and the effects (not only legal or similarly significant are under the AI definition). At the same time the AI definition seems narrower for what concerns the technology: automated decision-making can also be based on very simple algorithms (not based on machine learning or similar technologies).

In more specific terms, in the new proposed AI Act, some AI systems would be deemed to produce unbearable risks and would be thus prohibited. This blacklist would include, e.g.: dark patterns and manipulative online ads producing physical or psychological harms to consumers or exploiting their vulnerability on the basis of their age or disability; social scoring producing disproportionate or de-contextualized detrimental effects; and remote biometric identification systems used by law enforcement authorities in public spaces (where their use is not strictly necessary or when the risk of detrimental effects is too high).[62]

Other AI systems are considered 'high-risk'. For these systems, the providers and the commercial users should perform several duties, including: risk management, data management plans, human oversight measures, notification to a Supervisory Authority, conformity certification and corrective actions in case of non-conformity. There is already a list of high-risk systems (including certain AI systems used in critical infrastructures, in educational, employment or emergency contexts; in asylum and border contexts; in social welfare or for credit scoring or law enforcement or judicial purposes),[63] but the European Commission (on the basis of the severity and probability of impact of AI systems on fundamental rights) could update that list, in line with the proposal.[64]

For some AI systems (AI producing deep fakes like videos or images;[65] emotion recognition systems and AI interacting with humans) there would be general transparency obligations (Art 52 of the Proposed Regulation). For all the other AI systems (low-risk AI systems) there would be only general guidelines, including the possible use of codes of conduct.

An important aspect of the proposed Regulation concerns explainability and accuracy of high-risk AI systems. The text tries to go beyond the traditional safeguards about accountability and fairness of automated decision-making that are, e.g., in the GDPR as analysed in the previous sections.[66] In particular, the proposed Regulation would impose human oversight

---

[62] Art 5 of the Proposed Regulation on AI.

[63] See Annex III of the Proposed Regulation on AI.

[64] See Art 7 of the Proposed Regulation on AI.

[65] Robert Chesney and Danielle Keats Citron, 'Deep Fakes: A Looming Challenge for Privacy, Democracy, and National Security', SSRN Scholarly Paper (Rochester, NY: Social Science Research Network, 14 July 2018), https://papers.ssrn.com/abstract=3213954; John Fletcher, 'Deepfakes, Artificial Intelligence, and Some Kind of Dystopia: The New Faces of Online Post-Fact Performance', *Theatre Journal* 70, no. 4 (2018): 455–71, https://doi.org/10.1353/tj.2018.0097.

[66] About the limits of the traditional discourse on explainability of AI see Bryan Casey, Ashkon Farhangi, and Roland Vogl, 'Rethinking Explainable Machines: The GDPR's 'Right to Explanation' Debate and the Rise of Algorithmic Audits in Enterprise', *Berkeley Technology Law Journal* 34, no. 2019 (19 February 2018), https://papers.ssrn.com/abstract=3143325; Ronan Hamon et al., 'Impossible Explanations? Beyond Explainable AI in the GDPR from a COVID-19 Use Case Scenario', in *Proceedings of the 2021 ACM Conference on Fairness, Accountability, and Transparency*, FAccT '21 (New York, NY, USA: Association for Computing Machinery, 2021), 549–59, https://doi.org/10.1145/3442188.3445917; Andrew D. Selbst and Solon Barocas, 'The Intuitive Appeal of Explainable Machines', *Fordham Law Review* 87, no. 2018 (2 March 2018): 1085.

duties, according to which high-risk AI providers should always build or foresee an implementable model for understandable, interpretable, 'correctable' and contestable machine learning systems, through the mandatory participation of two 'humans in the loop' for the testing of high-risk AI models.[67] In addition, while in general the accuracy of data processing was just mentioned as a general principle in the EU, the proposed Regulation on AI seems to go further. The accuracy of results is reached through different parallel methods: the AI providers need to critically assess the results of AI that could be the 'biased' input of new AI activity; the system should be resilient to inaccuracies and inconsistencies (through, e.g., some 'backups' or 'fail-safe' plans). In general, the provider should prepare an adequate data governance plan for data used for training, validation or testing of the algorithmic model. This plan should include an analysis of the adequacy of the input data sets, address eventual 'data gaps', contextualize the AI system in the specific social setting where it should be used and prevent any machine bias.[68]

IX. CONCLUSION

As noted above, profiling algorithms and automated decision-making are a growing reality in the actual data-driven society. Policymakers, scholars and commentators are more and more concerned with the risks of AI and automatic decisions in every field of our public or private life.

The 1995 Data Protection Directive had already provided a general regulation for such decisions, but the GDPR (as well as the 'modernized version' of Convention 108 of the Council of Europe) has provided more specific tools for protecting individuals against automated decision-making: a right to receive/access meaningful information about logics, significance and envisaged effects of automated decision making processes; the right not to be subject to automated decision-making with several safeguards and restraints for the limited cases in which automated decision making is permitted.

In section II we described human and machine biases in automated decisions; while in section III we addressed the status of algorithmic decision-making before the GDPR (in particular, in Arts 12 and 15 of the Data Protection Directive). In section IV we focused on the specific regulation of automated decision-making in the GDPR (Arts 13–15 and Article 22). Consequently, section V addressed possible interpretations of the GDPR provisions, mentioning the academic debate. In addition, section VI discussed the specific safeguards that data controllers should take when performing automated decisions, in particular following WP29 Opinion interpretation of profiling in the GDPR. Finally, section VII has mentioned automated decision-making regulation in the new version of Convention 108 of the Council of Europe. Completing the overview, the new perspectives on the regulation of automated decision-making as emanating from the European Commission's proposal for an AI Act have been discussed.

---

[67] Art 14 of the Proposed Regulation on AI.

[68] See Art 10 of the Proposed Regulation on AI.

BIBLIOGRAPHY

Article 29 Working Party. *Guidelines on Automated Individual Decision-Making and Profiling for the Purposes of Regulation 2016/679*, 3 October 2017.

Barocas, S, and A D Selbst. 'Big Data's Disparate Impact'. *California Law Review* 104 (2016): 671. https://doi.org/10.2139/ssrn.2477899.

Boyd, D. 'Networked Privacy'. *Surveillance & Society* 10, no. 3/4 (22 December 2012): 348–50. https://doi.org/10.24908/ss.v10i3/4.4529.

Bygrave, LA. 'Minding the Machine: Article 15 of the EC Data Protection Directive and Automated Profiling'. *Computer Law & Security Review* 17, no. 1 (1 January 2001): 17–24. https://doi.org/10.1016/S0267-3649(01)00104-2.

Casey, B, A Farhangi, and R Vogl. 'Rethinking Explainable Machines: The GDPR's 'Right to Explanation' Debate and the Rise of Algorithmic Audits in Enterprise'. *Berkeley Technology Law Journal* 34, no. 2019 (19 February 2018). https://papers.ssrn.com/abstract=3143325.

Chesney, R, and D Keats Citron. 'Deep Fakes: A Looming Challenge for Privacy, Democracy, and National Security'. SSRN Scholarly Paper. Rochester, NY: Social Science Research Network, 14 July 2018. https://papers.ssrn.com/abstract=3213954.

Citron, D, and F Pasquale. 'The Scored Society: Due Process for Automated Predictions'. Faculty Scholarship, 1 January 2014. https://digitalcommons.law.umaryland.edu/fac_pubs/1431.

Comandè, G. 'Regulating Algorithms' Regulation? First Ethico-Legal Principles, Problems, and Opportunities of Algorithms'. In Transparent Data Mining for Big and Small Data, edited by Tania Cerquitelli, Daniele Quercia, and Frank Pasquale, 32:169–206. Studies in Big Data. Cham: Springer International Publishing, 2017. https://doi.org/10.1007/978-3-319-54024-5_8.

Crawford, K, and M Whittaker. 'The AI Now Report - The Social and Economic Implications of Artificial IntelligenceTechnologies in the Near-Term', 2016. https://ainowinstitute.org/AI_Now_2016_Report.pdf.

Edwards, L, and M Veale. 'Enslaving the Algorithm: From a 'Right to an Explanation' to a 'Right to Better Decisions'?' *IEEE Security & Privacy* 16, no. 3 (2018): 46–54.

Edwards, L, and M Veale. 'Slave to the Algorithm? Why a 'Right to an Explanation' Is Probably Not the Remedy You Are Looking For'. *Duke Law & Technology Review* 16, no. 1 (4 December 2017): 18–84.

Eubanks, V. *Automating Inequality: How High-tech Tools Profile, Police, and Punish the* Poor. New York, NY: St Martins Pr, 2018.

Ferrer, X, T van Nuenen, JM Such, M Coté, and N Criado. 'Bias and Discrimination in AI: A Cross-Disciplinary Perspective'. ArXiv:2008.07309 [Cs], 11 August 2020. http://arxiv.org/abs/2008.07309.

Fletcher, J. 'Deepfakes, Artificial Intelligence, and Some Kind of Dystopia: The New Faces of Online Post-Fact Performance'. Theatre Journal 70, no. 4 (2018): 455–71. https://doi.org/10.1353/tj.2018.0097.

Gillespie, T. 'The Relevance of Algorithms'. In *Media Technologies*, edited by T Gillespie, PJ. Boczkowski, and KA Foot, 167–94. The MIT Press, 2014. https://doi.org/10.7551/mitpress/9780262525374.003.0009.

Goodman, B, and S Flaxman. 'European Union Regulations on Algorithmic Decision-Making and a 'Right to Explanation''. *AI Magazine* 38, no. 3 (2 October 2017): 50–57. https://doi.org/10.1609/aimag.v38i3.2741.

Grimmelmann, J, and D Westreich. 'Incomprehensible Discrimination'. *Cornell Law Faculty Publications*, 1 March 2017. https://scholarship.law.cornell.edu/facpub/1536.

Hammond, K. '5 Unexpected Sources of Bias in Artificial Intelligence'. *TechCrunch* (blog). Accessed 27 May 2021. https://social.techcrunch.com/2016/12/10/5-unexpected-sources-of-bias-in-artificial-intelligence/.

Hamon, R, H Junklewitz, G Malgieri, P De Hert, L Beslay, and I Sanchez. 'Impossible Explanations? Beyond Explainable AI in the GDPR from a COVID-19 Use Case Scenario'. In *Proceedings of the 2021 ACM Conference on Fairness, Accountability, and Transparency*, 549–59. FAccT '21. New York, NY, USA: Association for Computing Machinery, 2021. https://doi.org/10.1145/3442188.3445917.

Hildebrandt, M. 'Privacy as Protection of the Incomputable Self: From Agnostic to Agonistic Machine Learning'. Theoretical Inquiries in Law 20, no. 1 (23 January 2019). https://www7.tau.ac.il/ojs/index.php/til/article/view/1622.
Hildebrandt, M. 'The Issue of Bias: The Framing Powers of ML'. In *Machine Learning and Society: Impact, Trust, Transparency*, edited by Marcello Pelillo. MIT Press, 2021.
Information Commissioner's Officer. 'Explaining Decisions Made with AI'. ICO, 19 May 2021. https://ico.org.uk/for-organisations/guide-to-data-protection/key-data-protection-themes/explaining-decisions-made-with-artificial-intelligence/.
Janssen, HL. 'An Approach for a Fundamental Rights Impact Assessment to Automated Decision-Making'. International Data Privacy Law. Accessed 10 April 2020. https://doi.org/10.1093/idpl/ipz028.
Kaminski, M. 'The Right to Explanation, Explained'. Berkeley Technology Law Journal 34, no. 1 (13 May 2019): 189. https://doi.org/10.15779/Z38TD9N83H.
Kaminski, ME and G Malgieri. 'Algorithmic Impact Assessments under the GDPR: Producing Multi-Layered Explanations'. International Data Privacy Law, no. ipaa020 (6 December 2020). https://doi.org/10.1093/idpl/ipaa020.
Kaminski, ME and G Malgieri. 'Multi-Layered Explanations from Algorithmic Impact Assessments in the GDPR'. In Proceedings of the 2020 Conference on Fairness, Accountability, and Transparency, 68–79. FAT* '20. Barcelona, Spain: Association for Computing Machinery, 2020. https://doi.org/10.1145/3351095.3372875.
Kaminski, ME and G Malgieri. 'Multi-Layered Explanation from Algorithmic Impact Assessments in the GDPR'. In FAT 2020 Proceedings. ACM publishing, 2020.
Kroll, J, J Huey, S Barocas, Edward Felten, Joel Reidenberg, David Robinson, and Harlan Yu. 'Accountable Algorithms'. University of Pennsylvania Law Review 165, no. 3 (1 January 2017): 633.
Lucilla Sioli and Roberto Viola. 'European Commission: 'Here Lies the True Strength of Our AI Regulation''. Agenda Digitale, 30 April 2021. https://www.agendadigitale.eu/cultura-digitale/european-commission-here-lies-the-true-strength-of-our-ai-regulation/.
Malgieri, G. 'Automated Decision-Making in the EU Member States: The Right to Explanation and Other 'Suitable Safeguards' in the National Legislations'. Computer Law & Security Review 35, no. 5 (1 October 2019): 105327. https://doi.org/10.1016/j.clsr.2019.05.002.
Malgieri, G. 'Réglementer l'intelligence artificielle : "Le nouveau modèle s'appuie de plus en plus sur la responsabilisation des entreprises"'. Le Monde.fr, 13 May 2021. https://www.lemonde.fr/idees/article/2021/05/13/reglementer-l-intelligence-artificielle-le-nouveau-modele-s-appuie-de-plus-en-plus-sur-la-responsabilisation-des-entreprises_6080117_3232.html.
Malgieri, G, and G Comandé. 'Why a Right to Legibility of Automated Decision-Making Exists in the General Data Protection Regulation'. International Data Privacy Law 7, no. 4 (1 November 2017): 243–65. https://doi.org/10.1093/idpl/ipx019.
Mantelero, A. 'AI and Big Data: A Blueprint for a Human Rights, Social and Ethical Impact Assessment'. Computer Law & Security Review 34, no. 4 (1 August 2018): 754–72. https://doi.org/10.1016/j.clsr.2018.05.017.
McDuff, D, R Cheng, and A Kapoor. 'Identifying Bias in AI Using Simulation'. ArXiv:1810.00471 [Cs, Stat], 30 September 2018. http://arxiv.org/abs/1810.00471.
Mortier, R, H Haddadi, T Henderson, D McAuley, and J Crowcroft. 'Human-Data Interaction: The Human Face of the Data-Driven Society'. ArXiv:1412.6159 [Cs], 6 October 2014. http://arxiv.org/abs/1412.6159.
Obermeyer, Z, B Powers, C Vogeli, and S Mullainathan. 'Dissecting Racial Bias in an Algorithm Used to Manage the Health of Populations'. Science 366, no. 6464 (25 October 2019): 447–53. https://doi.org/10.1126/science.aax2342.
Pasquale, F, *The Black Box Society: The Secret Algorithms that Control Money and Information*. Cambridge: Harvard Univ Pr, 2015.
Powles, J, and H Nissenbaum. 'The Seductive Diversion of 'Solving' Bias in Artificial Intelligence'. *Medium*, 7 December 2018. https://onezero.medium.com/the-seductive-diversion-of-solving-bias-in-artificial-intelligence-890df5e5ef53.
Regulation (EU) 2018/1725 of the European Parliament and of the Council of 23 October 2018 on the protection of natural persons with regard to the processing of personal data by the Union institutions, bodies, offices and agencies and on the free movement of such data, and repealing Regulation (EC)

No 45/2001 and Decision No 1247/2002/EC (Text with EEA relevance.), Pub. L. No. 32018R1725, 295 OJ L (2018).
Roselli, D, J Matthews, and N Talagala. 'Managing Bias in AI'. In *Companion Proceedings of The 2019 World Wide Web Conference,* 539–44. WWW '19. New York, NY, USA: Association for Computing Machinery, 2019. https://doi.org/10.1145/3308560.3317590.
Selbst, AD, and S Barocas. 'The Intuitive Appeal of Explainable Machines'. *Fordham Law Review* 87, no. 2018 (2 March 2018): 1085.
Selbst, AD, and J Powles. 'Meaningful Information and the Right to Explanation'. *International Data Privacy Law* 7, no. 4 (1 November 2017): 233–42. https://doi.org/10.1093/idpl/ipx022.
Veale, M, and L Edwards. 'Clarity, Surprises, and Further Questions in the Article 29 Working Party Draft Guidance on Automated Decision-Making and Profiling'. Computer Law & Security Review 34, no. 2 (1 April 2018): 398–404. https://doi.org/10.1016/j.clsr.2017.12.002.
Wachter, S, B Mittelstadt, and L Floridi. 'Why a Right to Explanation of Automated Decision-Making Does Not Exist in the General Data Protection Regulation'. *International Data Privacy Law* 7, no. 2 (1 May 2017): 76–99. https://doi.org/10.1093/idpl/ipx005.
Wachter, S, B Mittelstadt, and C Russell. 'Counterfactual Explanations without Opening the Black Box: Automated Decisions and the GDPR'. *Harvard Journal of Law & Technology*, 2018. http://arxiv.org/abs/1711.00399.
Whittaker, M, et al. *Disability, Bias, and AI*, 2019.
Zarsky, T. 'Understanding Discrimination in the Scored Society'. *Washington Law Review* 89, no. 4 (1 December 2014): 1375.

Index